Harper's Weekly

SOUTH CAROLINA DURING
RECONSTRUCTION

LET US HAVE PEACE.

Harper's Weekly

A NAST CARTOON OF THE SOUTH CAROLINA LEGISLATURE. BASED ON AN
ACCOUNT GIVEN IN THE CHARLESTON NEWS

SOUTH CAROLINA DURING RECONSTRUCTION

BY

FRANCIS BUTLER SIMKINS, Ph.D.

Associate Professor of History, State Teachers College, Farmville, Virginia

ROBERT HILLIARD WOODY, Ph.D.

Instructor in History, Duke University

GLOUCESTER, MASS.

PETER SMITH

1966

To

MARGARET LEONA WOODY
AND TO THE MEMORY OF
SAMUEL McGOWAN SIMKINS

PREFACE

TO South Carolina, as to other Southern states, the consequences of the Civil War meant a distinct break in the continuity of the state's history. Abruptly destroyed, the economic, social, and political structure of the Old South could not immediately be replaced by a new order. And especially was that true when the conquerors attempted to impose upon the conservative commonwealth of South Carolina advanced concepts of what was considered the national ideal of political and social democracy. The vanquished were perfectly willing to admit defeat at arms, but they would not or could not accept the doctrines of political and social democracy as preached by what they considered arrogant politicians and mistaken philanthropists. The traditionally dominant element of the state demanded the right to enjoy their hereditary privileges. The descendants of those who had conquered and settled the land demanded the right to remain its lords, politically, socially, and economically, as well as the privilege of continuing provincial differences. The intimacies of political and social relations, it was felt, should be determined by leaders who arose within the borders of the state.

However, the prestige as well as the strength of the victors united with the so-called moral forces of the North to override that goodly portion of Southern tradition, especially in respect to the Negro, which was on the side of the white South Carolinian. The clash of these forces created within the state situations as grotesque and as bizarre as the annals of revolutionary efforts usually afford. Venal politicians, a frenzied and powerful Negro electorate, and projects of extreme reform were the rule and not the exception. The story of these revolutionary phenomena must play a conspicuous part in this narrative. But in our opinion the process of reconstruction involved other events less showy and of a more constructive significance. For this reason we forego the temptation of following in the footsteps of historians who have interpreted the period as only a glamorous but tragic melodrama of political intrigue.

Believing that present-day South Carolina has been affected more by Reconstruction than by any other single phase of her history, we propose to give our discussion a broader scope than is usual in the histories of Southern states during the period. The destruction of the ancient economic system of the state and attendant losses, together with the changes in the form and extent of wealth and the rise of a new economic class, should cause one to ponder the economic condition of the state during Reconstruction. Therefore we are interested in the new basis of agriculture and the problem of free labor. Likewise we inquire into the nature of commerce and manufactures as well as transportation and the public finances. On the other hand we are confronted with a new social class which casts its lights and shadows on many phases of social life, including the church and education. In other words, our purpose is not to confine ourselves to the political story, but, within practical limitations, to recreate the life of a people during a short span of years.

No one realizes more fully than the authors the shortcomings of their attempt to develop so ambitious a theme. A variety of limitations has prevented its actual accomplishment. No doubt we have left untold many things which some may regard as necessary for an adequate understanding of the period. This was done to prevent a story of perhaps not the highest importance from growing to absurd proportions and because of the limitation of the authentic source-material at our command. Most of the voluminous literature on the period is narrowly political. The sparse memoir material is dominated by the Southern sense of reticence. Most of the diaries and letters and many of the newspaper files have been destroyed or were not found. The travelers who visited the state and left written records were few and undistinguished; and what most of them wrote is confused by preconceptions. The journalism of the period, when frank, was sensational and not altogether reliable. Moreover, to secure clarity we have found it necessary to tear apart the hodge-podge of interests which was the life of the people and to regiment the fragments into chapters. Life in the living is confused, but books must attempt to be ordered. We have been forced to discuss the educational apart from the political, and the industrial apart from the social, although in the original we found them mixed together.

Acknowledgments are made in the footnotes and bibliography to those who have written in the field. Miss Ellen M. Fitzsimmons of the Charleston Library Society and Professor R. M. Kennedy and Miss Elizabeth English of the Library of the University of South Carolina have extended every courtesy in the use of the numerous sources of information in their charge. Professors Yates Snowden and Rion McKissick of the University of South Carolina and the late August Kohn of Columbia have put their excellent private collections at our disposal. The late Joseph W. Barnwell of Charleston subjected portions of the manuscript to a critical reading. Professor O. F. Crow of the University of South Carolina read the chapter on education. Professor Holland Thompson of the College of the City of New York has lent valuable suggestions. The Honorable John Gary Evans of Spartanburg, Mr. Frank P. Gary of Columbia, and Mr. William Sheppard, formerly of the New York *World,* have pointed out sources of information. Professor William K. Boyd of Duke University and Mr. Warren Candler Sledd, formerly of Duke University, Mr. Bob White Linker of the University of North Carolina, and Professor J. Milton Ariail of Columbia College (S. C.) have corrected portions of the manuscript. Edna Chandler Simkins and Mr. Theodore M. Jones have aided with the reading of the proofs and the making of the Index. A subsidy from the Social Science Research Council of New York City has made it possible for the researches to be completed much sooner than would have been the case otherwise.

F. B. S.
R. H. W.

Columbia, South Carolina
June, 1931

CONTENTS

ILLUSTRATIONS

SOUTH CAROLINA DURING
RECONSTRUCTION

CHAPTER I

THE HERITAGE OF WAR

A NY attempt to rebuild South Carolina society after the Civil War had to take into account several significant results of that war. A great amount of property had been destroyed; the Negro had been made free; and the Negro and the Northern white man for the first time had become able to compete with the native white man for the control of many aspects of local life. Accordingly, this narrative must begin with descriptions of war losses, of the freeing of the Negro, and of the ambitions and relative strength of the native white man, the Negro, and the Northern conqueror. Then the way will be open to narrate the first act of the Reconstruction drama, the attempt of the native whites to build a new political society out of the wreck of the old.

The first experience with the destructive influences of war came when Northern forces in November, 1861, captured the Port Royal area. Its entire white population fled in such haste that household belongings and slaves were left behind. The conquerors gave the Negroes freedom and allowed them to plunder their former masters' property. The freedmen occupied houses and smashed or appropriated the contents. They tore down churches and used the lumber to build cabins for themselves, and they broke open church organs and blew the pipes in the streets.[1] A hint of the fate of the property of the planters is revealed by the reports of Northern residents. A schoolmistress found a Negro cabin she visited in 1862 "elegantly furnished" with straw matting and a mahogany bureau,

[1] *Report to the Episcopal Convention of Churches Damaged and Destroyed*, pp. 4-5, and "Tilmonah," in *Our Women in the War*, p. 469.

and her servant carried a silver thimble and a bit of embroid-
ered curtain as a handkerchief.[2]   A labor superintendent had
this to say of the house he occupied: "The force pump is
broken and all the bowls and their marble slabs smashed. . . .
Bureaus, commodes, and wardrobes are smashed in, as well as
the door panels. . . . We kindle our fires with chips of polished
mahogany, and I am writing on my knees with a piece of
flower-stand across them for a table."[3]

Sherman's army, in its march through the state in February,
1865, destroyed on a much vaster scale.   A path forty miles
wide was thoroughly pillaged.   The correspondent of the *New
York Herald* with the army wrote: "I hazard nothing in saying that three-fifths (in value) of the personal property of the
counties we passed through were taken by Sherman's army.
. . . As for wholesale burnings, pillage and devastation committed in South Carolina, magnify all I have said of Georgia
some fifty-fold, and then throw in an occasional murder, 'jis
to bring an old, hard-fisted cuss to his senses,' and you have a
pretty good idea of the whole thing."[4]   General Carl Schurz,
who visited the state in July, 1865, said: "The track of Sherman's march in South Carolina, at least, looked for many
miles like a broad, black streak of ruin and desolation—the
fences all gone; lonesome smoke stacks, surrounded by dark
heaps of ashes and cinders, marking the spots where human
habitation had stood; the fences along the roads wildly overgrown by weeds. . . . No part of the South I then visited
had indeed suffered so much from ravages of war as South
Carolina."[5]

The crowning act of vandalism of Sherman's men was the

[2] *Letters and Diary of Laura M. Towne,*
pp. 4-5. Contemporary writers did not
ordinarily capitalize such words as "negro," or "democrat." These words, however, have been capitalized in this book
to conform with modern usage, in order
to avoid an apparently meaningless inconsistency.

[3] E. S. Philbrick in letter of Mar. 9,
1862, in Elizabeth Ware Pearson, *Letters
from Port Royal,* p. 8.

[4] Captain David P. Conyngham, *Sherman's March through the South,* p. 314.

[5] *Reminiscences,* III, 167.

destruction of Columbia. "It had been a beautiful city," wrote the effusive correspondent of the *New York Herald*. "It was famed for its fine public buildings, its magnificent private residences, with their lovely flower gardens which savored of oriental ease and luxury."[6] "The eighteenth of February," added this witness, "dawned upon a city of ruins. . . . Nothing remained but the tall, spectre-looking chimneys. The noble-looking trees which shaded the streets, the flower gardens that graced them, were blasted and withered by fire. The streets were filled with rubbish, broken furniture and groups of crouching, desponding, weeping women and children." Actually two-thirds of the town, eighty-four of its 124 blocks, lay in ashes. This included 445 stores, the old state house, eleven banking establishments and six churches.[7] Every house except those on the campus of the state college had been pillaged.[8] The only important edifices not destroyed were the unfinished State House, the state college, the Methodist woman's college, the lunatic asylum, and the home of William C. Preston.[9]

Charleston had suffered terribly from a series of disasters. The fire of December 11, 1861, had cut a wide belt across the city from river to river. How this area appeared in 1865 was described as follows: "The tall chimneys, grim and charred, the dilapidated walls overgrown with moss, and cellars rank with grass, the streets without pavements, and ankle-deep with sand."[10] The lower portion of the city showed the scars of the Federal bombardment. An English visitor described its effect as follows: "Here there was hardly a house which had not suffered more or less. To some the damage seems at first sight to be trifling; a small hole knocked in the wall is apparently the extent of the mischief, till an examination of the interior shows the injury which has been done by the bursting of shells. . . .

[6] Captain Conyngham, p. 331.
[7] [William Gilmore Simms], *The Sack and Destruction of Columbia*, pp. 58-76.
[8] *Autobiography of Joseph LeConte*, p. 226.
[9] Simms, p. 52.
[10] *Trip of the Steamer Oceanus to Fort Sumter and Charleston*, p. 39.

In the next house, may be, the outside has suffered; every pane of glass is broken, the doors battered in and the handsome pillars broken short."[11]   A shell had scarred the steeple of St. Michael's Church and another had demolished the altar; the interior of the Huguenot Church had been entered by shells which had shattered the chandeliers and left piles of stones on the floor.[12]   A third disaster had devastated the upper portion of the city at the time of the Confederate evacuation—the explosion of the Northeastern Depot and the fire which followed.   Some two hundred persons were killed, and "the fire spread across the city, destroying millions of dollars worth of property."[13]

Impressions of the plight of the city are conveyed by Northern travelers.   "I shall never forget," wrote General Carl Schurz, "my first impression of Charleston. . . . There was no shipping in the harbor except a few quartermaster's vessels and two or three small steamers.   We made fast to a decaying pier constructed of palmetto-logs.   There was not a human visible on the wharf.   The warehouses seemed to be completely deserted.   There was no wall and no roof that did not bear eloquent marks of having been under fire of siege guns.   I was informed that when our troops first entered the city, the wharf region was overgrown with luxuriant weed, giving it the appearance of a large swamp. . . . The crests of the roofs and chimneys were covered with turkey buzzards, who evidently felt at home, and who from time to time lazily flapped their wings and stretched forth their hideous necks."[14]

Sidney Andrews wrote: "A city of ruins, of desolation, of vacant houses, of widowed women, of rotten wharves, of deserted warehouses, of weed-wild gardens, of miles of grass-grown streets, of acres of pitiful and voicefull barrenness—this

---

[11] John A. Kennaway, *On Sherman's Track*, pp. 178-79.
[12] *Trip of the Steamer Oceanus*, pp. 121-22.
[13] George Walton Williams, *History of Banking in South Carolina*, p. 13.
[14] *Reminiscences*, III, 164-65.

Trowbridge, *A Picture of the Desolated States*

LEAVING CHARLESTON ON THE CITY'S BEING BOMBARDED

is Charleston."[15] The churchyard of St. Phillip's, where Calhoun was buried, "symbolizes the city of Charleston. Children and goats crowd through a convenient hole in the front wall, and play at will among the sunken graves and broken tombstones. There is everywhere a wealth of offal and garbage and beef-bones. A mangy cur was slinking among the stones, and I found a hole three feet deep which it had dug at the foot of one of the graves. . . . The whole yard is grown up to weeds and bush, and the place is desolate and dreary as can be."

Sections of the state outside of Charleston and the path of Sherman showed the ravages of war. Raiding parties combed the low-country on missions of pillage and destruction. Many of them were made doubly terrible to the inhabitants because of the presence of Negro troops. A member of the Sinkler family gives an illustration of the conduct of these Negroes as enacted on her family estate, "Belvidere," at Eutaw Springs: "They broke open the smokehouse, storerooms and barns, and threw out to the Negroes all the provisions and things that they could find." Several went into the house and "began throwing things about, cursing and swearing, lashing carriage whips about our heads, and saying 'Damned rebels' very often; also kicking open doors, and thrusting their bayonets into closets and wardrobes, tearing off desk doors and evidently looking for wine and silver."[16] Many houses were burned after being sacked.[17] The fate of St. Andrew's Parish is thus described by a committee of clergymen: "The demon of civil war was let loose in the parish. But three residences exist in the whole space between the Ashley and Stono rivers. Fire and sword were not enough. Family vaults were rifled, and coffins of the dead forced open in pursuit of plunder."[18]

Confederate troops were guilty of some destruction. On

[15] *The South Since the War*, pp. 1, 10-11.
[16] Elizabeth Allen Coxe, *Memories of a South Carolina Plantation*, pp. 44-46.
[17] *Two Diaries from Middle St. John's, Berkeley*, pp. 11, 19, 22-23.
[18] *Report of the Destruction of Churches in the Diocese of South Carolina*, p. 8.

evacuating a position they usually destroyed cotton and other supplies and were unable to restrain the predatory instincts of the rabble. For example, on the eve of Sherman's occupation of Columbia cotton was fired in the streets;[19] the bridge over the Saluda was burned; Wheeler's men pillaged stores; and due to the carelessness of a band of plunderers, the South Carolina Railroad Depot took fire.[20] Moreover, Confederate raiding parties were active. "From Augusta to Hardeeville," wrote a citizen concerning the conduct of Wheeler's troops, "the road is now strewn with corn, left on the ground unconsumed. Beeves have been shot down in the field, one quarter taken off and the balance left for the buzzards. Horses are stolen out of wagons on the roads, and by wholesale out of stables at night. . . . It is no unusual sight to see these men riding into camp with all sorts of plunder. Private houses are visited; carpets, blankets and other furniture . . . are taken by force in the presence of the owners."[21] "I am sorry to say," remarked a lady of the low-country, "that Wheeler's men have done us more damage than the Yankees. . . . I do blame them very much for their wanton destruction of property they ought to protect. It is a shame and they ought to be exposed."[22]

*   *   *   *   *

The description of the effect of fire and shells on property is only a partial measure of the evil influences of war on South Carolina. There were other causes which injured economic and social life. First, there was the influence of the blockade; second, the necessities of war had prompted the neglect of processes of production essential to the normal functioning of the community; third, there was a great sacrifice of man power; fourth, most of the surplus wealth was expended in the cause

[19] According to the testimony of Major Chambliss, a Confederate ordnance officer.—James Ford Rhodes, *History of the United States*, V, 91-92.

[20] Simms, pp. 11-12.

[21] "Omega" to J. A. Siddon, Dec. 31, 1864, cited in *Courier*, Jan. 13, 1865.

[22] Charlotte St. Julian Ravenel, April 4, 1865, in *Two Diaries from Middle St. John's, Berkeley*, p. 42.

of the Confederacy and the defeat blasted hopes of its future redemption; fifth, the social discipline of the community was disrupted by the destruction of slavery.

The cutting off of most foreign trade by the Federal blockade had an evil effect upon a state so dependent for many of its necessities upon the exchange of cotton. Charleston, which had been the leading seaport of the southeast, lost its air of prosperity. "We have suffered severely; we are suffering now," said the *Charleston Daily Courier,* November 25, 1861. "Property represents painfully uncertain sums. Business of all kinds is prostrated, fortunes have been swept away, and we have been forced to restrict our wants within the limits of mere comforts." Although the profits of blockade-running were high, success was rare and promoted so much speculation and extravagance that many held that more harm than good was done.[23] Many ordinary commodities became very scarce. Patriotic citizens had felt the necessity of offering window weights and church bells to supply the deficiency of metals for war purposes, and in 1863 an advertisement announcing that no orders for a particular almanac could be filled unless fifty reams of printing paper could be purchased.[24] "Tea," said the *Charleston Daily Courier,* "is beyond reach."[25] The Reverend A. Toomer Porter told of children with yellow fever pleading for ice when none could be had.[26]

The plight into which the ordinary conveniences of living fell is illustrated by the fate of means of communication. Early in the struggle the use of artificial waterways was given up, and roads and causeways, because of neglect or overuse, fell into disrepair. Toward the end of the war a few army wagons and ambulances were about the only vehicles which remained fit. Horses and mules, and the provender necessary for their support, became "scarce and dear." The railroads fell

[23] Rhodes, V, 399, 401-2.
[24] *Ibid.,* 358.
[25] Apr. 2, 1862.
[26] *Led On! Step by Step,* pp. 149-50.

into disrepair and cars and locomotives became dilapidated.[27]
The hardships of railroad travel are illustrated by the experiences of a traveler from Richmond to Charleston. This journey, which can be made today in ten hours, then took forty-one.
At Florence the traveler's train was detained by the breakdown
of another, and when his was ready to move, he was forced to
fight his way "into some desperately crowded cars."[28]

A fundamental element of decay was the deterioration of
the soil. This was caused by too great a concentration on
staple crops, without sufficient attention either to renewal by
means of fertilizers, or to soil conservation by means of such
ditching and terracing as would prevent the washing away of
top soil. Grass was allowed to take the fields, gates and bars
tumbled down, ditches caved in, and plows became worn.
Cotton seed, because of the failure to maintain the proper system of selection, became "generally defective and unreliable."[29]
These circumstances account in part for a general decline in
land values of 60 per cent between 1860 and 1867,[30] and for
the fall in value of all farm properties, according to the defective census of 1870,[31] from $169,738,630 to $47,628,175 during
the ten years following 1860.

Another deplorable loss, even if considered only from an
economic viewpoint, was the sacrifice of man-power made in
the cause of the Confederacy. Of the state's arms-bearing population of 55,046, some 44,000 volunteered; and ultimately some
71,000, including those over and under age, entered the service.
The state lost 12,922 killed in battle or died of wounds. This
was 23 per cent of its arms-bearing population—a sacrifice
greater than that of any other state and most appalling when

[27] W. L. Trenholm, in *Handbook of
S. C., 1883*, p. 637.
[28] The experiences of A. J. L. Free-
mantle, in Rhodes, V, 387.
[29] "Juhl" (J. J. Fleming), *Courier*, May
4, 1866, and "S," in *Southern Cultivator*,

XXV (May, 1867), 140-41.
[30] *Annual Report of the Commissioner
of Agriculture, 1867*, pp. 105-19.
[31] As given in the *Census of 1910*, VII,
494-95.

compared with the 10 per cent average loss of all Confederate armies and the 5 per cent average loss of all Union armies.[32] When it is considered that these losses came from actual or prospective breadwinners, from the fathers and sons of families most of whose women were not accustomed to the pursuit of gainful occupations, and at a time when baffling social and economic problems demanded every ounce of energy, no further elaboration is needed to realize the tragic consequences. This statement is made without attempting to estimate the deleterious effect of the cutting off of the flower of white manhood on the hereditary qualities of future generations. Perhaps it can be concluded that the lack of distinctive achievements by South Carolinians since the war is in no small measure due to this loss.

On the top of other calamities was the collapse of the financial resources of the state. "It is difficult for those who are away," said the *Charleston Daily Courier*, "to understand the utter pecuniary prostration in which the war has left this section of the country. . . . It is as if at a single word and in a single moment the issues of every state and national bank and of the government should prove without value or effect, and the people, instead of currency, should find that they had as representative of toil and years of labor and hard-earned competency, pieces of waste paper. . . . Nearly every mode of investment shared the same fate. Confederate securities had absorbed the greater part of the gold, and almost every representative of value. . . . All that was practically left of the wealth in the country was the mere lands."[33] The *Charleston Daily News* said in a survey[34] that $15,000,000 in bank stock,[35] the endow-

---

[32] William F. Fox, *Regimental Losses in the American Civil War*, pp. 554-55. Other estimates are *Handbook of S. C., 1908*, p. 22, and John Johnson in *Centennial Edition of News and Courier*, p. 93.

[33] July 7, 1865.

[34] Cited in Winnsboro *Tri-Weekly News*, Sept. 12, 1865.

[35] Governor Orr in 1867 estimated that the banking resources of Charleston had fallen from $14,000,000 to $400,000, that is, to one thirty-fifth of its former value, *News*, Apr. 3, 1867. Later another writer said this decline was to one twenty-sixth, "Mercador," *ibid.*, Dec. 5, 1868.

ments of colleges and charitable institutions, and all of the resources of the state's three insurance companies, as well as the
$200,000,000 invested in the state's 400,000 slaves, had been lost.
This newspaper estimated that the gross property values of the
state had shrunk from $400,000,000 to $50,000,000 since 1860,
that is, to one-eighth.[36] No wonder the *Charleston Daily
Courier* said, "The condition of things has been like the dead
sea fruit—fair and bright in appearance, but within full of
bitterness and ashes."[37]

*   *   *   *   *

Added to these losses was the partial disruption of the
state's social and industrial economy caused by the sudden
breaking of the ties which bound more than half its population
—402,406 in number in 1860—to the habits and industries of
slavery. This was a loss which can be only partly estimated in
figures. Slavery was the driving force of the state's industrial
and social life; it was the institution which made South Carolina different from the states of the North; it was the principal
reason why the white manhood of the state had fought so desperately. The confusion caused by its destruction left an impression upon the community more lasting than that left by
the pillaging and burning already described. The latter involved the destruction of physical objects and their replacement
by ordinary efforts; the abolition of slavery involved the destruction of habits and emotions and their replacement by new
habits and emotions, creative labor difficult alike to ex-master
and ex-slave.

It is a remarkable fact that during the war the blacks manifested no general desire to become free. The only occurrence

[36] Governor Orr, *ibid.*, July 11, 1868,
estimated that during the war one-half of
property values had been lost and that in
the three years following there had been
a loss of one-half the remainder. The
census of 1870 gave the property values
at that time as $183,000,000 as compared
with $480,000,000 in 1860, but Professor
R. Means Davis estimated the "true
shrinkage" within those dates from about
$550,000,000 to a little over $100,000,000,
that is, to one-fifth.—*Handbook of S. C.,
1883*, p. 535.

[37] July 7, 1865.

which had a suggestion of servile insurrection was that of runaway slaves firing on Confederate pickets on Edisto Island in 1862. But if their object was insurrection it is not apparent from the evidence adduced at the trial.[38] The flight of the "Planter," a boat used by the Confederates in Charleston Harbor, into the lines of the Federal blockade squadron, under the command of Robert Smalls, is usually cited as evidence that slaves were willing to go to great risks to gain freedom. But, said a Northerner resident at Port Royal, "the secret of such exploits as the crew of the 'Planter' have lately performed lies in the fact that the men were forcibly taken from this region last November and wanted to get back home. If their old homes had been Charleston, they would not have left it at the risks incurred."[39] Certain of the hymns or spirituals composed at this time have been interpreted as indicating a longing for freedom; but, said a close student of these compositions, they expressed "nothing but patience for this life— nothing but triumph in the next."[40] All slaves, except a few which fled to the Union lines, remained faithful to their masters. "The Negroes," said a woman who passed the winter of 1862-1863 in the low-country, "were perfectly subordinate, and worked as steadily as though no gunboats were at the mouth of the river."[41]

Why were the Negroes so hesitant in accepting opportunities for freedom? They had reason to fear dire punishment from their masters if they revolted.[42] Slavery had many features which commended itself to the Negroes. It was closely intertwined with their religion, morality, and ways of making

[38] Rhodes, V, 460.
[39] E. S. Philbrick in letter of June 3, 1862, in Pearson, *Letters from Port Royal*, p. 63.
[40] Thomas W. Higginson, *Army Life in a Black Regiment*, p. 202.
[41] Claudine Rhett, in *Our Women in the War*, p. 13.

[42] On Mar. 26, 1865, while the army of invasion was enforcing freedom, twenty-seven slave insurrectionists were executed by the Confederates near Pooshee Plantation in Berkeley District.—*Two Diaries from Middle St. John's, Berkeley*, p. 40.

a living. They felt that the adventure in freedom involved many hardships which would not have come had there been no disturbance of the social order. They knew, said a friend of freedom, that these changes were full of tremendous import to them, and they were watchful and anxious. They, in their ignorance and helplessness, were crying out in agony, "What will become of us? ... O Lord, if it so please Thee, do we pray Thee, tuck care o' we."[43]

But freedom was forced upon them by the presence of abolitionist troops, or by the knowledge that such troops would be used to break the bond unless the masters took the initiative. Soon, through an interplay of circumstances, the Negroes became endowed with the emotions of free men. Some even learned to talk the language of New England liberals. How this change was effected is one of the most interesting phenomena in South Carolina history.

The principal circumstance which contributed to this end was the dramatic suddenness with which the abolitionist troops imposed themselves and their doctrines upon the state. One morning in November, 1861, while the Negroes of the Port Royal area were picking cotton, they were startled by the firing of guns at Bay Point. Then, said Northern observers, "there was a scene of hurried flight, with wringing of hands and wailing voices; and in two days the white population vanished, leaving ... in most cases the colored people in their houses. ... Thus without a moment's notice, with no debating on the part of friends, no opposition from enemies, with no exertion and no anticipation of their own, at the boom of a gun, five thousand slaves lifted their heads and were free!"[44] "A terrible 'army with banners,' clad in blue, burnishing blades and well polished guns, an endless stream of soldiers—infantry, cavalry and artillery," marched into the interior of the state in

---

[43] Elizabeth H. Botume, *First Days amongst the Contrabands*, pp. 191-92.

[44] [Edward Everett Hale and W. C. Gannett], *North American Review*, CI (July, 1865), 15.

1865, encouraging the Negroes to engage in pillage, fraternizing with them, and telling them that they were free.[45]   The occupation of Charleston was preceded by fires and explosions which reddened the sky by night and darkened it by day, while "crowds of frightened women and children, white and black," ran wildly about the streets.[46]   The first troops who entered the city were headed by a black soldier bearing a banner inscribed with the word "Liberty." Then came the colored regiments led by the famous Fifty-fourth Massachusetts singing "John Brown's Body." Every house in the city was searched by Negro troops for the purpose of proclaiming freedom and seizing firearms and "abandoned" property.   The so-called slave pens were inscribed with mottoes from Isaiah, John Brown, and William Lloyd Garrison, and the steps of the so-called auction block were sent to Boston to excite contributions for Negro education.[47]

"It was but human nature," remarked a Columbia woman of the Negroes, "when freedom came to them so suddenly, that they should receive it so extravagantly, and go with outstretched hands to welcome their deliverers."[48]   "The Negroes became wild with joy at the defeat of the rebels," said an observer at Port Royal. "They believed the day of Jubilee had come."[49] One Negro declared, "The differences in time are so great as if God had sent another Moses and a great deliverance—that it was heaven upon earth and earth upon heaven."[50]   Illustrative of the demoralization at Columbia was the conduct of an old mauma.   As the army was leaving, she was seen seated in a stolen carriage drawn by stolen horses, dressed in an enormous headgear of ante-bellum style; and though it was Feb-

[45] Simms, pp. 51-52, and Captain Conyngham, pp. 320-21.
[46] *Courier*, Feb. 20, 1865.
[47] *N. Y. Herald*, July 19, 1865, and W. P. and F. J. Garrison, *William Lloyd Garrison*, IV, 134.
[48] Mrs. S. A Crittenden, in *South Carolina Women in the Confederacy*, I, 329-30.
[49] Botume, pp. 12-14.
[50] *Letters and Diary of Laura M. Towne*, pp. 16-17, 50. Cf. Whitelaw Reid, *After the War*, p. 116.

ruary she was fanning herself with a huge palmetto fan. A
white woman asked, "Aunt Sallie, where are you going?" "La,
honey," she replied, "I'se gwine back into the Union."[51]   At
Plantersville a certain officer traveled "in an open carriage, followed by a throng of Negroes, whooping and yelling with
joy; in response to his announcement that they were free and
that everything belonged to them." They entered vacant houses
and took what they wanted. The next day they sang a strange
song:

> "I free, I free!
> I free as a frog!
> I free till I fool!
> Glory Alleluia!"

Then they revolved around some lady's carriage, "holding out
their shirts and dancing—now with slow, swinging movements, now with rapid jig motions, but always with weird
chants and wild gestures." As they brandished their sharp and
gleaming rice hoes, they cried, "No, no, we won't let no white
pusson een, we'll chop um down wid hoe; we'll chop um to
pieces sho'."[52]

The work of the army was immediately followed by many
public gatherings at which the excited freedmen were impressed with the opportunities and duties of their new state.
Great crowds in gala dress eagerly marched to convenient oak
groves to celebrate Emancipation Day or the Fourth of July,
or to listen to memorial services in honor of the War Dead or
the Martyred Liberator. The Negroes listened eagerly to the
"beautiful preachments" of army officers, visiting clergymen,
distinguished politicians, and precocious members of their own
race, on patriotic and moral themes. They heard, for example,
Henry Ward Beecher, standing on the parapet of Fort Sumter,
exult over the fall of Charleston, denounce the so-called ruling

[51] *S. C. Women in the Confederacy*, I,
330.
    [52] Elizabeth W. Allston Pringle, *Chron-
icles of Chicora Wood*, pp. 254-73.

class of South Carolina, and affirm the morality of the cause which had just triumphed in battle. There was "no reserve or restraint in the general flow of tears" when William Lloyd Garrison addressed the freedmen at Charleston. "I am here in Charleston, South Carolina," he said. "The chalice has been put to her lips, and she drank it to the dregs. . . . I have been a friend of the South, and in the desire to save her from greatest retribution, demanded in the name of the living God that every fetter should be broken, and the oppressed set free." As he left for the North, the Negroes loaded him with roses, jasmins, honeysuckles, and cakes.[53]

A circumstance fortunate for both races was that in large sections of the state, mostly to the west of Sherman's line of march, the freeing of the Negroes was accomplished without display or violence. The slave masters of those areas, knowing what had happened in sections visited by the Federal troops, wisely acquiesced in the inevitable. "When the crisis came," said William Henry Trescot, "it found the master ready to meet it in a spirit of kindness to his former slaves." On the other hand, when the Negroes heard that freedom was coming, added Trescot, "There was no impatience, no insubordination, no violence. They have received their freedom quietly and soberly. They remained pretty steadily on the farms of their masters, a very general disposition being manifest to adjust the terms of compensation on a reasonable basis."[54]

*　　*　　*　　*　　*

Under the prevailing circumstances it was inevitable that the plight of the white people of South Carolina should have been in many respects deplorable. Their cause had been de-

---

[53] Accounts of these meetings in Pearson, pp. 68-69 and 128-29; Botume, pp. 75-76; *Courier*, Apr. 15, 1865; *Littell's Living Age*, XXIX (May 6, 1865), 183-202; *Trip of the Steamer Oceanus*, pp. 41-

70; W. P. and F. J. Garrison, *op. cit.*, IV, 136-50.

[54] *DeBow's Review*, N. S., I (Mar., 1866), 550-52.

feated, a large portion of their property had been destroyed, and they feared that their conquerors would be vindictive.

The most pressing difficulty of many was acute destitution. "I heard," said a foreign visitor to Charleston, "of one gentleman, who before the war had been unable to spend the whole of a large income, being a porter of a dry goods store; and of another, who formerly possessed everything which riches could buy, dying in such penury that his family had to ask their friends to contribute for the funeral."[55] General Richard H. Anderson was forced, until he could find more congenial employment, to work as a day laborer in the yards of the South Carolina Railroad.[56] General M. C. Butler said that he came out of the war "twenty-nine years old, with one leg gone, a wife and three children to support, seventy emancipated slaves, a debt of $15,000, and in his pocket $1.75."[57] "Poor Timrod," wrote William Gilmore Simms of the principal poet of the state, "is the very Prince of Dolefuls, and swallowed up in distresses. . . . He can earn nothing where he is [Columbia], has not a dollar, and goes to bed hungry every night, and suffers from bad health. It is the mortifying thing to all of us, *that none of us can help him.* Bruns and myself are both living from hand to mouth, and not infrequently the hand carries nothing to the cavernous receptacle."[58] "Many hundreds of our citizens, who have been accustomed to all the luxuries," wrote a nun from Charleston, "have been compelled to live on government rations. . . . Could you but see these delicate ladies in houses void of furniture, reduced to the wash-tub and the cook-pot your heart would bleed; still more when you reflect that they have no means of securing the bare necessities of life. . . . The planting population around Charleston is destitute of

[55] F. Barham Zincke, *A Winter in the U. S.*, p. 97.

[56] Irvine Walker, *Life of Anderson*, p. 241.

[57] Myrta L. Avary, *Dixie after the War*, pp. 160-61.

[58] William Peterfield Trent, *Simms*, pp. 279-93.

everything. God only knows the full tide of misery which has set in on these people."[59]

If the upper classes suffered, it was inevitable that the hardships of the common people were greater. "No one, unless having visited the hovels of the suffering poor," said the *Charleston Daily Courier,* "can form an idea of the abject poverty which prevails in our midst. . . . Hundreds of mortal beings are perishing around us each day for want of food and raiment. . . . There are numbers of white families who know not where to get their next meal."[60]

The disappointment over the outcome of the war was perhaps more depressing than the experiences of physical want. "In the remembrance of all that the South had loved and lost —loved so well and lost beyond recall," said the *Charleston Daily News,* "there were keener pangs than any that could arise from ruined fields and desolated hills."[61] "We are shattered and stunned," wrote Mrs. Chesnut, May 16; "the remnant of heart left alive within us filled with brotherly hate. We sit and wait until the drunken tailor who rules the United States of America issues a proclamation, and defines our anomalous position." Two days later she added: "A feeling of sadness hovers over me now, day and night, no words of mine can express." June 12, she wrote: "We are shut up here, turned with our faces to a dead wall. We are cut off from the world, here to eat our hearts out."[62] Lee's surrender, said another woman, spread gloom over Charleston, and "bands of brokenhearted soldiery began to stagger into the city."[63]

A favorite pastime of Northern excursionists was to contrast the exultant spirit of Charleston in 1861 with the gloom which prevailed four years later. Whitelaw Reid wrote, "For

[59] Sister M. Helen in letter to *Philadelphia Enquirer* cited in Winnsboro *Tri-Weekly News,* Aug. 29, 1865.
[60] June 29, 1865.
[61] Dec. 25, 1867.

[62] Mary Boykin Chesnut, *Diary from Dixie,* pp. 390, 400.
[63] Carolina Joachimson, in *Our Women in the War,* p. 40.

the flush of victory we have utter despondency. The restaurants are closed and the shutters are up; the occupants of the club rooms are dead, or in prison, or in exile. . . . Beauregard is a prisoner. . . . Huger is dead. Barnwell Rhett is in exile. . . . Governor Pickens has vanished into the dim unknown of the interior. . . . In the course of a whole afternoon's driving about the city, I do not see a single one whom I could have supposed belonged to a leading family."[64] "Here is," wrote Sidney Andrews, "enough of woe and want and ruin and ravage to satisfy the most insatiate heart. . . . One marks how few young men there are, and how generally the young women are dressed in black."[65]

The most profound pessimism prevailed concerning the possibility of satisfactory existence with the Negroes as freedmen. It was generally believed that the Negro, although a human being, innately lacked the qualities necessary to exercise the privileges of freedom on the level of a people with European civilization. "The Negroes," ran a typical opinion, "can only become and continue a Christian people while in close connection with and under the control of a superior race."[66] "From all history," said a philosophically inclined South Carolinian, "we infer that God has given the Negro a tendency to thrive and multiply in a condition of servitude. . . . In freedom he has shown a tendency to deteriorate."[67] General Carl Schurz, in his journey through the state in 1865, was told by all whites whom he met that the Negro without compulsion would not perform manual labor, the one function thought proper to him.[68]

* * * * *

From what has been said it should not be assumed that the whites lacked weapons of defense against their conquerors.

[64] *After the War*, pp. 66-68.
[65] *The South Since the War*, pp. 2, 9-10.
[66] *The Land We Love*, II (Nov., 1866), 9.
[67] Gabriel Manigault, *ibid.*, V (Aug., 1868), 300-1.
[68] *Reminiscences*, III, 159-62.

Not all were without material resources. They inherited a tradition of social and economic dominance, and ultimately, through a subtle interplay of patriotism, hopefulness, adaptability, and craftiness, were able to outplay the conqueror in his endeavor to impose outside reforms.

Indeed, their material resources were extensive. In spite of threats at confiscation, except at Port Royal they remained the owners of the land. An unfolding of new agricultural possibilities was a partial compensation for the great decrease in land values. All the tools of production were not destroyed. Charleston was only a partial wreck, and the great up-country had been scarcely touched by the hand of the invader. The railroads, although greatly injured, were not a total loss. Many miles in the eastern and western part of the state had not been touched, and where Sherman had done his work, the roadbeds remained as bases on which the work of rebuilding could be readily pushed. Eleven of the eighteen cotton factories of the state had not been demolished, and the demands of war had in a measure stimulated the textile industry.[69]

Certain circumstances tended to ameliorate the fact that the accepted medium of exchange had suddenly become worthless. The sale of the 130,000 bales of cotton[70] which had been saved from destruction was a means of replenishing the coffers of many penniless persons. Many, especially in the up-country, had hoarded gold and silver because of suspicion of Confederate currency and because of inability to buy what they desired from the outside world. The Federal garrisons and the Negroes, who were receiving wages and the benefits of Northern charity, added to the supply of money by purchasing freely in the local markets.

As a consequence of these facts trade began to revive as early as June, 1865. "Purchasers of cotton and rice," declared

[69] Marjorie Potwin, *Cotton Mills of the Piedmont,* p. 28, and Rhodes, V, 422-23.

[70] Estimate of *Courier,* June 13, 1865.

the *Charleston Daily Courier,* "appear to be reaping a rich harvest. . . . Men of capital are coming from the North by every steamer in view of investing in cotton and rice. We are glad to see such a lively trade in South Carolina; it benefits everyone."[71]   George W. Williams, an enterprising merchant of Charleston, was able to resume business operations which bid fair to make him wealthy. The Reverend A. Toomer Porter demonstrated the possibilities of trade. He journeyed from Charleston to Anderson with a quantity of "Yankee notions," and so eager were the people to buy that, in an improvised store, he was able to take in $800 in one day.[72]

The whites faced their difficulties with a superb courage. "The plucky way in which our men keep up," wrote Mrs. Chesnut, "is beyond praise. There is no howling, and our poverty is a matter of laughing."[73]   A correspondent of a Northern newspaper said of the people of South Carolina, "While clouds were dark and threatening, I do not believe there was ever in the world's history a people who bear their afflictions with more philosophy and Christian fortitude than those unfortunate people."[74]   Women cheerfully turned to the kitchen and men to manual labor. A philosophy of hard work and close economy was preached, and every expedient which might lead out of the impasse of poverty and social stagnation was suggested. When it became evident that the new day would afford new opportunities, men became so optimistic that they predicted the development of a new society which would afford more wealth and happiness than the one which had been destroyed.

The experiences of the white people of South Carolina fitted them admirably for the adjustments which Reconstruction forced upon them. During the war the men had become used to the hardships of camp life, and the women had learned to

[71] June 24, 1865. Cf. *ibid.,* May 27, June 30, and July 16, 1865.
[72] *Led On! Step by Step,* p. 203.
[73] *Op. cit.,* p. 380.
[74] *N. Y. Express* quoted in *Fairfield Herald,* Jan. 9, 1867.

manage the plantations, maintain the slave discipline, and endure privations.   Certainly there were no grounds for the conventional belief, fostered by the romantic friends and enemies of the South, that the whites of South Carolina emerged from the war a lazy people given to lolling in hammocks and helpless unless administered to by faithful blacks.

But their patience and adaptability were limited by the consciousness that they had strength.   Of course all recognized that the Southern armies were defeated, that the Negro was free, and that the Union was restored.   A considerable number, under the fear of summary punishment, were willing to repudiate the Confederacy with unseemly haste.[75]   A very few— the first scalawags—were willing to adopt the beliefs of the conquerors.   For the great majority, however, the tragic outcome of the war but increased the hatred of the Yankees, made Southern doctrines more dear, and invested the war leaders with the aureole of heroism.   Only the minimum demands of the foe were to be submitted to, and as soon as it became clear that the North was not going to be as vindictive as some imagined, every reform suggested from the outside was contested with all the strength at hand.

In this struggle the whites generally had competent leadership.   From the old régime they inherited leaders who were experienced and who had lost many of their "fire-eating" qualities through the sobering influences of defeat.   They were usually able to hold the passions of their followers in check.   When these passions broke loose, usually to accomplish purposes with which the leaders were sympathetic, they knew how to avoid punishment from Washington by making the worse appear the better.

Perhaps the principal strength of the whites lay in the assertiveness of the common country people.   From early days this

[75] For evidence of this see Capt. Conyngham, pp. 312, 319-20, and Winnsboro *Tri-Weekly News,* Sept. 28 and Dec. 2, 1865.

class had dwelt on lands of their own, had developed a contempt for the Negro except as a menial, and had never been deferential, in the manner of European peasants, to the slave-holding leaders. Although for the most part indifferent to literary culture, they had a thorough understanding of local conditions and were possessed of gifts of imagination and character responsible for much of the enterprise and stability of the commonwealth. They had proved their capacity for endurance and bravery in the Confederate army. They stood ready to terrorize Yankees or Negroes when members of either class had the temerity to attempt to upset traditional social arrangements.

*   *   *   *   *

The Negro's equipment for the experiences of Reconstruction was far less adequate than that of the white man. It is true that the war had been won for his supposed benefit; that he did not have cause to mourn the loss of relations and property; and that he could rejoice in the gain of some things. Nevertheless, he was wretchedly deficient in many of the assets necessary for the competent exercise of the rights of freedom.

In the first place, he was very poor. He inherited no property from slavery, and, as we shall see, the attempts to endow him with lands created little else but confusion and false hopes. The utter poverty in which many Negroes emerged into freedom is conveyed by the following description of a band of refugees. They were, said a Northerner, "partly covered with every conceivable thing that could be put on the back of a biped. Some of the women had on old, cast-off soldiers' coats and 'crocus bags,' fastened together with their own ravellings, for shirts, and bits of sailcloth for head-handkerchiefs. Many of the men had strips of gay carpeting, or old bags, or pieces of blanket, in which they cut arm-holes and wore as jackets.

Their pants were tied below and above the knees and around the waist with pieces of rope to keep them on."[76]

Perhaps a greater weakness of the freedmen than poverty was their previous lack of the experience necessary to exercise with sagacity the opportunities which a great revolution had brought to them. Under slavery there had been no illicit social clubs, no hoarding of wealth, little training in the exercise of individual initiative. This meant that many phases of the institutional life of the race had to be built from the ground up. It was inevitable that much confusion would be created from the following of false suggestions and that much of the rejoicing with which freedom was celebrated would be but an effervescence which hid feelings of bewilderment. That the race was able to survive the ordeal of freedom was due more to its large numbers and to the blind instinct of self-preservation than to acquired social habits.

But it should not be concluded that the Negro was altogether devoid of qualities helpful in his new situation. He was capable of hard manual labor and had a knowledge of farming and certain industrial crafts. His taste for strong drink was not so avid as that of the whites, and he knew how to live on little. In a restricted sense he had the white man's powers of adaptability; he had been moved about as a slave and knew how to make the most out of that hardship. He possessed temperamental qualities which were helpful. Whatever may have been his boasts in moments of excitement, the Negro was usually too wise or too timid to attempt actions beyond his powers. He was seldom vindictive, failing to let blood in situations which would have provoked the white man to violence. He was not likely to go to such extremes in contests as to endanger the friendship between the two races to a degree

[76] Elizabeth H. Botume, p. 32. Cf. J. T. Trowbridge, *The South*, pp. 537-38; General Rufus Saxton, in *Courier*, Jan. 31, 1866; and W. P. and F. J. Garrison, *op. cit.*, IV, 149.

which would make him intolerable to the dominant race. He was capable of an almost pathetic loyalty to old associations. Moreover, he was contented under conditions which would have made a more sensitive race miserable. He knew how to dance and sing in the midst of physical distress; and he could almost turn a funeral into an occasion of joy; he could give rags the semblance of a fancy dress.

Nor was the race altogether devoid of the higher equipment of civilization. A majority of the 9,914 free persons of color in the state in 1860 knew how to read and write, and many of those in the city of Charleston had acquired considerable property.[77] A small number of the slaves—about 5 per cent—knew how to read and write. The race was adept in imitating the whites—in dress, in manners, and in speech. A few exhorters had had experience as religious leaders. Others had closely observed the habits of white politicians and, when the occasion arose, were going to prove political organizers and orators of ability.

*   *   *   *   *

At the end of the war Northern agents were ready to use their power over the conquered state to carry out their programs. At first blush it looked as if the measures to be adopted would be severe punishment for the community which more than any other was held responsible for the alleged crimes of secession and slavery. When Phillips Brooks heard of the destruction of Columbia he wrote, in a letter to his brother, "Hurrah for Columbia! Isn't Sherman a gem?"[78] Henry Ward Beecher said at Fort Sumter, "We look upon this shattered fort and yonder dilapidated city with sad eyes, grieved that men should have committed such treason, and glad that God hath set a mark upon treason, that all ages shall

[77] Out of the 3,237, 337 paid $12,015 in taxes on property assessed at $888,650. —Theodore D. Jervey, *The Slave Trade, Slavery and Color*, pp. 327-28.
[78] Rhodes, VI, 98.

dread and abhor it."[79] The New York *Independent* said, "Boastful and braggart Charleston. . . . Terrible is the self-inflicting retribution which an All-Wise Providence has decreed against this cockatrice's den. . . . O fallen Babylon! O elegant city of lies, rear a monument to thy shame."[80] The *Chicago Tribune* breathed vengeance. "If ever a people deserved extermination and banishment," it said, "it was the unprincipled, obstinate, ignorant and treacherous ruling class of South Carolina."[81] Moreover, many were dubious over the possibility of reforming the rulers of the state. "Perhaps it would be accurate to say," remarked Whitelaw Reid, "few could be found less treasonable than the majority of South Carolinians."[82]

One might infer from such language that it was the purpose of the victors to impose vengeance for vengeance's sake on the unhappy commonwealth. But their intentions were more benevolent. They merely wished to eradicate the supposed sins of the state and substitute New England liberalism. No one was to be punished unless he stood in the way of the program of regeneration. Almost all the harsh words quoted in the preceding paragraph were accompanied with advice as to how the happiness of the state could be promoted. It was suggested that the New England concepts of morality, small farms, and free schools be adopted; that the landed aristocracy be eliminated; that all semblances of secession, slavery, and class distinctions be eradicated; and that universal political democracy be inaugurated.

But the application of this program was scarcely less trying on the vanquished than would have been a policy of outright vengeance. The sweeping accusations made against the state's standard of civilization; the tactless manner in which it was

---

[79] *Littell's Living Age*, XXIX (May 6, 1865), 194.

[80] Cited in *Southern Christian Advocate*, Apr. 6, 1865.

[81] Cited in *Courier*, Dec. 20, 1865.

[82] *After the War*, 75. Similar statements in New York *Nation*, III (July 12, 1866), 31; Sidney Andrews, *The South Since the War*, 37; and citations in *Courier*, July 29, 1865.

proposed that the reforms be applied; the breaking of social ties which these reforms would involve—all this seemed to South Carolinians the cruelty and insolence of a hypocritical foe. Better perhaps, they felt, would have been the sort of peace the victor would have imposed before the age of humanitarianism and social reform. Such a peace would have demanded as its price an indemnity and the heads of some leaders; but it might not have involved chronic meddling with long established social institutions.

Several important weaknesses can be detected in the program of the conquerors. As has already been shown, the whites had greater powers of resistance than was imagined, and the Negroes were incapable of living up to expectations. The proposals for the regeneration of the community were far too simple for a state with as complicated a social history as South Carolina. And perhaps they were not what the state needed. Moreover, the North was confused in counsels. There was always danger of the Democrats' regaining power and undoing what had been accomplished. The interference of the national government in the internal affairs of a state violated a cherished constitutional principle; sooner or later this principle was bound to reassert itself. Lastly, the motives of the interventionists contained the seeds of their undoing. Those who acted from self-interest became corrupt and lost Northern support. Those who were disinterested either joined the self-seekers or retired from the field when their emotional enthusiasm subsided. No vital motives of self-interest sustained the interest of the North as a whole in the affairs of the state. It was easy for the average Northerner to forget South Carolina when the war emotions began to subside and when it was realized how difficult were the problems of Reconstruction.

CHAPTER II

PROVISIONAL RECONSTRUCTION

SHORTLY after the surrender of the Confederate armies
General Q. A. Gillmore, the Federal commander at Hilton
Head, made determined efforts to establish his authority over
the state. He informed Governor Magrath that the governor's
efforts to restore the government which had existed under the
Confederacy would not be recognized and that his attempts to
distribute Confederate stores "among persons, who by persistent treason on the part of their leaders, have been reduced to
a condition of abject pauperism," was a "senseless and fruitless
attempt at revolution."[1] A few days later the governor was
arrested by a party of troops sent to Columbia and thrown into
prison at Fort Pulaski, where he remained for seven months.[2]
The state was divided into nine military sub-districts in which
were placed garrisons sufficient for emergencies. Provision
was made for the trial by military commissions of persons accused of serious crimes; those accused of the lesser offences were
to be tried by the provost courts created in each military sub-
district and composed of an army officer and two "loyal" local
citizens. To look after the problems of the Negroes, the Freedmen's Bureau was created and the state was divided into six
districts of that agency, over each of which was placed an official known as sub-assistant commissioner. General Rufus Saxton, who had been in charge of the freedmen at Port Royal,
was made the state chief of the Bureau with the title of assistant
commissioner. His headquarters were at Beaufort.[3]

The satisfactory manner in which the troops reëstablished

---

[1] *Courier*, May 19, 1865.

[2] *Ibid.*, May 29, 1865, and LeRoy F.
Youmans, *Sketch of Andrew Gordon*

Magrath, pp. 8-9.

[3] See Gillmore's order of June 27, 1865,
in *Courier*, July 7, 1865.

public order excited general admiration. All persons well disposed toward the national government were assured protection and the people were asked to reopen schools, churches, and shops.[4] Fifty teams and two hundred laborers were employed to clean the Charleston streets, and by June 25, some thirty thousand loads of garbage had been removed.[5] Colonel William Gurney, who was in command at Charleston, warned the large number of freedmen who had congregated in that city of the necessity of returning to the farms, and when his advice did not produce the desired results, he asked ward committees to report "the names of all able-bodied idle persons" so that they might be put to work on the streets.[6] When riots broke out between Negro troops and local whites, weapons were seized and white troops armed with clubs, were detailed to keep the Negroes in order.[7] "The troops on garrison duty at this post," was a typical comment from the interior, "are gentlemanly and courteous, and by their conduct entitle themselves to the good opinion of the citizens."[8]

Both the Freedmen's Bureau and the army made strenuous efforts to relieve physical distress. In Charleston a committee composed of George W. Williams, ex-Governor Aiken, and Albert G. Mackey was appointed to distribute army stores, and Northern charitable agencies sent supplies for the relief of the stricken city.[9] By the end of September the Freedmen's Bureau was distributing rations to 10,644 persons of both races in Georgia and South Carolina.[10] Stranded persons were sent home. Those able to walk were sent on foot, but those unable to do so were sent on government transports and com-

[4] Ibid., Feb. 20, 27 and 28, and Mar. 10, 1865.

[5] Ibid., Mar. 31 and June 26, 1865.

[6] Ibid., Apr. 5 and June 2, 1865.

[7] N. Y. Herald, in Winnsboro Tri-Weekly News, July 29, 1865.

[8] Ibid., June 20, 1865.

[9] Courier, Feb. 20 and Mar. 14, 1865.

[10] House Ex. Doc., 39th Cong., 1st Sess., No. 11, pp. 26-29. During the eleven months following June 1, 1865, the Bureau gave 987,703 rations to the freedmen of the state and 124,144 rations to the whites.—Laura J. Webster, The Operation of the Freedmen's Bureau in S. C.

NEGRO CHILDREN BEING FED BY THE MILITARY AUTHORITIES AT HILTON HEAD

mandeered trains.[11] By December, sixteen physicians and twenty-nine attendants were busy attending the sick in several hospitals, with a capacity of 1,530 patients, and as many as 9,000 blacks and 1,600 whites were reported to have received medical attention.[12]

Other actions of the Federal government, however, were of a type which did not meet the approval of the local whites. They were told that the national authority must receive their primary allegiance. "All persons expressing disloyal sentiments," General A. S. Hartwell told the people of Orangeburg, "will expect summary punishment and no favors."[13] The wearing of Confederate uniforms was prohibited, and all persons were directed to give up arms in their possession.[14] So-called loyalists were given office in preference to persons held in greater local esteem.[15]

The greatest dissatisfaction was manifest over the seizure of property. The Port Royal plantations were sold to satisfy part of the $363,570.67 tax imposed upon South Carolina under the act of Congress levying a direct tax upon the property of the nation.[16] Since at the end of the war these lands had yielded only $11,523.61 of the state's apportionment, Charleston and its environs were made subject to the direct tax, and by February 10, 1866, had been forced to contribute $185,000.[17] Under act of Congress authorizing the seizure of "abandoned property," that is, property from which "the lawful owner thereof shall be voluntarily absent therefrom, and engaged . . . in aiding or encouraging the rebellion,"[18] considerable property was taken possession of when Charleston

[11] A correspondent of the N. Y. *Nation* reported in November that some 250 were moved each week.—*Ibid.*, 139-40.

[12] *House Ex. Doc.*, 39th Cong., 1st Sess., No. 11, pp. 19-21.

[13] *Courier*, June 8, 1865. Cf. Feb. 23 and 28, 1865.

[14] *Ibid.*, Feb. 24, 1865.

[15] Dr. Albert G. Mackey became collector of the port of Charleston and Frederick A. Sawyer collector of internal revenue.

[16] *Stat. U. S.*, XII, 422-26, and report of Direct Tax Commissioner W. E. Wording in *Courier*, May 14, 1866.

[17] *Ibid.*, Feb. 16 and May 20, 1866.

[18] *Stat. U. S.*, XIII, 375-78.

was occupied, and turned over to treasury agents. The most extensive seizures were effected under the famous Field Order No. 15 of General Sherman. By it all the sea islands from Charleston to Port Royal, and the adjoining lands to the distance of thirty miles inland, were set aside for the use of the Negroes who had followed his army.[19]

The Federal cotton policy was very trying on the people. Treasury agents were authorized to seize cotton which had belonged to the Confederate government. But since they were allowed 25 per cent on the returns of their catches, they took full advantage of the confusion of the times and the difficulties of establishing titles, seizing much cotton which belonged to private persons.[20] Another hardship was a Federal tax on cotton ranging from two to three cents a pound for a period of three years. In 1866 it was estimated that this tax was equivalent to an annual tribute of three dollars each on all the inhabitants of the state.[21]

Along with these exactions went meddlesome interferences into types of inter-racial relations which heretofore had been regulated solely by the whites. Efforts were made to prescribe the conditions under which the Negroes worked, to give them literary instruction, and to inspire them with social and political ambitions. The last of these topics will be discussed presently; the other two are reserved for future chapters.

*   *   *   *   *

Smarting under the burden of military rule, the whites pursued a policy designed to get relief from President Johnson. First, they became thoroughly peaceful. "Not one among the marvelous events of the war," said a correspondent of the New York *Nation* in July, "seems to me more marvelous than the almost perfect tranquillity into which South Carolina has

[19] Order in *Records of the Rebellion*, Ser. I, Vol. XLVII, Pt. 2, pp. 60-62. Sherman's explanation of its meaning in letter to President Johnson cited in *Courier*, Feb. 7, 1866. See below, p. 227.
[20] *Ibid.*, July 6, 1866, and Walter L. Fleming, *Sequel to Appomattox*, pp. 9-11.
[21] *Fairfield Herald*, Oct. 24, 1865.

returned."[22] Second, there was a frank acknowledgment of the defeat of the Confederacy and the restoration of the Union. "We have failed to establish our nationality," wrote James L. Orr in May, "and there can be no wrong or disorder in our accepting facts as they exist, and yield obedience to national authority."[23] That this expressed the opinions of the majority was attested by Northern visitors.[24] Third, meetings were held in various localities asking the President to restore civil government. He was told, "We admit that the principle for which the late war was waged failed, and that we have gone under. . . . The deprivation of civil government opposes the energies of the people, creates distrust and diminishes commercial enterprise."[25] The Charleston gathering appointed a committee, headed by Judge Edward Frost, to go to Washington to ask the establishment of provisional civil government such as the President had given other Southern states. The committee told him that the South was "defeated and conquered by the North," and that "the old delusion" of slavery and states' rights was no more.[26]

President Johnson responded graciously to the overtures of the South Carolinians. On May 20, he issued a proclamation extending amnesty to former Confederates who took the oath to support the Constitution and the Union and the presidential proclamations respecting slavery. From this pardon, however, were excepted fourteen classes of persons, the most notable of whom were those who were worth as much as twenty thousand dollars, or who had held high military or naval rank under the Confederacy. But those in the excepted classes were de-

[22] I (July 27, 1865), 106. "There certainly was no government," said the late Joseph W. Barnwell, "but it [the state of the country] was not so bad as one would think."

[23] To W. W. Boyce, in *Southern Christian Advocate*, June 29, 1865.

[24] Sidney Andrews, *The South Since the War*, p. 93, and Carl Schurz, *Reminis-*

cences, III, 159.

[25] Accounts of these gatherings in Winnsboro *Tri-Weekly News*, June 20 and 30, 1865; *Columbia Daily Phoenix*, June 14, 1865; and, *Courier*, May 12 and 25, and June 6, 17, 18, and 23, 1865.

[26] Northern newspapers' accounts of interview in Winnsboro *Tri-Weekly News*, July 8, 1865.

clared subject to individual pardon.[27] The President next
appointed provisional governors in five of the formerly rebel-
lious states with powers to assemble constitutional conventions
chosen by the "loyal" element of the population of their respective states. The test of loyalty was the taking of the oath
embodied in the amnesty proclamation.[28] W. W. Boyce, ex-
Governor Aiken, and James L. Orr, South Carolinians of
moderate views, were called into conference by the President,
and they returned home with glowing accounts of his indul-
gent attitude toward the state.[29] He asked the aforementioned
Charleston delegation to submit a list of names from which
he might select a provisional governor. From this list the
President selected Benjamin F. Perry, and on June 30, he issued
a proclamation prescribing a method for the restoration of
civil government to South Carolina identical with that already
prescribed for other Southern states.[30]

After several interviews the President and the provisional
governor came to an understanding as to how the President's
policy should be applied to South Carolina. It was agreed that
the state constitutional convention should declare slavery abolished, nullify the Ordinance of Secession, and provide for the
popular election of governor and presidential electors. The
President objected to the proposal that in the apportionment
of representation in the convention the parish arrangement of
the low-country, as well as the division of representation
equally between population and property, be respected; but he
yielded when the governor said that prudence prompted the
continuance of these traditional practices.[31] Accordingly, Perry
applied the President's reconstruction policy to South Carolina
in his proclamation of July 20. It declared in force the laws

[27] James D. Richardson, *Messages and
Papers of the Presidents*, VI, 310-12.

[28] *Ibid.*, VI, 312 ff.

[29] Winnsboro *Tri-Weekly News*, June
27 and 29, 1865.

[30] *Ibid.*, July 8, 1865; Perry, *Reminiscences of Public Men, Sec. Ser.*, p. 244;
and Richardson, VI, 326-28.

[31] Account of these interviews in Perry,
pp. 246-56.

of the state which had been enacted prior to secession and restored all state officials who had been in power at the time of the collapse of the Confederacy if they had taken the President's amnesty oath. He set the first Monday in September as the day for the election of delegates to a constitutional convention, which should meet in Columbia on September 13.[32]

What were the qualifications of Perry, the man on whom the President imposed the difficult task of bringing South Carolina back into the Union? His principal asset was that for years he had been the fiery opponent of the disunionist sentiments of his state. Upon his appointment he willingly accepted the opportunity of enlightening South Carolina concerning the wisdom of the Tennessee Unionist who had appointed him. He loudly spoke of "the madness of the Southern states in commencing the revolution" of 1860-61, and of the "fanaticism" then prevailing in the South. On the other hand, he had never been sufficiently radical to lose the respect of the Secessionists. He had adhered to the cause of the Confederacy, accepting three important civil offices under it. Moreover, he had personal qualities which were distinct assets. A man of energy, enthusiasm, and self-esteem, he accomplished the task of organizing a civil government with dispatch. His sterling character and patriotism made him immune to the opportunity for personal gain by turning scalawag.

Nevertheless, the Governor was largely responsible for the fact that his and the President's attempt to reconstruct the government of the state was one of the most dismal failures in the annals of the commonwealth. For this difficult crisis in its history the state needed an opportunist possessed of a self-effacing tact; instead it had a bigoted legalist. Perry had an absurd faith in the personal strength of Johnson, failing to appreciate the great power which the President's enemies had

[32] Winnsboro *Tri-Weekly News*, July 29, 1865.

obtained as the result of the outcome of the war and the circumstances under which Johnson had taken office. In an address delivered at Greenville shortly after he took office, Perry boldly asserted that Johnson was far more able than Lincoln to deal with the problem of reconstruction. He believed that South Carolina at that time enjoyed the immunity from outside interference which a member of the American Union ordinarily enjoys. He conceived the task of reconstruction as a simple constitutional problem involving the resumption of the traditional relation between state and nation with the sacrifice of slavery and a few legal practices. When the manifestation of new forces clearly proved that he had incorrectly read the tendencies of the times, he was too self-righteous, too passionately dedicated to what he considered right, to sacrifice principles in the interest of easy solutions.[33]

The Governor followed his proclamation of July 20 by moves which pointed to the reëstablishment of complete civil government in a short time. He convinced Hampton, and other Conservative leaders, of Johnson's magnanimity and was soon convinced that he had the backing of well-nigh all the whites of the state. When trouble was caused by the refusal of the military authorities to recognize the old judicial officers and by the objectionable conduct of Negro garrisons, he got Generals Meade and Gillmore to withdraw the Negro troops to the coast and to allow the courts jurisdiction in matters in which Negroes were not involved. Public order was assured by the organization of volunteer militia companies to supplement the work of the national troops.[34] He took energetic measures which made possible the participation of the maximum number of the former electorate in the election of del-

[33] Sketches of Perry in Winnsboro *Tri-Weekly News*, July 11 and 15, 1865; *News*, Apr. 24, 1867; and A. B. Williams in *Eminent and Representative Men of the Carolinas*, I, 69-75. His views in Winnsboro *Tri-Weekly News*, Aug. 17, 1865, and Perry, *op. cit.*, pp. 238-41.

[34] *Ibid.*, pp. 260-62, 270-73 and 285-86; *Courier*, Sept. 5, 1865; and Winnsboro *Tri-Weekly News*, Sept. 9, 1865.

egates to the constitutional convention. When the military tried to prevent local magistrates from carrying out his instructions to administer the oath, Governor Perry appealed to Washington and got an order restraining military interference. Largely through his efforts the President extended special pardons to 845 South Carolinians who were in the classes excepted from the amnesty proclamation.[35]

The election of delegates to the constitutional convention created scarcely as much interest as a legislative election in normal times. Only one-third of the normal vote was cast in Charleston, and in five parishes of the low-country and in many precincts of the up-country no elections were held.[36] There were no protests in Conservative circles, since the electorate which had held power in 1860 was protected in its privileges and clearly understood the necessity of electing only those leaders who understood the realities of the hour. The new political influences which within two years were to make politics turbulent found little expression. The only delegate who favored a plan of reconstruction more radical than that suggested by the President was elected by the Northern residents of St. Helena Parish. A ticket representing this view was presented in Charleston, but it was overwhelmingly defeated.[37]

*   *   *   *   *

The constitutional convention assembled in the Baptist Church at Columbia on the appointed day, September 13. It was composed, said Perry, of "the ablest, wisest and most distinguished men of South Carolina." Four of the members, F. W. Pickens, James L. Orr, Samuel McGowan, and Alfred Huger, enjoyed national reputations. Among the others were judges, chancellors, ex-governors, and ex-members of Con-

[35] Perry, pp. 264-88.

[36] *N. Y. Herald*, Sept. 13, 1865, and Sidney Andrews, *The South Since the War*, p. 38. Cf. "Juhl" (J. J. Fleming), in *Courier*, Sept. 6, 1865.

[37] *Ibid.*, Sept. 5, 1865, and *Journal of the Convention of 1865*, p. 159. (Hereafter referred to as *Convention Journal*.)

gress. One had been a member of the Confederate Congress, twelve had sat in the Secession Convention, twenty-five or thirty had been officers in the Confederate army, including four generals and six colonels. About twenty were either young or very old, but the majority were between forty-five and fifty-five years of age.[38]

The leaders of this body did not let personal feelings or pride lead them into the belief that this convention of "the people of South Carolina" was free to do its sovereign will in the manner of its more famous predecessors. Scant patience was shown the handful of delegates who counseled inaction in order "to await calmly the time and opportunity to effect our deliverance from unconstitutional rule." "It doesn't become South Carolina," was the wise admonition of Pickens, "to vapor or swell or strut or brag or bluster or threat or swagger. . . . She bids us bind up her wounds and pour on the oil of peace."[39] When a resolution was introduced petitioning the President to extend clemency to Jefferson Davis, "our former chief magistrate" for whose blood "the fanatics of the North . . . are shrieking," it was not passed until the inflammatory phrases were deleted.[40]

The Governor's suggestion that the Ordinance of Secession be nullified was fulfilled within two days after the assembling of the convention. Pickens' motion to this effect received the assent of 105 delegates; only A. P. Aldrich and two other delegates from Barnwell voted in the negative.[41]

Perry told the convention that slavery was "gone, dead forever, never to be revived or hoped for in the future," and that the recognition of this fact was necessary for the members of the body to redeem their amnesty oaths.[42] The committee to

[38] Perry, p. 274, and Andrews, pp. 38-40. The roll of the body in *Convention Journal*, pp. 3-4, and John S. Reynolds, *Reconstruction in S. C., 1865-1877*, pp. 15-16.

[39] Andrews, pp. 43-45.
[40] *Ibid.*, p. 55, and *Convention Journal* pp. 29-30.
[41] *Ibid.*, pp. 27-29.
[42] *Ibid.*, pp. 11-12.

whom the Governor's recommendation was referred reported a provision recognizing without qualification the *fait accompli*. But a determined minority suggested that the declaration be accompanied by the demand that the slave-owners should be compensated for their losses and that the legislature should restrain the Negroes "from engaging in any species of traffic and in any department of labor other than manual service." In answer to these proposals, Orr informed the body, on the authority of the Governor, that the President would not remove the troops or Congress receive the representatives of the state unless the unqualified abolition of slavery was recognized.[43] Accordingly, the proposed amendments were set aside, and the convention, by vote of ninety-eight to eight, simply declared: "The slaves in South Carolina having been emancipated by the action of the United States authorities, neither slavery nor involuntary servitude . . . shall ever be reëstablished in this state."[44]

The convention failed to fulfill the third obligation which the President imposed upon the states under process of reconstruction.[45] It refused to repudiate the war debt. Perry did not recommend that this be done, and the body willingly fell into his way of thinking. When Secretary of State Seward, in the name of the President, called the Governor's attention to the omission, he replied that no action could be taken since the convention had adjourned.[46]

The Governor was very much interested in making the political order of the state more representative of the white democracy. "It is a reproach to South Carolina abroad," he told the convention, "that her constitution is less popular and republican in its provisions than that of any other state in the

[43] Debate in *Courier*, Sept. 22, 1865, and Perry, p. 227.
[44] *Convention Journal*, pp. 59-61.
[45] See his instructions to Governor Holden of North Carolina in Fleming, *Sequel to Appomattox*, p. 77. South Carolina was the only one of these states which did not repudiate the war debt .
[46] Correspondence between Perry and Seward in *Courier*, Dec. 13, 1865.

Union." He suggested that the election of governor and presidential electors be taken from the legislature and given to the people; that secret voting in the legislature be done away with; and that the "parish system" of representation in the state senate be abolished. Under this arrangement, each of the parishes into which the judicial districts of the low-country were divided was given a senator, while the middle and upper districts, which had no parishes, were given only one senator each. A parish with twenty or thirty votes, said Perry, had as much representation as Edgefield District with three thousand votes. He favored one senator for each judicial district, except Charleston, which should have two. But in fairness to the low-country he advocated that the practice of apportioning half the representation in the lower house according to population and half according to property be continued.[47]

These proposals reopened the historic controversy between the up-country and the low-country. A lively debate took place when a Charleston member's proposal that the convention "restrict itself to such action as is essential to restore the state to her former position in the Federal Union" was defeated by the margin of one vote.[48] Encouraged by this victory, George Tillman, the leader of the up-country reformers, tried to carry the reform of the senate beyond Perry's suggestions. He proposed that the fourteen largest districts be given one senator each in addition to the one provided under the Perry apportionment; but a majority refused to listen to any modification of the Governor's plan. Sectional jealously was again aroused when low-country members proposed that the Negro population be counted in the apportionment of representation in the lower house. This would have given advantage to the low-country, where a majority of the Negroes lived. The proposal was defeated by a small margin, but this defeat would scarcely have come had there not been the feeling that the counting of

[47] *Convention Journal*, pp. 12-16.   [48] *Ibid.*, pp. 33-35.

the Negro in the apportionment suggested suffrage for that race.[49] It was provided that there should be one representative for every sixty-secondth part of the white population and one for every sixty-secondth part of the taxes paid.

The other reforms suggested by Perry were adopted with less debate. The direct election of presidential electors and governor was provided for. The term of the governor was increased to four years, and he was given a limited veto. Provision was made for a uniform system of taxation, the removal of property qualifications for members of the legislature, and the use of the viva voce method of voting in that body.[50]

The assembly shunned all suggestions that suffrage be given the Negro in any form. When a number of Charleston Negroes prepared a memorial on that subject, the convention refused to hear it. "It cannot but be the earnest desire of all members," said the *Charleston Daily Courier,* "that the matter be ignored *in toto* during the session."[51] The President did not demand that any action should be taken on the question, although the extension of suffrage to colored men of property and education would not have aroused his disfavor. Only a few South Carolinians like Wade Hampton, Professor Joseph Le Conte, the Reverend A. Toomer Porter, and Judge Edward Frost felt that suffrage laws which excluded all Negroes and included all whites regardless of educational and property qualifications were unwise.[52] The white democracy, especially that of the up-country, felt that a restricted suffrage which took no account of racial discriminations would disfranchise a large portion of the white vote and give the large landowners an unfair influence through their control of Negro votes.[53] That

---

[49] Andrews, pp. 69-73.

[50] Admirable summaries of these reforms in *Courier,* Sept. 29, 1865, and by Perry in *House Journal, Ex. Sess., 1865,* p. 14.

[51] Sept. 26, 1865.

[52] *Ku-Klux Conspiracy, S. C.,* p. 1222; Porter, *Led On! Step by Step,* p. 224; and Le Conte, *Autobiography,* p. 236.

[53] M. C. Butler, in *Ku-Klux Conspiracy, S. C.,* p. 1217.

there was need of placating in some manner the sentiment gathering in the North in favor of Negro suffrage seems not to have occurred to members of the convention. "It may safely be said," wrote the Columbia correspondent of the *Charleston Daily Courier,* "that the views and opinions of Sumner, Thad Stevens, Wilson, and some other Northern Radicals have been considered too unworthy to be seriously commented upon by members of the convention. It is well known that the sentiments of those gentlemen are extremely unpopular in the North."[54]

But the body did pass a resolution providing for the appointment by the governor of a commission to devise laws defining the social and economic status of the freedmen. Provision was also made for the creation of a system of courts to hear cases in which colored persons were involved. Only three votes could be mustered in favor of giving them the right to testify in cases other than those in which they were involved.[55]

Matters not a subject of controversy were attended to with the utmost dispatch. All laws and contracts made before and after secession and not inconsistent with the Constitution were declared in force. Provision was made for the election of a governor, a legislature, and members of Congress; the legislature was asked to pass laws encouraging immigration; and the governor was given authority to appoint a commission to push the recovery of seized lands.[56]

The Governor felt highly pleased over the work of the convention. Practically all the reforms he had suggested were enacted and the President informed him that he was satisfied with the copy of the constitution which the Governor sent him. Provision had been made for a more adequate expression of the power of the white democracy without doing violence to traditions; provision had been made for the political and social

[54] Sept. 26, 1865.   [56] *Ibid.*, pp. 54, 176-78.
[55] *Convention Journal*, pp. 103, 121-23.

subordination of the Negro without remanding him to slavery; the traditional right of the state to regulate its own internal affairs was reasserted without doing violence to the principles of federalism. The Governor felt that the state, under the leadership of its most experienced statesmen, stood on the brink of an era of prosperity.[57]

*   *   *   *   *

Before adjourning, the members of the convention signed a petition requesting James L. Orr to become a candidate for governor. This nomination would have been given Hampton had he been willing to accept. But he was preoccupied with private affairs and wisely felt that his election would have been inexpedient because he had held high rank in the Confederate army. But in spite of repeated assertions that he was not a candidate, his friends insisted on voting for him. He was very popular and there was much resentment against Orr as the candidate of the convention which in the same breath inaugurated the popular election of governor and attempted to designate who should be elected. Out of the 19,000 votes cast, Orr's majority was only between seven and eight hundred. Two-thirds of the voters refused to vote. In Sumter District Orr got only three votes to Hampton's 270; in Greenville Hampton's vote was twice as great as Orr's and in Orangeburg, seven times as great. Had not Hampton's home district, where his authority was immediate, gone for Orr by an almost unanimous vote, Hampton would have been elected. So chagrined was the governor-elect over the outcome, that he seriously considered not taking office; but at the urgent request of Perry he overcame his misgivings and took office November 27, 1865.[58]

---

[57] Perry's estimates of the work of the convention in *House Journal, Ex. Sess., 1865*, p. 14, and *Reminiscences, Sec. Ser.,* pp. 276-77.

[58] The election is analyzed by Orr in *Ku-Klux Conspiracy, S. C.,* pp. 12, 18; by Perry, in *Reminiscences, Sec. Ser.,* p. 278; and by *Courier,* Sept. 28 and 29, and Oct. 3, 18, 23 and 31, 1865.

Perhaps no other man in the state was as capable as James L. Orr of guiding the commonwealth through the difficulties which lay before it. Commanding in personal appearance and possessed of fluent powers of speech, he had had a distinguished career in the public service. At one time he had been speaker of the national house of representatives. Like Perry, he had long been a champion of the rights of the common white man and had opposed the extreme views of the Secessionists. As a member of the Confederate Senate, he had advocated a negotiated peace, foreseeing that the fall of the Southern government was inevitable. But he had not lost the respect of the dominant element in the state. When he saw that resistance to secession was useless, he signed the famous ordinance. Moreover, he had one practical virtue possessed by no other South Carolinian of his day eminent in public life. He was able to change his mind on fundamentals when his sound sense of realism told him that this was necessary. But defects in his character were partly responsible for the fact that his attempt to lead the state out of its difficulties was destined to be as great a failure as that of Perry. He became a man without a party when the whites refused to follow the devious policies he advocated. The historian cannot fail to recognize elements of a wise opportunism in Orr's espousal of many of the doctrines of the Radicals; but he must also recognize that those who elected Orr to office were correct in believing that he was not free from motives of self-aggrandizement. He had held public office since he reached his majority and he was willing to compromise principles to the degree necessary to make it possible for him to hold public office until the day of his death.[59]

The most immediate concern of the legislature which met

[59] Sketches of Orr in *Cyclopedia of Eminent and Representative Men of the Carolinas*, I, 112-17; J. T. Trowbridge, *The South*, p. 568; Andrews, *op. cit.*, pp. 49-50; and *Courier*, Dec. 4, 1865, and Aug. 13 and 18, 1867. See also the incisive analysis of his character in Perry, *Reminiscenses, First Ser.*, p. 179.

under Perry and Orr was to devise means to meet the financial obligations of the state. Provision was made for an ad valorem property tax, for a poll tax, a tax on sales and the issue of bills receivable of the state. The merchants of Charleston complained bitterly against the sales tax, the poll tax proved unsatisfactory due to popular misunderstanding, the property tax was not equitably assessed, and there were combinations formed in the up-country to resist sheriffs' sales.[60] Nevertheless, sufficient funds were raised to meet the modest requirements of the government. During the fiscal year ending October 1, 1866, $477,255 was raised, and when Orr left office in July, 1868, he reported a balance of $95,546 in the state treasury.[61]

The Orr administration was less successful in relieving the distress caused by the outcome of the war and the crop failures of 1866 and 1867. As late as April, 1867, the Governor reported that there were more than one hundred thousand people in the state who had not tasted meat in thirty days and that thousands had no bread for their starving children.[62] At his suggestion the legislature which met in special session in September, 1866, provided for the issue of $300,000 in bonds to purchase 300,000 bushels of corn. The Governor appointed D. Wyatt Aiken purchasing agent, but Aiken refused to accept the charge since the instructions of the legislature were impossible of fulfillment. The bonds could not be sold at par and the corn could not be had at one dollar a bushel.[63] Other types of relief were suggested, but all proved abortive. The credit of the state was not considered strong enough for the assumption of such novel burdens; the Freedmen's Bureau could be relied upon for the relief of some suffering; and better crops soon brought better conditions.

[60] *News,* Nov. 19, 1867, and Jan. 7, 1868.

[61] *Ibid.,* July 8, 1868, and *Reports and Resolutions of the General Assembly, 1866,* pp. 3-9, 28-29.

[62] *News,* Apr. 23, 1867.

[63] Orr, in *House Journal, Ex. Sess., 1866,* p. 14, and *House Journal, Reg. Sess., 1866,* pp. 28-29.

The legislature was no more successful in bringing relief to the large number of debtors created by the distress of the times. "Property is being sacrificed on the auction block," said the Spartanburg *Carolina Spartan*. "The widows of our brave soldiers ... have been thrust from their homes and their household goods have been knocked down for a paltry sum, while the poor women, weeping with their children, have stood among the sympathetic crowd, imploring in vain for relief from the law which made them beggars."[64] To meet this condition the "stay law" of 1861 was continued in a modified form under the act of December 21, 1865. It provided for the suspension of executions for indebtedness created prior to this enactment until the next regular session of the legislature, provided the debtor paid one-tenth of the amount due.[65] The law was bitterly opposed by commercial interests and was declared unconstitutional by the courts of appeals.[66] The popular clamor for relief continued, and the legislature in September, 1866, passed an act suspending the terms of the courts of common pleas until the following spring.[67] In this manner the executions against mortgages were delayed. It was believed that constitutional difficulties had been obviated because of the power of the legislature to fix the terms of the courts it had created. But the court of appeals again came to the rescue of the creditors, declaring the act unconstitutional in the spring of 1867.[68]

Governor Orr next had recourse to a power beyond the control of the courts. He induced General Sickles, in his General Order No. 10 of April 15, 1867, to abolish imprisonment for debt; to suspend judgment for actions arising between December 19, 1860, and May 15, 1865; to suspend all procedure · for the recovery of money the consideration for which was the

---

[64] Cited in *Fairfield Herald*, Oct. 17, 1866. The *Sumter News*, Aug. 24, 1867, declared that in the previous April 40,000 suits for debt were pending in the courts of the state.

[65] *Stat. S. C.*, XIII, 285-86.
[66] *Courier*, May 16, 1866.
[67] *Stat. S.C.*, XIII, 366^17-366^19.
[68] *Fairfield Herald*, Mar. 20, 1867.

purchase of slaves; to stop foreclosures for twelve months; and to reserve for the debtor in the sale of property under execution a dwelling house, twenty acres of land and five hundred dollars in personal property.[69] This brought some measure of relief. "But for your General Order No. 10," wrote Orr to Sickles, "I believe an increase of troops would have been necessary to guard the public records and insure the safety of sheriffs and other officials against popular violence."[70]

In spite of poverty and unsettled conditions, the Orr administration effected some needed public improvements. A state penitentiary was erected at Columbia large enough for three hundred convicts, and at the end of Orr's term of office 180 were reported as usefully employed therein.[71] A somewhat pathetic attempt was made to repay the Confederate soldiers for their sacrifices. Twenty thousand dollars was appropriated to provide artificial limbs for those who had lost limbs in the war, and some two hundred artificial legs were distributed.[72] The lunatic asylum was repaired and placed under efficient management, and adequate provision was made for the reception of colored patients.[73] It was hoped that the ingress of capital and labor would be encouraged by acts limiting the rate of interest and establishing a bureau of immigration.[74] Other constructive measures to which the Governor could point with pride were the repair of county buildings, the reorganization of the executive department of the government, and the reopening of the state college and other schools. These measures by no means fulfilled the requirements of a state which had recently been through a great ordeal; but considering the uncertainty of the times, and the meager resources at hand, they were as much as could have been expected from the prudent rulers of the commonwealth.

[69] *News*, Apr. 15, 1867.
[70] *Ibid.*, Sept. 27, 1867.
[71] *Ibid.*, July 8 and Dec. 31, 1868, and *Stat. S. C.*, XIII, 366²⁸-366²⁹.
[72] *Stat. S. C.*, XIII, 401, and *News*, July 9, 1868.
[73] *Ibid.*, Dec. 13, 1868, and *Reports and Resolutions, 1866*, p. 89.
[74] *Stat. S. C.*, XIII, 429, and see below, p. 244.

Overshadowing the other accomplishments of the state government was the enactment by the legislature, at its special session of September, 1865, of the so-called "black code" designed to regulate the status of the freedmen. Governor Perry told the General Assembly that "humanity and justice, as well as the imperative necessities of society" compelled it to make immediate provision for the protection and government of the ex-slaves. "The Negro," he added, "is innocent of all that he has gained and all that you have lost, and he is entitled to your sympathy and kindness, your protection and guidance."[75] Already the Governor had appointed Armistead Burt and David L. Wardlaw members of a commission to devise these laws. They were experienced lawyers noted for their moderate views. The legislature without hesitation enacted their recommendations.[76]

"Persons of color" were defined as those individuals possessing more than one-eighth Negro blood. Other persons were deemed white. Colored persons were given certain rights. The regulations of slavery were declared no longer in force, the Thirteenth Amendment was ratified, and colored persons were to be allowed to acquire property, sue and be sued, receive the protection of the law in person and property, testify in cases in which they were involved, and enter into marriage contracts. Their children were given the status of legitimacy. Provision was made for the care of indigent colored persons. The owners of plantations were not to be allowed to evict them from their property prior to January 1, 1867. They were to be supported by their relations or by fines and poll taxes imposed on the able-bodied of their race.

On the other hand, a series of restrictions attempted to assign colored persons to the position of an inferior caste. Intermarriage between the races was prohibited. Unless licensed to do so, no colored person was to be allowed to follow any

[75] *House Journal, Ex. Sess., 1865*, p. 15.   [76] *Stat. S. C.,* XIII, 245-85.

employment—on his own account—except that of farmer or servant. Those licensed to engage in other employments were required to prove their fitness and to pay an annual tax ranging from ten to one hundred dollars. Under no circumstances were colored persons to be engaged in the manufacture or sale of liquors. Colored persons entering the state were to be required to give bonds guaranteeing their good behavior. Capital punishment was provided for colored persons guilty of willful homicide, assault upon a white woman, impersonating her husband for carnal purposes, raising an insurrection, stealing a horse, a mule, or baled cotton, and house-breaking. For crimes not demanding death they might be confined at hard labor, whipped, or transported; "but punishments more degrading than imprisonment shall not be imposed upon a white person for a crime not infamous." Colored persons were not to sell farm produce without a written permit, were not to be members of the militia, keep any weapon except a fowling piece, or hire to another person when already engaged. Judicial officers were authorized to hire to farmers colored vagrants or those engaged in a variety of undesirable employments.

Elaborate provision was made for contracting colored "servants" to white "masters." The servants must work from sun to sun with reasonable intervals for meals, be quiet at night, and not leave the premises or receive visitors without express permission. They could be discharged for cause and have their wages forfeited when departing from the service of their masters. The masters were given the right to whip "moderately" servants under eighteen. Others were to be whipped on authority of judicial officers. These officers were given authority to return runaway servants to their masters. The servants, on the other hand, were given certain rights. Their wages and period of service must be specified in writing, and they were protected against "unreasonable" tasks, Sunday and night work, unauthorized attacks on their persons, and inadequate food.

Colored children over two years of age could be apprenticed to competent white or colored persons by their fathers, or by districts judges when the fathers were dead or incompetent. Males over twelve years of age and females over ten could assume this obligation on their own initiative. The master was required to teach the apprentice a trade, furnish wholesome food, and if there was an approved school within convenient distance, send him there at least six weeks in every year after he became ten years of age. At the expiration of his term of service, the apprentice was to receive from his master as much as sixty dollars. The master was authorized to chastise the servant and capture him in case of flight.

A special court was to be created in each district to administer the law in respect to persons of color. The petit juries of these courts were to consist of only six men. The local magistrate "shall be specially charged with the supervision of persons of color in his neighborhood, their protection, and the prevention of their misconduct." Public order was to be secured by the organization of forty-five or more militia regiments.[77]

The chief reason why this legislation was enacted was the desire to establish order out of the confusion which the outcome of the war had left. The rulers of the state were sincere in their belief that they were attempting a statesmanlike solution of the chief difficulties of the times. They felt that the grant of definite privileges to the Negro was a generous concession and that the obligations imposed would be as beneficial to the Negro as to the white man. To them the only social order proper to South Carolina was one which assigned the black man to an inferior position. This had always been his status, and there was little in the changes which the war brought to

[77] *Stat. S. C.,* XIII, 300-34.

indicate that, in the near future at least, he was going to manifest qualities to justify a radical alteration in his traditional position.[78]

Nevertheless, the interests of both races would have been better served had there never been a "black code." The legislature was dwelling in a fool's paradise when, without study or debate,[79] it followed the Governor's suggestions, believing that the Negro laws would "remove all pretense for military rule in the State, as well as facilitate its speedy restoration to the Union."[80] The provisions for corporal punishment, the vagrancy and apprenticeship laws, the use of the terms "master" and "servant," and the clear-cut manner in which the Negro was adjudged the member of an inferior caste, meant to the victorious North that South Carolina, a few months after its defeat, was attempting to reëstablish slavery. The legislature was highly impolitic in not making itself aware that it was flaunting a red flag in the face of the conqueror.

Moreover, what was done would have been unwise had there been no Northern sentiment to take into account. The laws were economically impractical since they attempted to place the Negro in a position inferior to that which competition for his labor among white landlords would have given him regardless of legal expedients.[81] Neither humanity nor expediency demanded such sharp distinctions between the races in imposing punishments. The restriction of Negro testimony to cases in which the race was involved was not common sense. The free admission of such testimony in all cases would not have involved the surrender of power by the whites since they were to be the judges and jury. The occupational restrictions, instead of tending to restore order, created the impression that the dominant race desired to exclude the blacks

---

[78] Governor Perry, in *House Journal, Ex. Sess., 1865,* p. 15.

[79] According to the recollections of Joseph W. Barnwell.

[80] Perry, in *House Journal, Ex. Sess., 1865,* p. 15.

[81] See below, p. 241.

from useful employment. It was impractical for a poverty-stricken commonwealth to have projected such elaborate
schemes of judicial and military reorganization. The great
defeat should have impressed the state with the fact that its
military career was over, and the courts already provided for
were ample for all cases. "Many believe," said a sagacious contemporary, "that under the circumstances it would have been
better to have made no such ostentatious legal and judicial distinctions between the races, but to have modified slightly the
common law. . . . This would have been less expensive and
onerous to the people, and certainly less offensive to those
whose renewed antagonism it were folly to invoke."[82]

*   *   *   *   *

In the meantime, forces were at work which were going
to shatter completely the Johnson-Perry plan of restoration.
Events at the North and in the Southern states, to which those
in South Carolina were only a contributing factor, were making this outcome inevitable. They lie beyond the scope of this
work. Here only the phases of those events which had a direct
bearing on South Carolina will be discussed.

In the first place, every step which Perry took was subjected
to hostile criticism. When he made known his intention of not
allowing the Negro to participate in the political life of the
state, the New York *Nation* declared, "The doctrine that 'this
is a white man's government and intended for white men only,'
is, as the Perrys profess it, as monstrous a doctrine as was ever
concocted." To allow the state to reorganize on this basis, the
same weekly added, "will make the very name of American
democracy a hissing and a byword among the nations of the
earth. . . . To have this theory of the nature of our government
boldly thrust in our faces now, after the events of the last four
years, by men who have come red-handed from the battle field,

[82] "Juhl" (J. J. Fleming), in *Courier,* Jan. 3, 1866.

and to whose garments the blood of our brothers and sons still clings; and to know that the President, who owes in part at least his ability to be President to the valor and blood of colored troops, concurs with them in this scandalous repudiation of democratic principles, are things which the country, we trust, will find it hard to bear."[83] The Governor was accused by the powerful *New York Tribune* of hatred of the Northerners. "It is scarcely good taste," this newspaper affirmed, "for the just-pardoned governor, addressing a half-pardoned convention, to cast an imputation on the purposes of the loyal states, and to arraign a great dominant political party in those states for its views on national policy. . . . We assure him in all kindness that South Carolina must present herself at the doors of the House next December with words quite other than this on her repentant lips."[84]

It was held that South Carolinians were unfitted to exercise the authority which ordinarily devolves upon the inhabitants of a state. General Carl Schurz, after a tour of the state, said that he found no influential class whose loyalty to the nation was more than a reluctant submission to force.[85] "I do believe," said General Saxton, "that a large majority, probably nine-tenths, of the people of South Carolina, are opposed to the government, and look to their connection with it as the greatest calamity which could befall South Carolina. . . . In their own words, they are overpowered, not conquered, and they regard their treason as a virtue, and loyalty as dishonorable."[86] In the light of these and similar opinions the *Charleston Daily Courier* sorrowfully concluded: "A large, active, and unhesitating party are, through the speeches of their orators and the powerful lever of their press, using every exertion and straining every nerve to inflame the public mind to the con-

[83] I (Sept. 28, 1865), 390. Cf. *N. Y. Herald*, Sept. 20, 1865.
[84] Sept. 20, 1865.
[85] *Reminiscences*, III, 159-73.
[80] *Report of Joint Committee on Reconstruction*, Pt. II, p. 217. Cf *N. Y. World*, June 21, 1865.

clusion that the South is not prepared to accept the principles of Reconstruction, and thus pave the way for their votes and efforts against the readmission of her respective states into the Union."[87]

Much attention was given to so-called "rebel outrages" committed in South Carolina. The practice of driving freedmen from plantations was declared to be "almost universal." In instances these expulsions were said to have been accompanied by acts of revolting cruelty. For example, from Barnwell came the report of a woman who was "tied with her clothes over her head and her naked person whipped so violently as to inflict severe wounds, and then driven from the plantation without pay and threatened with death if she told the authorities." An army officer claimed that he overheard a man say that unless the national government was conciliatory "poison and the knife would take the place of the bayonet and the sword, and that it was not difficult to make away with Northern officers through a pane of glass."[88]

Representatives of Northern sentiment concluded that the only remedy for such abuses was to enfranchise the freedmen. Chief Justice Chase, the most distinguished Northern visitor to the state, declared to the freedmen of Charleston, "I believe there is not a member of the government who would not be pleased to see universal suffrage";[89] while Major Martin R. Delany, the most distinguished Northern Negro in the state, declared in a letter to President Johnson, "What becomes necessary to secure and perpetuate the Union is simply the *enfranchisement* and recognition of *political equality* of the power that saved the nation from destruction—a recognition of the political equality of the blacks with the whites in all their relations as American citizens."[90]

[87] Sept. 26, 1865.

[88] Testimony of General Saxton and Capt. Alexander P. Ketchum in *Report of Joint Committee on Reconstruction*, Pt. II, pp. 223-35.

[89] *American Annual Cyclopedia, 1865*, p. 765.

[90] Frank H. Rollin, *Life of Delany*, p. 279.

These opinions were accompanied by demands of local Negro leaders for political rights. As early as May, 1864, the Negroes of Port Royal had taken part in a meeting which elected delegates to the National Union Convention which met in Baltimore the following month, and among the sixteen delegates elected were Robert Smalls and three other colored men.[91] The Colored People's Convention met in Zion Church, Charleston, in November, 1865, to protest against the work of the constitutional convention and legislature. It marked the beginning of concerted political action by the Negroes of the state since those who were later to play leading parts in politics were present. They were Robert C. DeLarge, A. J. Ransier, J. J. Wright, Beverly Nash, Francis L. Cardozo, Delany, and Richard H. Cain. The novel character of the assembly was appreciated by those present. A resolution declared that it was "an extraordinary meeting, unknown in the history of South Carolina, when it is considered *who* compose it and for what *purposes* it was *allowed* to assemble." Bitter complaint was lodged against the action of the state authorities in depriving the colored race "of the rights of the meanest profligate in the country," and Congress was asked to place "the strong arm of the law over the entire population of the state," to grant "equal suffrage," and to abolish the "black code."[92]

Congress signified its approval of these sentiments by taking steps which ultimately resulted in the undoing of the Johnson plan of reconstruction and the substitution of a plan radically different. When the members-elect from South Carolina and the other Southern states applied for admission to Congress, in December, 1865, they were refused seats.[93] This was followed by the creation of the famous joint committee on the condition

[91] W. C. Gannett, in Pearson, *Letters from Port Royal*, 267-68. The Port Royal delegates were not admitted to the convention.

[92] *Proceedings of the Colored People's Convention Held in Zion Church, Charleston, November, 1865*, pp. 24-31.

[93] Letter of Perry in *Courier*, Feb. 23, 1865.

of the states of the late Confederacy with power to recommend whether any of them was entitled to representation in Congress. Thus Congress, through the exercise of its right to determine the qualifications of its members, signified its intention of not recognizing the legitimacy of the government which the President had created in South Carolina, and it became necessary to reconstruct this government, since under the American system a state can scarcely be said to exist without representation in the national body. South Carolinians tried to console themselves by pointing out the logical inconsistency between this behavior of Congress and its previous tacit recognition of the legitimacy of the state government by accepting its ratification of the Thirteenth Amendment. But in their hearts they knew that Congress was not under the obligation of logical consistency; they were rudely awakened from their dreams that the rights of the states were inviolate; they knew that unless there was a change in Northern politics the governmental structure which they had created was doomed.[94]

Another circumstance which impressed the people of the state with the fact that it was not the intention of the national authorities to leave them in control was the activities of the resident Federal troops. On January 1, 1866, 352 officers and 7,056 enlisted men were on duty in various parts of the state under the vigilant command of General Daniel E. Sickles. Their presence was in part induced by the necessity of maintaining order. Sickles believed that "the fortunate exemption of this department from the riots and collisions which have occurred elsewhere" was in no small degree due to the vigilance of his troops.[95] The *Charleston Daily Courier* said that "in case of resistance to the laws of the state, there was no power to be invoked ... except the United States army."[96]

[94] See comments of *Courier*, Dec. 12 and 15, 1865.

[95] *Annual Report of Secretary of War, 1866-1867*, pp. 59, 63.

[96] Feb. 21, 1866.

Top left: BENJAMIN FRANKLIN PERRY, PROVISIONAL GOVERNOR, 1865. *Top right:* JAMES LAWRENCE ORR, GOVERNOR, 1865-1868; MINISTER TO RUSSIA, 1873. *Bottom left:* GENERAL DANIEL E. SICKLES, MILITARY COMMANDER, 1866-1867. *Bottom right:* MAJOR GENERAL E. R. S. CANBY, MILITARY COMMANDER, 1867-1868.

But Sickles did not confine himself to the preservation of order. He took measures against the assertion of "disloyalty" and to protect the freedmen against alleged oppression. In a general order of January 1, 1866, he declared the entire "black code" null and void. "All laws," he decreed, "shall be applicable alike to all inhabitants." He demanded that colored persons be given the same judicial rights as whites, that all occupations be open to them, that no special taxes be imposed upon them, that they be allowed to move about with the same freedom as whites, and that no discriminations be made in the application of the vagrancy and pauper laws. Corporal punishment was prohibited and all loyal men were given the right to bear arms. In abolishing the labor laws he promised that the military authorities would enforce fair labor contracts.[97]

The actuality of the power he exercised was made clear by several instances. Military force prevented the carrying out of an order of Judge A. P. Aldrich that a white man be lashed.[98] Federal Judge Bryan adjudged Sickles in contempt of court when the General refused to appear in answer to a writ of habeas corpus issued in favor of four men convicted by military commission for the murder of three soldiers. The General demonstrated the superiority of his power by refusing to allow himself to be arrested.[99] He arrested some of the leading citizens of Edgefield, took them to Columbia on charges of complicity in the murder of a soldier, and threatened to remove the freedmen of Edgefield, Laurens, and Newberry, and provide for them at the expense of those districts, unless they were treated more reasonably.[100] These actions were followed by threats against the editor of the Columbia *South Carolinian* for commending ceremonies in honor of the war dead at which a Confederate flag was displayed.[101]

[97] Order in *Courier*, Jan. 23, 1866.
[98] Full correspondence in this controversy *ibid.*, Mar. 7, 1866.
[99] *Ibid.*, July 6, 7 and 16, 1866.
[100] *Ibid.*, Mar. 27 and 30, 1866.
[101] Sickles to F. G. De Fountaine in *Courier*, July 19, 1866.

These and similar actions brought forth indignant but helpless protests from local leaders. Armistead Burt used the following moving words in protesting against the right of a military commission to hear cases: "I feel the painful consciousness that I stand in the presence of a military court, organized for the administration of military law—a court whose members are strangers alike to the witnesses, the accused, and the counsel. . . . Instead of the scales of Justice, I see displayed before me the sword. . . . Instead of a hall dedicated to justice, I find a military camp. . . . This fearful trial by mandate of a conqueror is held in a conquered country and a captive city."[102]

*   *   *   *   *

Realizing the futility of the policy they had been pursuing, the South Carolina leaders modified their conduct in hopes of averting the doom which Congress seemed to have in store for them. They revised the "black code" and militantly championed the cause of President Johnson in his battle with Congress. When these expedients failed, they offered no further compromises, resolving to submit to the will of Congress with the understanding that they did so through compulsion.

When Governor Orr proposed that the "black code" be modified, he struck a responsive chord. In commenting on Sickles' nullification order, the *Charleston Daily Courier* said that the code was "universally regarded as utterly impractical" and that "few of its apparent benefits are more than illiberal concessions."[103] The Governor told the legislature which met in extra session in 1866 that the restriction of the testimony of persons of color to cases in which they were involved "cannot be reconciled with sound policy or just discrimination." He asked that colored persons be accorded the same civil rights and criminal liabilities as the whites.[104]

The legislature without delay agreed to his suggestions.

[102] *Ibid.*, Feb. 24, 1866.
[103] Sept. 7, 1866.
[104] *House Journal, Ex. Sess., 1866,* pp. 9-12.

First, Negro testimony was declared competent in all cases.[105] After a "discussion which continued several days with unabated interest,"[106] an Act to Declare the Rights of Persons Lately Known as Slaves and as Free Persons of Color became law. It gave to such persons rights to property and personal liberty and security "as white persons now have," and declared that colored persons "shall not be subjected to any other or different punishments . . . than such as are prescribed for white persons." Although the legislature felt itself obligated to carry out the constitutional mandate to create district courts, no attempt was made to give these courts special jurisdiction over colored persons.[107] At the regular session of December the legislature decreased the number of capital crimes.[108] The Governor frustrated an attempt to continue some of the trappings of slavery. He vetoed a bill repealing certain sections of the patrol act of 1839 on the ground that partial repeal implied that the other sections were still in force. He held that all such laws had been declared void by an ordinance of the convention of 1865.[109]

The legislature had gone a long way toward the repudiation of what it had done the year before. But what it did was not as radical as it might have been. The previously declared definition of colored persons remained in force as did the act against the intermarriage of the races; the vagrancy and domestic relations laws were not tampered with.[110] The lawmakers were willing to give the Negro only legal equality; if reforms of a radical social and political character were to be introduced, the lawmakers by their silence let it be known that it must be done by other hands.

The revision of the laws brought sympathetic response from

[105] *Stat. S. C.*, XIII, 366⁸-366⁹.
[106] *Courier*, Sept. 22, 1866.
[107] *Stat. S. C.*, XIII, 366²¹-366³⁰.
[108] *Ibid.*, pp. 376-78.

[109] *Senate Journal, Reg. Sess., 1866,* pp. 129-31.
[110] *Stat. S. C.*, XIII, 366.

the national executive authority. By proclamation of April 2, 1866, the President declared that the rebellion no longer existed, and that in South Carolina and the other former insurrectionary states, "the law can be sustained and enforced therein by the proper civil authority." The troops were gradually retired from the state. Between January 1 and November, 1866, the number of soldiers was reduced from 7,408 to 2,747. By March of that year all military taxes were abolished. By October General Sickles turned the jails and all law cases over to the civil authorities except on the sea islands.[111] Moreover, he commended the manner in which the civil courts went about their duties. "Among the numerous matters of complaint disposed of during the year," he said, "the cases are exceptional and inconsiderate in number that seem to furnish just occasion for censorious comment or criticism, upon the manner in which the civil authorities, and especially the superior tribunals, have fulfilled their novel functions to the freedmen as citizens."[112]

South Carolinians observed with keenest sympathy the efforts of the President to sustain his reconstruction policy in the face of congressional opposition. When the news of his veto of the second Freedmen's Bureau Bill arrived, they acknowledged him "as the man who will eventually work out to a happy end the vexed problems of social and political rights."[113] When the shifting of political alignments gave them an opportunity to lend him a helping hand in the approaching congressional elections, they did their utmost. They took steps to be represented at the National Union Convention which was to meet in Philadelphia on August 14. The calling of this convention was prompted by the fact that the President

---

[111] *Fairfield Herald*, July 10, 1866, and *Courier*, Oct. 8, 1866.

[112] *Annual Report of Secretary of War, 1866-1867*, p. 66.

[113] *Courier*, Mar. 1, 1866.

had been deserted by the Union Republican party and needed
some sort of organization to sustain him. On the initiative of
Governor Orr, the National Union Club of South Carolina
was organized and a state convention was called to elect delegates to the Philadelphia convention. This was, said Orr,
the first opportunity which the state had had since the war to
be represented in the councils of the nation and "to oppose the
unjust schemes of the Radicals in their systematic effort to
humiliate the state."[114]   All but four of the districts were represented at the state convention. Orr was elected at the head
of the delegation to go to Philadelphia. No instructions were
imposed upon the delegates. It was felt that the only tactful
policy for them to follow was to stand ready to give Johnson
an earnest and quiet endorsement.[115]

The part played by the South Carolinians at Philadelphia
did not reflect credit on their state or the cause which the
President carried before the people of the North in the fall
elections. The spirit of cordiality which it was assumed existed between the sections was typified by the South Carolina
and Massachusetts delegates, on the first day of the gathering,
marching into the hall arm-in-arm amidst cheers, and both
groups rising and cheering, on the third day, resolutions declaring slavery abolished forever and that the Negro should
receive "equal protection of every right of person and property." Governor Orr was delegated by some of his Western
friends to persuade Vallandigham, the famous copperhead
from Ohio, of the propriety of his not taking a seat on the
floor. These actions were scarcely sincere and gave the enemies of the President occasion for jibes. South Carolina,
which had been denied seats in Congress, was gratuitously
taking part in the canvass for the election of members of that

---

[114] *Ibid.*, July 7, 1866.   Aug. 2-4, 1866, and *Fairfield Herald*,
[115] Proceedings of convention, *ibid.*,   Aug. 29, 1866.

body. Perry aptly remarked, why should a representative of South Carolina ask Vallandigham, because of his sympathy for the South, to exclude himself from a convention in which South Carolina was represented? The *Charleston Daily News* commented as follows: "We saw much we did not like. There was an obsequiousness on the part of many of the delegates from the South, a too evident desire to comply with every demand. . . . A proper dignity would have prompted a different course."[116] Orr himself was soon to see the folly of his course, and the fall elections put the Radical party in Congress in a better position to do what it liked.

South Carolina's reply to the refusal to heed its offers of conciliation was a hearty rejection of the Fourteenth Amendment. In submitting that proposal to the legislature Orr said, "History furnishes few examples of a people who have been required to concede more to the will of their conquerors than the people of the South." South Carolina, he continued, had even consented to "obliterate the constitution which had been made and hallowed by such hands as Rutledge, Pinckney, Marion, and Sumter"; it had ratified the Thirteenth Amendment; its citizens had practised "a true and thorough loyalty" to the national constitution; and it had given the blacks equal rights in person and property. He believed that no Northern state, if like South Carolina it had forty-one black men to every thirty white men, would ratify a constitutional amendment conferring the vote on the blacks. "Do sensible, fair and just men at the North," he asked, "desire that these people [the Negroes], . . . steeped in ignorance, crime, and vice, should go to the polls and elect men to Congress who are to pass laws taxing and governing them?" "If the constitutional amendment is adopted," he concluded, "let it be done by the irre-

[116] Cited in *Fairfield Herald*, Aug. 29, 1866. The proceedings of the convention described *ibid.*, Sept. 4, 1866; Rhodes, *History of the U. S.*, V, 614-16; and Perry, *Reminiscences, Sec. Ser.*, pp. 297-307.

sponsible power of numbers, and let us preserve our self-respect, and the respect of our posterity, by refusing to be the mean instrument of our shame." The legislature agreed with the governor. The house rejected the amendment by vote of ninety-five to one and the senate registered the same verdict without a record vote.[117]

[117] Orr's address in *House Journal, Reg. Sess., 1866,* pp. 32-35. The vote, *ibid.,* 284, and *Senate Journal, Reg. Sess., 1866,* p. 230.

Chapter III

CONGRESSIONAL RECONSTRUCTION

THE congressional plan of reconstruction was given thor-
ough-going expression in acts of March 2 and 23 and
July 19, 1867.[1] They declared that "no legal government or
adequate protection for life or property" existed in the unre-
constructed states, and that such governments as they had were
declared "subject to the paramount authority of the United
States at any time to abolish, modify, control, or supersede the
same." These states were divided into five military districts
each under the command of a general. North Carolina and
South Carolina became the Second Military District. The
military commanders were required to supervise the steps
which Congress prescribed as necessary for the states to be
represented in that body. They were: a constitutional convention must be held in each state, consisting of delegates
"elected by the male citizens . . . of whatever race, color, or
previous condition," exclusive of those disfranchised by the
proposed Fourteenth Amendment; a constitution granting the
suffrage to "the male citizens . . . of whatever race, color, or
previous condition" must be framed by this convention, ratified by the same electorate and approved by Congress; and a
legislature elected under this constitution must ratify the Fourteenth Amendment. After vainly attempting to stay this
legislation by use of the veto, the President ceased official
opposition and appointed the military commanders.

The command of the Second Military District fell to General Sickles, who, it will be remembered, had already had extensive experience in South Carolina. He formally assumed

[1] *Stat. U. S.,* XIV, 428-429, and XV, 2-4, 14-16.

command on March 21, 1867, with headquarters at Charleston. But his rule did not last long. By a presidential order of the following August 31, he was removed from the command and Major General Edward R. S. Canby was appointed. The President and Sickles had clashed over the latter's interference with the action of a Federal court in North Carolina.[2] The press of the state[3] was apprehensive over the change. But subsequent happenings proved that Canby was more congenial to the whites than his predecessor. He was a Southerner, a native of Kentucky, and had demonstrated a high order of administrative ability as commander of a portion of Louisiana. Temperamentally he was neither as petulant nor as unyielding as Sickles and consequently was not guilty of so many acts that caused resentment.

In an order published on the day he took command, Sickles made clear the power the military commander intended to execute. He declared that for the time-being the civil officials of the state would be protected in their functions as long as they did not interfere with the duties of the military, and that he hoped that occasions for military interference would seldom arise. But the civil government was declared provisional, the state was divided into eleven military districts, among which were distributed about two thousand troops, and the commanders of these districts were authorized to arrest civil officials whom they deemed derelict.[4] "The order," was the *Charleston Daily News'* accurate interpretation of its purport, "places before our people, not harshly but very distinctly, the fact that from today we are under military government. The commanding general possesses over a brave, a sensitive and a

[2] J. P. Hollis, *Early Period of Reconstruction in S. C.,* pp. 70-71.

[3] See comments of *Anderson Intelligencer, Newberry Herald,* and *Greenville Enterprise* in *News,* Sept. 14, 1867.

[4] Order in *News,* Mar. 25, 1867. Rhodes, VI, 76, citing the report of the adjutant general for Sept. 30, 1867, gives the number of troops on duty as 1,679 and the number of places occupied as twelve.

suffering people a more absolute authority than is wielded by any but one of the absolute monarchs of Europe."

Circumstances connected with the execution of the recon- struction policy tended to reduce friction to a minimum. In the first place, the whites, having abandoned all hope of stay- ing the hands of Congress, conducted themselves with moder- ation. They showed no tendency to resist the military. Shortly after his arrival, Sickles was visited by a committee of respon- sible Charlestonians with proffers of coöperation, and he was given an opportunity to explain his intention before the Charleston Board of Trade.[5] Governor Orr abandoned the uncompromising position he had assumed when he presented the Fourteenth Amendment to the legislature. He wisely felt that a perverse policy would have endangered the existence of his government and that with his aid the process of recon- struction would be more intelligently executed. So well did he get on with Sickles that when the General was removed, the Governor commended "the wisdom and success" of his admin- istration.[6] The attitude assumed toward General Canby was as conciliatory. The *Charleston Daily News* spoke of "the en- larged liberality of his views" and his determination "to make military supremacy as lenient and as equitable as military supremacy can be."[7]

The second cause of lack of friction was that the com- mendation bestowed upon the command was deserved. The troops stationed in the state were regulars under excellent dis- cipline and without the volunteer's zeal to impose innovations beyond their instructions. It is significant that among the "numerous acts of oppression" ascribed to the soldiers by the historian Reynolds there was no murder or other act of violent oppression.[8] The worst conduct of the troops was an occa- sional act of disorder induced by drunkenness. The following

[5] *News,* Mar. 27 and Apr. 4, 1867.   [7] Sept. 1, 1867.
[6] *Ibid.,* Sept. 20, 1867.   [8] *Reconstruction in S. C.,* pp. 64-72.

report from Darlington was a typical contemporary comment on their conduct: "The men are said to be orderly and under excellent discipline; the commander is spoken of among the citizens as a high-toned gentleman."[9] In truth, if the soldiers may be said to have in any way veered from the letter of their instructions, it was more often to favor the whites and oppress the Negroes than the opposite. "Among the regulars, 'rank and file,'" said a correspondent of the New York Tribune, "many acts of cruelty and oppression are constantly perpetrated. Whenever they can and dare they maltreat and abuse the freedmen."[10] We are told of "a fierce conflict" between drunken soldiers and Negroes in Edgefield and of a furious brickbat battle between the two elements in the streets of Charleston.[11]

The military commander seems always to have kept the public welfare in mind. He readily accepted the advice of the Governor in important matters. At the Governor's suggestion, as has been shown,[12] Sickles allayed the distress of the people by an order staying the execution of legal processes. Instead of making the tax burden onerous, Canby, in 1867, continued the tax measures of the legislature of the previous year with a few modifications in the interest of efficiency and equity. Both commanders were sparing in the removal of civil officers. Sickles, in a report issued four months after the beginning of his administration, said that only twelve persons in this class had been removed in both Carolinas and that all of them were acted against because of misconduct. Those appointed to office were seldom obnoxious. For example, William S. Hastie was appointed sheriff of Charleston. Although not a native of the place, he was a prominent merchant and his administration of the office gave satisfaction.[13] The appointment of General

[9] "Traveler," in News, July 12, 1867.
[10] Cited ibid., May 28, 1867.
[11] Ibid., Mar. 30 and Apr. 9, 1867.
[12] See above, pp. 46-47.
[13] News, Aug. 27, 1867.

W. W. Burns as mayor of Charleston caused popular dissatisfaction; but he soon won favor because of his very efficient administration. He punished the "bellicose Negro" and the "dubious woman," cleaned the streets, and put the municipal finances on a firm basis.[14] The restrictions which Sickles imposed upon the manufacture and sale of liquors were beneficial. A greater degree of public order was secured and more grain became available for the feeding of the undernourished.[15]

These evidences of accord between the civil and military elements should not, however, lead to the assumption that there was a tendency to execute the Reconstruction acts in a manner less thorough than Congress intended, or that local white sentiment willingly acquiesced in what was done. They merely indicated that all concerned, knowing that the enforcement of the will of Congress was inevitable, had the good sense to accept the situation. It is now our purpose to show that the military commander's duty to maintain law and justice as interpreted by Congress caused much resentment from the local whites and only a most unwilling acquiescence.

The first instance in which the feelings of the whites were in conflict with military decree was when Sickles ordered that a United States flag be carried in the parade on April 27, 1867, of the Charleston fire companies. It was the custom of the companies to carry only their own colors, and the order was only obeyed to prevent the arrest of leaders. "Since the bombardment of Fort Sumter," said a correspondent of the *New York Herald,* "no event has aroused the public mind to a greater degree of excitement." This feeling was accentuated by the arrest of a young man who, angered by the order of Sickles, had mutilated a national flag used to decorate a fire truck. He was confined for a month without trial and then publicly reprimanded.[16]

[14] *Ibid.,* Feb. 27 and Mar. 6, 1868.
[15] *Fairfield Herald,* July 10, 1867, and *Senate Docs.,* 40th Cong., 1st Sess., No. 14, p. 69.
[16] *N. Y. Herald,* May 5, 1867, and Reynolds, p. 66.

Of a more serious nature was Sickles' interference with the administration of justice. Police officers were required to make monthly reports to the military authorities, and a corps of detectives was employed to ferret out outlaws. A provost court was created in Aiken with jurisdiction over most matters in which colored persons of Barnwell and Edgefield were involved. It was felt that these persons could not get justice in those districts.[17] The military was almost as busy as the civil authorities in administering justice. Within seventeen months the army arrested 526 whites and 611 blacks in the two Carolinas, and 368 whites and 182 blacks were tried by military commission.[18]

Much ill feeling was engendered by the punishment of two Columbia youths for assaulting, in a Columbia barroom, J. Q. Thompson and William J. Armstrong, Northern visitors whose political activities had been offensive to the whites. Although the youths were arrested and released on bail by the civil authorities, and a group of citizens apologized for their conduct, Sickles resolved to make an example of this evidence of "political intolerance." This intolerance, "illustrated in countless affrays," he said, "was long permitted in Southern communities, to hunt down with cruel violence persons venturing to maintain opinions not in harmony with local sentiment." The culprits were sentenced to six months in Fort Macon, and the magistrate who had released them on bail was removed from office.[19]

The most conspicuous case of military interference with the ordinary process of justice was the annulment of a decree of the court of chancery refunding to the donors $8,797 which had been contributed before the end of the war by public subscription for the remounting of Hampton's cavalry. The money

---

[17] *News*, Apr. 29, 1867.
[18] A comprehensive review of the results of military justice in *Annual Report of Secretary of War, 1867-1868*, I, 308-9,

and *ibid., 1868-1869*, I, 350-53.
[19] *News*, Aug. 3 and 13, 1867, and Reynolds, pp. 67-68.

had not been used. Sickles declared that the decree was a fraud upon the rights of the United States since it violated an act providing for the confiscation of property used in the late insurrection. It was intimated that the attorneys in the case, and even Chancellor Henry D. Lesesne, were engaged in a conspiracy to hide the proceedings.[20] This conduct was regarded as arbitrary. The war had on April 2, 1866, officially been declared over, and neither the state nor Confederate government had ever had its hands on the money. Public opinion especially resented the aspersions on the honor of reputable lawyers and the judge. "It is safe to say," remarked Reynolds, "that no act of any military commander in the South ever gave greater offense than this order did."[21]

The commanders gave the state concrete examples of the rights congressional justice demanded for the freedmen. Sickles abolished discrimination between the races in public conveyances and made an example of the master of a ship who refused to allow a mulatto woman to ride as a first-class passenger. The ship master was fined $250.[22] Much consternation was created by Canby's order requiring that Negroes be allowed to serve on juries. The courts were told to revise their jury lists so as to include all persons assessed for taxes and qualified to register as voters.[23] The Governor protested to the President, and lawyers said that verdicts given by juries on which Negroes sat could not stand. But the courts generally accepted the decree. Christopher Haynesworth, a Columbia barber, was the first colored man selected for this novel function and others were selected after him.[24]

But all judges were not so acquiescent. Judge A. P. Aldrich, in his charge to the Edgefield grand jury, let it be known that he would not obey the order of Canby. He claimed that

---

[20] See his order in *News,* Oct. 2, 1867.
[21] The money was finally returned to its donors under military directions. See Reynolds, pp. 66-67, and Hollis, p. 70.

[22] Reynolds, p. 67, and *News,* June 4, 1867.
[23] *Ibid.,* Oct. 3, 1867.
[24] *Ibid.,* Oct. 12, 16, and 17, 1867.

it conflicted with an act of 1831 which said that juries should be composed exclusively of white men. Several days later, as he was preparing to open court at Barnwell, he received an order from Canby suspending him from office. Indignant, he laid aside the robes of office and delivered the following address: "Gentlemen of the jury, for the present farewell; but if God spares my life I will yet preside in this court, a South Carolina judge whose ermine is unstained. My brethren of the bar, be patient; be loyal to the constitution; be true to yourselves. . . . Mr. Sheriff, let the court stand adjourned while the voice of justice is stifled." The speech created a profound impression; South Carolinians have ever since regarded it as a classic defense of the judiciary against military tyranny.[25]

* * * * *

Meanwhile the military authorities were directing the reconstruction of the state government under the specifications of Congress. The state was divided into 109 registration precincts and a board of three men was appointed in each of these districts with authority to conduct the registration of voters. Practically all native whites were excluded from these boards since an oath was required saying that one had not borne arms against the United States or held office under an authority hostile to it. To protect the freedmen in their rights to register, punishment was provided for persons causing disorder at the places of registration, and to deprive a citizen of employment for having registered was declared an offense punishable by military court. All persons presenting themselves for registration were required to swear that they had never held office under any state or the United States and afterwards engaged in rebellion against the United States. This excluded an important class of whites.[26]

[25] Full report of this controversy in *Annual Report of Secretary of War, 1867-1868*, I, 304-7, and *ibid., 1868-1869*, I, 348-50. Aldrich lived to return to the bench after the restoration of white supremacy.

[26] See orders of May 8, July 19, and Aug. 1, 1867 in *News*, May 10, July 21, and Aug. 3, 1867.

So thoroughgoing had been the work of registration that
by November 19, 1867, 127,761 persons had been listed. There
were 80,832 blacks and 46,929 whites. In only ten of the
thirty-one counties were there white majorities. These majorities in most cases were slight. On the other hand, the black
majorities in the twenty-one remaining districts were decisive.
In most of them they were twice as great; in Berkeley and
Georgetown they were six times as great, and in Beaufort nine
times.[27]

In an order issued October 16, General Canby decreed that
on November 19 and 20 the registered voters should vote "For
a Convention" or "Against a Convention," and should vote for
delegates to this convention, which should be held in case a
majority of the registered voters participated in the election,
and a majority of this majority voted favorably. The 124 delegates to the proposed convention were apportioned among the
several counties according to the number of registered voters.[28]

Before giving the results of this election it is necessary to
retrace our steps in order to explain how the political interests
of the Negro were aroused to the degree necessary to bring
about the remarkable results which those figures disclosed. In
the months in which Sickles applied the acts of Congress to the
state, the Negro, in spite of a past devoid of political experience,
became anxious to embrace the widest political opportunities
which came his way. Moreover, he became possessed of the
resolution to act in political matters independent of, and if
necessary in opposition to, his former master. That he was
able to assume this unusual rôle is of course partly explained
by the fact that he was no longer a slave. The assumption of
political liberties was in a measure the result of the fact that
he had learned to exercise social and economic liberties. But
it should be noted that the degree of social and economic lib-

[27] *Annual Report of Secretary of War,*   [28] Order in *News,* Oct. 17, 1867.
1868-1869, I, 520-21.

erty he attained was never as great as his political liberties. In fact, as is shown elsewhere,[29] throughout Reconstruction he was content to remain socially and economically inferior to the white man. He would have manifested the same sort of subservience in politics but for the stimulus of outside influences.

The most immediate influence which induced the Negro to enter politics was the fact that the national government, through the strength of its armed forces and the gratitude it engendered because it had effected his liberation, persuaded him to enter politics. The ingenious thoroughness of the Reconstruction acts, in both letter and execution, gave him no better opportunity than the white man to escape from their demands. Moreover, the fear that the white man might chastise him for exercising political privileges was allayed by the presence of Federal troops.

But the acts of Congress and the military command only gave form and discipline to the Negro's political actions. Other forces were necessary to arouse the fervent interest in politics which he actually acquired. This was inspired by new leaders who now appeared upon the scene. They were the "carpetbaggers," the "scalawags," and a few native Negroes. As is well known, the carpetbaggers were outsiders, usually white men from the North, who had entered the state on various missions connected with the problems of reconstruction. Some were army officers; others were employees of the Freedmen's Bureau; a considerable number were religious or educational leaders; a few were agriculturists; and some came with the original purpose of engaging in politics. The Negro, without adequate leadership of his own, turned to them—they were the representatives of the nation, the dispensers of charity and protection; and they, seeing opportunity for personal aggrandizement or the application of principles for which they had fought, accepted this leadership with alacrity.

[29] See below, p. 356.

The scalawags were native whites or Northerners who had lived in the state before the war. They were impelled to forego feelings of race prejudice and local attachment in order to win office or plunder through the Negro vote. They enjoyed several notable advantages over the carpetbaggers. They were local white men who knew how to control the Negroes, and opportunists who never allowed mere faith in doctrines to lead them into extravagances.

The native Negro political leaders, who were less important than either of the classes already mentioned, were the few among the race who had had opportunities to equip themselves for leadership. Some had been free persons of color with property and some education; others because of inherent aptitude had imbibed political knowledge from the master class. That they were of the same race as a majority of the voters may have worked to their advantage; but this was not always true, for the race, even in this period of innovations, never got over its habit of following white leadership.

The political leaders of the Negroes were not content with the usual methods of the American politician. They infused into their work the zeal of the missionary and adopted innovations designed especially to charm the ex-slave. They introduced a secret oath-bound political society known as the Union League, held numerous political meetings, and organized a political party.

The Union League of America, as is well known,[30] was organized in the North during the war to promote patriotism. It followed the army into the South, enlisting the sympathy of Unionists and arousing the political interest of the Negroes. It is not clear, from the sources examined, when it first entered South Carolina; but there is proof that its activities had assumed significant proportions late in 1866, that is, when it

[30] See especially Fleming, *Sequel to Appomattox*, pp. 174-95.

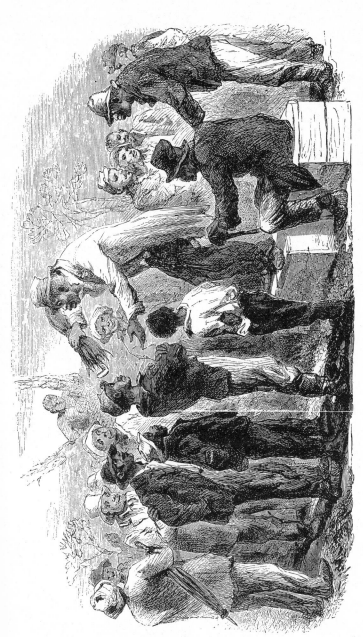

FREEDMEN DISCUSSING THEIR POLITICAL RIGHTS

Trowbridge, *A Picture of the Desolated States*

became known that the Negroes were going to be enfranchised.[31] It reached the height of its activities in 1867 and 1868, that is, when there was greatest need of stirring the Negroes into political activities.

The Union League, with modifications to suit local conditions, was just the sort of organization to bind the Negro to the Republican party. Just as the Ku-Klux Klan, because of its appeal to lawless and romantic emotions, racial pride, and moral idealism, was destined to have a strong hold upon the imagination of the white man, so the Union League made a special appeal to the colored man. His desire for club life, which had been rigidly denied under slavery, and which since Reconstruction has been gratified by numerous societies, was satisfied. The nocturnal secrecy of the gatherings, the weird initiation ceremonies, the emblems of virtue and religion, the songs, the appeal to such patriotic shibboleths as the Declaration of Independence, the Constitution, the Flag and the Union, the glittering platitudes in the interest of social uplift—all these characteristics of the League had an irresistible appeal to a ceremony-loving, singing, moralistic, and loyal race. That the purposes of the order, when reduced to the practical, meant that the Negro had become the emotional and intellectual slave of the white Radical did not dull the Negro's enthusiasm; he was accustomed to be a slave to the white man. That the high-sounding phraseology, when translated into ordinary language, meant that he was bound hand and foot to vote the Republican ticket was no handicap; he believed that the continued success of the party which had given him freedom was necessary for his happiness.

[31] Judge R. B. Carpenter, *Ku-Klux Conspiracy, S. C.,* p. 267, said that the League became active in Laurens in 1866. The *Yorkville Enquirer,* Feb. 9, 1871, said that it had been active in York "some years." Henry Johnson, president of the Winnsboro council of the order, said that it entered Fairfield in 1866.—*Ku-Klux Conspiracy, S. C.,* p. 320. The *News,* Oct. 19, 1867, said that there were then 88 League organizations in the state and that "every Negro almost in the state" was enrolled in them.

The constitution of the order which was circulated in the state[32] called for elaborate ceremonies when members were admitted into local councils. Around an altar on which was displayed an open Bible, the Declaration of Independence, the Constitution, and such symbols of industry as the anvil, were grouped the president, the chaplain, and other officers. The session was opened by a prayer asking for the protection of the "loyal people of the United States of America" against "foreign foes and domestic traitors." Amidst mysterious noises the candidates for membership were admitted and then encircled by those already present. The president addressed the initiates as follows: "Worthy sons of America! We bid you welcome. This circle of freedom and equal rights now encircling you must never be broken by treachery." Afterwards the candidates, with hands upon the open Bible, repeated the oath of membership. It obligated them to support the Declaration of Independence and the Constitution, to strive for the maintenance of liberty and for the education of the people in the duties of citizenship, to practise charity and friendship, to vote "for those who advocate and support the great principles set forth by this League," and not to divulge its secrets. This was followed by a round of songs, prayers, and addresses on the benefits of democracy. Then all circled around the "fire of liberty" and swore to elect only true Union men to office. Next came a long address from the president on the purposes of the society. "Its present purpose," he said, "is to secure the complete ascendency of the true principles of popular government —equal liberty, education, and the elevation of the workingmen of the Nation, and the security of all by means of the elective franchise." The ceremonies were closed by a communication of the secret signs of the order. They were the four L's,

---

[32] In a pamphlet entitled *Ritual, Constitution, and By-Laws of the National Council. U. L. of A., Together with all Necessary Information for the Complete* *Working of Subordinate Councils*, which was republished in *Ku-Klux Conspiracy, S. C.*, pp. 949-60.

Liberty, Lincoln, Loyal, and League, the utterance of each of which was to be accompanied by special movements of the arms.

The League strove to have in each election precinct a council which should hold a weekly meeting and "enlist all loyal talent in the neighborhood." The local councils were united in a state council, which was subordinate to the national council. The officers of the state council in 1870 were F. L. Cardozo, president; T. J. Mackey and H. W. Purvis, vice-presidents; E. W. M. Mackey, secretary; and R. H. Gleaves, treasurer. Its executive committee consisted of two representatives from each county. The state council was supposed to meet once a year. Its principal duties were to supervise local councils and to issue charters to them when there were as many as eight prospective members in a community.[33]

It is not certain that the League functioned in South Carolina with the perfection for which its constitution called. It was a vital force in politics only during 1867 and 1868; it played a minor rôle in the canvass of 1870.[34] During the winter of 1870-71 many councils were destroyed by Ku-Klux raids.[35] In 1868 and 1869 there were no meetings of the state council,[36] and after 1870 the meetings seem to have had little more than a ceremonial significance. As we shall see,[37] by that time the militia companies had become the agency through which the politicians kept up the morale of the Negroes, and it was against them, rather than against the League, that the energies of the Ku-Klux Klan were directed.

[33] The officers listed in *News,* July 29, 1870.

[34] W. D. Simpson, a well informed white, said in 1871: "The Union League had been broken up to some extent before the election of 1870. . . . In 1868 . . . a good many had wandered from it, got tired of it."—*Ku-Klux Conspiracy, S. C.,* p. 1308.

[35] Testimony of Henry Johnson and Alberry Bonner, *ibid.,* pp. 320, 444; S. B. Hall, *A Shell in the Radical Camp,* p. 74, declared in 1871: "It was not our fault that we had no Leagues in York. . . . But the K. K's said there should be no Leagues."

[36] F. L. Cardozo, *Address before the Grand Council of the Union League,* July 27, 1870, p. 3.

[37] See below, p. 452

The few accounts of the meetings of councils which have come under our observation indicate that the elaborate ritual of the order was not adhered to, or that if it were, it was not fully understood by those for whose instruction it was intended. Members subjected to searching questions failed to show that they knew much about the order. All that a Spartanburg Negro could tell was: "We took a pretty solemn oath, held up our hands and kissed the Book."[38]   A Pickens Negro could not tell the name of the officers of his council; all that another knew was that a "white gentleman" read a paper which the Negro could not understand.[39]   A white member from York who wrote a book to expose the secrets of the order does not give evidence that much attention was paid to the ritual. He merely says that the meetings were opened with the singing of an initiatory ode, the reading of the obligation, and the singing of "Rally 'Round the Flag," and that they were closed with prayer.[40]

But the fact that the League was a vital force for only a limited time, and that its ceremonies were not applied efficiently, should not be interpreted as evidence that it did not accomplish the purpose for which it was intended, namely, that of binding the Negroes to vote as the Republican leaders bade. The years in which it was active were the crucial time in which the political habits of the Negro were formed for the entire Reconstruction period. The decline of the order after 1868 was due to the fact that it had already accomplished its purpose and that its work could be carried on by the militia companies. The militia enjoyed state subsidies and was controlled by the same politicians who organized the League.[41]   More-

---

[38] Albert Bonner, in *Ku-Klux Conspiracy, S. C.*, pp. 443-44.

[39] Testimony of William Perry, Alexander Brown, and Clarke Cleveland, Sr., in *Annual Report of Secretary of War, 1868-1869*, I, 403, 393-95.

[40] Hall, *A Shell in the Radical Camp*, pp. 5-13.

[41] That leagues often became militia companies was attested by M. C. Butler and D. T. Corbin in *Ku-Klux Conspiracy, S. C.*, pp. 77 and 1203.

over, the failure to enforce the letter of the ritual is not proof that the purposes of the order were defeated. It was possible for the Republican bosses to convince the Negroes of the necessity of following them without much attention to ceremonious niceties.

All contemporaries, both friendly and hostile, testify to the effectiveness of the Union Leagues. S. B. Hall, a renegade member, has made the most extensive affirmation of this effectiveness. He wrote: "Every member we initiated would be compelled by oath and obligation to vote for those nominated by the order. . . . These Leagues were intended for no other purpose than to carry the elections, and impose upon the ignorant that they were compelled to support the nominations or else be exposed. . . . Some were threatened to be reported to the President of the United States, and that, after freeing them, he would take back their freedom and place them in slavery again. Others would tell them that you swear to do this, and that if you do not carry out your obligations, you will be liable for perjury and perhaps sent to the penitentiary.

"Everything that could be brought to bear upon the mind of the ignorant colored man was shown up by parties seeking office. Inflammatory speeches were generally made the topic of the night by most of the office-seekers—telling the colored man who was his friend and who was not; at the same time giving their [former] owners a general raking, and instructing them that their former owner merely wanted their votes to place them back in slavery as soon as the Democratic ticket was elected. . . . They were told that the Yankee was their only friend—he had fought and bled on the battlefield for their liberation."[42]

[42] *A Shell in the Radical Camp*, pp. 22-23. His assertions are affirmed by F. L. Cardozo, *Address before the Grand Council of the Union Leagues, July 27, 1870*, pp. 3-4; R. H. Cain, in *News*, Sept. 29, 1867; T. W. Woodward, in *Fairfield Herald*, Aug. 28, 1867; and M. C. Butler and Wade Hampton, in *Ku-Klux Conspiracy, S. C.*, pp. 1192, 1203, and 1228.

That the Leagues voted the Negroes like "herds of senseless cattle"[43] is amply confirmed by the Negro members themselves. A Pickens County Negro explained why there were no differences in political opinions among the Negroes as follows: "Why, Lor' bless your soul, massa, we swore to do that in the League." Another member from the same county explained that the League was the "place where we learn the law."[44] The only explanation which many, who appeared before an investigation committee, could give for their political affiliations was that they were "pledged" to stand by "principles." Said one, "We swore to stick to one another and vote the Radical ticket."[45] A Negro when asked by a band of Ku-Klux raiders why he voted Republican replied, "I can't read, and I can't write, and I can't much more than spell. How can a black man get along without there is some white gentleman or other with him? We go by instructions. We don't know nothing much."

Occasionally the League manifested itself in external activities. Political catechisms were issued instructing freedmen how to vote.[46] "Iscariots" in politics were denounced and subjected to trials for "not being sufficiently strong in the faith."[47] Sometimes the members engaged in acts of violence. Certain leagues undertook the arrest of whites against whom they had grievances. For example, a white man wounded a Negro at Fort Motte. The leaguers assembled three hundred strong, surrounded the house of the culprit, and would have dealt violently with him, had not a detachment of troops come to the rescue.[48] Influenced by the enthusiasm of their meetings, the leaguers often marched through the streets of villages at late

[43] N. Y. Herald cited in Fairfield Herald, Nov. 20, 1867. Cf. Ku-Klux Conspiracy, Reports of Committees, p. 524.

[44] Annual Report of Secretary of War, 1868-1869, I, 403.

[45] Ku-Klux Conspiracy, S. C., p. 321.

[46] Fairfield Herald, Nov. 6, 1867, and Reynolds, pp. 63-64.

[47] News, Mar. 12, Apr. 27, May 14-16, and June 19, 1869.

[48] Ibid., Jan. 4, 1868. Cf. ibid., Oct. 10, 1867, and Annual Report of Secretary of War, 1868-1869, I, 370 ff.

hours, disturbing the inhabitants by curses and the firing of guns. Their worst crime was house burning in retaliation for alleged wrongs.[49]

During the campaigns of 1867 the work of the Leagues was supplemented by a series of political gatherings of a frequency and intensity almost unparalleled in the history of the state. For these occasions the freedmen assembled in large numbers, willing to listen all day or half the night to what was said and always ready to approve the sentiments uttered. "The blacks," said the Sumter correspondent of the *Charleston Daily News,* "are kept in a state of camp meeting excitement. Meetings are held everywhere. Traveling disorganizers . . . visit all points, . . . and the wildest and most reckless whip the disaffected in line."[50] These meetings were usually orderly; the only complaints lodged against the participants were for whooping, singing, and shooting afterwards, and for raiding the Charleston street cars as the freedmen returned from an enthusiastic assemblage.[51]

A sample of the sort of doctrine propounded at these gatherings was the speech which Senator Henry Wilson delivered at Charleston on May 3 to five thousand blacks. "After four bloody years," he cried, "Liberty triumphed and slavery has died to rise no more. . . . The creed of equal rights, equal privileges and equal immunities for all men in America is hereafter to be the practical policy of the Republic. . . . Never vote unless you vote for the country which made you free. Register your names. Vote for a united country. Vote for the old flag. Vote for a change in the constitution of the state that your liberties may be consummated."[52]

The efforts of the Union Leagues and the political orators were accompanied by the organization of a state branch of the

[49] *News,* Dec. 31, 1867, and Jan. 6, 1868, and *Ku-Klux Conspiracy, S. C.,* pp. 192-193.
[50] Oct. 31, 1867.
[51] *News,* Apr. 1, 2, 18, and 25, 1867.
[52] *News* and *N. Y. Herald,* May 3, and 4, 1867.

Union Republican party. The first formal steps in this direction were taken at two meetings held in Charleston on March 7 and 21. At the first gathering a committee of thirteen, of which only two were whites, was designated to draft a platform. At the second gathering the platform was presented. It gave enthusiastic endorsement to the Reconstruction measures of Congress and declared that the Republican party was the savior of the country. Its program of local reforms called for universal education without distinction of race, the prohibition of corporal punishment and imprisonment for debt, the abolition of large estates, the protection of the newly-enfranchised in their rights, and the election to office of "only those who are truly loyal, honest, and capable, irrespective of race." The whites were told that if they wanted the political coöperation of the blacks, "let them come with us, and stand here, side by side, cheek by jowl, and fight for the liberties of this great nation." The assemblage completed its work by calling for a permanent organization of the Republican party and the meeting of a state convention of its members at a later date.[53]

The so-called first state convention of the Union Republican party met in Charleston on May 7. Only nine of the thirty-one counties were represented by sixty-nine delegates. Because of the slim attendance, the convention adjourned after a three-day session, making arrangements for a larger assembly at Columbia in July. But this was a forward step. The leaders were stirred to the necessity for greater action, and opportunity was given for novices to try their hands at parliamentary law and for speakers to denounce the compromises which Governor Orr was then suggesting.[54]

The Columbia convention was gratifying to the Republican leaders. Nineteen counties were represented by some seventy delegates. Its directing spirits were Northerners of both races

---

[53] *News,* Mar. 11 and Mar. 22, 1867.   [54] *Ibid.,* May 8-10, 1867, and *N. Y. Herald,* May 19, 1867.

and Thomas J. Robertson, a native white man of wealth who had come out for a platform "broad enough to accommodate the human race." The suggestion that in the interest of compromise a white man be made president of the body was brushed aside, and the honor fell to R. H. Gleaves, the mulatto who had been president of the preceding Charleston convention. One delegate even took up the suggestion of Wendell Phillips that a Negro be made Republican vice-presidential candidate, but no action was taken on his proposal. A platform was adopted embodying the same ideas as the one approved at the previous Charleston gathering. The work of the convention was completed by calling for a permanent organization of the Union Republican party and the appointment of a central committee to give reality to this ambition. Their work done, the delegates retired to various sections of the state to explain the platform and organize Union Leagues.[55]

*   *   *   *   *

When Negro suffrage became a certainty, a few of the more moderate whites made an effort to control the colored voters. Among those was Governor Orr, who, although regretting the radical turn of affairs, professed to believe that the Negroes needed representation in Congress and that Negro suffrage offered a tolerable way out of the impasse of military rule. Of the Reconstruction acts he said, "I will accept their terms, humiliating as they may be, and openly, fairly and squarely urge their adoption by our people."[56]

Another group of compromisers was under the leadership of Wade Hampton. It was far more influential. Hampton thought he saw the opportunity to turn the Reconstruction acts to the purposes of the whites without offering any tangible concessions to Radicalism. He would do this by inducing the

[55] Accounts of proceedings in *News*, July 25-29, 1867; *Fairfield Herald*, July 31, 1867; and *N. Y. Herald*, Aug. 17, 1867.

[56] Address before Charleston Board of Trade in *News*, Apr. 3, 1867.

Negroes to vote as their former masters bade. The *New York Herald* summarized his views as follows: "He appeals to the blacks, lately his slaves, as his political superiors, to try the political experiment of harmonizing with their late white masters before going into the political service of strangers. . . . The broad fact that the two races in the South must henceforth harmonize on a political basis to avoid a bloody conflict is the ground covered by Wade Hampton."[57]

To promote this sort of coöperation, public meetings were held at which Negroes were invited to listen to speakers of both races. To make the gatherings attractive to the Negroes, they were allowed to march in procession to the place of assemblage, members of their race were appointed as a special police force to supplement the regular white force, and a free barbecue was provided. The white orators stressed the advantages of the close bonds which had existed between the races and the disasters which would come if they were broken. Northern cupidity, they asserted, had been responsible for slavery, and the good in that institution had come from the benevolence of Southerners. Then came the colored orators. They were amiable persons who were always willing to wait until after the whites had spoken and who lectured their race on the wisdom of moderation and honesty. When these gatherings broke, after sturdy repasts of barbecued lamb and kid had been enjoyed, everyone was in the best of spirits and it seemed as if kindly coöperation were going to heal sores left by the war.[58]

But this augury was false. The powerful outside stimuli already described were driving a political wedge between the native whites and the Negroes which appeals to traditional affinities could not arrest. However cordial the social intercourse between the races may have continued to be; however large may have been the crowds which gathered to eat bar-

[57] Cited in *News*, Apr. 4, 1867.
[58] Accounts of these meetings in *Fairfield Herald*, July 10 and 17, 1867, and in *News*, Mar. 23, Apr. 13, May 2, and 25, and July 20, 1867.

becue of the other race; and however pleased the Negro may have been with the kindly sentiments of his former master, the call of the Republican agitators was too alluring not to get all the black man's political sympathies. Were not the whites adhering to the doctrine of universal suffrage because it had been forced upon them by the Republican friends of the Negro? Why should the Negroes follow after men who, in exchange for their votes, gave only nebulous promises of fair play without the promise of public office? Why should they follow leaders who demanded that they speak first and eat their barbecue at a separate table? Better far, the Negroes agreed, to follow leaders who would give the race some of the offices and banquet cheek by jowl with them.

The advocates of non-recognition of the Negroes' political rights found vigorous leaders in ex-Governor Perry and Thomas W. Woodward, a former Confederate officer from Fairfield. "Strange to say," wrote Perry, "there are many persons in the Southern States whose high sense of honor would not let them adopt the Fourteenth Amendment, who are now urging the people to swallow voluntarily the Military Bill, regardless of honor, principle, or consistency." If the state were forced to acquiesce in the tyranny of Congress, he added, "she need not embrace the hideous thing. . . . If we are to wear manacles, let them be put on by our tyrants, not ourselves." He argued the folly of attempting to control the Negro vote. "General Hampton and his friends," he asserted, "had just as well try to control a herd of wild buffaloes as the Negro vote."[59] Woodward was violent in denouncing the compromisers. "Why, oh why, my Southern nigger worshippers," he cried, "will you grope your way through this worse than Egyptian darkness? Why not cease this crawling on your bellies and assume the upright form of men? . . . Stop, I pray

[59] Letters in *News,* Apr. 24, May 18, and Aug. 3, 1867.

you, your efforts at harmony, your advice about conventions, your pusillanimous insinuations about confiscations, etc., or you will goad these people by flattery to destruction, before they have a chance to pick out the cotton crop."[60]

Perry and Woodward had something definite to offer the whites in addition to the saving of pride. Cherishing a faith in the traditional Southern interpretation of the Constitution, they looked to the courts for a remedy. When they failed, they advised the whites to register and vote against the constitutional convention. If they succeeded in this, military rule would continue; but they believed that that was a thousand times better than Negro rule and would give opportunity to await the revival of the Democratic party.[61]

The realization of the futility of the attempt to get the co-operation of the Negroes forced all white leaders, with the single exception of Orr, into agreement with Perry and Wood-ward. In a letter to sixty whites who asked his advice, Hampton wrote, "Recent events show that there is no longer a possibility of that entire harmony of action among our people for which you and we have heretofore hoped and striven." Although he continued to favor restricted Negro suffrage, he declared the Reconstruction acts "illegal, unconstitutional and ruinous."[62] Other advocates of compromise soon expressed agreement with Hampton.[63]

The restored unity of white sentiment was expressed in a convention which met in Columbia a week before the question of the constitutional convention was submitted to the electorate. Twenty-one of the thirty-one districts were represented, and James Chesnut, Jr., a moderate with views like those of Hampton, was made president, and Hampton and Perry were among the vice-presidents. Although this convention expressed a willingness to live under a state constitution like that of any

[60] *Fairfield Herald*, Aug. 28, 1867. See also *ibid.*, May 15 and 29, 1867.

[61] *News*, Apr. 24, 1867, and *Fairfield*

Herald, May 29, 1867.

[62] *News*, Aug. 29, 1867.

[63] *Ibid.*, Oct. 5 and 22, 1867.

Northern state, the Reconstruction acts were declared illegal and designed to "sow the seeds of discord in our midst and place the best interests of society in the hands of an ignorant mob." "The fact is patent to all," it was affirmed, "that the Negro is utterly unfitted to exercise the highest function of a citizen. . . . We protest against this subversion of the social order, whereby an ignorant and depraved race is placed in power and influence above the virtuous, the educated, and the refined." The nation was informed that the white people of South Carolina "would never acquiesce in Negro equality or supremacy."

The convention agreed that no recognition should be given to the proposed constitutional convention. No candidates for membership in that body were suggested, and the registered white voters were asked not to vote in the approaching referendum. It was hoped that the combination of all the whites, with such Negroes as would naturally stay away from the polls, would result in a majority of the electorate's not voting and thereby bring about the defeat of the convention call. It will be remembered that one of the Reconstruction acts stipulated that the convention should not meet unless a majority of the electorate voted.[64]

The policy adopted by the convention had several significant results. The frank manner in which the Reconstruction acts and Negro suffrage were condemned, dissipated all hopes of getting the coöperation of the Negroes under those acts. The refusal to participate in the election of delegates to the constitutional convention meant that that body was to meet without the aid of those who for all times past had been rulers of the state. This gave ground for the charge that the whites, because of their inaction, were in a measure responsible for the extremes to which the Negro-dominated government went.

[64] Proceedings of convention in *News*, Nov. 1 and 9, 1867, and *Courier*, Nov. 9, 1867.

Chesnut, the president of the white convention, characterized the conduct of his associates as follows: "Filled with adjectives and epithets which can only increase animosity, we shall put a weapon in the hands of our enemies."[65]

*   *   *   *   *

The spirit in which the freedmen fulfilled their voting privileges illustrates the effectiveness of the forces which have been described. Their enthusiasm over the opportunity to register their names was perhaps increased by their ignorance of the true significance of that act. "Many of our new-found brethren," said a correspondent of the *New York Herald,* "had no idea what registration meant, and as a natural consequence the most ludicrous scenes took place. Quite a number brought along bags and baskets 'to put it in,' and in nearly every instance there was a great rush for fear we would not have registration 'enough to go around.' Some thought that it was something to eat; others thought it was something to wear; and quite a number thought it was a distribution of confiscated land under a new name."[66] Yet "their eyes beaming with anxiety were constantly turned in the direction from whence the registrars came: . . . after their names were taken they went on their way rejoicing."[67]

The conduct of the freedmen on election days was but a confirmation of their previously shown enthusiasm and ignorance. Everywhere the polls "were thronged with eager crowds of Negroes." At some places there was "wrangling, scrambling, fighting, almost suffocation in the eager rush to be first." Much confusion was caused by the fact that many voters had forgotten the names under which they had registered.[68]

---

[65] *News,* Nov. 9, 1867.

[66] Sept. 24, 1867. Cf. "A," in *News,* Aug. 22, 1867.

[67] *Yorkville Enquirer* cited in *News,* Aug. 26, 1867. Cf. Elizabeth H. Botume, *First Days amongst the Contrabands,* p. 230.

[68] This confusion was of course largely due to the fact that many had been forced to improvise surnames when they registered, since under slavery they had been known only by Christian names.

Some said that they had come to vote for the "Invention," the "Inspection," or for the picture of Lincoln which appeared on the ballots. All were led to believe that they had no choice but to vote "For a Convention."[69]

As may have been expected the election resulted in a decisive Republican victory. The following are the figures:[70]

	Whites	Blacks	Total
Total Registration	46,882	80,550	127,432
"For a Convention"	2,350	66,418	68,768
"Against a Convention"	2,278	0	2,278
Not Voting	42,354	14,132	56,486
Majority "For a Convention"			66,490

All but a handful of the delegates elected to the constitutional convention were Republicans. Since a majority of those registered voted, and a majority of those who voted favored a convention, General Canby ordered that body to assemble in Charleston on January 14, 1868. He named the delegates elected and furnished each of them with credentials.[71]

[69] Accounts of election in *News*, Nov. 20-27, 1867, and *Fairfield Herald*, Nov. 27, 1867.

[70] These figures are from Rhodes, *History of the U. S.*, VI, 83-85. Those in the *Annual Report of Secretary of War, 1868-1869*, I, 521, are slightly different.

[71] See order in *News*, Dec. 29, 1867.

CHAPTER IV

THE INAUGURATION OF THE RADICAL GOVERNMENT

THE "convention of the people of South Carolina," which assembled at Charleston on January 14, 1868, "for the purpose of framing a constitutional and civil government," attracted more attention than any other body which has assembled in the state since the memorable Secession Convention of 1860. The great interest which the whites had always taken in a convention of the people was intensified by the fear that this sovereign body might go to extremes. Might it not resort to tyrannical proscriptions? Might it not by law abolish those social restraints which, it was felt, alone made life tolerable in South Carolina? "The demagogue is to rule the mass, and vice and ignorance control the vast interests at stake," said the *Charleston Daily News*.[1]

If fear heightened the interest of the heretofore dominant element, hope of what might be done gave the articulate portion of the Negro majority a fervent interest. After a year's labor on the part of agitators, the Negroes had been taught to think as a unit in political matters and to believe that, as a result, all sorts of revolutionary benefits would come their way. Inevitably they expected much from a convention which was seemingly possessed of the power to remedy many of the ills which rested upon them.

The presence of representatives of Northern newspapers proved that the outside world had interest in the doings of the convention. Many saw in this assemblage an opportunity to gratify their craving for the sensational and bizarre. The more serious saw in it an opportunity to secure for the state, in per-

[1] Jan. 20, 1868.

manent form, those benefits of democracy which had heretofore been so sternly resisted. Negro rule, it was argued, might
have dangers, but they could be no worse than the example of
government which the state's slaveholders had already given.
Moreover, the interest of practical politicians was excited. The
convention was scheduled to create political institutions which
would definitely tie the state to the Republican party.

The atmosphere of the body impressed the observer with
the fact that it was unique among the many assemblies which
had met to determine the destinies of the state. On the opening day spectators "dressed in the fragmentary style of the
Charleston Negroes" packed the hall, talking politics and equal
rights, paying no attention to the delegates, and spitting around
as though they were not aware that they were not white men.[2]
For the first time in the history of the state the Negro was
represented in an official body.[3] Seventy-six of the 124 delegates
were colored. Only Louisiana, among the Southern states
which were holding conventions at this time, had such a large
proportion of black delegates. Of the seventy-six, two-thirds—
one authority gives the number as fifty-seven[4]—had only a few
years before been slaves, and it is scarcely necessary to add that
illiteracy was one of their most distinguishing characteristics.

The ex-slave delegates, however, deserved little praise or
blame for the work of the convention. For the most part they
maintained a bashful silence, participating in the proceedings
only to the extent of voting as the more sophisticated delegates
directed. Observers said that they wore their best clothes and
tried to be dignified. The native whites felt, said the correspondent of the *New York Times,* that the destinies of the
state were safer in the hands of the unlettered Ethiopians than

[2] Carl Benson, in *New York Times,*
Jan. 27, 1868, and *News,* Jan. 15, 1868.

[3] The five previous constitutional conventions had been composed exclusively
of whites and there were only six Ne-

groes in the constitutional convention of
1895.

[4] Hollis, *Early Period of Reconstruction
in S. C.,* p. 88.

in those of the whites of the body. "Beyond all question," was
the effusive comment of the *Charleston Daily News*, "the best
men in the convention are the colored members. Considering
the influences under which they were called together, and their
imperfect acquaintance with parliamentary law, they have displayed, for the most part, remarkable moderation and dignity.
. . . They have assembled neither to pull wires like some, nor
to make money like others; but to legislate for the welfare of
the race to which they belong."[5] One of this group, Francis L.
Cardozo, was destined to play a leading part in the proceedings.

Of course the nondescript character of their origin was at
times betrayed by absurd conduct. For example, Abram
Dogan, a delegate from Union, was jailed when articles belonging to a fellow-member were found in his trunk.[6] One
evening a group excited by over-indulgence in champagne and
vomiting and using violent language, entered the leading hotel
of Charleston to serenade Thomas J. Robertson.[7] Some of
the reforms proposed by colored delegates were born of ignorant self-assertiveness; for example, the suggestion that landlords be required to pay wages from January 1, 1863, and that
they be required to give their tenants one-half of the crops.[8]

If judged by antecedents and motives, the twenty-seven
Southern members of the convention deserve more condemnation than the Negroes. Their apostasy from the white race
was induced either by hopes of personal aggrandizement or
by pique for some misfortune suffered at the hands of the
heretofore dominant element. In fact, many had before the
war been ardent champions of many things they now affected
to despise. J. M. Rutland, a delegate from Fairfield, had made
up a purse to buy a cane for Preston Brooks after the latter's

[5] Jan. 31, 1868. See also *ibid.*, Jan. 15,
1868, and Benson, in *N. Y. Times*, Jan.
20 and 21, 1868.
[6] *Fairfield Herald*, Mar. 25, 1868, and
J. B. Steadman in *Ku-Klux Conspiracy*,
S. C., pp. 1015-1016.
[7] *Charleston Mercury*, Mar. 11, 1868.
[8] *Proceedings of the Convention of 1868*,
p. 867.

famous assault on Sumner; Franklin J. Moses, Jr., had assisted in hauling down the Union flag from Fort Sumter; Joseph Crews had been a Negro trader; and another delegate had prayed for the sinking of the Yankee fleet. Some of them, notably Crews, J. P. F. Camp, and C. C. Bowen, had been accused of grave crimes, and Moses had already given evidence of a bad character.[9] "There is scarcely a Southern white man in the body," said the correspondent of the *New York Times,* "whose character would keep him out of the penitentiary." In fact there were only two men of outstanding ability in this group. They were Thomas J. Robertson, a wealthy business man willing to be cordial toward the Negro majority, and Dr. Albert G. Mackey, who had gained a national reputation on account of his Unionist sentiments and writings on Masonic subjects. As presiding officer of the convention, Mackey was in no small degree responsible for its most constructive work.

Aside from Mackey, Robertson, and Cardozo, the leading spirits of the convention were a group of non-Southern adventurers of both races. They were Daniel H. Chamberlain, the Reverends B. F. Whittemore and Richard H. Cain, B. F. Randolph, J. K. Jillson, R. B. Elliott, J. J. Wright, A. J. Ransier, C. P. Leslie, and Niles G. Parker. The character, attainments, and antecedents of these men were most varied. A few were incorruptible and sincerely convinced of the necessity of raising South Carolina to the level of Massachusetts. Others were bent upon making the most out of their opportunities. Ignorance was not among their weaknesses since most of them were lawyers, preachers, teachers, and army officers. Perhaps they were as learned as the leaders of any similar body which has met in the Southern states since 1865.

The learning of the leaders bore fruit in a constitution written in excellent English and embodying some of the best

[9] John J. Leland, *A Voice from South Carolina,* p. 52; *News,* Jan. 15, 1868; *N. Y. Times,* Jan. 23, 1868; and *N. Y. World,* Apr. 10, 1868.

legal principles of the age. In letter it was as good as any other
constitution the state has ever had, or as most American
states had at that time. This assertion is supported by the practical endorsement which a subsequent generation of South
Carolinians gave it; the Conservative whites were content to
live under it for eighteen years after they recovered control of
the state government, and when in 1895 they met to make a
new constitution, the document they produced had many of
the features of the constitution of 1868.

But the leaders of the convention of 1868 lacked a practical
acquaintance with the peculiar problems of the state and the
restraint born of extensive vested interest in the community.
As a consequence, they succumbed to the temptation of trying
to legislate into the political complex of the state innovations
which were repellent to its traditions. They created a situation
which made revolution against their decrees inevitable. But
for the touch of practical venality—the members had their own
political futures to look after—the constitution they produced
might have been copied from some manual or improvised by
a board of experts sitting in some distant city. It had the ear-
marks of theoretical perfection. But, as every student of government knows, a constitution which does not agree "with the
humor and disposition of the people in whose favor it is established" could not inspire permanent confidence.

The irresponsible character of the convention is demonstrated by certain facts concerning the origin and property-
holding qualifications of its members. Only twenty-three of
the forty-eight white delegates were natives of the state. Four
were born in other Southern states, seven in Massachusetts,
eight in other Northern states, five in Europe, and the origin
of one is unknown. Seventeen of the seventy-six Negro delegates were non-native. Four were born in other Southern
states, six in the North, one in Dutch Guiana, and the origin

of six is unknown.[10] Five of the delegates were not, at the time of their elections, residents in good faith of the counties from which they were elected.[11] The researches of a group of Conservative contemporaries[12] show that forty-seven white delegates paid only $761.62 in taxes. Of this amount all but $252.76 was paid by one Conservative. This meant that the remaining forty-six averaged less than six dollars each. In fact, twenty-three paid no taxes whatever. The colored delegates made even a less respectable showing. Of the seventy-four listed, one, William McKinley of Charleston, paid $83.35 in taxes; the remainder paid $32.35, or an average of less than fifty cents each. Fifty-nine paid no taxes whatever.

* * * * *

On the first day of the convention, Robertson, the temporary chairman, announced the purpose of the body. It was, he said, "to frame a just and liberal constitution that will guarantee equal rights to all, regardless of race, color, or previous condition."[13] That this purpose was accomplished, in the opinion of the guiding spirits of the deliberations, was attested by A. G. Mackey, the permanent chairman, in his valedictory. He affirmed that for the first time manhood suffrage had been written in the laws of the state and all vestige of serfdom removed; that arrangements had been made for universal education; and that all dangers of rebellion had been removed by the obliteration of "that most pernicious heresy of state sovereignty." "We do not claim," he concluded, "a preëminence of wisdom or virtue, but we do claim that we have followed in the progressive advancement of the age; that

[10] Reynolds, *Reconstruction in S. C.,* pp. 78-79. The figures of the *N. Y. World,* Apr. 10, 1868, are slightly different.

[11] Reynolds, p. 69.

[12] In a pamphlet entitled *An Appeal to the Honorable Senate of the United States in Behalf of the Conservative People of South Carolina, etc.,* which was republished in *Ku-Klux Conspiracy, S. C.,* pp. 1238-49.

[13] *Proceedings of Convention,* p. 60.

we have been bold and honest enough and wise enough to trample obsolete and unworthy prejudice under foot."[14]

The most important concern of the body was the regulation of suffrage and office-holding. The committee on franchise and elections proposed universal suffrage under certain qualifications. It suggested that every male citizen of the United States, "without distinction of race, color, or former condition," who was a resident of the state at the time the constitution was adopted, or thereafter a resident of the state for one year and the county in which he applied for voting for sixty days, should be entitled to vote, with the exception of those who should come of age after 1875 without knowing how to read and write, if physically able to fulfill this qualification, and of those who were disqualified by the national constitution. Others proposed that the payment of a one dollar poll tax be an additional qualification for voting.[15] The residence proposal fitted in with the migratory habits of the Negro and the carpetbagger and was more liberal than any the state had ever had; the educational and poll tax proposal fitted in with the optimistic hopes concerning what was going to be done for popular education. All of these restrictions could have been adopted without preventing universal suffrage from becoming an immediate actuality.

But the convention was determined that there should be no restrictions whatever upon the political power of those who gave it being. The right to vote, said Ransier in a discussion of the proposed educational restriction, "belongs alike to the wise and the ignorant, to the virtuous and vicious. . . . I hope that the music of the nineteenth century will inspire every man upon this floor to view it in the light of progress and reason, and strike out every word that puts a limitation upon the manhood of the citizen, so far as regards the right to vote."[16]

[14] Ibid., pp. 925-26.
[15] Ibid., pp. 709, 824.
[16] Ibid., p. 829. Cf. Cain and S. G. W. Dill, ibid., pp. 823, 829.

Supplementing this fustian were more practical arguments. Elliott pointed out the inconsistency of the convention's attempting to limit the suffrage of those who gave it being, and Cardozo pointed out the impossibility of inaugurating an adequate system of schools before 1875 and that as a consequence the proposed limitation of suffrage would prove fatal to the work of the convention.[17] The educational provision was deserted by its sponsors and defeated by vote of 107 to 2.[18] "You strike at the freedom of South Carolina," said Moses of the poll tax proposal.[19] "You will allow power to go again in the hands of the aristocratic element." It was rejected by vote of 81 to 21.[20] Universal manhood suffrage was adopted without material restrictions.

The convention did not stop here in its enthusiasm for political democracy. Larceny was omitted from the list of crimes for which the legislature might disfranchise. It was a crime of which the freedmen were frequently guilty. Moreover, no persons could be disfranchised for crimes committed while a slave. There should be no property qualification for office holding, and representation in the lower house of the legislature was no longer to be divided between property and white population but was to be apportioned according to the whole population. Provision was made for the popular election of presidential electors, the governor, other state officers, and the county officers including justices of the peace. Although the election of judges by the legislature was continued, their responsibility to public sentiment was made certain by the abolition of life tenure. Justices of the peace were to be elected for six years and circuit judges for four. The four congressional districts were strung out in long lines of counties so as to secure "a majority of loyal voters in every con-

[17] Ibid., pp. 826, 827-28.
[18] Ibid., p. 834.
[19] Ibid., p. 735.
[20] Ibid., pp. 737-38.

gressional district." There were also to be two congressmen-at-large.[21]

The steps taken in the direction of social equality were more nebulous than those in the direction of political equality. An elaborate declaration of rights of forty-one sections superseded the modest declarations of eight and nine sections respectively of the constitutions of 1790 and 1865. It declared that slavery and imprisonment for debt should never exist again in the state. Dueling, the sport of gentlemen, was outlawed. No person was to be disqualified as a witness, prevented from enjoying property rights, hindered in acquiring an education, or subjected to any other legal restraint or disqualification "than such as are laid upon others under like circumstances." As in Louisiana, race lines were abolished by law. "Distinction on account of race or color in any case whatever," the constitution affirmed, "shall be prohibited, and all classes of citizens shall enjoy equally all common, public, legal and political privileges." Only two definite steps, however, were taken towards applying the equality which this dictum implied. Public schools were to be open to all persons regardless of race and no provision was made for the separation of races in the militia. An attempt was made to legislate out of existence the terms by which the whites referred to Northerners and members of the inferior caste. T. J. Coghlan, a white delegate from Sumter, proposed that steps be taken "to expunge forever from the vocabulary of South Carolina the epithets 'negro,' 'nigger,' and 'yankee' as used in the opprobrious sense," but this suggestion was tabled as impractical, as was the resolution to abolish crime and poverty and establish concord.[22]

Efforts were made to establish phases of economic equality. The landless, it was felt, should be aided in the acquirement of property and the landed aristocracy discriminated against.

---

[21] Speech of Whipper, *ibid.*, p. 809. The apportionment is given *ibid.*, p. 886.
[22] *Ibid.*, pp. 205, 208.

STEPS TOWARD ECONOMIC EQUALITY 99

It was proposed that Congress be petitioned to lend the state one million dollars to be used in the purchase of land for the colored people; that the legislature be required to appoint a land commission; that homesteads up to a certain value be exempt from the levy of processes; and that all contracts the consideration of which was the purchase of slaves should be declared null and void.

The fact that Congress would not be likely to listen to a petition asking its aid in the purchase of lands did not dampen the enthusiasm with which the convention debated that question. It offered a golden opportunity for the more loquacious members to display their liking for demagoguery and reform. It was a popular measure among the land-hungry blacks. It was argued that the possession of land was a certain means of raising the new electorate to the level of responsible citizenship. "You cannot make citizens out of these people," declared Moses, "unless you give . . . land; give them houses. They deserve it from the people of South Carolina."[23] The petition was passed by a great majority; but on the receipt of a telegram from Senator Wilson saying that it was impractical, the motion was dropped.[24] The convention had to be content with a substitute calling on Congress to give to the freedmen lands which had been taken for non-payment of Federal taxes and with instructions to the legislature to create a commission to buy additional lands and sell them to the freedmen.

The debate over the proposal to invalidate slave contracts gave opportunity for the display of feelings against the former slaveholders. Instead of taking the statesmanlike view that it was best to say little of the errors of the past, the majority could not let pass the opportunity to rebuke the former master class. "A few years ago," declared Elliott, "the popular verdict of the country was passed upon the slave seller and the slave buyer, and both were found guilty of the enormous crime

[23] *Ibid.*, p. 434.   [24] *Ibid.*, pp. 438-39.

of slavery. The buyer of the slave received his sentence, which was the loss of the slave, and now we pass sentence upon the seller." The ordinance passed by vote of ninety-six to nineteen.[25] But two circumstances prevented the rebuke from being other than moral. Punishment of the slave seller was neutralized by the freeing of the slave buyer of a debt; and it is hard to determine which of the two was the greater sinner in the eyes of the anti-slavery moralist. Second, there was great likelihood of the law's being declared unconstitutional on the ground that it impaired the obligation of contracts. This actually happened.[26]

An act of greater sagacity was the introduction of the principle of protecting homesteads up to a certain value against the processes of creditors. The members were practically unanimous in desiring such a law, but they differed over what the amount of the exemption should be. Some opposed making it as high as two thousand dollars for fear of protecting large land holdings. The provision adopted placed the exemption on lands and buildings at one thousand dollars, in addition to furniture and personal belongings to the value of five hundred dollars.[27]

The legal foundations were laid for a system of universal free education, the nature of which will be discussed elsewhere.[28] It is sufficient to say here that for the first time the fundamental law of the state carried the obligation of universal education and demanded the creation of a school system like that of Northern states.

The rights of women were enlarged. The property of married women was declared not subject to levy or sale for their husbands' debts and to be disposed of as though the wives

[25] *Ibid.*, pp. 227, 248-49.
[26] *Calhoun* vs. *Calhoun*, 2 S. C., p. 283.
[27] *Proceedings of Convention*, pp. 882, 888-89.
[28] See below, pp. 434 ff.

were not married.[29] For the first time in its history the state was given a divorce law.

The principle of national unity was given a sufficiently emphatic recognition to set at rest forever the old South Carolina doctrine of state sovereignty. "Every citizen of this State," it was declared, "owes paramount allegiance to the Constitution and Government of the United States, and no law or ordinance of this State in contravention or subversion thereof can have any binding force." It was further declared, "This State shall ever remain a member of the American Union, and all attempts . . . to dissolve the said Union shall be resisted with the whole power of the State." All members of the bar, public officials, and members of the General Assembly were required to take an oath recognizing the supremacy of the national law.

Perhaps the convention's achievement of greatest permanent importance was the reform of local and judicial administration. Thereafter the judicial districts were to be called counties, the county of Oconee was created out of a part of Pickens District, and provision was made for the creation of other new counties out of areas of not less than 625 square miles.[30] Greater vitality was given to the units of local government. Boards of county commissioners were created with jurisdiction over the highways and the supervision of the collection and disbursement of public funds. A court of probate was instituted in each county with all of the powers of the former ordinary and some of those of the commissioner in equity. A new importance was given justices of the peace by conferring on them jurisdiction in cases involving penalties or judgments not over one hundred dollars. The counties were divided into school districts and townships. All county officers were to be elected by popular vote. This was designed to stimulate the sort of interest in local affairs which Anglo-Saxons had been taught to believe would promote civic virtue.

[29] *Ibid.*, p. 788.   [30] *Ibid.*, pp. 101-4, 842.

The reforms in judicial administration, with the possible exception of the abolition of life tenure of judges, were salutary. A state Supreme Court of three justices was continued, but no provision was made for a separate court of errors. Circuit courts were continued in their old form with a few modifications. Judges were assigned to distinct districts and given jurisdiction in both chancery and common law matters. No provision was made for separate equity judges, or for the district courts of the constitution of 1865.

Not the least among the earnest considerations of the convention was the creation of devices to meet the financial obligations of the government. A committee of Conservatives estimated that $2,230,950, instead of $350,000 as had been the case before the war, would be necessary to meet for the first year the expanded functions of government outlined in the constitution.[31] Although there is no evidence that the constitution-makers contemplated such a radical increase, they were determined to endow the state with thoroughgoing fiscal powers. Provision was made for a uniform tax on all real and personal property and for the levy of taxes by municipalities, counties, townships, and school districts. The government was obligated to make an adequate valuation of lands and improvements by 1870 and every five years thereafter. A commission composed of Chamberlain, Moses, Robertson, DeLarge, and J. M. Allen was created to investigate the financial status of the state for the guidance of the legislature.[32] The new school system, which was expected to be the largest item of expense, was guaranteed an annual levy on all property and a poll tax.

Two acts of omission on the part of the convention were freighted with sinister possibilities. No limit was placed upon the amount of indebtedness the legislature was allowed to contract and upon the agencies to whom the credit of the state

[31] *News*, May 22, 1868.
[32] *Proceedings of Convention*, pp. 1907-8.

might be extended. The committee on finance and taxation suggested that the indebtedness be limited to $500,000 and that the legislature be not allowed to extend credit to private organizations. But these suggestions were voted down.[33] Delegates professed to see visions of industrial progress through state aid. They declared that railroads, schools, and poorhouses must be built and lands distributed among the people. In a progressive age, said Wright, the legislature must do its part, and the responsibility of that body to the people was sufficient check against extravagance.

The official duties of the convention were completed with the enactment of an ordinance prescribing means to put the constitution into effect. It was ordered that an election be held on April 14, 15, and 16, at which the electorate should express their approval or disapproval of the document and choose state officers and legislators and members of Congress. Five days before the adjournment of the convention, General Canby issued an order calling the prescribed election.[34]

* * * * *

An analysis of the proceedings of the convention makes clear how its limitations in circumstances and personnel were reflected in its work. More heed was paid to the arguments of the champions of universal suffrage living in other climes than to the consequences of the application of this principle to the illiterate and poverty-stricken manhood of South Carolina. The efficacy of the plans for universal education was never doubted, although they involved the shattering of traditions, the sending to school of persons who had the least use for book learning, and the imposition of an unprecedented tax burden upon a state recovering from disaster. In deference to the arguments of English economists, it was suggested that the lands be broken into small proprietorships; no inquiry was

[33] Ibid., pp. 656-60.
[34] Ibid., pp. 800-4, 814-22, and News,

Apr. 16, 1868. The text of the constitution of 1868 is in Stat. S. C., XIV.

made as to whether this would promote the prosperity of the state. In obedience to the equalitarian philosophy of the age, steps were taken toward the eradication of the caste system of the state. Doubts concerning the wisdom of such reforms, or the ability of a mere legislative assembly to change the social order, were not entertained. More attention was paid to the contemporary doctrines of economic progress than to the financial ability of the government to meet the obligations which such doctrines involved. In order to satisfy the forces which had triumphed in the war, stinging declarations against slavery and states' rights were adopted; the injured feelings of the by no means impotent white minority were not considered.

But it must be admitted that there was some justification for the behavior of the convention. Universal suffrage, its most radical innovation, was forced upon it. Congress demanded this reform as the principal prerequisite for the readmittance of the state into the Union. Qualified suffrage would have meant a white majority and the return to power of those who would have made short shrift of the convention's work. The suffrage provisions adopted were not so objectionable as those of the constitutions being adopted at this time in other Southern states. South Carolina, unlike these states, did not require the prospective voter to swear to accept the political and civil equality of all men and not to attempt to deprive any persons of any privilege; and it did not disfranchise persons for political causes.[35] The *Charleston Daily News* declared, "The constitution framed by the Reconstruction convention is more liberal in regard to the right of suffrage than any other constitution in the Southern states made under the authority of the Congressional legislation."[36] Moreover, as we shall see,[37] universal education was not the mere inspiration of cloistered reformers;

[35] Cf. the constitutions of Georgia, Arkansas, Alabama, Mississippi, Florida, Louisiana, and Virginia as digested in McPherson, *History of Reconstruction*, pp. 327-35.

[36] June 20, 1868.

[37] See below, pp. 426 ff.

it registered a sincere and persistent desire of the Negroes. The plan to increase public expenditures satisfied more than the demands of doctrinaire optimists and office-seekers. The rebuilding of a shattered commonwealth and the inauguration of a liberal democracy required more money than had the government of the parsimonious oligarchy which had ruled the state before the war.

The manner in which the convention went about its work was almost exemplary. It finished its labors within fifty-three days, foregoing the temptation to enjoy for a longer time the eleven dollars per diem allowed each member. President Mackey and the able carpetbag leaders, assisted by the competent advice of such outsiders as D. T. Corbin and D. C. Melton, disciplined the members to their proper tasks. The loquacious were restrained, and when a member made improper mileage claims, he was reprimanded by the president. The office of chaplain was dispensed with when several members opposed "digging unnecessarily into the state treasury." An incompetent sergeant at arms was discharged.[38] Moreover, the delegates did not create "the Negro bedlam" which tradition has associated with them. President Mackey said that he had "no unpleasant reminiscences of those acrimonious bickerings which, in all deliberative assemblies, are often incidental to the excitement of debate and the attrition of antagonistic minds."[39] Insults were avoided in referring to the whites; there was even an inclination to respect the feelings of "the brave men" who had been defeated. The only occasion on which there was disorder was when the reporter of the *Charleston Mercury* was expelled from the floor. The newspaper had been engaged in scathing attacks on members of "the ringed, striped and streaked" convention. When an attack on the president was published, E. W. M. Mackey, his

[38] *News,* Jan. 18, 1868, and *Proceedings of Convention,* pp. 19-21, 58-62, 582.   [39] *Ibid.,* p. 924.

son, assaulted the reporter, and after a scene characterized by threats of mob violence, the convention voted to exclude all representatives of the newspaper.[40]   On the other hand, the *Charleston Daily News* and the *Charleston Daily Courier* were praised for the fairness of their accounts of the proceedings, and their representatives were extended every courtesy.   The convention received warmly an address which Governor Orr delivered before it, and probably would have listened to other Conservatives had they been amenable.

*   *   *   *   *

One week before the adjournment of the constitutional assembly, a convention of the Republican party met to make nominations for the state officials and congressmen to be elected in the approaching election.   This convention was largely composed of delegates to the constitutional convention, and all but two of the fourteen nominees of the party were members of the convention.[41]

The Republican convention was followed by mass meetings in the various counties which endorsed the nominees of the party and nominated candidates for the legislature and county offices.   The enthusiasm engendered at these meetings was illustrated by the following account of the one held at Georgetown: "The freedmen from their respective plantations assembled *en masse* to participate in the selection of their representatives in the general assembly. Prior to the meeting, groups were to be seen in every direction on Bay Street, holding their caucuses and discussing the merits and demerits of the respective candidates for nomination. The shrill shriek of the fife, however, soon summoned them to their rendezvous where a hot contest ensued between the friends and supporters of the several candidates."[42]

[40] *Proceedings of Convention*, p. 187, and *News*, Jan. 17, 1868.

[41] This convention is described in *News*, Mar. 2, 9-2, 1868, and *Courier*, Mar. 2-12, 1868. The names and char-

acter of the nominees are given in Chap. V.

[42] *News*, Apr. 9, 1868. Cf. *ibid.*, Mar. 28, and Apr. 3 and 14, 1868.

"I SHALL DISCHARGE EVERY NIGGER WHO VOTES TO ADOPT THIS RADICAL YANKEE CONSTITUTION"

Trowbridge, *A Picture of the Desolated States*

Republican victory in the approaching election was made more certain by the conduct of General Canby. By a series of orders,[43] he endeavored to protect the voters in the exercise of their right and to insure a maximum participation in the election. He warned that any attempt to interfere with the voting would involve the full penalties of the law, and military commissioners, with troops at their command, were charged with supervision of the election. He set aside five days in which qualified persons previously unregistered might register, and allowed persons who had moved from the precinct in which they had registered to vote at the one nearest them.

To meet the Republican onslaught, the whites abandoned their policy of inaction. Even if they could not save the state from Radical domination, they felt that there should be a concerted expression of white opinion and that delegates should be elected to the national Democratic Convention, a body in which they never lost hope. "Fellow citizens of Sumter District," ran a typical Democratic exhortation, "arouse from your lethargy. Think of your wives and children. Let the love of them stimulate you to action."[44] Democratic clubs were organized in many counties late in March.[45]

A convention of these clubs was held in Columbia on April 2. It gave expression to the well-nigh unanimous sentiment of the white race when, in a series of pronouncements, it roundly condemned the recently published constitution and the political activities of the Negroes. The constitution was said to be "the work of sixty-odd Negroes, many of them ignorant and depraved, together with fifty white men, outcasts of Northern society, and Southern renegades, betrayers of their race and country." Its franchise provisions were declared to be designed to further the ambitions of "mean whites"; its judicial system "repugnant to our customs and habits of thought"; the home-

[43] *Ibid.*, Mar. 16 and 24 and Apr. 7, 1868.

[44] *Sumter Watchman* cited *ibid.*, Mar. 26, 1868.

[45] *Ibid.*, Mar. 25-31, 1868.

stead provision "a snare and deceit"; and "the stupendous school arrangement" "a fruitful source of peculant corruption." The Negroes were told that their political activities, if persisted in, would bring ruin to them and the state.

Nevertheless, this convention made one significant concession. The colored population was recognized "as an integral part of the body politic," and the whites were pledged "when we have the power, to grant them, under proper qualifications as to property and intelligence, the right of suffrage."

Moreover, the mistake of political inaction was recognized. A recent congressional enactment had removed all possible advantages which might be derived from non-participation in the approaching constitutional referendum. It said that the constitution would be effective if a majority of the voters favored it regardless of whether or not a majority of those registered took part in the election. The voters were urged to vote against the constitution. A full state ticket, headed by W. D. Porter, a Charleston moderate who had been lieutenant governor under Orr, was nominated. Although the making of nominations for offices under the new constitution may be interpreted as a recognition of the legality of that document, the convention was careful to assert the contrary. It declared, "In voting for officers under the constitution we put on record our protest against its validity." It is likely that the nominations were made without any hope of electing the candidates, but as adjunct to the main purpose of defeating the constitution.

Several additional acts completed the work of the assembly. As many delegates as the number of the state's representation in Congress were elected to the national Democratic Convention. The fact that the state was entitled to double this number seems to have been overlooked.[46] The organization of Conservative clubs to enlist the support of Negro voters was urged. An executive committee, with Hampton as its chair-

[46] Reynolds, p. 101.

man and John P. Thomas as its leading spirit, was organized to direct activities and to protest to Congress against the new constitution.[47]

The efforts of the Democrats to stem the rising tide of Republicanism were unsuccessful. The colored voters turned a deaf ear to the suggestion that they put trust in "old friends," who had treated them "humanely and justly," and repudiate the politicians who had been "cruel slave-owners."[48] The constitution was ratified by vote of 70,758 to 27,228. The entire Republican state and congressional ticket was successful. Only six of the thirty-one senators and fourteen of the 124 representatives were Democrats. This party had been able to carry only Horry and the nine hill counties.[49] Moreover, Congress failed to heed the representations of the whites made against what was taking place. When their committee told the congressional committee on reconstruction that the whites of South Carolina "would never submit quietly to Negro rule," Thaddeus Stevens replied, "What the protest claimed as grievances were regarded as virtues."[50] Congress accepted the state constitution, and South Carolina, by the omnibus bill of May 22, 1868, was declared entitled to representation in Congress as soon as its legislature should have approved the Fourteenth Amendment.[51] This was soon done. On July 7 the senate, with only five votes in the negative, ratified the Amendment, and on the next day the house followed suit by vote of 108 to 10. Shortly afterwards two United States senators were elected. Then the South Carolina delegation was admitted to both houses of Congress. On July 24, Canby announced that all authority conferred on him by the Reconstruction acts was

[47] Accounts of those proceedings in the *News* and the *Courier,* Apr. 2-6, 1868. The officers and nominees listed in Reynolds, pp. 88-89.

[48] Speech of Col. A. C. Haskell, *News,* Apr. 11, 1868.

[49] Reynolds, pp. 93, 106-8.

[50] *News,* May 9, 1868.

[51] McPherson, *History of Reconstruction,* pp. 337-38.

remitted to the civil authorities. Thus in the eyes of Congress, the process of reconstruction was completed.[52]

*   *   *   *   *

But the whites gained some comfort from the course of events. They had been able to elect legislators in half a dozen counties; and they carried half the counties in the election of June 2 and 3 for the choice of county officers.[53] They had hopes of doing better in future elections.

Then, too, the whites showed no tendency to adjust doctrines and feelings to the new conditions. This was evident in the refusal of W. D. Porter to accept the nomination for governor from the convention which had approved qualified Negro suffrage and in the demand that there be another white convention to repudiate the declaration of the aforementioned convention. Accordingly a convention was held in Columbia on June 8. It adopted a resolution favoring "a white man's government" and elected delegates to the national Democratic Convention. Through the mediation of Hampton, conciliation was effected with a representation of the April convention. The executive committees and delegations to the national convention of both were combined, and it was generally understood that the April declaration on Negro suffrage had been repudiated.[54]

The feelings of the whites in the spring and summer of 1868 toward the government then going into operation were made clear. "The maddest, most unscrupulous and infamous revolution in history," ran a typical comment, "has snatched the power from the hands of the race which settled the country . . . and transferred it to its former slaves, an ignorant and feeble race."[55] The Euphradian Society, a debating club of the University of South Carolina, took revenge on two of its

---

[52] *House Journal, Ex. Sess., 1868,* pp. 3. 50, and 81, and *News,* July 21, 1868.
[53] See comments of *News,* June 12 and 15, 1868.
[54] *News,* June 10-12, 1868.
[55] *Fairfield Herald,* Apr. 29, 1868.

members who dared be prominent in the councils of the new régime. Thomas J. Robertson and Franklin J. Moses, Jr., were declared to have "in all respects lowered their dignity and station as true gentlemen of Carolina," and their names were declared to be "no longer an ornament to or a jewel in the honorary roll of this society." They were expelled.[56] These and similar declarations indicated the true feelings of the whites even before the new government had a chance to try its hands.

[56] Reynolds, p. 99.

CHAPTER V

THE RADICAL GOVERNMENT

THUS was South Carolina restored to the Union, her freedmen given the suffrage, and her former ruling oligarchy deprived of political power. As the result of religious, philanthropic, or partisan zeal, new men and new measures were to have their way for a few troublous years. Viewed from almost any angle, Reconstruction was a failure. Perhaps one may say that the Negro race itself lost more than it gained; certainly parties and politics played ignoble rôles. From the beginning, congressional reconstruction was doomed by both sectional and racial antagonisms, and many prophets foretold as much. That South Carolina would consent to be ruled by alien whites and native blacks was unthinkable; and that the rule of such people would not coincide with the interests of the native whites was equally certain. Thus in 1868 was begun a struggle which was to last for nine years; not until 1877 did a political minority triumph over a majority. Broadly speaking, one may say that the carpetbag and Negro government fell because it was too weak to withstand a well-organized, determined minority which was fighting for what it firmly believed to be its social, economic, and political existence. Even in its palmiest days the Radical government felt secure only when protected by Federal troops. Had that government been more capable, more efficient, and more honest, no doubt a different story could be told.

The failure of the Radical government, supported almost until the end by the strong arm of the Federal government and operating under a modern, and in most respects excellent, constitution, was due not so much to its organization as to its personnel. To the native Carolinian, a carpetbagger was a contemptible parasite, a Negro was properly a servant and not a fit creature to rule, and for a scalawag the Conservative native had a perfect antipathy. Some important figures in the Radical personnel will be examined more closely.

Robert Kingston Scott, governor of South Carolina from 1868 to 1872, first entered Charleston as a prisoner of war.[1] From his native state of Pennsylvania he migrated to Ohio and thence to California, where he engaged in mining and the practice of medicine. Before returning to Ohio and setting up as a physician, realtor, and merchant, he made a prospecting tour in Mexico and South America. He was the organizer and colonel of a regiment of Ohio volunteers. Later he was brevetted a major general and in January, 1866, he was made assistant commissioner of the Freedmen's Bureau for South Carolina, a position he held until inaugurated governor.[2]

As a Westerner it was thought that he would not arouse the prejudices of the native whites as much as a New Englander. His first message to the legislature appears to have given more satisfaction than was expected, the *Charleston Daily News* stating that it was "reassuringly moderate in sentiment," and seemed to indicate that Scott was "anxious to gain the good will of the respectability and intelligence of the State."[3] In this message Scott recommended that the General Assembly memorialize Congress to relieve every citizen of the state from all political disabilities,[4] and by his appointments he earnestly endeavored to appease the former ruling class.[5] But with all his disposition to act fairly,[6] Scott possessed neither the courage nor the ability to control the unscrupulous men who surrounded him. And the legislature was quite beyond his influence.

[1] *Senate Journal,* 1872-73, p. 33.

[2] *National Cyclopedia of American Biography,* XII, 175-76; *Phoenix,* Sept. 1, 1868; *News,* Nov. 9, 1868, Aug. 3, 1870, Aug. 22, 1872; Columbia *State,* Aug. 15, 1900.

[3] July 10, 14, 1868.

[4] *Courier,* July 10, 1868.

[5] Last message, *Senate Journal, 1872-73,* pp. 29, 30.

[6] *News,* Sept. 12, 1868.

Some of its leading members, both black and white, denounced him very bitterly, and in 1871 he was impeached by the House for "high crimes and misdemeanors" in connection with a large over-issue of bonds.[7]

This first Republican governor of South Carolina, who found himself confronted with the many perplexities of a great political and social revolution, was not corrupt at heart nor was he devoid of common sense. But he was notoriously weak and pliant and was incapable of withstanding the cool and deliberate strategy of his associates. He was "subject alike to alcoholic and female allurements," and on one occasion the scheming state officials gave a star of the burlesque stage a percentage commission to induce the drunken governor to sign an issue of bonds.[8]

Important in the tangled financial history of the state during Reconstruction was Niles Gardiner Parker, state treasurer during the two administrations of Scott.[9] Coming to the state as a captain in a regiment of colored volunteers, Parker settled in Charleston as a planter and merchant. Later he became proprietor of a small hotel. In 1867 he was a member of the city council, and in 1868 he was prominent in the constitutional convention as chairman of the finance committee.[10] Like Scott, he was by temperament frank and genial but pliable. By training and by character he was not fitted to supervise the revenues of the state or to pass through his hands millions of dollars in bonds.

Comptroller-General John L. Neagle was little better. Sent to Davidson College in his native state of North Carolina to

---

[7] *House Journal, 1871-72*, pp. 181 ff.; *News*, Dec. 20, 21, 23, 1871; Jan. 21, 26, 1872.

[8] E. P. Mitchell, *Memoirs of an Editor*, p. 326.

[9] 1868-1872. By the constitution of 1868 the governor was elected biennially and the treasurer, comptroller-general,

attorney-general, secretary of state, and superintendent of education were elected quadrennially. In 1874 an amendment made all elections biennial.

[10] *News*, Mar. 9, 1868; *Mercury*, Feb. 21, 1868; *N. Y. Nation*, May 26, 1870; *N. Y. World* as quoted in *Keowee Courier*, Sept. 20, 1877.

Top left: ROBERT KINGSTON SCOTT, GOVERNOR, 1868-1872. *Top right:* REVEREND
BENJAMIN FRANKLIN WHITTEMORE, MEMBER OF THE CONSTITUTIONAL CONVEN-
TION, 1868; CONGRESS, 1868-1870; STATE SENATE, 1870-1877. *Bottom left:* MAR-
TIN R. DELANY, EDITOR, PHYSICIAN, CANDIDATE FOR LIEUTENANT-GOVERNOR ON THE
UNION REFORM TICKET IN 1874. *Bottom right:* ROBERT SMALLS, MEMBER OF THE
HOUSE OF REPRESENTATIVES, 1868-1870; STATE SENATE, 1870-1874; CONGRESS,
1875-1879, 1882-1887; CONSTITUTIONAL CONVENTION, 1895.

prepare for the Presbyterian ministry, he was soon expelled for stealing; then he read medicine with a physician. After serving as an assistant surgeon in the Confederate army, he settled at Rock Hill, South Carolina, where he kept a store; it was as a delegate from York County that he was sent to the constitutional convention.[11] More honest than Parker, he was usually excluded from any profits in the manipulations of the Financial Board and the Bond Ring.

The most interesting character in South Carolina during Reconstruction was Daniel Henry Chamberlain, attorney-general under Scott, 1868-1872, and governor of the state, 1874-1876. A native of Massachusetts, he was educated at Phillips' Academy, Amherst, Yale, and Harvard. In 1864 he entered the war as a lieutenant, and two years later he went to South Carolina; he became first a planter and then a politician. Representing Berkeley District in the constitutional convention of 1868, he proved to be one of the leading delegates. Calm, cool, and temperate in manner, with a voice sharp and clear, his argumentative, decided speech betrayed his educated training and marked him as a polished orator. In appearance he was a little below the average height, with a compact, elastic, and well poised figure. His head was prematurely bald and his eyes and face were expressive and full of quick intelligence. As a cold, elegant man of refined habits, cultivated tastes, and undoubted intellectual force, he often seemed to be more a critical scholar than a Republican partisan.[12]

In 1874 Chamberlain was elected governor, and the reforms which he inaugurated were so extensive that a large portion of

[11] *Mercury*, Feb. 22, 1868; *News*, Mar. 9, Aug. 8, 15, 1868. March 15, 1870, the *News* described Neagle as "A physician by profession, comptroller-general by authority of Governor Scott, and a sneaking looking white man by gift of nature."
[12] *News*, Mar. 9, 1868; *Phoenix*, Aug. 21, 1872; *News and Courier*, May 22.

1877, April 14, 1907; A. B. Williams in Columbia *State*, Sept. 19, 1926; [Belton O'Neall Townsend], *Atlantic Monthly*, XXXIX (Feb., 1877), 182; James Green, *Personal Recollections of Daniel Henry Chamberlain, passim*; Walter Allen, *Governor Chamberlain's Administration in South Carolina*, biographical sketch.

the whites hailed him as a savior. But before that date his love for reform had not been preëminent. With Scott and Parker he was a member of the financial board, and his transactions with Kimpton, the financial agent of the state, were questionable.[13] In 1877 a legislative investigating committee had "not a doubt" that Chamberlain paid $2,500 for the purpose of securing a favorable decision for his client in the case of *William Whaley* vs. *Bank of Charleston* before the Supreme Court.[14] Whether or not Chamberlain actually profited from any personal malfeasance in office, it is certain that he could not have been oblivious to the corruption which surrounded him. Young and ambitious, perhaps he did not feel that he should shoulder the burden of reform alone. But his position in the government would have given him vast influence. Always he posed individually as a reformer, though never joining a "reform" party. His knowledge of political science and his thorough understanding of the forces at work during Reconstruction qualified him for a place which he never assumed.[15]

Francis Louis Cardozo was the most prominent Negro to hold an administrative office. He was secretary of state under Scott, 1868-1872,[16] and treasurer under Governors Moses and Chamberlain, 1872-1876. A free-born mulatto, he was reputed to have been the son of J. N. Cardozo, a Jewish economist of Charleston, by a half-Negro, half-Indian mother. He grad-

[13] *Reports and Resolutions, 1877-78,* Fraud Report. The report cited was the work of several commissions and committees appointed by the Democratic legislature of 1877 to investigate the various frauds of the Radicals. The voluminous report is based on sworn testimony and private documents. See pp. 920-25, 932-33 for testimony of Parker alleging that he, Scott, Chamberlain, and Kimpton were to make certain divisions of state money fraudulently secured. See pp. 1576-81 for Chamberlain's connection with the Greenville and Columbia Railroad fraud.

[14] *Reports and Resolutions, 1877-78,* Fraud Report, pp. 1769 ff.

[15] See Chamberlain's letter admitting the failure of the Radical government, *News,* May 8, 1871. See also his defense in *News and Courier,* Aug. 20, 1874, and the *Atlantic Monthly,* April, 1901. For a more favorable estimate of Chamberlain see *Dictionary of American Biography,* III, 595.

[16] Oct. 31, 1871, he resigned to accept a professorship in Howard University, but apparently the resignation was not accepted.—*Reports and Resolutions, 1871-72,* p. 193.

uated with distinction from the University of Glasgow, and after two years at a theological school in London he became a Presbyterian minister and returned to New Haven to accept a church. After the war he went to Charleston as principal of Avery Institute and then entered politics. He was a handsome man, almost white in color, and with his tall, portly, well groomed figure and elaborately urbane manners, he soon made himself a power in politics and became head of the Union League. He was an expert accountant; on several occasions he refused to put the state seal on fraudulent bonds. In 1875 there was a movement to impeach him, and the General Assembly presented a petition to Chamberlain for his removal. Irregularity and misconduct in office were charged but not proved.[17]

*   *   *   *   *

Having inquired as to the manner of men who were to be largely responsible for the administration of a new government in a new society, let us glance briefly at some of the more important representatives of this sovereign state in Washington. On July 9, 1868, the state had been admitted to the Union as entitled to four representatives, elected by popular vote, and two senators elected by the General Assembly.

B. Frank Whittemore of Malden, Massachusetts, was said to be a graduate of Amherst College and to have traveled in Europe and South America. As a minister of the Methodist Episcopal church, he was sent to South Carolina by the Freedmen's Bureau to organize schools. Possessed of a stentorian bass voice, he could address large audiences and sing well at meetings and soon became extremely popular with the Negroes. After serving in the constitutional convention, he was elected to Congress from the first district, and was seated July

[17] *News*, Nov. 11, 1867, Mar. 9, 1868; *News and Courier*, Feb. 25, Mar. 3, 6, 8, 10, 11, 12, 22, 1875; *Phoenix*, July 25, 1873; *News*, Aug. 10, 1872; Chicago *Herald*, June 21, 1884; *Keowee Courier*, Sept. 20, 1877; Columbia *State*, Mar. 18, 1906; Williams in Columbia *State*, Nov. 21, 1926.

18, 1868. The *Charleston Daily News* described him as a cunning demagogue who had ingratiated himself with the Negroes by social intercourse, falsehoods and blandishments, and who could "control more Negro votes than any other white man in the State."[18]   When expelled from Congress for having been "influenced by improper pecuniary considerations in making appointments to the Military and Naval academies," his constituents promptly returned him to that body by a vote of 11,101 to 2,548 for his competitor.[19]   When he presented his credentials a second time, the House declined to allow him to be sworn.[20]   He was then elected to the state Senate where he played a conspicuous part throughout Reconstruction.

It would be difficult to imagine a more corrupt and degraded rascal than Christopher Columbus Bowen who represented South Carolina in Congress from July 20, 1868, to March 3, 1871.   From his native Rhode Island he went to Georgia, where he made a living as faro dealer and gambler. Shortly after his dismissal from the Confederate army by a court-martial, he instigated the murder of his commanding officer.   From the Charleston jail he was released by the general delivery which followed the invasion of the city by Union troops.   Bowen became a champion of the rights of the freedmen and was one of the organizers of the Republican party in the state.   After two terms in Congress, he was elected sheriff of Charleston County as well as a member of the General Assembly.   In February, 1871, he was acquitted of a bigamy charge.   Four months later, however, he was convicted on another charge and sentenced to two years in Albany; he was pardoned by President Grant.[21]

[18] Sept. 12, 1868.

[19] He was not actually expelled by Congress but resigned the day before expulsion would have come, Feb. 24, 1870.

[20] *News*, Jan. 15, Feb. 17, 1868; *N. Y. Times*, Jan. 23, 1868; *News*, Mar. 17, 18, 1870; *News*, Feb. 22, June 2, 1870; *News*

and *Courier*, Jan. 29, 1894; *Biographical Congressional Directory, 1774-1911,* pp. 1107, 254, n. 2.

[21] His wife, who stood faithfully by him during the trial, was Mrs. Susan Petigru King Bowen, daughter of James L. Petigru.—*Biographical Congressional*

The other members of the House, Manuel S. Corley and James H. Goss, were South Carolinians. They were of little influence and were soon dropped from office. No Negro senators ever represented the state, and it was not until 1870 that Joseph H. Rainey, the first Negro to sit in the House of Representatives, was sent to Congress to fill the vacancy caused by Whittemore's being refused his seat. In 1871 the state sent two Negroes, Rainey and Robert B. Elliott, to the House and a third, Robert C. DeLarge, contested for a seat; the next Congress had four South Carolina Negroes, Rainey, Elliott, Alonzo J. Ransier, and Richard H. Cain; one of them, Elliott, resigned to return to his state and become speaker of the House; Rainey and Robert Smalls represented the state in the last Congress before the overthrow of Radical rule.

The senators elected by the General Assembly in 1868 were men of worth and ability. Thomas J. Robertson was a native, a graduate of South Carolina College, and one of the wealthiest business men in the state. He was one of the first prominent persons in South Carolina to join the Republican party.[22] Robertson was elected for the short term but was reëlected and served until March 3, 1877. Frederick A. Sawyer, elected for the long term, was a native of Massachusetts but had come to Charleston in 1859 to take charge of the Normal School. A very honest and capable gentleman, he soon lost favor with his party, and in 1873 he was replaced by John J. Patterson of

Directory, p. 489; A. G. and T. J. Mackey, *The Political Record of Senator F. A. Sawyer and Congressman C. C. Bowen of South Carolina*, pp. 11-23; *News*, April 13, 1869; Feb. 17, Nov. 28, June 2, Feb. 14, June 16, 1871; Jan. 10, 20, 25, 1873; *News and Courier*, Oct. 21, 23, 1874; *Courier*, Sept. 4, Nov. 18, 1872; *Fairfield News and Herald*, April 3, 1878; James M. Morgan, *Recollections of a Rebel Reefer*, pp. 351, 353-59. The *News* did not exaggerate when on May 6, 1868, it said: "Not gifted, but bold; not discreet, but voluble; not learned, but swaggering; not particular, but ambitious; not black, but comely—this Georgia Confederate Captain wormed himself into the ring, into the convention, into the nominating mouth and over the heads of worthy men into the saddle for a seat in Washington, and by the will of reconstructed South Carolina is declared the choice for the same."

[22] *News*, Jan. 15, Mar. 9, July 29, 1868; *Phoenix*, April 15, 1868; Columbia *State*, Oct. 14, 1897.

Pennsylvania, perhaps the most notorious man in the state during Reconstruction.[23]

* * * * *

Perhaps the most important body in the state was the General Assembly. To it was given the authority of carrying into effect the provisions of the new constitution. Laws, therefore, must be passed regulating and supervising the functions of the administrative officers, a judicial system must be established, the laws codified, local government reordered, the state institutions provided for, the peace and harmony of the citizens maintained, internal improvements encouraged, the debt of the state diminished and its credit improved, and all the citizens, without regard to race, color, or previous condition, given equal justice. For all those purposes money must be raised and disbursed in the interests of the taxpayers and citizens. The success or failure of Reconstruction in South Carolina was to depend to a very great degree upon the efficiency, honesty, and intelligence of the General Assembly. Would it be equal to the task of establishing a new government in an old commonwealth in which existed strange and heretofore unknown political and social conditions?

The legislature which assembled in Janney's Hall in Columbia on July 6, 1868, in special session, presented a sad and peculiar spectacle to the former rulers of the state. Through the action of a Radical Congress and the aid of the military power of the United States, an alien people and a former sub-

[23] *Biographical Congressional Directory,* p. 977; *Courier,* June 14, 1865; *N. Y. Times* and *N. Y. Herald* in *News,* July 21, 1868; *News,* July 6, 14, 15, 17, 1868; Aug. 27, 1872; Mar. 19, 1873. In 1873 Sawyer became assistant secretary of the Treasury and continued in government service for most of his life. Sawyer defeated A. G. Mackey of Charleston in the senatorial race. There was a movement to elect a Negro to the position. It was said that Charles Sumner had written a letter expressing "regret that the golden opportunity should be lost of making a colored citizen senator . . . a colored senator would be as good as a constitutional amendment, making all backward steps impossible." Prominent Negroes, however, declared that the safety of the state depended upon the election of Sawyer because he had the confidence of the Conservatives, and Conservative votes aided in his election.

ject race were placed in control against the will of a majority
of the white people. And from those white people the legislature was to have a determined and rigid opposition throughout its entire existence. Of the 157 legislators, 84 were colored
and 72 were white; of the whites, 7 in the Senate and 16 in
the House were Conservatives.[24] It was said that the comptroller's report showed the total taxes paid by the members of
the legislature to be $700.63, and of this amount six members
paid $391.62, leaving the balance paid by all others at $309.01.[25]

The first legislature was not greatly different from succeeding ones. The proportion of black and white, Radical and
Conservative, varied, but always there was a large Radical
majority. Even in the legislature of 1874-1876, where there
was a white majority of three, the Radicals had a majority of
73. The composition and character of the legislature never
improved; if anything it got worse.[26]

Naturally the Conservative press of the state heaped abuse
upon this assemblage. The files of the leading newspapers of
the time are full of the most scathing, cutting words that a pen
could write. One unfamiliar with the situation would think

[24] *Phoenix*, July 25, 1868.
[25] *Ibid.*, May 10, 1868. Williams in
Columbia *State*, Aug. 8, 1926, said only
three Negro Senators paid taxes and the
total was $2.10. Fifty-eight Negro rep-
resentatives, he said, were not tax-payers.
John S. Reynolds, *Reconstruction in South
Carolina*, p. 108, gives the following
statistics: Average tax of Republican members was $3.12 and 91 paid no tax what-
ever. The senators and representatives
from Charleston—twenty in all—paid a
tax of $84.35, of which all but a dollar
(paid by F. J. Moses, Jr.) was paid by a
colored man. By Art. I, Sec. 32 of the
constitution of 1868 no property qualification was necessary for the holding of
any office.
[26] For the composition of succeeding
legislatures the following are the statistics as nearly as they can be ascertained:

1870, House: 49 white, 75 colored; 22
Reformers, 1 Independent, 101 Radicals;
Senate: 20 white, 10 colored (two having
died); 24 Radicals, 5 Reformers, 1 Independent. 1872, House: 80 colored, 101
Radicals, 23 Conservatives; Senate: 16
colored, 17 white, 25 Radicals, 8 Conservatives. 1874, House: 50 white, 74
colored, 92 Radicals, 32 Conservatives;
Senate: 16 colored, 17 white, 26 Radicals,
7 Conservatives. As given in the rolls of
the House and Senate there were in the
General Assembly of 1870: 10 lawyers,
31 farmers, 9 physicians, 17 clergymen,
12 teachers, 16 planters, 13 merchants, 3
merchant tailors, 3 clerks, 2 masons, 8
builders, 1 engineer, 1 marble dealer, 8
carpenters, 2 hotel keepers, 1 druggist, 1
bookkeeper, 1 wheelwright, 4 coach makers, 1 tanner, 2 mechanics, 1 chemist, 1
auditor, 1 hatter, 1 blacksmith, 1 tailor.

that the editors and their correspondents had gone crazy with anger or were obsessed with some fearful mania, so great was the ridicule, contempt, and obloquy showered upon the representatives of the state. With the deepest scorn for a scalawag, with all the Southern hatred for an adventuring Yankee, and with either sympathy or shame for the ignorant, misled Negro, the press, the aristocracy, the poor whites, the up-country, the low-country—all with one voice protested against the "unlawful assembly" in Columbia, maintained in power, they said, by the Federal bayonet. The *Fairfield Herald* battled "against the hell-born policy which has trampled the fairest and noblest States of our great sisterhood beneath the unholy hoofs of African savages and shoulder-strapped brigands—the policy which has given up millions of our free-born, high-souled brethren and sisters, countrymen and countrywomen of Washington, Rutledge, Marion, and Lee, to the rule of gibbering, louse eaten, devil worshipping barbarians, from the jungles of Dahomey, and peripatetic buccaneers from Cape Cod, Memphremagog, Hell, and Boston."[27]

Northern observers visited the capital to record their impressions. Andrew D. White found the State House "a beautiful marble building, but unfinished without and dirty within." He found the door of the House of Representatives "guarded by a Negro, squalid and filthy," who "evidently reveled in his new citizenship." With his chair tilted back against the wall, his feet high in the air, the doorman was "making everything nauseous about him with tobacco." When finally admitted to the House, White beheld "one of the most singular deliberative bodies ever known—a body composed of former landed proprietors and slave-owners mixed up pell-mell with their former slaves and with Northern adventurers." The speaker was "a bright, nimble, voluble mulatto," and when a "gentleman of one of the most historic families of South Carolina, a family

[27] Nov. 20, 1872.

RADICAL MEMBERS OF THE SOUTH CAROLINA LEGISLATURE

From left to right beginning at the top:

1. Dusenberry, McKinlay, Dickson, Winder, Hoty, Randolph, Harris.
2. Mayes, Jillson, Lomax, Jackson, Thomas, Webb, Bozeman, Tomlinson, Wright.
3. Demars, Brodie, Hayes, Cain, Maxwell, Martin, Cook, Miller.
4. Rivers, Duncan, Boozer, Smythe, Wright, Moses, Sanders, Nuckles.
5. Miteford, White, Barton, Boston, Shrewsbury, Mickey, Henderson, Howell, Hayne, Mobley, Hudson, Nash, Carmand.
6. Smith, Pettengill, Hyde, Lee, Simonds, Chesnut, McDaniel, Williams, Gardner.
7. Swails, Perrin, Majes, Johnston, Wimbush, Hayes, Farr, Meade, Thompson, Rainey.

which had given to the State a long line of military commanders, governors, senators, and ambassadors, rose to make a motion" he was "at once declared . . . out of order."[28]

The classic description of the legislature is that by James S.
Pike, a Northern Republican who had served under Lincoln
as ambassador to the Hague. He visited the state in February
and March, 1873, and wrote the following:

The members of the Assembly "issued forth from the State-
House. About three-quarters of the crowd belonged to the
African race. They were of every hue, from the light octoroon
to the deep black. They were such a looking body of men as
might pour out of a market-house or a court-house at random
in any Southern State. Every Negro type and physiognomy
was here to be seen, from the genteel serving-man to the rough-
hewn customer from the rice or cotton field. Their dress was
as varied as their countenances. There was the second-hand
black frock-coat of infirm gentility, glossy and threadbare.
There was the stove-pipe hat of many ironings and departed
styles. There was also to be seen a total disregard of the pro-
prieties of costume in the coarse and dirty garments of the
field; the stub-jackets and slouch hats of soiling labor. In some
instances, rough woolen comforters embraced the neck and hid
the absence of linen. Heavy brogans, and short, torn trousers,
it was impossible to hide. The dusky tide flowed out into the
littered and barren grounds, and, issuing through the coarse
wooden fence of the inclosure, melted away into the street beyond. These were the legislators of South Carolina. . . . 'My
God, look at this!' was the unbidden ejaculation of a low-country planter, clad in homespun, as he leaned over the rail inside
the House, gazing excitedly upon the body in question. . . .
The Speaker is black, the Clerk is black, the door-keepers are
black, the little pages are black, the chairman of the Ways and

[28] Andrew D. White, *Autobiography*, I, 175.

Means is black, and the chaplain is coal-black. At some of the desks sit colored men whose types it would be hard to find outside of Congo; whose costume, visages, attitudes, and expressions, only befit the forecastle of a buccaneer. . . . The whole thing is a wonderful novelty to them as well as to observers. Seven years ago these men were raising corn and cotton under the whip of the overseer. Today they are raising points of order and questions of privilege. They prefer the latter. . . . It is the sunshine of their lives. It is their day of jubilee. It is their long-promised vision of the Lord God Almighty."[29]

White carpetbaggers, scalawags, Negroes, both native and foreign, and native whites composed the legislature. In the beginning, "the enfranchised freedmen were utterly at sea in politics; they needed leaders. The Southern whites refused the opportunity, though it is doubtful if they could have secured it, with scorn. The carpetbagger seized it."[30] Many Negro leaders warned against the carpetbagger. "They will only stand by us so long as they can use us, and when they have no more axes to grind they will cast us aside. Defunct outcasts in the North . . . hasten South among the poor ignorant freedmen. . . . These same men, as if the colored men of the South are devoid of common sense, are constantly urging them not to place a certain class on their tickets . . . yet they never hint of the propriety of placing on their tickets men of their own complexion."[31] Of the carpetbaggers it was said that "Neither labor, nor property, nor population, nor learning, nor civilization, can claim them as representatives."[32]

The carpetbaggers constituted the head and front of the Radical government. More aggressive than the Negro, more numerous and usually more trusted by the Negro than the

[29] James S. Pike, *The Prostrate State*, pp. 10 ff.

[30] [Belton O'Neall Townsend], *Atlantic Monthly*, XXIX (Feb., 1877), 177.

[31] *The Leader*, Charleston Negro weekly quoted in *N. Y. Herald*, April 22, 1867.

[32] *Two Letters from the Hon. James B. Campbell . . . on Public Affairs and Our Duties to the Colored Race.*

scalawag, their superior training and larger experience gave them places of leadership. As members of the state administration there were Scott, Parker, Chamberlain, Neagle, and J. K. Jillson from Massachusetts, the latter superintendent of education from 1868 to 1876. Perhaps the outstanding carpet-bag legislator was David T. Corbin, a well trained lawyer from Vermont. He first appeared as a provost judge on Wadmalaw Island in 1865, and later as state senator.[33] He was city attorney for Charleston, prosecuting attorney in the Ku-Klux trials, and undoubtedly a shrewd lawyer.

Other carpetbaggers of influence can only be mentioned. C. P. Leslie of Brooklyn, New York, who came to South Carolina in 1865 as a revenue spy, was a member of the constitutional convention and was elected senator. He was said to have been a member of the New York legislature as well as a fugitive from justice. A sharp talker who had little regard for the personal feelings of the Negroes, he was once expelled from the Senate for his remarks about Negro supremacy.[34] Timothy Hurley, a jovial Irishman from Connecticut, was owner of a Negro newspaper[35] in Charleston before he went to the legislature and became a noted lobbyist. He was a "shrewd, shameless little scamp, respected by nobody, liked by everybody."[36] John B. Dennis from Connecticut was a former tinker and an officer in the Union army;[37] T. C. Dunn of Massachusetts was formerly a seaman and had been in business in Wisconsin before he went to South Carolina in 1865 to enter the lumber and turpentine business;[38] Reuben Tomlinson of Pennsylvania went South as a missionary, then became superintendent of

[33] *News*, July 8, Aug. 27, 1872.

[34] *Mercury*, Feb. 21, 1868; *News*, Sept. 19, 21, 24, 1868; Oct. 26, 1869; Mar. 9, 1870; *Phoenix,* Sept. 9, 10, 1868; *Senate Journal, 1868-69,* p. 104.

[35] *The Leader.*

[36] *News*, Jan. 15, 1868; Mar. 17, July 13, 1870; May 17, Nov. 10, 1871; *News*

and Courier, Dec. 17, 1874; *Ku-Klux Conspiracy, S. C.,* p. 740; Williams in Columbia *State,* Jan. 30, 1927.

[37] *News*, Mar. 11, 1870; *News and Courier,* April 15, 1875, Jan. 4, 1877.

[38] *News and Courier,* Oct. 3, 13, 1874, Mar. 24, July 26, Nov. 3, 1875; *Union Herald,* Nov. 3, 1873.

education for the Freedmen's Bureau, and was state auditor for a time; in 1872 he was the defeated gubernatorial candidate.[39] Some of the carpetbaggers were men of undoubted ability, but in their efforts to win the Negro vote they broke into political factions; the abilities and talents of the few honest ones were not sufficient for the occasion.

As to the scalawags—the native Southerners who joined and openly supported the Radical party—it was not believed that any of them had gone over to that party "from pure and simple philanthropy," and even "men of good character who instructed Negroes in their legitimate political rights suffer[ed] obloquy at the hands of the whites"; all who took office had their motives impugned.[40]

An almost perfect type of the conventional conception of a scalawag was Franklin J. Moses, Jr. His father was an able lawyer, a member of the state Senate before secession, a circuit judge in 1865, and chief justice of the state supreme court from 1868 to 1877. He was honored and respected alike by Radicals and Conservatives. The junior Moses withdrew from South Carolina College in 1855, and four years later he married the daughter of J. S. G. Richardson, a distinguished lawyer. In 1860 he began his public career as private secretary to Governor Francis W. Pickens. Because of his magnetic personality and zeal for the secession policy, he soon became an influence in politics. Moses was admitted to the bar in 1866, and during 1866 and 1867 he was editor of the *Sumter News,* a newspaper which favored Johnson's reconstruction plans.

But in 1867 he suddenly became a renegade. For Radical writings he was dismissed from the editorship, and it was discovered that he was closely affiliated with the Union League. Possessed of ingrained moral weaknesses and a gift of honeyed oratory, he could not let pass the opportunity of leading the

[39] *News,* Aug. 6, 1868; Mar. 15, 1870; N. Y. *Nation,* Aug. 29, 1872.   [40] *Ku-Klux Conspiracy, S. C.,* pp. 456-57.

Harper's Weekly

FREEDOM AND PARDON FROM GOVERNOR MOSES

Negro voters. His success was immediate. Elected a delegate to the constitutional convention, he was chairman of an important committee of that body, and his speeches advocated just those measures which would please the Negro. Under the Radical government he held simultaneously the offices of speaker of the House, adjutant and inspector general, and trustee of the state university. In 1872 he was elected governor. As a public officer he was thoroughly unscrupulous. As speaker he issued fraudulent pay certificates, and accepted bribes for influencing legislation. As adjutant general he misappropriated funds designed for the purchase of arms for the militia. As governor he received money for approving measures of legislation, for pardons, and for official appointments. His extravagant and immoral manner of living caused public scandal.[41]

In contrast to Moses was James L. Orr whose career through the governorship has already been traced. In September, 1868, he was elected judge of the eighth judicial circuit by the Radical legislature. A man of unquestionable ability and integrity, he was a far-seeing politician and cast his lot with the Radicals because he thought it was important for prominent men to identify themselves with that party for the purpose of controlling its actions and preventing mischief in the state.[42]

Like Orr, S. W. Melton was a native lawyer and was regarded by all as a man of intellect and substance who would work for the good of the state. In 1872 he was elected attorney-general; he resigned in May, 1876. During most of this time he was a law partner of Chamberlain. His service to the state would have been more worthwhile had his hands not been tied

[41] Sumter News, Sept. 21, 1867; files of News, Courier, News and Courier, and Phoenix during Reconstruction. See sketches in Columbia State and News and Courier, Dec. 12, 1906.
[42] Courier, Dec. 5, 1865, Aug. 26, 1872; Phoenix, Feb. 11, 1872; News and Courier, May 7, 1873, Feb. 28, 1902; B. F. Perry, Reminiscences of Public Men, Sec. Ser., pp. 197-98. In 1872 Grant appointed Orr Minister to Russia, where he died in May, 1873.

by the legislature; neither he nor Orr was a member of the Reconstruction legislature.[43] Joseph Crews, on the other hand, was a man of mediocre ability but of considerable influence in the legislature. He had failed in business before the war, had been a slave trader, "and was a good hearted fellow, very accommodating, although people had little confidence in his integrity." He was on important committees in the legislature and was noted for incendiary speeches.[44]

But the majority of the voters of the state were Negroes and in every session but one that race had a majority in the legislature. They outnumbered, and in many cases outshone, their carpetbag and scalawag contemporaries. They sent seven men to Congress; for a total of six years two Negroes were lieutenant governors; and for four years two Negroes were speakers of the House. A mulatto was secretary of state and treasurer for eight years; a Pennsylvania Negro was associate justice of the Supreme Court for five years; another member of that race was adjutant and inspector-general for four years. Without knowing something of the quality of leadership these men exhibited both in and out of the state legislature and Congress, it would be difficult to understand the nature and actions of the legislature and difficult to imagine the political situation which kept the Radical government in power for eight years.

The Negroes were conspicuous in the General Assembly. Orr said that a large proportion of them were former slaves and that at the time of emancipation two-thirds or three-fourths of them could not read. At the time of his testimony in 1871, however, most of them were able to read; "most of them have learned to write their names, and some of them

[43] *Courier*, Aug. 27, 1872, Jan. 1, 1873; *South Carolinian*, Nov. 7, 1872; *News and Courier*, April 18, 1876; Charleston *Sunday News*, Mar. 26, 1899.

[44] *News*, Mar. 11, 1870, April 27, 1872; *Ku-Klux Conspiracy, S. C.*, pp. 1307, 1314, 1329; John A. Leland, *A Voice from South Carolina*, pp. 52 ff. In 1875 Crews was ambushed and killed.—*News and Courier*, Sept. 10, 11, 15, 1875.

have made more progress than that; very considerable progress, the younger portion of them."[45] The Union Leagues had given them their first notions of parliamentary law and debating. Then they were encouraged to attend court as spectators, were inducted into jury and military service, and their prominent men were elected to office. The legislature, particularly the lower house, was, as might be expected, the scene of much disorder and confusion. The excited Negroes were very voluble and the orators were subject to all sorts of interruptions. Soon the imitative black man acquired confidence, joined in debate, and with his ready flow of words criticized the measures proposed. They were "to the last degree good-humored unless persistently opposed," and many of them exhibited a practical "get-at-the-facts disposition" which was "a near approach to that sterling English quality, common sense." The Negro was not the type to be abashed by criticism, and it was said that when he got a sentence tangled, or could not follow the thread of his own thought in words, he would "gravely open a book— the statutes, or some other ponderous volume lying before him —and after seeming to consult it for some minutes," would resume. He had been "gaining time for a new start."[46] While many of the more illiterate and less intelligent Negroes were tiresome speakers, some of the blacks were of real force and eloquence. The better men were sent to the Senate, and some of the colored members "spoke exceedingly well, and with great ease and grace of manner; others were awkward and coarse."[47] One observer recorded that "The President of the Senate and the Speaker of the House, both colored, were elegant and accomplished men, highly educated, who would have creditably presided over any commonwealth's legislative assembly."[48]

[45] *Ku-Klux Conspiracy, S. C.*, pp. 8-12.
[46] Edward King, *The Southern States of North America*, pp. 461 ff.; [Belton O'Neall Townsend], *Atlantic Monthly,* XXXIX (Feb., 1877), pp. 192-94.
[47] King, *op. cit.*, p. 461.
[48] *Ibid.*, p. 460.

Of course many of the colored legislators were mulattoes, quadroons, and octoroons. Opinions differed as to the relative merits of the darker and lighter-hued members. One correspondent believed that the "black men were as a class as well educated as their lighter-hued brethren; made better speeches and were better qualified for their duties"; he even asserted that "the colored men generally were superior in decency and ability to the majority of the native white Radical legislators."[49] Another observer would place second to the leading spirits of the Senate "the bob tailed white men [mulattoes] like Ransier and Hayne." And to him it was clear that the blacks were restive under "this combined mulatto and carpetbag domination"; and as a general thing, he said, "the quadroons and octoroons of the Senate are infinitely superior in personal appearance to their white Yankee and native compeers."[50]

The first colored lieutenant governor, elected in 1870, was Alonzo J. Ransier. A native freedman before the war, he was noted as an advocate of equal rights in 1865. Following the constitutional convention, he became a member of the legislature, chairman of the state Republican executive committee, and auditor of Charleston County; in 1872 he was elected to Congress. In the state Senate he was a good presiding officer; his dignity and cleverness were traced to the fact that he was nearly white.[51] Richard H. Gleaves succeeded Ransier as lieutenant governor, 1872-1876. Gleaves came from Pennsylvania to South Carolina in 1866. He was made a commissioner of elections, trial justice, probate judge, and then lieutenant governor. He was a mulatto of prepossessing appearance and was undoubtedly intelligent and well posted in parliamentary law.[52]

[49] *News*, Mar. 17, 1870.
[50] *News*, Mar. 10, 1871.
[51] *News*, Mar. 10, 1871, Mar. 15, 1870; *Biographical Congressional Directory*, p. 944. Ransier lost influence with the Radicals and his last employment was as a laborer on the streets.—*News and Courier*, Aug. 19, 1882.
[52] *Union Herald*, Oct. 28, 1872; *Courier*, Aug. 27, Nov. 28, 1872.

The first Negro speaker of the House was Samuel J. Lee, elected in 1872 and serving until 1874. He was a native of the state, a farmer and sawmill worker, who by his own efforts had prepared himself for admittance to the bar in 1871. Even the enemies of this light-colored mulatto legislator admitted that he was intelligent, courteous, and one of the most creditable lawyers in the state for his age.[53]

Lee's successor was Robert Brown Elliott, a native of Massachusetts and a graduate of Eton College. He studied law and became a lawyer of the first rank. He first went to Charleston as editor of the Negro journal, *The Leader;* after a period in the constitutional convention and the legislature, he was elected to Congress in 1870. He resigned his seat in January, 1873, to become sheriff; again elected to Congress in 1872 he resigned in November, 1874, to enter the state legislature where he became speaker of the House during Chamberlain's administration. Although a very black man with the typical features of his race, there was no evidence of the African dialect. He was of commanding presence and was perhaps the best Negro orator in the South. His reply to Alexander H. Stephens on the Civil Rights Bill was highly praised for its constitutional arguments. In 1876 he was candidate for attorney-general.[54]

Other leaders in the legislature who should be mentioned here were Cain, DeLarge, Swails, Nash, and Smalls. Richard Harvey ("Daddy") Cain of Virginia, Ohio, Iowa, and New York left his church in Brooklyn in 1865 to come South as a missionary. He became editor of the *Missionary Record,* the most influential Negro paper ever published in South Carolina; from the constitutional convention he went to the state

[53] *Union Herald,* Dec. 4, 1873; *Courier,* Nov. 28, 1872; *News,* Nov. 27, 1872; *News and Courier,* July 21, 1873.

[54] *Biographical Congressional Directory,* p. 627; G. W. Williams, *History of the Negro Race in America,* p. 581; John W. Cromwell, *The Negro in American History,* pp. 179-87; *News,* July 26, 1867, Aug. 17, 1868, Mar. 11, Nov. 10, 1870; *News,* Sept. 12, 1868, Feb. 25, 1871; *South Carolinian,* Jan. 4, 1873, April 7, 1873; Williams, in Columbia *State,* Nov. 14, 1926.

Senate and from there to Congress for two terms. He was a man of intellectual endowments and of great energy and organizing power. An effective preacher who had gone into politics, he was usually in any reform movement which he thought would improve his race and protect them from carpet-baggers.[55]

Robert C. DeLarge, a light mulatto tailor from Charleston, had been an agent of the Freedmen's Bureau and graduated to the constitutional convention, the legislature, and Congress. In South Carolina he was successively chairman of the Ways and Means committee of the House, commissioner of the sinking fund, and state land commissioner. He lacked education but was shrewd and tricky; the *Charleston Daily News* said it was difficult to assign a reason for his influence, but it was almost unlimited.[56]

Stephen A. Swails of Pennsylvania went South with the Union troops, remained to become an agent of the Freedmen's Bureau, a free school teacher, a member of the constitutional convention, a senator and president pro-tem of the Senate in 1872. He was a light, good-natured mulatto with a reputation for integrity. With only a common school education, he was a good parliamentarian and a forcible speaker.[57]

One of the most influential Negro senators was Beverly Nash from Richland County. A slave before the war and for a time a waiter in a Columbia hotel, he had learned to read and was said to write a passable hand. Nash was as black as charcoal but of pleasing appearance and equipped with a keen

[55] D. A. Payne, *Recollections of Seventy Years*, p. 332; *Biographical Congressional Directory*, p. 522; Williams, *History of the Negro Race in America*, pp. 580-81; *A. M. E. Church Review*, III, 337-50.

[56] *Biographical Congressional Directory*, p. 601; Williams, *History of the Negro Race in America*, p. 581; *News*, Sept. 12,

1868; Mar. 11, Nov. 10, 1870. He died in 1874. *News and Courier*, Feb. 16, 1874.

[57] *Mercury*, Feb. 6, 1868; *News*, Mar. 10, 1870; *Courier*, Nov. 28, 1872, Jan. 10, 1873; *Union Herald*, Oct. 29, 1873; *News and Courier*, May 19, 1900.

mind; he was always ready with a story or anecdote which carried the audience with him.[58]

Another native of prominence was Robert Smalls, pilot of the ship "Planter" which he had turned over to Federal authorities during the war. He was self educated and was a ready, self-possessed speaker who was extremely popular with his own race. He was a member of the constitutional convention, a state representative and senator, and a member of Congress in 1875 and after Reconstruction.[59]

The few Conservative members of the legislature were not men of distinction. They were usually from the up-country and were not active in the deliberations of the assembly. Glum and scornful amid the mass of black speakers, they sat together in one section of the house of which they were members. Their committee appointments were unimportant and occasionally, when on investigating committees dominated by Radicals, they refused to serve; they sometimes attacked the integrity of members of the General Assembly and frequently recorded protests in the legislative journals. Since it was almost always a vain gesture to vote for the appointment of a Conservative to any position of importance, they generally threw their vote to the more capable or less corrupt of the Radical candidates. Sometimes a division of the legislature would give the Conservatives a controlling voice, but on any question concerning race or affecting the control of the dominating element the Radicals usually voted *en masse*.

The Reconstruction legislatures were not distinguished for notable legislation or constructive achievements. They were composed of Northern adventurers, most of them totally unqualified for the positions to which they aspired; scalawags

[58] *News,* Aug. 13, 1867; Jan. 15, 1868, Mar. 9, 1870. Louis Post, "A 'Carpet-bagger' in South Carolina," in *Journal of Negro History,* X (Jan., 1925).

[59] *Biographical Congressional Directory,* p. 1002; *Union Herald,* Nov. 1, 1873; Sir George Campbell, *White and Black; The Outcome of a Visit to the United States,* p. 346; *Mercury,* Feb. 18, 1868.

who, with a few exceptions were of mediocre talents and indifferent morals; and Negroes, many of whom had been slaves and most of whom were devoid of any systematic education. Not that they were totally lacking in ability and even talent. But whatever political or legislative skill they possessed was frequently misdirected, not always of their own accord but by the forces of the social and political revolution around them. It must not be forgotten that "the bottom rail was on the top," and that the former ruling oligarchy, which, if it had not always been actuated by motives of the highest idealism, had furnished a strong and economical government, was now displaced by those who represented neither the wealth nor the traditions of the state. Furthermore, as we shall see later, the whites were in almost constant opposition to the measures and men of the new order.

*   *   *   *   *

Let us glance behind the scenes of legislative action. From the nature and composition of the legislature, it is not surprising to know that from the very first session in July, 1868, money was used freely and soon openly to purchase the votes of the legislators. The charges of fraud and corruption made by the Conservative press were seldom denied; even the *Charleston Daily Republican* and Cain's *Missionary Record* raised their voices against corruption. The *Charleston Daily Republican* of March 18, 1871, stated that for their votes "one man was promised $1,000; another man more than ten times that amount in cash; some sold themselves for gold watches; one poor member sold himself for the paltry sum of $21";[60] and Cain declared that "For the last two years a certain set of unmitigated scoundrels have dictated to the mass of voters of the State."[61]

To one reading the press of the period for the first time, it is impossible to believe that bribery was as extensive and open

[60] *Ku-Klux Conspiracy, S. C.*, p. 773.   [61] *Ibid.*, p. 774.

as was claimed. It is easier to believe that editors of reputable newspapers had become so blinded with partisan prejudice that they resorted to shameless and brazen falsehood to discredit the opposition. But such was not the case. Practically all the charges made by the Conservative press were later substantiated by an investigating committee appointed by the Democratic legislature in 1877. The chairman of this committee was a Republican who had been a member of the Reconstruction legislature. The report of the committee was based on documents, official papers and letters, diaries, and the sworn testimony of many who had participated in the frauds. The evidence is incontrovertible and will not be dwelt upon in detail.

As stated above, the Conservative and even the Radical press made open charges, frequently naming the men involved. Much corroborative testimony was taken by a Radical Congressional investigating committee which came to the state in 1871 to investigate Ku-Klux activities; and even Governor Scott accused the legislature of "all sorts of villainies." He spoke of committee members asking large sums of money to recommend a bill; he told of injunctions being filed to restrain state officers from selling bonds, but, he said, the injunction would have been removed for $25,000; "I want to say," concluded the Governor, "do you suppose that if our Savior would come here with a bill ever so good . . . do you suppose he wouldn't be crucified again if he didn't pay something to prevent it?"[62] Senators usually cost more than representatives; the latter, however, organized a group commonly known as the Forty Thieves. It became necessary to expend large sums of money to get important bills passed, the amount increasing as time went on and varying from a few dollars or some gift to several thousand dollars. Bills having to do with important business enterprises, railroads, bonds, and financial

[62] *Ku-Klux Conpsiracy, S. C.*, p. 477.

settlements were always expensive. The phosphate bill, for example, which gave to the incorporators a practical monopoly on the phosphate deposits of the state, was said to have cost $60,000 to pass over the veto of the governor.[63]

Perhaps the most noted case of bribery was the election of John J. Patterson to the United States Senate in the winter of 1872. Patterson was a native of Pennsylvania and a person of unsavory reputation. He had been a newspaper man, a member of the Pennsylvania legislature, and a henchman of Simon Cameron. He came to South Carolina in 1869 and became interested in various financial transactions and railroad developments. In order to secure his election over Robert B. Elliott and ex-Governor Scott, Patterson rented an elaborately furnished caucus room and spent an unknown sum, reputed to have been $40,000, to get votes. Numerous members were given sums ranging from one or two hundred to several thousand dollars. Usually, but not always, this was done through agents of Patterson. One agent was commissioned to offer Elliott $10,000 if he would withdraw from the race. After Patterson's election, he was arrested on affidavits made by men who had been bribed. Patterson was released by a trial justice, but later surrendered and was held to bail to appear before the court of general sessions. At this court, Chamberlain, a reputed secret attorney for Patterson, moved to quash the jury on the ground that the jurors had not been drawn a proper number of days before the court. This was done on behalf of Chamberlain's client, one Robert Cooper. The judge, R. B. Carpenter, who had just been elected by the same body that

[63] See *Reports and Resolutions, 1877-78*, Fraud Report, pp. 1676 ff. S. J. Lee, Speaker of the House, testified that Chamberlain gave him $250 or $275 for his vote on the phosphate bill. Timothy Hurley was the principal lobbyist for this bill, as he was for many others. It became known that he wanted to give some members one price and others a different one for their votes. So a committee of the House told Hurley that they must be paid equally and required him to deposit the sum necessary (about $7500) with Moses, Speaker of the House. Afterwards it was divided equally.

elected Patterson, granted the motion and Patterson was never brought to trial but was admitted to the Senate where he served a full term.[64]

Along with bribery went increased extravagance and accompanying fraud. The length of the legislative session was unduly drawn out in order to increase the per diem of $6;[65] unnecessary clerks were employed; and it became customary to vote the speaker a gratuity of several hundred dollars. For a time there was a saloon in the State House which was open to all members and their friends; expensive wines and the best of whiskey as well as fine cigars and other luxuries were supplied in never failing quantities. When the House of Representatives was moved from Janney's Hall to the partially completed State House, it was fitted with the finest furnishings in the most modern style. The Democratic investigating committee found that there had been paid out within four years for furniture alone over $200,000. But in 1877 an appraisal of the prices paid for the furniture showed that the value of the furniture remaining in the State House amounted to only $17,715. A number of committee rooms were furnished outside the State House as well as a number of private rooms at the boarding houses of the members; and it appears that many of those rooms were furnished each time the legislature met. Furthermore, the evidence proved conclusively that a majority of the members of the House combined against the merchants who furnished the goods and demanded to be paid for voting the proper appropriations. Benjamin Byas, chairman of the

[64] *Reports and Resolutions, 1877-78,* Fraud Report, pp. 626-42; *News,* Nov. 27, 1872; Feb. 6, Mar. 6, 1873. In December, 1869, the legislature passed an act providing that every "executive, legislative or judicial officer who corruptly" accepted a gift or gratuity should be punished by imprisonment in the state penitentiary at hard labor "not exceeding ten years, or by fine not exceeding five thousand dollars, and by imprisonment in jail not exceeding two years." A similar penalty was provided for jurors, umpires, jailors, sheriffs, etc.—*Stat. S. C.,* XIV, 308-11. Apparently this act was never enforced.

[65] In March, 1872, it was enacted that each member should receive an annual salary of $600 and twenty cents mileage.—*Stat. S. C.,* XV, 216.

committee which reported favorably on a raised claim, received a legislative certificate to the amount of $12,319.50. From a single New York and Paris firm were purchased 206 cuspidors, "richly decorated and marked House of Representatives," amounting to $1,800; six "tulip toilet sets, 11 pieces, green, and marked House of Representatives" amounted to $473.50; six "fine black Belgian marble" clocks, "with best French movement," amounted to $885.00; one "large carved walnut time-piece" for the House was billed at $600; five "walnut and gilt mantel mirrors" for committee rooms amounted to $2,137.50, and one "walnut and gilt mantel mirror for Speaker's room, carved, with palmetto, shield and eagle" cost $960.00.[66]

Under the head of "Supplies" was embraced what the legislators chose to order. "At first the orders were moderate, and included only stationery and postage stamps, but they gradually increased until they assumed gigantic proportions. In the commencement of this business of furnishing members they gave orders on the clerks to deduct the amount from their pay, but very soon the orders largely exceeded their pay, and the accounts were then included in the report of the Committee on Contingent Accounts, and pay certificates thus issued for almost every description of merchandise."[67] Hear the report of the investigating committee: "If the simple statement were made that Senators and members of the House were furnished with everything they desired, from swaddling clothes and cradle to the coffin of the undertaker, from brogans to chignons, finest extracts to best wines and liquors, and all *paid for by the State,* it would create a smile of doubt and derision; but when we make the statement, and prove it . . . all will with sorrow admit the truthfulness of this report."[68]

Pay certificates, issued by the presiding officer of the House

[66] *Reports and Resolutions, 1877-78,* Fraud Report, pp. 1136-38.
[67] Testimony of Josephus Woodruff,
Clerk of the Senate, 1868-1877, in *ibid.,* pp. 1019-20.
[68] *Ibid.*

AN AMATEUR ARTIST'S CONCEPTION OF SCOTT'S ADMINISTRATION, 1868-1872

University of South Carolina Library

or Senate, became valid claims against the state and were a large item of fraud. A. O. Jones, the mulatto clerk of the House, 1868-1877, testified that "The issue of certificates was enormous in number and amounts, and the pressure upon the presiding officers by members of the Senate and House to have certificates issued to their friends, political and otherwise, for sinecures and gratuities, increased at every session. The issue ran to the highest point at the session of 1871-72, when the orders on the state treasurer, drawn by the Speaker of the House, amounted to over a half million of dollars, two-thirds of which were for sinecures and gratuities."[69] As a result of the fraudulent pay certificates issued to members, and to clerks and porters who never served, as well as those drawn to fictitious persons, and for similar reasons, the legislative expenses were enormous, as the expenses for the following sessions indicate:

1870-71	$ 822,608.83
1871-72	1,533,574.78
1872-73	908,855.00
1873-74	922,536.00
1876-77	84,096.00

In addition to the "legislative ring" there was the "printing ring" which constituted a large drain upon the treasury. The Carolina Printing Company, organized by Scott, Chamberlain, Parker, and others, owned the *Columbia Daily Union* and the *Charleston Daily Republican* and also got contracts for the public printing. Pay certificates were drawn and issued to senators and members of the committee on printing for their approval of printing bills. Later the Republican Printing Company was formed by Josephus Woodruff and A. O. Jones, clerks of the two houses. It was the duty of the clerks to let contracts for the public printing, and these contracts they let to themselves as being the sole members of the Republican

[69] *Ibid.*, p. 1407.

Printing Company. To get the large appropriations for that company passed and approved, large sums were spent as bribes and commissions. It cost more than $98,500 to get through an appropriation for $250,000 in 1872, and for the passage of a similar bill the next year Woodruff and Jones paid $124,969.[70] In a like fashion "huge frauds were committed under the head of newspaper advertising," Republican newspapers and interested senators getting the bulk of the money. All this, of course, was at the expense of the state. It is not necessary to mention in detail other frauds of a similar nature such as those concerning the Ku-Klux rewards, the militia and the purchase of arms, the constabulary and armed force of the state, contingent funds, and fraudulent claims of one sort or another. Some of these will be referred to in other places.

Such, then, was the legislature of South Carolina. Nearly all the leaders mentioned, and many others, were concerned in, and in many cases directly responsible for, the frauds mentioned. Little wonder is it that upon the adjournment of one of the legislatures the *Charleston Daily News* exulted: "It has faded away like a nubilous shadow—dissolved like a noxious exhalation. In life it has been unlovely, and in death it has not belied its record. As it lived, it has died—an uncouth, malformed and abortive monstrosity, its birth a blunder, its life a crime, and its death a blessing."[71]

* * * * *

Something must be said about the judicial division of the Radical government. By the constitution of 1868, a Supreme Court was to replace the court of appeals at law and in equity.[72] All books of records, files, and property of the court of appeals, of law and equity, and of the court of errors, existing under the provisional government, were to be transferred to the Supreme Court, as well as all cases pending in

[70] *Ibid.*, pp. 1221-1396.   [72] Art. IV.
[71] Mar. 15, 1872.

the courts of the provisional government.[73] The Supreme Court was to have appellate jurisdiction only in cases of chancery, and was to constitute a court for errors at law.[74] The legislature in September, 1868, passed an act organizing the Supreme Court which was to consist of a chief justice and two associate justices, to be elected by the legislature for a period of six years.[75]

The constitution provided also that the state should be divided into convenient circuits and that for each circuit a judge should be elected for a period of four years by the legislature. Each circuit was to have a court of common pleas which was to sit twice in each judicial district during the year and hear civil cases and have jurisdiction in all matters of equity. The court of general sessions was to sit three times yearly in each district and was to have jurisdiction in criminal cases.[76] By the act of August 20, 1868, organizing the circuit courts, all suits in equity which had not been disposed of by the chancery courts of the provisional government by January 1, 1869, were to be transferred to the court of common pleas. The act furthermore provided that there should be eight judicial circuits, each circuit to consist of a certain number of counties.[77]

The constitution further provided for a court of probate which should replace the ordinary's court and should have jurisdiction in all matters testamentary and of administration, and in business appertaining to minors and the allotment of

[73] *Stat. S. C.*, XIV, 73-74.
[74] Constitution of 1868, Art. IV, Sec. 4. For details see *The Code of Procedure*, approved March 1, 1870, Pt. I.
[75] *Stat. S. C.*, XIV, 73-74.
[76] Art. IV, Sec. 16, 18.
[77] *Stat. S. C.*, XIV, 5 ff. There had been for a long while a struggle in the state to make the judicial and election districts the same in fact as well as in name. The constitution of 1865 made each judicial district an election district except in the case of the city of Charleston where there were to be three election districts known as St. Philip's, St. Michael's, and Berkeley. The constitution of 1868 made all counties judicial districts and also declared each county an election district.—John P. Thomas, Jr., *The Formation of Judicial and Political Sub-divisions in South Carolina*, pp. 22-24.

dower in cases of idiocy and lunacy, and persons *non compotes mentis*.[78] Both probate judges and justices of the peace were to be chosen by popular vote. In the former case they were so elected, but, in the latter, courts of the justices of the peace were never organized. In September, 1868, an act was passed providing for the temporary appointment by the governor of "magistrates." In February, 1870, an act was passed providing for the appointment of "trial justices" by the governor, and the act regarding magistrates was repealed.[79] The jurisdiction of the justices of the peace, of the magistrates, and of the trial justices was practically the same. But by organizing the court of the trial justice rather than that of the justice of the peace, the justice could be appointed by the governor rather than elected as the constitution provided for the justice of the peace.

In 1868 the white people opposed the new constitution because it destroyed their "admirable judiciary" by introducing a new system which was "repugnant to our customs and habits of thought." The system, they feared, would entail added expense and would give justices of the peace too much control.[80] Furthermore, said the Conservatives, judges could not charge the juries in respect to matters of fact but could only state the testimony and declare the law.[81] And it was also claimed that the election of the Supreme Court and circuit judges by the legislature would destroy the independence of the judiciary.

But as a matter of fact the judicial system worked as well as could have been expected under the circumstances. Franklin J. Moses, Sr., father of the notorious speaker and governor, was elected chief justice in July, 1868, and took his seat after the removal of his political disabilities by Congress in Decem-

[78] Art. IV, Sec. 20. This court was organized Sept. 21, 1868. *Stat. S. C.*, XIV, 76 ff.

[79] *Stat. S. C.*, XIV, 99 ff., 376-77.

[80] *Phoenix*, April 7, 1868. Justices of the peace had decision of all cases, civil and criminal, under $100.

[81] Constitution of 1868, Art. IV, Sec. 26; *Phoenix*, Apr. 19, 1868.

ber. He was a man of recognized ability and served with distinction until his death in March, 1877.[82]

Elected at the same time was Associate Justice A. J. Willard, a well trained lawyer from New York who came South as a lieutenant colonel of colored troops. He had charge of the military courts in Charleston in 1865. Later he was appointed judge advocate general of the second military district. In 1867 he took charge of the Bureau of Civil Affairs and acted in that capacity until the removal of the military. "His opinions in important cases evidenced careful preparation and laborious research."[83] After the overthrow of the Radical government, he succeeded Moses as chief justice and remained on the bench until 1880.[84]

Solomon L. Hoge, the third justice, was a graduate of the Cincinnati Law School and a former officer in the army. At the close of the war, he was assigned to duty on the staff of Scott as adjutant and inspector-general, and afterwards as judge advocate. He possessed very little experience at the bar, and without having written a single decision he resigned his position after eighteen months' service to enter Congress.[85]

His successor was Jonathan Jasper Wright, a colored lawyer from Pennsylvania who was said to have been the first Negro admitted to the bar in that state. Wright had been an adviser to the Negro in the Freedmen's Bureau, a member of the constitutional convention, and a state senator. First elected February 1, 1870, to fill out the term of Hoge,[86] he was reëlected in December, 1870, for a full term and served until his resignation was accepted by Governor Hampton in August, 1877. Although he lisped, Wright was a good speaker, decidedly

[82] *News*, Aug. 25, 1868; *Courier*, Sept. 11, 1868; *News and Courier*, Mar. 7, 1877.

[83] John S. Reynolds, in Columbia *State*, May 7, 1900.

[84] *Courier*, Aug. 1, 1868; *News*, Aug. 1, 1868; June 3, 1872.

[85] *Courier*, Aug. 1, 1868; *News*, Aug. 1, 1868; Apr. 5, 1869; *Courier*, Aug., 27, 1872; *Biographical Congressional Directory*, p. 732.

[86] Who had been elected for the short term—two years.

intelligent, and generally said to be the best fitted colored man in the state for the position.[87]   In spite of the fact that the Supreme Court was composed of a scalawag, a carpetbagger, and a Negro, its administration was fair and its decisions equitable.

All the circuit judges elected and seated during Radical rule were white and most of them were natives.   With a few exceptions they were excellent lawyers and judges and were honest men.   Some of them were Conservatives but the majority were Radicals.   The circuit judges were commissioned in the fall of 1868, and after a belated start the courts appear to have functioned in an orderly fashion.

The act regulating the manner of drawing juries[88] provided that all persons qualified to vote for representatives in the General Assembly should be liable to be drawn as jurors, except those usually exempted.   The selectmen of each town (which was the local unit of government introduced under the constitution of 1868) were to prepare annual lists of citizens qualified to serve, "being persons of good moral character, of sound judgment, and free from all legal exceptions."   Any person "convicted of any scandalous crime, or guilty of gross immorality" should be disqualified.   In March, 1869, this act was amended so that the number of colored and white citizens on the jury list should be in proportion to the whole number of voters of the two races.[89]   A third act provided that a jury commissioner should be appointed by the governor with the approval of the Senate. The jury commissioner with the county auditor and chairman of the board of county commissioners formed a board of jury commissioners for the county.[90]

It will be seen, then, that the jurors were to be of both races, somewhat in proportion to the number of voters.   And there were no property or tax qualifications.   In the low coun-

[87] News, July 26, 1867, Jan. 15, Mar. 9, 1868; Jan. 22, 1870; Weekly News and Courier, Feb. 25, 1885.

[88] Stat. S. C., XIV, 119 ff.
[89] Ibid., p. 236.
[90] Ibid., p. 690.

ties it was said that the juries were about equally divided between the two races,[91] while in the up-country there would
naturally be a predominance of white jurors.[92] Objection to
Negro jurors on the part of whites does not seem to have been
very strong. Perhaps this was because the Negro jurors were
quiet and easily controlled by the white jurors.[93] However, it
was said by experienced lawyers that race prejudice interfered
with the impartiality of a jury, and many important cases with
mixed juries resulted in mistrials.[94] Judge Orr, on the other
hand, found no fault with mixed juries and said that colored
jurors convicted colored prisoners without hesitation. In fact,
he said, more indulgence was shown toward a colored man by
a white jury, for they realized the former's lack of experience.[95]

The greatest criticism of the judiciary was directed against
the trial justices. As before stated, they were appointed by the
governor with the consent of the Senate. It was almost universally conceded that many of the appointments were bad.
Many uneducated, unqualified Negroes were appointed, frequently because no one else would accept the position. Governor Scott stated that he had been thrown, unfortunately,
almost exclusively upon members of one political party for
choice of trial justices, and that, in many cases, "persons without the requisite qualifications have been recommended."
There was reason to believe that persons appearing before trial
justices were charged extravagant fees; and in many instances
the costs charged and collected were not returned to the
state. The Governor insisted that "knowledge of elementary

[91] *Ku Klux Conspiracy, S. C.,* p. 87.

[92] The *Charleston Daily News,* June 12, 1869, cited an instance in Williamsburg County in which of the 31 petit jurors 23 were Negroes and 8 white; of the grand jury 12 were black and 7 white. Another instance, May 7, 1869, in Sumter County: "On the right of the Judge the grand jury was seated; consisting of nine Negroes and three white men, on the left a petit jury consisting of eight Negroes and four whites; a Negro constable on each side of the entrance to the bar, and a Negro crier."

[93] *Ku-Klux Conspiracy, S. C.,* pp. 808-9.

[94] *Ibid.,* pp. 60, 69. Testimony of Judge Willard and D. T. Corbin, Radicals.

[95] *Ibid.,* p. 5.

branches of education" be made "an indispensable requisite to appointment for office of a higher grade of service."[96]

We have examined the personnel of the administrative, legislative, and judicial branches of the government and have endeavored to give some idea of the nature of the Radical government. The workings of that government will be illustrated in subsequent chapters.

[96] *House Journal,* 1870-71, p. 24. For instances of ignorance or outrageous conduct on the part of trial justices see, Myrta Lockett Avary, *Dixie After the War,* pp. 192-93; James M. Morgan, *Recollections of a Rebel Reefer,* pp. 326-27.

Chapter VI

PUBLIC DEBT AND TAXATION

THE period of Reconstruction in South Carolina was characterized by a mismanagement of the public funds and the practice of fraud and deception by state officials. Public opinion condemned those who defrauded the state; yet the public debt continued to increase. State officials could not show value received for the new debt, but through their control of the Republican party and the Negro voters they remained in office. The state debt increased rapidly, the interest was seldom paid, and the credit of the state was almost wiped out; yet with one or two exceptions the offenders were not brought to justice. To unravel in detail this tangled skein of fraud is neither pleasant nor necessary; but to understand something of the financial history of the period and the consequent economic difficulties of the people, we must delve into dark deeds and almost inexplicable actions.

Before the Civil War the credit of the state was good, the bonded debt was only $4,046,540.16, and the interest payments were made promptly. Bonds issued to restore Charleston after the disastrous fire of 1838, to aid the Blue Ridge Railroad, and to build a new State House were readily subscribed. The Bank of the State, which had been chartered in 1812 and in which the state was the only stockholder, was prosperous. During the war, bonds were issued for the military defense of the state and for the payment of the Confederate war tax. Another loan was authorized for the purpose of continuing the construction of the State House. On September 30, 1865, the comptroller reported that the public debt totaled $8,013,636.97, and that assets amounted to the nominal sum of $8,306,772.63.

Nearly $3,000,000 of this debt was later repudiated as a war debt.

During the administration of Governor Orr and the military government, the debt of the state was kept at a minimum. Under the act of December 21, 1865,[1] the treasurer was authorized to borrow, for the year commencing in October, 1865, and to be payable in not more than twelve months after date, a sum not exceeding $100,000, and to deposit such collateral securities as might be received and transferred to the state by the Bank of the State for that purpose. On the same day the issue of bills receivable in payment of indebtedness of the state to the amount of $500,000 was authorized.[2]

The special session of the legislature passed a funding act[3] to meet accrued interest and matured bonds. This act authorized the issue of bonds or stocks, one-half to be payable January 1, 1887, and the other half in 1897, and to bear interest from July 1, 1867, at the rate of 6 per cent.[4] Under these acts and on account of the inability of the state to pay interest, the debt stood at $8,378,255.64 on October 1, 1867. By an ordinance of the constitutional convention of 1868,[5] the faith and credit of the state was pledged for the payment of bonds or other obligations of the state except those created "for the purpose of aiding the rebellion, and for maintaining a hostile government to the laws and authorities of the United States." The war debt being thus repudiated by "the People of South Carolina, in Convention met," the total state debt was reduced to $5,407,306.27.[6]

*   *   *   *   *

Thus with the inauguration of the Radical government in

---

[1] *Stat. S. C.*, XIII, 5.

[2] *Ibid.*, p. 45. Under act of Sept. 20, 1866, the treasurer was authorized to redeem the bills receivable in treasury notes of the U. S. or the notes of any national bank. *Ibid.*, pp. 383-84. Repealed Mar. 3, 1874.—*Ibid.*, XV, 569.

[3] Sept. 21, 1866, *ibid.*, XIII, 391-92.

[4] This act was amended and extended Dec. 20, 1866.—*Ibid.*, pp. 421-23.

[5] *Ibid.*, XIV, 27-28.

[6] *Reports and Resolutions*, 1868-69, pp. 24-26.

July, 1868, the debt of the state was comparatively small and could have been paid in a reasonable time had the new régime administered the funds with honesty and efficiency. The great increase of the debt took place in the years 1868-1872, during the administration of Scott. Parker was treasurer, Neagle, comptroller-general, Chamberlain, attorney-general, and H. H. Kimpton financial agent of the state in the city of New York. Under the guidance of these men the debt increased to an unwarranted degree and the credit of the state sank to a low ebb. We shall pass in review the legislation which increased the state debt during this period and which placed the control of the bonds and stocks of the state in the hands of untrustworthy men.

1. By the act of August 8, 1868, the governor was authorized to negotiate a loan of $125,000 and to use as collateral security bills receivable, bonds, stocks, "or other securities owned by the State."[7]

2. In the same year the governor was authorized to borrow on the credit of the state, on coupon bonds, within twelve months, a sum not exceeding $500,000 to redeem the bills receivable, said bonds to bear interest at 6 per cent, payable semi-annually, and to be redeemable within twenty years.[8] The bonds were to be sold by the state's financial agent at a price fixed by the governor, treasurer, and attorney-general, and a special tax was to be levied to pay the interest and redeem the bonds.

3. August 26, 1868, the governor was authorized to borrow on coupon bonds, within twelve months, a sum not exceeding $1,000,000 to pay the interest on the public debt. The other terms of the act were the same as above.[9] The amount of bonds to be issued was not definitely stated, only the amount of the loan being named. Subsequently some of the state officers

[7] *Stat. S. C.*, XIV, 2.
[8] *Ibid.*, p. 27. The time limit for issuing the bonds was later extended to two
years. *Ibid.*, p. 258.
[9] *Ibid.*, p. 18.

claimed that the act authorized a sufficient amount of bonds to *realize* $1,000,000, while others said only $1,000,000 of bonds could be issued.

4. On September 15, 1868, under an act to close the operations of the Bank of the State, the legislature provided for the funding of all bills of the corporation which had been issued prior to December 20, 1860. Bonds of the state, payable in twenty years, with interest at 6 per cent, were to be issued for bills of the bank which were presented to the treasurer before January 1, 1869. All acts which rendered the bills of the corporation receivable for taxes were repealed.[10]

5. On February 17, 1869, authority was given to borrow on coupon bonds, within twelve months, a sum not exceeding $1,000,000 for the relief of the treasury, said bonds to date from January 1, 1869, with interest at 7 per cent, payable semi-annually, and redeemable at any time, at the option of the state, within twenty years. The bonds might be used as collateral for loans by the financial board or sold for a sum not less than that fixed by the governor, attorney-general, comptroller-general, and treasurer. An annual tax sufficient to pay the interest was to be levied.[11]

6. Under an ordinance of the constitutional convention of 1868,[12] a land commissioner was appointed who should hold office at the pleasure of an advisory board consisting of the governor, comptroller-general, treasurer, secretary of state, and the attorney-general. It was the duty of the commissioner "to purchase or cause to be purchased any lands in any portion of the State, improved or unimproved, at such price as the said Advisory Board may determine, not to exceed in the aggregate amount in any one fiscal year the par value of the public stock

---

[10] *Ibid.*, pp. 21-22.

[11] *Ibid.*, pp. 182-83. As in the case of the bonds for the payment of interest on the public debt, a question arose as to whether the act provided for the issue of an amount sufficient to raise $1,000,000 in cash or for the issue of bonds with a face value of $1,000,000.

[12] Mar. 7, 1868. *Stat. S. C.*, XIV, 34.

of this State created by the General Assembly for this purpose." The treasurer was authorized to issue to the land commissioner bonds of the state in the sum of $200,000, bearing 6 per cent interest, payable in twenty years. Lands thus bought were to be sold to actual settlers on terms at 6 per cent interest. The revenue thus raised was to be used to pay interest on the bonds and as a sinking fund.[13] By an amendment of this act of 1869,[14] bonds of the state to the additional sum of $500,000 were to be issued to the land commissioner to negotiate in such form and manner as the advisory board should determine, and an annual tax sufficient to pay the interest accruing was to be levied.

7. Under an act to provide for the "conversion of state securities," passed March 23, 1869, the treasurer was authorized to issue, on the application of any person holding stock of the state, coupon bonds bearing 6 per cent interest and payable within twenty years. Likewise bonds were to be converted into stock in the same manner. This will be hereafter referred to as the conversion act.[15]

8. Under the act of August 26, 1869, to pay the interest on the public debt, the governor, treasurer, and attorney-general were authorized to appoint "some responsible bank or banker in the city of New York" to act as financial agent of the state, such agent to be subject to their direction and control.[16]

9. An act to create a debt known as the Sterling Funded Debt was passed March 7, 1871. It authorized the governor to borrow on coupon bonds of the state bearing 6 per cent interest and payable semi-annually, the sum of 1,200,000 pounds sterling, the proceeds to be used exclusively in exchange for, or in payment of, the existing public debt. No new debt was to be

---

[13] *Ibid.*, pp. 275-76.

[14] Amended Mar. 1, 1870.—*Ibid.*, pp. 385-86.

[15] *Ibid.*, p. 241. The treasurer was authorized to charge a fee of $1.00 for each certificate of stock or bond exchanged and a further fee of 50c for each blank used in the transaction.

[16] *Ibid.*, p. 18.

created until this was paid.[17] This act aroused great opposition in the state; it never went into effect and was repealed a year after its passage.[18]

*   *   *   *   *

When the Radical government was inaugurated in July, 1868, there was only $45 in the treasury, and since there was a large bonded and floating debt which had to be provided for, it was necessary to borrow on the securities of the state until money could be realized from the tax levy. Governor Scott proceeded to New York to select a financial agent. After conferring with several leading banks, all of which declined the agency, alleging that the duties were arduous and the time of payment uncertain, H. H. Kimpton, a young classmate of Attorney-General Chamberlain at Yale and a man of less than two years' banking experience, was appointed agent and permitted to go his own security for $50,000 while in charge of over $2,000,000.[19]

With the bonds authorized and the financial agent appointed, the state was ready to dispose of its securities. Some bonds were sold outright in the market; others were hypothecated or deposited as collateral security for loans, some of them subject to call and all at a high rate of interest. These transactions were unfortunate, to say the least, and resulted in an expensive debt. In January, 1868, during the military rule, state stocks and bonds were selling at 22 and 25 cents on the dollar; in July, when restoration to the Union was assured, they were worth 62 to 66 cents, and interest rates had decreased from $2\frac{1}{2}$ or 3 per cent per month to $\frac{3}{4}$ to 1 per cent per month.[20] When Scott in the fall of 1868 went north to negotiate a loan, he predicted that in a short time South Carolina's

[17] *Ibid.,* pp. 616-18.

[18] Mar. 13, 1872.—*Ibid.,* XV, 193.

[19] Scott's message, Nov. 28, 1871. *House Journal, 1871-72.* Scott's statement of the amount in the treasury in-

July, 1868, does not agree with Orr's figures. See above, p. 45. It is impossible to say which was correct.

[20] Orr, in *News,* July 11, 1868.

credit would stand foremost among the states of the Union;[21] in November bills receivable were selling at 85.[22]

But what appeared to be a revival of state credit was seen in a different light after a few weeks' session of the legislature.[23] The financial agent was sent $500,000 for the redemption of bills receivable and $1,000,000 in bonds for the payment of the interest on the public debt. At first he was unable to borrow on the bonds. In November, the governor and his friends secured a loan of $100,000 on bonds at 25 cents on the dollar, at a percentage of 18 or 20.[24] After the payment of interest on July 1, 1869, bonds reached 70, at which price the financial board instructed Kimpton to sell some of the bonds for the redemption of bills receivable and for the payment of the interest on the public debt.[25] A small number of conversion bonds were sold by the financial agent in 1871 at about the same price; and a portion of the bonds for the payment of the interest on the public debt, a portion of the bonds for the relief of the treasury, a portion of the land commission bonds, and the remainder of the conversion bonds, were sold under forfeiture for non-payment of loans in 1871 or after at various prices, making a general average of nearly 43 cents on the dollar. From the sales of these bonds, amounting to $8,057,500, there was derived the sum of $3,442,127.39.[26]

Thus the bonds and stocks of the state were not good securities. As the market value declined, the financial agent was instructed not to sell state securities but to hypothecate them

[21] *Ibid.*, Nov. 9, 1868.

[22] *Ibid.*, Nov. 26, 1868.

[23] *Courier*, Aug. 17, 1868.

[24] Scott said: "It was regarded as a wild speculation to loan money on South Carolina bonds." Special message, Jan. 9, 1872; testimony before committee to ascertain what bonds of the state were pledged as collateral for state loans, *Reports and Resolutions, 1874-75*, p. 731.

[25] *Reports and Resolutions, 1874-75*, pp. 727, 732.

[26] *Ibid.*, p. 727. In December, 1869, it was enacted that interest should be paid in gold or silver coin; and in 1870 trustees "and all other persons holding funds in trust for investment," were authorized to invest the same in bonds of the state, and they were "relieved from all responsibility for said investment, except for the safe keeping of the bonds," and it was provided that there should be "no order of the Court directing a different investment."—*Stat. S. C.*, XIV, 303, 404.

for loans, which he usually did for about 40 cents on the dollar.[27] In order to take up these loans and stop interest and expenses, he urged the financial board to authorize him to sell at about 68 or 70. This he was not permitted to do. As the price of bonds fell, more bonds were required as collateral, while, at the same time, the difficulty of selling bonds became greater and greater. While the bonds went down, the loans went up, and the result was, in 1872, that the price and credit of the bonds had reached such a point that they could not be sold even at a forced sale to extinguish the loans.[28]

Chamberlain and Parker, members of the financial board with Scott, agreed with Kimpton and thought that the low price for bonds would have been largely offset by saving interest and expenses on loans frequently renewed. Scott thought the bonds would reach a permanent value of 80 or more. Old bonds (those issued before 1868) had sold as high as 95, and the new bonds on one occasion reached 86, but the market was limited at such prices. In the fall of 1871 old bonds were at 75 and new bonds at 50.[29] Scott claimed that the decline in prices was partly due to the fact that the opposition press threatened repudiation and denounced the securities as bayonet and scalawag bonds.[30] Holders frequently called for more collateral which could not be furnished by Kimpton, and collateral securities were put on the market at a very low figure and so increased the public debt.

Thus in two years there were various classes of securities outstanding against the state. Some of these had been sold by the financial agent; others had been sold by holders of collateral for loans when the market dropped and no more collateral could be had from the financial agent. The exact amount of the debt was not known; the figures from the reports of the treasurer, comptroller-general, and financial agent did not

[27] *Reports and Resolutions, 1874-75,* p. 732.
[28] *Ibid.,* p. 744.
[29] Test. of Kimpton, in *Reports and Resolutions, 1871-72,* pp. 258-59.
[30] *News,* Oct. 23, 1871.

agree; and it was claimed by the opposition press and even by some of the state officials that there were large issues of fraudulent bonds on the market, and that certain of the state officials had profited thereby. The comptroller-general's report at the close of the fiscal year ending October 31, 1870, showed the public debt to be $7,665,908.98; in May, 1871, the taxpayers' convention put it at $10,665,908.98; in September, 1871, Governor Scott informed a congressional committee that it was $9,528,964.10; in October, 1871, the governor placed the debt at $11,994,908.98; in November, Treasurer Parker issued a report which showed the debt to be $12,013,908.98; and in December an investigating committee of the House put it at $15,767,908.98.

During the whole of Scott's two administrations the public press charged corrupt and fraudulent mismanagement of the public funds. These charges were very plain and specific, were not successfully denied by the officials concerned, and were later found to be substantially correct. While the Conservative press continually reviled the Radical government, on no topic was it so prolific or bitter as that of finances and taxation. The public demanded an investigation, the legislature did likewise, and in 1871 there were some startling disclosures.

It had been freely stated that there had been an over-issue of some $6,000,000 of conversion bonds under the act of March, 1869. There were many complaints of the burden of taxation under the corrupt legislature, and when on March 7, 1871, the legislature passed the Sterling Funded Debt Act which provided for the issue of 1,200,000 pounds sterling to fund the public debt and reduce interest, there was a strong protest against any further issue of bonds that might be mishandled. In the latter part of March the Charleston Chamber of Commerce met to consider the financial situation of the state. This body resolved that the majority of property holders and taxpayers were excluded from any power in the legislature; that the money raised by taxation was corruptly used; that the credit of the state had been illegally pledged, and that the legislature proposed to pledge the credit of the state for further loans. Therefore it declared that any bonds issued without legal sanction, and the so-called sterling loan or any other bonds, would not be binding. Furthermore, the Chamber of Commerce would in every way and at all times resist the payment thereof, or any tax to pay the same, "by all legitimate means within our power."[31] It warned all persons not to receive any such bonds "as they will be held null and void by us." It was resolved that a convention of taxpayers be held in Columbia, the convention to investigate the accounts of the comptroller and the financial agent and to determine the amount of the public debt with a view to such further action as might be necessary for the protection of public creditors and taxpayers.[32]

This convention met in Columbia on May 9 and continued in session through May 12. Thirty counties were represented and the delegates comprised some of the most influential citizens of the state. James Chesnut said it was the "best body that I have seen assembled in South Carolina, except the secession convention of 1860." There were four ex-governors, two ex-lieutenant governors, three ex-United States senators, five ex-congressmen, one ex-chancellor, one ex-secretary of the Confederate treasury, forty-three ex-members of the House of Representatives, sixteen state senators, eleven generals, and five bankers.[33] Governor Scott was admitted to the floor, and Attorney-General Chamberlain was third vice-president. One of the secretaries was a Radical and two or three Negroes were in attendance. The *Columbia Daily Union,* a staunch Radical paper, said that so far as its public operations were concerned

[31] *News,* Mar. 31, 1871; *Phoenix,* Apr. 1, 1871.

[32] *Ibid.* These resolutions were also adopted by the Charleston Board of Trade.

[33] *News,* May 9, 1871; *Orangeburg News,* May 13, 1871. The more distinguished men present included J. P. Richardson, M. L. Bonham, John L. Manning, Johnson Hagood, W. D. Porter, George A. Trenholm, James Chesnut, M. C. Butler, M. W. Gary, and W. H. Trescot.

the convention was non-political.[34] W. D. Porter was elected president. In his address he spoke of "the fearful and unnecessary increase of the public debt," the "reckless and profligate" applications of the public moneys, and the logical result of "excessive taxation."

One of the prime causes of the taxpayers' convention was the threatened issue of the sterling loan bonds. The executive committee of the convention denounced the sterling loan "or any other bonds or obligations, hereafter issued, purporting to be under and by virtue of the authority of this State, as at present constituted," and recommended to the people of the state, "in every manner and at all times, to resist the payment thereof, or the enforcement of any tax to pay the same, by all legitimate means within their power." Likewise they warned "all persons not to receive, by way of purchase, loan, or otherwise, any bond or obligation hereafter issued by the present State Government, or by any subsequent government, in which the property-holders of the State are not represented."[35]

The most important committee having to do with the finances of the state was that appointed under a resolution of M. C. Butler. It was to inquire of the governor the amount and disposition of bonds issued and to investigate the extent to which the state and county officers had unnecessarily increased since the organization of the government in 1868.[36] The committee conferred with the governor and made "a very casual and hasty examination" of the records of the comptroller and treasurer "and expressed themselves satisfied that the records there were all correct."[37] When the committee visited the governor (the treasurer, comptroller, and the financial agent being present also), Scott observed that notwithstanding the rumors

[34] May 15, 1871. See *Proceedings of the Taxpayers' Convention*, May 9-12, 1871.

[35] *Ibid.*, p. 86.

[36] *Ibid.*, pp. 19, 20.

[37] Test. of Neagle, comptroller, before the committee on public frauds, in *Reports and Resolutions, 1876-77*, Fraud Report, p. 904.

that an illegal and irregular manipulation of the public funds had taken place, nothing had been done involving the credit of the state which was not strictly according to law, and he stated that he had signed no bonds other than those set forth in the printed statement of the funded debt which had been furnished to the convention by the comptroller-general.[38] By the comptroller's statement, $7,665,908.98 was "the total funded debt." To which the committee added $800,000 in cash advanced by the financial agent and for which he had hypothecated $1,800,000 in bonds, and the further sum of $400,000 for bonds sold by Kimpton. The total debt, then, as reported by G. A. Trenholm, was $8,865,908.98, to which should be added the $1,800,000 hypothecated bonds, making a grand total of $10,665,908.98.[39]

The comptroller's statement was "confirmed by the Governor, who united with the Treasurer, Mr. Parker, in giving to the committee every assurance of its correctness." And it appeared to the committee "that the several issues and sums of bonds described" were "of unquestionable legality and force as obligations of the State."[40]

Although the governor in his next message to the legislature said that this "highly respectable body of citizens" had all the records of the several bureaus in the executive department "unreservedly laid open" to them,[41] it subsequently appeared that the committee had been misled by the governor and others. Parker testified that it was the aim of the financial board to conceal the fact of the issue of conversion bonds amounting to about five millions. He affirmed that the statement presented to the committee was prepared in his office by Chamberlain and submitted to Scott before exhibition to the committee.[42] Subsequent reports of the treasurer and financial agent showed

[38] *Proceedings of the Taxpayers' Convention, 1871*, pp. 102-3.

[39] *Ibid.*, pp. 108-10.

[40] *Ibid.*, p. 111.

[41] *House Journal, 1871-72*, p. 34.

[42] *Reports and Resolutions, 1877-78*, Fraud Report, pp. 926-27.

that there had been a large over-issue of conversion bonds at that date. "After the convention was through, Scott, Chamberlain, and Kimpton laughed at the manner in which they had succeeded in deceiving the members."[43]

The committee of the convention had no doubt "that frauds the most flagrant, and corruption the most dangerous and demoralizing" had been perpetrated by many of the state officials; yet it had no power to make a thorough investigation.[44] It recommended that the governor request the attorney-general to inquire into all cases of alleged fraud, and adopted instructions to the legislature suggesting methods of making safe the funds of the treasury and securing increased revenue.[45] Finally, on the strength of the report of the committee, the convention adopted a resolution stating that the funded debt of the state as reported by the committee was a valid debt, and that the honor and funds of the state were lawfully pledged for its redemption.[46] The *Columbia Daily Union*[47] admitted that there were abuses which needed reformation, but thought that on the whole "the Republican party has much reason to feel gratified with the result of the Convention." It was the general consensus of the press that the convention was a failure.[48]

Meanwhile, another examination, more thorough and extensive, of the financial condition of the state was being made by committees of the legislature. Under a resolution of February, 1871, a joint committee was "appointed to make a complete and thorough examination of all the accounts of the State Treasurer, Comptroller General, and Financial Agent, since their induction into office."[49] After considerable delay due to the reluctance of the state officials, including the governor, to submit to an investigation, the committee made its

---

[43] Test. of Neagle, *ibid.*, p. 904.
[44] *Proceedings of the Taxpayers' Convention, 1871*, p. 105.
[45] *Ibid.*, pp. 105-8.
[46] *Ibid.*, p. 115.
[47] May 15, 1871.
[48] *New York Sun*, Feb. 1, 1878.
[49] *Reports and Resolutions, 1871-72*, p. 867.

report in December, 1871.[50] The members from the House concluded that the entire bonded debt of the state was $15,767,-908.98, and had been created in accordance with the law. It was of the opinion that there had been no over-issue of bonds for the reason that no act of the General Assembly limited the amount to be issued.[51] However, a special committee appointed to inquire into the matter of an over-issue concluded "after a careful investigation and close scrutiny" that there had been an over-issue of $6,314,000 in bonds. The committee found that up to October 31, 1870 there had been, according to the comptroller's report, an issue of $3,000,000 of new bonds. And although the treasurer had since that date made monthly reports to the comptroller as required by law, he had failed to give any account of a further issue of bonds; yet according to his sworn statement there were then signed and outstanding $9,514,000 of new bonds, $6,314,000 of which in the judgment of the committee, had not been issued according to law.[52]

The joint special financial investigating committee in its report of December, 1871, scathingly denounced the officials who were connected with the state's finances. It denounced the work of the land commission as a "gigantic folly," it revealed fraud and extravagance in connection with the militia and armed force; many doubts were cast upon the financial board, the financial agent, the sinking fund commission, and other related agencies. The committee found that appropriations had been diverted from their intended and specified purpose, but that the "inexhaustible funds" of the state, "like a never-failing fountain," were sufficient for every demand when it was in the interest or pleasure of the heads of the financial departments. The public money was deposited in a bank which was controlled by state officials, no interest was paid as

[50] The investigation extended over a period of several months. The elaborate report presented is found in *Reports and Resolutions, 1871-72.*

[51] *Reports and Resolutions, 1871-72*, p. 871.

[52] *Ibid.*, pp. 901-3.

required by law, pay certificates and other claims were cashed by the bank only after a large discount, and the committee questioned "the propriety of State officials forming themselves into a Banking Association (The South Carolina Bank and Trust Company), and depositing the State funds with themselves, drawing out of the Treasury with one hand, and paying out of the bank with the other . . . and charging heavy per cents for the privilege."[53] The failure of this bank in 1875 stopped the interest on the public debt and cost the state about $200,000. The bank had never been financially secure after its organization in 1870.[54]

The committee found that the American Bank Note Company had printed bonds and certificates of stock to the amount of $22,540,000 which was at the disposal of the state officials. The printed reports of these officials claimed that there had been destroyed, cancelled, or deposited for safe keeping, or were on hand in the treasury, bonds to the amount of $13,-026,000, which would leave the real bonded debt at $14,921,-306.27. From this was deducted the old bonded debt of $5,407,306.27, which left the new bonded debt, created since July, 1868, at $9,514,000, which was just the amount which was represented to have been delivered to the financial agent.[55] By adding to this amount the old debt, plus $1,259,000 of bonds issued in 1869 for funding bills of the Bank of the State, plus certain bonds purchased by Kimpton from the proceeds of the college land scrip, which could not be less than $200,000, the committee arrived at "a total Confessed Debt of $16,371,-306.27." To this, they said, might well be added the sterling loan bonds for $6,000,000 (£1,200,000), of which $3,500,000 had already been signed and made ready for issue, which would give an aggregated old and new bonded debt of $22,371,306.27.

[53] Report of the Financial Investigating Committee, *ibid.*, pp. 1-23.
[54] *News and Courier*, July 3, 5, Sept. 17, Oct. 23, 25, 1875; *Reports and Resolutions, 1875-76*, pp. 389 ff.
[55] *Reports and Resolutions, 1871-72*, p. 266.

To this add the contingent debt of $6,687,608.20 and the entire indebtedness of the state was $29,158,914.47. The committee affirmed that there was "indisputable evidence that all the Financial officers of the State, as well as the Governor himself, in their State and official papers, have hitherto disguised the true condition of the debt, as well as the issue of bonds,"[56] and it was on the basis of this evidence that C. C. Bowen, then a legislator from Charleston, introduced on December 18, 1871, a resolution to impeach Scott and Parker for high crimes and misdemeanors. These two officials became much alarmed and by issuing fictitious warrants on the Armed Force Fund[57] to the amount of $48,645 and by giving $15,000 to Speaker Moses, bribed members of the legislature and stopped the proceedings.[58]

The impeachment proceedings and legislative investigations came to naught; but great doubt was entertained as to the validity of some of the bonds and obligations of the state, and on March 13, 1872, a validating act was passed. It declared that the bonds and obligations issued on behalf of the state, as mentioned and set forth in the report of the treasurer, on October 31, 1871, were duly and lawfully issued in conformity with the true intent and meaning of the acts of the General Assembly and an annual tax should be levied to pay the interest.[59]

[56] *Ibid.*, p. 267.

[57] A fund at the disposal of the governor by a joint resolution authorizing him to employ an armed force for the preservation of the peace. *Stat. S. C.*, XIV, 285.

[58] *House Journal, 1871-72*, p. 181; *Reports and Resolutions, 1877-78*, Fraud Report, pp. 1595 ff; *Columbia Daily Union*, Jan. 17, 1872, said that the impeachment scheme, instituted "solely for the purpose of gratifying private malice and personal hatred," had cost not less than $50,000.

[59] *Stat. S. C.*, XV, 278-81. The issues validated were issued under the following acts: "An Act to authorize a loan to redeem the obligations known as the Bills Receivable of the State of South Carolina," approved Aug. 26, 1868; "An Act to authorize a State loan to pay interest on the public debt," approved Aug. 26, 1868; "An Act to provide for the appointment of a Land Commissioner, and to define his powers and duties," approved Mar. 27, 1869; "An Act to amend the last named Act, and for other purposes," approved Mar. 1, 1870; "An Act to authorize a loan for the relief of the Treasury," approved Feb. 17, 1869; "An Act to provide for the conversion of state securities," approved Mar. 23, 1869; and "An Act to authorize the Financial Agent . . . to pledge State bonds as collateral security. . . ," approved Mar. 26, 1869. It was further provided that "neither the sum or sums realized from any sale or sales of any of the bonds of this State, shall in any manner

Harper's Weekly

GOVERNOR MOSES VIEWING THE PROMISED LAND FROM
MOUNT RUIN

Meanwhile the credit of the state was almost entirely destroyed. With well-founded rumors of fraudulent bonds upon the market, with a corrupt and extravagant legislature, and with an empty treasury, the state could not raise funds to maintain its schools or institutions of charity. The demands for funds for educational purposes were met with "No money"; the state institution for the deaf, dumb, and blind was almost destitute and the superintendent had to raise money through charity; the superintendent of the insane asylum mortgaged his private property to the extent of $15,000 so that his charges might not suffer.[60] Governor Moses stated in December, 1872: "There is no money in the Treasury with which to meet either the current expenses of the State Government, or its large and outstanding liabilities. The necessities of the several charitable, educational, and penal institutions, which have been so extremely urgent for many months past, still remain unsatisfied."[61]

The taxpayers' convention and the legislative investigations did not correct existing evils. The taxpayers' investigation was not sufficiently thorough, and the legislative reports exhibiting fraud on the part of state officials were smothered. Yet all the investigators as well as the press united in condemning the work of the financial agent and the financial board. The financial agent, knowing that his period of usefulness was past and possibly fearing further examinations of his financial manipulations, sought to secure a settlement with the state. After a number of the legislators had been bribed for the purpose, an act was passed in the spring of 1872 authorizing the financial board, Scott, Parker, and Chamberlain, to settle the claims and demands of the agent and "to execute and deliver

affect or impair the validity and obligation thereof." The treasurer's report for Oct. 31, 1871, put the debt at $11,994,908.98.

[60] *News,* April 24, 1871, May 3, 4, 1872, May 25, 1872, July 6, 1872. Many of the state officers had not received their salaries for several months.

[61] *Senate Journal, 1872-73,* p. 83.

to him a full release and discharge for all liability to this State."[62] This was done and Kimpton received a due bill for over $139,000 for the remainder of commissions due him.[63] Some efforts were made to secure a reputable New York banking house as financial agent, but no other agent was appointed.

* * * * *

By 1872 there was much discussion of repudiation. There was little doubt in the public mind that much of the debt was illegal; it had increased constantly; the interest could not be paid; and from the point of view of the state officials as well as the taxpayers, some financial adjustment was imperative.

Talk of repudiation was not new. By most of the state press the Radical legislature of 1868 was held to be unconstitutional and its acts void from the beginning. No "bayonet" bond, issued by a bogus legislature, would be paid. The *Charleston Daily News* said, July 17, 1868: "Would New York or Boston touch these bonds, issued by authority of a horde of Negroes, and in face of the protest of the white people of the State?" Northern capitalists were warned that they might as well throw their dollars into the sea as lend them to the usurping body in session in Columbia. Declared the *News:* "No bonds issued by this so-called Legislature will ever be paid. . . . No loans . . . recognized. . . . No bills receivable, issued by the so-called Governor of the State, with the sanction of the pretended Legislature, to carry on an illegal government, will be permitted to be received in payment of the taxes of the State. . . ."[64]

[62] *Stat. S. C.,* XV, 277-78.

[63] It appears that the financial board and agent were anxious to make a settlement to cover up their manipulations. According to Parker the agent's commissions were to be divided equally between Kimpton, Parker, and Chamberlain. *Reports and Resolutions, 1877-78,* Fraud Report, p. 1629.

[64] Aug. 17, 1868. Yet the same paper was soon saying that the state was in a sound and solvent condition and that Scott should be sustained in his efforts to restore public credit. Dec. 1, 1868. A year later the *News* felt that the debt could be paid as it stood, but feared that another year of Radical rule might swell the total to the extent that the people would repudiate at the first opportunity every dollar of debt contracted after the war. Dec. 1, 1869.

Meanwhile the administration found its financial legislation attacked by investigating committees and colored politicians. In the spring of 1871, a short while before the taxpayers' convention, there was talk of a new political party. Colored statesmen were its leaders—Robert C. DeLarge, William Beverly Nash, Lucius Wimbush, Robert Smalls—and they made a proposal to the Charleston Chamber of Commerce and the Board of Trade to repudiate the state debt.[65] In January, 1872, it was reported that the debt was to be scaled at the rate of fifty cents on the dollar, bonds issued before 1868 to be scaled at seventy-five. The Union Trust Company of New York was to be appointed agent, was to guarantee the fulfillment of the contract, and was to advance money sufficient to redeem hypothecated bonds.[66] A little later New York bondholders prepared a bill providing for the scaling of the debt at seventy-five,[67] and by December, 1872, the recently elected governor, Moses, proposed to have a committee call on the bondholders to get them to accept a new issue which would reduce the debt to seven or eight millions.[68]

In February, 1873, a Conservative member of the legislature proposed that the debt be scaled at thirty cents providing the holders were willing to do so voluntarily,[69] and Senator Nash proposed a bill providing that "the State shall not be legally bound for the payment of any debt contracted by any public officer under and by authority of an act of the General Assembly."[70]

In order to pass a tax levy which had been declared mandatory by the supreme court, and to "take into immediate consideration the condition of the public debt," a special session of

[65] News, April 6, Nov. 13, 1871. They said they wanted a party based on intelligence and integrity.

[66] News, Jan. 18, 20, 1872. Scott apparently took active steps to put this scheme through but failed.

[67] Orangeburg News, Feb. 17, 1872.

[68] Courier, Dec. 6, 1872.

[69] News, Feb. 1, 1873.

[70] News, Feb. 13, 1873; Senate Journal, 1872-73, p. 495.

the legislature was convened October 21, 1873.[71] Moses in his message to the special session stated that with the exception of $2,189,000 bonds which were quoted at twenty-three cents on account of a recent court decision,[72] both the old and new bonds were quoted at fifteen cents. It was evident that it was to the interest of every bondholder that the debt be reduced to a reasonable amount so that interest payments could be resumed.[73]

Nothing was done at the special session, but at the regular session immediately following an act was passed to "reduce the volume of the public debt and provide for the payment of the same."[74] This act authorized and required the state treasurer to receive from the holders willing to surrender the same the certificates of stock and bonds enumerated in the act. In lieu of bonds and stocks so surrendered he was to issue to the holders either coupon bonds or certificates of stock as they desired, equal in amount to 50 per cent of the face value of the bonds or certificates of stock surrendered. The bonds and stocks and coupons and interest orders thus specified as exchangeable, amounted to $11,480,033.91. The remainder of the apparent funded debt of the state, consisting of what were known as "conversion bonds," and amounting to $5,965,000, were declared to have been "put upon the market without any authority of law" and were "absolutely null and void." The new consolidation bonds and certificates of stock were to bear upon their face the declaration that the payment of the interest and the redemption of the principal were secured by the levy of an annual tax of two mills on the dollar upon the entire taxable

---

[71] *News and Courier*, Oct. 11, 1873. The consensus of opinion was that the legislature would do nothing. Said the Radical *Union Herald:* "If the legislature would be able, honestly and fairly, to dispose of our debt, find out what we owe and don't owe, then it might be well."—

Quoted in *News and Courier*, May 31, 1873.
[72] Case of Morton, Bliss, Company, *Mandamus.*
[73] *House Journal, Spec. Sess., 1873,* pp. 24, 33-36.
[74] Dec. 22, 1873. *Stat. S. C.;* XV, 518-23.

property of the state. This declaration was to be considered a contract entered into between the state and every holder of said bonds and stocks. The act declared, however, that no tax should ever be levied to pay the interest or principal on any of the bonds or stocks mentioned in the act as long as such bonds or certificates should remain outstanding in their present form. The consolidation bonds and stocks were to bear interest at the rate of 6 per cent, payable semi-annually, the principal to be payable within twenty years from the date of the passage of the act, and were to be dated January 1, 1874. All coupons or interest orders were made receivable "in payment of all taxes due the State during the year in which they mature, except for tax levied for the public schools." Provision was made for a fund, to be kept separate from all other funds, to be applied to the interest and to the extinguishment of the principal. The act contained provisions for the public registry of all the new bonds and stocks, and provided heavy penalties for any dereliction of duty on the part of any officer in the execution of the law.

To safeguard further the public funds, an amendment to the constitution was ratified. This amendment provided that no further debt or obligation, "either by the loan of the credit of the state, by guaranty, endorsement or otherwise, except for the ordinary and current business of the state," could be created by the General Assembly unless two-thirds of the qualified voters of the state should be in favor of a further debt.[75]

While the *News and Courier* did not question the fact that the "stigma of illegality and probably fraud" attached to a large number of the bonds of the state issued since the war, it did not believe the consolidation act could be made operative. It believed that there was not sufficient confidence in the state authorities to cause the holders of genuine bonds to surrender them for doubtful security at 50 per cent off.[76]

---

[75] *Stat. S. C.*, XV, 295, 466-67.   [76] *News and Courier*, Dec. 30, 1873.

Nevertheless, the funding of the debt went steadily forward. The total amount funded up to October 31, 1875, was $7,220,512.65.[77] The operation of the consolidation act was severely criticized. In 1874 a legislative committee charged that $978,500 of the bonds funded belonged to a class which, "in the united judgment of the Senate, should not have been funded at all"; Treasurer Cardozo was accused of "a singular want of vigilance in guarding the public interests," and he came near being removed.[78] Another investigating committee showed that "a very large amount" of coupons maturing between July, 1867, and October 1, 1871, had been funded, "although the records of the Treasury prove that they had been previously paid."[79] The consolidation bonds became a good buy in the market, and by 1875 there were very few offered in New York. Since no taxes were to be levied for the old bonds, there was an advantage in buying the old bonds at a low figure and consolidating them under the act. The old bonds rose from twenty-five to forty cents, and the rate at which the unconsolidated bonds sold fixed the value of the consolidated bonds. To the large taxpayer the consolidated bonds had the advantage that they could be bought at sixty and the coupons used to pay taxes, thus saving forty cents on every dollar of taxes paid.[80]

A determined effort for retrenchment and reform was made by Governor Chamberlain in 1874-76, but he was opposed and thwarted by the legislature. Chamberlain was anxious to raise the credit of the state and win the support of Conservatives. He sought to prevent extravagant and fraudulent legislative

[77] *Reports and Resolutions, 1875-76*, pp. 3-4.
[78] *Reports and Resolutions, 1874-75*, pp. 625-26.
[79] *Reports and Resolutions, 1875-76*, pp. 3-4.
[80] *News and Courier*, Jan. 4, 18, 1875. At 40 per cent $10,000 of old bonds would cost $4,000. In exchange for them the owner could obtain $5,000 in consolidated bonds, also consolidated bonds for accrued interest to Jan. 1, 1874. The interest, averaging two years at six per cent, would equal, on $10,000, a sum of $1,200 which at 50 per cent would give $600 in bonds. For $4,000 the investor would have $5,600.

expenses, he reformed the system of taxation by providing specific levies for specific purposes, and he made some attempt to punish offenders against the state. Proceedings were instituted against Kimpton, the former financial agent, to recover a large amount of funds placed in his hands by the sinking fund commission and the board having charge of the agricultural college land scrip. Attorneys were hired to conduct the cases in New York against Kimpton, but appropriations by the General Assembly were not sufficient to pay the expenses: "Indeed, the inference was plain that the General Assembly desired the litigation to be discontinued, and it has accordingly been done."[81]

Former Treasurer Parker was brought to trial. He was arrested for having received $28,100 from the sinking fund commission and applying it to uses other than those prescribed by law. In a short time suit was also instituted against him for the embezzlement and fraudulent appropriation of interest coupons.[82] It was charged that when paying interest coupons on valid bonds he put aside $450,000 of such coupons uncanceled and in their place as vouchers put coupons which could be cut off from conversion bonds which had already matured and could not be paid. Those valid coupons were later funded at the treasury.[83] The jury decided that Parker had taken $150,000 in coupons and had defrauded the state of $75,000, the amount for which they were fundable.[84] Parker escaped jail,[85] was rearrested, illegally released on a habeas corpus,[86] and made his way north.

After the failure of Chamberlain's reforms to win him Conservative support, the credit of the state was still very low. Wade Hampton, the Democratic governor who succeeded Chamberlain, said that the credit of the state must be restored to its "ancient high character" and hoped that "under no

[81] Attorney-General Melton, in *Reports and Resolutions, 1875-76,* p. 383.
[82] *Ibid.,* pp. 379 ff.
[83] *News and Courier,* April 23, 1875.
[84] *Ibid.,* July 21, 1875.
[85] *Ibid.,* Aug. 5, 10, 17, 1875.
[86] 6 S. C. 472.

circumstances will repudiation, direct or indirect, be coun-
tenanced." He recommended that a special tax of one-half
mill should be levied to buy state bonds while they were selling
at 25 to 30 per cent below par.[87]

*   *   *   *   *

After assuming control of the state in April, 1877, the Democrats were anxious to remove any doubt or suspicion attached
to claims against the state and to give reasonable assurance to
the creditor that the state intended to meet her obligations.
To accomplish this and to satisfy the taxpayer that steps would
be taken to adjust and provide for the public debt, the General
Assembly, by joint resolution, June 8, 1877,[88] appointed a commission to investigate the indebtedness of the state, and also to
ascertain "whether there is in the state treasurer's office, on file,
as vouchers, canceled bonds, coupons, and certificates of stocks
of the issues described" in the consolidation act of 1873, which
were issued in accordance with law, and to report whether
any stocks, bonds, or coupons had been unlawfully or otherwise improperly issued under said act, together with the evidence upon which the illegality or nonconformity to law rested.

The commission sat from August 1, 1877, until February 5,
1878. In its report to the legislature[89] the commission stated
the total amount of bonds and certificates of stock outstanding
to be $4,396,290.41.[90] Of the $8,792,779 of vouchers on file in
the treasury,[91] the commission found that $5,184,062 were
"issued in accordance with law" and authorized to be consolidated, and that the remaining $3,608,717 vouchers were not
"issued in accordance with law" and not authorized to be consolidated.[92]

The committee found that certain detached coupons from

---

[87] Senate Journal, 1877-78, p. 14.
[88] Stat. S. C., XVI, 318.
[89] Report of the Commission to investigate the Indebtedness of the State, in Reports and Resolutions, 1877-78, Fraud Report, pp. 859 ff.

[90] Ibid., p. 864.
[91] The vouchers representing the outstanding stocks and bonds funded at 50
per cent.
[92] Ibid., pp. 866-67.

relief of the treasury bonds had been consolidated although the bonds in question had never been issued as a charge against the state. Similarly, certain detached coupons from conversion bonds had been consolidated although they had matured before the bonds to which they were originally attached were issued from the treasury. Also certain detached coupons maturing on or before July 1, 1871, were held to be invalid. In each case it was a matter of legislative and judicial record that all matured coupons were cut off from bonds before the latter were issued from the treasury or financial agency. The presumption was that uncanceled coupons had been illegally removed from the treasury or financial agency and funded by parties interested. In fact, the testimony was clear that Parker and Scott had procured about $331,996 in such coupons from Kimpton and had funded them at the state treasury through agents.[93] Bonds and coupons to the amount of $2,166,039 had been illegally hypothecated by the financial agent;[94] the land commission bonds to the amount of $700,000 had not been issued according to law;[95] and there had been an over-issue of bills receivable to the amount of $71,000.[96]

Finally, under the act of August 26, 1868, which authorized the governor to borrow, on the credit of the state, on coupon bonds, within twelve months, a sum not exceeding $1,000,000 for the payment of interest on the public debt, an excess of $1,000,000 bonds had been issued. The first issue of $1,000,000, printed in September, 1868, was indorsed as "loans to pay interest on the public debt." Since these bonds caused distrust in the market, a second issue of $1,000,000 was printed in August and November, 1869, and indorsed as "issued under act approved August 26, 1868." The testimony of the governor and the treasurer showed conclusively that $2,000,000 in bonds had been put upon the market contrary to the terms of the act,

[93] Ibid., pp. 871, 932-38.
[94] Ibid., pp. 872-76.
[95] Ibid., pp. 880-2.
[96] Ibid., p. 883.

and the commission concluded that the whole of the second issue was fraudulent and placed upon the market without authority of law.[97]

On the basis of the report of the investigation commission the legislature created a "court of claims" with authority "to hear and determine any case or cases made up or brought to test the validity of any of the consolidated bonds, coupons and certificates of stock," or any of the various classes of them mentioned in the report of the commission as resting on vouchers not issued in accordance with law. The court was to consist of three circuit judges of the state to be selected by the General Assembly.[98]

The cases brought before this court involved constitutional questions as well as questions of fact, and upon the latter the proof was convincing as to the illegal funding of certain coupons. The cases were appealed to the state Supreme Court and there consolidated and determined.[99]   On September 29, 1879, the court rendered the following decision:

That all the bonds issued under an act entitled "an act to reduce the volume of the public debt and provide for the payment of the same," were valid obligations of the state, except as follows: (1) Such as were issued in exchange for bonds issued under the act entitled "an act to authorize a loan for the relief of the treasury,"[100] or for the coupons of said bonds. (2) Such as were issued in exchange for the second issue of bonds under an act entitled "an act to authorize a state loan to pay interest on the public debt,"[101] or the coupons of such bonds. (3) Such as were issued in exchange for either of the two classes of bonds last mentioned, viz., bonds for the relief of the treasury, and the second issue of bonds to pay interest on the public debt, or in exchange for the coupons of *such* conversion bonds.

The court decided that the bonds issued under the act for

[97] Fraud Report, p. 878.
[98] *Stat. S. C.*, XVI, 669-73.
[99] 12 S. C. 202-13.

[100] Act of Feb. 17, 1869.
[101] Act of Aug. 26, 1868.

the relief of the treasury were not valid obligations of the state because the act was in conflict with Section 7 of Article IX of the state constitution.[102] The court held that the act was liable to two constitutional objections: (1) It purported to create a debt which was not "for the purpose of defraying extraordinary expenditures"; and (2) the debt therein sought to be created was not "for some *single* object," and such object was not "distinctly specified therein." "We think, therefore, that . . . every bond, together with its coupons, issued under the authority of this act is absolutely void, even in the hands of a *bona fide* holder, because issued without any authority whatever, and hence every consolidation bond resting upon such bonds or coupons, is, to the extent that it does rest upon such bonds or coupons, not a valid debt of the state of South Carolina."[103]

In determining the question as to the validity of the second issue of bonds under the "act to authorize a state loan to pay interest on the public debt," the court said: "In the case of the second issue . . . there does not seem to have been the shadow of authority of any kind, and which [bonds], therefore, are absolutely void, no matter in whose hands they may be."

The court further decided that "If any consolidation bond rests wholly upon any of the three objectionable classes of bonds or coupons . . . mentioned, then it is wholly void; but if it rests only in part upon such objectionable bonds or coupons, then it is only void to the extent which it does rest upon such objectionable bonds or coupons, and for the balance it is a valid obligation of the state."

At the next session of the legislature a special commissioner was appointed whose duty it was to ascertain and establish the validity, or the percentage and amount of validity, of each

[102] Which says in part: "For the purpose of defraying extraordinary expenditures, the State may contract public debts; but such debts shall be authorized by law for some single object to be distinctly specified therein."

[103] 12 S. C. 288.

consolidated bond and stock certificate under the decision of the Supreme Court.[104]   By the report of this commissioner the total invalidity in bonds and stocks outstanding February 12, 1880, was $1,126,762.99; the total valid consolidated debt at the same time was $4,479,048.05.[105]

By "an act to provide for the settlement of the consolidated debt of the State in accordance with the decision of the Supreme Court,"[106] it was provided that every holder of consolidated bonds or stocks or of the interest coupons of the same, due and unpaid before July 1, 1878, reported by the special commissioner as wholly or partially valid, might exchange the same for new consolidated bonds bearing 6 per cent interest, and equal in amount to the valid portion of the bonds, stocks, and coupons surrendered.   Old securities still outstanding were to be funded also.   By an amendment to this act,[107] the privilege of exchanging or refunding was extended to detached coupons and interest orders due on or before July 1, 1878, and provision was made for funding interest due on or before July 1, 1878.

The settlement of the floating or unfunded debt incurred before November 1, 1876, was provided for in an act approved March 22, 1878.[108]   From time to time the floating debt had been enormously increased by a reckless legislature through the connivance of state and legislative officials.   But during the administration of Chamberlain this debt had been reduced and further increases guarded against.   The final settlement was by a court of claims which had power to adjudicate upon all claims which were in existence on November 1, 1876, and which had not been funded in bonds or stocks.   These claims included the bills of the Bank of the State, so much of the funded debt as was known as the "Little Bonanza," the war-

---

[104] Act of Dec. 23, 1879. *Stat S. C.*, XVII, 221.

[105] *Census*, 1880, VII, 578.

[106] Dec. 23, 1879. *Stat. S. C.*, XVII, 104.

[107] Feb. 19, 1880.

[108] *Stat. S. C.*, XVI, 555-56.

rants drawn by the comptroller in pursuance of an act in 1875 providing for the settlement and payment of certain claims against the state, and the liability of the state by guarantee of the Spartanburg and Union Railroad bonds. "Deficiency" bonds were issued in settlement of such claims; the amount outstanding October 1, 1881, was $562,577.50.[109]

* * * * *

During the entire period of Reconstruction, South Carolina protested against the burden of taxation. This burden, said the white people of the state, had been placed upon them by a corrupt legislature which did not represent the wealth and intelligence of the state. The Radical government put the state heavily in debt, increased three-fold the ordinary expenditures of the government, levied heavy taxes to meet this increased expense, and prevented, to a considerable degree, the economic development of the state. The people of property who had formerly controlled the government were deprived of a voice in state affairs and were compelled to support a dishonest and inefficient government.

While taxation increased, property valuation decreased. In 1860 the assessed value of the property of the state was $489,-319,128;[110] in 1866 it was $90,888,436, a decrease of nearly $400,000,000.[111] Taxation in 1860 was $1,280,386; in 1870, $2,767,675, an increase of over 100 per cent. Yet the decrease of the total assessed valuation of property amounted to 62.4 per cent.[112] In per capita wealth South Carolina stood third in 1860, fortieth in 1870.[113]

Taxes were not levied under the provisional government of Perry; under Governor Orr and Major General Canby they were nominal. The amount levied for the year commencing October, 1865, was $419,668.71; yet only $327,637.25 was paid

---

[109] *Census,* 1880, VII, 579.
[110] The true valuation was estimated at $548,138,754.
[111] *Census,* 1870, III, 10.
[112] *Ibid.,* pp. 8-11.
[113] *Ibid.,* p. 7.

into the treasury.[114]   The amount collected for the years 1866 and 1867 was not much greater;[115] yet it was the occasion for great complaint.   Charleston merchants claimed unjust discrimination.   The income of merchants was taxed $5 on $100, a professional man $2 on $100, and sales were taxed 60 cents per $100.[116]   Charleston said its people were taxed in every form—tax on incomes, sales, payment for certain privileges, articles of luxury, telegraph, gas and express companies—but the most hated was that on sales, part of which went to provide free schools, free roads, and public buildings.   The total state and city taxes amounted to nearly $1.58 per $100.[117]   The act to raise supplies for the year commencing October, 1865,[118] provided for a tax of 15 cents ad valorem on every $100 on lands, lots, buildings; $2 on male residents between the ages of twenty-one and sixty unless incapable of procuring a livelihood; 60 cents per $100 on factorage, employments, faculties, and professions, excepting clergymen; 60 cents per $100 on amount of commissions received by brokers, vendue-masters, and commission merchants; $1 per head on each and every dog; 40 cents per $100 on capital stock of gas light companies; $1 on $100 on premiums taken by insurance companies incorporated within the state, $2 on $100 for those incorporated without the state; $1,000 on all express companies doing business within the state; 20 cents per $100 on sale of goods, $1 per $100 if sale made by a transient; $1 on articles manufactured in the state for sale, barter, or exchange; $20 per $100 on spirituous liquors; $1 on every $100 of cotton on hand October 1, 1865; a tax on rosin and turpentine.   Governor Orr, in his farewell message, July, 1868, said that the people had encountered "extreme difficulty" in meeting the demands of the state.[119]   He pointed to the fact that in the past year only $375,000 had been collected and recommended that taxes for

[114] Orr, in *Phoenix*, Nov. 28, 1866.
[115] *News*, Mar. 16, 1869.
[116] *Ibid.*, Jan. 5, 1867.
[117] *Ibid.*, Nov. 19, 1867.
[118] *Stat. S. C.*, XIII, 3-6.
[119] *Courier*, July 8, 1868.

the present year be curtailed by the reduction of salaries and otherwise.

With the advent of the Radical government, a new system was inaugurated. The act of September 15, 1868, provided for a uniform rate of assessment of all property at its fair money value.[120] This new system was a radical departure from the ante-bellum system which had been light on land and slaves, while the mercantile, professional, banking, and similar secondary interests bore the brunt. Comptroller-General Neagle estimated that the ante-bellum merchant paid five or six times as great a tax as the planter. In 1859 Attorney-General I. W. Hayne wrote T. J. Pickens that the valuation fell so far short of the "positive actual value of the taxable lands of the State that it has ceased to approximate to a fair estimate." In 1859 the total tax value of lands in the state was $10,257,727, whereas the value of the lots and buildings in Charleston was $22,274,-175.[121] The report of the comptroller-general for 1860 stated that "the tax on all the land of the State, amounting to 17,558,-401 acres, produced only $82,515.51, which is less than an average of five cents per acre."[122] Before the war there had been a poll tax of $1.26 on each slave and a tax of $3.00 on each free Negro, mulatto, or mestizo between the ages of fifteen and fifty except those who were incapable of procuring a livelihood.[123] The new system met with many obstacles. It was difficult to find competent administrators who were sympathetic with the government; some of them as well as the taxpayers imagined difficulties in the system; and a large class of persons, which at first "included the whole press of the State," raised objections to the law and its execution. In regard to the valuation of real property the taxpayers and assessors had in their minds the old valuations, and when the former

[120] *Stat. S. C.,* XIV, 27-67.
[121] *Reports and Resolutions, 1869-70,* pp. 193-207.
[122] Quoted in message of Moses, *House Journal, Spec. Sess., 1873,* p. 41.
[123] *Stat. S. C.,* XII, 837.

assessment had been raised from 20 to 50 cents per acre they were satisfied.[124]

Governor Scott predicted that under the new assessment there would be returned not less than $300,000,000 of property as a basis for taxation.[125] But only $114,953,467 was returned.[126] No matter what the return of property, the board of equalization usually raised it to about $180,000,000. As the amount of property returned decreased, the rate of taxation increased. The total value of all taxable real estate and personal property in 1869 was $181,095,262; in 1877 under the Hampton government it was $101,229,090. There had been a gradual decrease. Under the Radicals the average rate of taxation for the first four years was nine mills, for the second four years more than eleven mills.

The white people of the state were soon in vigorous opposition to what they called excessive and oppressive taxation. It was frequently asserted that the Negro government wanted to raise taxes to the point of confiscation. The Conservative members of the legislature had no voice in the tax apportionment, and the whites were gradually being dispossessed of their property, either by taxation or by sheriff's sales. In 1871 the *Union Times* suggested that the people of each county have a mass meeting to determine what should be done about the unreasonable taxes. If payment were refused, no violence to the law would be done, "for the people are a law unto themselves. The *Greenville Mountaineer* said: "We have seen delicate women and decrepit old men selling the provisions which were absolutely necessary to keep their children from starvation, in order . . . to pay their taxes."[127] A letter to the *Charleston Daily News* (Mar. 28, 1871) signed, "One hundred men who fought under Lee," said that if the land were sold for refusal to pay taxes the *first* purchaser *certainly* wouldn't

[124] *Reports and Resolutions, 1869-70,* pp. 196-200.
[125] *House Journal, 1868-69,* p. 21.
[126] *Reports and Resolutions, 1869-70,* p. 199.
[127] Quoted in *News,* Mar. 27, 1871.

get it; and if the people of the North wanted to expend their blood to keep the Radicals in power, they should have a chance at it.[128] It was being suggested in the up-country that the people refuse to pay taxes until the expenses of the government were reduced and the character of the legislation changed. The difficulty of course was that the lands would be sold for taxes and there would be a risk of their falling into the hands of native Negroes or Northern speculators. But those who could not pay would be no worse off, and those who were able to pay could redeem the land within two years by paying the penalty.[129] Property sold for taxes could be redeemed within the first year by paying the amount the land sold at, together with subsequent taxes and a penalty of 25 per cent. In the second year the penalty was 50 per cent. It was suggested that the sheriff be enjoined from selling property for taxes; if the judges would not take notice of the fraud upon which the levy was based, time would be gained at any rate.

As we have seen, a taxpayers' convention met in May, 1871. It urged proportional representation which would give the 60,000 taxpaying voters proportionate representation in the legislature with the 90,000 voters who paid no tax.[130] The convention accomplished no immediate good. Although advocated by several of the state officials, including Chamberlain, proportionate representation was not adopted.

In the fall of 1872 an injunction was granted restraining the county auditors and treasurers from collecting taxes which had been authorized by Comptroller-General Neagle. Due to the confusion created by changing the time for the payment of taxes, two taxes had been levied for one year. This was held to be unconstitutional.[131]

[128] Ibid., Mar. 28, 1871.
[129] News, April 13, 1871.
[130] Proceedings of the Taxpayers' Convention, 1871, pp. 68-69. In March, 1871, C. G. Memminger urged a constitutional convention to change the constituency that elected the legislature. He proposed reading and tax-paying qualifications for voting.—News, Mar. 30, 1871.
[131] Sumter Watchman, Nov. 27, 1872; South Carolinian, Nov. 15, 19, 24, 1872.

The Radical government could not raise a respectable portion of the taxes levied. Out of a total state levy for 1870 of $1,670,063.66, more than $524,000 was uncollected. During the three years, 1868-1870, the total delinquent taxes plus the penalty amounted to $1,137,457.51.[132] Certain counties especially complained of excessive taxation. In Darlington County the grand jury stated that the suggestions of intelligent citizens were ignored and the assessments were increased far beyond their actual value by boards of equalization, and that 50 per cent had been arbitrarily added to the already exaggerated assessments on property in incorporated towns and villages.[133] A memorial to the legislature from Marion stated that the assessments of the county had increased $1,140,745 in one year.[134]

The newspapers were full of reports of sheriff's sales. In 1872, 2,900 acres of "estate lands" were sold in Orangeburg County for $425.00, being $16.92 less than was due for taxes.[135] In September, 1870, over 74,000 acres were advertised for sale for taxes in Darlington County.[136] In the same month, the *News* reported 86,000 acres for sale in Williamsburg County and 45,000 in Fairfield.[137] The *Beaufort Republican*[138] contained in one issue fourteen columns of delinquent land tax sales for Beaufort and Colleton counties. The *Edgefield Advertiser* contained two and one-half columns of the same matter, and other papers throughout the state published a greater or lesser quantity.[139] In May, 1874, there were advertised for tax sales 4,977 acres of land in Lancaster County, 13,982 in Greenville County, 19,999 acres in Fairfield County.[140] In one

[132] *House Journal, 1871-72,* pp. 7-8. Scott said that if taxes had been paid as they should, the state would have been saved at least $2,500,000 of bonded debt.

[133] *Reports and Resolutions, 1869-70,* p. 1542.

[134] *Reports and Resolutions, 1873-74,* pp. 967-68.

[135] *Orangeburg Times,* May 29, 1872.

[136] *News,* Sept. 24, 1870.

[137] *Ibid.,* Sept. 26, June 30, 1870.

[138] Feb. 22, 1872, in *Sumter Watchman,* Mar. 6, 1872.

[139] *Sumter Watchman,* Mar. 6, 1872.

[140] *News and Courier,* May 19, 1874.

week more than 2,000 pieces of real estate in Charleston were forfeited to the state for non-payment of taxes.[141] These are typical examples.

Thus the state was unable to collect the amount of taxes levied and was forced to sell the property of its citizens. Meanwhile, the state debt was increasing and interest was not being paid on its bonds. In April, 1873, Morton, Bliss and Company, New York bankers who had come into possession of a large sum of state bonds, made a demand on the comptroller-general to levy a tax to pay the interest on such bonds.[142] That official refused and the matter was taken to the courts.[143] The Charleston Chamber of Commerce decided that the taxpayers should be represented, and the citizens of Columbia retained Armistead Burt, M. C. Butler, and A. B. DeSaussure. Morton, Bliss petitioned for a mandamus to compel the levy of a tax to pay the interest on the state bonds. The attorneys of the tax payers alleged that a large portion of the conversion bonds which the plaintiff possessed were fraudulent, and a circuit judge granted a temporary injunction restraining the fiscal officers of the state from levying or collecting any tax for the purpose of paying the interest upon certain bonds mentioned.[144] The mandamus proceeding was brought in the Supreme Court. The return filed by the attorney-general in behalf of the comptroller, besides the technical questions presented, challenged the validity of the bonds and put in issue the liability of the state to pay them. In any event it was insisted that the right to levy the tax had not been delegated to the comptroller but remained with the General Assembly. The opportunity of inquiring into the facts bearing upon the validity of said bonds was not allowed by the court; the court held that the comptroller was charged by law to levy a tax, and a peremptory mandamus was issued requiring him to levy

---

[141] *Ibid.*, May 22, 1874.
[142] D. H. Chamberlain was the leading attorney for Morton, Bliss and Company.
[143] *News and Courier*, Apr. 25, 1873.
[144] *Ibid.*, May 6, 31, June 4, 5, July 10, 1873.

a tax sufficient to pay interest due in July, 1873, and October, 1874.[145]

Governor Moses immediately called a special session of the legislature to meet in October,[146] and at that session a bill was passed which deprived the comptroller of power to levy taxes. Thus the mandamus was defeated.[147]

A second taxpayers' convention met in February, 1874. On November 27, 1873, the *Orangeburg Times* called for a convention to "make an effort to arrest this outrageous spoliation, before you are hopelessly and ignominiously enslaved. . . . Protest at Washington against further taxation, under such a filthy, disgusting, loathsome State government and ask to be made a territorial dependency, or a conquered province, anything rather than the football of Moses and his crew." After further urging by the press and the Charleston Chamber of Commerce,[148] the executive committee of the taxpayers' convention of May, 1871, called a convention of those who were opposed to "the frauds and corruptions which prevail," and who were in favor of "honest government with exact and equal justice to all."[149]

Meanwhile, the state legislature had scaled the debt 50 per cent, and it was thought by some that little good would result from the convention.[150] But the *Union Herald,* a strong Republican paper in Columbia, approved of the convention.[151]

This gathering, like that of 1871, was more distinguished for its membership than its accomplishments. The customary resolutions were passed, an address was made to the people, a memorial was presented to the legislature, and a committee was dispatched to confer with the authorities in Washing-

---

[145] 4 S. C. 430; *Reports and Resolutions, 1873-74,* pp. 732-33; *News and Courier,* Aug. 29, 1873. The bonds in question amounted to $3,549,000.

[146] Before the comptroller was required to levy the tax, Nov. 15.

[147] *Stat. S. C.,* XV, 479-80; *News and Courier,* Oct. 22, Nov. 24, 1873.

[148] *News and Courier,* Dec. 27, 31, 1873.

[149] *Ibid.,* Jan. 14, 1874.

[150] *Keowee Courier,* Jan. 9, 1874.

[151] *Union Herald,* Feb. 17, 22, 1874.

ton.[152] The latter committee presented its memorial to the House, and was received by Secretary Fish and President Grant.[153] A committee of the state legislature presented a counter-memorial. The Judiciary Committee of the House made a report, but no relief to the taxpayers was forthcoming from Congress.[154]

The convention sent a communication to the legislature which stated that the tax law was "cumbrous, obscure, and intricate." The assessments were made "without method, without discrimination between productive and unproductive property, and in many cases without any knowledge of the property assessed, very frequently in secret." The only motive of the county auditor and the board of equalization seemed to be to raise as much money as possible. With the credit of the state "utterly ruined," with corruption in nearly all the departments of the government, the taxpayers were the only source for ill-gotten gains.[155]

The legislature made reply by citing figures to show that the cost of government had increased only 38 cents per capita. The appropriations for free schools had been increased, the lunatic asylum was now supported by the state, a penitentiary had been built and supported, colored orphans were cared for, and the public debt had been increased only $5,000,000 under the Republican régime. The taxpayers' convention, said the legislature, was composed of the former ruling class which simply desired to regain the power which they lost by the folly of secession.[156]

The only constructive work of the convention was the formation of tax unions composed of the taxpayers of the various counties. There was to be a central state organization

---

[152] See *Proceedings of the Taxpayers' Convention of South Carolina, February 17-20, 1874.*

[153] *News and Courier*, Mar. 27, 30, 31, 1874.

[154] *Ibid.*, April 1-3, 7-9, 1874.

[155] *Reports and Resolutions, 1873-74,* pp. 972-74.

[156] *Ibid.*, pp. 983-90.

with subordinate county unions. The purpose of the organization was to see that taxes were fairly assessed and collected, that the money was expended economically and wisely by county officers. Dishonest officials were to be persecuted. The organization was to be supported by the taxpayers. This plan was suggested by the *Port Royal Commercial,* a Republican paper, before the convention.[157]

During the spring and summer of 1874 tax unions were organized in various counties, and by August 22 it was reported that there were 181 subordinate unions and nine county unions.[158] The *Orangeburg News,* a Republican paper, said it was the purpose of the tax union to defeat the Radicals in the election of 1874. All over the state the cry was heard: "Old men in the Tax Unions and young men in the Rifle Clubs."[159]

The tax union held two or three state conventions but failed to have any important effect on taxation or politics. In September, 1874, delegates from 27 counties met in Columbia. General James Chesnut was president. It was his purpose to have the tax unions nominate candidates for state offices if the Radical state convention did not nominate honest men. The convention adjourned, however, without taking any action in that direction. At conventions held in November, 1874, and December, 1875, committees were appointed to confer with the governor and request low taxation and the appointment of honest officials.[160]

During the administration of Chamberlain the collection of taxes improved, but the amount levied did not decrease. Chamberlain apparently made determined efforts to run the government honestly and economically. Many Democrats

---

[157] *News and Courier,* Jan. 26, 1874; *Phoenix,* Jan. 28, 1874.

[158] *News and Courier,* April 3, 6, 16, June 5, 18, 22, Aug. 1, 22, 1874.

[159] *Orangeburg News,* Aug. 15, 1874.

[160] *Ibid.,* Nov. 26, Dec. 5, 1874; Nov. 8, Dec. 1, 2, 15, 16, 1875; *Fairfield Herald,* Dec. 8, 22, 1875; *Keowee Courier,* Dec. 24, 1875; Columbia *Register,* Dec. 17, 1875; *Orangeburg News and Times,* Dec. 18, 25, 1875.

came to his support, and he was able to appoint more capable county officials. But he could not control the legislature, and if he vetoed an excessive appropriation it was usually passed over his veto.[161] It was not until the inauguration of Hampton that tax rates decreased sharply. Tax unions and taxpayers' conventions no longer functioned.

[161] *News and Courier,* March 31, Dec. 1, 1875.

CHAPTER VII

RAILROADS AND TRANSPORTATION

HAND in hand with efforts to revive prosperity went renewed attempts to improve transportation facilities. To penetrate the interior of the state and to bring to Charleston for export the products of the up-country was not a novel scheme; and an outlet for Charleston imports was not a new necessity. The state could never have a great port unless there were economical means of transporting goods into the interior and to regions beyond. Thus, as old as railroads in the United States, was the plan to build roads which would terminate at Hamburg, Columbia, Camden, and Cheraw, exactly the four points which a century and a quarter before had been the outposts of European civilization. The idea had been to connect every part of the state with Charleston, through which distributing point the produce of the state would flow. The construction of a road to Greenville was to get the trade of that section instead of giving it to Augusta and Hamburg on the Savannah River. Furthermore, the western trade from North Carolina, Tennessee, Virginia, and Kentucky would be intercepted and carried to Charleston instead of to Augusta and Savannah. The Northeastern Railroad extending to Florence was to grasp the North and form a link between New York and Florida. The South Carolina Railroad looked westward toward the Blue Ridge and to the cotton sections of the southwest. In a like manner were to be tapped the resources of the Gulf region.

Since the time of Hayne and Calhoun there had been ambitious projects looking to the connecting of the great west with Charleston. The Charleston and Memphis road via Chattanooga and the Charleston, Louisville, and Cincinnati road were calculated to feed the great port of Charleston and unite the South and the West. After the failure of the Charleston to Cincinnati project, it was proposed to build the Blue Ridge Railroad through the Rabun Gap in northeast Georgia and connect with the Tennessee lines at Knoxville. This road would commence at Anderson, one of the western terminals of the Greenville line, and would penetrate the copper, coal, and iron region of east Tennessee. Other roads were to progress from Knoxville to Danville and from there to Covington, which would complete the connection with Cincinnati. By this route Knoxville was 103 miles nearer to Charleston than to Savannah, and 46 miles nearer to Charleston than to Richmond.

Such ambitious schemes received ample encouragement from the state in the way of liberal charters, the endorsement by the state of bonds issued to finance the roads, and the purchase by the state of a considerable amount of stock in the new corporations. Columbia, Charleston, and other towns along the proposed routes subscribed liberally to such stock. Before the war, Charleston had subscribed $500,000 toward the Nashville and Chattanooga road and $250,000 to the Memphis and Charleston road. Later the city fathers subscribed $1,000,000 to the Blue Ridge Railroad. After the war complaint was made that new roads were bisecting the state and cutting at right angles into lines running to Charleston, thus carrying goods to Augusta, Savannah, or Wilmington rather than to the South Carolina port.

With the close of the war South Carolinians once more set themselves to the task of carrying out ante-bellum railroad projects. It was hoped by many that a manufacturing state would develop. Slavery had been abolished and there was no reason to cling to the old agricultural system. It seems that the whole thought of the people was set on reviving prosperity along industrial lines. True, there was great interest in agriculture and the high price of cotton was not a thing to which the people could be indifferent. But the leading editorials in the newspapers had to do with the industrial possibilities of the state and with the great need of railroads. The two were inevitably linked together, for they both offered unknown possibilities. Plainly, the old system of living and working had failed; the state was not, and could not be, self-sufficing. There must be a new departure not only politically but also economically.

It was confidently expected that the legislature would again come to the rescue of worthy railroad enterprises. And such was to be the case. The legislatures called under the Johnson plan of reconstruction continued to give state aid to internal improvements. The Radical legislatures were even more lavish in their use of the credit of the state. In South Carolina, as in other states of the Union, there was a railroad fever that knew no checking. It was not confined to the Radicals and those who were attempting to defraud the state; it was general in extent and worthy, but was destined to accomplish little permanent good.[1]

The decade preceding the war was notable for progress in railroad building. In 1850 the total mileage in South Carolina was 289; in 1860 it was 973. During the war, however, only a few miles were built, and those just before peace came. In 1864 the mileage was still 973; in 1865 it was 1,007, at which point it remained stationary for three years. By 1868 there was an increase of 69 miles and there were further small increases in the years immediately following.[2]

At the close of the war the railroads of the state were in a deplorable condition. Track had been torn up and bent and twisted so as to make it entirely useless; trestles, bridges, depots,

[1] For a discussion of the early history and economic importance of railroads in the South see, U. B. Phillips, *A History of Transportation in the Eastern Cotton Belt to 1860*, Chaps. III, IV, VIII, IX; John G. Van Duesen, *Economic Bases of Disunion in South Carolina*, Chap. VI.

[2] *The Railway Monitor*, in *The Commercial and Financial Chronicle*, Jan. 13, 1872, p. 51; cited in *Ku-Klux Conspiracy, Report of the Joint Select Committee*, pp. 221-22.

machine shops, and way-stations had in many cases been destroyed by fire. The rolling stock had been worn out, lost, or destroyed. "The cars for passengers are outrageous, and utterly to be condemned; they are without glass or blinds. When it rains the passengers are soaked." This on the Union and Spartanburg. The cars on the Greenville and Columbia were not much better; "one gentleman had to raise his umbrella" when it rained.[3]

Sherman's army had been very destructive. This will be discussed in some detail when a description is given of the reconstruction and operation of some of the more important railroads of the state. Perhaps one can form a clearer idea of the situation by consulting statistics. There were a number of small roads in the state which we shall not attempt to discuss in detail. But the important facts about all the roads will be shown in the accompanying tables, and their extent and location may be readily seen on the map. The roads as they existed in 1867 were as follows:[4]

NAME OF ROAD	LOCATION	EXTENT
Blue Ridge	Anderson to Walhalla	33. mi.
Branch:	Main Line to Hayne's Quarry	1.5
Charleston and	Charleston to Savannah	103.5
Savannah	In operation: Charleston to Coosawhatchie, S. C.	60.
Charlotte & South Carolina	Charlotte, N. C. to Columbia, S. C.	109.6
Cheraw & Darlington	Cheraw to Florence	40.
Greenville & Columbia	Columbia to Greenville	143.25
Branches:	Cokesbury to Abbeville	11.5
	Belton to Anderson	9.5
Leased:	Blue Ridge Railroad	33.
King's Mountain	Chester to Yorkville	22.5
	(Destroyed during war)	

[3] *News*, Aug. 14, 1867.
[4] H. V. Poor, *Manual of the Railroads of the United States 1868-69.* Hereafter cited as Poor's *Manual*. Consult Index under name of road for page references.

Laurens	Newberry to Laurensville (Not in operation. Iron carried off during war)	32.
Northeastern	Charleston to Florence	102.
South Carolina	Charleston to Hamburg	137.
Branches	Branchville to Columbia	68.
	Kingsville to Camden	38.
Spartanburg & Union	Alston to Spartanburg	68.
Wilmington & Manchester	Wilmington, N. C., to Wateree Junction	171.

The following table gives statistics of operation expenses and the debt:[5]

NAME OF ROAD	GENERAL BALANCES	GROSS EARNINGS NET EARNINGS	
Blue Ridge	$204,000—portion of an intended issue of 7% bonds, secured by first mortgage to amount of $2,500,000, dated 1854, and maturing in 30 years		
Charleston & Savannah	Capital stock, $1,000,000; bonds guaranteed by state, $505,000	Gross: Net:	$ 46,252 1,847
Charlotte & So. Carolina	Capital stock, $1,500,000; funded debt, $334,000	Gross: Net:	$273,725 76,579
Cheraw & Darlington	Capital stock, $391,222; funded debt, $261,600	Gross: Net:	$ 61,013 14,145
Greenville & Columbia	Capital stock, $1,510,374; funded debt, $1,550,000	Gross: Net:	$251,931 137,245
King's Mountain	Not in operation		
Laurens	Not in operation		
Northeastern	Capital stock, $1,053,950; funded debt, $1,101,086	Gross: Net:	$317,775 55,907
South Carolina	Capital stock, $5,819,275; funded debt, $3,767,944	Gross: Net:	$1,316,006 613,777
Spartanburg & Union	Not known	Not known	

[5] Poor's *Manual*, 1868-69.

Wilmington & Manchester	Capital stock, $1,147,018; funded debt, $1,026,000	Gross: $402,340 Net: 122,824

From the net earnings were paid, usually, the interest on the debt, damages, money for stock killed, etc. The residue, if any, was applied to the reduction of the debt and to construction. During the entire Reconstruction period only one road paid any dividends whatever: the South Carolina Railroad paid 1 per cent one year and 2 per cent another year.

* * * * *

It is our purpose to discuss in the remainder of this chapter the construction, operation, and financing of some of the more important companies. We shall see the form and the extent of aid given by the state; we shall try to discover what profits accrued to the state and its citizens from the railroads; and we shall investigate the management, or mismanagement, of certain state aid roads. Perhaps our exposition will account for the fact that little progress was made even though the state extended its credit to the roads to an unwise degree.

The Charleston and Savannah was incorporated December 20, 1853,[6] and the estimated cost of linking the two ports by rail was $2,000,000. Capital stock of $1,000,000 was subscribed, and under an act of 1856[6a] the company issued 6 per cent bonds guaranteed by the state to the amount of $505,000. Up to this time the stock and bonded debt of the road was $1,505,000. This was increased in January, 1858, by the issue of bonds to the amount of $1,000,000, secured by a second mortgage of the road, including all the property it possessed, which, with all the property it would in future acquire, was solemnly pledged, first for the debt of $505,000, and then for the payment of the $1,000,000. The company was conveyed by deed of trust to three trustees to secure the payment of the 7 per cent interest bearing bonds. After exhausting the proceeds of the second mortgage bonds, the road, which was finished in the fall of

[6] *Stat. S. C.*, XII, 271.   [6a] *Ibid.*, p. 543.

1860, had a floating debt of about $500,000, which it was proposed to fund by another issue of bonds, secured by a third mortgage, to be called equipment bonds.[7]

When the war ended, the road was almost completely destroyed, but the rolling stock was saved and it was estimated that $300,000 would reopen the road. This the company could not raise as it had no security to offer. The state had first claim on the property of the road, and since it was evident that the property in its present condition was valueless, the legislature of 1865 authorized the company to borrow $500,000 upon a first mortgage on its property, and for this purpose the legislature postponed the lien of 1856 and directed that it should be a second lien, provided that bondholders and creditors consented.[8]

This plan of effecting a loan failed, due to the general lack of credit and the unsettled condition of affairs with prospects of military rule. The road was insolvent; on November 20, 1866, the trustees under the deed of January, 1858, foreclosed, and the mortgaged premises were sold; subject, nevertheless, to the lien of the state by act of 1856. The advertisement stated that the bonds secured by that lien amounted to $505,000, unpaid interest of about $140,000, and the principal with interest at 6 per cent due March 1, 1877. George W. Williams and other second mortgage bondholders purchased bonds of $505,000, with accumulated interest, for the nominal sum of $30,000.[9]

In December, 1866, the road was incorporated by its new owners as the Savannah and Charleston Railroad.[10] The new company retired the $1,000,000 of second mortgage bonds and issued in lieu thereof certificates of stock representing $1,000,000, thus invalidating the whole original issue of stock, and reducing the issues of the second mortgage bonds to stock for

[7] *Courier*, Dec. 15, 1868; *News*, Dec. 7, 1868; 12 S. C. 314 ff. The average cost of construction was $30,000 per mile.

[8] *Stat. S. C.*, XIII, 368.

[9] 12 S. C. 314 ff.; *Courier*, Dec. 15, 1868.

[10] *Stat. S. C.*, XIII, 438.

the same amount in the new company. At this time, with a debt of $1,000,000, and the original state guaranteed bonded debt of $505,000, the interest of which had reached $200,000, the guarantee bonds were selling in the market at forty cents on the dollar. Only 62 miles of road remained, worth about $12,000 per mile, a total of some $744,000. Without a loan, the company could not repair and put into operation enough of the road to yield a revenue sufficient to pay the interest on its debt; and it could not get a loan so long as the state held the prior lien of 1856. In 1869, therefore, the company presented a memorial to the legislature praying that it might secure, by a mortgage which would take priority over the state statutory lien, a new loan of $500,000 if so much was necessary to rebuild and complete the road and pay off arrears of interest. Although it was argued that this scheme would work great injustice to first mortgage state guaranteed bondholders, the attorney general said the state had a right to postpone the lien. The merchants of Charleston also memorialized the legislature, and in January, 1869, the much sought after act was passed. It provided (in addition to the consent for a loan of $500,000 and the postponement of the first to a second lien to cover the whole of the road) that the road should be completed by January 1, 1870 and that an amendment to the charter should subject the company to taxation by the state.[11] July 1, 1869, the company issued bonds to the amount of $500,000, and later issued bonds to pay interest due September 1, 1869. On February 8, 1871, the stockholders authorized the directors to issue bonds to the amount of $300,000, payable twenty years after date with interest at 8 per cent.[12]

As we have said, the Charleston and Savannah at the close of the war was "a mere wreck; every bridge and trestle was destroyed, including the magnificent and costly bridges over

[11] Stat. S. C., XIV, 201; Courier, Dec. 15, 1868; News, Dec. 7, 9, 12, 1868; Courier, Jan. 11, 1869; 12 S. C. 314 ff. The act was passed without the approval of Governor Scott. [12] 12 S. C. 322.

the Ashley, Edisto, and Savannah rivers; the depot in Charleston was burned, as well as the depots and buildings at eleven of the way stations, and nearly the whole track torn up."[13] The rolling stock, estimated at $94,450, was leased to the South Carolina Railroad for $8,000 to $12,000 per month on a lease which ended August, 1866. By May, 1869, the road reached Coosawhatchie; the remainder of the road to Savannah, some forty miles, was destroyed or made useless. It was first reconstructed to Salkehatchie (or Saltketcher) with money obtained from the hire of all rolling stock to the South Carolina road, and as far as Coosawhatchie by iron, or sale of iron, taken from the road beyond that point.[14]

It was not until March 2, 1870, that the road carried passengers to Savannah. And then it entered Savannah on three miles of the track of the Central Railroad of Georgia; also it used the Central's depot. After a dispute with the Central in 1875, the Charleston and Savannah rented a track entering Savannah from the Atlantic and Gulf road.[15] The road had originally contemplated a bridge across the Ashley on the west side of Charleston. The bridge, built shortly before the war by the Charleston Bridge Company and used by the railroad was destroyed; during Reconstruction railroad passengers crossed the river by boat.

The company was not prosperous; it was not long until it defaulted on the interest of all classes of its bonds and went into the hands of a receiver. In 1868 its expenses exceeded earnings by nearly $100;[16] by 1873 it had outstanding a bonded debt of $1,427,800, and it was understood that it had not paid interest on the debt since September, 1873.[17] The state owned stock in the road to the amount of $270,000, and had guaran-

---

[13] *The Trade and Commerce of Charleston.*

[14] 12 S. C. 319.

[15] *Ibid.*, pp. 322-26.

[16] *Reports and Resolutions, 1868-69,* p. 35.

[17] Poor's *Manual, 1876-77,* p. 343. The company refused to furnish information concerning its condition or operations.

teed a large amount of bonds, the interest on which had not been paid. In April, 1874, the circuit court transferred possession of the road to a receiver and an advisory board, the road to be operated for the benefit of its creditors and stockholders.[18] In 1875 another circuit judge ordered its sale for $1,500,000.[19] The Supreme Court decided that the state should take charge of the road pending the litigation between the creditors, the assets of the road to be subject to the direction of the court.[20]

* * * * *

The South Carolina Railroad was the oldest in the state. A part of the original Charleston to Cincinnati scheme, it was chartered in December, 1827, and opened to Hamburg, a distance of 137 miles, in 1834. The Charleston to Cincinnati project did not materialize; in 1840 the stockholders in Tennessee and North Carolina withdrew from the company and it was reorganized under the name of the South Carolina Railroad. In a few years it was paying handsome dividends which for several years before the war ranged between 6 and 10 per cent. In addition to the main line from Charleston to Hamburg, there were branches from Kingsville to Camden and from Branchville to Columbia, giving a mileage total of 242.

Of the period from January to June 19, 1865, when the road was restored to its owners by the Federal military authorities, little is known. Only the upper lines were in possession of the company previous to this date, and these, for all practical purposes, were valueless—chiefly from the irregular disposition of the means of transportation, and the lack of paying business in the disorganized condition of the company. On February 17, 1865, under an imperative military order, all the locomotives, cars, and movable property of the company in Charleston were withdrawn, and after being hauled from point to point,

[18] 8 S. C. 207; News and Courier, April 30, 1874.
[19] News and Courier, May 3, 1875.
[20] Reports and Resolutions, 1877-78, pp. 1010-11. Two years later it was still in the hands of a receiver.—Ibid., 1879-80, p. 493.

as circumstances demanded, were finally located on the Camden branch, beyond which they could not be carried because of the destruction of the Wateree bridge. About the 20th of April an expedition from the coast under General Edward E. Potter destroyed or rendered entirely useless 15 of the locomotives and 147 of the cars.

On the approach of Sherman's army to Columbia, all the property capable of being moved was withdrawn to the Charlotte road and was left there until the spring of 1866. Beyond the natural deterioration from exposure and occasional depredations, against which it was impossible to guard when property was strung along a line of fifty miles, this property sustained no injury. But the damage inflicted upon what was left at Columbia, and upon the line above Orangeburg on the Columbia branch, and above the Edisto River on the Hamburg division was "painfully great." At Columbia all the shops, depots, and buildings of every description, including new and valuable tools and materials, were "utterly destroyed." On the line of road between the points indicated, "with rare exceptions," the entire wooden structures, cross-ties, culverts, station houses, and water tanks, experienced a like fate; and the rails were burnt, twisted, and bent into shapes utterly baffling all efforts at restoration.[21]

On the 19th of June, after constant and urgent applications on the part of the officers of the company, the road, by order of General Gillmore, was turned over to the directors of the company, with the understanding that the work of repairing the line to Columbia should be prosecuted with the utmost energy in order that connections might be established with Charleston at the earliest practicable date. At that time the

[21] *Proceedings of the stockholders of the South Carolina Railroad Company . . . in the city of Charleston on the 13th and 14th of February, 1866. Report of the President and Directors, and Report of the Superintendent.* For a detailed history of this railroad during the Civil War and Reconstruction see S. M. Derrick, *Centennial History of the South Carolina Railroad,* chaps. XXIV and XV.

University of South Carolina Library

MAIN STREET FROM THE STATE HOUSE

University of South Carolina Library

FREIGHT DEPOT OF THE SOUTH CAROLINA RAILROAD

COLUMBIA AFTER SHERMAN'S VISIT

company was disorganized, without a dollar of available funds, and, in view of its heavy losses, heavy debt, a large portion of which was nearly due, and the thorough disorganization of the country, without credit. Without wishing to postpone the work until the experiment of negotiating a large loan in the North could be made, General Gillmore authorized the removal of the rails from the Camden branch to be used in rebuilding the Columbia line. The Camden road stood entirely isolated and could not be worked in connection with either Charleston or Columbia. The original purpose had been to repair the Hamburg and Columbia divisions simultaneously, but the Hamburg force was withdrawn. On October 16 Columbia was regained and work was then commenced on the Hamburg division; it was hoped that Blackville would be reached by February, 1866.[22]

In 1860 the rolling stock consisted of 62 locomotives, 59 passenger cars and 790 freight cars.[23] Of the 44 locomotives remaining in 1866, 5 were under repairs and 19 were awaiting repair, the work requisite in some cases being almost equal to the building of new engines; of first and second class passenger cars there were 28, and of freight cars there were 252.[24] Whereas in 1860 the road carried 314,619 bales of cotton and 36,179 bushels of grain, in 1865 it carried of those commodities only 35,536 bales and 7,424 bushels respectively.[25]

The road was not in a prosperous condition. Many of the repairs were only temporary and had to be replaced out of the earnings of the road. Although the gross earnings in 1865 were $1,600,982.30 (part of that doubtless in Confederate currency), and although the net earnings from 1866 through 1875 were from $450,000 to $600,000 yearly, the company was not

[22] Ibid.; Courier, Mar. 1, 1866. The Courier rejoiced that although the Camden branch was not yet restored nor the Columbia depots rebuilt, 100 miles of road had been repaired and 4 bridges built and the credit of the company maintained.

[23] Poor's Manual, 1868-69, p. 295.
[24] Proceedings of the stockholders . . . 13th and 14th February, 1866. Report of the Superintendent.
[25] Poor's Manual, 1868-69, p. 295.

able to escape its creditors and after Reconstruction went into the hands of a receiver.[26]

The condition of the company's finances in 1866 demanded the "earnest and undivided attention" of the stockholders. Not only had the means and property of the road been seriously impaired, but a large portion of the debt had matured. To the foreign debt of $2,000,000 and the domestic debt of $234,000 there was added the $495,000 accrued interest. In anticipation of the maturity of the foreign debt, held mostly in England, and, in fact, "in view of the utter impracticability of any other arrangement," the board addressed a memorial to the legislature, praying a renewal of the state's guarantee upon the new bonds which they designed to offer to the bondholders in substitution of those past due, and the accrued interest.[27] The application to the legislature was successful,[28] and the bondholders accepted new bonds due at the same time as the old ones (twenty years) and at the same rate of interest (5 per cent). On January 1, 1867, the auditor of the company announced that he was prepared to pay interest on bonds due at that date.[29]

By 1868 the aggregate sterling debt was $2,275,310.86, and the domestic debt was $1,492,632.92.[30] In 1875 the total liabilities were as follows: stock $5,819,275, bonds, $4,590,089.91, debts, etc., $1,820,023.[31] Yet in 1870 and 1871 dividends of 2 and 1 per cent, amounting to $116,388, and $58,194, were paid; there was chronic complaint that for several years the road had been in receipt of large profits without paying proper dividends.[32]

In 1872 the Greenville and Columbia was bought by the South Carolina Railroad under foreclosure and proceedings in

[26] Reports and Resolutions, 1879-80, p. 493.
[27] Proceedings of the stockholders . . . 13th and 14th of February, 1866.
[28] Acts, 1865, p. 104.
[29] News, Jan. 1, 1867.
[30] Poor's Manual, 1868-69, p. 296.
[31] Ibid., 1875-76, p. 432.
[32] Proceedings of the Stockholders . . . 1877; Phoenix, Mar. 15, 1873.

bankruptcy. This road, depending entirely upon local business for its income, was on the decline—a situation that was explained by "the peculiar condition of things in the State, which for months past has reduced the consumptive demand of our own interior people to the merest minimum, and their wants to the satisfaction only of absolute necessities."[33]   The South Carolina road excused its lack of earnings by references to the "financial revulsion of unprecedented extent," of 1873, and by the fact that "in all these years, a competitive strife for our business, waged with four powerful lines of transportation," had sapped the financial resources.[34]   During the entire period, the road was in the hands of William J. Magrath, president, and prominent Conservatives such as George A. Trenholm, William A. Courtenay, James S. Gibbes, and George W. Williams.

The South Carolina Railroad was the most important one in the state, because of its location and the amount of business done. It handled more through freight and did more local business than any of the other roads. The following comparative statement of the cotton, grain, flour, and naval stores brought to Charleston by the road will illustrate the part it played in the commerce of the state.[35]

	Bales cotton	Barrels flour	Bu. grain	Naval stores
1865	35,536	. . . .	7,424	1,293
1866	94,097	2,495	20,293	10,923
1867	155,455	10,948	93,662	11,912
1868	184,544	5,830	801,284	17,093
1870	246,679	23,821	61,676	17,550
1872	264,625	30,150	105,952	37,671
1874	343,786	72,659	218,427	48,956
1876	336,814	71,330	371,166	52,185

[33] *Proceedings of the Stockholders . . .* 1877.

[34] *Ibid.*

[35] *Ibid.*, p. 33, Table A, No. 2.

The number of live stock transported jumped from 381 in 1865 to 12,133 in 1875; and bales of merchandise jumped from 2,523 in 1865 to 24,375 in 1875. The average expense of moving a ton of freight in 1872 was $2.46, in 1873 it was $2.35.[36]

*   *   *   *   *

The Greenville and Columbia Railroad, running between the two towns, with branches to Abbeville and Anderson, was not begun under auspicious circumstances, nor was it ever prosperous. Its post-bellum vicissitudes were numerous, the most unfortunate being that it fell into the hands of a group of sharpers and Radical politicians who used it to defraud the stockholders and the state. After tracing the early history of the road, we shall look into the fraudulent operations of the so-called Railroad Ring.

Incorporated by the legislature in 1845-46, the company finally, in 1849, began laying track from Columbia to Greenville, a distance of 143 miles. The line was completed to Anderson in June, 1853, and to Greenville in the following December. The length of the Anderson branch was 9.5 miles, the Abbeville branch 11.5 miles. The roadbed was poorly made; the president's report of 1855 alluded to the opinion among the public "that this is a rickety road, exposed constantly to the danger of being swept away by freshets." The road was built through a broken country, with three river crossings, at a cost of less than $14,000 per mile.[37]

The financial resources of the company had been strained to the utmost; a 20 per cent assessment was made upon the original subscribers to the stock, and the gross amount of capital paid in, including the assessment, was $1,293,464 in 1854.

---

[36] Annual report of president and directors, *News and Courier*, April 14, 1874. For a time the cotton freight was conducted at the rate of $1 per bale to Charleston, without being particular as to the weight, or "a handful of miles of transport."—Robert Somers, *The South-* *ern States Since the War*, p. 61. At another time the rate was $1.50 per bale from Augusta to Charleston; the same rate applied from Augusta to Savannah. —*News,* Nov. 13, 1869.

[37] Phillips, *Transportation in the Eastern Cotton Belt*, pp. 344-45.

That same year the company executed to Charles M. Furman, trustee, a mortgage of their entire road to secure bonds of the company to the amount of $800,000 for the purpose of completing the road. Since the bonds were about to fall due in 1862, 1863, and 1864, and a further extension of time was desired, the General Assembly provided that the debt might be enlarged to $900,000 and the time for payment extended twenty years. The debt was to be secured by a guaranty of the state, the state being given a lien in substitution of a first mortgage on the road.[38]

For fear that there might be some difficulty about bonds issued during the war which carried the caption "Confederate States of America," the legislature of 1866 determined to reissue them with another caption. The authority of the act of 1861 was to be renewed by issuing $200,000 of bonds which had not been previously issued, and by putting into the form of certificates of indebtedness the interest which had accrued, amounting to $350,000. In addition, there was a provision for the funding of a new debt of $600,000 by a compromise of one for three, and to that end $250,000 in certificates of indebtedness was authorized.[39] This, with the original guarantee of $900,000 made the total liability of the state $1,500,000. In 1867 the company executed a second mortgage on the entire property to Cyrus D. Melton, as trustee, to secure bonds to the amount of $1,500,000. The state neither authorized her guarantee nor declared a statutory lien to secure these bonds, the mortgage declaring that the mortgage "is to be subject to the first mortgage and the statutory lien aforesaid."[40]

Meanwhile, 1865 and 1866 had been eventful years. A freshet in January, 1866, had washed away or made unfit for use some forty miles of track. The invasion of the state by a Federal army had led to the destruction of the principal depot

[38] Act of 1861, *Stat. S. C.*, XII, 185; 13 S. C. 228 ff.

[39] *Stat. S. C.*, XIII, 395, 427.

[40] 13 S. C. 239.

and office building, twelve miles of road, five bridges, and several engines. As in the case of other roads, the surrender of Lee and the fall of the Confederacy had swept away the investments and profits; for five years the road had been subject to the requisition of the Confederacy and as compensation for its services had the bonds and notes of a fallen government. Finally, the Federal government had seized the road, and while it was justly liable for the payment for transportation of troops, no vouchers could be obtained to present to Washington.[41] From September 1, 1866, when the road was reopened, to April, 1867, the gross income was $251,931.19; expenses $144,730.37, with a net income of $107,200.82.[42] This, of course, was not sufficient to rebuild and equip the road, much less take care of interest on the debt. There were many complaints on account of slowness in moving freight; in 1868 there were twenty-three locomotives (all old), fifty-eight freight cars, fourteen passenger cars, and two mail and baggage cars.[43]

On February 17, 1869, there was passed over the veto of Governor Scott an act to indorse the bonds and certificates of indebtedness of the Greenville and Columbia Railroad to the amount of $50,000. This act was passed in the name of the act of 1866 which it validated.[44] The act was not to become of force until the corporation consented to the taxation of its property by the state.

Scott vetoed the bill on the ground that it was unconstitutional and inexpedient. He said that the act of January 28, 1861, upon which the acts of 1866 and 1869 were based, was unconstitutional, and that subsequent legislation indorsed a debt contracted during the war which was specifically prohibited by the state constitution. The railroad company, from the time the Confederate legislature gave the indorsement of the state to its bonds, had not paid a dollar of the debt, principal

[41] *Phoenix*, May 3, 1866.

[42] *News*, April 25, 1867; Report of the president in *News*, April 29, 1867.

[43] Poor's *Manual, 1868-69*, p. 113.

[44] *Stat. S. C.*, XIV, 183.

or interest, but had been annually accumulating a floating debt. Scott admitted that assistance might safely be rendered to the company by a new act, giving the state indorsement, under proper restrictions, but if it were understood by corporations or individuals that "the success of their schemes" could be assured by presenting to the legislature a bill embracing whatever provisions they deemed most conducive to their interests, and "by assiduous lobbying and other questionable means force[ing] it through," the state capitol would be constantly "infested with the paid agents and advocates of every conceivable project by which speculators may hope to obtain control of the people's money."[45]

* * * * *

During the Radical régime there were many successful schemes for getting "the people's money." One of the schemes was commonly called the Greenville and Columbia fraud. The purpose of certain state officials, legislators, and unscrupulous carpetbaggers in fraudulently securing control of the Greenville and Columbia may best be explained by the letter of Attorney-General Chamberlain to Kimpton. From his office in Columbia, Chamberlain, on January 5, 1870, wrote a letter to Kimpton:

. . . Do you understand fully the plan of the G & C enterprise? It is proposed to buy $350,000 worth of the G & C stock. This with the $433,000 of stock held by the State will give entire control to us. The Laurens branch will be sold in February by decree of court, and will cost not more than $50,000, and probably not more than $40,000. The Spartanburg and Union can also be got without difficulty.

We shall then have in G & C 168 miles, in Laurens 31, and S & U 70 miles—in all 269 miles—equipped and running. Put a first mortgage of $20,000 a mile on this—sell the bonds at 85 or 90, and the balance, after paying all outlays for cost and repairs, is immense, over $2,000,000. There is a mint of money in this or I am a fool.

[45] *Senate Journal, 1868-69*, pp. 262 ff.

Then we will soon compel the South Carolina Railroad to fall into our hands and complete the connection to Asheville, N. C.

There is an indefinite verge for expansion of power before us. . . .

Harrison [President of the Blue Ridge Railroad] shall be attended to at once. I don't think Neagle will make any trouble. Parker hates Neagle, and magnifies his intentions. . . .[46]

In this ring were included John J. Patterson, George W. Waterman, brother-in-law of Governor Scott and representing his interests, Treasurer Parker, Reuben Tomlinson, state auditor, Comptroller-General Neagle, Chamberlain, F. L. Cardozo, mulatto secretary of state, C. P. Leslie, land commissioner, Kimpton, Joseph Crews, chairman of the House committee on railroads, and Representative Timothy Hurley.[47] The leader of the ring appears to have been John J. Patterson. Patterson was also connected with the Blue Ridge Railroad fraud, and in 1872 secured by bribery his election to the United States Senate.

The most direct method of securing the controlling interest of the road was to procure legislation authorizing the sale of the stock held by the state in the Greenville and Columbia road. To this end a bill was prepared under the direction of Chamberlain providing for the creation of a sinking fund commission, the commission being composed of the governor, attorney-general, comptroller-general, the chairman of the committee of ways and means in the House, and the chairman of the committee on finance in the Senate, the purpose of the commission being to sell "all such real or personal property, assets and effects belonging to the State as is not in actual public use."[48] This bill became a law on March 1, 1870. Ostensibly, its purpose was to dispose of the damaged granite, marble, and other material lying around the State House grounds. The real

[46] Quoted in John S. Reynolds, *Reconstruction in South Carolina*, p. 465.

[47] *Reports and Resolutions, 1877-78*, Fraud Report, pp. 1575-88.

[48] *Stat. S. C.*, XIV, 388; *Reports and Resolutions, 1877-78*, Fraud Report, test. of Neagle, p. 1580.

purpose of the act was accomplished by the sale of 21,698 shares of stock in the Greenville and Columbia Railroad Company; stock which cost the state $20 per share aggregating $433,960 was sold to the ring at $2.75 per share, aggregating $59,969.50. The first meeting of the commission was held the day the act was approved, and the sale of the stock was nominally agreed to on that day, but it had been decided that a bid would not be acted upon the day it was received; so the transaction was not concluded until the next day.[49]

Private parties as well as the state suffered at the hands of the ring. The state stock did not give a controlling interest in the road; therefore ex-Governor Orr and J. P. Reed were appointed as agents to buy stock from private parties. This they did by paying the stockholders $1.75 to $2.00 for shares worth $25.00 at par. The stockholders did not know to whom they were selling; they were selling to agents who represented an unknown body of men, and in some instances they were in doubt whether to sell or not. Orr and Reed, who were all along directors in the company, received $20,000 for their trouble.[50]

Not only had the state stock been purchased from the members of the sinking fund commission who were also members of the ring, but that stock as well as that secured from private parties was paid for by the funds of the state. The stock was divided among the members of the ring who had formed a co-partnership. There were twelve shares, each worth $20,000, making a total of $240,000. In order to raise this sum, the ring had recourse to their partner, Kimpton, who as financial agent of the state had on hand bonds of the state for sale or hypothecation. Kimpton was under the direction of a financial board composed of Governor Scott, Treasurer Parker and At-

[49] *Reports and Resolutions, 1877-78,* Fraud Report, test. of Neagle, p. 1580; *ibid.,* p. 1576.
[50] *Ku-Klux Conspiracy, S. C.,* test. of C. H. Suber, pp. 160-61; test. of E. W. Seibels, pp. 111-12, 137, 165-66, 255-56; Hurley, a member of the ring, in *Phoenix,* May 18, 1871.

torney-General Chamberlain, all of whom were members of the ring. And although the proceeds from state bonds were applicable only to the purposes of the state, the accounts of the financial agent revealed that they were diverted for whatever purposes the financial board chose to direct. Since the members of the financial board, the sinking fund commission, and the financial agent all were members of the ring, it was natural that the proceeds of state bonds should be used in paying for railroad stock which had been purchased from the state and individuals. This was the scheme, and "It was understood by Kimpton and the Financial Board that the amount of these expenditures and many others should be realized from the state bonds and covered by the difference between the actual amounts for which the bonds were sold by Kimpton and the amount which he should report that he had sold for."[51]

The ring having thus got control of the road, the stockholders on April 28, 1870, elected the following as directors: John J. Patterson, J. W. Harrison, Niles G. Parker, James L. Orr, Timothy Hurley, D. M. Porter, Joseph Crews, H. H. Kimpton, James M. Allen, A. J. Ransier, George W. Waterman, and F. L. Cardozo. Patterson became vice-president and Reuben Tomlinson treasurer.[52] And it was alleged that the new directors issued a large amount of guaranteed bonds without complying with the terms and conditions imposed by law.[53]

Another scheme was brought into play in the shape of a "Bill relating to the Greenville and Columbia Railroad Company," a bill which had been prepared by Chamberlain and introduced by Hurley, both members of the ring. It was claimed that the purpose of the bill was to authorize a further issue of bonds and give them a value in the market. The bill

[51] *Reports and Resolutions, 1877-78*, Fraud Report, test. of Parker. The evidence of Parker was sustained by Kimpton's report, for there was no itemization of the amount or rate of sales for nine-tenths of over $8,000,000 bonds.
[52] Poor's *Manual, 1871-72*, p. 313.
[53] 13 S. C. 240.

included several impracticable provisions, authorizing the extension of the road in several directions, and a consolidation with the Blue Ridge Road upon certain conditions, and the title was changed so as to read "An Act to promote the consolidation of the Greenville and Columbia Railroad Company and the Blue Ridge Railroad Company." This bill was passed with arguments "metallic, not oral," and Governor Scott was so conscious of its objectionable character that he deemed it necessary to communicate to the General Assembly his reasons for approving it.

The real purpose of the Act was found in its fifth section.[54] The state then held a lien for indemnity against her indorsement upon $1,500,000 of guaranteed bonds of the Greenville and Columbia, so that subsequent bonds would be of little or no value and could not be sold by the ring. By this section the lien was postponed to bonds to be issued under a second mortgage, thus enabling the ring to put their bonds upon the market.[55]

Meanwhile the "cherubic Kimpton" in New York was selling bonds "as rapidly as possible preparatory to our railroad interests" and was "working here for the best interests of all." He was optimistic: "We must *not* enlarge our railroad circle, but control all ourselves. It is sure of success."[56] Nine days later, however, the bonds were selling on the street at 55, and it was openly said that Kimpton was carrying money for the railroad ring. "The whole matter seems to be known here, as I feared."[57] Another letter stated that although "they seem to know things about our affairs which should not be known . . . our railroad matters will come out all right. . . . We have parties now in Europe who are working for us."[58] By mid-

[54] *Stat. S. C.*, XIV, 591.

[55] *Reports and Resolutions, 1877-78*, Fraud Report, p. 1577.

[56] Kimpton to Parker, Jan. 9, 1871. All the correspondence is cited in *Reports and Resolutions, 1877-78*, Fraud Report.

[57] Kimpton to Parker, Jan. 18, 1871, Fraud Report, p. 1585.

[58] Kimpton to Parker, Jan. 21, 1871, *ibid.*, p. 1586.

summer, however, the January coupons on a second mortgage could not be paid, and Kimpton conceded that "Our railroad matters are in a very unsatisfactory condition."[59]

Matters went from bad to worse. The Laurens road was acquired, but in June, 1872, the ring was trying to sell the Greenville and Columbia to the South Carolina Railroad for $700,000 of its bonds, which was considered a large amount.[60] It was later rumored that the Greenville and Columbia had been bought by the Pennsylvania Central,[61] but in 1872 it was bought by the South Carolina road under foreclosure and proceedings in bankruptcy.[62] W. J. Magrath became president of both roads. The Greenville and Columbia road never prospered and in 1880 it was sold by order of the court to W. A. Courtenay and associates for $2,963,400.[63]

* * * * *

A road with an even more checkered history was the Blue Ridge which ran from Anderson to Walhalla, a distance of thirty-three miles. Begun in 1851-52 as a revival of the old Louisville, Cincinnati, and Charleston project, it secured charters from South Carolina, North Carolina, Georgia, and Tennessee. The holdings of the companies in the three latter states were assigned to the South Carolina Blue Ridge company, and state aid was given by South Carolina and Tennessee. It was virtually a South Carolina enterprise and little help could be expected from other states which had competing lines. The Charleston influence in the legislature secured the indorsement of $1,000,000 of bonds in 1852, and the comptroller-general was directed, when one million dollars in stock was taken by individuals and corporations, to subscribe $500,000 on behalf of the state, and when a further sum of $500,000

---

[59] Kimpton to Parker, July 6, 1871, ibid., p. 1587.

[60] Ku-Klux Conspiracy, S. C., test. of E. W. Seibels, pp. 111-12.

[61] News, July 3, 1871.

[62] Phoenix, Jan. 23, 1872; 18 S. C. 87.

[63] 14 S. C. 385.

should be subscribed by individuals or corporations to sub-
scribe an additional $500,000.

A contract was let, and the work of construction began in
the fall of 1854. Difficulty with the contractor and his successor followed, resulting in the loss of time and money estimated at $1,000,000. In 1856 the president of the company
asked the legislature to repeal the condition governing the
additional state subscription and to vote it unreservedly. This
measure was opposed by William Gregg and others, but the
company was able to raise $220,000, which was the amount
needed for a second subscription from the state, and thus an
additional $500,000 was secured from the state. In 1858 the
Blue Ridge asked for an additional state subscription; although
it was supported by an eloquent speech from C. G. Memminger the measure was defeated, as was a similar measure of
1859. However, the friends of the company did raise the
$310,000 necessary to complete the road to Walhalla.[64]

During the war nothing was done toward completing the
road, but it was still an ambitious project and was in the
hands of Conservative citizens of the state who urged its completion.[65] In 1867 the board of directors included J. W. Harrison, president, G. A. Trenholm, Edward Frost, Henry Gourdin, Charles Furman, Charles Lowndes, and J. H. Holmes.
They were anxious to extend the road and were supported in
this desire by Governors Orr and Scott. Just before Orr gave
way to Scott in July, 1868, he stated to the legislature that the
financial and commercial interests of the state in the Blue
Ridge could not be overestimated. The state held stock
amounting to $1,310,000 which it was in danger of losing if the
project was not completed; and stocks in roads whose prosperity depended upon the completion of the Blue Ridge would

[64] Phillips, *Transportation in the East-
ern Cotton Belt*, pp. 375-80; Van Deusen,
*Economic Bases of Disunion in South
Carolina*, pp. 249-54.

[65] See G. A. Trenholm, in *Debow's Review*, N. S. II (Sept., 1866), 314-16;
Keowee Courier, June 30, 1866.

depreciate. Orr said much of the grading and masonry work in South Carolina, Georgia, and North Carolina had been completed, and it was estimated that $3,500,000 would complete the road to Knoxville and stock it with cars and motive power. Orr pointed out that the bonded debt was only $230,000 (the $1,000,000 in bonds indorsed by the state had not been used), but since the road terminated upon the edge of the mountains and stopped short of any connecting lines, it did not yield a sufficient revenue to pay even the interest upon the bonds. Fortunately the bondholders had not yet entered suit, and it would be most unfortunate if the state allowed the road to be lost to strangers for the paltry sum of $230,000, a road that had cost the state, the city of Charleston (which owned stock to the value of $1,048,000) and a few private stockholders over $3,250,000.[66]

Orr had recommended that the $230,000 of bonds be promptly renewed, by substituting bonds guaranteed by the state for the principal and interest, and that steps be taken to resume work on the road. Governor Scott in his first message included a report of Harrison, president, which stated that all the Blue Ridge expected of the state was that she should guarantee bonds for $3,000,000 to be issued as the work required, and that the state should provide for the payment of the interest on the bonds while the road was being built. Harrison estimated that by the expenditure of $420,000 to pay the bond interest, to be raised by taxation in three years, the road could be completed to Knoxville, a distance of about 195 miles. And the state would have as guarantee a first mortgage on a road well located, costing $7,500,000, with a debt of only $3,000,000.[67] Scott was more favorable toward the Blue Ridge enterprise than any other, "feeling confident that it is the only railroad enterprise that will develop our resources." In August, 1868, he was interviewed by William Aiken, representing

[66] *Courier,* July 8, 1868; Orr to Harrison, *Courier,* April 9, 1868.

[67] Scott's message, July 6, 1868.

the city of Charleston, and W. A. Courtney and Henry Gourdin, representing the Charleston Board of Trade and Chamber of Commerce, and others, upon the condition and prospects of the road.[68]

Financial aid to the Blue Ridge was forthcoming from the state. On September 15, 1868, a special session of the legislature authorized additional financial support. Bonds to the amount of $1,000,000 were indorsed and as much of them as was necessary, not exceeding $300,000, should be applied to the existing bonded debt. Furthermore, the faith and funds of the state were pledged to secure the payment of bonds to the amount of $3,000,000, and as soon as the comptroller-general should indorse such bonds the possessions of the Blue Ridge in South Carolina, Georgia, North Carolina, and Tennessee should stand as a first mortgage to the state. It was further provided that the $3,000,000 bonds should not be used unless upon application to the Congress of the United States, or to private capitalists, the amount of $3,000,000 in currency, or as much of that sum as should be necessary, should be furnished in exchange or upon the security of the bonds. In other words, the bonds could be sold at par only. The act authorized the governor to advance the company $20,000 from the treasury to repair the road and keep it in working condition.[69]

It was thought that $4,000,000 in bonds would be sufficient to finish the project. But Harrison and others, after making "every effort," did not secure the assistance hoped for, and the road was left to its own resources. Nevertheless, the company advertised for bids for its construction, and on July 8, 1869, the contract was awarded to Creswell and Company.[70]

The details of the $1,000,000 bond indorsement are difficult

[68] *Courier,* Aug. 21, 1868.

[69] *Stat. S. C.,* XIV, 25.

[70] It was said that the Creswell bid of $10,000,000 was cut to $9,000,000 and accepted by Scott over the protest of two other members of the executive committee. It was claimed that one bid was as low as $7,500,000. "Lux," in *News,* July 17, 1869.

to unravel. That it was a result of bribery there is little doubt;[71] it was claimed that there was no intelligent effort made to raise money on the bonds, and that a whole year was spent in getting them printed.[72] Later it was said that "not one dollar of these bonds had been put upon the market," which could not, the investigating committee thought, be altogether correct. Certain it was that the bonds had been issued, and whether sold or not they had been pledged for loans and were under the control of the financial agent.[73]

At any rate, it was apparent that the four millions of first mortgage bonds fell far short of the funds necessary to complete the road, and it was estimated that four millions more would be required. In a message to the legislature in the fall of 1869, the governor referred to the fact that unless additional guarantees were provided the state would be the sufferer, for "the whole investment must remain as dead capital until the means are provided to finish the road." One of two things could be done: abandon the whole scheme of a direct railroad route to the west and lose the capital invested, or assist the company by such means as would be valuable to them and at the same time not injure the credit of the state. The executive committee, on which the governor represented the stock of the state, believed that the latter could be done by an indorsement of the first mortgage bonds by the state to an amount sufficient to complete the road and put it in running order. An arrangement had been made whereby the company should meet the interest on the bonds put upon the market until the road was completed, after which it was believed that a lease for a term of years might be given, by which the payment of the debt and interest would be guaranteed, thereby leaving the

---

[71] Report of investigating committee, *Reports and Resolutions, 1870-71*, pp. 815-20.

[72] D. T. Corbin, in *Senate Journal, 1871-72*, pp. 527 ff.

[73] Report of the Joint Special Financial Investigation Committee, in *Reports and Resolutions, 1871-72*, Appendix, p. 48.

THE BLUE RIDGE MORTGAGE

state without a risk of ever having to pay one dollar of her indorsed bonds of the road.[74]

However, practically nothing was done on the road. In the legislature of 1870-71 it appears that the friends of the Greenville and Columbia road prepared a bill whereby the state's indorsement of the Blue Ridge bonds should be withdrawn and $4,000,000 bonds indorsed for the Greenville and Columbia, since it was claimed that Greenville or Spartanburg would give better connections with the west. To prevent the passage of this bill, Harrison, president of the Blue Ridge, hastened to Columbia prepared to spend a half million dollars. By bribing some senators the bill was defeated. But both the Greenville and Columbia and the Blue Ridge corporations were in trouble. The Blue Ridge could raise no funds, for the condition of the state's indorsement restricted them to selling the bonds at or above par. The Greenville and Columbia was powerless to raise money because there was an existing lien on its whole property in favor of the state.

Under those conditions, the Greenville and Columbia proposed that since the Blue Ridge could not secure a loan sufficient to complete the road, and since the road did not furnish adequate security for further loans, the interests of the roads be consolidated. To this President Harrison agreed, provided: that the Blue Ridge be adequately represented upon the consolidation board, and that sufficient guarantee be given that the $4,000,000 would be expended upon the Blue Ridge. Thus on March 6, 1871, an act to promote the consolidation of the two roads passed the legislature.[75] By this act and "in view of the consolidation" the indorsement of the Blue Ridge bonds was ratified, and the making and execution by the Blue Ridge and "other Companies" (Greenville and Columbia) of a mortgage to Henry Clews, Henry Gourdin, and George S. Cameron, to secure the payment of the bonds, was confirmed, and the mort-

[74] *House Journal, 1869-70,* pp. 21-23.   [75] *Stat. S. C.,* XIV, 590.

gage was declared "to be a lien prior to that of the State on all property described in said mortgage, and on the entire line of the road aforesaid, and on all the properties of the said several Companies, or which they, or either of them, may hereafter acquire." Furthermore, in order that there might be no obstacle to an immediate or entire use of these bonds, which was restricted by conditions under the act authorizing their issue, the portion of the act of 1868 which provided that $3,000,000 of the bonds could be sold only at par or above, was repealed, and after consolidation the bonds held by the two companies were to be indorsed by the consolidated company.[76]

The taxpayers' convention of 1871 instructed its executive committee to inquire and report upon what terms and for what considerations the Blue Ridge mortgage to Clews, Gourdin, and Cameron had been executed and ratified by the legislature and the mortgage declared to be a lien prior to that of the state. The committee reported that "for some reasons unknown to your committee, the legislature has, without consideration, relinquished to private individuals the State's lien," and W. D. Porter and James Connor were instructed, if in their judgment it was necessary and practical, to prevent, by due process of law, "the consummation of this fraud upon the property holders of the State." W. H. Trescot, who was present in the convention and who was an attorney of the Blue Ridge, rose to defend the consolidation act. He defended Harrison and other "men whom the State in the past has delighted to honor," who were said to be involved in the swindle.[77] Trescot defended the act upon the ground that no statutory lien had existed when the mortgage was executed. The act of 1868 was not binding until the comptroller-general had indorsed the bonds, and by delays beyond the control of the

[76] Ibid.; Proceedings of the Taxpayers' Convention, 1871, pp. 75-99; Report of investigating committee, in Reports and Resolutions, 1870-71, p. 819.

[77] The evidence is conclusive that Harrison was using money to influence the legislature.

company, the bonds were not signed for months after the execution and record of the mortgage. And, he said, the mortgage was better security than a statutory lien; and, whether right or wrong, the action of the legislature had been completed and must stand. Trescot offered an amendment which provided for the immediate publication of the findings of Porter and Connor, but the resolution was laid on the table. Apparently, however, the work of the taxpayers' convention stopped at this point.[78]

We have seen how the state postponed its lien on the Blue Ridge in favor of other parties who held a first mortgage. At about the same time the financial board through the financial agent advanced to the company about $200,000 in cash, the agent supposedly having received bonds of the company as security. Then on July 22, 1871, the stock of the road held by the state was purchased from the sinking fund commission by a private corporation. Scott said that after "consulting many prominent business men," he recommended to the commission the propriety of disposing of the interests of the state to a private corporation.[79] The private corporation was composed of George S. Cameron, John J. Patterson, and Thomas Steers, and their associates. The associates of Cameron were Robert Adger, W. H. Inman, W. B. Smith, and W. B. Gulick. Patterson's associates were ―――― Binock, Harry Thomas, and M. W. Gary, and the associates of the contractor Steers were J. C. Cotteron, M. C. Butler, and J. B. Palmer. The corporation bought from the commission the 13,100 shares owned by the state at $1 each. This sale was made upon condition that the corporation would give $300,000 bond that the $4,000,000 secured by the state would be faithfully administered and expended, that the state would be paid $10,000 per year for five years after the completion of the road, and that if the road

[78] *Proceedings of the Taxpayers' Convention, 1871,* pp. 75-99.   [79] *House Journal, 1871-72,* p. 42.

were not completed within five years the stock of the company was to be transferred.[80] The validity of the sale was seriously questioned as not being within the authority of the sinking fund commission and not properly confirmed by the legislature. However, for all practical purposes the state had parted with its stock and had given control of the road and its bonds to a few private persons. It was further alleged that hundreds of thousands of the funds of the road had been applied to purposes and objects foreign to those indicated by the charter of the corporation. The city attorney of Charleston urged that legal proceedings be instituted to protect the honest creditors and the interests of the city.[81]

Whether or not the private corporation as it originally existed was acting in good faith cannot be determined. Some of its members were reputable citizens and highly regarded in the state. But John J. Patterson and others whom he later associated with himself in the company could not but be regarded with suspicion. In 1872 Patterson put through a scheme which was calculated to enrich himself and associates at the expense of the state. Evidently there were some members of the corporation who were not willing to go with Patterson, and in January, 1872, Colonel Cothran resigned the presidency and Gary, Gulick, Butler, and Palmer resigned from the board of directors.[82]

In the reorganization Patterson was elected president, Steers, the contractor of the road who had a lien on $2,000,000 of the bonds, vice-president, and F. S. Jacobs, a cashier of one of the Columbia banks who was involved in numerous fraudulent schemes, secretary and treasurer. C. D. Melton, George W.

[80] Testimony before committee to investigate transactions of the sinking fund commission, in *Reports and Resolutions,* 1873-74, pp. 755-65. The transaction was made by Scott, W. J. Whipper, and Neagle.

[81] *News,* June 26, 1872.

[82] *Phoenix,* Jan. 20, 1872. Some time later Gary denied that he had ever been connected with the fraudulent scheme and said he had never owned a bond of the Blue Ridge nor attempted to bribe any member of the financial board. *Phoenix,* Mar. 3, 1874.

Waterman, the brother-in-law of the governor, and James M. Allen were also elected to the board of directors, and it was understood that work on the road would be "pushed forward rapidly, all the necessary arrangements having been completed."[83]

It can scarcely be believed that Patterson and associates ever had any serious intentions of completing the road. The whole purpose of Patterson, Parker, Kimpton, H. G. Worthington and others was to enrich themselves at the expense of the state. Having obtained control of the road for the paltry sum of $13,100 and finding that the $4,000,000 bonds indorsed by the state were practically valueless because of the depreciation of state securities, resulting partly from that indorsement, Patterson caused to be introduced in the House of Representatives on February 3, 1872, a bill "to relieve the State of South Carolina of all liability for its guaranty of the bonds of the Blue Ridge Railroad Company by providing for the securing and destruction of the same." The bill set forth that the present condition of the finances of the state and of the company were such as to make the continuance of the bonds on the market inexpedient and inadvisable, and a serious injury and prejudice to the credit of the state, and that the existence of the guaranteed bonds created a large liability upon the state which the treasurer might be required to meet at an unforeseen and inopportune time. Therefore, upon the surrender to the state of the $4,000,000 indorsed bonds, the state treasurer was authorized and required to deliver in exchange to the president of the Blue Ridge treasury certificates of indebtedness (styled revenue bond scrip) to the amount of $1,800,000. If the company was not able to deliver all bonds, certificates of indebtedness should be issued in proportion to the amount of bonds delivered. The faith and credit of the state was pledged to redeem the scrip, and an annual tax of 3 mills was to be levied

[83] *Phoenix,* Jan. 20, 1872.

to retire one-fourth of the scrip annually. The scrip was to be receivable in payment of taxes and all other dues to the state, except any special tax levied to pay interest on the public debt; and the state treasurer might pay out scrip in satisfaction of any claims against the state, except for interest on the public debt. Upon the delivery of the bonds to the state the lien of the state was to be released.[84] The bill was vetoed by Governor Scott, but by the most shameless and free use of money the veto was overridden by a vote of 22 to 6 in the Senate and 84 to 18 in the House.[85]

Scott vetoed the act on the ground that the $4,000,000 indorsed bonds was a contingent liability only, and that the state could not be held responsible until the assets of the road had been exhausted, and it was "fair to presume that, before the twenty years had expired, the work would have been completed, and these bonds would have been a first mortgage upon the entire property, and hence a good security, independent of the state indorsement." The condition of the finances of the state did not warrant such an obligation, and the constitution of the state and of the United States clearly prohibited the state from issuing bills of credit. He stated that the bill had been on the calendar for more than a month, but that the entire press of the state had been silent on its merits, leading him to infer that it met the approval of all parties interested in the financial welfare of the state.[86]

Senator D. T. Corbin, of Charleston, said that by that act

[84] *Stat. S. C.*, XV, 79 ff.

[85] *Reports and Resolutions, 1877-78,* Fraud Report, pp. 1625 ff; see especially letter from Patterson to Barker authorizing the latter to pay Kimpton $42,859 in scrip at par for paying the expenses of passing the bill through the House. Kimpton deposited in the Central National Bank $30,000 for Josephus Woodruff, clerk of the Senate, to divide among six Senators; a similar deposit of $20,000 was to be divided between Senator Leslie and Senator Owens. Many of the transactions were handled through C. P. Leslie who was stakeholder; he got away to New York with some of the money and was followed by some duped and indignant Senators who failed to recover the thrice stolen cash. Senators always cost more than representatives. R. B. Elliott and S. J. Lee, two future Speakers of the House, were participants in the fraud.

[86] *Senate Journal, 1871-72,* pp. 572 ff. The message was written by T. J. Mackey.

the president of the Blue Ridge said to the legislature: "You have indorsed four millions of dollars of the bonds of my Company; now, release us of all obligation to you for the two hundred thousand dollars, and the twenty thousand dollars you have loaned me, and give us eighteen hundred thousand dollars more, and I will surrender and release to you your indorsement of the bonds of the Company."[87]

On petition of Edwin F. Gary, state auditor, Associate Justice Willard of the supreme court issued an injunction restraining the state treasurer and county treasurers from putting into circulation the certificates of indebtedness or bills of credit authorized by the legislature.[88]

In July, 1872, Judge Willard pronounced the Revenue Bond Scrip Act null and void, as contravening the clause of the Federal Constitution prohibiting the states from issuing bills of credit; the injunction previously granted against the receipt of the scrip for taxes, and against the issuing of it, was sustained. And since it was important to inquire whether the scrip that was actually issued was conformable to, and authorized by, the act, the injunction was continued until the final hearing and determination of the action.[89] The injunction cause was brought before Circuit Judge S. W. Melton in November and the injunction made perpetual.[90] In July, 1872, certain stockholders and creditors had brought action against the Blue

[87] Ibid., pp. 531-32.

[88] News, June 3, July 12, 13, 16, 24, 1872. Gary later said that he instituted the suit with the sanction of Scott to prevent circulation of the scrip. But after "the usual necessary inducements [had] been offered his Excellency, an effort was made by himself and others interested, to induce me to withdraw the suit. Ten thousand dollars in cash was offered me by one party the day that the case came into court; and an indirect offer of $25,-000 in scrip was subsequently made by another party, in case I would consent to withdraw the suit." Gary also refused to levy taxes for the bonded debt of the state, including a levy of 3 mills to redeem $450,000 of the scrip—one quarter of the entire issue. Gary lost his job. Letter from Gary in Orangeburg Times, Oct. 30, 1872.

[89] State ex relatione Edwin F. Gary, auditor, vs. Parker and others, state and county treasurers.—News, July 24, 1872.

[90] News, Dec. 6, 1872.

Ridge and asked that a receiver be appointed.[91] In January, 1873, action was brought by certain holders of the scrip to compel the comptroller-general to issue orders for the collection of a tax to provide for its payment. In April, Chief Justice Moses rendered the opinion that the scrip was "unequivocally illegal" and the mandamus to compel the raising of taxes to pay the scrip was not issued.[92] How much of the $1,800,000 of the scrip was issued is not known, but it appears that practically all of it was issued. It was alleged by a Conservative member of the legislature that $5,400,000 of scrip was issued.[93]

Before the decision of the Supreme Court against the scrip had been reached, a bill was introduced in the House to repeal the Scrip Act since it was unconstitutional.[94] This was described as an *ex post facto* attempt to lock the treasury vault after $1,800,000 had been taken from it. Later in the session Representative Robertson attacked the bill and said the Scrip Act constituted a contract and could not be repealed without violating that clause of the constitution which forbade the legislature to pass any law to impair the obligation of contract.[95] By the last of February an act repealing section four of the Revenue Bond Scrip Act which provided that a tax should be levied to redeem the scrip was passed. On March 8 the

[91] *Ibid.*, July 1, 1872. Case brought in county of Richland, court of common pleas. The complaint alleged that proceeds of bonds had been misapplied; that Parker in March, 1872, gave Patterson $1,979,000 in scrip on the surrender of the equivalent in bonds; that Patterson and directors in the conspiracy had pledged certificates of indebtedness to various trustees in S. C. and N. Y. to the amount of $1,157,000; that the sum received (about $410,000) had been converted to private use; that certificates of indebtedness had been paid out fraudulently and without any legal consideration to Hardy Solomons ($10,000), Niles G. Parker ($50,000), H. G. Worth-

ington ($20,000), and others; that Solomons, Jacobs, Worthington, and others owned no stock and were not legally qualified to act as directors.
[92] *News*, Jan. 10, 14, 17, Feb. 5, April 19, 1873. Moses, Jr., son of the chief justice and at that time governor, testified later that he was offered by Patterson $50,000 in scrip and $25,000 in money if he would agree to use his influence with the supreme court to secure a decree in favor of the scrip. *Reports and Resolutions, 1877-78*, Fraud Report, pp. 1656-57.
[93] *News*, Feb. 26, 1873.
[94] *House Journal, 1872-73*, p. 68.
[95] *News*, Feb. 26, 1873.

Charleston Daily News called on H. J. Maxwell, chairman of the senate committee on engrossed acts, whose duty it was to present the bill to the governor for his signature, to explain why the bill had not been presented. Subsequent investigation revealed that Patterson, upon being told by Governor Moses that he would certainly sign the act if it reached him, had promised Maxwell $1,000 if he would agree that the bill should not reach Moses.[96] It was not until the next session of the legislature that the act was signed.[97] This final act destroyed all value of the scrip, although in August a Columbia bank had sold at auction $25,000 of scrip for $375.[98]

In January, 1873, James P. Low, chief engineer of the road, filed in the United States district court a petition for involuntary bankruptcy against the Blue Ridge.[99] The petitioner alleged that the road had committed an act of bankruptcy in suspending payment on its commercial paper; it was further alleged that an act of bankruptcy was committed when the company suffered its property to be taken in legal process in favor of J. W. Green, of New York, upon a judgment of the Supreme Court of New York for the sum of $205,118.30, which judgment was entered by default.[100] On April 22 the road was declared bankrupt, and in July George W. Williams, James P. Low, and J. P. Southern were appointed assignees.[101] In 1875 there was an attempt to revive the road. It was proposed to have the bondholders sell their bonds to the company as low as possible and then memorialize the legislature for assistance. A committee was appointed to visit Washington and try to secure an appropriation from Congress. Governor Chamberlain, ex-Governor Perry, and Conservative leaders approved the enterprise, but nothing was ever accomplished.[102]

[96] *Reports and Resolutions, 1877-78,* Fraud Report, p. 1658.
[97] *Stat. S. C.,* XV, 479.
[98] *News and Courier,* Aug. 25, 1873.
[99] *News,* Jan. 23, 1873; *News and Courier,* Jan. 1, 1874.
[100] *News and Courier,* April 24, 1873.
[101] *Ibid.;* and *ibid.,* Jan. 1, 1874.
[102] *Spartanburg Herald,* Nov. 10, 1875; *News and Courier,* Nov. 3, 1875.

The road has never been extended, and the tunnel entering Stump Hole Mountain has fallen in.

In 1875 South Carolina had a total mileage of railroads built and in operation of 1,335, with a total investment per road-mile of $31,902. The net earnings per road-mile were $1,124, but no dividends were paid.[103]

*   *   *   *   *

In 1865 the steamship lines which before the war had connected Charleston with New York, Philadelphia, Baltimore, Boston, and Havana no longer existed. Some of the vessels had been seized by the Federal government, and others had been hired by the Confederate government. The lines of small steamers that plied between Charleston and Florida, Savannah, Beaufort, Georgetown, and the landings on the various rivers, shared the same fate.[104]

But by 1870 there were two lines of steamers to New York, one to Baltimore, one to Philadelphia, and one to Liverpool, and there were steamboat communications with nearly every important river town and with Savannah, Beaufort, and Georgetown.[105] In 1865 the New York and Charleston steamship line, established in 1845, was revived with the steamers "Manhattan," "Champion," "Charleston," and "James Adger." About 1870 W. P. Clyde, of New York, aided by several Charleston firms, had placed in operation the iron steamers "South Carolina" and "Georgia."[106]

In 1872 it was said that between Charleston and New York there was a tri-weekly line of eight fine steamers capable of carrying 30,000 bales of cotton per month. A "large number" of passengers could also be accommodated. To Boston there

---

[103] Poor's *Manual, 1876-77,* table of comparative statistics.
[104] *The Trade and Commerce of Charleston.*

[105] *News,* July 19, 1870.
[106] *Columbia the Future Manufacturing and Commercial Centre of the South,* p. 37.

were two steamers for freight only. It was estimated that the total tonnage in 1872 was no larger than that of 1860.[107]

After the war, when only one or two steamers could be had to run between Charleston and New York, passenger fare was as high as $50 and $60, and freight ranged from forty to fifty cents per cubic foot. But railroads were reopened and competition from other lines reduced the fare to $10 or $15. In 1867 passage on the best steamers to New York could be had for $10, while by land the cost was $26.[108]

To what extent each of the factors of unstable political conditions, fraud, mismanagement, trade conditions, and lack of financial resources hampered and restricted the development of transportation facilities it is impossible to know. But taken together they explain why the roads were not prosperous and why the amount of railroad built was negligible.

[107] *Trade and Commerce of Charleston;* Edward King, *Southern States of North America,* pp. 438-39; *News,* Jan. 1, 1872.

[108] *Letters and Diary of Laura M. Towne,* p. 180; *Trade and Commerce of Charleston.*

CHAPTER VIII

AGRICULTURAL PROBLEMS

THE settlement of the agricultural problems of Reconstruction was of utmost importance to the people of the state. The daily bread of the average inhabitant depended upon their satisfactory solution, and they were as much the subject of controversy as were the political problems of the day. The war had destroyed the state's system of labor, but it had settled irrevocably only one problem of the farm. The Negro was free. Both the whites and the freedmen were in hopeless confusion concerning the application of this freedom to farm problems. Who should own the soil? Under what conditions should the Negroes work? What wages should be paid and how should they be paid? All sorts of solutions were suggested and attempted—by the whites, by the Negroes, and by outsiders with powers and interests in the state. They varied from plans for the elimination from the state, of one or the other race, to compromises of a more practical nature. Finally, after much struggling, certain understandings were effected. It is true that these satisfied the full hopes of neither race, but they were tolerated by both to a degree which made a return to ordered production possible.

Had there been no vexing problems of race and labor, the reconstruction of the state's agricultural life would have been difficult because of the immediate effects of the war. As has already been pointed out,[1] there was a general decline in farm values and in the quality of the soil and of cotton seed. The old sources of credit had been destroyed, and there was little capital available for agricultural purposes. The principal pros-

[1] See above, p. 10.

pective source of credit was partly destroyed by the Federal government's confiscation of and tax on cotton. The fact that the war ended so late in the spring meant short crops in 1865 even for those who saw the necessity of an energetic resumption of farm operations. In 1866 and 1867 there were crop failures due to bad weather conditions.

A disturbing factor in agricultural life was the feeling among the freedmen that it was possible to live without hard labor. They were told that freedom carried solid benefits, and they set about enjoying these benefits in the most realistic fashion. To their simple minds slavery was synonymous with work and freedom with not working. They were not able to make the fine distinction between labor for the benefit of others, as had been the case under slavery, and labor whose benefits would devolve upon them at some remote time when the crops were harvested or when a better civilization should have evolved. It is true that they listened patiently to the platitudinous advice on the advantages of industry which the agents of the Freedmen's Bureau gave them.[2] But to their way of thinking their Northern friends, through the good things they dispensed, gave proof that it was easier to live in idleness than by hard work.

From the occupation of Port Royal to 1868 gifts of clothing and victuals were widely distributed among the freedmen by Northern charitable agencies. These gifts were necessary to relieve absolute distress and were approved by white contemporaries. Nevertheless they had a demoralizing effect upon the freedmen. The hope of receiving them was the principal reason so many laborers left the plantations in 1865 and wandered about aimlessly. This condition was accentuated by the Freedmen's Bureau policy of giving away army clothing and rations and furnishing free transportation. "Their [the Negroes'] idea

[2] See, for example, General Saxton's address of Aug. 16, 1865, in *Report of Joint* *Committee on Reconstruction*, Pt. II, pp. 230-231.

of freedom," wrote a correspondent of the *New York Herald,* "is that they can live as they have been accustomed to see the white people do, and that the government will feed them."[3] The case is on record of a freedman who walked a hundred miles to receive half a bushel of corn from the Bureau, whereas by honest effort he could have earned nine times the value of the corn in the time it took him to go for it.[4] Mary Ames was furnished with clothes by New England agencies to distribute among her "filthy and nearly starving students" on Edisto Island. Their distribution created so much demoralization that the Negroes, though repulsively ill with smallpox, overcrowded her school.[5] The impulsive General Saxton was far too free with government supplies.[6] Although General Scott was more circumspect, he did not let his desire to secure order stand in the way of his ambition to please the Negroes in such a way as to make his political success possible.

The most immediate desire of the freedman was to enjoy those physical comforts and pleasures which had previously been denied him. He would acquire a horse, a buggy, a dog, and a gun, and his wife would acquire showy clothing and leave the field in order to look after the home.[7] From this home was dispensed "a prodigal hospitality while a pound of bacon and a bushel of sweet potatoes remains."[8] Extravagance has ever since remained the Negro farmer's besetting sin. Inheriting a capacity to labor unceasingly, and surrounded by opportunities common to all Americans—relatively high wages and the opportunity to purchase lands cheaply, he has spent

[3] June 21, 1865. Cf. statement of Radical editor in *Courier,* May 21, 1865, and *Harper's Magazine* cited *ibid.,* Nov. 4, 1868.
[4] Told by Col. U. R. Brooks in Laura J. Webster, *The Freedmen's Bureau in S. C.,* p. 124.
[5] Mary Ames, *A New England Wom-an's Diary in Dixie,* pp. 23, 69, 90 ff.
[6] See report of Generals Fullerton and Steedmen, investigators for the secretary of war, *Courier,* Feb. 12, 1866.
[7] *Rural Carolinian,* VII, 131 (Mar., 1876).
[8] *Annual Report of Commissioner of Agriculture, 1867,* p. 420.

TRANSPORTATION IN THE LOW-COUNTRY

what he has earned in a manner incomprehensible to the more thrifty descendants of European peasants.[9]

One of the most persistent ambitions of the Negro was to wrest the control of the land from the whites. This ambition grew out of the war policy of the Federal government on the sea islands. The capture of Port Royal and the flight of the landowners gave the national authorities possession of 195 rich plantations and the opportunity to employ more than ten thousand abandoned or refugee Negroes in the production of sorely needed cotton. Early in 1862 these Negroes were put to work under labor superintendents imported from the North.[10] Had this been all that was done, there would have been little ground for the belief that the government intended to confiscate lands for the benefit of the Negroes. But on June 7, 1862, Congress held such portions of the states in rebellion responsible for a direct tax upon the lands of the nation.[11] Accordingly, when the absent landowners of Port Royal failed to pay the tax, their properties were sold to satisfy this obligation. Most of these lands were bought by Northerners, but some were sold to Negroes at nominal prices.[12] A more radical step was taken by General William T. Sherman when, on January 16, 1865, he issued his famous Field Order No. 15.[13] It provided that the sea islands, from Charleston south, which had not already been disposed of by the government, and the rice plantations bordering them to the distance of thirty miles inland, should be set aside for the use of the Negroes who had followed the General's army. They were to be given "possessory" titles pending their final disposal by Congress. This order was confirmed by a provision of the act creating the Freedmen's Bureau. It

[9] Sir George Campbell, *White and Black*, p. 336, described as follows the spending qualities of a typical group of rural Negroes: "They seldom save. After they have made a little money they like to go and spend it."

[10] Charles Nordhoff, *The Freedmen of South Carolina*, pp. 2-3, and Edward L. Pierce, *Atlantic Monthly*, XII, (Sept., 1863).

[11] *Stat. U. S.*, XII, 422-26, 589-92, 540.

[12] Webster, *op. cit.*, p. 78.

[13] *Official Records of the Rebellion*, Ser. I, Vol. XLVII, Pt. II, pp. 60-62.

assigned to refugees and freedmen forty-acre tracts from the lands which had been confiscated or abandoned. The national government, the provision said, would provide "such title as the United States can convey."[14]

These measures were executed with vigor by General Rufus Saxton. Possessed of generous feelings for the Negro, he took possession of 485,000 acres of land, divided them among some forty thousand Negroes, prohibited whites from coming on this reserve, and induced the Negroes to begin planting operations early in the spring of 1865.[15] A handsome and striking figure, he impressed the Negroes with his oratory. "I came to tell you to get the land," he told an enthralled audience at Charleston.[16] "I wish every colored man, every head of a family in this department to acquire a freehold, a little home that he can call his own."

Inevitably the Negroes developed an avid desire to own land and became convinced that the national government was going to gratify this desire to the fullest extent. Sidney Andrews reported in September, 1865: "There is among the plantation Negroes a widely spread idea that the land is going to be given them by the government, and this idea is at the bottom of much idleness and discontent. At Orangeburg and Columbia, country Negroes . . . asked me 'When is de land goin' to be dewided?' Some of them . . . believe that the plantations on which they have lived are to be divided among themselves. . . . There is a widespread idea that the whites are to be driven out of the lower section of the state, and that the Negroes are to live there by themselves."[17] In other sections they were possessed of "the wildest notions and were wandering over the country in a state of idleness."[18] So great was the

[14] *Stat. U. S.*, XIII, 508.
[15] *Report of Joint Committee on Reconstruction*, Pt. II, p. 221, and Webster, pp. 94, 96.
[16] At Zion Church, May 2, 1865, *Courier*, May 13, 1865. Cf. *Official Records of the Rebellion*, Ser. III, Vol. IV, Serial 125, p. 1025.
[17] *The South Since the War*, pp. 97-98.
[18] "Juhl" from Sumter in *Courier*, July 24, 1865.

number which congregated at Charleston that the public authorities had to provide a camp for them.[19] Their credulity was taken advantage of by unscrupulous strangers. Throughout the up-country land stakes painted and numbered were sold at one or two dollars apiece. The Negroes believed that all that was necessary to secure the coveted forty acres was to mark the land of their choice with the stakes.[20]

They threatened for a time to override all measures of restraint which the alarmed authorities imposed. They asked, "What's the use of giving us freedom if we can't stay where we were raised, and own our houses where we were born, and our little pieces of ground?"[21] A party of landlords, who visited Edisto Island to repossess their lands, were told by the leader of a group of squatters, "You had better go back to Charleston, and go to work there, and if you can do nothing else, you can pick oysters and earn your living as the loyal people have done—by the sweat of their brows."[22] When others were asked on what terms they would contract with their former landlords, they replied, "Gov'ment drap we here. We can't go 'till Gov'ment take we off."[23] There were on record cases of freedmen who refused to yield lands they had possessed even at the request of the Freedmen's Bureau, keeping intruders away with clubs.[24]

In the midst of these actions the Federal government decided to restore most of the lands which had been assigned to Negroes. The prime mover in this policy was President Johnson. In his proclamation of amnesty and pardon of May 25, 1865, he provided easy means through which all property could be restored, except of course property in slaves and the Port Royal lands which had been legally sold for taxes.[25] Under

[19] Webster, p. 121.
[20] M. C. Butler, in *Ku-Klux Conspiracy, S. C.*, pp. 124, 134.
[21] N. Y. *Nation*, I (Sept. 28, 1865), 393. Cf. Webster, p. 95.
[22] *Courier*, Feb. 6, 1866.
[23] John T. Trowbridge, *The South*, pp 542-43.
[24] *News*, July 23 and 24, 1867.
[25] See above, p. 33.

his instructions General Howard issued a circular providing means through which the seized lands could be restored to all persons who could show proof of title and pardon and who had made provision to compensate the freedmen for improvements. On October 17, 1865, he arrived in Charleston "to effect arrangements mutually satisfactory to the freedmen and the planters."[26]

The difficulties experienced in effecting the restoration of lands were illustrated by happenings on Edisto Island. Accompanied by representatives of the planters, Howard went there two days after his arrival in Charleston. He told two thousand freedmen assembled in a church that their former owners had been pardoned, that the lands would be restored, and that he desired the freedmen to make labor contracts. "At first," said a witness, "the people hesitated, but as soon as the meaning struck them that they must give up their little homes and gardens and work for others, there was a general murmuring of dissatisfaction."[27] They insisted that they could not work again "for the Secesh." A few days later they drew up an illiterate petition to the President, expressing "sad feelings" over his decree, and begging that each of them be given an acre and a half of land. But Howard proceeded with his instructions. He issued an order for an agent of the Freedmen's Bureau to constitute himself and "two other citizens"—one a landlord and one a freedman—as a board with power to make labor contracts. But no sooner had Howard left, than fresh difficulties arose. The planters objected to a freedman serving on the board as he was not a "citizen." Howard yielded and the board was made up of the agent and two planters. But the freedmen now refused to contract unless they were given an acre of land each. The result was a deadlock, with the planting season of 1866 near at hand.

[26] Webster, pp. 97-98.   [27] Ames, *A New England Woman's Diary in Dixie*, pp. 97-103.

Fresh difficulties were created when the Second Freedmen's Bureau Bill was introduced in Congress in January, 1866. It proposed the validation of the titles given by Sherman's order. Although it failed to become law because of the President's veto, it naturally created false hopes among the freedmen.

Matters were finally clarified, however. In January, 1866, Saxton was dismissed as head of the state branch of the Freedmen's Bureau and the more conciliatory Scott was appointed in his place. The military authorities took the management of affairs out of the hands of the hesitant Howard. Negroes who refused to make contracts were summarily evicted.[28] This was followed by the enactment on June 16, 1866, of the Third Freedmen's Bureau Bill, which confirmed the titles to the land at Port Royal sold for taxes but required the freedmen to vacate other lands.[29] Under Scott's direction all of these lands were restored by November, 1868.[30]

The vacillating land policy of the national government created the impression that there was a deliberate conspiracy to create disorder. But this was not true. The contradictory policy was due to the unfortunate quarrel existing between the President and other agencies of the government. Moreover, it should be remembered that the government never committed itself to a policy of permanent confiscation; the primary reason why the lands were seized was to provide for refugee Negroes who could be disposed of in no other way during the war emergency. It was unfortunate that the Negroes and certain government agents should have given these actions such a broad interpretation.

Should the government not have attempted to provide means through which the Negroes could have become permanent owners of the soil? Would that not have been the

---

[28] *Ibid.*, pp. 99-103; Webster, *op. cit.*, and *House Executive Document, 39th Cong. 1st. Sess.*, No. 11, pp. 1-10.

[29] *Stat. U. S.*, XIV, 173-77.

[30] Webster, pp. 102-3.

most effective means of endowing them with the obligations of citizenship? Although there were many arguments in favor of such a policy, practical difficulties stood in the way of its success had it been tried. It would have failed because the type of government agents sent to South Carolina at this time were not capable of executing a difficult economic policy. Moreover, the freedmen were incapable of exercising the function of land ownership with sagacity. "I haven't yet found a single man on any of my places," wrote an abolitionist with wide experience, "who wants to risk buying land. They all say that they had rather stay where they are and work for me. The most intelligent foresee many difficulties in owning land, such as having no access to the marsh or woodland, no capital for livestock, plows, harness, carts, etc., and they don't like the idea of having to wait a whole year to get their pay for planting the cotton crop."[31] Of course there were Negroes capable of owning and managing land, but they demonstrated this capacity by making purchases at the low prices prevailing. Those who let this opportunity pass showed thereby that they did not have the qualities necessary for competent proprietorship.

Very detrimental to the success of the Negro as a farmer were his migratory habits. Traditions of long endurance did not attach him as a slave to a particular community, and he never forgot the habits of moving about formed in 1865. The mad character of his movements during that year was illustrated by the following report from Abbeville: "The able-bodied men and women, in many instances, abandoned the farm on which they were employed, leaving behind them the children and old people. . . . In some instances husbands have deserted wives and children, and we have known instances of both father and mother abandoning their infants to the care of

[31] E. S. Philbrick, in Pearson, *Letters from Port Royal*, pp. 246-47.

others."[32]   Although conditions were never again as bad, the habit of moving from one farm to another at the end of the planting season became established. In January, 1866, the Negroes were reported "in a state of anxious locomotion, changing homes, moving luggage, hunting places and making arrangements for the current year. A directory which might have located them a month ago would scarcely enable you to find one of them now."[33]   Each January thereafter this movement was repeated, and the landlord always felt insecure lest his tenants desert their crops during the growing season.

Many Negroes moved to the Southwest from sound motives of self-interest. There, wages were higher and the climate and social conditions like those to which they had been accustomed.[34]   During the winter of 1866-67 it was estimated that thousands of Negroes, discontented because of crop failures or the inability to make satisfactory contracts, emigrated to Florida.[35]   The following was a typical press comment on the movements after 1867: "A party of some sixty Negroes . . . passed through Laurensville during the Christmas holidays en route for Alabama. They were moving in wagons, had fair mules and horses, and were generally well equipped for the journey."[36] These movements created such a profound impression that many believed the state was losing its colored population. Indeed the census of 1870 reported that 97,492 colored persons born in South Carolina were living in other states; in 1880 this number was 93,489.[37]   But these movements failed

[32] Winnsboro *Tri-Weekly News*, July 23, 1865. Cf. *Courier*, Sept. 23, 1865.

[33] *Ibid.*, Jan. 9, 1866. Cf. *ibid.*, Feb. 18, 1866, and Jan. 18, 1867.

[34] Wages paid male agricultural laborers in South Carolina in 1867 and 1876 were less than those paid in any of the ten cotton states.—*Annual Report of Commissioner of Agriculture*, 1876, p. 131. See also tables in Edward Young, "Labor in Europe and America," *House Ex. Doc.*,

44th Cong., 1st Sess., No. 21, pp. 740-47.

[35] Webster, *op. cit.*, p. 140; *Fairfield Herald*, Dec. 16, 1866, and Jan. 21-29, 1867; *News*, Jan. 21, 27 and 29, 1867.

[36] *Ibid.*, Jan. 11, 1870. Cf. *ibid.*, Mar. 30, 1870, and Jan. 17, 1873.

[37] *Handbook of S. C., 1883*, p. 389. In 1880, 16,294 of the 93,489 were living in Georgia, 14,537 in Alabama, 16,117 in Mississippi and 11,688 in Florida.—*Census of 1880*, I, 488.

to neutralize by a wide margin the natural increase of the colored population which remained at home.

Another disturbing factor in the agricultural life of the state was the quixotic idea of many Negroes that they could improve themselves by emigrating to Liberia. "We do not believe," said a leader of this movement, "it is possible, from past history and from the present aspect of affairs, for our people to live in this country peaceably, and to educate and elevate our children to the degree which they desire."[38] In 1866 the African Colonization Society offered to transport emigrants from Charleston free of cost. During that and the following year some two thousand made the passage in ships of this society.[39] Another notable departure was that of 274 by way of Baltimore in 1867.[40]

In spite of the great unrest created by this agitation scarcely more than twenty-five hundred black South Carolinians actually made the venture. The average Negro loved his home state too well to make a good settler in a foreign country. Yeasty sentiments about being one's own master in the African Fatherland were not a fitting substitute for living under the only climate and social conditions which he had been used to. Those who went to Liberia were disappointed. A professor in a Liberian college wrote as follows to the newspaper of the town in which he had been a slave: "I long to get back to your town where I can see my old friends . . . and eat once more bacon, hominy and sausage at Christmas time." He expressed aversion for "the Yankee white man" with whom he had been thrown, and for the naked Liberians with their fish, fruits, yams and plantains.[41] Others experienced disaster. "The unhappy people who went," remarked Sir George Campbell,

[38] Rev. Elias Hill, in *Ku-Klux Conspiracy, S. C.*, p. 1410.

[39] *News*, Nov. 16, 1866, and Feb. 27, May 21 and Nov. 18, 1867.

[40] Benjamin Brawley, *Social History of the American Negro*, p. 197, and [A. B. Williams], *The Liberian Exodus*.

[41] James Ruffin, in *Fairfield Herald*, Oct. 30, 1867.

"found themselves worse off than if they had remained at home."[42]

Another disturbing factor in agricultural life was the feeling of the Radical politicians in charge of the state government that it was possible to improve the conditions of the laboring classes through artificial regulations. A state labor convention met in Columbia in November, 1869, under the presidency of Robert B. Elliott. Inquiry was made into the wages and treatment of agricultural laborers, and it was declared that such persons should receive one-half the share of the crop or a minimum daily wage of seventy cents to one dollar. This body said that a commissioner should be appointed by the legislature to supervise labor contracts, to reduce rents and to prohibit the postponement of suits to recover portions of crops due for services.[43] Repeated efforts were made in the legislature to secure laws to prevent the discharge of laborers until paid, and to provide against the removal of crops before satisfactory settlements had been made.[44]

More practical was the demand of the freedmen that the system of working plantations in gang units be abolished. They wanted to lease farms. The planters were opposed to this demand. The leasing of land to Negroes, said a planter, "is ruinous. Improvement is almost impossible; depreciation of property almost certain; it makes the laborer too independent; he becomes a partner and has the right to be consulted."[45]

But the Negroes were insistent. "There is but one opinion expressed," wrote a Northerner from the sea islands as early as 1862. "I don't want no driving either by black or white man.... There will be a difference in the land, sir, but we can't

---

[42] *White and Black*, p. 332. Cf. *News*, Nov. 1, 1867, and Apr. 3, 1868, and Brawley, p. 197.

[43] *Phoenix*, Nov. 25, 1869; *Charleston Daily Republican*, Nov. 30, 1869; and *News*, Nov. 25-29, 1869.

[44] *News*, Aug. 13, 1868. Cf. Moses in *Senate Journal, 1873*, p. 250.

[45] William Alston in *Rural Carolinian*, I (Feb., 1870), 317. Cf. Wyatt Aiken, *ibid.*, II (Jan., 1871), 194-95.

help dat; each work his and do as well as he kin."[46]   This
inclination increased in later years.   An observer reported in
1866: "There is a strong desire, amounting almost to a passion,
on the part of a large number of the more enterprising blacks
to obtain land by lease."[47]

The result was the breaking up of many plantations into
small farms.   In some cases the farms were sold to persons of
both races, but more often they were leased to Negroes.   The
size of the average farm in the state decreased from 488 acres
in 1860 to 233 in 1870.[48]   The Negroes abandoned the cabins
clustered around the "big house" and took up their abode in
cabins scattered over the land.   These changes, said the United
States commissioner of agriculture,[49] meant more to the Negro
"than any of the post-bellum amendments to the constitution."

They were possible because of the law of supply and demand.   There was a decrease in labor supply due to the decline
in the efficiency of colored labor, the withdrawal of many colored women from the field, and the removal of many of both
sexes to the towns or to areas of higher wages.   On the other
hand, there was an increase in the demand for labor due to
the stimulus given to the production of cotton by high prices
and to the fact that the landowners, because land was the principal resource which the war had left them, were forced to
give greater attention to its exploitation.   They attempted to
obviate their difficulties by importing outside labor, but, as will
be shown, this attempt ended in failure.

The Negro's insistence on land divisions did injury to the
agricultural interests of the state.   The United States commis-

[46] C. P. Ware, in Pearson, p. 113.   Cf.
ibid., pp. 109, 148.

[47] General Charles H. Howard in Report of Joint Committee on Reconstruction, Pt. III, p. 36.   Cf. General O. O.
Howard in House Ex. Doc., 39th Cong.,
1st Sess., No. 11, p. 7; and Edward King,
Southern States of North America, p. 464.

[48] Between these years the number of

plantations over one thousand acres decreased from 482 to 129 and the number
between one thousand and five hundred
decreased from 1,350 to 461; whereas
the number of farms under one hundred
acres increased from 19,961 to 44,183.
—M. B. Hammond, The Cotton Industry,
p. 129.

[49] Annual Report, 1876, p. 34.

sioner of agriculture said, with some exaggeration, that it was "the best possible plan to destroy fertility and profit and demoralize labor."[50]   It forced an undue concentration on cotton as the only certain means of securing rent. The prosperity of large sections of the low-country was dependent upon large-scale production, and when this was abandoned they fell into decay. The inexperienced Negro was capable of efficient production only under the immediate direction of the white man. As the manager of his own farm he was guilty of every conceivable crime against good farming. Contemporary documents are filled with tales of Negroes who worked only long enough to secure bare sustenance; of those who resorted to wholesale stealing; of those who flooded merchants with orders, never thinking of debts they were accumulating; and of those who neglected their farms in order to spend two or three days at a political meeting.[51]

So great was the injury done by the inefficiency of the labor that whole sections of the low-country suffered blows from which they have never recovered. Conditions there nine years after the war were vividly described by Edward King as follows:

The undoing of the old relation between races has been the ruin of certain sections of the lowlands. Neither race seems likely to resume operations on anything like the old scale of grandeur. . . . Today, the majority of those engaged in planting at the outbreak of the war are pitifully poor. . . . The enforced poverty of many is even bitterer than at the close of the war. . . . Along the Ashley the old manorial houses and estates, like Drayton Hall and Middleton House, stand like sorrowful ghosts lamenting the past; on James Island one can wander among rich cotton plantations now overrun with the maze of fortifications. . . . There is a wide belt of forsaken plantations near the Cooper River, along the famous Goose Creek. . . . Along Charleston Harbor are deserted and bankrupt towns

[50] *Ibid.*, p. 131.
[51] *Courier*, July 24, 1866; *News*, Aug. 27 and 30, and Nov. 8, 1867, and Feb. 1, 1868; Botume, p. 273.

. . . filled with moss-grown and rotting houses whose owners are fled unless they are too poor to get away.[52]

These observations are confirmed by the statistical findings of Major Harry Hammond. According to him, the coast region, excluding the city of Charleston, had under cultivation in 1880 only 1.5 acres per inhabitant, as compared with 3.8 for the state at large, and only 62 acres of improved land per square mile, as compared with 135 for the state at large. It grew only 11 bushels of grain and 92 pounds of lint cotton per capita. The fact that 83 per cent of the people of this area were colored was significant. Conditions were almost as gloomy in the upper swamp area, where the Negro population was also dominant. Lands had been allowed to return to their original state, and a typical farm which had produced 35 bushels of corn per acre before the war was not producing enough of this grain to feed its Negro inhabitants.[53]

* * * * *

It should not be assumed that all the farm difficulties of Reconstruction were the fault of the Negro. The white man had almost as much difficulty as the Negro in adjusting himself to free labor. He was subject to ambitions almost as wild and he showed a reluctance almost as great to accommodate himself to inevitable trends.

In the first place, the typical white South Carolinian thought it impossible to make successful use of the free Negro as a farm laborer. The freedmen, Sidney Andrews was told in 1865, "are always a nuisance, and you'll find them so in less than a year. They'll be idle before winter. . . . I would not give ten cents apiece for them."[54] So sagacious a leader as C. G. Memminger declared that the effect of the experiment of free labor

[52] *Southern States of North America,* pp. 428-31, 458. Cf. *Rural Carolinian,* VI (May and Oct., 1875), 405-6, 406-7 and 741-42.
[53] Harry Hammond, "Report on Cotton Production in South Carolina," *House Misc. Doc.,* 47th Cong., 2d Sess., Pt. 6, pp. 447, 479-86.
[54] *The South Since the War,* p. 25.

"will be the abandonment of the Negro to his indolent habits and the relapse of a large portion of the country to its original forest condition."[55]   As late as 1872 Stephen Powers heard "for the thousandth time" an accepted truism that the Negro was incapable of ordered effort without a master. "The nigger, sir," a planter said, "is a savage whom the Almighty Maker appointed to be a slave. A savage! with him free, the South is ruined, sir, ruined. . . ."[56]

In the face of these gloomy forebodings and the actual distress in many aspects of agricultural life, the first impulse of many planters was to emigrate to some foreign country. During the summer of 1865 General Wade Hampton received numerous requests to lead such an expedition.[57] Some planned to go to Mexico, where ex-Confederates were receiving lands and political preference. Others were attracted by Venezuela. The government of that country had authorized C. R. Bryce, a prominent citizen of Columbia, to issue as many as 2,500 land grants of 2,500 acres each to persons in South Carolina.[58] But the country which most attracted South Carolinians was Brazil. It offered liberal land grants, had for years been attractive to white immigrants, still tolerated Negro slavery, and its southern provinces had a climate similar to that of South Carolina. A committee of planters composed of Dr. J. McF. Gaston of Chester and Robert Meriwether and H. A. Shaw of Edgefield visited the provinces of Pernambuco and Sao Paulo and brought flattering accounts of conditions in the latter territory.[59]   The newspapers told of enthusiastic receptions given Southerners in Rio de Janeiro—bands playing "Dixie," the pealing of bells, and land at twenty-two cents an acre.[60]

These emigration projects, however, ended largely in talk.

[55] Letter to President Johnson in H. D. Capers, *Life of Memminger*, pp. 373-74.
[56] *Afoot and Alone*, pp. 27-28, and 25.
[57] See his letter to *Phoenix* in *Courier*, Aug. 1, 1865.
[58] *Ibid.*, Mar. 10, 1866.
[59] Report in *DeBow's Review*, N. S., II (July, 1886), 30-38, and in Gaston, *Hunting a Home in Brazil*.
[60] *Courier*, Mar. 7, 1866.

So far as can be ascertained no South Carolinians went to Venezuela, a few went to Mexico, and a slightly larger number, mostly from Edgefield and Chester, went to Brazil.

The reasons why more did not go are not far to seek. Agricultural conditions at home were not so bad as some imagined; certainly they were better than any Latin-American country could offer. The social and political changes at home did not involve inconveniences comparable to those which would have arisen had South Carolinians attempted to adapt themselves to the strange languages and attitudes toward colored peoples prevailing in Latin America. The friendly imperial régime in Mexico soon collapsed, and, in the words of the *Charleston Mercury,* was supplanted by "an anarchial despotism" friendly to the United States.[61] Brazil, according to this newspaper, was bound to go through an ordeal of emancipation like that which South Carolina had experienced. Moreover, patriotism was appealed to as a reason why South Carolinians should not desert their state. Hampton, in his eloquent reply to those who asked him to lead an emigration, said: "The very fact that our state is passing through so terrible an ordeal as at present should cause her sons to cling more closely to her. . . . The Roman Senate voted thanks to one of their generals because in the darkest hour of the Republic he did not despair. Let us emulate the example of the Romans, and thus entitle ourselves to the gratitude of the country."[62]

But no such barriers stood in the way of emigration to the western part of the United States. There, cheap lands and social conditions like those at home existed, circumstances of more weight than the objections to living under the American flag. The patriotic appeal to cling more closely to South Carolina did not in this case act as a restraint. South Carolinians were already in the habit of moving west, for, in 1860, 256,868

[61] Cited in *Fairfield Herald,* Mar. 25, 1868.   [62] *Courier,* Aug. 1, 1865.

of the 470,257 natives of the state then living were residing elsewhere in the United States than South Carolina. This movement continued after the war. In 1870, 148,574 of the 418,825 white natives of the state were residing in other states; in 1880 these figures were 137,418 and 500,994 respectively.[63] But emigration did not mean that the white race was escaping contacts with the Negroes; for throughout Reconstruction the proportions of the two races remained about the same as in 1860.

The whites attempted to put their labor in order through the labor provisions of the famous "black code" of 1865. But these laws would have been a failure even if they had not been nullified by General Sickles. They failed to take into account that the freedman was free of all artificial devices which attempted to impose restrictions upon the right of the laborer to sell his services to the highest bidder. The competition of the planters among themselves for his services guaranteed him working conditions far more liberal than those which the laws aimed to establish.

Another scheme of the planters to escape from their labor difficulties was to sell plantations to Northerners. Many people both in the North and the South believed that the freedmen could best be managed by those who had given them freedom and that the thrifty New Englander could transform potentially rich but degenerate South Carolina into another Massachusetts. Moreover, the low price of land and the high price of cotton were inducements to capital.

Immediately after the war Northerners purchased South Carolina lands. The newspapers were filled with advertisements of "first class plantations" which "offered unprecedented bargains as strangers to the climate can remain on them the entire year."[64] "There is a large number of old planters,"

---

[63] *Handbook of S. C., 1908*, p. 526.   [64] *Courier*, Dec. 14, 1865. Cf. *ibid.*, Feb. 10, 1866.

wrote a Northerner who had made purchases, "who are offering their lands at very low rates, and so many tempting chances are offered Northern men."[65] Interest in these offers was widespread, and half the passengers aboard the Charleston steamers were said to be Massachusetts men seeking their fortunes in the South.[66]

But this was no solution of the state's agrarian problems. Most Northerners found sufficient opportunities at home for the investment of their surplus capital. The low price of South Carolina lands was a symptom of decay rather than opportunity. The lands offered for sale were mostly along the coast, where adjustments were most difficult and the climate not the best. Many prospective immigrants, living in an age which exaggerated the drawbacks of a southern climate, were driven away by fear of the swamp malaria.[67] Others, fearing disorderly Negroes, were induced "to pack up their valises and embark on the first train home."[68] Those who actually took up planting were seldom of the type that could be successful. Some were adventurers who turned from farming to store-keeping or politics in order to get rich as soon as possible. Others were high-minded persons interested in proving that free Negro labor was a success. The last named class were not actuated by the motive which usually induces emigrants to seek a new home—the desire to improve individual fortunes. As soon as their emotions were cooled by actual contact with the Negro, they gave up farming and returned North where easier fortunes awaited them.

The disappointments in store for these immigrants were borne out by their experiences. The following report was made concerning the plantations on which they attempted the

[65] E. S. Philbrick in letter of Oct. 15, 1865, in Pearson, *Letters from Port Royal*, p. 317.

[66] *Boston Post* cited in *Courier*, Dec. 21, 1865, and Sidney Andrews, pp. 3-4.

[67] See opinions of Stephen Powers, *Afoot and Alone*, p. 44, and Henry Latham, *Black and White*, p. 199.

[68] *Courier*, Mar. 2, 1866. Cf. the flight of four Pennsylvanians from James Island, *ibid.*, Feb. 1, 1866.

difficult task of growing sea island cotton: "Not only has the quality of the labor deteriorated in the absence of proper and intelligent direction, but the lands have undergone a degree of positive injury and sterility."[69] A certain Colonel Chadwick rented the Sinkler plantation "Belvedere," and believed that he had found a home for life. But soon tales of cruelty and insubordination reached the owners. Chadwick acknowledged that he could not get the Negroes to agree to contracts and he was dismissed.[70] Henry Lee Higginson and two others invested $27,000 in lands in Georgia near Beaufort. He gave up planting operations after realizing only $10,000 out of an investment of $20,025 in the first year's crop. He and his wife had become utterly discouraged over the conduct of the Negroes. "It is discouraging," wrote Mrs. Higginson, May 9, 1867, "to see how utterly wanting in character these people seem to be, and how much more hopeful they appear at a distance than near to. . . . I shall leave this place with a sense of utter failure, . . . failure to manage the blacks well and quietly as servants."[71]

While some were trying to solve their labor difficulties through selling their lands to Northerners or through emigration, a far larger number of South Carolina landowners were stirred by the hope of inducing European immigrants to come to the state and work their lands. Many hoped and believed that the Negro was being eliminated from the state in such large numbers as to make the substitution of foreigners imperative. "A few short years and their race in this country will be run," was the typical opinion of the Negro. "To be put in competition and on a level with the white race to make a living, is starvation to the Negro. Already we feel that their numbers decrease in our midst with rapid bounds—sickness from uncleanliness and vice, with emigration to richer fields

[69] T. C. W., *ibid.*, Sept. 23, 1865.
[70] Elizabeth A. Coxe, *Memories of a South Carolina Plantation*, pp. 67-70.
[71] Bliss Perry, *Life and Letters of Henry Lee Higginson*, pp. 251-66.

and sunnier climes, will soon cause the place that once knew them to know them no more."[72]

Many planters thought they saw positive reasons why immigrants should come to the state. They knew that the previous failure of the South to attract immigrants had been a cause of its inferiority to the North in wealth and population, and that the abolition of slavery had destroyed many prejudices which had prevented the entrance of outsiders. They felt that through free labor the state would become prosperous and that the plantations would break into small proprietorships, for which immigrants were supposed to have a predilection. There were thousands of unoccupied acres previously worth forty to fifty dollars each which could be had for five or ten dollars each. The state was rich in natural resources, and with the exception of certain sections of the lowlands, had a climate suitable for Europeans. Moreover, most of the immigrants coming to America at that time fitted in with the South Carolinian's notion of a good people. They were the blond Irish, and if the Irish did not exactly fit, on account of their Catholicism, there were the Germans. They were blond and Protestant, and a successful colony of them had been established at Walhalla shortly before the war.[73]

With such ideas in mind, the legislature created the office of commissioner of immigration, and Governor Orr appointed John A. Wagener to this position. Wagener had been largely responsible for the establishment of the colony at Walhalla and, being a native of Germany, had a special knowledge of conditions in that country.[74] An attractive pamphlet, *South Carolina: A Home for the Industrious Immigrant*, was published

[72] *Laurensville Herald* cited in *Fairfield Herald*, Sept. 13, 1867. Cf. Winnsboro *Tri-Weekly News*, July 1, 1865; *DeBow's Review*, N. S., II (Sept., 1866), 285; and *Courier*, May 15, 1866.

[73] These views were given by Governor Perry, *House Journal, Ex. Sess., 1865*, pp.

14-15; John A. Wagener, *South Carolina: a Home for the Industrious Immigrant*, and Mr. Easley in *Courier*, Jan. 30, 1866.

[74] Act of Dec. 20, 1865, *Stat. S. C.*, XIII, 380-81; Orr to Willy Wabach in *Courier*, Mar. 6, 1866; and *Keowee Courier*, Aug. 31, 1876.

in English, German, and the Scandinavian languages, agents were sent to Germany and the Scandinavian countries, and 332,660 acres were listed for sale. The German Land and Trading Company was organized in Charleston in 1865. Immigration societies were organized in various places, notably in Columbia, Newberry, Edgefield, and Winnsboro, and some planters promised to give fifty acres of land to each immigrant head of a family who would put fifty dollars in improvements upon the gift.[75] In 1869 the South Carolina Improvement and Trust Company was promoting the breaking up of plantations into small farms and the establishment of a colony of immigrants in Chesterfield County. A convention held in Charleston in 1870 proposed that a line of steamers be inaugurated between Europe and Charleston to encourage settlers and that societies be formed to offer them free lands. Similar agitations were carried on by the State Agricultural and Mechanical Society and by the taxpayers' convention of 1874. In 1871 Generals Butler and Gary formed a company to establish a lottery which was to raise money to buy lands for immigrants and furnish them steamer passages. In 1874 there was talk of organizing the Coöperative Colonization Bank of South Carolina with a capital stock of $5,000,000, an immigration bureau was established in Charleston under the direction of Frank Melchers, and Edward King felt that he saw a change in the attitude of the population which would make immigration more successful.[76]

These efforts bore fruit in the arrival at Charleston on November 28, 1867, of the German bark "Gauss" with 152 immigrants aboard, and in the report of Wagener that by June 19, 1868, he had induced four hundred Europeans to settle in the

[75] *Courier*, Aug. 21, and Oct. 30, 1867, and June 20, 1868; and E. J. Watson, in *Handbook of S. C.*, 1908, p. 513.

[76] *News*, May 6, 1869, and Feb. 20 and June 22, 1871; *Phoenix*, Jan. 24, 1874;

Rural Carolinian, I (June, 1870), 572-73, and V (Mar., 1874), 306-7; *News and Courier*, Feb. 21, 1874; and *Proceedings of Taxpayers' Convention, Feb., 1874*, pp. 45-46.

state. The taxpayers' convention of 1874 reported that Melchers had introduced eight hundred immigrants and that the Reverend Tilman R. Gaines, who maintained an immigration office in New York City, had induced four hundred to come to the state. Other agencies were able to report scantier successes.[77]

But the immigration movement had little effect upon the trend of the state's population. In 1880 only 7,686 of the state's white population were foreign-born, which was less than 1 per cent of the total and 2,300 less than the foreign-born population in 1860. This was truly a scant counterbalance to the 137,418 white South Carolinians living in other states in 1880. Moreover, only 6 per cent of the 7,786 immigrants were engaged in farming. It is evident that immigration had been no solution of agricultural difficulties.[78]

There were numerous reasons why immigrants did not come to South Carolina in larger numbers. In the first place, the Radical government did not favor the idea. Wagener's office was abolished in 1868. The Negroes complained of the desire of the whites "to bring foreigners to your country, and thrust us out or reduce us to a serfdom intolerable."[79] In the second place, the whites did little of a concrete nature to further immigration. Racial sympathy did not lead planters to give foreigners better conditions of employment than Negroes. Indeed we have every reason to believe that the planters preferred Negro labor. "Experience has taught the world," said the sagacious Wyatt Aiken, "that the successful cultivation of cotton is a science only appreciated by the Southern-born planter and their former slaves. The wants of the Negro laborer are a warm back and a full belly. These supplied, he

[77] *News*, Nov. 29, 1867, Aug. 3, 1868, and Oct. 9, 1870.

[78] *Handbook of S. C., 1883*, pp. 389-91.

[79] *Proceedings of the Colored People's Convention Held at Zion Church*, p. 25.

Cf. *News*, Oct. 15, 1868; Moses in *Senate Journal, 1872-1873*, p. 231; and commissioner of agricultural statistics, in *Reports and Resolutions, 1870-1871*, pp. 663-64.

is capable of wonderful endurance. The wants of the white laborers are manifold. . . . Fresh meat, sugar, coffee, flour, a feather bed, are necessary for his contentment."[80] The immigrants who came were not liked. They were subjected to espionage and surveillance and excited the jealousy of the small white farmer with whom they competed. The traditional aversion for the outsider as a possible abolitionist was transferred to the outsider as a possible carpetbagger.[81]

Neither immigrants nor prospective immigrants were pleased with South Carolina. Those who arrived on the "Gauss" hastily departed, saying that the state was "extremely unhealthy and inhabited by Negroes and half-civilized whites." Others objected to bad housing, bad roads, few public schools, thieving among the blacks, and "in some sections ignorance, prejudice, and superstition among the masses." Others were not willing "to settle down and live on bacon and corn bread" and the low wages offered.[82]

Yet the whites did find a means of partly ridding themselves of the monopoly of Negro labor. They began producing with their own hands a much larger share of the state's cotton crop than had been their habit. We are told of white youths who had been reared in a counting house being "jerked and jostled about to the infinite amusement of grinning darkies" when they first attempted plowing, but who persisted in this endeavor and were successful.[83] It was estimated that 32 per cent of the cotton crop of 1875 was produced by white labor as compared with only half that amount in 1860.[84] Major Harry Hammond said that in 1880 in certain sections of the

[80] *Rural Carolinian,* IV (Mar., 1873), 291-294. Cf. *News,* Nov. 26, 1868.

[81] N. Y. *Nation,* III, (Nov. 8, 1866), 370, and *Rural Carolinian,* I (Aug., 1870), 713.

[82] *News,* Nov. 30, 1868; B. W. Jones in *Rural Carolinian,* II (Aug., 1871), 605-6; B. O. D., in *ibid.,* II (Aug., 1871), 638-39. Cf. Ludwig Lewisohn's vivid portrayal in *Up Stream* of the shock a family of cultivated German Jews experienced on the first contact with the comparative barbarities of the state.

[83] J. S. J., of Richmond, in *Southern Cultivator,* XXVI (Sept., 1868), 260.

[84] *Annual Report of Commissioner of Agriculture, 1876,* p. 136.

up-country the proportion of whites in the fields was greater than that of the Negroes.[85]

This change was due to a variety of reasons. Negro labor had become less efficient, and economic distress forced many whites to turn to manual labor. But the principal cause was the rise of the up-country, where the greater proportion of the whites lived, and the decline of the low-country, where the greater proportion of the Negroes lived. Aside from factors which have already been suggested, the rise of the up-country was due to the more extensive use of commercial fertilizers in the years after the war.[86] In 1880 the up-country, with one-third the area of the state, was producing 53 per cent of its total cotton crop.[87]

[85] *Op. cit.,* p. 521.
[86] See below, p. 258.

[87] Harry Hammond, p. 499.

Chapter IX

COMPROMISE AND PROGRESS IN AGRICULTURE

AGENTS of the Federal government were leaders in efforts to bring about conditions which would make possible the resumption of ordered production. They relieved physical distress,[1] and the services of the troops in keeping order in rural areas were recognized by white contemporaries.[2] But the most helpful efforts of the national agents were directed toward inducing both races to enter into labor contracts.

Early in 1865 army officers were reported negotiating labor agreements.[3] General Saxton told the Negroes "not to let a day pass ere you find some work for your hands to do." He supplemented this advice by appointing, in each Freedmen's Bureau district, a board consisting of a Bureau agent and representatives of the planters and freedmen, to arrange contracts. He prepared model contracts which specified general obligations, but wisely left the determination of rates of wages or shares of the harvest to the individuals concerned. The Bureau agents were empowered to settle disputes arising over contracts.[4] So strenuous was Saxton in urging the freedmen to forget previous promises of land allotments, and to enter into contracts with landlords, that he won the commendation of many whites.[5] The manner in which his agents went about their work is illustrated by the case of Major Delany, who operated in the neighborhood of Beaufort. In the beginning the

---

[1] See above, p. 30.

[2] Both the Sumter correspondent of the *Courier*, Oct. 6, 1865, and the military affairs committee of the legislature, *House Journal, Ex. Sess., 1865*, p. 63, suggested that the garrisons be retained.

[3] Laura J. Webster, *The Freedmen's Bureau in S. C.*, p. 106.

[4] *Ibid.*, p. 110.

[5] See, for example, *Courier*, Jan. 6, 9, and 11, 1866.

planters distrusted him, but soon he was able to convince them of the benefits of the labor which his contracts offered.[6] "The Freedmen's Bureau," said one of its agents, "has been a great blessing to both, because it has been a mediator between the two classes; it has endeavored to persuade the freedman to trust his employer, assuring him that the Bureau would see justice done him; and it has urged the master to give up his prejudices and treat the Negro fairly."[7]

The usefulness of the Bureau was enhanced by the appointment of Scott in the place of Saxton as the head of its branch in the state. The new commissioner modified provisions of Saxton's model contract which were objectionable to the planters, and he was able to report, three months after he took office, that the Negroes "had entered into contracts with a willingness and unanimity beyond the expectations of the most sanguine persons in the state." During 1867 and 1868 the agents of the Bureau reported that their offices were thronged with planters and freedmen calling on them to settle differences and divide crops, and that there was a growing cordiality between the two classes in the areas of their operations.[8] One of Scott's measures directly bearing upon the problem of agricultural rehabilitation was the furnishing of supplies to freedmen whose landlords were not able to do so. The last-mentioned action was declared to be "humane and judicious" and of "great and substantial benefit to the planters"; while Scott was declared to have conducted the general affairs of the Bureau "with judgment and sound discretion."[9]

But the Freedmen's Bureau, like other artificial agencies with similar purposes, was not the means of reëstablishing agricultural order. The first circumstance which worked against its success was the unwise actions of its agents. Sax-

---

[6] Rollin, *Life of Delany*, pp. 242-71.

[7] *Report of Joint Committee on Reconstruction*, Pt. II, p. 230.

[8] Webster, pp. 114-17.

[9] For these and other expressions of approval, see *Courier*, Feb. 1, 1866; and *News*, Feb. 2 and 10, 1866, Dec. 24 and 28, 1867, and Dec. 14, 1868.

ton's land policy created a hatred for which a subsequent wiser policy was no compensation. Many of his subordinates were inexperienced or corrupt. Some of them accepted fees for such actions as inducing strikers to work, settling disputes, and flogging Negroes.[10] Another circumstance which militated against its success was that it operated only in limited areas and that its labor-regulating activities did not continue beyond 1868. Its agents largely confined their activities to the coast, and even there, they were too few in number for detailed attention to the many complications which arose from farm contracts.[11]

There was, moreover, a fundamental reason why the Bureau could never have been successful as a labor-regulating agency. It aimed to enforce abstract principles of justice which ignored social and economic realities. Actually the landlords, who were the owners of the land and the inheritors of many social privileges, were in a position to sit in judgment in agrarian matters. They successfully resisted the attempt of the Bureau to inject the judicial dogma of equality into economic concerns. Their irritation was expressed by Judge A. P. Aldrich: "We are greatly embarrassed in the management of our domestic affairs by the interference of the Freedmen's Bureau. I believe that if the delicate problem of organizing the labor of our former slaves was entirely left to us . . . we would very soon regain their confidence."[12] Of course, as has been shown, the Negro agriculturists gained many privileges which the landlords did not wish to concede; but they came through the working of economic law.

* * * * *

In truth, the reorganization of labor through the necessary coöperation of the two classes was proceeding at a steady pace,

[10] For these and other examples of inefficiency or corruption see Webster, Chap. III, and Sidney Andrews, *The South Since the War*, pp. 22-24.

[11] In 1868 there were only forty-nine agents in the state.—*South Carolina Almanac for 1868*, p. 35.

[12] Address to grand jury of Richland, *Fairfield Herald*, Oct. 16, 1866.

in spite of the conflicting forces which we have already described. When it was realized that the necessities of existence forced the two races to work the soil together, each began to see virtues in the other and to cherish hopes of mutual happiness. It was not only possible to live under such conditions, but it was also possible to make high profits through the growing of cotton. Consequently, the demoralizing ambitions which we have described tended to disappear, and freedmen and planters entered into contracts which promised profits for both.

Indeed the chasm which existed between Negro and white farmers was not so wide as some imagined. They ate the same food, loved the same homes, and were accustomed to working the same crops with very much the same methods. "The relations existing between us and the Negroes," said the *Charleston Daily News,* "are old, kindly, and in some respects very strong. . . . The influences we have with them began in the cradle and their interests and ours are identical."[13]

The planters, however bitterly they deplored the changes the war had brought, showed generally an admirable adaptability to the new conditions. Some, said a correspondent of the *New Orleans Delta,* "are as sanguine of as much success in planting under the new system as under the old."[14] The *Charleston Daily News* came to the conclusion after three years' experience that "to hire a Negro at reasonable wages . . . is cheaper for the planter in the long run than to run the risk of his cost when owned, and to assume the responsibility of his clothing, doctor's bill, and his support when disabled by disease and old age."[15] General Hampton begged his fellow-planters to help the Negro. "Deal with him frankly, justly, kindly, and my word for it," he said, "he will reciprocate your kindness."[16]

[13] Mar. 15, 1868.
[14] Cited in *Courier,* July 15, 1865.
[15] Dec. 29, 1868.

[16] Speech at Walhalla, Sept. 22, 1866, in *Courier,* Oct. 10, 1866.

The Negroes as a whole soon realized that it was necessary to perform the tasks of the farm with much of the old-time efficiency. Governor Orr declared as early as 1866: "The experiment of free labor, whilst it is not entirely satisfactory, is far from proving a failure. . . . Suddenly relieved from the controlling will of others, . . . they have performed during the present year an amount of voluntary labor which may excite surprise."[17] Nine years later the leading writer in the state on farm problems was inclined to ascribe the "hard times" of that day to faulty farm management rather than to the Negro's lassitude or political aberrations. "The labor of the South," he affirmed, "is as reliable as that of the North, and more efficient and less expensive."[18] These conclusions were confirmed by a foreign observer. "There is no question," wrote Sir George Campbell in 1878 of the Negroes, "that for a certain time no workmen can be more steady and effective. . . . They are, as a rule, good labourers and very tolerable cultivators."[19]

There was always one incentive which could get work out of the Negro. That was economic necessity. The complaint that the sea islanders would not work, said a careful observer, was quite absurd, since by 1867 many were face to face with an exacting poverty which made them willing to walk ten miles to earn fifty cents.[20] The Negroes on the Santee estate of Captain Thomas Pinckney, who cherished extravagant notions of their rights to the land, were soon forced by fear of starvation to resume work on Pinckney's terms. "Cap'n, I 'clar' 'fo' Gawd, suh," said an humbled field hand, "I ain' got no vittles fur my wife an' chillun, I ain' got a day's rations in my cabin. I'se been willin' fur right smart while to work. I

[17] *House Journal, Reg. Sess., 1866*, pp. 20-21. Cf. "Juhl" in *Courier*, Mar. 22, 1866.

[18] D. Wyatt Aiken, *Rural Carolinian*, VI (Feb., 1875), 227-30. Cf. *ibid.*, II (July, 1871), 572-74, and *ibid.*, V (June, 1874), 486-87.

[19] *White and Black*, pp. 156-59.

[20] Elizabeth H. Botume, *First days amongst the Contrabands*, pp. 235-36.

ain' nuvver seed dis way we been doin' wuz zackly right."[21]

Moreover, it should be remembered that in most of the up-country the transition from slavery to a condition of ordered free labor was made with the minimum friction. There the majority of blacks, after some aimless wandering, entered into labor agreements with their former masters during the first year of freedom. "In the main," a citizen told Whitelaw Reid in 1865, "the niggers are working just as they used to. . . . A few have been hired by the day; and some others have gone to work for a specified share of the crops. In many instances the planters have told them to work ahead, get their living out of the crops, and what further share they are entitled to should be determined when officers who approve contracts come."[22]

The conditions under which the Negroes became agriculturists were various. Some became wage hands; others became proprietors; a notable minority became renters; the system which ultimately attracted the largest proportion was the share crop arrangement.[23]

As has been indicated,[24] the planters preferred the wage system. It seems to have been the prevailing system during the first years after the war, and has since played an important part in farm life. Harry Hammond said that in 1880 it prevailed in the lower pine belt, notably in Colleton and Williamsburg counties. Although it made greatest appeal to the less provident, the Negroes who submitted to it were by no means miserable. They were relieved of the responsibility of crop management, were given an extensive holiday at Christmas, and enjoyed fruits of their labor not taken into account by their monthly wage of ten or twelve dollars. Hammond said, "In most cases they are given shelter, rations, firewood, and al-

---

[21] Pinckney, in M. L. Avary, *Dixie after the War*, pp. 341-45.

[22] *After the War*, p. 84. Cf. Gov. Perry in *Courier*, Feb. 23, 1866.

[23] The census estimated in 1880 that 49.7 per cent of the farms were operated by owners (and managers); 26.9 per cent by share and share-cash tenants; and 23.4 per cent by cash and non-specified types of tenants.

[24] See above, pp. 235-37.

most invariably a garden, and the privilege of raising some stock, a cow or a pig. The work commences at sunrise and is over with at sunset, no night work of any kind being required; the time allowed for meals varies, but dinner is from one to three hours, according to the length of the day. All exposure to rain or bad weather, even in pressing exigencies, is scrupulously avoided, and during exceptionally chilly weather little is obtained or expected of Negro laborers."[25]

The ambition of a large group of Negroes, seeking the maximum freedom from the control of their former masters, was to rent lands in return for a stipulated amount in money or produce (usually cotton). Although the planters were suspicious of such arrangements, they granted them to Negroes who demonstrated capacities for independent operations. Wyatt Aiken, forced to rent his land because of the competition of other planters, found this arrangement highly satisfactory. In 1875 he wrote: "I have repeatedly seen farms in South Carolina of from one to five hundred acres sell for from five to twenty-five hundred dollars, and no sooner had they changed hands than they were leased to Negro farmers for 25 per cent on the investment. . . . To my mind no people ever had a fairer chance of becoming lordly landowners . . . than have the Southern planters at the present time."[26]

Negroes in various parts of the state became landowners. This achievement was possible because of the low price of land as compared with the high rental value, and the opportunity

[25] "Report on Cotton Production in S. C.," *House Misc. Doc., 47th Cong., 2d Sess.,* Pt. 6, p. 521. Edward Young, "Labor in Europe and America," *House Ex. Doc., 44th Cong., 1st Sess.,* No. 21, pp. 740-47, gives the following scale of monthly wages in South Carolina:

	1860	1870	1874
Experienced hands in summer with board	$ 9.28	11.67	12.00
Experienced hands in winter with board	8.57	10.30	5.00
Common labor other than farm work	10.33	12.00	8.00
Female servants	5.28	7.40	8.00

[26] *Rural Carolinian,* VI (June, 1875), V (June, 1874), 486-87. 455. Cf. *ibid.,* III (Dec., 1872), 114, and

to accumulate capital due to the high price of cotton. That not more than 5 per cent of the Negro farmers were in this class at the end of the Reconstruction period was due to bad economy. The type who became landowners was represented by a certain Edward Hill, who lived in an unnamed interior county. Immediately after emancipation, he became a share cropper on the lands of his former master. Although his horse died, at the end of the first year he had enough money to pay his debts and buy supplies for the next season. With the proceeds of his second crop he bought his first lands. Nine years after the war he was the owner of a large tract of land and he and his family produced twenty-five bales of cotton annually. His success had been due to wise economy, unceasing industry, and his refusal to become involved in politics—he voted Democratic.[27]

The share crop arrangement represented a compromise between landlord and tenant. It provided for a division of the control of the land. Each Negro family was allotted twenty-five or more acres which were to be operated as a unit distinct from the rest of the plantation. On this farm the family took up residence in a cabin erected for that purpose. But the degree of independence given the tenant was not as great as that given those who rented outright. The landlord reserved the right to prescribe what crops should be planted and to supervise the growing crop. A high degree of interest on his part was prompted by the fact, that, instead of a fixed rental, he received a specified percentage of the total produced.

Share crop contracts were often so intricate that they defy general description. The one proposed by a laborer in the upper pine belt represented the evolution from the wage system to the share system proper. This laborer became possessed

[27] [John P. Green], *Recollections of the Carolinas*, pp. 51-55. Cf. story of Limus, in Pearson, *Letters from Port Royal*, pp. 37-38.

of the idea that he should work five days of each week for the landlord, and that in return he should receive one-fourth of the harvests which resulted from this work, in addition to a house and food, three acres of land and a mule to work on Saturdays, and sixteen dollars at the end of the year. This plan, with modifications the following years through which the freedmen worked fewer days for the landlords and furnished an increasing proportion of the supplies, became popular. The share crop system fully developed has been described by Chancellor Johnson as used on his lands in Marlboro County in 1880: "I furnish the stock, the food for it, pay one-half of the blacksmith, fertilizer, bagging and ties account, and furnish ginning facilities. The tenant has his garden and potato patch free, and does all the work, from repairing fences and ditches to preparing the crop for market. My advances are repaid, and the crop is equally divided."[28] In general, it may be said that one-third of the produce went to the tenant in return for labor; one-third to the landlord as rent; the remaining third was divided between the two in proportion to the supplies each furnished. With the passing of years, there was a tendency for the tenant to furnish an increasing share of the supplies. Often, however, he received little or nothing in cash because he had already mortgaged his third or half to the landlord or a merchant for supplies which had been necessary for himself and family through the growing season.

Contrary to popular impression, there was a steady rise in the output of South Carolina farms following the war. In 1870, 224,500 bales of cotton were produced. This represented a vast increase over the 30,000 produced in 1865 and was not an unfavorable comparison with the 353,412 bales of 1860. The crop of 1876 was only 43,000 bales less than that of 1860; the crop of 1880 was far greater than that of 1860.[29] During Re-

[28] Harry Hammond, p. 519.   [29] *Handbook of S. C., 1883,* p. 359.

construction, the state actually produced a larger proportion of the nation's cotton crop than before the war.[30]

Although there was a pronounced concentration on cotton, other interests were not neglected. In 1875 only one-third of the cultivated area of the state was in the fleecy staple, which was less than the acreage devoted to Indian corn.[31]

That the farms were on an upward grade during Reconstruction, is indicated by the following estimates of the increases in the state's number of livestock:[32]

	1868	1870	1871	1873
Number of horses........	39,427	51,300	53,800	55,300
Number of mules........	30,429	40,700	42,300	45,300
Number of oxen and other cattle.......	151,657	167,700	174,400	179,600
Number of milk cows...	137,773	140,500	147,500	541,800
Number of hogs.........	200,592	308,000	317,200	332,000

A variety of circumstances was responsible for the recovery of the farms. Chief among these was the increased use of commercial fertilizers. This was possible because the high price of cotton made the use of Peruvian guano profitable, and because of the discovery of the use of the state's phosphate deposits. Under the stimulus of commercial fertilizer, it became profitable to grow cotton on worn hill lands and even in foothill areas where previously the plant had matured too slowly for the short season. Hammond declared in 1880: "Since the introduction of commercial fertilizer . . . good crops have been produced on lands . . . formerly considered of little value. As a consequence, some of these lands near a railroad, which were sold in 1858 at $3.00 an acre, have recently brought as much as $30 and even $40 an acre."[33]

[30] *Annual Report of Commissioner of Agriculture, 1876*, pp. 118-19, said that its percentage was 6.4 in 1859 and 7.4 in 1869.

[31] *Ibid.*, pp. 120-21, said that 35 per cent was in cotton, 44 per cent in corn, and 21 per cent in other crops.

[32] *Ibid.*, *1867*, pp. 92-94; *1869*, pp. 47-48; *1870*, pp. 47-48; and *1872*, pp. 43-44.

[33] Harry Hammond, p. 491.

Moreover, there were some improvements in the technique of farming. Replies to a series of questions addressed to representative farmers in 1876 indicated "a change in the closer copying of model practice, and especially in a more general use of improved implements. If the old form of implements are retained, there is a marked improvement in the grace of outline and perfection of finish, as well as in the economy of material and power."[34]

During Reconstruction enterprising leaders and organizations strove for agricultural adjustments and improvements. Foremost among the leaders was D. Wyatt Aiken, editor of the *Rural Carolinian,* a monthly magazine published from 1869 to 1876. Aiken was a learned and forceful writer, who had much success as a practical farmer; although he was a zealous reformer, he was a constructive critic and devoted to the interests of the white farmers. It was largely through his efforts that the Patrons of Husbandry, which will be discussed presently, was introduced into the state.

An important organization was the South Carolina Agricultural and Mechanical Society, organized in 1869 as a revival of an ante-bellum society. The annual reports of its meetings contained thoughtful papers on the means of improving farm practices. Its most important activity was the holding of an agricultural fair at Columbia in 1869 and every year thereafter. The model exhibits at the fairs stimulated progress. The most active of the local agricultural societies were the South Carolina Agricultural Society of Charleston, the Pomological and Farmers' Club of Society Hill, and the Cheraw Farmers' and Mechanics' Club. The experiments of Aiken, Johnson Hagood of Barnwell, and W. C. Coker of Darlington did much to guide the mass of farmers toward better practices. Professors Francis S. Holmes and Charles U. Shepard, Sr., of Charleston did much

[34] *Annual Report of Commissioner of Agriculture, 1876,* p. 127.

to make the phosphate deposits of the state available; while Thomas G. Clemson, the son-in-law of Calhoun, as early as 1867, was being heard as the advocate of scientific agricultural education.[35] Later his ideas were to bear fruit in the college which bears his name.

Many writers were of the opinion that the farmers of South Carolina made a mistake in concentrating to such a high degree on the production of cotton. By 1876 almost as much cotton was produced as in 1860, without a similar recovery in other lines. Undoubtedly the farmers suffered from this absorption. The greater and greater cotton crops produced in South Carolina and the other Southern states after 1865 led to a steady fall in price; in other words, the efforts of the farmers resulted in the destruction of the very conditions they wished to enjoy. Moreover, they suffered from irritating debts contracted in the purchase of the large amounts of fertilizer and provisions which the concentration on cotton made necessary. The following was a typical criticism of these practices: "We made cotton to buy Yankee trash; to buy western corn, meat and mules, heedlessly destroying our homesteads by the most barbarous system of agriculture; our cotton fields are hideous wastes—monuments to a people's folly."[36]

But it is likely that the farmers were wiser than their critics. What satisfactory substitutes could they have found for cotton? Some advocated the establishment of factories, but such developments were impossible due to lack of capital. Viniculture, fishing, and other industries wholly out of keeping with the practices of the people were advocated. The most sagacious advocate of diversification suggested that olives and bananas be grown along the coast![37] Aside from corn and sweet potatoes, which were produced in ample quantities, the state made

---

[35] See his papers in *Land We Love*, II (Feb., 1867), 245-52, and in *Proceedings of the Agricultural and Mechanical Society, 1869.*

[36] *News*, Jan. 23, 1867.

[37] Harry Hammond, p. 475.

a poor showing in its attempts to produce the other great food staples. Its average yield per acre of wheat, rye, oats, barley, hay and Irish potatoes was nearly always less than that of any other state in the Union.[38] The relative meagerness of forage, due to excessive heat and dryness, made the raising of cattle in competition with the West and North impractical. On the other hand, conditions made the cultivation of cotton profitable. The quality of the soil, and the moderate rainfall and excessive heat of summer, the very characteristics which hindered diversity, made South Carolina one of the regions of the world almost ideal for the difficult art of cotton culture. The decline in prices, due to so-called overproduction, was the inevitable result of the return of the South to normal conditions. This decline was not so rapid as some imagined; prices did not fall to the level of 1868 until 1878.[39] The decline was not without advantages; it tended to destroy foreign competition.

It was largely through the profits from cotton that the economic rehabilitation of the state was effected. In 1873 William M. Shannon, after extensive observations, proved that larger profits could be derived from cotton than from corn, and he told of instances in which cotton farmers, out of the proceeds of one year's harvest, were able to purchase the land on which their cotton was produced. "Spite of old complications; spite of fraud, corruptions, unequal, unjust and burdensome taxation, and in spite of the inefficiency of labor," he concluded, "the farmers have prospered by and through the cotton plant."[40]

Under such conditions, it is not surprising to find that the profits from investments in farms were high. A writer in the *Rural Carolinian* showed that the investment of $47,091,709 in South Carolina farms in 1873 brought a gross return, after

[38] *Annual Report of Commissioner of Agriculture, 1869*, pp. 27, 35-37; *1870*, pp. 29, 37-38; *1872*, p. 25; etc.
[39] Frederick W. Moore, *The South in* the Building of the Nation, VI, 402-4.
[40] *Rural Carolinian*, IV (Aug., 1873), 567-71. Cf. D. Wyatt Aiken, in *Fairfield Herald*, Apr. 17, 1867.

reducing what was paid for wages, of $34,680,524, which was 73.8 per cent; whereas, the corresponding figures for Illinois for the same year were $955,082,933 and $192,859,600, which was a return of only 20.18 on the investment.[41] A survey made seven years later showed that the annual production of South Carolina farms was worth 47 per cent of the capital outlay, as compared with 18 per cent for the whole United States.[42]

* * * * *

It was inevitable that so spirited a class as the white farmers should protest against the new agricultural credit system which is described elsewhere.[43] The poverty inherited from the war filled them with a spirit of jealousy and disappointment which was almost as likely to be expressed in hatred for the upstart tradesmen, who were succeeding at their expense, as against upstart Northerners and Negroes. There was, as has been shown, a clamor for "stay laws" in 1866 and 1867. In the latter year mobs threatened the executors of legal processes, and soon bitter protests against the lien system began to appear.

These protests came to a head in 1871, when a national organization, which promised to eliminate this and other agricultural evils, was introduced into the state. It was the Patrons of Husbandry. Its leaders were Aiken and Colonel D. H. Jacques, the joint editors of the *Rural Carolinian*. The Grange, as the Patrons of Husbandry was called for short, said Aiken, "is a secret association of persons, males over eighteen and females over sixteen, interested in agricultural pursuits and bound together by mystic ties for the purpose of mutual benefit and protection. . . . It proposes to impress upon the farmer the mournful, but long since patent truth, that he had been the pack-horse for all other parties; that he has been the dupe, the very scapegoat of speculators and middlemen of every shape,

---

[41] *Rural Carolinian*, VI (Dec., 1874), 151. Cf. Aiken, *ibid.*, VI (June, 1874), 455.

[42] *Handbook of S. C., 1883*, p. 573.

[43] See below, pp. 273-75.

size, color and description; that he has rights which, from ignorance, he has never dared maintain." The already-existing agricultural societies, according to Aiken, only gave information on the practice of farming; whereas, the Grange would give protection against fraudulent merchants and high freight rates and provide such mutual benefits as nursing the sick, assisting poor members, and furnishing coöperative buying and selling agencies.[44] It did not court disunity by engaging in politics. The order was, on principle, opposed to such activities, and the whites were in no humor to tolerate the injection of new issues into politics at a time they were trying to rid the state of Radicals.

In the years following its introduction, the Grange grew rapidly. In January, 1873, the first state convention of the order was held. One hundred and eleven local granges were represented. By 1875 the number of local granges had risen to 350, and the state organization was said to have been the most powerful in the South.

It is not exactly clear what the activities of the order were. In the beginning the farmers doubtless got much pleasure from its social activities—the speeches, the ritual, the opportunity to meet each other. Some coöperative purchasing was undertaken.[45] There was talk of establishing cotton factories, banks, and even coöperative villages in the pine lands of the lowlands, from which steam plows would haul the farmers to the fields!

The Grange, however, was not destined to play a lasting part in the agricultural life of the state. As early as 1874 local granges were in decay because "captious and impatient mem-

[44] *Rural Carolinian*, II (Apr., 1871), 390, III (Dec., 1871), 115-118, and III (June, 1872), 449-51.
[45] The Sandy Spring Grange was said to have saved its members $4,000 through the coöperative purchase of fertilizers.—

Ibid., VII (June, 1876), 267; and the Sumter Grange was said to have been just as successful in the coöperative purchase of flour and cotton ties.—*Ibid.*, IV (Oct., 1872), 37.

bers say they receive no benefits."[46]   After 1875 the number of local granges declined more rapidly than they had previously increased.[47]   The causes of this decline were numerous.   The members became dissatisfied when the fanciful promises of the leaders were not redeemed.   The central office was abolished in 1876, because the salaries received were deemed extravagant. The attempts at coöperative buying were mismanaged by farmers turned business men.   There was far more talk than action. Moreover, the farmers lacked the resources with which to free themselves from their merchant-creditors.   They had little or no savings, and in the face of falling prices, little chance of accumulating any.   The opportunity of turning the organization into a political machine, as had been done in the West, was withstood for fear of endangering white unity.

What was left of the Grange joined hands soon after Reconstruction with the Agricultural and Mechanical Society to hold sessions at courthouse towns each summer.   The philosophy of the older organization dominated these meetings. About the only definite post-Reconstruction achievements of the order were to induce the Conservative legislature to create the office of commissioner of agriculture and to pass very moderate laws regulating railroad rates.   But since the credit system against which the Grange had complained survived the organization's period of militancy, it was natural that in later years its principles should have been revived.   This came in 1890 with the political triumph of the Farmers' Alliance under Ben Tillman.

In summary, it should be said that the Reconstruction period was characterized by changes notable in the agricultural history of the state.   It was then that a new system of labor was given form and order and the plans for the slow recovery of ante-bellum prosperity were laid.   This recovery may be

[46] "Payson," *ibid.*, VI (Nov., 1874), 90.
[47] John A. Barksdale, *ibid.*, VII (Dec., 1876), 557.

said to have been achieved between 1900 and 1910, for it was then that the value of all farm property reached the level of 1860.[48]   Other notable developments were the breaking of the plantations into small units of management, and the rise of a new credit system and of the small town with its new merchant aristocracy.

But it should not be assumed that the agricultural life of the state was entirely made over during Reconstruction. Some had predicted that the Negro would dominate the agricultural life of the state, becoming the owner of the soil. Others predicted that the rising energy of the new white democracy would drive the black man from the state. But neither of these predictions materialized. Both races remained in about the same proportions and in about the same relative positions as before the war. The Negro continued to be the tiller of the soil and the white man continued to be the owner. Moreover, the prediction that freedom would mean less interest in the cultivation of cotton and the breaking of the plantations into small proprietorships, did not come to pass in anything like the degree expected. Cotton and large proprietorships continued to dominate the agricultural life of South Carolina.

[48] *Census of 1910*, VII, 494.

CHAPTER X

TOWNS, CREDIT, AND COMMERCE

THE efforts of South Carolinians to revive prosperity were many and varied; in some cases considerable success was achieved, but the story of the results is not a happy one. Those who dreamed of a New South were disappointed; yet their efforts were not wholly unavailing and are worth our attention.

Some few were prompt to say that the emancipation of the slaves, even though attended by a disorganized system of labor, was a blessing. Joseph LeConte said "an intolerable burden" had been lifted from his shoulders. To the astonishment of his friends, he asserted that the freeing of the slaves was not necessarily a loss of property, certainly not a loss in the sense in which the burning of a house was. This was only saying that slaves were not property, or chattels, in the sense in which other things were. The right claimed was to their labor and the change was simply from a slave-system to a wage-system. He contended that if the labor remained reliable, the market value of the slaves would be transferred bodily to the land, for the income from the land would be certainly as great as ever; and the value of the land, "as in every other investment," was "determined wholly by the income."[1]

A premature prophet of the New South was Governor Perry. He saw a vision of a diversified agricultural and industrial South Carolina. Pointing out the weaknesses of the ante-bellum régime—the drain on the energies of the state by the removal of wealth and population to the southwest, the neglect of manufactures, the contempt for commerce, the suspicion of foreign immigration, the failure to establish diversified agricul-

[1] *The Autobiography of Joseph LeConte,* pp. 232-33.

ture—he said that immigration should be encouraged,[2] everything used on the farm should be raised at home, those who had spent their lives in ease and luxury should become tradesmen, manufacturers, and artisans; this would be the making of an "independent people."[3]

An anonymous writer in *DeBow's Review*[4] saw evidence of hope for the future of South Carolina. Taxes were low, free schools would soon be opened, the constitution was liberal toward immigrants, there were one thousand miles of railroad, steam packets plied between Charleston and Savannah and Northern cities, and energetic mechanics were in great demand. He saw forests invaluable for lumber and turpentine; he spoke of the economic possibilities of the persimmon, a "most delicious fruit," which could be dried like a fig, or distilled into brandy, or made into "a very refreshing and agreeable beer." Aiken had many advantages as a health resort, many railroad projects were under way, saw mills were profitable, and there was an extensive paper mill at Bath. A traveling agent for the *Review* noted an "active spirit of enterprise," especially in his native city of Charleston, and the din of improvement, he said, was heard everywhere.[5]

The newspapers carried many optimistic comments. Wrote "Marlboro" in 1868: "What is there to prevent the return of prosperity to the South? It is here now! Even the Negroes have rolls of bank bills in their hands, and the stores are crowded with them. . . . Lands are appreciating in value; cotton lands are sought with avidity. Proprietors are no longer anxious to sell—their pockets are getting full, and they do not know what to invest in."[6] In Camden merchants had made their calculations for a large trade, cotton was coming in freely,

---

[2] It was proper to break up the plantations by selling to Northerners and immigrants. Instead of a population of 700,000 the state could support 7,000,000, said Perry.

[3] *House Journal, Extra Sess., 1865*, pp. 14-15.

[4] Second series, II (July, 1866), 38-49; *ibid.* (Sept., 1866), 262-74.

[5] *Ibid.*, 111.

[6] *News*, Nov. 13, 1868.

and the streets were often crowded as in the "good old days of Adam and Eve."[7] And indicative of a little relaxation in the stringency of the times was the fact than many of the Methodist ministers who went to the annual conferences wore new coats.[8]

A correspondent of the Baltimore *Gazette* observed: "What with carpet-bag officials, scalawag judges, and Negro representatives and jurymen, there is but one liberty left South Carolina. That is the liberty of making money, and of this the Carolinians are bent on availing themselves."[9] In 1872 an editorial in the *Charleston Daily News* stated that "in spite of the rapacity and tyranny" of its rulers, South Carolina was better off than at any time since the war.[10]

In the efforts to revive the prosperity of the state, cotton was not forgotten. In May, 1865, it was felt that there would be a brisk trade in cotton between Charleston and the towns of the interior. A number of Charleston merchants had taken stocks of goods to points on the Northeastern and South Carolina railroads and offered to take cotton in exchange for merchandise; people in the country wanted dry goods and groceries but had no cash. With the cotton situation made easier by increased production and good prices, the people needed better facilities for transportation since wagons and mules were scarce.[11] The purchasers of cotton and rice were reaping a rich harvest, and after the 25 per cent tax was taken off cotton, that article went "forward to market in large quantities."[12] By every steamer Northern men of capital were coming to invest in cotton and rice. The result of this trade would be that in a

[7] *Ibid.*

[8] *Ibid.*, Dec. 18, 1868.

[9] Quoted in *News*, April 9, 1869.

[10] July 20, 1872.

[11] *Courier*, May 27, 1865.

[12] *Ibid.*, June 24, 1865. A tax of 25 per cent was levied on cotton by a Treasury regulation in force during 1865. Treasury regulations, May 9, 1865. Heavy taxes were levied on cotton by acts of Congress: Mar. 3, 1865, a tax of 2½c per lb.; this was increased to 3c July 13, 1866; on Sept. 1, 1867, by act of Mar. 2, 1867, the tax was reduced to 2½c, and a year later the tax was discontinued on all cotton raised after the crop of 1867.

few short years the state would be "in a more prosperous condition than ever."[13]   The Sumter correspondent of the *Courier*
wrote: "The three g's—gold, greenbacks, and groceries—bring
out the cotton and put the King once more in lively motion.
. . . He seems quite respectable still, and his society is courted
and his drafts honored at sight."[14]

* * * * *

It is interesting to note the number of South Carolinians
who were excepted from the benefits of the amnesty proclamation of May 29, 1865, because the estimated value of their taxable property was over $20,000.   The total number was at least
638,[15] but this does not compare favorably with the number in
Virginia and Georgia, which states had excepted 2,070 and
1,228 respectively; yet the number of exceptions in North Carolina was only 482.[16]   Provisional Governor Perry said that, of
the two or three thousand pardon applications which he approved, most were from persons worth more than $20,000.[17]   It
is not known whether or not this post-bellum estimate was
based on an ante-bellum valuation of land and other property.

Among the few very wealthy individuals in the state was
George W. Williams.[18]   Immediately after the war, he and
his associates resumed business and erected in the "burnt
district" of Charleston fifteen large brick warehouses at a
cost of $100,000 for the storage of cotton, merchandise, and
fertilizers.   He also rebuilt the Charleston Iron Works and
established a large cotton press.[19]   His company had bought
sterling exchange at 103 in 1861 with Confederate money; they
sold it in 1865 at 225.   Their New York brokers sold six hun-

[13] *Courier,* June 24, 1865.

[14] "Juhl," Aug. 11, 1865.

[15] *House Ex. Docs., 39th Cong., 1st Sess.,* No. 99, p. 54.

[16] *Ibid.,* p. 17.

[17] B. F. Perry, *Reminiscences, Sec. Ser.,* p. 288.

[18] A native of North Carolina, Williams was very successful in the wholesale busi-ness in Augusta, Georgia, and in 1852 es-tablished a business in Charleston. See sketch in *Cyclopedia of Eminent and Rep-resentative Men of the Carolinas of the Nineteenth Century,* I, 362.

[19] George W. Williams, *History of Banking in South Carolina, 1812-1900,* p. 13.

dred thousand sterling exchange for them, and invested in United States government 7 per cent bonds at less than par. Thus Williams and his associates were able to establish the National Bank of Charleston immediately after the war at a capitalization of $500,000.[20]

Gradually money conditions became easier, and in 1869, after the sale of marketable produce at a net profit of between $8,000,000 and $10,000,000, the statement was made that there was "more hard money in South Carolina today than there was at any time before the war."[21] Bank shares which before the war had been worth twenty-five dollars each were consolidated at two dollars and fifty cents each.[22] This consolidation enabled many banks to resume business,[23] and in 1868 there was established the Bureau of Agricultural Statistics "for the encouragement of Industrial Enterprises, and to invite capital . . . for the development of the resources of the State."[24] But due partly to the uncertain political future, capital was slow to come, and in 1870 the report of the comptroller-general listed only three banks which had resumed business since March, 1869, two others which were redeeming their bills but had not resumed business, and ten which were in the hands of receivers.[25]

In 1872 there were in Charleston three national and four state banks with a total paid up capital of $2,930,000, an increase of $2,530,000 since 1866.[26] In addition there were four savings banks with deposits of $1,155,990. This, with the cur-

[20] *Ibid.*, p. 14. This bank paid more than 12 per cent per annum to its stockholders. Arthur Mazyck, *Guide to Charleston*, p. 145. In 1866 Williams furnished $10,000 capital to a co-partner to establish a banking and brokerage business in Columbia, and two years later a profit of $8,000 was divided. This partner of Williams, Edwin J. Scott, with a capital of $75,000 furnished by his associates, made a profit of $25,000 or more during 1870-72 "without dealing harshly or illiberally with any customer."—Edwin J. Scott, *Random Recollections of a Long Life, 1806-1876*, pp. 199, 207, 208.

[21] *Orangeburg News,* Aug. 14, 1869.
[22] *Stat. S. C.,* XIV, 622-23.
[23] See *News,* Nov. 24, 29, Dec. 1, 1869.
[24] *Stat. S. C.,* XIV, 118-19.
[25] *Reports and Resolutions, 1870-71,* p. 7.
[26] *The Trade and Commerce of Charleston.*

rent deposits in the other city banks, made a total deposit of $2,745,990, only $1,419,625 less than the total deposits in all the banks of the state in 1860;[27] yet the banking capital of the city had been cut from $13,000,000 to less than $3,000,000.[28]

The banking situation in Columbia was similar. In 1872 there were four banks in Columbia and also the private banking house of Edwin J. Scott. Before the war the banking capital had been about $2,300,000—estimating the capital of the Bank of the State as $1,000,000—but was now reduced to only $605,000.[29]

The panic of 1873 was not especially severe in South Carolina. Three of the state banks in Charleston suspended currency payments, but were undoubtedly solvent, and the remaining banks paid all demands.[30] In Columbia, however, the National banks suspended payment for sums exceeding $100, and the Citizens' Savings Bank went into bankruptcy.[31]

Of importance to the colored population was the National Freedmen's Savings Bank and Trust Company, established in December, 1865, as a branch of the National Freedmen's Savings Bank, which was under government control. The Freedmen's Bank served a very useful function until the failure of the parent bank. The Charleston branch in 1866 had deposits of $18,000, most of which belonged to the wealthier class of colored men.[32] In 1870 there were deposits of $165,000,[33] and

[27] Ibid.; Edward King, The Southern States of North America, p. 439.

[28] Ibid. In an address to the New England Society, Dec. 22, 1873, Richard Lathers put the banking capital of the state at $200,000 in 1865 and $4,000,000 in 1873; the total bank deposits he put at $200,000 in 1865 and $2,750,000 in 1873. On May 2, 1877, M. W. Gary in a speech in the state Senate listed the 19 banks existing in 1860 with an aggregate capital of $19,500,000; the 20 banks of 1877 he gave an aggregate capital of only $3,750,000.

[29] Phoenix, Jan. 7, 1872; for an estimate which reduced the banking capital of $5,000,000 in 1860 to half that amount in 1871 see, Columbia, The Future Manufacturing and Commercial Centre of the South, p. 60. Columbia presented "an almost unrivalled field for converting small cash into very large profits."

[30] News and Courier, Sept. 27, 1873.

[31] Scott, Random Recollections of a Long Life, p. 208.

[32] News and Courier, Aug. 1, 1873.

[33] Robert Somers, The Southern States Since the War, 1870-71, pp. 54-55.

in 1873 the Charleston branch had nearly $350,000 on deposit belonging to 5,500 depositors. Only about 200 depositors were white; the rest were colored people whose accounts varied from five cents to one thousand dollars. The bank paid 6 per cent interest, compounded in January and July of each year.[34]

Unhappily for the freedmen, the parent bank in Washington failed in 1874, and the Charleston and Beaufort branches were closed without depositors being paid. The Charleston branch owed its 5,296 depositors a total of $253,168.35; the Beaufort branch owed its 1,200 depositors a total of $77,216.79.[35]

The laws of the state against usury had been repealed in 1866,[36] and the price of money immediately soared. In 1870 a traveler found complaints of the usurious rates charged for money quite general in the farming communities. Twenty-five and 30 per cent was taken by banks and people who had money to lend.[37] In the towns rates were not so exorbitant, but the banks turned over money at 18 to 24 per cent.[38]

In 1869 the South Carolina National Bank in Columbia issued certificates of deposit drawing interest at the rate of 7 per cent on sums deposited to remain thirty days or more.[39] Charleston considered herself fortunate to be able to borrow money for 7 per cent whereas a few months previous it had been 18 and 12 per cent.[40] In 1870 an attempt to revive the usury law failed. The *Charleston Daily News* opposed the bill because it failed to cheapen money—efforts to compel a bank to take $7.00 for what was worth $12.00 only made money harder to obtain.[41] Perhaps such a condition helps to explain the fact that in 1867 there were 541 cases of bankruptcy in the

[34] *News and Courier*, Aug. 1, 1873.

[35] *News and Courier*, Dec. 30, 1874. This paper carried on a vigorous campaign for Congress to reimburse the freedmen. Cf. W. L. Fleming, *The Freedmen's Saving Bank*.

[36] *Stat. S. C.*, XIII, p. 462.

[37] Somers, *The Southern States Since the War*, p. 57.

[38] *Ibid.*, p. 45; speech of M. W. Gary in state Senate, May 2, 1877.

[39] *Tri-Weekly Phoenix*, Dec. 2, 1869.

[40] *News*, June 29, 1869.

[41] *Ibid.*, Dec. 28, 1870.

Charleston district.[42]   In 1873 it was said to be impossible to raise money in Columbia.   All the banks had ceased discounting notes, even upon the best collaterals.   They already had out every dollar they could spare with safety, and borrowers offering 2 per cent per month, with good security, went begging.[43]

Closely connected with the monetary situation was the system of farm credits inaugurated with the change from slave to free labor.   Under the old régime, credit and farm supplies had been furnished to farm managers through factors dwelling in Charleston and Augusta.   The freeing of the slaves and the collapse of the financial arrangements of the Confederacy well-nigh destroyed this system.   Yet after the war there was a great demand for credit.   Land and labor remained as almost the only forms of wealth, and the necessity of making a living stimulated the search for capital with which to put the land and labor to work.   Since the changes of emancipation had broken the plantations into small units of management, there was a demand for small credit.   To meet this demand the merchants were forced to devise the crop lien system.   Because the farmers were unable to pay cash for the supplies necessary to run their farms, the merchants had to secure their investments by mortgages on the prospective crops.   Such an expedient was of great service in the years immediately following the war, since it was a means through which labor without capital could begin farming on its own account.   But this system continued in later years and even grew stronger in spite of the steady increase in the productive capacity of the state.

[42] *Ibid.*, Dec. 9, 1870.
[43] *News and Courier,* June 5, 1873.   In 1877 in a speech on a bill to regulate the the rate of interest, M. W. Gary said that bankers had borrowed money in New York and other commercial centers at six and seven per cent and "loaned it to our poor farmers and planters at from twenty to forty per cent."   "The drawing in of money into a State, upon rates of usury, is not an acquisition to the capital of the State; but, on the contrary, it is a loss of capital, for the original principal will eventually revert to the foreign owner, with the addition of usurious interest, the State being the loser, in the end, the amount of interest charged and collected."   —Speech of May 2, 1877.

It put the farmer at the mercy of the merchant, who dictated what should be planted and who charged extortionate rates on the advances made. The merchant demanded that cotton, which could be turned into cash most readily, be planted even when the interests of a sound economy demanded diversification.

The extent and nature of the new credit system is made clear by the survey made by Harry Hammond in 1880. It was so prevalent that in the eleven counties of the Red Hill Belt (excluding Union) there were 30,205 liens on the farms, a number almost equal to the number of farms in that area. However, it is not probable that more than half of the farms were under lien, since many carried more than one. The advances made by the merchants consumed from one-third to seven-eighths of the crop, leaving the farmer so depleted of resources that he was forced to mortgage the crop of the following year. Conditions in typical low-country counties were described by Hammond. Of Williamsburg he said, "The system of credit and advances on the growing crop prevails largely, from one-half to three-quarters of the farmers, black and white, receive such assistance." Of Clarendon he said, "The liens for advances . . . for the year number 2,716, or one for every farm save nine, and aggregate $283,317.18." The exact nature of these mortgages was described as follows: "The lien is a bond for the payment of a specific amount—usually about $100—given to the storekeeper by the farmer, and pledging the growing crop as collateral security. On this acknowledgment of indebtedness—which by act of the legislature covers the entire crop of the party giving it—the farmer receives from time to time during the crop season such supplies as may be agreed on between him and the storekeeper. These liens, bonds, or mortgages on the growing crop are recorded in the office of the clerk of court. . . . This record gives these debts precedence of other indebtedness. The collection of these liens is equally simple, cheap, and prompt. On affidavit of the lien holder that he believes his debtor means to avoid payment, the clerk of the court orders the sheriff to seize the crop, and sell the whole, or so much of it as will pay the debt with costs, and to devote the proceeds to these purposes."[44]

That such a system survived the degree of agricultural prosperity already described was due to several causes. The farmers of the state failed to practise that close economy which agricultural people the world over seem to find necessary. The normal tendency of the farmers to be extravagant[45] was accentuated by special circumstances. The fact that they realized their earning shortly before Christmas, the great holiday season, and that they knew they could get additional advances after New Year's, made them careless in expenditures. Borrowed money, which seemed to come easily, was spent easily. The white farmers, sharing with the freedmen the errors just mentioned, were in some respects less economical. Cherishing the hope of wealth through concentration on cotton, they often invested too heavily in lands and fertilizer, only to have their visions of profit turn into a reality of increased debt because of a crop failure or fall in prices. Inefficiency in farm management likewise reduced profits and increased the burden of the credit system.

Another reason for the perpetuation of the lien system was the high rate of interest which the merchant was able to exact. Hammond estimated in 1880 that the prices charged by the merchants for goods sold to farmers under the lien law were twenty to one hundred per cent in advance of the cash

[44] Harry Hammond, *Report on Cotton Production in S. C.*, *House Misc. Doc.*, *47th Cong., 2d Sess.*, Pt. 6, pp. 517-22.— *Census*, 1880, Vol. VI. These practices were defined by the law of Sept. 20, 1866, and after the failure of efforts to repeal this enactment in 1873, they were more fully defined. *Stat. S. C.*, XVI, 265, 410, 713, etc.

[45] See below, p. 320.

prices. "When the cash price of corn is seventy-five cents," he said, "the credit price is not infrequently $1.25 and upward."[46] According to the *Rural Carolinian* a barrel of flour which cost the merchant $8.00 was sold to the farmer for $12; a pound of bacon which cost twelve cents was sold for eighteen; and a gallon of molasses which cost forty cents was sold for seventy-five cents.[47] Thus an interest of 50 per cent was exacted from goods sold in the spring and paid for in November. According to an authoritative writer, the planter who borrowed $1,000 with which to purchase supplies was forced to pay $300 to the commission merchant who bought the supplies; another $300 when the goods were sold; $120 interest on the money; and a commission of $25 for selling the cotton, the returns of which were to satisfy the indebtedness.[48] Under such conditions many planters sank deeper and deeper into debt; the Negro, careless and philosophical as he was, soon came to regard indebtedness as his natural fate. Some even became peons when they refused to resist the pressure of creditors who forced them to work out what they owed.

There were two main reasons why such high rates of interest were in effect. As has been indicated, there was a great scarcity of capital coupled with a great demand for that which was available. This demand grew out of the prevailing desire to plant cotton and the great increase in the number of farm operators. Secondly, it was a tremendous risk to lend money on crops before they were planted. There was much likelihood of the creditor's losing in the bargain—through a crop failure, a fall in the price of cotton, and the flight of the tenant before harvest time or his making away with the crop at night. The rural white, perhaps to a greater degree than the Negro, was generally inclined not to pay his debts unless forced to do so by

---

[46] Hammond, *Report on Cotton Production in S. C., House Misc. Doc.,* 47 Cong., 2 Sess., pp. 517-18.

[47] VII (April, 1876), 178-79.

[48] "Paysan," in *Rural Carolinian,* V (Sept., 1874), 643-44.

law; especially was this true after they became convinced that the merchants were cheating them.[49]

It has been maintained by local agrarian agitators and Northern friends of the Negro that the merchants were in a conspiracy to keep the farmers in debt to them. That is hardly true. It was regarded as a favor for the merchant to make a loan to a farmer, and probably most merchants would have preferred to sell their goods for cash at the market price; and doubtless on such a basis their profits would have been greater. As the situation was, the merchant had to be a very sound realist to make even a minimum profit; for losses were almost as frequent as profits. Although many of them became rich according to local standards, none became very wealthy, and many failed where the few succeeded.

* * * * *

A phenomenon of the Reconstruction period was the rapid increase in the number of towns; and the towns found their center in the cross-roads store which became an important factor in the organization of labor and the distribution of wealth. Perhaps the chief reason for the development of the town and country store was the break-up of the old plantations into small farms, largely a result of a changed labor system. By 1880 the 33,000 plantations of 1860 were divided among 93,000 small farmers.[50] The following table[51] will illustrate this:

| | Number of Farms | |
Size of Farm	1860	1870
Under 10 acres	352	10,474
10 to 19 acres	1,219	9,146
20 to 49 acres	6,695	16,415
50 to 99 acres	6,980	8,148

[49] "The farmer learns before he lays the crop," said D. Y. Aiken, "that he is losing at such an operation, and before the harvest time nature's first law begins to work on him, and he is not solicitous as to the morality of the thing."—*Rural Carolinian*, VII, (April, 1876), 178.

[50] *Handbook of South Carolina, 1883*, p. 660.

[51] O. C. Stine and O. E. Baker, *Atlas of American Agriculture*, Pt. V. Sec. A., "Cotton," p. 22.

100 to 499 acres......................	11,369	7,112
500 acres and over...................	1,841	594

The country store was first established as an adjunct to industries other than the plantation, as a commissariat for farm hands and for those employed in saw mills and in turpentine or phosphate works. But with the destruction of the plantation system the small farmers, absorbed in their struggle with the soil and the seasons, intrusted their trading interests to the care of the country storekeeper. Near the store settled the blacksmith, the wheelwright, and the justice of the peace; eventually churches and schools were opened for the community.[52]

In 1860 there were in South Carolina only sixteen places which the census rated as towns; by 1870 this number had increased to thirty-three, an increase of over 100 per cent.[53] At the end of the next decade the same authority designated 110 towns and villages, while Harry Hammond in the same year put the number of towns and trading points at 493.[54] Of the towns enumerated by Hammond, 244 or 49 per cent, were in the piedmont region; the upper pine belt had 20 per cent, the lower pine belt 16 per cent, the coast 7 per cent, the red and sand hill regions 6 per cent, and the alpine region 2 per cent.[55] These towns contained 15 per cent of the aggregate population of the state, and the wealth of the storekeepers of the state was estimated at $40,156,000.[56]

There were only three towns in 1880 with a population over 4,000. These were Charleston, Columbia, and Greenville. The destruction and losses of the war, the changed industrial system, and the new methods of trade kept their population almost stationary.

The rebuilding of Columbia went forward slowly, although

---

[52] *Handbook of South Carolina, 1883,* pp. 659-60.
[53] *U. S. Census,* 1870, I, 258.
[54] *U. S. Census,* 1880, I, 92; *Handbook*
of *South Carolina, 1883,* p. 661.
[55] *Handbook of South Carolina, 1883,* p. 661.
[56] *Ibid.*

in the fall of 1866 workmen were observed "busily plying the trowel and the plane in every direction."[57]   The night traveler had only a few shop lights as guide.   A monument to the invader's triumph was the long rows of ruined houses and unsightly piles of chimneys that still covered a large portion of the capital city;[58] the city's finances and the poverty of its citizens prevented improvements.[59]   A carpetbagger observed in 1870 that "Main Street, a vista of ruins, had been but half rebuilt, mostly after the shack models of a frontier town."   Of the old bridge over the Congaree only naked piers remained, and crossings were effected on flat boats.   "As the city and its environs then appeared, Columbia needed no voice to proclaim her a conquered place."[60]   By 1877 the town had been rebuilt to a large extent, and many of the better houses were for sale cheap since their carpetbag owners were disappearing.[61]   In the early years of Reconstruction, real estate in Columbia was said to have risen 100 per cent in value,[62] the taxable real and personal property totaled $2,768,407, and non-taxable property consisting of public buildings, churches, and so on, was valued at $2,367,000.[63]   Good houses, containing four or six rooms, could be rented for two to four hundred dollars per annum, and "elegant and capacious mansions, possessing all modern conveniences," could be had for $600 per annum.[64]   There were five "leading" hotels, having accommodations for about 425 guests.[65]

Charleston, much more the center of wealth and trade than Columbia, never quite regained its commercial eminence of

[57] *Fairfield Herald*, Sept. 12, 1866. See also J. F. Williams, *Old and New Columbia*, pp. 125-37.

[58] *News*, Jan. 7, 1867.

[59] *Ibid.*, Jan. 7, Aug. 30, 1867.

[60] Louis Post, "A 'Carpetbagger' in South Carolina," in *Journal of Negro History*, X (Jan., 1925), 14; for an English traveler's impression see Somers, *The Southern States Since the War*, pp. 56-57.

[61] Sir George Campbell, *White and Black*, pp. 318-19.

[62] *News*, Jan. 5, 1869.

[63] *Courier*, Mar. 4, 1869.

[64] *Columbia, The Future Manufacturing and Commercial Centre*, p. 51.

[65] *Ibid.*; for a discussion of the industries of Columbia, see below, pp. 295-96.

ante bellum days. The city debt in 1865 was $4,715,058 and by 1870 had increased to $5,241,709,[66] whereas the value of real estate had fallen from $25,690,000 in 1861 to $18,121,200 in 1870; by 1871 it increased $531,385.[67] However, the city set to work to rebuild its fortunes and undoubtedly made much progress. New constructions were soon under way, streets and buildings were repaired and rebuilt, merchants and factors noted a gradual revival of business, the Chamber of Commerce was active, and many old establishments again became centers of trade. Among the constructions was a street railway, completed in December, 1866, and inaugurated by the mayor and William Gilmore Simms midst the flow of wines and liquors.[68] Railroads were repaired and the city put in communication with every part of the country;[69] the Northeastern Railroad built a new depot and was the first to resume night trips.[70] Sidewalks were repaved and protected from carts by strong wooden curbs, and it was hoped that soon one would be able to travel at night without fear of falling into a bog hole.[71] By 1869 the 222 streets, courts, and lanes were lighted by 290 lamps at an operating cost of $23,460 per annum.[72]

Improvements were noted in the wholesale district on East Bay Street. The wharves were crowded with cotton, and the consequent travel of loaded drays, in spite of desperately muddy streets, was almost what it was in the palmiest days.[73] King Street still preserved its character as a fashionable promenade and the number of ladies who frequented it was a gladsome sight to the storekeepers.[74] New stores were in the course of erection and old ones were being remodeled, blackened walls were disappearing,[75] some wholesale houses were working at

[66] *Report of Subcommittee on Debt and Elections of the Late Insurrectionary States*, p. 125; *Charleston Year Book, 1881*, p. 1.
[67] *Ibid.*
[68] *Courier*, Dec. 17, 1866.
[69] *News*, Feb. 15, 1867.
[70] *Courier*, Feb. 2, 1867.
[71] *News*, Jan. 29, 1867.
[72] *Ibid.*, Aug. 31, 1869.
[73] *Ibid.*, Jan. 5, 1867.
[74] *Ibid.*, Jan. 10, 1867.
[75] *Ibid.*, Nov. 15, 1867.

night;[76] an evidence of prosperity was the many planters who visited the city, secured credit, and ordered guano, corn, salt, and agricultural implements.[77]

While prospects for trade looked brighter, the destruction of property and the collapse of the railroads turned trade to other places with which Charleston was in no condition to compete.[78] Yet the *Charleston Daily News* felt that "notwithstanding the depression of trade incident to a small cotton crop, bad debts, and unpaid loans, we have moved steadily forward until the contrast between 1865 and 1868 has become marked and well defined."[79]

An improvement in Charleston municipal affairs was noted in 1868. The balance in the city treasury August, 1867, had been $37,987 with $12,000 city bills in circulation, but a year later the treasury balance was $81,713 with no city bills in circulation.[80] Municipal politics, however, were by no means pleasant, and even when a fusion Democrat, John A. Wagener, was elected mayor, the city remained in control of Republicans.[81]

Charleston found her progress toward prosperity slow and painful. Thurlow Weed found it "impossible . . . to remain insensible to the destitution and sufferings of her most wealthy . . . most estimable families,"[82] and a correspondent of the *New York Tribune* thought it "singular to see parsley and wild grass growing up through flagging, and rising to the door sills of wholesale houses in streets strictly devoted to commerce."[83] In 1868 a member of the Charleston bar said that the most fortunate of his colleagues had scarcely done more than make a

[76] *Ibid.*, Feb. 10, 1867.
[77] *Ibid.*, Feb. 28, 1867.
[78] *Ibid.*, July 27, 1867; July 14, 1868.
[79] June 17, 1868.
[80] Report of city treasurer for Aug. 31, 1868, in *News*, Oct. 26, 1868.
[81] *Charleston Year Book, 1881*, pp. 255-

63. In May, 1868, the board of aldermen was composed of 11 whites and 7 Negroes. *News*, May 26, 27, 29, 1868; King, *The Southern States of North America*, pp. 447-48.
[82] *News*, Feb. 2, 1869.
[83] *Ibid.*, July 8, 1869.

living. There was perhaps a little more money in circulation in Charleston than in the interior, but "clearly we are on the descending scale. Our merchants are gloomy, trade is stagnant, and every interest is suffering." Three years later during a yellow fever epidemic the city presented a "gloomy and deserted appearance; stores closed, and labeled to let. . . ."[84]

Nevertheless the people were not discouraged and signs of prosperity continued to appear. In 1870 there were two lines of steamers to New York, one each to Baltimore, Philadelphia, and Liverpool, and steamboat communications with Savannah, Beaufort, and Georgetown.[85] The discovery of phosphates was adding millions to the wealth of the people, banks were flourishing, and the hotels were full of tourists.[86] Somers found the men "with the steady fire of Anglo-Saxon courage in their eyes, attending to affairs like men determined to conquer fortune even in the depths of ruin and on the brink of the grave." The quays and wharves were busy; new ones, to meet new branches of trade, had been built with files of counting-rooms to suit; the cotton presses were again at work; "lorries laden with the staple products of the interior pour the livelong day along the streets towards the river"; and at least one handsome buggy of a dry-goods man from the North was seen on the street.[87]

The Charleston wholesale merchants had a steadily increasing business. They handled dry-goods, drugs, boots and shoes, hardware, crockery, groceries, hats and caps, fancy and millinery goods, paints and oils, tobacco, clothing, toys, and liq-

[84] Mary Doline O'Connor, *Life and Letters of M. P. O'Connor*, p. 33.

[85] *News*, July 19, 1870.

[86] *Ibid.*, July 19, 1870, Mar. 3, 1870.

[87] Somers, *The Southern States Since the War*, p. 38. In 1873 a census found Charleston with 282 grocers, 154 commission merchants, 73 dry-goods merchants, 92 lawyers, 72 doctors, 64 keepers of bar-rooms, 62 shoemakers, 61 factors, 61 fruit dealers, 45 confectioners, 37 bakers, 31 apothecaries, 29 auctioneers, 25 barbers, 23 blacksmiths, 24 builders, 22 clothiers, 27 grain merchants, 16 grist mills, 25 jewellers, 24 junk shops, 20 millinery stores, 32 tobacco and cigar dealers, 20 wood factors, 9 coal dealers, 13 music teachers, and "about 300 miscellaneous trades."—*News and Courier*, May 17, 1873.

uors.[88] The following statistics will show approximately the extent of the jobbing trade:[89]

Commodity	Per cent of increase of sales, 1871-72	Total sales
Dry goods	25	$3,000,000
Boots and shoes	12	1,200,000
Hardware	15	700,000
Clothing	25	400,000
Drugs	30	300,000
Hats and caps	15	175,000
Steam machinery and fixtures	25	. . . . . .

Charleston real estate probably reached its lowest prices in 1871. After the war there was a brisk demand for houses and vacant lots due to an unreasonable confidence in the immediate recovery of the city. The natural reaction in prices was accelerated by political troubles and by heavy taxes levied upon property. Then followed three years of unsuccessful planting, which drove many planters on the coast into bankruptcy and threw a large amount of real estate upon the market.[90] By 1872, however, the sale of vacant lots for building purposes had increased, and fair and even prices were paid.[91] There were few dwelling houses to rent in Charleston in 1872, although small houses properly located yielded a good profit; dwelling houses ranging in price from $3,000 to $5,000 were in steady demand and buildings of that class rented at rates which returned 15 to 20 per cent upon money invested.[92] During 1872, $473,800 was spent for new buildings and repairs in the city, and $177,509 was spent for similar work on Sullivan's Island.[93]

[88] *News and Courier,* Aug. 1, 1874.

[89] *The Trade and Commerce of Charleston,* p. 25.

[90] *Ibid.,* p. 27.

[91] *News,* Jan. 1, 1873.

[92] *The Trade and Commerce of Charleston,* p. 27.

[93] *Ibid.* In 1875, however, Andrew D. White visited Charleston and observed "on all sides ruins, due not only to the Civil War, but to the more recent fire and earthquake." To him it seemed "as if the vengeance of Heaven had been wrought upon the city; . . . in the days gone by a noble hospitality had centered there, but all was now silent and distressed."—Andrew D. White, *Autobiography,* II, 384-85.

A large portion of the ante-bellum wealth of South Carolina was from the production and sale of staples such as rice and cotton. The factors and merchants in the port of Charleston handled a major portion of this trade, and before the war Charleston was the principal seaport of the South Atlantic States. Naturally Charleston wished to regain the commercial prestige which had been lost during the war, and for that reason the building of railroads and the establishment of steamship lines were encouraged; the towns of the interior as well as the city merchants took a keen interest in the revival of the port of Charleston. It is worth while to note the extent of post-bellum exports of rice and cotton as well as phosphates, naval stores, and lumber, the principal exports. Elsewhere we have discussed the production of cotton[94] and the manufacture of phosphates, naval stores, and lumber. Here we are primarily concerned with these commodities only as they affected exports.

The amount of rice produced in 1866 was 12,415 tierces as compared to the 70,000 to 85,000 tierces produced previously; the acreage dropped from 30,000 to 12,950,[95] and the state which had furnished the world with the choicest rice was brought to the necessity of importing rice from India.[96] The rice exported from 1850 to 1860 was valued at $24,619,009,[97] but after the war many large rice plantations were abandoned. An English traveler heard of an estate which had been worth $500,000 before the war; after the war an offer of $275,000 was refused but by 1878 the estate had wholly broken down and was bought for $6,000.[98] The cost of reclaiming and fitting rice-lands for culture was about $100 per acre before the war, but more than half that sum was spent after the war in rehabilitating the lands, and the annual cost of cultivation per acre had increased

---

[94] See above, pp. 257, 260-61.

[95] *The American Annual Cyclopedia,* 1886.

[96] *News,* June 11, 1867.

[97] King, *The Southern States of North America,* p. 433.

[98] Campbell, *White and Black,* p. 324.

ON THE CHARLESTON WHARF

Photo Cook

from about ten to thirty dollars.[99] The rice industry gradually declined as a result, largely, of lack of financial resources, uncontrollable Negro labor, and the growing competition of wheat and oats. Competition with other rice producing countries could not be met, and the absence of sufficiently high protective duties reduced prices.[100]

The following table shows the total receipts of cotton at the port of Charleston during the Reconstruction period:[101]

Year	Bales	Price, Sept. 1 of each year
1865-66	111,714	36 @ 38
1866-67	165,316	30 @ 31
1867-68	246,018	24½ @ 25½
1868-69	206,764	28 @ 28½
1869-70	250,761	32
1870-71	256,544	17½
1871-72	282,086	18
1872-73	386,128	17¾
1873-74	437,035	15½
1874-75	419,947	13¾
1875-76	396,812	10 @ 11

The following tables show the amount of rice, naval stores, phosphates, lumber, and cotton goods exported from Charleston:[102]

RICE

Year	Tierces
1865-66	4,019
1866-67	15,337
1867-68	22,451
1868-69	35,541
1869-70	38,528
1870-71	44,017
1871-72	42,677

[99] King, *The Southern States of North America*, p. 435.
[100] *News and Courier*, May 1, 16, 1876.
[101] *News and Courier*, Sept. 1, 1876.
[102] *Ibid.*, Sept. 1, 1873, Sept. 1, 1876.

1872-73	48,943
1873-74	43,667
1874-75	46,796
1875-76	45,367

NAVAL STORES

	Barrels
1865-66	32,136
1866-67	54,026
1867-68	62,852
1868-69	72,279
1869-70	79,156
1870-71	90,297
1871-72	151,553
1872-73	225,683
1873-74	221,000
1874-75	276,222
1875-76	280,282

LUMBER

	Feet
1865-66	8,389,171
1866-67	19,831,103
1867-68	17,958,615
1868-69	18,558,652
1869-70	13,205,066
1870-71	15,728,467
1871-72	18,490,139
1872-73	20,769,280
1873-74	21,000,000
1874-75	5,242,238
1875-76	4,080,511

PHOSPHATES

Year	Tons
1872	
crude	42,153
manufactured	37,759
1873	
crude	49,838
manufactured	56,298

1874
    crude 56,413
    manufactured 46,302
1875
    crude 51,546
    manufactured 49,500
1876
    crude 52,917
    manufactured 47,381

The other principal exports were cotton goods and yarns, and vegetables. Between 1872 and 1876 over 80,000 bales of cotton goods and yarns were exported, and about 125,000 packages of vegetables were shipped annually.[103] Miscellaneous articles such as hides, porcelain clay, and wood products were also shipped.

The following table shows the total value of exports and imports by decades:[104]

	Exports	Imports
1860	$21,170,273	$1,500,570
1870	10,772,071	505,609
1880	19,590,827	202,790

Undoubtedly the commercial prosperity of South Carolina was slowly reviving; the hope of the people, though exaggerated, had not been without some foundation. However, the increase in wealth and banking capital was very slow, the new towns were not yet well established, Charleston had lost its commanding position, and manufactures were coming very haltingly.

[103] *Ibid.,* Sept. 1, 1876.   [104] *Handbook of South Carolina, 1883,* p. 680.

CHAPTER XI

THE STATUS OF MANUFACTURES

THE lack of ante-bellum industrial development in South Carolina and other Southern states, has been attributed to a variety of causes. Although in 1810 the manufactures of the Carolinas, Georgia, and Virginia surpassed those of all the New England states, long before 1860 the South was predominantly agricultural. The South relied upon the North and West and England for its provisions and manufactured articles, not because it was deficient in raw materials and manufacturing power; the chief drawback was the institution of slavery and the resultant monopoly of land by large landholders. The economic system was adjusted to the production of one staple product, cotton, and the profits from its culture were —or were thought to be—large. Moreover, it was more profitable to purchase British or New England manufactured articles than to make them at home; hence opposition in the South to a high tariff and hence nullification in South Carolina.

Nevertheless, there were a few men, such as James H. Hammond and William Gregg, who urged the establishment of manufactures and the diversification of industry within the state. Though these efforts in the main failed, some cotton factories and a few other enterprises were begun. Political leaders who feared for their pet theories on the tariff were opposed to the industrial movement, and there were pertinent economic reasons which retarded industrial development. For example, it is pointed out that the capital made available by the planters was insufficient, plants were too small for the profits to absorb overhead expenses, reliable labor was difficult to obtain, home manufactures were not patronized because goods could be bought cheaper in England or the North or because it was thought that foreign products were of better quality, and the periodic high price of cotton hindered the manufacture of that commodity.[1] In fact, between 1850 and 1860 there was an actual decline in cotton manufactures. Although the number of manufacturing establishments decreased by only one during that decade, there was a decline in the amount of capital invested of more than 7½ per cent. The number of pounds of cotton consumed decreased more than 10 per cent, and there was a corresponding decline in the value of the products and the number of hands employed.[2]

During the Civil War the resources of the state were directed into military channels. There was some increase in manufactures, especially in those necessary to the prosecution of the war, but the close of the conflict found the remaining factories in disrepair and short of capital with which to rebuild and meet the economic emergencies of the period. The partial industrialization of the state during Reconstruction is insignificant as compared with the later movement, and the little that was accomplished was done in spite of innumerable difficulties. It was not until the eighties that any important industrial expansion became generally apparent. In fact, the capital employed in 1870 was less than that of 1850. (Should the monetary figures for 1870 be reduced to a gold basis, the decrease would be about 25.3 per cent.) There were only 154 more establishments in 1870 than in 1850.[3] Furthermore, neither

[1] For an elaboration of these points see John J. Van Deusen, *Economic Bases of Disunion in South Carolina, passim,* and especially Chap. VII; Broadus Mitchell, *William Gregg, Factory Master of the Old South, passim,* and especially Chap. II.

[2]

	1850	1860
Establishments	18	17
Spindles		30,890
Capital	$ 857,200	$ 801,825
Hands employed	1,019	891
Pounds cotton consumed	4,468,050	3,978,961
Value of products	$ 842,440	$ 713,050

—*U. S. Census,* 1880, II, 542-47.

[3]

	1850	1860	1870	1880
No. establishments	1,430	1,230	1,584	2,078
Capital	$6,053,265	$6,931,756	$5,400,418	$11,205,894

the capital invested nor the value of the manufactures compared favorably with North Carolina or Georgia. In 1870 the capital invested in manufactures in North Carolina was $8,140,473, and in Georgia $13,930,125, as compared with $5,-400,418 in South Carolina. Similarly, the value of the products in North Carolina and Georgia was $19,021,327 and $31,196,115 respectively, as compared with $9,858,961 in South Carolina.[4]

To just what extent Reconstruction was responsible for the non-development of manufactures it is impossible to say. One must consider such factors as the economic losses of the war, the scarcity of capital, the unsettled political conditions, and the fear of Northern investors to send their money into the state. One must remember also that many prejudices against manufactures and their concomitants still persisted. It is generally true, however, that the newspapers and the publicists of the period favored the encouragement of manufactures and the development of the natural resources of the state. Industrial enterprises were given considerable space and fulsome praise in the newspapers, and editors never ceased to predict a prosperous state. However that may be, the "Prostrate State" was in no position to help itself and had fallen apparently so low that no one else wished to help it.

There were those who contended that the small amount of capital in the state should be turned to the development of agricultural resources. Manufactures, they said, must necessarily be carried on in competition with the North and England; the North demanded a protective tariff to compete with foreign countries, and it was impossible for the South to compete with the North. The population was too small; capital had to accede to labor; and in the South the cost of labor was higher than in England.[5]

Hands	7,066	6,994	8,141	15,828
Wages $1,127,712	$1,380,027	$1,543,715	$ 2,836,289
Cost of material $2,787,534	$5,198,881	$5,855,736	$ 9,885,538
Value of products $7,045,447	$8,615,195	$9,858,981	$16,738,008

[4] *Ibid.*, p. 16.   [5] *Winnsboro News*, Dec. 1, 1866.

But in general there was little opposition to manufactures; there was only the question of how they could be induced and where the necessary capital could be secured. Some objected to the infiltration of Northern capital; they were afraid that Charleston and Columbia might become Yankee cities; better to seek aid in Europe rather than humiliate oneself by receiving Northern capital.[6] Indeed, Northern gentlemen who inquired about the difficulties of investing in Southern property were dissuaded by the uncertainty of labor, the high price of supplies, the possible future low price of cotton, and the uncertainty as to what course political Reconstruction would take.[7]

Naturally if manufactures were to be developed it must be by private enterprise, but the state also sought to encourage such activity. For example, the Conservative legislature of 1865 in enacting a tax law provided that assessments for taxes on property used in manufacturing, or for railroad purposes, should not include the value of machinery, but only the value of the lots and buildings "as property merely."[8] In the first Radical legislature a resolution was passed by the House which provided that a special committee should report, if they deemed advisable, a plan whereby the "manufacture of cotton and other staples may be promoted . . . and whether it may be necessary or advisable to extend the faith and credit of the State to the development of manufacturing enterprises."[9] While the *Charleston Daily News* in general opposed such subsidies, it could not say too much in "praise of the spirit which prompted such enterprise."[10]

Governor R. K. Scott, in his second message to the legislature, submitted "for consideration" the propriety of exempting from taxation, for five years, all capital thereafter invested in the state.[11] Scott's successor, F. J. Moses, Jr., recommended

[6] Carl Schurz, *Reminiscences*, III, 166-67.
[7] *Charleston Daily Courier*, Feb. 22, 23, 1866.
[8] *Acts, 1865*, p. 4.
[9] *House Journal, 1868-69*, pp. 80, 129.
[10] December 10, 1868.
[11] *House Journal, 1869-70*, p. 36.

the "speedy passage" of a law providing that cotton and wool manufactories receive a "bonus" equal to the state tax, such bonus to be continued for five years after the factory went into actual operation.[12] In December, 1873, the legislature passed an act to "aid and encourage manufactures." This act provided that capital invested in the manufacture of "cotton, woolen and paper fabrics, iron, lime, and of agricultural implements" should be exempt from state, county, and municipal taxation, with the exception of two mills for school purposes, for the space of ten years. Enterprises completed since January 1, 1872, or improvements added since that date, and all vessels of one hundred tons measurement or upwards built and owned within the state, were included in the provisions of the act.[13]

* * * * *

In spite of this legislative encouragement and the efforts of its citizens to engage in profitable manufactures, the state made no great strides forward. Industrially, at least, South Carolina was noticeably behind the neighboring states. Its five leading industries were the production of flour and grist mill products, lumbering, tar and turpentine manufacturing, cotton milling, and the fertilizer and phosphate business. These industries, according to the census of 1880, furnished 78 per cent of the aggregate products of manufactures in the state.[14]

The products of the flour and grist mills amounted to 22 per cent of the products of all manufactures. For at least two decades the milling industry had been developing consistently, and there was a rapid increase in the number of establishments during the war and Reconstruction.[15] This is doubtless ac-

---

[12] *Senate Journal, 1872-73,* p. 240; *Phoenix,* December 18, 1872; *Charleston Daily News,* January 15, 1873.

[13] *Stat. S. C.,* XV, 513-14.

[14] *Handbook of South Carolina, 1883.* p. 607.

[15]

	1860	1870	1880
No. establishments	270	624	720
Capital	$ 639,525	$ 835,814	$1,339,262
Hands	355	1,138	1,052

counted for by the break-up of the large plantations and the establishment of more towns and villages with numerous centers of trade.

The sawing of lumber was a considerable industry and formed 12 per cent of the manufactured products of the state in 1880. It is interesting to note, however, that during the period between 1860 and 1870, the census reports a decrease of 37 per cent in the number of establishments, 61 per cent in the amount of capital, 4 per cent in the number of hands, but a 7 per cent increase in the value of the products. There were about 20,000 square miles in the lower part of the state timbered in pine. The next most important timber was the cypress; other trees included the live oak for shipbuilding, hardwoods, such as the persimmon, for cogs of motive wheels, the dogwood for shuttles, and the white oak for staves.[16]

Likewise, the Reconstruction period marked a sharp decline in the tar and turpentine industry of the state. The capital invested in that industry in 1870 was only 78 per cent of what it had been in 1860, and the value of the manufactured product was off nearly 30 per cent. By 1880, however, the number of tar and turpentine establishments exceeded that of 1870 by more than thrice, and the value of the products had more than doubled.[17]

Wages	$ 66,424	$ 109,386	$ 139,352
Materials	$1,517,366	$2,663,423	$3,265,485
Products	$1,757,174	$3,180,247	$3,779,470

—U. S. Census, 1880, II, 183; U. S. Census, 1870, 568; Handbook of South Carolina, 1883, p. 603.

[16]

	1860	1870	1880
No. establishments	361	227	420
Capital	$1,145,116	$ 583,425	$1,056,265
Hands	1,263	1,212	1,468
Wages	$ 219,361	$ 209,806	$ 221,963
Materials	$ 498,290	$ 581,499	$1,237,361
Products	$1,125,640	$1,197,005	$2,031,507

—U. S. Census, 1880, II, 173; U. S. Census, 1870, III, 569; Handbook of South Carolina, 1883, p. 605.

[17]

	1860	1870	1880
No. establishments	95	54	192
Capital	$ 931,270	$205,425	$ 565,290

It is interesting to note that South Carolina "furnishes the only instance in the history of the country of a state having wholly abandoned the manufacture of iron." In 1856 the state had eight furnaces—one in York, one in Union, and six in Spartanburg County, the old "iron district." Four of these furnaces were then in operation, producing 1,506 tons of charcoal iron, but three others had been out of repair for twenty years, and the remaining furnace had been abandoned. In 1856 there were also three small rolling mills in the state—one on the Pacolet River, in Spartanburg County; one on the Broad River, in Union; and one on the same river in York County. Their joint product was 640 tons of blooms.[18] The census of 1870 indicated that iron manufactures still survived,[19] but the census of 1880 showed no activity whatever in that business.

The five machine shops or "iron-works" in Charleston in 1872 furnished employment to 272 hands, represented $460,000 capital and produced $410,000 worth of manufactured articles. All these shops had foundries attached, in which the "heaviest castings" were made.[20] Columbia in 1871 had four iron works. The Congaree Iron Works had been rebuilt after the fire of 1865 and were manufacturing "steam engines of all kinds, smut machines, bells, iron and brass castings, etc." The Phoenix shops established in 1865 employed about 25 hands and used annually about 200 tons of imported Scotch pig iron.

Hands	1,432	876	4,619
Wages	$ 150,124	$123,645	$ 555,460
Materials	$ 619,555	$422,378	$ 666,179
Products	$1,096,974	$774,077	$1,893,206

—*U. S. Census*, 1880, II, 184; *U. S. Census*, 1870, II, 659; *Handbook of South Carolina, 1883*, p. 606.   [18] *U. S. Census*, 1880, II, 833.

[19]

	No. establishments	Capital	Products
Iron blooms	2	$12,000	$ 8,475
forged and rolled	2	20,000	22,190
pigs	2	20,000	8,200
castings	7	64,251	119,750

—*U. S. Census*, 1880, II, 568.

[20] Arthur Mazyck, *Guide to Charleston*, p. 98; *The Trade and Commerce of Charleston*.

Iron store fronts were made, as well as "large quantities of iron railings for gardens, verandas, and cemeteries." They also manufactured steam engines, mills, castings, and a patented cotton press. The City Iron Works were not so extensive as the others; the Palmetto Iron Works, rebuilt in 1868, made "all kinds of machinery" of the "highest order."[21] Spartanburg established a foundry in 1875.[22]

There were several planing mills in Columbia and Charleston which appear to have been fairly prosperous. In 1866 P. P. Toale established a door and sash factory in Charleston. He later built a larger factory and employed fifty or sixty workmen in making all sorts of building materials.[23] By 1875 there were five such industries in the city. They represented a capital of about $187,000 in buildings, grounds, machinery, and cost of operating, and turned out nearly $250,000 worth of material per year. A company was also established to manufacture ready-made houses and churches.[24] In Columbia there were Wing's and Allen's saw and planing mills; Allen's occupied nearly two acres of ground and was run by an engine of forty-five horsepower.[25]

In 1870 E. P. Alexander, Johnson Hagood, John Bratton, and other business men of the city, incorporated the Columbia Oil Company "for the purpose of extracting and manufacturing oil from cotton seed, and other seeds or grain."[26] The capital was $30,000 and they erected a factory near the South Carolina Railroad which was capable of producing 3,000 gallons of oil per week. The three grades manufactured were Southern yellow, which was a good paint oil; salad oil, "equal to the best imported olive oil," and one-third cheaper than lard; and white oil, a substitute for linseed oil. Since the cot-

[21] *Columbia, the Future Manufacturing and Commercial Centre of the South*, p. 46.

[22] *Spartanburg Herald*, June 9, 1875.

[23] *News and Courier*, Sept. 4, 1875.

[24] *The Trade and Commerce of Charleston.*

[25] *Columbia, the Future Manufacturing and Commercial Centre*, p. 48.

[26] *Stat. S. C.*, XIV, 333-34.

ton seed hulls were not valued for stock food, they were used as fuel and the ashes recommended as top dressing for turnips. The cake, however, was used for stock food.[27]   Two years later the Beaufort Manufacturing and Improvement Company was incorporated by certain of the Negro members of the legislature and their friends for the manufacture of oil.[28]

Near Columbia was a broom factory employing about thirty hands; the brooms were made from straw grown in the West. The car shops of the Charlotte, Columbia and Augusta Railroad occupied about four acres of ground and manufactured locomotives, passenger and freight cars, and various kinds of machinery.   The brewery of John C. Seegers was said to manufacture beer equal to that of Philadelphia or Cincinnati; the same plant made 8,000 pounds of ice per day which retailed at one cent per pound.[29]

Charleston had a bagging factory and also the tin factory of H. A. Duc, which made pan handles, bucket tops, milk pans and other articles from sheet tin "by a single stroke of huge machinery."   Fifty dozen half-gallon buckets, seventy-five dozen pint cups, or four hundred dozen seamless tin pans could be made in one day; miniature tin cups sold at nineteen cents per dozen, and quart coffee pots at ninety cents per dozen.[30]

During the Reconstruction period about fifty mining and manufacturing companies were incorporated by the legislature. Most of these, however, remained unproductive and many of them never went into operation.   Several gold mining companies were formed, but they were unsuccessful.[31]   Statistics

[27] Ibid.; Columbia, the Future Manufacturing and Commercial Centre, 48; Williams, J. F., Old and New Columbia, p. 136.

[28] Stat. S. C., XV, 113-15.

[29] Columbia, the Future Manufacturing and Commercial Centre, p. 49.

[30] The Rural Carolinian, IV, (July, 1873), 539.

[31] It was said that the mountains were rich in resources but that the people had neither the requisite capital nor skill to work them.   Northern and foreign capitalists were prevented from investing because of the enormous valuations placed on the property.—Keowee Courier, April 19, 1872.

found in the United States census of 1870 show the number of establishments and the value of the products of some of the principal industries of the state,[32] as well as the general location and extent of the mechanical and manufacturing industries. Of the nine leading manufacturing counties of the state, six were in the middle or up-country.[33] With the exception of Barnwell, Charleston, and Georgetown counties, there was little manufacturing in the coast region or lower pine belt.

* * * * *

The manufacture of cotton was destined to be the chief industry of South Carolina and the foundations for this development were laid during the Reconstruction period. Prior to 1860 cotton manufactures had not been looked upon with favor, although the cotton industry in the South appeared to have great possibilities. Its rivers and streams would furnish abundant and cheap water power; raw materials were easily acces-

[32]

	No. establishments	Value of products
Blacksmithing	147	$151,329
Boots and shoes	60	93,843
Bread, crackers, etc.	17	142,045
Carpentering and building	64	313,350
Carriages and wagons	77	186,114
Machinery (not specified)	11	286,550
railroad repairing	1	116,552
Printing and publishing, Newspapers..	11	237,930
Saddlery and harness	15	40,493
Sash, doors, and blinds	3	40,500
Ship building, repairing, etc.	7	45,650
Tin, copper, and sheet-iron ware	20	87,294

Products of flour and grist mills, cotton factories, fertilizer factories, lumber and turpentine industries are not included.—*U. S. Census,* 1870, III, 568-69.

[33]

Counties	No establishments	Value of products
Anderson	78	$ 534,677
Barnwell	154	325,391
Charleston	224	2,431,763
Edgefield	64	1,316,807
Georgetown	12	376,575
Greenville	48	351,875
Richland	69	536,992
Spartanburg	95	437,152
Union	55	318,076

—*U. S. Census,* 1870, III, 568.

sible and could be secured at a lower cost than elsewhere due to savings in transportation and handling; and labor was cheap and plentiful. Few of the mills which had been established had proved successful, however, and even the example of the Graniteville and Vaucluse mills could not counteract the fact that much money had been invested and lost.

With the close of hostilities in 1865, however, a new attitude was apparent. No doubt the emergencies of war had forced the state to see its need, and the revolution in the system of labor made a diversified industry imperative. The newspapers of the period are full of editorials and letters pleading for the establishment of manufactures, particularly cotton mills. Building materials were cheap, labor was plentiful and cheap, water power was abundant, and New England mills could not compete with those who manufactured the raw material where it was grown. The Charleston *News and Courier* was the leading protagonist of these ideas. "Ten years ago," it said, February 10, 1880, "the *News and Courier* formulated what is now an accepted truth, in declaring that the remedy for commercial distress in the North and the secret of sure fortune in the South was to bring mills to the cotton." There were those who doubted that the million spindles of wealthy New England could be brought to the sparsely settled districts of the cotton states. The *News and Courier* replied that a spinner in Columbia made number 20 yarn at five cents less than the lowest estimate of the cost of making it in New England; this paper concluded that the mills must come to the cotton.[34] The only question was, should they come from New England or Old England? By 1875, in fact, all spinners had felt the general dullness of trade, and in New England some had closed their doors and many were working only part time. The Southern mills, on the other hand, continued steadily at work although it was necessary for them to reduce dividends.[35]

[34] Aug. 1, 1873.   [35] *Ibid.*, July 7, 1875.

The state sought to "aid and encourage" cotton and woolen manufactures. "For the purpose of inducing the investment and employment of capital" in such industries, an act was passed in 1870 providing that the tax upon the "property, or capital employed directly and exclusively" in the manufacture of cotton and woolen goods should be returned annually to the investors. The act was to be in force for a period of not more than four years.[36] Certain improvement companies were incorporated "for the purpose of purchasing lands, houses, plantations and rights of way, mill sites, water powers, and for building of houses, mills, trainways, factories, machine shops, and operating the same,"[37] but apparently nothing ever came of them. Many of the incorporators were prominent Negro legislators.

As is well known, the rapid development and expansion of the cotton mill industry in South Carolina did not come until after 1880. Nevertheless, it is clear that the way for this expansion was prepared during the Reconstruction years. Between 1860 and 1870 the amount of capital employed in the cotton mill industry increased 33 per cent, although the number of spindles increased by only 13 per cent. The number of mills actually decreased, but in spite of that fact there was an increased consumption of cotton and the value of the manufactured products increased by nearly 72 per cent. The increase in the amount of capital, the cotton consumed and the value of the products between 1870 and 1880 was, of course, even more phenomenal.[38] During Reconstruction the psychological and

[36] Stat. S. C., XIV, 411. [37] Ibid., pp. 233-35, 263-64, 311.

[38]	1860	1870	1880
No. establishments	17	12	14
Spindles	30,890	34,940	82,334
Capital	$ 801,825	$1,069,600	$ 2,776,100
Hands	891	1,123	2,018
Wages	$ 123,300	$ 206,143	$ 380,844
Cotton consumed, lbs.	3,978,061	4,756,823	15,601,005
Value of products	$ 713,050	$1,223,940	$ 2,895,769

—U. S. Census, 1880, II, 542-47.

material foundations for the future extension of the cotton mill industry were laid. In some respects, at least, cotton was still King to the survivors of the Confederacy. However, the lack of capital together with the uncertain political conditions created obstacles too great to overcome in one decade.[39]

The mills that survived the period of the war did not find the new era hopeful. Buildings and machinery had deteriorated and the earnings made during the war, which were in some cases very large, had been paid in depreciated currency. There was not sufficient capital to be had to rebuild the plants properly or to carry on the business.

One of the most famous mills was that established before the war by William Gregg and known as Graniteville. It had been quite prosperous during the war and was probably in a better condition than any other mill in the state to meet the trials of Reconstruction. Its earnings during the year 1865 were $288,125.09, and on January 1, 1866, there was a total surplus of $101,986.09, a large part of which was represented by cotton valued in gold at about 35 cents. "The new year, however, brought a different story. Cotton, and consequently cloth, fell in price, so that between January 1 and May 22, 1866, the company lost (as expressed in currency) $42,537.46."[40] Other mills must also have been in a precarious state. Nevertheless it was reported in 1866 that the proprietors of seven mills in the upper part of the state were rebuilding and repairing their factories. New machinery had been placed in factories at

[39] Again it is interesting to make a comparison between South Carolina and her neighbors. The following table illustrates the situation in 1874:

	No. mills	Spindles	Cotton used (bales)
Georgia	42	137,330	39,920
South Carolina	18	62,872	15,376
North Carolina	30	55,498	14,726

Labor in Europe and America, 44th Cong., 1st. Sess., House Ex. Doc. No. 21, p. 748.

[40] Broadus Mitchell, *William Gregg,*   clearly the difficulties that confronted even Chap. XI, *passim.* The chapter shows   a well-established mill.

GRANITEVILLE COTTON FACTORY ABOUT 1870

The Rural Carolinian

Batesville, Crawfordsville, and Bivingsville. The burned Saluda factory had been reconstructed with new machinery from the North, and the Vaucluse factory had been enlarged.[41] William Gregg had gone to Europe to purchase new and improved machinery for Graniteville.[42]

Early in 1867 the *Charleston Daily News*[43] said that between ten and twelve cotton factories, operating 32,000 spindles, were in successful operation in different parts of the state.[44]

Despite small establishments and lack of capital, some of the mills were undoubtedly quite prosperous. The Graniteville company found its surplus capital wiped out by the decline of prices in 1866. Large sums were expended for English machinery, and a considerable outlay of capital was required to support the working force while the new machinery was being installed. Nevertheless, by January 1, 1867, the capital deficiency of $221,000 in May, 1865, had been wiped out, dividends of $36,000 had been paid, and there was on hand a credit to profit and loss of $1,800—a net gain in 19 months and 8 days of $257,800. And "at the commencement of the year, the company had a cash mercantile capital, clear of debt, of $55,000—an amount as large as the average cash capital during the decade preceding the war."[45]

This operating capital was not sufficient for the mill's needs, and rather than let the company become dependent upon commission houses which would advance capital and give credit in return for a practical monopoly on the products of the mill, money was borrowed at as high as 12 per cent. In August, 1867, after the dam had broken, the whole loan indebtedness,

[41] *The American Annual Cyclopaedia, 1866,* p. 709.

[42] Mitchell, *William Gregg,* pp. 236-37, 240-41.

[43] Jan. 29, 1867.

[44] For list of mills with their location and number of spindles see *News,* Jan. 29, 1867, Dec. 9, 1868; Walker's *Almanac* for 1867; August Kohn, *The Cotton Mills of South Carolina.*

[45] Mitchell, *William Gregg,* pp. 247-48 and Chap. XI, *passim.*

with interest, amounted to $156,700, and there was a possibility that the mill would have to close.[46]

Upon the death of Gregg, H. H. Hickman, the treasurer, was elected president pro tempore. In less than a year, Hickman had been able to pay off most of the obligations which Gregg had been forced to contract at 12 per cent, and by March 1, 1868, the loan debt had been reduced to $100,208. In addition to this liquidation, the company had been able to pay two dividends amounting to $14,330.[47]

From 1868 to 1872 inclusive the company paid annual dividends of 8 per cent; in 1873, 10 per cent; in 1874, 15 per cent; and in 1875, 11½ per cent. Further, the company paid $153,090.25 for 1,160 shares of stock which it bought and cancelled, reducing the capital to $116,000. About 40 operatives' houses had been built and the $200,000 spent on the mill increased production from 120,000 yards to 217,000 yards a week. According to newspaper reports, the company had in 1875 a cash capital of over $300,000 over and above the amount paid for dividends, improvements, and cancelled stock. The stock was rated at $160 per share.[48]

The Langley Manufacturing Company, which had been incorporated in 1868 with a capital stock of $300,000,[49] got into full operation in Edgefield County in April, 1872. The capital stock had been increased to $400,000, although actually $411,192 had been expended, and by 1875 two annual dividends of 10 per cent each had been paid. After charging to profit and loss the $11,192, the company then had a surplus of $112,662 which if divided would have given over 27½ per cent more to stockholders. The mill employed 325 persons.[50]

In January, 1866, a mill in Anderson County was sold to John W. Grady, O. Hawthorne, and William Perry for $28,000. Perry was deeded the mill and operated it until November,

---

[46] *Ibid.*, pp. 254-55.
[47] *Ibid.*, p. 257, n. 34.
[48] *Fairfield Herald*, June 2, 1875.

[49] *Stat. S. C.*, XIV, 2-3.
[50] *Fairfield Herald*, June 2, 1875.

1868, when he deeded one-half interest in it for $22,000.[51] William Perry was also successful in operating the Pendleton Factory. He estimated that an outlay of $110,000 would be necessary to erect fire-proof buildings of brick and purchase and place in operation machinery for a "good sized" factory. The profit on the investment would be 22½ per cent. He spoke with authority for he had been operator, manager and owner of factories for thirty years; and for the last five years his Pendleton Factory had paid dividends of 26½ per cent.[52]

Another successful operator was Henry P. Hammett. In 1870 he resigned his position as president of the Greenville and Columbia Railroad to build the Piedmont Cotton Mills. He had it well under way when the panic of 1873 caused him to suspend operations. By 1876, however, he had succeeded in raising the capital and starting the mill with 10,000 spindles and 300 looms. This was said to be the first mill in the South to make 36-inch sheetings, three yards to the pound, for the export trade. "The Piedmont mill was designed, built and equipped after strictly modern plans," whereas most of the others were conducted on the old lines, with more or less old machinery.[53] The net profit from the operation of the mill for the six-months period from July 1 to December 30 was $12,689.58, and after paying all interest and other charges there was a net balance of $9,674.09.[54]

Although the Columbia *Phoenix* by 1873 had reached the conclusion that farming in South Carolina scarcely paid 5 per cent interest and that manufactures in some localities were paying from 15 to 20 per cent,[55] investors eager for profits did not dot the land with mills. Even though "Rusticus" pointed to a net profit of $187,631.48 made by the Graniteville mill, mill

[51] Louise Ayer Vandiver, *Traditions and History of Anderson County*, p. 291.

[52] *Orangeburg News*, Sept. 20, 1873. In 1873, Perry established another factory of 30,000 spindles in Anderson County.— *Phoenix*, May 11, 1873.

[53] D. A. Tompkins, *Cotton Mills, Commercial Features*, p. 189.

[54] *News and Courier*, Jan. 30, 1877, from *Greenville Daily News*, Jan. 24, 1877.

[55] *August 19, 1873.*

sites and water power went unused.[56] The constant, active movement of machinery was said to exert a sympathetic influence upon the human organization, "promoting to more energetic, methodical, indefatigable, cheerful labor." Moreover, it was said, the moral and social benefits of mill life showed themselves in the enlarged educational facilities, the "literary and religious influences," and the stimulus given to "higher culture and greater excellence."[57] But not even for humanity's sake were mills established.

The great drawback was the lack of capital. A mill site on Lyon's Creek was offered gratis to anyone who would erect a cotton factory on it.[58] The dam was already complete, the fall of water constant, and the climate healthy. To raise capital it was proposed that a joint stock company should be formed, and those who were able should contribute at least one bale of cotton.[59] The citizens of Anderson County talked of reviving the People's Manufacturing Company which had been inactive since 1871. The plan was to raise a capital of $250,000 and establish three mills, one devoted to weaving and two to spinning.[60] Another coöperative enterprise was that fostered by the English Manufacturing Company. The Company purchased 3,000 acres in Spartanburg County which it proposed to subdivide into tracts of six acres each and sell to English and American settlers, men of small capital, who were also to take stock in the company. Steps were taken to erect a lumber and saw mill, and machine shops, preparatory to building the plant.[61] The state Grange also promoted coöperative manufacturing.[62]

[56] *The Rural Carolinian*, III (Mar., 1872), 314-17.

[57] *Ibid.*

[58] *Ibid.*, pp. 217-18.

[59] *Orangeburg News*, Jan. 30, 1869.

[60] *Keowee Courier*, Sept. 12, 1873.

[61] *News and Courier*, Sept. 10, 1875; *Columbia Register*, Oct. 3, 1875.

[62] In 1875 some 2,500 people gathered at Erwin's Mill on the Saluda River to hear J. N. Lipscomb, Grange lecturer, propose that a subscription of $35,000 be made to build a cotton factory at that place. The capital stock was to be fixed at $50,000, and shares at $25.00 each might be taken by others than members of the Grange. *Columbia Register*, Sept. 4, 1875; *News and Courier*, Sept. 6, 1875.

The coöperative establishments never became numerous, however, and only the well established and well managed companies were profitable.

* * * * *

The discovery of phosphate deposits in South Carolina in 1867 added materially to the prosperity of the state. The deposits were quite large, and numerous companies engaged in the mining and manufacture of phosphate fertilizer. The state granted franchises to companies engaged in the mining of phosphate rock in the navigable streams and waters of the state, but through lack of careful supervision the revenue from the royalty which the state received was not commensurate with the value of the franchises.

It had been known for some time that extensive marl beds existed in the state, and in 1843 Edmund Ruffin of Virginia, who had been employed to make a geological and agricultural survey of the state, reported that the marl deposits were richer in carbonate of lime than those of Virginia.[63] His successor, Professor M. Toumey, devoted part of his report of 1846 to the calcareous manures of the state, and in 1859 Professor Charles U. Shepard, Sr., in an address before the Medical Association of South Carolina, said: "As the supply of guanos from abroad fails, we shall be looked to to fill the vacuum . . . and it would not be strange if a few years hence Charleston, besides supplying her own state, should ship more casks of phosphatic stone to the North than she now receives of ordinary lime from that region."[64] In 1860 Lewis M. Hatch began mining the marl deposits but suspended operations on account of the war.[65]

In November, 1866, Dr. St. Julien Ravenel began an association for the manufacture of fertilizer (not from phosphate

There was also a plan to establish a shoe factory at Hodge's. $2,300 was subscribed in the neighborhood and $1,600 in another community.

[63] Francis S. Holmes, *Phosphate Rocks of South Carolina and the Great Carolina Marl Bed*, pp. 56-57.

[64] Philip E. Chazal, *A Sketch of the South Carolina Phosphate Industry*, pp. 34-35, 39.

[65] *Ibid.*, pp. 40-41.

rock, however), and early in 1867 a factory was established. In August, 1867, Dr. Ravenel handed to Dr. N. A. Pratt, of Georgia, a phosphate nodule for examination. It was found to contain about 60 per cent of phosphate of lime, and Dr. Pratt, at the suggestion of Professor F. S. Holmes, went to a site on the Ashley River where a deposit of similar nodules was found.[66]

Professor Holmes and Dr. Pratt undertook to raise money in Charleston to form a mining company, but after six weeks of effort they felt obliged to resort to Northern cities for aid. Two Philadelphians, George T. Lewis and Frederick Klett, furnished the necessary capital and on November 29, 1867, the Charleston, South Carolina, Mining and Manufacturing Company was organized with a paid-in capital of $1,000,000.[67] The new company speedily secured for itself a large area of phosphate lands on both sides of the Ashley, above Bee's Ferry and Ten Mile Hill. Meanwhile, Dr. Ravenel and associates organized the Wando Fertilizer Company. They relied entirely on local capital, and their efforts were much restricted; they were prevented from making any attempts to secure a large acreage of phosphate property.[68]

On December 4, 1867, John R. Dukes, president of the Wando Company, shipped the first small sample of rock to New York. Twelve days later the Charleston Mining and Manufacturing Company sent its first shipment, a sample lot of sixteen tierces, to Baltimore, whence it was forwarded to Philadelphia, and the first lot of super-phosphates was manufactured by Messrs. Potts & Klett of that city. The first cargo, of 100 tons, was shipped to Baltimore on April 14, 1868, by the Wando Company. On April 22, the schooners, "T. G. Smith" and "Anna Barton," sailed for Philadelphia, carrying

[66] Holmes, *Phosphate Rocks of South Carolina*, pp. 64-68; Chazal, *Sketch of the Phosphate Industry*, pp. 42-25.

[67] Holmes, *Phosphate Rocks of South Carolina*, p. 69; *News*, Nov. 30, 1867, July 2, 1868.

[68] Chazal, *Sketch of the South Carolina Phosphate Industry*, p. 49.

ACID WORKS

PHOSPHATE PLANT OF THE WANDO MINING AND MANUFACTURING COMPANY ON THE ASHLEY RIVER, 1870

The Rural Carolinian

the first cargoes (296 and 329 tons) of the Charleston Mining Company.[69]

The price fixed for this first contract was $14 per ton, netting about $10 per ton, f. o. b. This price was not remunerative and the contract was cancelled. The chief cause for this lay in the way the rock was mined. The nodules were found several feet under the earth in layers eight to thirty inches thick or in the beds of streams where they had been carried and deposited. Thus there was "land mining" and "river mining." The first mining was on land and consisted of digging a series of separate small pits. The amount of labor was thereby greatly increased, and the output per acre was greatly reduced by the amount of ground left undug. The rock was very dirty and until washing machines were constructed the only cleansing it received was by hand brushes in convenient creeks. It was first dried in the sun and later in kilns. As the industry developed, however, improved methods were applied, and dredges were used to recover the phosphate from river beds. The labor was done nearly always by Negroes who were accustomed to manual labor and could withstand malaria. In fact, it was said that this employment had saved many sea-island Negroes from being thrown upon the county for support or left to starve.[70]

The phosphate region lay along the coast, and practically parallel to the shore line, for a distance of about seventy miles, extending from the Wando River, on the north, to the Broad River, on the south, and at a distance of from ten to twenty miles from the ocean. The principal subdivisions of the phosphate beds were the following: Wando River, Cooper River, Northeastern Railroad and Mount Holly, Ashley River, Five Stores, Edisto and Ashepoo, Coosaw, and Beaufort. The Beau-

---

[69] Holmes, *Phosphate Rocks of South Carolina*, p. 76; Chazal, *Sketch of the South Carolina Phosphate Industry*, p. 49.

[70] For a discussion of mining methods see A. R. Guerard, *A Sketch of the History, Origin and Development of the South Carolina Phosphates, passim; Reports and Resolutions, 1877-78*, pp. 548-72; *Handbook of South Carolina, 1883*, pp. 48-52; Chazal, *Sketch of the South Carolina Phosphate Industry*.

fort beds were extensive but were scarcely rich enough for profitable mining.[71]

The Charleston, South Carolina, Mining and Manufacturing Company was the first and for a long while the most successful of the enterprises. Many difficulties had to be surmounted. The field was new; much money was spent in experiments; and the unskilled Negro accomplished little in a day's work. By 1870, however, the company was on a firm basis. The capital of the company was reduced to $800,000, and $150,000 had been paid out within the year for buildings, wharves, mills, machinery, railroads and locomotives, besides making two dividends to the stockholders.[72]

The Wando Company was well managed and succeeded in paying a dividend of 30 per cent, thereby encouraging phosphate digging and manufacture.[73] By 1870 there were thirteen companies engaged in mining and manufacturing the material into fertilizers.[74] The original idea had been to mine the phosphate rock and send it North for manufacture into fertilizers. It was not long, however, before Charleston companies had their own sulphuric acid vats. The phosphate of lime was treated with sulphuric acid, by which the phosphate of calcium was decomposed, sulphate of calcium formed, and the phosphoric acid converted into a soluble acid calcium salt, a superphosphate, or else reduced to the free state. The more important plants manufactured their own sulphuric acid with sulphur imported from Sicily.[75]

By 1874 there were five phosphate companies in active op-

[71] Ibid., pp. 1-2.

[72] Holmes, Phosphate Rocks of South Carolina, p. 75.

[73] Robert Somers, The Southern States Since the War, 1870-71, p. 47; Edward King, The Southern States of North America, p. 450.

[74] Some of these companies were not in operation. The U. S. Census of 1870 lists only 2 establishments, capitalized at $350,-000, employing 825 hands, and producing material valued at $425,000; see Holmes, Phosphate Rocks of South Carolina, pp. 73-74, for a list of the companies.

[75] For a description of the manufacture of commercial fertilizers see Guerard, Sketch of the History, Origin and Development of the South Carolina Phosphates, pp. 12-13.

ATLANTIC PHOSPHATE COMPANY'S WORKS, ON THE ASHLEY RIVER NEAR CHARLESTON, 1871

The Rural Carolinian

eration, and the manufacture of commercial fertilizers was said to give employment to upwards of $12,000,000. The Etiwan Company claimed to have the largest acid chamber in the United States, and in the Wando, Etiwan, Pacific, Guano, Atlantic, Stono, and Wappoo mills, four or five millions of dollars had been invested since 1866.[76] The phosphate trade was said to be the largest and most profitable trade in South Carolina, and the demand for commercial fertilizers exceeded the supply.[77]

The state pursued an uncertain and indefinite policy in regard to the operation of river mining companies. It claimed jurisdiction over the phosphate beds in the navigable streams and waters, but the charters which it granted to certain individuals and companies were neither calculated to encourage efficient mining nor to produce a proper revenue for the state.

On March 1, 1870, the state granted to George W. Williams, William Birnie, and others, the right to dig and mine in the beds of the streams of the state for the term of twenty-one years. This "gift and grant" was made upon the condition that a royalty of one dollar be paid the state for each ton of phosphate rock mined and removed.[78] Governor Scott vetoed the bill. He urged that a most valuable franchise, estimated as worth many millions of dollars, the consideration for which was a contingent one, had been granted without a single guarantee that the corporators would at any time remove a single ton of deposits, "and consequently could not be required to pay one cent into the Treasury; but could prevent all others from doing so." He remembered also that several leading corporators in the bill already had large investments in phosphate deposits and the land which they had purchased and leased and the buildings and machinery which they had erected would

---

[76] Mazyck, *Guide to Charleston*, p. 98; King, *The Southern States of North America*, p. 450.

[77] *News*, April 2, 1873, quoting *New York Daily Bulletin*. The price was about 30 per cent less than guano.—Somers, *The Southern States Since the War*, p. 47.

[78] *Stat. S. C.*, XIV, 381-82.

be greatly diminished in value if the submarine deposits were brought into competition with them. In other words, the bill granted a monopoly which would prevent fair competition.[79] The bill passed over his veto, however, and fifteen days later the Marine and River Phosphate Mining and Manufacturing Company was formed. The company claimed exclusive rights to mine in the waters of the state, and therefore it decided to work only those of the highest grade.[80]

However, the Coosaw Mining Company began to operate in competition with the Marine and River Company, and the latter's claims were set aside by the courts. The proper policy of the state would have been to have the territory properly examined and sub-divided and exclusive rights to mine in the various subdivisions given to responsible individuals and companies.[81] The state was never successful in getting proper returns from some of the companies.[82]

In 1878 the Democratic legislature repealed all charters previously granted to river mining companies, and fifteen companies were incorporated by an act which amply protected the rights and interests of the state.[83] Two sorts of rights were granted, "exclusive" and "general." In the former, exclusive rights were given in a certain restricted territory; in the latter, general rights were given to mine and remove phosphate deposits in territory not granted exclusively to other companies. In either case the operators paid a royalty of one dollar per ton.

[79] *House Journal, 1869-70,* pp. 512 ff.

[80] Chazal, *Sketch of the South Carolina Phosphate Industry,* p. 53; Holmes, *Phosphate Rocks of South Carolina,* p. 82.

[81] It was claimed that the Phosphate Bill was passed by bribing members of the legislature, and doubtless this was true. See *Reports and Resolutions, 1877-78,* Fraud Report, 1676-78. In 1871 the legislature granted a charter similar to that of the Marine and River Mining and Manufacturing Company. The capital stock was $2,000,000 and the company was

composed of prominent Negro legislators, carpet-baggers, and scalawags.—*Stat. S. C.,* XIV, 688-89.

[82] Report of state inspector, in *Reports and Resolutions, 1872-73,* pp. 316 ff; Report of the special joint committee to investigate mining and removing of phosphates, etc., in *Reports and Resolutions, 1871-72,* pp. 996 ff; Governor's message, Jan. 14, 1873, *Senate Journal, 1872-73,* p. 288.

[83] *Stat. S. C.,* XVI, 615 ff.

DIGGING PHOSPHATE ROCK

Photo Cook

In 1880 there were in the state 21 establishments, capitalized at $2,071,300, employing 2,485 hands, and mining 211,377 tons of phosphate valued at $1,123,823.[84]

In South Carolina, as in other Southern states, the Reconstruction era was not one of commercial prosperity and industrial expansion. While the North was going forward by leaps and bounds, the maimed and battered South was trying manfully to preserve an integral existence. Suffering from economic, social, and political maladjustments, the Old South had not yet given place to the New.

[84] *U. S. Census,* 1880, p. 1008.

The following table gives the total number of long tons mined, and the royalty paid the state:

Year	Total Tons	Royalty
1867	6	$ .....
1868	12,262	......
1869	31,958	......
1870	65,241	1,989
1872	58,760	22,502
1874	109,340	57,716
1876	132,784	81,910
1878	210,322	97,700
1880	190,763	65,151

Chazal, *The Century in Phosphates and Fertilizers,* in *Centennial edition of the News and Courier,* 1904, p. 70.

Chapter XII

DARKER PHASES OF SOCIAL LIFE

THAT South Carolina society during "the dark days of Reconstruction" was unwholesome in many of its aspects, was vividly revealed by travelers describing the accommodations furnished them. The train which conveyed Louis Post from Chester to Yorkville in 1871 "consisted of a locomotive, a freight car and a passenger car. There was a partition across the middle of the latter, primarily to divide white smokers from other whites and incidentally to prevent racial promiscuity. Its wheels rolled on strap rails, but not very fast, for they were more than two hours in rolling us the twenty miles from Chester to Yorkville."[1] Carlyle McKinley said that in 1875 trains were so slow that it took all night to go from Columbia to Charleston and all day to go from Columbia to Greenville, Spartanburg, or Abbeville.[2] George Rose, in 1868, found the dining car service out of Charleston the "worst ever set before travelers in a so-called civilized country." The fare "consisted of some boiled fowl's bones, with nothing on them, some filthy bacon and cabbage, and a dish of raw onions, so strong and so heartily devoured as to render the railroad car untenable for the remainder of the day."[3] "I recall vividly the long, shabby, crowded car and its peculiar reek of peanuts, stale whiskey and chewing tobacco," said Ludwig Lewisohn of a journey out of Charleston some years later. "Half of the passengers were burly Negroes who gabbled and laughed weirdly. The whites wore broad-rimmed wool-hats; whittled and spat and talked in drawling tones. I very distinctly shared my

[1] Post, *Journal of Negro History*, X (Jan., 1925), 42-43.

[2] *Centennial Edition of News and Courier*, p. 29.

[3] *The Great Country*, p. 174.

parents' sense of the wildness, savagery and roughness of the scene, their horrified perception of its contrast to anything they had ever known or seen."[4]

The travelers were astonished by the means of conveyance through the streets of the towns. "Such wagons and such horses," said Whitelaw Reid, "were surely never seen. Each rivaled the other in corners, in age, in protuberance, and shakiness and in general disposition to tumble down and dissolve."[5] The hack which conveyed Sidney Andrews from the Orangeburg railroad station to a hotel, was a "rickety old short-boxed spring wagon, with two rough board seats, on the back of one of which was a wornout cushion, over both being a canvas supported on sticks nailed to each corner of the box. This establishment was drawn by a scrawny lame mule."[6]

The condition of the streets was deplorable. "It requires some agility in the stranger," said the Viscountess Avonmore, "to ride in a buggy in Charleston streets, the seats being no more secure than a dog-cart, while the ruts are both deep and sudden."[7] George Rose found that a rain storm had made the streets of the city "like a vast bath of mud, so deep that it seemed as though it would be impossible for the horse to drag the omnibus from the hotel to the station."[8] In fact, so real were the dangers of street travel that the public authorities of the city cautioned persons to look out for lights put over holes.[9] "Not a yard of street," said Carlyle McKinley of Columbia, "was paved or surfaced with any kind of hard material. After a good spell of rain, Main Street was a long clay bog, and few of the others were any better, save where the sand was deep. . . . There were no stone flaggings on the sidewalks anywhere, except for a few yards in front of hotels, and two or three other favored public buildings."[10]

[4] *Up Stream*, pp. 36-37.
[5] *After the War*, pp. 69-70.
[6] *The South Since the War*, pp. 15-16.
[7] *Teresina in America*, I, 57.
[8] *Op. cit.*, p. 174.
[9] *News*, Feb. 10, 1869.
[10] *Centennial Edition of News and Courier*, p. 29.

The state was noted for its bad hotels. "South Carolina," said an exasperated correspondent of the *New York Herald,* "is characterized by the meanest hotels which were ever dignified by that name. They are mainly places where cleanliness is no virtue and huge buildings where the furniture is lilliputian. . . . For board in such a miserable abode the lazy proprietor . . . coolly demands four dollars a day. Fifty cents is charged for extra lights. . . . The Northern man who trusts himself in the clutches of the hotel keepers of South Carolina may take warning in time and bring with him on the trip a bale of greenbacks."[11] Sidney Andrews has left a detailed description of such an establishment. The hotel at Orangeburg, he said, although enjoying an extensive patronage, was a place of disgusting squalor. In the yard were five "gaunt and wolfish dogs," nine "half grown and very long of nose" hogs wallowing in mud, bits of wood and crockery, scraps of old iron, wisps of straw and fodder, old rags, broken bottles, stones, bones, and so on. The "missus" of the house prepared to greet the stranger by washing her hand in the water with which a Negro boy had been scrubbing the steps. He was invited into a drawing room whose furniture consisted of three old chairs, a rickety table, a wreck of a piano and several pieces of a carpet. The room to which he was assigned was partitioned off with rough pine boards with pieces of cloth over large cracks. The ceiling was covered with wasp nests and sooty cobwebs. The bed had a dirty mattress without sheets. Nights were made miserable by the presence of bed bugs, mice and mosquitoes. The table remained spread for three days. The only articles of food "passably good" were tea, eggs and waffles; the biscuits and bread were "sour and laden" and the meats were "swimming in strong fats."[12]

Sanitary conditions in Charleston were not always the best. "One's impression, regarding its sanitary condition," said Rose,

---

[11] Apr. 15, 1867.   [12] *Op. cit.,* pp. 15-21.

"is not favorable: nor are the sights and smells one encounters in the streets, calculated to inspire confidence on this point." There was, he continued, "a nasty-looking market" with buzzards acting as scavengers.[13] The city registrar complained of the presence of cow yards and the nightly transportation of the contents of privy vaults through the streets. Most of the street drains, he added, "may be regarded as so many extensive lines of cesspools, which receive from year to year the sewage of houses and privies and deleterious matter from the street surfaces, all of which are never discharged, owing to the improper constructions and undulations of the drains."[14]

Portions of the city gave the appearance of decay. Although there was some reconstruction work in the years following the war, many ruined or dilapidated buildings remained untouched. Especially was this true of the "burnt district," the belt across the city left by the fire of 1861. The condition of many houses in the best portions of the city became worse, due to the inroads of the weather and the neglect of poverty-stricken or careless tenants. "King Street, from the Battery to the confines of the burnt district," said a patriotic pamphlet, "is infested by Negroes; . . . one of the most disagreeable and dirty portions of the city."[15] The Viscountess Avonmore said, "The roofless houses, the paneless windows, the stagnation reigning over a city once so beautiful, wealthy and full of vitality, could not but strike one with a sense of desolation, and even awe."[16]

The well disciplined social order of the older city gave place to a society featured by poverty and parasitism. "The burden of charity," said Edward King, "is by no means small. The alms-house has more than sixteen hundred regular 'outdoor

[13] Op. cit., pp. 171-72. For the uses to which the buzzards were put, compare Julian Ralph, Dixie, or Southern Scenes and Sketches, p. 264, and Premium List of the South Carolina Institute, pp. 58-59.

[14] Robert Lebby, in News and Courier, Feb. 6, 1875.

[15] Premium List of the South Carolina Institute, pp. 36-37.

[16] Op. cit., I, 43-44.

pensioners,' that is, poor residents who receive 'rations or half-rations' regularly. The city and main hospitals are filled with colored patients."[17] Symptomatic of decay was the fact that the number of junk shops had by 1868 grown from one or two to forty licensed ones. They throve on the loot which chiffoniers were able to gather from decaying property.[18] Stephen Powers, who visited the city in 1872, made the following analysis of some of its social grades: "Charleston is a city, first, of idle, ragged Negroes, who, with no visible means of support, nevertheless send an astonishing multitude to school; second, of small dealers, laborers and German artisans, starving on the rebel custom; third, of widows and children of planters keeping respectable boarding-houses, or pining in hopeless and unspeakable penury; fourth, of young men loafing in the saloons, and living on the proceeds of their mothers' boarding-houses; fifth, Jews and Massachusetts merchants doing well on the semi-loyal and Negro custom; sixth, of utterly worthless and accursed political adventurers from the North, Bureau leeches and promiscuous knaves, all fattening on the humiliation of the South and the credulity of the Freedmen."[19]

But Charleston, if noted for its social and moral decay, at least had an active life. This was not true of some of the smaller towns which had known prosperity before the war. Edward King thus described Beaufort, the most notable place in this class, as it appeared in 1874: "The long street by the water side was as still when I entered it as if the town was asleep. The only sign of life was a Negro policeman dressed in a shiny blue uniform, pacing up and down. There was not even a dog to arrest. On the pretty pier in front of the Sea Island Hotel two or three buzzards were ensconced in sleep. . . . I wandered through the town. It was evidently once very beautiful, and even now there were remains of the ancient beauty. But

[17] *Southern States of North America*, p. 464.
[18] *News*, Feb. 18, 1868.
[19] *Afoot and Alone*, pp. 43-44.

the silence of the grave reigned everywhere. Many of the mansions were closed or fallen into decay. . . . A wealthy and highly prosperous community had been reduced to beggary."[20]

Many of the commercial villages which had come into being after the war were touched by an atmosphere of semi-barbarism. "In 1890," said Ludwig Lewisohn in writing of a typical town of the middle counties, "the village of St. Mark's in South Carolina was raw; it had more than a touch of wildness and through its life there ran a strain of violence. It consisted of two principal streets, running diagonally to each other and half a dozen lesser streets that trailed off into the cotton-fields and pine-forests. There was a cotton-seed oil mill, a saw mill and twenty to thirty general merchandise stores. Three or four of these were housed in one-story buildings of red brick. For the rest, the village was built of wood and many of the houses were unpainted, showing the browned and weather-beaten boards. There was a Methodist Church and a Baptist Church, each with a graveyard behind it. North of the village straggled a Negro graveyard, its graves decorated with colored pebbles, bits of iridescent glass and the broken shards of cheap vases. Here or there, behind houses or in chance lanes were small, black one-roomed huts inhabited by Negro women."[21]

The village loafers kept the place from having the appearance of utter abandonment on week days. They sat under the eaves of the court house, on merchants' counters, or in the shade in front of their shops. A contemptuous observer described them as follows: "In front of stores and groggeries on benches were invariably to be seen lounging many inferior specimens of humanity smoking clay pipes with long reed stems, squirting tobacco juice, whittling pine sticks and 'spinning yarns'."[22]

A feature of the landscape, especially in the low-country,

[20] Op. cit., pp. 426-28.
[21] Up Stream, Chap. I.
[22] [J. P. Green], Recollections of the Carolinas, pp. 50-51.

was the decay of many of the mansions which had been the chief glory of ante-bellum society. Stephen Powers, in his walk from Charleston to Savannah in 1872, found only two mansions standing. In place of planters' houses towering above "the tender green" of the rice-fields, and surrounded by the splendors of Southern gardens, he found heaps of ashes, blackened chimneys, gardens eaten by mules, and former masters presiding over country stores.[23]   A correspondent of the *News and Courier* said that the only life extant on "a once baronial estate" were two plowers, a man with a horse and a woman with a mule. Within the house "the stuccoed ceiling lay all around, the frieze moldings were hanging in decay, the carved balustrade was a wreck, the staircase had found its way to the cellar. What had been a wine vault now held a one-horse wagon; a pile of manure was heaped up close to the window of the parlor; a calf was penned under the carved porch. The gloom that pervaded with pressless [sic] force was startled by a venerable rooster, who was perched with lordly dignity where wealth, fashion and happiness once ruled amidst the sanctity and reservation of a Carolina home."[24]

With the mansion, passed much of the elegance of the South Carolina gentleman. Many of the families, not immediately prostrated by the war, said Belton O'Neall Townsend, a local commentator, tried to keep up old styles—carriages with outriders, the giving of dinners, the handing of wines to visitors. But, added this critic, "gradually they descended. They became their own drivers, they opened their own gates. . . . The horses were spoiled by plow service, and the only vehicles were those preserved throughout the war. The carriages of the best-off citizens were lumbering, shabby, old, ante-bellum coaches, drawn by either two mules or a mule (with a shaved tail) and a regular Rozinante. The harness would be patched,

[23] *Op. cit.,* pp. 44-47.   [24] "Quelquefois," in issue of Mar. 17, 1875.

the whip worn down one half and turned into a handle for a leather lash."[25]

Gentlemen were no longer required to engage in extravagant conduct. Townsend remarked that there had not been more than eight or ten duels in the eleven years following the war, which was hardly less than the number fought in a single year previous to that event. "Men will rarely fight duels," he affirmed, "when death may mean starvation to their families; and I ought to add that for the same cause pistols are not drawn as quickly as of old, and the tendency is to brandish rather than shoot, so little can our hot bloods now afford the expense of a legal trial." Men felt obliged to be careful how they spent their money. "Southerners still make largesses to servants, stand treat, game and run in debt," said Townsend; "but they can ill afford to be lavish with their money. Fees and bets are small in amounts, and the aristocrat, who of old would not wait to receive change, or would pocket it without looking at it, will now count it over when handed him. Treats are as often invited as proffered, and cheaper refreshments are selected than formerly. . . . Merchants, who used to rival each other in seeking the patronage of influential families, became cautious in dealing with them."

The poor discipline of society was illustrated by the quality of the servants tolerated in most white homes capable of employing them. "Washer-women," said Townsend, "badly damage the clothes they work on, iron-rusting them, tearing them, breaking the buttons off, and burning them brown." The cooks were notorious for their wastefulness and uncleanliness. "Inconceivably vast quantities of excellent material, flour, meats of every description, fresh and salted, etc.," declared Dr. F. Peyre Porcher, "have been and are ruined in the preparation of the table."[26] D. Wyatt Aiken said that the seven

to ten dollars a month and board paid cooks were just the beginning of what they cost. Husbands and tribes of little ones
must be fed from the master's table and kept warm from his
wood pile. Time, added Aiken, did not enter into their consideration. "The cook spends her time hunting up wood and
water, and looking after her 'chillun,' except when standing
over a kitchen fire, built of a cord of wood, and hot enough
for a smelting furnace." She was "systematically filthy," adept
at hiding dirt. Housewives were ashamed to have strangers
visit their kitchens, for the slops had been thrown through the
cracks, the egg shells and bones were in the corners, and the
tables smeared with dirty dish rags. "Is it any wonder," concluded Aiken, "that each of us eats his peck of dirt before we
reach our teens?"[27]

Perhaps the principal reason why servants were allowed
such licenses was because every family with any pretensions to
social position felt that it was dependent upon them. "To be
waited upon is the normal arrangement of Southern life," said
Aiken. "A servant to black my boots as well as to harness my
horse, to fetch me a pitcher of water or to build me a fire, to
go on errands, or otherwise consume valuable time, is a per-
plexing luxury too frequently indulged in by men who confess
their poverty, and are ever ready to lament their condition."

Lack of intelligence in the conduct of the home was in
some respects most glaring among families too humble to employ outside help. Dr. Porcher said that in the up-country bad
biscuits were among the three scourges which have "afflicted
this country with countless woes." The inhabitant of that section, he added, "does not comprehend or practice in perfection
one single art of cookery—he can stew or fry, it is true, but he
can neither boil nor bake, nor roast. He eats and drinks without discrimination."[28] Dyspeptics resulted from its extreme

[27] *Rural Carolinian*, VI (Nov., 1874),   [28] *Op. cit.*, pp. 1138-41.
81-84.

profusion, its procession of hot breads, its inordinate use of fats in the form of ham and bacon, and its equally inordinate coffee and spirit drinking.

Little sense was used in the construction and upkeep of houses. Porcher complained of up-country cottages contaminated by bad air because of small window space, contracted rooms and lack of proper sanitary devices. Aiken said of the farm houses in general: "There is nothing in the house either as to size, shape or plan that suggests economy, convenience or comfort." Where a sitting room should have been was a windy hall blocked by a lumbering staircase; there were piazzas and shed rooms which because of their low ceilings and flat roofs were hot in summer and cold in winter; there were great fireplaces before which one scorched his shin while his back was freezing, and from which nine-tenths of the heat escaped up the chimney; and no respect was shown for topography or the points of the compass in the choice of dwelling sites.[29]

The failure of the white males to observe ordinary prudence in personal habits was illustrated by their excessive indulgence in strong drink and tobacco.

The drinking of hard liquors in South Carolina had always been attended by special evils. It had let loose the slumbering emotions of lawlessness inherent in a people recently removed from the frontier. Its evil effects on health had been accentuated by the warm and malarious climate. Influences manifested after the war increased these evils. "Many Southerners," wrote Townsend in 1877, "were driven to drink deeply by their misfortunes, and drunkenness (with all the family misery it entails) is deplorably prevalent to this day."[30] Such innovations as the wider distribution of ready cash and the growth of the country store and the commercial village greatly stimulated drinking. The country stores were said to be "disguised whis-

---

[29] *Rural Carolinian*, VI (Dec., 1874), 137-40.

[30] *Loc. cit.*, p. 469. Cf. "Juhl," *Courier*, Oct. 31, 1865.

key shops" and the numerous saloons of the villages were said to sustain "an army of drunkards."[31]

On Saturdays the otherwise quiet streets of the villages became bedlams. Farmers spent their money as readily for drink as they did for family necessities. Men, law-abiding at other times, became profane and noisy and tumbled in ditches in helpless stupors; while those of worse character drew pistols and knives and sometimes committed crimes. The pent up anger of the white man toward the Negro flared, under the stimulus of drink, into acts of violence because the Negro was assuming new liberties. So real were the dangers that it became traditional for ladies and children not to venture on the streets on Saturday afternoons. "I believe," said a prosecuting officer, "drunkenness to be the cause, on the average, of not less than nine-tenths of the crimes of violence prevailing among the whites since the war."[32]

A less harmful but cruder habit of the males was the chewing and spitting of tobacco on all occasions without apparent consciousness that the finer sensibilities of anyone were being offended. Homes, offices, churches, and courthouses, wherever men congregated, were equipped with spittoons. But these receptacles seldom served a useful purpose, for the doughty chewers paid no attention to them, spitting on walls and floors. Ludwig Lewisohn, as is noted elsewhere,[33] discovered that it was the normal custom of his teachers to emit "amazing streams of repulsive brown juice" and that the railroad cars reeked with the smell of this liquid. Mrs. Chesnut said that these cars were "usually floating an inch deep in liquid brown juice."[34] "Five cents a day," said Aiken, "is less than the average tobacco-chewer pays for the pleasure of squirting 'amber' all over the floor, whether in church or store."[35] The limits to

[31] News, Dec. 5, 1868, and Temperance Advocate, Dec. 1, 1884.
[32] J. B. Kershaw, ibid., Dec. 1, 1885. Cf. W. C. McGowan, ibid., Feb. 16, 1885.
[33] See p. 422.
[34] Diary from Dixie, p. 375.
[35] Rural Carolinian, VII (Apr., 1876), 154.

which tobacco-chewers were capable of going were illustrated by an occurrence in Charleston against which there were protests. White boys who congregated at night around Hibernian Hall spat so carelessly that the skirts of passing ladies were ruined.[36]

Accompanying these vices were social attitudes which retarded progress in the direction to which post-war conditions inevitably pointed. Chief among these was the disinclination of an important element of the able-bodied white men to work. A sight painfully frequent, said a correspondent of the *Sumter Watchman,* was young men "loafing about towns and villages and drinking whiskey and smoking segars at other people's expense."[37] The editor said in comment, "In too many instances the cry is, 'The worthless Negro, he won't work,' when the example set before him is in no way calculated to improve his habits of industry. Young men who have nothing to depend on except their own energies and labor, too frequently expect to realize a living from their father's farm, or a small planting interest of their own, on which they never put a hand to plow. . . . This even with some of the sober industrious [sic] class, while the lazy and liquor drinking party . . . is yet in more perfect dependence on Negro labor." One of this class, comparing his attitude toward labor with that of North Carolinians, told Stephen Powers, "You see, sir, the Tar-heels haven't got no sense to spare. . . . They haven't no more sense than to work in the field, just like a nigger. If you work with a nigger, he despises you for equalizin' yourself with him. Any man is a dog-goned fool to work, when he can make a nigger work for him."[38]

The fundamental cause of this behavior, as has just been hinted, was the failure to recognize the full significance of the outcome of the war. It was difficult to believe that the legen-

[36] *News,* Mar. 13, 1869.   [38] *Afoot and Alone,* pp. 38-40.
[37] June 24, 1874.

dary ease of the old régime was no more, and that the Negro was made for any other purpose than to serve the white man. A few even dreamed of the time when "the landed aristocracy will, in a measure, be reinstated in their position of independence and influence." "An elevated race . . . based upon landed proprietorship," it was argued, "is the life and light of society."[39]

The number of persons who claimed aristocratic privileges for themselves and their families increased. This was in spite of the fact that slaveholding and the possession of public office and military rank, which had been the bases of the state's aristocracy, passed with the fall of the Confederacy. But the fact that a person, or his ancestors, had held such prerogatives remained the grounds for claims to aristocracy, and since to establish one's claims, it was no longer necessary to possess the realities of class distinctions, it became easier for unworthy persons to convince themselves and the public of their exalted birth. The number of persons who were reputed to have been generals, colonels, and majors in the Confederate army, or who had owned a hundred or more slaves, became legion. Because of this reputation some demanded exemption from many of the ordinary obligations of human beings. A few refused to work.[40]

"Southern chivalry" assumed that women were burdened with the frailties of the heroines of the romances of Sir Walter Scott, and they were therefore hedged about with all sorts of artificial privileges and restrictions. Aiken complained of the quietness and seclusion which were forced upon girls. "If they give way to their natural instincts, and run, jump, climb fences and roll and tumble on the ground," he said, "they are quickly rebuked. One of the most fruitful causes of the prevailing delicacy of the female sex is the deprivation of sun-

[39] J. W. Trotti, in *Southern Cultivator,* XXVIII (May, 1870), 132.

[40] Cf. Ludwig Lewisohn, *Up Stream,* p. 46; and Sir George Campbell, *White and Black,* p. 340.

light." Some women, he added, sat in dark parlors for fear of ruining their complexion.[41] "The Southern lady," said Townsend, "is usually far more helpless and fragile than her Northern sister. She is never allowed to do a thing if a gentleman is with her. Socially and politically the state of woman in the South is much less advanced than in the North. Nor is there much prospect of an amelioration. The idea of females voting or speaking in public is extremely distasteful to Southern whites, and even more so to women than to men. Southerners traveling in the North, and seeing ladies participate in public meetings, come back disgusted."[42]

Another handicap to wholesome development was the extreme aversion of the average white for the pretentious Yankee or Negro. A planter told Stephen Powers, "Never, sir, . . . will any high-toned Southron consent to remain any longer than brute force compels him in a Union controlled by the nutmeg-eyed, muslin-faced Yankee. . . . Live in alliance with pump-handle makers and cheese-pressers! Honor is dearer to every Southron than the ruddy drops which visit our sad hearts."[43] This feeling was more intense among the women. "They will prove in the end," said Townsend, "the chief obstacles to reconciliation with the North. . . . Every young man is afraid, if he associates with a Yankee or a Republican, that his sweetheart will cut him, or his mother and sisters look grieved."[44] Toward Negroes in whom they had no sentimental attachment, this author affirmed, the conduct of the whites "is sullen and reckless; and for the rights of the race at large they have no consideration whatever, save what springs from compulsion." Whites, he added, often did not resent an insult from members of their own race. "But let a colored person insult them, and their nature seemed wholly altered.

---

[41] *Rural Carolinian*, IV (Dec., 1872), 165.
[42] *Loc. cit.*, pp. 667-78.
[43] *Op. cit.*, p. 36. Cf. J. T. Trowbridge,

The South, pp. 572, 575, 577.
[44] *Loc. cit.*, 677. Cf. Sidney Andrews, pp. 10, 12-14, and *Autobiography of Joseph Le Conte*, p. 237.

Accordingly, the whites do not think it wrong to shoot, stab, or knock down Negroes on slight provocation. It is actually thought a great point among certain classes to be able to boast that one has killed or beaten a Negro."[45]

If poverty and other unfortunate social maladies afflicted the upper and middle sections of white society, improvement could have hardly been expected in the lot of the "poor whites." Their poverty and misery had been a reproach to Southern society in the palmiest days of the old régime. This condition had been caused by isolation or poor soil or lack of industrial opportunity due to slavery. They lived in the piedmont, in the pine barrens, and in the sand hills. The stress and poverty of Reconstruction increased their degradation and predatory habits. A correspondent of the *New York Herald* thus described the state of those dwelling in the sand hills north of Columbia: "Here and there has been a clearing, and from the uncongenial soil, by dint of hard grubbing, the occupant has been able to obtain a subsistence. A wretched log hut or two are the only habitations in sight. Here reside, or rather take shelter, the miserable cultivators of the ground, or a still more destitute class who make a precarious living by peddling 'lightwood' in the city. . . . These cabins . . . are dens of filth. The bed, if there be a bed, is a layer of something in the corner that defies scenting. If the bed is nasty, what of the floor? What of the whole enclosed space? What of the creatures themselves? Pough! Water in use as a purifier is unknown. Their faces are bedaubed with the muddy accumulation of weeks. They just give them a wipe when they see a stranger to take off the blackest dirt. . . . The poor wretches seem startled when you address them, and answer your questions cowering like culprits."[46]

[45] *Loc. cit.,* pp. 469-70. Cf. *ibid.,* pp. 191, 676; *N. Y. Times,* June 15, 1868; *Sumter News,* Oct. 3, 1872; etc.

[46] May 7, 1867. Cf. Townsend, *loc. cit.,* p. 679; [J. P. Green] *Recollections of the Carolinas,* p. 210; and Stephen Powers, p. 42.

The degradation of the women was greater than that of the men. "The husband is always gone," said the correspondent of the *New York Herald,* "and the wife is left in the sad plight of having to shift for herself and the young ones." Their children were described as "puny, unwholesome-looking creatures, with tangled whitish hair and a complexion of a dingy straw color."[47] When the women came to town they purchased the strongest Scotch snuff, and with sticks ten inches long in their mouths, went about the streets to gad and talk.[48] A few of them committed the crowning sin of Southern society: they co-habited with Negro men. Stephen Powers said that in his travels he found six cases of such "unnatural unions" in South Carolina, but never more than one in any other state. "In every case, without exception," he added, "it was a woman of the lowest class, generally a 'sand-hiller,' who, having lost in the war her only supporter, 'took up with a likely nigger' to save her children from absolute famine."[49] When such intimacies took on the formality of marriage, there were protests in the newspapers.[50]

Many of the whites, as has been shown, retained objectionable social attitudes. On the other hand, some attempted to throw off some of the engaging aspects of the civilization of the Old South. Many advocated the abandonment of both the big plantation and the concentration on cotton, and the substitution of the Northern formulas of small farms, immigration, and diversification of industry. Puritanism and humanitarianism, which in the opinion of the ante-bellum South Carolinian, were New England abominations, began to be accepted as social ideals. Even the principle, if not the practice, of political democracy became axiomatic. Apologists for the old régime emphasized the respects in which it approximated the progressive standards of the nineteenth century and min-

---

[47] N. Y. *Nation,* I (Nov. 23, 1865), 652.
[48] [J. P. Green], *op. cit.,* pp. 159-60. Cf. Chesnut, *Diary from Dixie,* pp. 400-1.
[49] Pp. 40-41.
[50] E.g., *News,* Apr. 23 and June 21, 1869.

imized the peculiarities of the Southern moral and social order. The gospel of labor and thrift was preached with a New England fervor. The vernacular in architecture, those subtle modifications of Georgian standards through which peculiarities in landscape and climate had been expressed, gave way to rigid but modest imitations of houses popular among the rich men of the North. The mansard roof, jig-saw work, piazza posts of fantastic shape, observatory towers, clumsy porticoes, and other conventions of an age of helter-skelter in architecture, were appropriated by South Carolina merchants, the only class which could afford to have decorative homes.

The lack of creative energy in South Carolina civilization was best illustrated by the quality of the literature produced. "I do not suppose," said Ludwig Lewisohn, "that in any age or any country the division between literature and life was ever more complete." There was, he adds, only a poetry of "smooth sentiments and sonorous verses," "the rhythms of an outworn music" uttered by "gentle dignified rhetoricians."[51] George Herbert Sass, the leading poet after Timrod and Hayne, was, in the opinion of Lewisohn, "a tall, elegant, repressed personality. He hardly dared face his bolder thoughts." Over him brooded "the hush of old-fashioned seemliness." "I think," concludes our authority, "that Sass was a much better poet potentially than he ever dared to be." William Gilmore Simms, the most eminent author the state has ever produced, had lived a full life touched by the hardships of the war and its aftermath; but only once in the six years remaining to him after the war did he direct his prodigious energy toward the recording of the realities he had lived. He wrote a passionate pamphlet on the burning of Columbia. Otherwise he busied himself writing vague romances about mountaineers far re-

[51] *Cities and Men*, pp. 85-87. His "The Books We Have Made: A History of Literature in South Carolina," in fourteen chapters, appeared in *News and Courier* July 5, 1903, and every seventh day thereafter until Sept. 20, 1903. It is the only critical appreciation of the letters of the state extant.

UNCLE ABE'S CABIN

Photo Cook

moved from the things he was feeling. Literature to be accepted had to be moralistic and polite. There was no recognition of the axiom that art should be closely related to the feelings and environment of the artist.

* * * * *

The social maladies of the Negroes were of course more intense than those of the whites. It is true that the blacks did not suffer some of the misfortunes of the other race. They experienced no disappointment over the outcome of the war; their gains were obvious and their losses not always apparent. Nevertheless, they were face to face with the obligation of reconstructing their moral and social order.

The most obvious failing of the Negroes was the poor quality of the houses they were able to provide for themselves. The cluster of cabins around the "big house," in which a few continued to live, lost the orderly and well kept character which the slave masters had been able to enforce. The cabins which were erected for them on their farms, or in the "nigger town" sections of the villages, were usually log structures of one or two rooms with wooden shutters and mud chimneys. The almost universal absence of window panes enforced darkness when it was necessary to keep the cold air out. The dwellers were often at the mercy of the elements because of the absence of ceilings, and because of the numerous cracks in the walls and the roofs. The worst houses were described as follows: "These huts consisted of four rough posts from six to eight feet high, with sides of planks. The pine boughs were laid on the top for a roof, and this was covered with a thick coating of mud from the swamps. There was no floor and no chimney. The dwellers sat and slept on the ground, and built their fires on one side, letting the smoke go out of the cracks. When it rained the place was flooded, and when the sun came out, the steaming mass sent out most noxious gases."[52]

[52] Botume, *First Days amongst the Contrabands,* p. 239.

An English observer wrote in 1876: "Exceptions may occur, but as a rule, the colored people under freedom live in worse houses and eat less hearty food. A man sucks more canes, and chews more quids; yet eats less wholesome food, and occupies less wholesome rooms."[53] Townsend wrote: "The food of the Negroes is coarse and barbarously prepared. . . . Their dwellings . . . have usually but one room, in which they sleep, cook, eat, sit, and receive company. . . . They eat either directly out of the cooking instruments, or employ tin pans and cups, and (when they can afford it) thick-grained crockery painted with red flowers. . . . Their food rarely includes more than hominy, corn-bread, rank fat bacon sides, coffee and cheap molasses for breakfast. . . . At dinner they have corn-bread, rice—if thrifty—pork 'sides,' and vegetables slimy with grease. At supper the same articles appear as for breakfast, minus the meat. On Sundays a plate of wheat bread, either biscuit or hoe-cake, is prepared for breakfast as a luxury, and what is left is warmed over for dinner and supper, and the coffee is rendered more palatable by a modicum of exceedingly coarse brown sugar. The gardens of the Negroes contain only a few specimens of plants: sweet potatoes, Irish potatoes more rarely, peas, beans, watermelons and collards. . . . A family that can afford it keeps a pig impounded during the year, fattening it to kill at Christmas. . . . Many of them have invested their earnings in a cow, and most of them rear fowls. But side by side with this tendency may often be descried the fatal disposition which has been the curse of Ireland: The desire to burrow in a hole. They will buy an acre or two, build a cottage, move in, and live in sloth and filthiness on what they can raise on their half-cultivated lot."[54]

As may have been expected of a people so recently out of slavery, the Negroes were poor respecters of the obligations of

[53] W. H. Dixon, *White Conquest,* II, 139. Cf. *News,* Sept. 15, 1868.   [54] *Loc. cit.,* pp. 678-79.

marriage. "Chastity is the exception among them," said Townsend. "Tens of thousands of Negroes live together as man and wife without marrying. The married ones are every day quitting each other and taking up with illicit partners."[55] Although their moral sense was sharpened by religion, circumstances militated against the application of the moral law to sexual problems. The natural sensuality of the African had been encouraged by the communal life of the slave quarters. The disruptive influences of freedom promoted the gadding about of the male, which led to the neglect of family obligations and the tendency to meddle with those of others. Forced by the migratory habits of their mates to shoulder the responsibilities of the family, the women showed a self-assertiveness worthy of the most sanguine feminists of the twentieth century. They earned the bread of the family, consorted with any man who struck their fancy, and by the use of their sharp tongues and strong fists protected themselves against masculine discipline. Many Negresses, like Scarlet Sister Mary, the heroine of Julia Peterkin's novel, satisfied their instincts to the limit and reared families without once bending their necks under the yoke of masculine tyranny.

The relations existing between the Negro parent and child seemed barbaric to persons accustomed to the traditions of the North European family. There was a decline in parental discipline. "The children," said Miss Botume, "ran more at large and acquired bad habits. In former times the elders had unquestioned authority over the younger people, from whom they exacted implicit obedience."[56] "The Negro females," wrote Townsend, "are very roughly handled by the males, and colored children are treated by both their fathers and mothers in a way that would make Pestalozzi, Froebel and Herbert Spencer shudder."[57] "It is no uncommon occurrence," said

[55] *Ibid.,* p. 474. Cf. *Letters and Diary of Laura M. Towne,* p. 24, and Edward King, *The Southern States of North America,* p. 430.
[56] *Op. cit.,* p. 277.
[57] *Loc. cit.,* p. 678.

the *Charleston Daily News,* "to find mere infants whipped until blood flows freely, or a girl of tender years lashed for a quarter of an hour."[58] Infants were shut up in houses all day while parents were at work or pleasure and were put to work as soon as they were old enough to handle a hoe.

The working clothes of the Negroes showed no improvement over those they had worn as slaves. Townsend described them as follows: "The dress of the Negroes is simply disgusting; their clothes are stiff with mingled grease and dirt. It is unpleasant to have one of them approach within ten feet of you."[59] Sometimes they purchased brogan shoes, ready-made clothing, cheap calico prints and unbleached cloth from country merchants. But when possible they bought or begged the cast-off garments of the whites. Their passion for this sort of raiment was so strong that Miss Botume said that they "seemed to delight more in an old garment than in a new one."[60] The whites were not willing to part with their garments until they were well worn. "It is often impossible," said Townsend, "to discern the original piece of coat or pair of pants, or its intended color, owing to the number of party-colored patches." The shoes which they got from the whites were often full of holes; if this were not true, holes were cut in them to make room for larger calloused feet. If adults dressed thus, what could one expect of the children? Most of them wore rags. "The Negro children in isolated places," affirmed Townsend, "hardly ever wear more than a shirt, and it is not so startling a thing to see them playing about naked."

A fundamental weakness of the Negro was disrespect for law and moral conventions. His most frequent offenses were lying and stealing, which were heritages from slavery. The demoralizing influences of Reconstruction accentuated these

[58] Sept. 15, 1868. Cf. W. H. Dixon, *White Conquest,* II, 139-40, and [Edward E. Hale and W. C. Gannett], *North American Review,* CI (July, 1865), 5-6.

[59] *Loc. cit.,* p. 680.

[60] *First Days amongst the Contrabands,* p. 263.

practices. "Lying is at this day," said Townsend, "the Negroes' worst failing. They are the most bare-faced perjurers ever seen in courts of justice; and especially are they expert in giving false testimony to save fellow blacks."[61] A Northerner sorrowfully summarized his experiences with the race as follows: "The satisfaction derived from the faithfulness and honesty of perhaps thirty is hardly sufficient to atone for the anxiety and distrust with which one regards the remaining ninety, who lie by habit and steal on the least provocation. . . . 'Wherefore he is called the everlasting Niggah.' "[62] "The amount of stealing done in this neighborhood," was a typical news report of the times, "is perfectly frightful, and is on the increase. Stores are repeatedly robbed in the most daring and cunning manner; but of all classes the farmer suffers most. . . . His fields, his gin house, his barn is robbed. . . . This indicates a state of vagrancy, idleness and immorality which is almost impossible to realize."[63]

Crimes of violence figured prominently among the Negroes' offenses against the law. By 1868 practically all possessed firearms, regarding them as a necessary attribute of freedom. Although fear prevented them from openly provoking encounters with white men, they did not hesitate when provoked to fire stealthily on members of the superior race, to deal brutally with women and other helpless persons, or to apply the torch to barns and gin houses. But the greater portion of their violence was directed against members of their own race. The usual cause was rivalry over women. "Jealousy," said Edward King, "is a terrible passion among these people, and sometimes leads to capital crime."[64] In their social relations, said Townsend, they were usually cordial, but when aroused fearful in revenge, resorting to murder, mutilation and wife-murder.[65]

[61] *Loc. cit.,* pp. 473-74.
[62] C. P. Ware, in Pearson, *Letters from Port Royal,* p. 227.
[63] From Lynchburg in *Sumter Watchman,* Dec. 22, 1875. Cf. Townsend, *loc. cit.,* p. 473, and *News,* Sept. 19, 1867.
[64] *Op. cit.,* p. 430.
[65] *Loc. cit.,* p. 474. Cf. *News,* Mar. 8, 1869.

The worst crime which the Negro committed against himself was the careless expenditure of his earnings. The country Negro, said Sidney Andrews, "is very often, and perhaps generally, idle, vicious, improvident, negligent and unfit to care well for his own interests."[66] "You all think," Wade Hampton told a committee of Congress, "that the Negro is actuated by the same feelings as the white man, but this is a mistake. They have no provision; they have no forethought at all; they are content to live from hand to mouth; they do not pretend to lay up anything."[67] Edward King said that the masses were satisfied with a bare living. He added, "They know little about markets, surplus crops, and the accumulation of riches, and care less. They love hunting and fishing. They revel in idleness, which they never knew until after the war."[68]

Perhaps no peasantry in history has ever had such a passion for the expensive luxury of traveling. They exhausted their work animals on pleasure trips, which habitually lasted until late at night. For the longer trips they employed the railroad. "They are literally crazy about traveling," said Townsend. "The railroad officials are continually importuned by them to run extra trains, excursion trains, and so on, on all sorts of occasions: holidays, picnics, Sunday-school celebrations, church dedications, funerals of their prominent men, circuses, public executions. . . . They attract whole counties of Negroes, and it is delightful to witness their childish wonder and enjoyment and behavior on the cars."[69]

Because of these and other weaknesses, the colored man, in spite of superiority in numbers, political power, and laboring ability, failed to rise economically and socially to the level of the white man. Sir George Campbell noted this fact in 1878 as the result of observations at Beaufort. The colored aristocracy of the town, he said, consisted chiefly of public officials

[66] *Op. cit.*, p. 22.
[67] *Ku-Klux Conspiracy, S. C.*, p. 1236.
[68] *Op. cit.*, p. 427. Cf. Ludwig Lew-

isohn, *Up Stream*, p. 38, and Sir George Campbell, *White and Black*, p. 336.
[69] *Loc. cit.*, p. 682.

and a few lawyers in the criminal practice. One or two tailor shops owned by colored men had survived the war, a member of that race owned a small harness-making establishment, and there were colored hack drivers and carpenters and one store-keeper. There had been one colored physician, but he had been accused of extortion and had left town. All other Negroes were engaged in unskilled labor. The white minority were the economic and social rulers of the town.[70] What was true of Beaufort was even to a greater degree true of other towns, where the opportunities of the freedmen were less.

The lawlessness of the Negro has often been ascribed to the laxity in the administration of justice characteristic of the period. But the fact that 239 out of 262 persons in the penitentiary at the outset of the Radical régime were colored, and that at the close of this period these figures were 325 and 355 respectively,[71] indicates that there was no marked tendency for the state to favor colored wrong-doers. This malady had a deeper cause. The Negro failed to impose social or moral penalties upon criminals. A Negro wrote as follows of the social morality of Sumter, a typical community: "I find a society among the colored people of this town which takes into full membership anybody be his or her character ever so bad. I find that persons living in this village can be guilty of burglary and larceny and at the same time be occupants of the highest rank in the so-called good society. A woman can live in a dissipated house and at the same time marry a man moving in the highest rank of society. . . . It seems to me that the wickedness practiced by the people of my color has grown to such a height that none but the God of the Universe can turn the tide thereof."[72]

The barbaric tastes of the Negroes were vividly illustrated by their interest in hangings, which attracted greater crowds

[70] *Op. cit.,* p. 355.
[71] *News,* Apr. 12, 1869, and Townsend, *loc. cit.,* p. 474.
[72] Shelton W. Lawton in Sumter *True Southron,* Mar. 12, 1874. Cf. Townsend, *loc. cit.,* p. 475.

than any other event. For days and even weeks prior to an execution, colored persons crowded around the cell of the condemned, singing, praying, and eagerly awaiting the expected confession. On the fatal day there was "a rushing, swelling and swaying" of the mass of several thousand colored persons who gathered around the county jail to witness the gruesome drama. "On the scaffold," said Townsend, "prayers are made, which extract groans of assent from the concourse, frenzied by the speech of the usually repentant and confessing criminal. Hymns are sung to wild airs, the colored spectators joining. A dead silence then ensues; this is broken by the falling of the drop, and as the doomed man is launched into eternity, a piercing and universal shriek arises, the wildest religious mania seizes on the crowd, they surge to and fro, sing, and raise the holy dance."[73]

The physical defects of the Negroes grew worse with the coming of freedom. Townsend wrote, "In consequence of their bad food and unhygienic conduct, they are usually diseased to a lamentable degree. 'How do you do this morning?' To such an inquiry, a colored person will never reply, 'First rate.' The invariable response is, 'Well, I am rather poorly,' 'I'm not so well this morning,' 'I'm sorter middling, sir,' or 'I'm jes' betwix and between.' The whites ridicule this as an affectation, but really half of it is not put on."[74]

The vital statistics of Charleston, which in the absence of other data may be regarded as illustrative of the entire state, show that the death rate among the freedmen was much greater than that among either the slaves or the whites. During thirty-six years previous to the war, the average annual death rate among each one thousand of colored population was only 26.45, which was only slightly greater than the corresponding figure of 25.60 among the whites; whereas, for

[73] Loc. cit., p. 682. Executions are described in profuse details in Sumter Watchman, Apr. 1, 1874; Sumter True Southron, Apr. 16, 1874; and News and Courier, Mar. 22, and Apr. 5, 1875.
[74] Loc. cit., p. 680.

thirty-nine years after the war this average among the colored population rose to 43.33 and fell among the white to 24.04.[75] All of the major diseases to which the human family is subject, with the exception of yellow fever and alcoholism, took a greater toll among the freedmen than among the whites.

"This contrast is not surprising," said the *Charleston Daily News,* "when one considers the squalor and filth in which a majority of the Negroes of this city live, to say nothing of their addiction to midnight carousals of every kind. . . . They are victims of want of cleanliness, lack of proper nutrition, and the absence of skilled medical attention."[76] Infant mortality and affections of the respiratory system took the largest toll. The city registrar ascribed the death of infants to carelessness, crude obstetrics and even murder. "From exposure, night reveling and dissipations of all kind, want of proper nutrition, clothing and bedding," he added, "the young and the middle-aged contract pneumonias and catarrhs, which finally terminate their lives by consumption."[77] Although the race was relatively immune to malaria, that disease took a large number because of the unhealthy location of dwellings. Even insanity, which had been almost unknown among the slaves,[78] became widespread. That the number of Negroes within the state did not suffer a relative decline, was due to a high birth rate and the emigration of a greater number of whites.

[75] Frederick L. Hoffman, *Race Traits and Tendencies of the American Negro,* pp. 53-54, and *Handbook of S. C., 1883,* pp. 675-76.

[76] July 11, 1868.

[77] Robert Lebby, in *News and Courier,* Feb. 6, 1875.

[78] Gen. D. H. Hill, in *Land We Love,* I (Sept., 1866), 349-60.

CHAPTER XIII

BRIGHTER PHASES OF SOCIAL LIFE

FACTORS other than misery and retrogression must be taken into account if a full picture of social conditions in South Carolina during the Reconstruction period is to be approximated. Important bases of the community life, if shocked, were not shattered by the effects of the war, and many had expectations of exacting the benefits which the changes of Reconstruction promised. The hopes of the period bore fruit in the recovery of traditional institutions, happiness grew out of the degree of contentment developed, and the foundations of the respectable civilization which the state has today were laid.

Many of the social manifestations whose darker side has been described had also a brighter side. The culture of the Old South glowed in mellow colors because it was in sunset. Gentlemen were more charming and restrained because they carried with them the memories of a great experience and had suffered defeat without losing honor. The "fire-eating" qualities of the South Carolinians were in abeyance. The caste pride of the whites had its virtues as well as its vices; it was a means of conserving the heritage of white civilization. The tendency of the Negro to work less and frolic more had its compensations. Perhaps he was fulfilling the legitimate craving of every free man for recreation; perhaps his wife deserted field work because she was busy with the tasks of setting up a home. To censure the Negro to a great degree for moral delinquencies involves the creation of arbitrary standards.

Moreover, many of the social practices for which there can be no apology were not universal. If country hotels were barbarous, this does not mean that those of Charleston were, or that there were not homes in which the economy was excellent. All Negroes were not boisterous and lawless; there were many who were meek and law-abiding. The whites who were considerate of the feelings of the Negroes were as numerous as those who lynched and whipped. In South Carolina society there were many sound qualities which asserted themselves over demoralizing influences.

There was one great influence which had a conserving effect upon both the external activities and the innermost feelings of the state's entire population—the distinctive characteristics of the climate and landscape. This was an influence which had not been affected by the war, which had been largely responsible for the unique aspects of South Carolina culture, and which, in the face of demoralization and the lure of new ideals, forced, after the war, the streams of human endeavor back into old channels. Its hardships repelled outsiders and blighted the plans of innovators; its charms and gifts satisfied those who followed after traditional customs consonant with it. It was the immutable force which conserved South Carolina for its native blacks and whites and for its established industries.[1]

A conserving influence more tangible if less universal than that of landscape and climate was what remained in actuality or in spirit of the ante-bellum house and garden. They were pretexts for the revival of old sentiments, places where the rhythms of a once spacious life could for a time reassert themselves. "Charleston," remarked a stranger, "is something of a city after all. . . . Few places in the country possess more of the elements of comfort."[2] If a Northern visitor found the city surrounded by destruction, such was not her discovery in the lower portion of the city. From the steeple of St. Michael's Church she looked down upon houses which retained much

[1] For the influences of the climate of the state see Mrs. Jane Pringle in *Our Women in the War*, pp. 350-51; William G. Simms, *Rural Carolinian*, I (July, 1870), 635; Viscountess Avonmore, *Teresina in America*, I, 57-59; and Ludwig Lewisohn, *Up Stream*, p. 39.
[2] *News*, Feb. 26, 1868.

of their traditional elegance. "Below," she said, "lay the city closely built. . . . Lights were twinkling from the windows of the old houses, built generally with narrow gable-end on the street, rising three stories high, with closed shutters and massive jealous garden walls. . . . We could see the long stretch of broad verandas adorning each story from ground to roof, and the mass of green in the hidden gardens, which, like Moorish courtyards, are for the dwellers within, and not for the passers-by."[3]   Edward King, who walked these streets, was impressed with their "novel appearance" and their "tall weather stained mansions . . . screened from the sun and from observation by ample wooden lattices and by trellised vines and creepers."[4]

Some of the country seats which had given character to ante-bellum society survived. One of the most notable of these was "Edgewood," the home of Lucy Holcombe Pickens at Edgefield. As was true of almost all rural places of the up-country, the house itself was not distinguished. It was a rambling one story affair, originally built from the remains of another house and added to from time to time. The interior adornments, however, portrayed the wealth and good taste of the ante-bellum planter and public servant. The paintings indicated ancestral pride and a residence in Europe. The vases, clocks, chandeliers, china, and glassware were of fine imported quality, and the furniture was in the best American tradition. But the principal charm of the place was its surroundings. For half a mile in every direction was a forest of primeval oak, hickory, and pine, which gave a touch of native wildness. The principal approach was through an avenue of interlocking cedars. The garden was an enticing adaptation of English tradition to local needs. There were formal walks bordered by hedges of the odorous boxwood and leading to shady parks.

[3] Constance Fenimore Woolson, in *Harper's Magazine*, LII (Dec., 1875), 1-24.   [4] *Southern States of North America*, pp. 441-43, 446.

There were mounds surmounted by cast-iron statues, and a profusion of roses, jasmine, sweet olives, and raspberry in sunny spots. Above all towered the great magnolia and other semi-tropical trees, which gave the garden a damp coolness and stale sweetness so satisfying in a sun-scorched climate.[5]

The rawness and bad architectural taste of the new towns was to some degree softened by the restfulness and beauty of shade trees and native shrubbery. They hid cheap and ugly houses. Marion was described as "a very quiet, pretty little village full of trees and gardens," and Edgefield as "a quiet but beautiful town," picturesque and full of trees. Edward King said of Columbia, "The broad, richly shaded avenues, the gardens filled with jasmines and japonicas, laurels and hawthorns and hollies, and perfect groves in which the live oaks, the pines, the magnolias and the oranges vie with each other in charm, give it an especial fascination."[6] As yet the craving for English and exotic forms of open landscaping, unsuited for the environment, had not come to expose unkempt actualities to the bleaching of the sun.

The ladies and gentlemen who survived had not forgotten the manners of the old régime. "The Southern *ladies,*" said a Northern resident, "were true to their antecedents. They bravely took up their duties without complaint, and never asked for help. . . . They lived in great seclusion, but when brought face to face with strangers always showed themselves courteous and refined."[7] Of the qualities of the gentlemen the Viscountess Avonmore wrote, "The South Carolinians seemed almost a different race. Tall, thin, well-formed, sinewy men, sallow complexioned, with large features, long, dark, straight hair, and deep-set eyes of a most peculiar gray. . . . They had a carriage differing far from the hurried, shuffling tread of the

[5] Descriptions in *Courier,* June 13, 1866, and *News and Courier,* July 10, 1926.
[6] N. Y. *Nation,* I (Nov. 9, 1865), 586;
Courier, June 13, 1868; and King, pp.458-59.
[7] Elizabeth H. Botume, *First Days amongst the Contrabands,* pp. 231-32.

business and money-making men of the North. . . . There is more dignity—more polish—about him than the Northerner. . . . Their long frock-coats and broad-leaved hats of straw or felt, are suitable to the climate, and the latter far more becoming than the hideous 'chimney-pot.' In the summer they wear no vests, and with their broad, white shirts and white trousers they only lack a *ceinture* for the dress to be really picturesque."[8]

In such a setting among such a people life soon became animated and gay. "I never knew," said Professor Joseph LeConte, "so much real social enjoyment in Columbia as in the years 1866 and 1867; society was really gay, the necessary result of the rebound from the agony and repression of the war. . . . As everybody was poor, the gatherings were almost wholly without expense, and therefore frequent, the hostess simply furnished lemonade and cake and the young men a Negro fiddler."[9] A typical item in the press ran as follows: "Sumter, with its floral wreaths and gush of merriment, is by no means an unpleasant place on the first of May. The air is laden with the delicious breath of a thousand flowers, and the dark shadows of anxious thought, which wear so heavily on heart and brain, are, for a time, dispelled by youthful loveliness in the rapture of its careless happiness."[10]

How the young ladies of Charleston were able to exact the maximum pleasure out of meager resources is revealed by Elizabeth W. Allston Pringle. Although many people thought it proper to be gloomy because of poverty and the death of relations in the war, there were, as early as August, 1865, delightful dances. For these occasions, we are told, the young ladies were "nicely dressed, for all the girls and their mothers had become expert dressmakers, with few exceptions. But the frocks were generally of the simplest muslin, sweet and fresh, but not such as would be worn in the great world to the full-

[8] *Teresina in America,* I, 48-49.
[9] *Autobiography,* p. 236.
[10] *News,* May 8, 1866. Cf. another dispatch from Sumter, *ibid.,* Sept. 23, 1865.

dress ball; and when these creations . . . burst upon us, we were filled with admiration and wonder."[11] Although nominally in mourning, Miss Allston managed to wear a "bleached pink paper cambric baby waist," exquisite lace on her bodice, and old Mexican silver—"a pair of broad silver bracelets like manacles of fish scales," a string of silver beads, and "carved silver earrings about three inches long." The young men were described in glowing terms. "They were," we are told, "such nice young men, who had fought through the war, and now were not ashamed to take any kind of work to help their mothers and sisters. They were literally butchers and bakers and candlestick makers, but all thorough, true gentlemen, and most of them beautiful dancers." They graciously consented to carry the girls' slippers and to wax the floors. "We were sure of good music," Miss Allston continues, "for there were four or five girls going in society that played delightfully for dancing." For the entertainments there was "a great big cool room . . . and a great wide piazza all around outside to walk in after dancing." The refreshments generally consisted "of rolls handed in dishes of exquisite China, and water in very dainty glasses. At one or two houses there was the rare treat of coffee, but that did not often happen, and when the rolls appeared just after the German, they were very welcome and greatly enjoyed, for we were all working hard, and living was none too high."

The war was scarcely over before South Carolinians began to revive the social organizations of peace times. A month after the firing of the last gun the Mansion House, a famous hotel of Charleston, announced that it was ready to serve its customers with viands and drinks as sumptuous as those before the war.[12] The young men of the countryside had scarcely laid aside the weapons of actual war before they took up the

[11] *Chronicles of Chicora Wood*, pp. 228, 300-3, 316-33.   [12] *Courier*, May 1, 1865, and Jan. 3, 1866.

mimic lances of the tournaments. In 1866 St. Patrick's Day was celebrated in Charleston by a lavish feast,[13] and banqueting soon became the custom of many clubs. Within a year the city had its first operatic performance and theatrical season. These were followed by numerous professional and amateur plays, amateur musicals, and lyceums. The exhibitions of traveling circuses, magic lantern shows and Negro minstrels became popular throughout the state. In 1869 the aristocracy of Charleston felt sufficiently recovered to resume the famous balls of the St. Cecilia Society, and in the same year the young men of the state organized the South Carolina Club, which gave annually a ball at the time of the state fair.[14] Dancing once more became a popular pastime. In 1873 the Camden Jockey Club revived its races; in the following year races were revived at the famous Washington Race Course near Charleston.[15] By that time the mineral springs, notably Glenn Springs near Spartanburg, had become the rendezvous of many in search of health and pleasure, and amateur baseball was enjoying much popular favor. Other sources of enjoyment were the gatherings of the Masons and other fraternities, and the countless picnics and other forms of outdoor pleasure in which South Carolinians seemed to be forever participating. So widespread did popular gatherings become that Belton O'Neall Townsend was able to remark at the close of the Reconstruction period: "Public entertainments, concerts, tableaux, county fairs, balls, etc., not to mention private parties and dances, have become as common as in normal times."[16] This was saying much, for South Carolinians already had reputations for immoderate indulgence in social pleasures.

The most widely chronicled form of entertainment was the tournaments, that is, the catching of suspended rings by mounted men armed with lances. The contestants assumed

---

[13] *Ibid.*, Mar. 19, 1866.
[14] Pringle, p. 326, and *News*, Nov. 18, 1869.
[15] *News and Courier*, Dec. 15, 1874, and Jan. 4, 20, and 22, 1875.
[16] *Loc. cit.*, p. 682.

the names and dress of medieval knights. The lady love of the most successful participant was crowned Queen of Love and Beauty, and after this ceremony there were dinners and dances. Although there was an element of absurdity in men dressing themselves in fantastic costumes and calling themselves "Disinherited Knights," "Knights of the Sword," and "Knights of the Lone Star," and pretending that the bestowal of a coronet on a young woman from a modest wooden house was the summit of earthly felicity, great crowds seem to have gained satisfaction from these ceremonies. Such an event held at Sumter in 1865, we are told, "was the grandest affair in the shape of a tournament which this country has ever witnessed. Some thirty knights, in splendid attire and magnificently mounted, contended for the prize in the presence of several thousand spectators. Music and beauty's smile graced the occasion, and fun and merriment were not wanting."[17]

Horseback riding and the chase had an almost instinctive appeal to a rural people endowed with a wealth of forest and open field. "Every man, white or black, rich or poor, aristocrat or plebeian," said Townsend, "keeps a gun or a pistol. The whites are nearly always first-class marksmen. . . . A mile's walk from a city will conduct you to game. . . . Deer, though thinned, are found in river swamps; foxes are often encountered, and wild turkeys, squirrels, raccoons, opossums and rabbits abound. . . . Every Southerner is also ambitious to own blooded stock, horses, dogs, hounds and game fowls. The white man is invariably a good, usually a graceful rider, and is fond of the exercise."[18] The ladies, we are told, were once famous for equestrian accomplishments, but owing to the inferiority of the horses had largely given up the habit. An old lady of Barnwell bitterly lamented that no more of "our fine girls and handsome women" could afford mounts; but she was gratified that those who appeared at the races rode well.

[17] *Courier*, Oct. 31, 1865.   [18] *Loc. cit.*, p. 681.

One young woman, she said, "rode upon the field well mounted, controlling her horse with the ease and grace of a practiced equestrienne"; while her escort, "a tall grenadier, rode his horse like an Arab."[19]

The people of the rural districts, at least those of the upper and middle classes, enjoyed dancing with even greater spontaneity than did the more polite circles of Charleston. Their dances were informal community gatherings to which all with the proper aptitude were admitted. The popularity of the diversion seems to have been little affected by the opposition of the evangelical clergy. The enthusiasm engendered is revealed by the extravagance into which the aforementioned lady of Barnwell fell in describing "the softly tinted picture of the fun-loving crowd" at the dance following the Barnwell races of 1868. The "fair young hostess," we are told, had a "matchless wealth of hair which fell in clusters around her snowy throat, recalling to every eye the gorgeous coloring which only portraits of old masters reveal." One of the guests was "the brightest of brunettes who well understands the effects of *coleur de rose* on a lissome figure"; another "cheered the hearts of many by her reappearance in her moire antique of shimmering blue"; and a third was like "a snow drop as she glided into the room in a dress of loveliest green." The gentlemen appeared "handsomely dressed and with polished manners, convincing me that war did not do harm either to their cultivation or their refinement."

South Carolinians demonstrated that they were capable of living up to the standards of an age which loved long and heavy feasting, and which had put no restrictions upon the variety or quantity of the drinks served. The high water mark of these indulgences was perhaps reached when the Hibernian Society of Charleston gathered in its hall to celebrate St. Patrick's Day, 1868. Nearly two hundred of the distinguished

¹⁹ *News*, Dec. 29, 1868.

citizens of the city and state, we are told, gathered around the table "in old fashioned dress with its ruffled wristbands and extravagant shirt fronts" for "the promotion and diffusion of felicity."[20] A prodigious feast was consumed, amidst a display of "much Irish enthusiasm" in the form of bombastic oratory and poetry. According to the published menu, it consisted of twelve courses, in addition to the drinks. First came oysters on the half shell, then cooter [terrapin] soup and two varieties of fish, followed by five boiled meats, four cold dishes, seven relishes and six varieties of roast meats; next came the game meats, consisting of wild turkey, venison, prairie hen, duck, pheasant, quail and snipe; added to this were eleven vegetables, fourteen flavors of pastry, and ten desserts. Thirteen dozen bottles of champagne, it was affirmed, were drunk in eleven minutes. So spirited was the drinking that "the rattle of small arms and the salutary detonations of champagne reminded one of a mimic engagement on a bloodless field."

Far more popular than banquets were community picnics given by churches, schools, political clubs, lodges and military companies, in oak or hickory groves convenient to springs. Ostensibly the primary purpose of these gatherings was to listen to sermons, school examinations, or oratory. But the main interest of all but the leaders was social intercourse with one's neighbors and the enjoyment of the bountiful feast of barbecued kid and shoat, and of such delicacies of the domestic larder as fried chicken, potato and lemon pie, and salads. A majority of the few who pretended to listen to the addresses carried on such a murmur of conversation that it was difficult for the handful of serious listeners to hear a word. "You might have seen," we are told of an occurrence of this character, "pedestrians and equestrians, buggies, barouches, carriages and wagons filled with ladies and gentlemen, walking, riding, roll-

[20] *News*, Mar. 20, 1868. Cf. *ibid.*, Apr.　*News and Courier*, Feb. 16, 1876.
16, 1868; *Courier*, Mar. 19, 1866; and

ing, rattling toward Salem Church" to enjoy "a table groaning under good things."[21] "Such a dinner," we are informed of another occasion, "has seldom been served in the South since the war. Five hundred were present, yet the preparations had been ample for two thousand."[22]

The fairs, concerts, and dinners given by the women to raise money for the building of monuments to the Confederate dead, or for some other public purpose, enjoyed wide popularity. For the fair, a hall was filled with brightly decorated booths from which sweets were sold and prizes raffled. For the fair of the Sumter Monument Association, the new town hall was "fitted up in handsome and tasteful style, and the tables, beautifully decorated in evergreens and artificial flowers, presented quite a gay appearance."[23] The ladies "coaxed the greenbacks out of many a vest pocket" to the sum of eight hundred dollars. The fairs were successful, for a monument rose on the square of practically every village and town.

The occasions which attracted the largest numbers of whites were for the revival of the memories of the late war. They were Monument Day, when the war memorials were unveiled or their cornerstones laid, and Memorial Day, when the graves of the departed heroes were decorated. For the latter ceremony, according to Townsend, "the whole white population of a town turns out in procession, headed by the Ladies' Memorial Association, and decorates the graves. Poems, too, are commonly recited, either specially written for the occasion by local bards unknown to fame, or such 'old, old stories' as Collins' ode, 'How Sleep the Brave.' "[24] For Monument Day at Sumter, we are told, a large crowd gathered, in the center of which was "an overflowing of as brilliant an array of beauty as was ever gathered to honor manly valor."[25] General J. B.

---

[21] At Salem School, Fairfield County. —*Fairfield Herald*, Aug. 8, 1866.

[22] A gathering of Patrons of Husbandry in Sumter County.—*Sumter News*, Nov 7, 1872.

[23] *Sumter News*, Jan. 9, 1873. Cf. *Courier*, May 4, 1866.

[24] *Loc. cit.*, p. 683.

[25] *Sumter Watchman*, May 13, 1874.

Kershaw, the orator of the day, "did full justice to the latent purposes and unbridled license of the North, which first saddled slavery upon us, and then was willing to destroy us to free the slaves!" His recital of the noble part which the sons of Sumter had played in the war, brought tears from many. This was followed by a series of tableaux illustrative of recent history. Each of the states of the former Confederacy appeared in mourning. "Louisiana," "Florida," and "Arkansas" appeared in chains to bring home the fact that they had not been redeemed from Republican rule. "South Carolina" appeared bound by a stalwart Negro, while her rich treasures were being despoiled by carpetbaggers and scalawags. Other scenes represented the Confederate soldier parting from his weeping family, and lying dead upon the battlefield shrouded in a Palmetto flag.

The whites paid little attention to the traditional national holidays except Christmas. Good Friday and Easter were observed by the small minority who belonged to the liturgical churches; the majority ignored them because of ignorance or because they were considered popish. Thanksgiving had too much of a New England flavor to arouse enthusiasm. On that day slimly attended religious services were held, but no turkeys were killed. New Year's was monopolized by the Negroes as Emancipation Day. The Fourth of July, which had once been lavishly observed, was studiously ignored since it had been made into a second Emancipation Day and an occasion for the manifestation of patriotic emotions objectionable to white Southerners.[26] Christmas, on the other hand, was celebrated with a week's holiday. But little attention was given it as a public or religious ceremony. The people stayed at home, feasting, firing a few rockets, and exchanging a few gifts.[27]

The agricultural fairs gave opportunities for social pleas-

[26] *Sumter News,* July 4, 1872.   [27] Townsend, *loc. cit.,* pp. 682-83, and *News and Courier,* Jan. 6, 1875.

ures. Thousands of visitors crowded the streets of Columbia and overran its hotels and boarding houses for the fair of the Agricultural and Mechanical Society, and hundreds came to the courthouse towns for similar occasions. The principal attractions, according to the critics, were the horse races, and the exhibitions "of fat women, giants and disgusting monstrosities, and the nameless hosts of gamblers and swindlers" furnished by the traveling carnivals.[28] But the pleasures derived from such diversions were as often innocent as vicious, and the educational value of agricultural exhibits was not neglected. Moreover, with political associations largely monopolized by Negroes and strangers, the fairs gave the whites their principal means of meeting each other.

During Reconstruction, baseball for the first time became a great popular diversion. "Amateur baseball clubs," wrote Townsend, "have sprung up everywhere. Public match games between nines from a distance, which lead to dinners and picnics are frequent."[29] A Fourth of July game at Orangeburg between the Orange Club of that town and the Carolina Club of Charleston illustrated how these contests were enjoyed. The Orangeburg organization, we are told, consisted of "plucky young men who have the hearty countenance of the more substantial citizens of the place."[30] Its challenge to the Charleston team created "a decided ruffle in the placid current of summer life in the village and surrounding country, and village belles and their sweethearts began at once to make arrangements to witness the game." A large crowd met the Charlestonians at the station and escorted them through the streets. The game lasted no less than three and one half hours and resulted in victory for the visitors by a score of 41 to 23. At exciting moments in the contest the men were said to have engaged in "mighty shouts," and the ladies, segregated at a respectable

[28] *Rural Carolinian*, IV (Dec., 1872, and Feb., 1873), 147-49, 256.

[29] *Loc. cit.*, p. 862.
[30] *News and Courier*, July 6, 1874.

distance from the heat of the fray, "waved their kerchiefs with delight." The festivities were completed with a banquet in honor of the visitors.

The patronage of public lectures and the theater by the better classes was evidence of the appreciation of the finer things of life. Although the lectures were stereotyped, they had an educational value and enjoyed a popularity unknown in later generations. Professor Francis S. Holmes, for example, created such a favorable impression on Charleston audiences by his descriptions of Mount Vesuvius and the Aurora Borealis that there were "numerous demands for repetition."[31] The lecture of "an eminent Virginia divine and fine belle-lettre scholar" was described as "truly unique, considered by all who have heard it as a matchless and delicate satire, flashing with wit and irresistible humor."[32] In many towns lyceum societies were organized in order to attract lecturers. The one at Sumter, which was typical, was said to have been an enlightening influence. The Catholic bishop of Charleston and a select group of native lawyers and divines were on its programs. It heard, for example, Judge A. P. Aldrich deliver "a finished and tasteful" exposition of *Hamlet,* and the Reverend David E. Frierson draw from "the volume of nature" and deliver a panegyric on the Bible, in a discourse entitled "The Office of Books."[33]

By 1868 theatrical and operatic seasons had become part of the social life of Charleston. The city demanded the best of the companies which made provincial tours. The audiences, said the hypercritical Townsend, "are highly intelligent and critical."[34] The local critics showed an originality and reserve seldom found in provincial theatrical notices. When the singers were adjudged poor, the comments were harsh. "There were," said the *Charleston Daily News* of those of 1867 and

[31] *Courier,* July 13, 1866.
[32] *Ibid.,* Mar. 10, 1866.
[33] *Sumter News,* June 3, 1872.
[34] *Loc. cit.,* 681.

1868, "the usual calf-less tenor, corpulent soprano, weazened contralto, and burly basso, but very few felt sufficient interest to do their very best."[35] But when the dramatic season reached its peak in 1875 with performances of *Maria Stuart, The Earl of Essex, Richelieu,* and *The Merchant of Venice,* there were appreciative audiences and warm praises.[36]

As has already been indicated,[37] the literature of the period lacked the vitality born of contact with the realities of contemporary life. But this was due less to the inability to attain this standard than to the dominance of another standard. Literature, the South Carolinians felt, should be a means of escape from contemporary misfortune and barbarism, and of conserving the ideals of a bygone day. "Literature to them," Ludwig Lewisohn aptly remarks, "was one of the graces of civilized life and not the vital affair. . . . It was the elegance and restrained beauty of Latin poetry and English prose of the eighteenth century which attracted Simms' contemporaries."[38] Within this limitation the state produced a literature of which it had a right to be proud.

In the field of imaginative efforts some contributions were made. William Gilmore Simms wrote a few of his less important novels between 1865 and his death in 1870, and in 1866 brought out his anthology of war verse. "The book," says Lewisohn of the anthology, "contains no work that approximates great poetry, except Timrod's, but in it ring the voices of men and women as high-souled in endeavor, as nobly devoted to the cause that was all in all to them, as magnanimous under defeat and desolation as any of whom a record is preserved among men." The two most famous poets the state has ever produced lived at this time. Henry Timrod, in the interval between the war and his death in 1867, wrote verse which showed a conscientious perfection of form. Paul Ham-

[35] May 8, 1868.

[36] *News and Courier,* Jan. 6, 7 and 12, 1875. Cf. *News,* Mar. 19, 1868, and Mar. 27, 1869.

[37] See above, p. 328.

[38] *News and Courier,* Sept. 6, 1903.

ilton Hayne, with his property destroyed, retired to the pine barrens near Augusta, Georgia, where until his death in 1886, he maintained a dignified existence and wrote competent verse. The other poets of the period, of merit, if not of fame, were George Herbert Sass, Carlyle McKinley, and John Dickson Bruns. Each of them published slim volumes.

The novel, aside from the work of Simms, was represented by Caroline Howard Glover and Susan Petigru King. What these women wrote was bound by the conventionalities of the age—"a Byronic prose, a plentiful sprinkling of 'withered hearts,' an evil delight in obvious French phrases." It has since been completely forgotten. But it at least demonstrated that South Carolina women were ambitious. Lewisohn says that Mrs. King was "a woman of clear and vigorous spirit, eagerly ready amidst a somewhat narrow social life, to think for herself, and not afraid to put her thoughts on record."[39]

The list of writers who made contributions to science and history was more extended. Professors Francis S. Holmes and Charles U. Shepard, Sr., made discoveries of practical value in connection with the development of the phosphate industry. Francis Peyre Porcher wrote comprehensively on botanical, medical, and literary subjects. The Reverend James Bachman, in addition to writings on religious and social questions, made significant contributions to the knowledge of American animals. The *Charleston Medical Journal and Review* gave evidence of the scientific attainments of the physicians of the state. Among the notable historical writers were John Henry Logan, the historian of upper South Carolina; Maximilian La Borde, the chronicler of the South Carolina College; John Johnson, who wrote accurately on the defense of Charleston Harbor; Edward McCrady, Jr., the scholarly but uninspired chronicler of the Colonial and Revolutionary history of the

[39] *Ibid.*, Aug. 30, 1903.

state; and William Henry Trescot, brilliant essayist and distinguished historian of phases of American diplomacy.

South Carolina writers on religious subjects stood well among their Southern associates. In addition to Bachman, there were James Petigru Boyce and Basil Manly, Baptist theologians; James Warley Miles, an Episcopalian; Patrick Nieson Lynch, Catholic bishop of Charleston; and Thomas Smyth, a learned Presbyterian theologian whose collected works make ten huge volumes. Columbia was the home of the *Southern Presbyterian Review,* the able exponent of Southern views on religion and other subjects.

The state's contributions in the field of the memoir were less significant. Benjamin F. Perry was the only man who achieved distinction. His series of recollections give an intelligent, if verbose, appraisal of the men and events of his life. The women left one notable volume, *Our Women in the War.* In this book a host of amateurs told naïvely and passionately of the stirring things they saw and did.

The *XIX Century,* which was published at Charleston from 1869 to 1872, was a brave if moribund attempt to revive an excellent tradition in literary journalism. Lewisohn believed that it was superior to *Russell's Magazine,* its more famous predecessor. He felt that the chastening influences of the war had been responsible for a greater simplicity in the manner of saying things and for a deepening of tone. "Throughout the *XIX Century,*" said Lewisohn, "we find work which gains a beauty and a dignity beyond its value as literature from the immediacy of its inspiration from the real and tragic world."[40]

The self-centered character of the state's life made possible the survival of newspapers of originality. No South Carolina journal was ever again to have a sectional appeal like that of the *Charleston Mercury* before the war; but the people of the state were not yet willing to have most of their daily reading

[40] *Ibid.,* Aug. 9, 1903.

composed by outsiders. They demanded and received newspapers composed for their special inspiration. In the numerous country weeklies, they had vivacious chronicles of the brighter happenings of the various counties. The Charleston *News and Courier* almost monopolized the field of the daily newspaper. Under the editorship of Francis W. Dawson, a brilliant Englishman who had served in the Confederate army, for years it was an accurate and vivid record of the political, social, and economic life of the state, and its bold editor had much to do with shaping public opinion along progressive lines.

*   *   *   *   *

Perhaps the most hopeful fact about Reconstruction society was the survival or development of good feeling between the races. This statement seemingly contradicts previous assertions, for we have already given numerous examples of racial conflict. But it should not be forgotten that interracial relations in South Carolina have always involved a paradox. Affection and hatred, coöperation and conflict, have existed side by side. Individuals of one race professed hatred of the other race and practised love; others professed love and practised hatred. There can be no explicit answer to the question, Did the races like or dislike each other? All that can be done is to give certain facts. In other chapters evidence of conflict is given. Here those of coöperation will be given. But we do believe that the reader, after reading the evidence, will conclude that the last-named manifestation was of more importance in making up the complexity of interracial relations.

The greatest potential cause of conflict was that the Negroes should challenge the position of a superior caste which the whites demanded for themselves. Conflicts of this character, while frequent, were for the most part artificially-induced incidentals of the political ambitions of the Negro. Normally he accepted the caste system. The rank and file did not even demand social equality with their white political leaders. Only in the high political circles of Columbia, among persons of non-native traditions, did manifestations of social equality have elements of spontaneity. The laws providing for the mixture of the races in schools, theaters and other public places were enacted more to do lip service to proclaimed principles than to effect any actual softening of the hard forms of caste. "I venture to say to my white fellow-citizens," said one of the principal promoters of this type of legislation, "that we, the colored people, are not in quest of social equality. I for one do not ask to be introduced in your family circle if you are not disposed to receive me there."[41]

Leading Negro advocates of the political rights of their race accepted as a matter of course a position of inferiority in social relations with native whites. When Beverly Nash visited a home in which he had served as butler, the daughter of the house called him "Beverly" and he replied with a "Miss Isabella."[42] When Robert Smalls entered the home of his former master, he ate at a separate table.[43] Nancy, the nursemaid who married Speaker Elliott, lived ostentatiously among the political circles of Columbia, but to her former employer she remained a nursemaid. "Nothing could induce her," said James Morrison Morgan, "to stop in front of Mrs. Heyward's house in that costume or in her carriage, but in the cool of the afternoon, Nancy, arrayed in the neat cap and apron of a nursemaid, would stop her carriage around the corner from her former mistress's home, and alighting would walk to the house and beg to take the children out. The people who had seen her gala attire in the middle of the day would behold the strange spectacle of the same Nancy, as demure as a novice, seated in the front seat of her own landau, with the children

[41] Congressman Rainey in *Congressional Record*, 43rd Cong., 2d Sess., p. 960. Cf. above, p. 98.

[42] Myrta L. Avary, *Dixie after the War*, p. 356.

[43] *Letters and Diary of Laura M. Towne*, pp. 240-41.

in the back seat."[44] Sir George Campbell went to Beaufort, expecting to find a "white hell." "To my great surprise," he said, "I found exactly the contrary. At no place that I have seen are the relations of the two races better and more peaceable. . . . White girls go about as freely and pleasantly as if no black had ever been in power."[45]

If such cordiality was expressed by Negro politicians, it was natural that among others it should have been greater. "The Negro men and women," said Edward King, "still maintain their old-time servility toward their former masters. When they meet them on the road the men always touch their hats, and the women, no matter how large the basket they may be happening to be carrying on their heads, courtesy profoundly. The word 'mas 'r' is still used, being so intimately associated in the Negro's mind with certain individuals, that he has no inclination to drop it."[46] A minister was surprised over the contrast between the political assertiveness of the Negroes and their conduct in other respects. "They are," he said, "modest, respectful and considerate in their behavior toward the whites. . . . I have not yet witnessed the slightest demonstration of colored insolence or presumption."[47] Even on public occasions of a non-political character the colored persons behaved as the whites would have them. "It was pleasant to see," wrote a lady from the Barnwell races, "with what propriety they conducted themselves, and how kind and genial seemed the intercourse between the Negroes and their former masters. It looked quite like old times, as every now and then some family servant would step up and respectfully say, 'Master, which horse do you think will win?' And when the heat was over, how they would shout and laugh as the horse they had bet on

[44] *Recollections of a Rebel Reefer*, p. 331.

[45] *White and Black*, pp. 176-78, 342.

[46] *Southern States of North America*, p. 430.

[47] J. R. Kendrick, former pastor of the Citadel Square Baptist Church, in *News*, Feb. 5, 1873.

came out ahead."[48] They were not even reluctant to place wagers on a horse named Ku-Klux.

In every family of any distinction there was at least one "uncle" or "daddy," or "mammy" or "mauma" on whom the most intimate affections were bestowed. The disturbances of the times in nowise affected these relations. The story of one of these saints has been told by members of the family whom she served. Maumer Juno scorned the opportunities of freedom, being adverse to receiving wages and unwilling to wear the new bonnets and gaudy dresses of the day. Although illiterate, she was intelligent and given to the use of the best English. She combined dignity with the refusal to sit in the presence of her superiors unless told to do so. A fervent Methodist, she carefully guarded the morals of the thirty-three children whom she nursed at various times. "We regarded her," said her biographers, "more as a venerated grandmother and as such honored her at her burial."[49]

In addition to maintaining cordial relations with the whites, the Negroes made progress in social relations among themselves. The most important manifestation of this type was the development of family life.

They responded with alacrity to the suggestion of the military commanders, the missionaries, and the "black code" that they enter into formal marriage. Miss Botume told of a couple who, after living together as slaves for forty years without a formal ceremony, were delighted to receive a marriage certificate from the Federal authorities; of those invested with a new dignity when they were given the certificate; of the "expectant look on the faces of the betrothed"; and of the general feeling that "none could live until they got married and got their certificates."[50] "They have," said Whitelaw Reid, "a

---

[48] *News*, Dec. 29, 1868.
[49] Mr. and Mrs. J. C. H., *Life of Maumer Juno of Charleston, S. C. Cf.*

the story of Daddy Ancrum in Pringle, p. 349.
[50] *Op. cit.*, pp. 157-60. Cf. Whitelaw Reid, *After the War*, p. 126.

great desire to enter its bonds fashionably. . . . At the Beaufort wedding . . . the bride wore a calico dress whose colors were as glowing as her own was swarthy; her hands were covered with white cotton gloves; as for her head, neck and shoulders, a true history will be forever at a loss to tell how they *were* clad."[51]

Another step in the assumption of the forms of family life was the acquirement of a surname to supplement the lone Christian name by which slaves had usually been designated. The procedure was simple: the family name of the former master was assumed. When, however, the master had not been liked, the name of a white neighbor was taken, or a distinguished name selected at random. It became common for such proud patronymics as Rhett, Middleton, Barnwell, Vander Horst, Drayton, Legaré, Grimké, and even Washington and Jefferson, to be borne by dusky South Carolinians. That they regarded themselves as more intimately connected with their former masters than with their liberators, is indicated by the fact that in almost no instances did they assume such names as Lincoln, Sumner, Garrison, and Phillips.[52]

Having assumed the trappings of family life, the Negro was confronted with the long and difficult task of achieving its substance. As has been made clear, his success was not all that was expected. But he did make progress. The setting up of homes scattered over the land meant that the wife and children of the colored farmer became distinct from the families of other Negroes.[53] Another advance was the tendency of the women to desert the fields to devote themselves to domestic duties. If this never extended far enough to satisfy the friends of Negro uplift, the mother has at least always had the right to devote her spare time to her children; and, we may add, the

---

[51] *Ibid.*, pp. 126-27. Cf. T. W. Higginson, *Army Life in a Black Regiment*, p. 258.

[52] Botume, *op. cit.*, pp. 46, 61, and Townsend, *loc. cit.*, p. 675.

[53] Rossa B. Cooley, *Home of the Freed*, pp. 80-81.

cotton field, with its wealth of sun and air, has not been the least ideal nursery.

The home life of the average Negro family was, as has been said, characterized by many gloomy circumstances. But in judging these conditions, one should not hastily apply Anglo-Saxon standards. The average Negro scarcely recognized these standards, and for him, if not for his white critics, his ways of living had compensations. He was able to be happy and contented in the environment he provided for himself. This is proven by the joyous and worldly songs he began to improvise. While others were struggling through hard work and education to reach exalted standards of living, the happy-go-lucky Negro was able to gratify his simple needs with a minimum of effort. All the education which he really needed came to him as the casual result of his environment. His life of physical exertion gave him the brawn necessary for his labors. Born and reared in the cotton patch, he easily learned how to cultivate the great staple. To grow Indian corn, squash, water-melons, collards, peanuts, okra, and other vegetables in quantities sufficient to satisfy his needs, was easy in so gifted a climate. Ample supplies of wild plums, blackberries, persimmons, and muscadines were free to all who took the trouble to gather them. Everyone owned a dog and a gun and early developed into a skillful hunter. The reward was ample catches of rabbits and opossums and a lesser quantity of the savory partridge. The lagoons and rivers of the low-country yielded much fish and other aquatic products, and the streams of the up-country, perch and catfish.

The houses of the Negroes, if fulfilling few of the requirements of the fully civilized, satisfied the ordinary ex-slave. About all he required of them was that they should be a place to eat and sleep. Great fires and the plastering of the walls with newspapers kept out some of the cold of winter. That this was not an environment in which sentiments about the home could readily develop, was no special hardship, for the need for such sentiments was not clearly felt. The fact that the one or two rooms of the house necessitated a hugger-mugger existence was not a discomfort to a race which had not yet developed much sense of modesty. That the house was usually ugly and dingy caused no difficulties; the occupants had not developed a sense of the esthetic. They got the joys which they desired most. They hunted and fished, shouted in church and made love to the "sisters" on the way home, wore old finery and bright calicoes, and ate molasses and the products of their farms.

The morals of the Negro gave his friendly critics deep concern; and, as has been said, here lay one of his greatest weaknesses. But there were compensations. The Negro, unlike the Anglo-Saxon, did not burden himself with an overdose of morality in order to catch himself in its meshes. He tolerated the foibles of his neighbor and did not pursue him with gossip. He sinned conveniently without much afterthought. His attachments were warm, but when by reason of a death or a quarrel, he lost a wife or a relation, he knew how to forget and rapidly to form other attachments.

Because of his moral opportunism it should not be assumed that the Negro was without morality. His intense profession of the religion of the white man forced upon him a vivid sense of right and wrong. Of course in many cases professions and practices were inconsistent. But the preacher was always telling the black man what sin was, and the black man was always trying to mend his ways. There was seldom an individual sufficiently sophisticated to regard himself as free from moral restraint. In some respects the Negroes lived up to standards of Christian virtue. They were charitable, affectionate, loyal, and not especially materialistic. They had reverence for a solemn oath; it took moral calibre to keep an oath as faithfully as they did that of the Union League. Certain writers found among them an absence of profane and lewd speech. "Their comparative freedom from swearing," said Colonel Higginson, "was partly a matter of principle. I once heard one of them say to another, 'Ha-a-a, boy, s'pose I be no Christian, I cuss you so!' "[54] Miss Elsie Clews Parsons noted a deliberate suppression of certain drinking songs, or "man's tales."[55] Tales of preachers with a Boccaccio-like turn were told, but always from the smug Baptist point of view.

It is very likely that the race was less subject to the evils of drink than the whites. "People here," said Sir George Campbell of St. Helena in 1878, "deny that there is much drinking among them [the Negroes]; in fact, until recently there was no whisky-shop at all upon the Islands."[56] A prosecuting officer asserted that drinking was much less a cause of crime among the blacks than among the whites. "Drunkenness," he added, "is not a very prevalent crime among the Negroes."[57]

Some Negro homes were dominated by standards of cleanliness and thrift. They could be detected by their whitewashed rail fences, their modest gardens of bright flowers, vines over their doors, the rows of potted plants on porches, and shining cooking utensils hanging out of kitchen windows. Such houses, usually whitewashed, consisted of two rooms with an open hall between. On entering, one got an impression of cleanliness. In one room were the beds and pallets of the family; in the other, the beds for the guests. The walls were decorated with newspapers cut in fancy designs, religious pictures and enlarged crayon portraits of members of the family. The meals served, especially if guests were present, were as plentiful as those of the rural whites, and in most cases more wholesome. Such a meal, according to an observer, consisted

[54] *Army Life in a Black Regiment*, pp. 253-58.
[55] *Folk-Lore from the Sea Islands, South Carolina*, pp. 19-20, 135.
[56] *Op. cit.*, p. 344. Cf. Higginson, p. 257.
[57] Solicitor J. B. Kershaw in *Temperance Advocate*, Nov. 14, 1884. Cf. statistics of Hoffman, *Race Traits of the American Negro*, p. 122.

of collards boiled in fat bacon, stewed chicken, sweet potatoes, corn bread, pickles, apple pie and coffee.[58]

Some of the street activities of this unique race excited the wonder and admiration of observers. Each town had its "Negro character," an old man who was half beggar and half porter, half foolish and half wise, half entertainer and half nuisance. Such a person was Old Shady who walked about Sumter. "Since emancipation," said an informant, "he has become quite a character, and holds a prominent place among existing institutions of Sumter, cultivating music, in which he has become quite proficient, and giving examples of elocution and rhetoric which are certainly not to be found in the books."[59] Unique among the street characters of Charleston were the chimney sweeps, called "ro-roos" because of the cry they made when they reached the top of the chimney. They were small Negro boys with musical voices, from whose sooty faces white eyes and teeth protruded.

The most picturesque of all street characters were the Charleston hucksters. These traveling venders, with baskets of fish or vegetables on their heads, were noted for their cries. "The streets of this quaint, old Southern city," remarked a Charleston woman, "are teaming with sights and sounds of interest. . . . To the stranger nothing is so amusing or unintelligible as the various cries of the hucksters as they ply their street trade. . . . They become well-known friends, their several cries familiar music."[60] They sold shrimp, fish, crabs, muskmelons, watermelons, yams, and other products of their little farms on James Island. The women were more interesting than the men. "On their red head-kerchiefs," said Ludwig Lewisohn, "they carried large flat wooden platters full of fresh, faintly coral-tinted shrimps to be boiled early and served with hominy at the white folks' breakfast table. In their rich un-

[58] [J. P. Green], *Recollections of the Carolinas.*

[59] "Juhl," in *Courier,* Mar. 1, 1866.

[60] Harriette Kershaw Leiding, *Street Cries of a Southern City.*

tutored voices, the women would cry their wares."[61]   "The 'vegetable maumas,' who move with a firm, swinging stride," said the aforementioned Charleston woman, "are wonderful, wide-chested, big-hipped specimens of womanhood that balance a fifty-pound basket of vegetables on their heads and ever and anon cry their goods with as much ease and grace as a society woman wears her 'merry widow' hat."

In the recesses of old houses, or on the street curbs on holidays, the Charleston "mauma" sat by her little stand, on which was spread a tempting stock of molasses and benne candy and "ground nut cakes"; beside it, in a cedar pail, were bottles of ginger pop and sassafras beer.   "A gaudy cotton kerchief, in which yellow and scarlet were the dominant hues," said an observer, "is crossed over her ample bust, and another is deftly wrought, over a stiff framework of paper, into the folds of her wonderful turban, as with automatic motion she waves a palmetto fly-brush over her luring sweets and dozes serenely, but with one wakeful eye for the penny bargains which build up her humble fortune."[62]

The festive character of evenings spent around cabin doors has been portrayed by the minstrel show, a famous American institution.   That the post-bellum South Carolina Negro carried on this rolicking tradition is evidenced by the following observation.   The Negroes, said a writer, "are pervaded with a certain amount of good humor and mirthfulness that follows them from the cradle to the grave. . . . It seems to be a physical impossibility for them to repress their laughter, songs, dancing and merry-making.   Many of them seem never to reach old age. . . . We not infrequently find old 'aunties' and 'uncles' who are just as playful and supple as in their youthful days."[63] Corn-shuckings and log-rollings were accomplished under the most joyous circumstances.   Whiskey was passed around, and

[61] The Case of Mr. Crump.   Ways of the Old South, p. 200.
[62] Robert Wilson, Half-Forgotten By-   [63] [J. P. Green], op. cit., pp. 182-84.

THE CELEBRATION OF EMANCIPATION DAY IN CHARLESTON

after the work was over, the dance was taken up to the rhythm of the fiddle and the patting of feet. No attention was paid to the time, and unless the good feeling was marred by a fight, the company did not break up until morning.

The Negro's Christmas, like that of the white man, was a season of rest and quiet. Some of the proceeds of the harvest was spent on new shoes and shirts, an ample supply of food, and on presents for friends.[64] The "laying-by" season was the time of camp meetings, political demonstrations, picnics, and fraternizing with neighbors over watermelons. What happened on Sundays is described elsewhere.[65]

New Year's and the Fourth of July, the two occasions on which Emancipation was observed, were celebrated ceremoniously. Illustrative of the spirit of these fêtes was the celebration at Charleston of New Year's, 1873, the tenth anniversary of the publication of the great Proclamation.[66] It was observed, we are told, "with all the fervor and gusto which is incidental in this latitude to the observance of this occasion." To witness the parade of the militia and other organizations, the streets were crowded "by throngs of colored people, mostly in gorgeous garments and all with smiling, expectant faces." The First Regiment of National Guards, five hundred strong, moved to the tune of "Yankee Doodle." Then came the Longshoremen's Association and the Union League. The members of the latter society carried batons and wore olive sprigs on the lapels of their coats. The paraders were followed "by a dense throng of colored men, women and children, who took possession of the sidewalks to the absolute exclusion of the non-interested." At the Battery Major Sam Dickerson read the Emancipation Proclamation "in stentorian tones that startled sleepy echoes in surrounding trees." Afterwards there were speeches on conventional patriotic themes. Then the crowds

[64] The Christmas of the Negroes of Fairfield was described in *News and Courier*, Jan. 6, 1875.

[65] See below, pp. 408 ff.
[66] *News*, Jan. 2, 1873.

dispersed in an orderly fashion. Thousands, said the *Charleston Daily News,* "seemed to have imbibed enough happiness to last until the next Fourth of July."

How this happiness was renewed will now be described. "Among the colored people of Charleston," said the *News and Courier,* "the Fourth of July, of late years, has become the holiday *par excellence.* The chimes peal out merrily as of yore, the suspension of business is as general as ever, and the refreshment stands of the old maumas are quite as multitudinous."[67] For the celebration of 1874 there were visitors from points as distant as Augusta. Again the feature of the day was the parade of the militia. "The Randolph Riflemen were uniformed in half-dress coats, instead of frock coats, and the Mishaw Zouaves wore moccasins and turbans. Several kinds of music and drum corps enlivened the line." The Union League, now a mere handful, followed the soldiers. The members were fancifully dressed. One carried an American flag and wore a gorgeous uniform. At the Battery the Declaration of Independence was read, speeches extolling Republicanism were made, and the crowd patronized the venders of cakes, sweet beer, peanuts, cold cuts, and ginger pop.

The traveling circuses drew the entire colored population of a community, as well as numerous whites. They visited the court house towns each harvest season. "The advent of the circus," said the *Sumter Watchman,* "is usually marked by the wildest abandon on the part of the people wonderful to behold. The plow is left in the furrow, the saw on the bench. . . . All who have the spare change hasten to the charmed circle, and those who have it not, borrow, beg or ——— the requisite amount."[68] Placards and advertisements telling fabulous tales heralded the coming of "the biggest show on earth." The public was expected to believe that there would be "a grand aviary," 1,050 animals, a museum, a Roman hippodrome, an

[67] July 6, 1874. [68] May 20, 1874.

Egyptian caravan, 750 men and horses, lions, panthers, tigers, elephants and camels![69] But the fact that performances did not come up to the promises seems not to have dulled popular enthusiasm.

* * * * *

Most whites fancied that all Negroes, without creating discomfort, could be placed in one great social class marked "colored"; and the whites have consistently refused to recognize different grades in this society. Nevertheless, these grades existed. The generalizations which have been made concerning the poverty, ignorance, and immorality of Negro society, should not be applied to all grades of non-white society. The colored race had some members who possessed superior culture and wealth and who because of this, set themselves above the great mass. "The Negroes," said Townsend, "have among themselves social rank and aristocracy outrageously severe and strictly discriminating. . . . The gradations are founded principally on official station, position in the church, possession of money or real estate, former ownership, and city birth. Those who have been trained up 'genteelly' in white families of the highest respectability, as waiting men, maids, drivers, and so on, of course pride themselves not a little on their polished deportment; and those who are able to work on their own account (for instance, to rent land and to farm, to keep a smithy, or be carpenters) hold themselves considerably above such as have to hire out as laborers."[70]

Miss Botume was astonished to find class distinctions even among the semi-barbarous sea islanders. "The clannishness of the freed people," she said, "was indescribable. Those belonging to one family or one master 'ganged' together, and were always ready to fight for one another. Little jealousies cropped out on different plantations. All were destitute and helpless,

---

[69] Advertisement in *Sumter News*, Aug. 29, 1872. [70] *Loc. cit.*, p. 677.

but there were class distinctions." Former house servants held "rice niggers," "low-down country niggers," and "only Georgia niggers" in contempt. Most of them regarded themselves as superior to the less favored members of the dominant class, calling them "po' buckra" and "po' white trash." Even the friendly Yankee at times was designated "po' white buckra, anyhow."[71]

Social preëminence was accorded to that portion of the mulatto population of Charleston who had never been slaves. This was the class, said the *News and Courier,* "who had long been equally distinguished for their high order of respectability and perfect devotion to their native city and state."[72] The changes of Reconstruction increased their importance at a partial sacrifice of the esteem of the whites. Before and during the war as owners of slaves, they had affiliated with the whites. Afterwards they took the part of the Negro in his struggle for political power. This step was induced by the refusal of the whites to accord them a social position superior to that of the black masses and by the political opportunities which were dangled before them. They secured an extraordinary number of lucrative positions; in proportion to numbers they held, in 1875, fourteen times as many offices as the blacks, and five times as many as the whites.[73]

The acme of social distinction ever obtained by colored South Carolinians was the right to participate in the official society of Columbia; that is, the opportunity to ride in fine carriages, to dress lavishly, and to be present at the balls, dinners, receptions, and races made possible by the swollen fortunes of the coterie who dominated the politics of the state. Some of these social manifestations were pervaded by an air of good taste. The Rollin sisters—Catherine de Medici, Charlotte Corday, and Louise Muhlbach—were the sisters-in-law of

[71] *First Days amongst the Contrabands,* pp. 120-21, 132-33.

[72] Mar. 9, 1875.

[73] *Diocesan Journal of the Episcopal Church, 1876,* p. 35.

Whipper. Their house in Columbia was equipped with "beautiful carpets, elegant furniture, tasteful pictures, a one thousand dollar piano; photograph albums filled with the choicest Rembrandts lay in profusion on an Italian marble table, and legislative documents bound in morocco." They conducted a sort of mulatto salon, entertaining political leaders of both races. Their enterprising mentality was illustrated by the fact that at their home, Governor Scott and other lights of the Radical régime were elected to a national woman's suffrage convention.[74] Another manifestation of good taste was a ball given by a colored militia captain. "The youth and beauty of colored society," we are told, "were present with a sprinkling of whites."[75] The captain was described as handsome and gracious and the music as excellent.

Other events of this society horrified the whites. Governor Scott, said a friendly critic, "makes no distinction among members of the legislature (125 of them are colored); all taken equally by the hand with the graceful urbanity for which his honor is distinguished. All alike crowd around his luxuriant refreshment tables, where, as his accomplished lady told me, no invidious distinctions are made."[76] Governor Moses of course outdid his more modest predecessor. "I remember—not once but on several occasions—," remarked James Morrison Morgan, "seeing a handsome landau drawn by a spanking pair of high-stepping Kentucky horses, and containing four Negro wenches arrayed in low-neck and short-sleeves, their black bosoms and arms covered with real jewels in the middle of the day, draw up in front of a barroom on Main Street. . . . Out of the saloon would come the governor, accompanied by several high state officials, followed by a servant bearing a waiter on which was champagne and glasses, and right there in the

[74] N. Y. Sun, cited in News, Apr. 3, 1871, and ibid., Nov. 12, 1872.

[75] N. Y. Sun, cited ibid., Apr. 18, 1871.
[76] Letters of J. W. Alvord to O. O. Howard.

public sidewalk enter into a perfect orgy with the dusky belles."[77]

Moses, bloated by corrupt gain, prodigal in expenditures, and a master of entertaining, gave a series of notorious receptions at the Preston Mansion, the finest house in Columbia. There he enveloped the colored belles and dandies in the garish splendors of an ostentatious age. A renegade Radical has described one of these occasions. "The colored band," he said, "was playing 'Rally 'Round the Flag'. . . . There was a mixture of white and black, male and female. Supper was announced, and you ought to have seen the scrambling for the table. Social equality was at its highest pitch. It was amusing to see cuffy reaching across the table and swallowing grapes by the bunch, champagne by the bottle, and turkey, ham and pound cake by the bushel."[78]

One of the most hopeful signs in Negro society was the development of clubs and societies, mostly of the type which had been prohibited among the slaves. Attention has already been given the Union League, the militia companies, and the political associations; presently religious organizations will be discussed. But there are a number of associations that fall into neither of these classes.

The most interesting of these associations was the Longshoremen's Protective Association of Charleston. In 1875 it was described as "the most powerful organization of the colored laboring class in South Carolina." The parade of five hundred of its eight hundred members was said to have been "exceedingly creditable, the members being well-dressed and a good looking body of men. Banners were displayed, and silver and gold badges were worn." It had to its credit a record of vigorously conducted strikes, and it was the only successful labor union which has ever been known among the blacks of the state.[79]

The most notable colored organizations which survived the war were the fire companies of Charleston. Four of them, composed of more than two hundred men, appeared in parade in 1868, and the fire chief said they were very efficient. Their engines were decorated in flags and flowers, and the men themselves wore gay uniforms. Some were "in dark blue frock coats with yellow facings and trimmings"; others were in "white flannel frock coats, blue cuffs, facings and trimmings, and black pants."[80]

Far more significant in the lives of the great masses were the burial aid societies. They took form in the years following the war and soon spread to every Negro community in the state. They exist today as one of the most successful experiments in coöperative societies ever known in the United States. They grew out of the inability of the Negro to provide out of his individual means the elaborate and respectable funeral each one of them most sincerely desired. This difficulty was overcome by the several members of the community agreeing to create a fund by each making a small and easily paid weekly contribution to a common treasury. In this manner enough money was gathered to meet the funeral obligations when they arose from time to time. Additional dignity was insured by requiring members of the society to attend the burial of a brother in white gloves and mourning costumes, and to carry banners and badges of the organization.

The importance of these societies in the life of the Negro community is made clear by the following report from Beaufort in 1880: "The colored people have a number of charitable organizations for the care of their sick and the burial of their dead. Some of these are the Benevolent Society of the First

[79] News and Courier, Dec. 23, 1875, and News, Jan. 5, 7, and 9, 1867, and Feb. 25, 1868.

[80] News, Dec. 23, 1868.

Baptist Church, the Workers of Charity, the Shekinak Society, the Sons and Daughters of Zion, the Knights of Wise Men, and an Independent Order of Odd Fellows. These societies have an aggregate membership exceeding one thousand, and own eleven buildings and lots valued at $12,000."[81]

[81] *Handbook of S. C., 1883,* p. 667. Andrew Simkins and Addison Childs, colored men of Edgefield, have furnished information on the history of the Simmons Ridge Burial Aid Society and the Mutual Aid Society of the Macedonia Baptist Church, two typical organizations.

Chapter XIV

THE CHURCH IN TRANSITION

DURING Reconstruction there were significant movements in the history of the South Carolina churches. Northern missionaries attempted to reform the religious institutions of the state and the Negroes set up churches of their own, independent of white control. These two topics will be the theme of this chapter. The next chapter will discuss topics scarcely less significant—the rebuilding of religious institutions shattered by the war and the internal progress made by the churches of the two races.

The churches had espoused the cause of the Confederacy as fervently as had the political and military leaders. They had seceded from the national churches. Their religious and moral enthusiasms had been in a large measure responsible for the thoroughgoing manner in which both races had accepted slavery and for the persistence with which the soldiers of the state had battled for Southern independence.

The churchmen came out of the war with their devotion to Southern principles intensified. Their hatred of the conqueror is illustrated by the comment of the Harmony Presbytery on Sherman's army. It said, "An enemy, cruel and relentless, professing to be Christian, but trampling on every principle of humanity, of right, of truth, of justice and of religion; . . . an enemy which respects neither age nor sex nor condition, has passed like a destructive tornado over her [the Church's] territory. Her congregations have been broken up. . . . In one instance . . . the sanctuary on the Sabbath day was used as a place of dancing and reveling. . . . Fondly anticipating the day when God will put down our haughty and wicked foes, we would take fresh courage."[1] The attitude toward Northern churches was expressed by a prominent Baptist minister. He said infidelity would spread in the North because of "the contempt of religion, and especially of the Christian ministry." "The Protestant pulpit of the North," he affirmed, "reeked with political garbage, and was clamorous for blood."[2] Theologians came forward with ingenious arguments to explain why God had let a just cause fail. "The providence of God," said a Presbyterian writer, "has sorely smitten them [the people of the South]. . . . But it does not follow that the Providence of God has decided against the justice of their cause. . . . Providence, for wise ends, may permit an ungodly nation to prosper for a time. . . . The people of the South, whilst submitting to the terrible rebuke of a Holy God for their sins, do not thereby surrender their well-established views and principles: political and moral: the first, supported by the constitution of the country; the last, protected by the Scripture of eternal truth. They have not been 'converted by the sword to Northern ideas.'"[3]

Ignoring these experiences and feelings, the Northern evangelical churches fancied that they could convert the South Carolina churchmen to their views. They believed that the Southern churches "had been so completely leagued with detestable sin that its representative ministers are incapacitated for the work of social and religious regeneration."[4] A Methodist bishop asserted that "the very conscience of the professedly religious portion of the South was debauched; that the ministry had been guilty beyond the power of language to describe in that they were debauchers, and I fear that both

[1] F. D. Jones and W. H. Mills, *History of the Presbyterian Church in S. C. since 1850*, pp. 100-1.

[2] Dr. J. L. Reynolds, in *Richmond Religious Herald*, cited in Philadelphia *National Baptist*, May 10, 1866.

[3] A. W. Miller, *Southern Presbyterian Review*, XXI (Jan., 1870), 61-62. For a similar view see statement of the Methodist bishop in charge of South Carolina in *Sou. Chr. Adv.*, Nov. 23, 1865.

[4] A New England conference of Methodists, cited in *Sou. Chr. Adv.*, Sept. 7, 1865.

University of South Carolina Library

CHRIST EPISCOPAL CHURCH

University of South Carolina Library

LUTHERAN CHURCH

COLUMBIA AFTER SHERMAN'S VISIT

preachers and people were backslidden into a depth out of which even the mercy of God might fail to lift them."[5]

It was felt that the triumph of the Northern arms would inevitably lead to the return of the Southern churches to the bodies from which they had seceded. Had not slavery and the principle of states' rights been destroyed, and were they not the causes which had led to the break in church unity? A leading Northern religious weekly said, "The tide turns in favor of loyalty and liberty, and the Methodist Episcopal Church . . . can fully meet the demands of the situation. Even the rebels and traitors will soon refuse to receive the Gospel except from those who have shown their fear of God by loyalty to the Nation. The mad-dog cry of 'abolitionist' becomes effete and ridiculous now that the doctrines of liberty blaze in splendor from all the starry folds of the flag of the Republic."[6]

The conditions under which the Southerners were to be readmitted were radical. They must give satisfactory assurance of their "loyalty to the national government and their approval of the anti-slavery doctrines of our Church."[7] Religious bodies must be organized by "loyal" churchmen. Those who had been in rebellion were to be admitted only after they had confessed their sins.[8]

The Negroes were of course declared a special subject for missionary endeavor. The President of the Baptist Home Missionary Society said of them, "We must educate them,—send missionaries to them, and make their religious fervor intelligent."[9] Moreover, they were to be enlisted in the fight for political and social revolution. Powerful religious bodies endorsed Negro suffrage, and it was suggested that "invidious

[5] Bishop Clark of Cincinnati, cited in *National Baptist*, Aug. 31, 1865. Similar citations *ibid.*, Apr. 5, 1865, and *Sou. Chr. Adv.*, Aug. 31, 1865.

[6] *Western Chr. Adv.*, cited *ibid.*, Aug. 31, 1865.

[7] Words of the General Conference of the Northern Methodist Church, cited *ibid.*, Sept. 7, 1865.

[8] Northern Presbyterian Assembly, cited *ibid.*, Aug. 31, 1865.

[9] B. M. Anderson, in *National Baptist*, May 25, 1865.

distinctions" of race be abolished and that Negroes should be admitted into churches as social equals.[10]

The Northern churches' actual work in South Carolina was not so extensive as their utterances seemed to suggest. Their most intense endeavors were in the Port Royal area where as early as 1862 Baptist, Methodist, and Congregational missionaries were active. When Charleston was captured church properties were seized, and for a time six of the principal pulpits of that city were occupied by Northern divines.[11] From them stern lectures were delivered to the populace. The necessity of all, declared the Reverend Charles Lowe from the Unitarian church, "is a real and uncompromising loyalty!"[12] An Episcopal minister who refused to read the prayer for the President of the United States was expelled from Charleston, his property seized, and his congregation warned.

But most of the churches of the North did not follow up these initial moves. In 1865 the Baptist Home Missionary Society was maintaining only nine missionaries in the state; in later years this number did not increase.[13] The most notable achievement of this body was the founding at Columbia in 1871 of Benedict Institute, a Negro school partly devoted to the training of ministers.

The Northern Methodists were much more active. After the Reverends T. Willard Lewis and Alonzo Webster had prepared the way, the South Carolina Conference of their church was organized at Charleston by Bishop Baker on April 2, 1866. Although only nine ministers were reported in service in the state, the church was adjudged "a living and efficient agent through which sinners are converted to God," and the establishment of a theological institute in the preceding year for the

[10] *Sou. Chr. Adv.*, June 29 and Sept. 7, 1865.

[11] *Ibid.*, Aug. 31, 1865; *Courier*, May 5, 1865, and June 2, 1866; and W. H. Lawrence, *A Centenary Souvenir*, p. 7.

[12] *Courier*, Apr. 29, 1865.

[13] *American Baptist Home Missionary Society, Annual Report, 1865-1876, passim.*

training of a native ministry was viewed with satisfaction. Resolutions were adopted "to ignore all those artificial distinctions of society founded on ungenerous prejudices." Stability was given to the work of the Northern Methodist church by the contribution of its mission board of from ten to fifteen thousand dollars annually, and by the establishment in 1869 at Orangeburg of Claflin University.[14]

It was inevitable that the attempts of the Northerners to win the white churchmen should fail. "There is nothing," was the comment of a wise Northern editor, "which irritates the Southerner so outrageously as the assumption, on which nearly all offers of reconciliation are based, that they have not only sinned, but sinned with the full knowledge that they were sinning—that they went into the war well knowing that they were about to commit a great crime. We accordingly not only look upon their defeat as a piece of retribution, but we expect them to see it in the same light, and to meet us as penitents in sackcloth and ashes, and take our advances to them as proofs of our magnanimity and forgiveness."[15] Knowing that they had their flocks behind them, the South Carolina churchmen scornfully rejected all proffers of reconciliation. They would recognize only the unmistakable achievements of the war—the reëstablishment of the Union and the abolition of slavery. Their views were made clear by a committee of Presbyterians. "How," their Northern co-religionists were asked, "will you justify, on Presbyterian principles, your intrusion in their [the Southerners'] field of labor, your scattering their flock, your use of military power to keep possession of their church property? By what authority does your committee intrude into the diocese of another? Are you lords over God's heritage among us? Did we lose our spiritual liberties in the war?"[16] The

[14] *Sou. Chr. Adv.*, May 25, 1866, and Lawrence, pp. 9-10.

[15] The N. Y. *Nation*, III (July 21, 1866), 31.

[16] *Courier*, June 2, 1866. Similar statements in *Sou. Chr. Adv.*, Aug. 31, and Nov. 25, 1865, and Dec. 4, 1868, and Dec. 3, 1874.

Northerners admitted defeat. "The native white population," wrote a correspondent of the *New York Christian Advocate,* "stand aloof, and usually do all in their power to hinder the work of the missionary."[17] The Northern branches of the Baptist, Methodist, and Presbyterian, the three most popular faiths in the state, acquired no white members, and down to the present all efforts at church union between the Northern and Southern churches have been unsuccessful.

But the Northern Methodists by persistent efforts did have some success in winning Negroes. This was largely due to the Reverend T. Willard Lewis. He won the allegiance of the colored portion of the congregation of Trinity Church, Charleston, as they sat in the gallery of that church. After they had heard white leaders plead with them to remain, he arose and said, "Brothers and sisters, there will be no galleries in heaven. Those who are willing to go with a church which makes no distinctions, follow me to the normal school." "The congregation," wrote a sympathetic observer, "rose to the man, and marched with enthusiasm to the normal school."[18] A separate church was organized, the Wentworth Street Baptist Church building was purchased with funds raised by the congregation and the Northern missionary board, and the so-called Centenary Church began its successful career. In a similar fashion other churches were organized in various portions of the state. By 1890 the Northern Methodist church in the state had grown to 43,000 members; in 1916 this number was 53,000.[19]

That the other Northern churches did not have as great a success with the Negroes was due to a variety of reasons. In the first place, these churches neglected their opportunities, failing to send sufficient missionaries. In the second place, many of the missionaries failed to appreciate the Negro's denominational prejudices. Congregationalists and Presbyterians

[17] Cited *ibid.,* Mar. 23, 1866.
[18] Lawrence, *op. cit.,* pp. 9-14.

[19] *Census of Religious Bodies, 1916,* I, 111.

attempted to minister to Negro Baptists, not realizing that their hearers were steeped in sectarianism. The Negroes gave them respectful attention, regarded what they said as good for the white man, and continued to adhere to the Baptist doctrines which they had inherited. Finally, on close contact neither group found the religion of the other congenial. The Northerners were liberal in their theology, restrained in their manner of worship, and inclined to enforce a prudish ethical code; the Negroes were theologically bigoted, were emotional in worship, and laid little emphasis on ethical practice. "I am bound to add after extensive observation," said a Northern churchman, "that no other people in Protestant Christendom show so imperfect a religious development. . . . Morals and religion are practically distinct. . . . Licentiousness and theft are still prevalent. . . . Most of the sermons we have heard have been the sheerest rhapsodies, incoherent in language and disconnected in thought, with the almost uniform desire to excite the hearers up to a white heat."[20] "Some of our missionary friends," wrote a Negro from Beaufort, "do more in the way of keeping farms and keeping our poor race in ignorance than anything else. They pretend, when they are in the North, that they would come down and do anything for our race in the way of enlightening them; but instead of this, when they see the cotton bag they forget about Christ and Him crucified. . . . All they wish to do is to pat the Negro on the shoulder with the left hand, while with the right hand they catch hold of his pocketbook."[21]

*　　*　　*　　*　　*

The Episcopal church took little part in the acrimonious debate which divided the other great branches of the Protestant church. The Northern Episcopalians, amidst cries of a

[20] Dr. Abel Stevens in *New York Methodist*, cited in *Sou. Chr. Adv.*, Feb. 4 and 25, 1874. Cf. Charles Stearns, *The Black Men of the South and the Rebels*, Chap. XXXIII.

[21] *Christian Record*, cited in *Sou. Chr. Adv.*, Aug. 21, 1867.

"divorce between patriotism and religion" from their evangelical brethren,[22] endeavored to dissipate the hard feelings which had grown up between the sections during the war. The anti-slavery element was in the minority in the General Convention of the church in 1865, and Bishop Hopkins of Vermont, the presiding officer, was a conservative, anxious for reconciliation on easy terms. He had written a kindly letter to the Southern bishops assuring them that they would be welcome as delegates. No test oath was required for membership in the body and several Southern states were represented.[23]

The South Carolina church soon reaffiliated with the Northern dioceses. The earlier inclination of Bishop Davis that there be an independent Southern church melted away. "The Providence of God," he said in 1866, "has determined otherwise. . . . I advise immediate return of the diocese into union with the Church of the United States. Let me say, too, that I have received the strongest memorials of kindness and affection from our brethren of the North."[24]   On motion of the Reverend A. Toomer Porter before the diocesan convention of 1866, this reunion was adopted unanimously and delegates were elected to the next national council of the church.[25] Since that time entire harmony has existed between the South Carolina church and the national church.

The plan of missionary relief resolved upon by the national church was the principal reason why the South Carolina Episcopalians were willing to reënter the national body. Like their evangelical brethren, the Northern Episcopalians were anxious to participate in the uplift of the Negro, but they resolved to send no missionaries to the South and to turn over the funds they had for this purpose to the Southern clergy.

[22] New York Independent cited ibid., Nov. 9, 1865.
[23] Ibid., Sept. 7 and Nov. 9, 1865, and Mark Mohler, "The Episcopal Church and National Reconciliation, 1865," Political Science Quarterly, XLI (Dec., 1926), 567-96.
[24] Courier, Oct. 21, 1865.
[25] Diocesan Journal, 1866, pp. 40-41, 50, and Courier, Feb. 17, 1866.

The Reverend J. S. Hanckel, a native white man, was appointed state agent of the Episcopal Freedman's Aid Commission, and Northerners agreed to aid financially in the reconstruction of the churches in the state along lines dictated by natives.[26] Accordingly when the Reverend Mr. Porter went to New York to solicit funds for the aid of both races he was cordially received and promised $66,000. How he was received by the secretary of the Church Mission Board is best told in his own words: "Doctor Twing opened his strong arms, and throwing them around me said, 'You blessed rebel, yes, there is plenty of coals here in my heart and the Holy Spirit will flame them into love!' And he gave me a squeeze that nearly took my breath away." At other places Porter was received with emotions almost as great: old port was opened, he was invited to preach, and after one sermon a man gave him five hundred dollars.[27]

The diocesan journal for the years immediately after the war was filled with expressions of gratitude for funds given by Northerners. "Generous Christian friends" in some of the Northern dioceses, it said, contributed funds for the projected reopening of the theological seminary.[28] "Our people," said the rector of the St. Helena Church, "have been generously aided by Northern people settled here." "Such evidences as these," said the rector of the church at Camden in comment on aid given by citizens of Pennsylvania and Delaware, "go far to convince us of the warm Christian interest manifested by many of our Northern church people toward us."

* * * * *

To introduce the second task of this chapter, the story of how the Negroes established independent churches, it is necessary to say something about their religion as slaves. The master class had shown great solicitude for their spiritual wel-

[26] *Diocesan Journal, 1867*, p. 23.
[27] Porter, *Led On! Step by Step*, pp. 212-22.
[28] *Diocesan Journal, 1867*, pp. 20, 60, and *ibid., 1868*, pp. 60-61.

fare. All vestiges of African superstition had ostensibly been eradicated and they had been indoctrinated with the beliefs of historic Protestantism. The white ministry gave half of their time to the slaves and ample accommodations were provided for them in the churches. The records of all the principal churches were filled with comments on the ready manner in which the slaves responded to the teachings of the white ministers. "The Blessed Redeemer," ran a typical report from a colored mission, "has smiled most graciously upon it, and as from the blackest stuff in the bowels of the earth the fairest and most costly gem is elaborated, so from the dark sons of Ham, has He, through His grace, elected many a jewel which shall shine conspicuously in His mediatorial crown."[29]

The result of this work is that there were probably as many Negro members of the principal churches of the state on the eve of the war as there were white members. The following is a comparative table based on incomplete returns of the several churches:[30]

	Year	White members	Colored members
Episcopal	1860	3,166	2,960
Presbyterian	1859	8,000	5,009
Methodist	1860	34,351	42,469
Baptist	1858	25,212	21,911
Totals		70,729	72,349

The most notable feature of ante-bellum church life was the almost absolute control which the whites exercised over the slave's religion. He was only allowed to attend churches in which whites were present and only ministers considered worthy of the confidence of the slaveowner were allowed to

[29] Jones and Mills, *op. cit.*, p. 48. Cf. *ibid.*, pp. 43, 48, 74; Bishop Theodore Bratton, *A Study in Negro Development*, pp. 185-91; W. P. Harrison, *The Gospel among the Slaves, passim*; John M. Burgess, *Chronicles of St. Mark's Parish*, p. 83; etc.

[30] *Diocesan Journal, 1860*, pp. 7-8, 70; Jones and Mills, p. 34; and *Minutes of the State Baptist Convention, 1859*, p. 38.

give him instructions. Most of these ministers were white; the so-called Negro exhorters were carefully selected and strict limits were placed upon their activities. Between 1832 and 1835 the leaders of the only independent Negro church were forced out of the state. Although the Negro derived great advantage from the interest of the whites in his spiritual life, an important cause of this interest was the desire to use the bondage of soul as a means of making more perfect the bondage of body. The churches were a mainstay of the slave system. They taught that the Negro was an inferior order of human being, that the Scriptures justified slavery, and that it was the duty of the servant to obey his master. The managers of the Methodist Missionary Society of the state made clear how this was done. "While our missionaries," they said, "have been unfolding to the Negro race the riches of the graces revealed by Jesus Christ, . . . they have likewise been teaching from the same inspired record that the way to the attainment of that life is by obedience and fidelity. . . . While the ravings of a misguided fanaticism have been threatening the subversion of government, . . . the labors of our missionaries have been strengthening our domestic ties, and advancing the best interests of society."[31]

The forming of independent churches by the Negro was an inevitable consequence of the coming of freedom. The whites were unwilling to revise radically their conception of the proper place of the Negro in their churches. If he continued his membership it must be as an inferior with no voice in the management. The Negroes, on the other hand, felt that they should have equality and freedom in their church life. This could only be obtained in churches of their own.

Naturally the whites did not willingly surrender their great power over the Negro's religion. In 1865 all the important

---

[31] *Minutes of the South Carolina Conference of the Methodist Episcopal Church, South, 1850*, p. 8. Cf. Harrison, *passim.*

church bodies of the state instructed their agencies to continue as heretofore their ministrations to the race. The colored people were reminded of the noble work which had been done in behalf of their spiritual uplift, were warned against innovation, and cordially invited to stay in their accustomed pews. "We regard," was a typical announcement, "our obligations to impart to them [the Negroes] the blessings of the Gospel as unimpaired and enjoin our ministers and churches to continue to instruct them by preaching, catechetical teaching and all other means of improving their spiritual condition."[32]

During the first years after the war the whites were able to report numerous responses of colored people to their ministrations. When Dr. Richard Fuller, a prominent Baptist minister, returned to the sea islands to preach to his former slaves, the following scene took place: "Men and women pressed forward indiscriminately; the good doctor, in a moment found both his hands busy, and stood, like a patriarchal shepherd, amid his flock. They pushed up against him, kissed his hands, passed their fingers over his hair, crowded about, eager to get a word of recognition."[33] The Negroes, said the *Minutes of the Baptist Convention* in 1868, "are now manifesting a renewed confidence in their former instructors and a praiseworthy desire to be guided aright."[34] For three years after the war the Methodists were able to report "the refreshing news" that many colored persons were joining mixed congregations.[35]

Yet, in spite of these manifestations, each year of freedom marked a steady decline in the number of Negroes who be-

[32] Harmony Presbytery, in Jones and Mills, p. 120. Cf. *ibid.*, pp. 130-131; *Minutes of the Baptist Convention, 1866*, p. 240; *Sou. Chr. Adv.*, Aug. 31, 1865, and Mar. 6, 1866.

[33] Whitelaw Reid, *After the War*, chap. III. Cf. the experiences of J. L. Girardeau, a Presbyterian minister, in *Courier*, Dec. 24, 1866.

[34] P. 288. Cf. Episcopalian records in *Diocesan Journal, 1867*, pp. 50-54; *ibid; 1869*, p. 30; *ibid., 1871*, pp. 52, 69.

[35] *Sou. Chr. Adv.*, Apr. 3, 1866, carried the news of the conversion of 50 black and 150 whites at Greenville; Nov. 8, 1867, that of 71 blacks and 118 whites at Edgefield; May 11, 1866, that of 6 blacks and 7 whites at Winnsboro; and Aug. 25, 1868, that of 42 blacks and 205 whites at Marion.

longed to churches controlled by the whites. By 1867 the 40,000 Negro membership of the white Methodist church fell to 8,275; by 1873 it had fallen to 653. Only 1,614 Negro Baptists remained in communion with the whites of that faith in 1874. The Presbyterians had similar losses. The Episcopalians, although not troubled by subversive influences from the North, had no better success. The number of colored Episcopalians fell from 3,000 at the close of the war to 262 in 1876.[36]

How powerful the independent Negro religious bodies became is indicated by a recent census. In 1916 one great Baptist group had 225,479 Negro members, which was 50,131 in excess of the number of white Baptists. In the same year six Negro Methodist bodies had 175,348 members, which was 70,042 more than the number of whites in the state of the same faith. There were 8,320 Negro Presbyterians and 3,017 Negro Reformed Episcopalians, while the orthodox Episcopal church had only 1,078 colored members.

The figures just cited indicate that Negro Christianity in South Carolina since the Civil War has largely been centered in independent Baptist and Methodist churches. We must therefore describe the origin of these churches.

The African Methodist Episcopal church, the leading colored Methodist body, began its career in the state with a great flourish. Daniel A. Payne, a minister who had been exiled from the state thirty years previous, returned to Charleston in 1865 as the bishop appointed to establish this church. He was, he said, "led by the triumphant genius of freedom" to enter a city smitten by "the hot indignation of God."[37] He opened the first conference of his church on May 15, with twelve native ministers and four from the North present. Richard H. Cain, one of the Northerners, expressed the hope of the assembly

[36] Minutes of the Annual Conferences of the Methodist Episcopal Church, South, 1865-1876, passim; Minutes of the State Baptist Convention, 1874, p. 28; and Diocesan Journal, 1865-1876, passim.
[37] Recollections of Seventy Years, pp. 162-63.

when he said that the time had come for the native colored man to play a part "in the great work of elevating their brethren, and that God's Providence had leveled the barriers and rolled away tyranny's mountain—the pathway was cleared, lit up by the sunlight of liberty and the presence of God." Resolutions asserting that a separate Negro church was necessary were adopted. Although his church was willing to recognize the brotherhood of man, said Payne, the day had not come when all men could worship at the same altar because of the prejudices of the white churchmen of both the North and the South. "Colored men who had admitted to a distinction in the House of God," he added, "had lost half their manhood." To spread this principle, provision was made for the dispatch of missionaries to the interior of South Carolina and to neighboring states.[38]

When the second annual conference of the African Methodist church met at Savannah in 1866, its leaders reported substantial progress. There were 22,388 members in South Carolina and surrounding territory, and $28,900 worth of property and thirteen ministers in the state. The most successful of the ministers had been Cain, whose unique powers have already been described.[39] He had built in Charleston, at the cost of ten thousand dollars, the great Emanuel Church with a seating capacity of two thousand. Wherever he went he was received by "a closely packed audience of the darker hue."[40] "Quite a parade of 'bishops, deacons and elders' had been indulged in," said a white layman. "Sambo, like the white man, is fond of office, and the temptation of being made a live bishop caused hundreds and thousands to join the African Methodist Church."[41]

Subsequent conferences of this church were able to report

[38] *Courier,* May 19 and 31, 1865.
[39] See above, pp. 131-32.
[40] *Sou. Chr. Adv.,* Nov. 2, 1865, and

May 25 and June 1, 1866; and *Courier,* Aug. 29, 1866.
[41] George W. Williams, in *Sou. Chr. Adv.,* Aug. 31, 1865.

rapid progress. In 1876 the value of church property was placed at $143,875, the number of ministers of various grades at one thousand, and the number of members at 43,746. The fact that the number of members was one thousand more than all Negro Methodists in 1860 is convincing evidence of the effectiveness of African Methodism.[42]

The lack of bitterness which characterized the secession of the Negro Methodists is a tribute to the spirit of Christian tolerance of both races. The white Methodists soon realized the inevitability of the withdrawal and accommodated themselves. The official organ of the white church was of the opinion that since the colored people "will not remain in any church organization that does not admit them to the legislative and pastoral relation," and that since "the social relations of the two races preclude the idea of such equality," independent Negro organizations were necessary.[43] The cordial reception of the fraternal delegates of the African church by the general conference of the Southern church was approved in South Carolina,[44] and the whites of Charleston extended the use of Trinity Church to the Negroes until they could complete a church of their own. This last act prompted Cain to express "fraternal feelings" toward the white church. In reply, the Charleston Quarterly Conference expressed its "continued desire . . . for the improvement of the colored people in education, morals and religion."[45]

The whites made provision for those Negroes who did not wish to join the African or Northern Methodist church or remain in the white church. Under the supervision of the bishops of the Southern church the Colored Methodist Episcopal Church of America was organized at Jackson, Tennessee, in 1870. It was given the status of an entirely independent church

[42] *Minutes of the South Carolina Conference of the A. M. E. Church, 1876,* pp. 31-33.

[43] *Sou. Chr. Adv.,* June 15, 1866.

[44] Letter of J. E. Evans, *ibid.,* June 15, 1866.

[45] These interchanges, *ibid.,* Nov. 2, 1865.

with authority to elect its own bishops. The white church leaders of that state ordained colored men as deacons and elders and organized separate Negro quarterly conferences.[46] By 1876 this church was enjoying prosperity.[47]

Very little friction was caused by the organization of independent Negro Baptist churches. There were several reasons for this. In the first place, the nucleus of an independent church and clergy already existed in the plantation prayer meeting and exhorter. Since Baptists did not stress clerical training or the character of church edifices, it was no difficult matter to declare informal Negro gatherings regular congregations. In the second place, the fact that each Baptist congregation was a law unto itself made possible the constitution of independent churches with the minimum of formalities. All that was necessary was to get the approval of the church from which the congregation was withdrawing, and the ordination of the minister could be had through the good offices of a few local ministers. There was no need, as in the case of the Methodists and Episcopalians, to wait on the approval of some central ecclesiastical body. In the third place, the Baptists were more willing than the other denominations that the Negroes should determine their own ecclesiastical destinies. Unlike the Presbyterians, they did not find it necessary to be solicitous concerning their orthodoxy, for the experiences of slavery proved that the Negroes were already thoroughly grounded in Baptist beliefs and ritual. Unlike the Methodists and Episcopalians, the Baptists had never regarded the Negroes as subjects for deliberate missionary endeavors. They had come into the church in much the same manner as whites; it was deemed proper that they should be allowed to form independent churches with the freedom accorded whites.

The ready manner in which Negro Baptist churches were

[46] *Ibid.*, May 29, 1869.   [47] See account of Limestone District Conference.—*Ibid.*, Sept. 12, 1876.

organized is attested by all available evidence. We learn of the dismissal from white churches of their colored members, of the public being asked to contribute toward the building of houses of worship for "these pious and worthy persons," and of fairs being held to raise funds for this purpose.[48] "As the house of worship could not hold the congregation that attended it," ran the report of a white assembly, "it was deemed best to constitute the colored members as a separate church, . . . and they are now known as the Pineville Colored Baptist Church. They have adopted the covenant and declaration of principles set forth by the Welch Neck Baptist Association."[49] The Negroes, until they could acquire the resources necessary to build a church of pine boards, were content with a shelter made of the branches of trees, a "bush harbor" as they called it. So great was the success of the independent church that on May 2, 1877, a state convention was organized by the ten or more existing regional associations.[50]

That the white Baptists approved what was done is indicated by authoritative utterances. "There is reason to believe that in certain localities, and under certain circumstances," said a committee of the white state convention in 1866, "the Negroes will prefer to be organized into separate churches. Where this desire is strongly felt, and there is any probability of their being able to maintain public worship among themselves, it seems to your committee the better plan to give them letters of dismission, to aid them in forming churches of their own, and then to assist them either by allowing them the use of the house of worship, or helping them to build."[51] The general agent of the church reported the following year: "There are a number of interesting churches and schools

[48] Florence A. Mims, *History of the Edgefield Baptist Church*, and *News*, June 27, 1866, and Jan. 18, 1867.
[49] *Minutes of the Charleston Baptist Association, 1868*, p. 4.

[50] *American Baptist Yearbook, 1878*, pp. 40-41.
[51] *Minutes of the State Convention, 1866*, p. 240.

among them, and some revivals of religion which seem to be true and genuine, with a tendency, however, to superstition."[52] When the Negroes organized their state convention, the whites expressed satisfaction and received cordially colored fraternal delegates.[53]

The experiences of Alexander Bettis of Edgefield, as related by one of his followers,[54] reveal the actual process through which independent Negro Baptist churches were constituted. Because of unusual native ability and piety, Bettis's considerate mistress had given him special recognition as a slave. He had been made a member of the Edgefield Village Baptist Church, a plantation exhorter, and manager of his mistress's business undertakings. Immediately after the war seventeen colored members of his church asked him to become their leader and he appeared before the Edgefield Baptist Association asking for ordination. This was refused. "The matter of conducting prayer meetings may be intrusted to some Negroes," he was told, "but we cannot afford to have them 'mommick' up the Gospel—a thing they cannot help doing, if empowered to preach." All the members of the association did not agree with this verdict. Three white preachers and a Negro who had been ordained in Georgia met with Bettis and the seventeen laymen, organized the Mt. Canaan Baptist Church, and ordained Bettis as its minister. The way was now open for the display of his unusual qualities. He organized more than forty churches, at one time was the pastor of ten, and continuously was pastor of four. Moreover, he had a notable career as an educator and assisted in the formation of regional associations and the ordination of many ministers.

The white Presbyterians did not have a clear understanding of the religious consequences of emancipation and steadily refused to recognize the separatist inclinations of the blacks.

[52] Ibid., 1867, p. 264.
[53] Ibid., 1877, p. 17.
[54] Alfred W. Nicholson, Life of Bettis, pp. 6-37, 52.

"They," affirmed the South Carolina Presbytery in 1865, "cannot bear the teachings of the Bible in reference to persons in their condition."[55] A negative attitude was adopted. The colored people, said the Harmony Presbytery in 1868, "were too unsettled politically and religiously to inaugurate any permanent plan of religious instruction among them separate from the old plan. . . . The Gospel was offered them, but they declined it as coming from us."[56] When in 1873 the General Assembly of the Southern Presbyterian church resolved upon the expediency of a separate Negro church, South Carolina whites obeyed reluctantly. The Charleston Presbytery "feared that the present intellectual and moral qualifications of this people were not such as to fit them for the successful management of such an undertaking."[57]

The result of this attitude was the alienation of the entire colored membership of the white church and a great relative decline in the number of that race professing any form of Presbyterianism. The limited autonomy allowed colored congregations, said a white minister, "was in no wise calculated to inspire a spirit of independent or vigorous Christian activity. . . . It involved a condition for its success which it was folly to expect, namely, that a race actually independent, and possessed of every social and civil right that we claimed, should consent to remain dependent and subordinate in their ecclesiastical relation."[58] The result was that all Negro Presbyterians deserted to the Methodists or Baptists, or joined the Northern branch of their church. In 1916 there were 8,300 colored South Carolinians in the last-named body.[59]

The Episcopalians tried to hold their colored members true to their faith. "As those who have been long associated with the race," said a committee of their church, "we of the South

[55] Jones and Mills, op. cit., p. 129.
[56] Ibid., pp. 122-23.
[57] Ibid., p. 119.
[58] G. W. Leyburn, Southern Presby-terian Review, XXV (Apr., 1874), 229-30.
[59] Census of Religious Bodies, 1916, I, 574.
[60] Diocesan Journal, 1866, pp. 46-49.

best understand their peculiar traits, habits and character, and are, therefore, best fitted to minister to their physical and mental and spiritual wants." They, it was held, must not be left "to the injudicious teachings of others or to the blind guidance of self-constituted, confident and ignorant guides of their own condition and class." It was suggested that a board be constituted to promote the education of the race, to select candidates for the ministry and to organize separate congregations. But no provision was made for an autonomous church.[60] Soon there developed colored congregations directed by ministers of their own race, and, as shown elsewhere,[61] the Episcopalians did notable work in the promotion of Negro education.

But these devices were not sufficient to keep the three thousand colored Episcopalians faithful. Many joined the Methodist or Baptist church, where they could manage their own affairs and indulge in extravagances in worship intolerable to the church from which they came. "Alas, for the changes in five or six years!" said a committee of the church.[62] "The Negroes have forsaken the way they had learned. . . . Fanaticism and extravagance rule in their religious assemblies to such an extent as to require the aid of the military to keep order and repress violence. There are indications of a return to African barbarism."[63]

In 1873 a heated controversy was started when St. Mark's, a self-supporting congregation of mulattoes, made application for representation in the diocesan convention.[64] The clerical delegates favored the admission of the delegates of this church, but the lay delegates held that color was sufficient grounds for exclusion. They asserted that mulattoes were more objectionable than blacks. "This is the class," they said, "in which miscegenation is seen and which attempts to miscegenate."[65] By

[61] See below, p. 424.
[62] Report of the Committee on the Destruction of Churches, p. 13.
[63] Diocesan Journal, 1869, p. 81; ibid., 1871, p. 88; ibid., 1872, p. 39; and ibid., 1873, p. 102.
[64] Ibid., 1873, p. 19.
[65] Ibid., 1875, pp. 25-43.

a close vote the petition was refused.[66]   But the question continued to be agitated in one form or another for a number of years. In 1887 the insistence of the clergy that a colored minister be accorded a seat on the floor of the convention resulted in the withdrawal of two-thirds of the lay delegates. The following year a compromise was effected. Provision was made for a separate colored convocation under the control of the white bishop.[67]   This settlement was agreeable to the whites who withdrew and the Negroes who remained within the church.

This controversy and other causes which have been suggested resulted in an independent Episcopal church entering the state in 1875 and receiving the allegiance of a majority of the colored Episcopalians. The new church, which had originated in Kentucky, was known as the Reformed Episcopal church. B. F. Stevens, a native white who was the leading missionary of the Episcopal church, induced most of the rural colored congregations to join the new body. His work has been permanent, for in our own day the colored members of the reformed church are thrice as numerous as the colored members of the older body.[68]

It was not many years after the war before the whites became indifferent or even hostile toward Negro religion. The principal cause was that the Negro ministers turned to politics. As early as 1867 it was noted that there had been "the development of sentiment among the leading men of the African M. E. Church which will drive from it the sympathy of the Southern Church. . . . When it turns the church into a political club . . . it should be rebuked."[69]   The activities of certain leaders of the Negro church were characterized as follows: "It is not

[66] Ibid., 1876, p. 63.
[67] Ibid., 1888, pp. 17-19, and ibid., 1889, pp. 16-20.
[68] Census of Religious Bodies, 1916, I, 574, and B. F. Stevens, Centennial Edition of the News and Courier, p. 80.
[69] Sou. Chr. Adv., June 7, 1867.

the gospel of salvation to perishing sinners they preach, but their own political rhapsodies."[70]

Moreover, many whites became as convinced as Northerners that the type of Christianity the Negroes practised was disreputable. "Instead of being quiet and orderly," ran a typical criticism, "the Negroes never preach, pray, or sing without yelling at the top of their voices, and adding to these acknowledged religious exercises a barbarous shouting, thus disturbing the neighborhood in the most intolerable manner up until midnight."[71] A Presbyterian writer scarcely exaggerated the respectable white man's conception of the Negro's religion when he said that many colored ministers were possessed "of bad personal character, licentious and dishonest, and ready to make the use of their ghostly powers for selfish and base ends."[72]

Many whites saw positive advantages to themselves from the withdrawal of the Negroes from their churches. Thereby they were relieved of financial burdens and their ministry of a great responsibility. "The withdrawal of the colored people from our church," said a Charleston minister, "has already operated in opening up for us a new and brighter prospect. We are relieved of a burden and what was a stigma. . . . The absorption of the church by them . . . placed us in a false light before the community."[73]

So thorough has become the separation of the races along religious lines in our own day that it is quite possible for a stranger to attend many religious meetings of either race without becoming aware that the other race exists in the state. In no other sphere are the races more rigidly separated. It has become such an immutable part of the social structure that most South Carolinians of today are not aware that conditions

[70] Anon., *Southern Presbyterian Review,* XIX (Apr., 1868), 273.

[71] *News,* Sept. 15, 1868.

[72] *Southern Presbyterian Review,* XIX (Apr., 1868), 273-74.

[73] E. J. Meynardie, in *Sou. Chr. Adv.,* Aug. 31, 1865.

were ever different. The two races, declared a writer as early as 1874, "have not in the past, nor will they ever in the future, mingle as one race together. . . . It is foolish to run our ecclesiastical laws in collision with the well known and long established laws of man's actual history and nature."[74]

The winning of religious independence by the Negro was perhaps the most momentous social change of Reconstruction. Not only was it a change in matters of most intimate concern, but it was also the most clearly defined change which has remained permanent. No one at the present ever dreams of challenging its existence. Those who with a heavy hand undid the political accomplishments of Reconstruction have never questioned its principal religious accomplishment.

[74] G. W. Leyburn, *Southern Presbyterian Review*, XXV (Apr., 1874), 233-34.

CHAPTER XV

ASPECTS OF RELIGIOUS LIFE

IT is probable that the churches of both races suffered as little as any institution from the consequences of the war. The assaults of the Northern churches, as has been shown, only gave occasion for the renewal of native faiths. The poverty and confusion of the times tended to make Christians cherish more fondly an institution which promised happiness in another world. The loss by the white churches of their colored members meant that the whites could give more attention to their own spiritual uplift. The winning of religious freedom by the Negroes made possible significant steps in their religious development. But war and its aftermath did handicap the churches in some respects, and before describing positive achievements it is necessary to describe some of the difficulties of the churches and how they were overcome.

All the white churches complained bitterly of material losses. In 1868 only fifty-three of the seventy-three parish organizations of the Episcopal church survived, and only ten of these held regular services. "Along the entire seaboard, where our church had flourished for more than a century," said a committee of that church, "there are but four parishes which maintain religious services; not one outside the city of Charleston can be called a living . . . ; the clergy were living by fishing, farming and the mechanic arts."[1] The endowments for missions, churches, and for the support of the bishop and the widows and orphans of clergymen were greatly reduced. Bishop Davis, blind and in tatters, said to A. Toomer Porter, "I am the dying bishop of a dead diocese."[2]

[1] *Report of the Committee on Destruction in the Diocese of S. C.*   [2] *Led On! Step by Step*, pp. 206-7.

University of South Carolina Library

THE CATHOLIC CONVENT

University of South Carolina Library

WASHINGTON STREET M. E. CHURCH

COLUMBIA AFTER SHERMAN'S VISIT

The losses of other church bodies were great. The Catholics had lost their cathedral, the episcopal residence, two orphan asylums, two convents, and several churches; and six clergymen had died.[3] "Our churches," said a Baptist report, "have suffered badly from the effects of the war. Some of them are nearly broken up; many of them are, to a great extent, without preaching; very few of them are able to sustain their ministers; and all of them are greatly crippled in their ability to do good. It is a time of great darkness and fear and trembling."[4] The number of Baptist ministers fell from 540 in 1860 to 302 in 1866.[5] The Reverend J. A. Broadus said that he knew of only one Baptist congregation in the state which adequately supported its pastor; one missionary said that he was forced to sell his horse to get food for his family, and another said that although his people wanted the Gospel preached, they were unable to buy food.[6]

The troubles of the Presbyterians and Methodists were similar. In 1868 there were only twenty-eight ministers to care for the fifty-three Presbyterian congregations. "It is feared," said a report, "that a number of these churches will soon perish, while others will soon be in rapid decline."[7] Many Methodist ministers were forced by necessity to resort to secular pursuits.[8] Their average annual salary for the four years following 1869 was about $600. This was meager because their families were usually large and because the itinerant character of their duties forced them to keep a horse and frequently prevented them from tending a garden or a farm. Some ministers were less fortunate. One was of the opinion that the thirteen

[3] Bishop P. N. Lynch, *Courier*, Mar. 8, 1866.

[4] *Minutes of the Charleston Baptist Association, 1868,* p. 7. Cf. *Minutes of the State Convention, 1865,* p. 220; *ibid., 1867,* pp. 261, 263; and J. L. Reynolds, in *Christian Index and Southwest Baptist,* May 28, 1868.

[5] *Minutes of the State Convention, 1860,* pp. 89-91, and *ibid., 1866,* p. 242.

[6] *Ibid., 1868,* p. 259, and *Christian Index and Southwest Baptist,* June 1, 1868.

[7] *News,* June 19, 1868.

[8] "Juhl," in *Courier,* Sept. 12, 1866.

dollars he was able to collect from his flock was not enough to shoe his horse, while others complained that they had to go about their duties on foot because they had to sell their horses to provide for their families.[9]

All the evangelical churches feared that the disorders caused by the war threatened the moral integrity of their organizations. The reverses of war, said a Baptist association, had produced "almost general demoralization, and a general apathy . . . is preying upon the vitals of religion itself." Young men were reported without employment, "brooding over blighted hopes and realizing for themselves the sad consequences of defeat, and we fear that not a few of them . . . have taken to their cups or to gambling shops, and are now to be seen on the plain highway to destruction."[10]   "Here as almost everywhere," wrote a Methodist minister from Horry, "the church has suffered terribly. Morals have become lax, backsliding frequent, and in some localities the church is in a condition to dishearten its ministers."[11]

Yet the churches succeeded in transmitting to the generations after Reconstruction the standards of religious and moral excellence which had existed before. That the church leaders acknowledged weaknesses and spoke out boldly against them was perhaps evidence of strength rather than weakness. They knew that the moral and religious enthusiasms of their flocks were too deeply engrained to be overcome by the misfortunes of the times. "I feel," said Bishop Davis, "that I can truly say that the Church has never had a stronger hold upon the hearts of her people than at the present moment. . . . The strong cords of faith and love have become stronger, mutual relations of clergy and people have been more established and upon

[9] *Sou. Chr. Adv.*, Aug. 3, May 24, and Oct. 11, 1867, and Apr. 9, 1874.

[10] John R. Logan, *Broad River and Kings Mountain Baptist Association*, p. 195.

[11] G. H. Wells in *Sou. Chr. Adv.*, Sept. 28, 1866. Cf. *ibid.*, Oct. 4, 1867, and Jones and Mills, *op. cit.*, p. 129.

purer principles."[12] A Methodist minister, although "stripped of every earthly comfort," was reported as "standing by the cross, unfurling the banner and shouting to the charge."[13] "The faith of our church," said a Methodist minister after an extensive tour, "is growing stronger by its trials—Christian sympathy is more fully developed—prayer is growing mightier and more prevailing."[14]

Indeed, the Methodist and Baptist churches succeeded not only in reëstablishing old standards, but also in emerging from Reconstruction as the dominant religious forces of the state. This was largely due to their ability to evoke the revivalistic spirit among a great portion of the inhabitants. Such emotional experience created in its subjects the desire to live the life of virtue and faith which would insure the happiness of heaven. What concern was it to them that their church was poor, their minister without formal training, and the world of Negro voters and politicians topsyturvy?

The Baptist revivals were held annually during the August "laying-by" season. Usually they lasted a week, but if the crowds were large and enthusiastic they might continue indefinitely. A few comments made during 1866 will give an idea of their effects. "A nine days' meeting with the Coranos Church resulted in the baptism of fifty-three rejoicing converts." "At the close of a protracted meeting at Florence nineteen hopeful converts were buried with Christ in Baptism." "A revival meeting is in progress in the Baptist Church of this town," said a report from Sumter. "From a meeting of days it is likely to be marked by weeks in duration. . . . The ordinance of Baptism was administered in the most impressive

[12] Diocesan Journal, 1866, p. 26. Cf. ibid., 1867, p. 40.
[13] Experiences of Lucius Bellinger, in Sou. Chr. Adv., Oct. 19, 1866.
[14] Whitefoord Smith, in ibid., June 28, 1867. Cf. ibid., Oct. 16, 1868; Minutes of the State Baptist Convention, 1867, p. 264, and Jones and Mills, op. cit., p. 120.

manner, and tears attested the sacred interest with which it was witnessed."[15]

The Methodist revivals were more spectacular and have been more extensively chronicled. The files of the *Southern Christian Advocate* leave the impression that throughout the Reconstruction period the churches were under the influence of these emotional outbursts. They were most numerous during 1866, a great revival year. Then Spartanburg County was "in a perfect blaze of revivals" due to the "language of melting tenderness" of a minister "whose face shown like that of Moses." In Greenville, the neighboring county, "the congregations gave way to old-time manifestations." "There were shouts in the camp," wrote a witness, "as of one that getteth victory—loud exclamations of 'Glory to God.' The spirit was with us, and the people of God had liberty to express their joy."[16] A year later from Walterboro a minister wrote the following: "Never did I witness such feeling, such interest and manifestations of divine power as here. The love-feast on Sunday morning was full of interest. . . . From Saturday the altar was crowded with weeping penitents, and 'the grand old woods' rang with shouts of new-born souls."[17] The spirit prevailing in 1873 is illustrated by the report from Lexington: "There was a most wonderful display of divine power. Suddenly, as from one voice, the people of God shouted for joy, and several penitents were happily converted. At the instance of this baptism of the Holy Ghost there was a rush for the altar of many who were heard earnestly crying aloud for mercy."[18]

[15] Philadelphia *National Baptist*, July 19 and Aug. 30, 1866, and "Juhl," in *Courier*, Oct. 11, 1866. Additional information of Baptist revivals cannot be given because the files of the *South Carolina Baptist* and the *Working Christian*, which promised much information, have not been found.

[16] Relations of W. H. Fleming and R. C. Oliver in *Sou. Chr. Adv.*, Sept. 19, and Nov. 2, 1866. Cf. *ibid.*, Aug. 3, Sept. 28, and Nov. 9, 1866.

[17] *Ibid.*, Oct. 11, 1867. Cf. *ibid.*, Sept. 20, 1867.

[18] *Ibid.*, Dec. 3, 1873.

Camp meetings had long been a powerful agency in the evangelization of Methodists. They were held in conveniently located groves where rude benches and a shelter of rough boards for pulpits were erected. A group of "tents," really wooden shacks, were provided for the overnight shelter of those who attended the week or ten days sessions. These "feasts of the Tabernacle" were adaptations to local demands of what supposedly had been the custom of the ancient Jews. They provided convenient opportunity for extended contacts of a people who normally lived in rural isolation.

During the war or immediately afterwards most of these assemblies were abandoned. But by 1868 many had been revived, and in 1875 there were approximately twenty-four in the state.[19]

The spirit of these gatherings is conveyed by witnesses. At Sandy Springs on the Pendleton Circuit in 1870, we are told, "the Holy Spirit was there in mighty power. The old people and the preachers say that they had never seen the like. Some of the scenes beggar description. One afternoon the services continued from the three o'clock sermon until midnight, giving the regular preacher no time to preach."[20] At Binnaker's in Orangeburg County, where for a long number of years "many ransomed sinners had been born to glory," there was a notable gathering in 1876. Of what happened a witness said: "It is hard to conceive of a more beautiful or touching spectacle than that of hundreds of people leaving their work for a few days to devote themselves to praise and prayer. . . . Every service was well-attended, every sermon seemed endowed with special power from on high and many were born to newness of life. . . . The communion service at night was a scene almost painful in its awful solemnity; the sacred vessels were on the rude table; there were deep Rembrandt shadows from which

[19] J. W. Kelley, *ibid.*, Oct. 27, 1875, said that there were from one to five in each of the eight district conferences. Taking three as a possible average, we arrive at the aforementioned number.

[20] *Ibid.*, Nov. 18, 1870.

would emerge a face radiant with a light which was not of this earth. . . . The presence of God was felt and acknowledged by the cheering of the cast-down, the comforting of the weary, the supporting of the weak, and triumphantly attested by the exultant songs of the new-born soul."[21]

In spite of what has been said to prove that the church's chief source of power during Reconstruction was its ability to move large sections of the population by emotional experiences, the post-bellum revivals were less intense and perhaps less frequent than those which shook the state before the war. "Certainly," said a writer, "Methodists are no longer given to the strange bodily exercise called the 'jerks,' which had been witnessed by the famous Bishop Asbury on his tour of the state in 1803."[22] There were even ministers, an old-timer deplored, who had since the war regarded shouting as undesirable.[23] Reports of the successful revivals frequently contained such sentences as this: "This was the most quiet meeting I ever enjoyed"; "The penitents have given little external evidence of concern"; "There was generally not much outburst of feeling."[24] Some deplored the fact that camp meetings did not create as much attention as before the war.[25]

The decline of the emotional side of the faith should not, however, lead to the conclusion that the church was losing power. This was due to the decline of the rudeness of the backwoodsman and to the increase of those types of virtue which the church, through its educational, moral, and social activities, always tried to impose on its converts. It is a truism of religious experience that the more intense the sin the more graphic is the process of conversion. Certainly it is hard to conceive a population more given to the sins which Methodists and Baptists deplored than the rustics from which, before the war, those churches drew their converts. "The pictures given

[21] I. D. M., *ibid.*, Sept. 19, 1876. Cf. *ibid.*, Aug. 21, 1868, and Dec. 15, 1875.
[22] *Ibid.*, Aug. 15, 1876.
[23] *Ibid.*, Oct. 9, 1866.
[24] *Ibid.*, Mar. 9, and June 28, 1876.
[25] *Ibid.*, June 10, and Aug. 29, 1876.

of society then were certainly not rose-colored," remarked one who had examined the records of the Old Wateree Conference. "Church people 'running for the bottle, getting drunk and turning up jack. A free fight at Carter's Meeting House on the expulsion of a member and the drunkard cursing in the religious assembly at Lancaster Village'.... Whisky and peach brandy so abounding that preaching was postponed until the drunkards had gone home."[26] After the war there were even towns like Spartanburg, Cokesbury, Anderson, and Greenville where the Methodists and Baptists dominated socially in the same manner as did the Episcopalians in Columbia and Charleston. In these places they were able to maintain themselves through routine educational and moral efforts without the emotionalism necessary during the formative period of their churches' history. The Sunday school and the weekly prayer meeting and the Sunday service directed by an educated minister became of primary significance.

The Episcopalians and Presbyterians, who were without notable manifestations of the revivalistic spirit, had to depend for their power on measures of routine discipline. Here they were on common ground with the Methodists and Baptists, and for this reason the disciplinary efforts of the four denominations will be discussed jointly.

For these efforts much more elaborate organizations were necessary than was needed to bring about conversions. Ministers had to be educated and paid and churches had to be built and maintained. For this, considerable funds were needed.

The manner in which the churches went about raising funds challenges attention. The church leaders refused to accept at their face value cries of poverty; they knew that Protestants had been always inclined to give less than they were capable of; they frequently drew comparisons between examples of worldly prosperity and the poverty of religious insti-

[26] *Ibid.*, July 25, 1876.

tutions. "Our Scotch Irish people," said a Presbyterian leader, "are a thrifty, temperate, hospitable race, but we are too canny. We are too close and we often pinch a six pence until it squeals."[27] Suffering, he paradoxically held, because it was evidence of God's punishment, should induce gifts to the church. The Baptists were boldly told by their leaders that they spent more for tobacco than they did for the Gospel.[28] "Forty-nine fiftieths of the Methodists," said a minister of that faith, "have not paid a cent this conference year. . . . The people seem in other respects to love their preacher very much. . . . They give me the best they've got when I go to see them, yet contribute no money. . . . I am willing to do all that I can to assist them into getting into heaven. Still when money is required they do not respond."[29] It was asserted that excuses for not paying church dues were "in many instances weak and frivolous," since there were persons crying poverty who presented "most respectable appearances to the public, and their tables were still crowned with an abundance of substantial food."[30]

It was inevitable that these and similar appeals should have had success among a pious people. "It would do the soul good to see," was a typical report, "the old, the young, even the little boys and girls, walking up to the box with one, five, ten, twenty-five and fifty cents, and the beautiful smile on their faces."[31] Steady increases in the salaries of ministers[32] made possible progress in the raising of that calling from an amateur to a professional standing. Churches destroyed by the war were rebuilt and primitive ante-bellum meeting houses were replaced by more substantial edifices. Increased revenues made possible the founding of a Methodist college at Williamston

[27] J. B. Adger, cited in Jones and Mills, op. cit., pp. 134-35.

[28] Convention Minutes, 1869, p. 301.

[29] R. C. Oliver in Sou. Chr. Adv., Aug. 3, 1866.

[30] Report of Columbia Quarterly Conference, ibid., July 10, 1868.

[31] Christian Index and Southwest Baptist, Mar. 21, 1867.

[32] In 1870 the South Carolina Presbytery reported that the average salary of its ministers was double that of 1860.—Jones and Mills, op. cit., pp. 132, 134.

in 1872, the reopening of Columbia Female College in the following year, and the establishment of Methodist and Presbyterian orphanages. By 1870 the estimated value of all church properties in the state had almost reached the level of 1860—$3,276,982 in 1870 and $3,481,236 in 1860. The wealth of the Methodists was greater in the latter year.[33] Even the revenues of the Episcopal Church rose from $12,809 in 1867 to $87,439 in 1873.[34]

The churches did not forget their duty of enforcing personal and social morality. Conversion was not taken as a full assurance that the member would live as a Christian should; he was continually reminded what his conduct should be, and the sins of individuals and groups were exposed with a frankness which would be startling to church-goers of later times. Complaints were lodged against dancing, card-playing, theatrical performances, Sabbath breaking, drinking, extravagant dressing, and even baseball and foot races. A typical clerical opinion of dancing was the following: "Let the sexes promiscuously indulge in this fascinating art and see at once the tendency to dissipation and lasciviousness."[35] Watch was kept over members with the view of expelling the transgressors.[36] Church fairs were frowned upon because they promoted raffling and extortion, although a tolerance of them meant profits.[37]

The most vigorous efforts of the religious moralists were directed against the drink evil. Here the difficulties were great. Even Methodists were disposed to manufacture and sell intoxicants and to have "strange chronic diseases for which they took bitters." It was charged that the entire membership of only two Methodist churches in Greenville County were free

[33] Ninth Census, I, 506-25.
[34] Diocesan Journal, 1874, p. 64.
[35] Henry M. Mood, in Sou. Chr. Adv., Nov. 18, 1874.
[36] Ibid., Aug. 3, 1866, and Florence A. Mims, op. cit.
[37] See Methodist resolutions in Sou. Chr. Adv., Dec. 24, 1869.

of this habit.[38] The Tagalo Baptist Association admitted that "many charges were being made against members of the Baptist Church for the crime of intoxication."[39] The Baptists were more individualistic than the Methodists and laid emphasis on Biblical tolerance of drinking and were therefore less inclined to heed the suggestions of reformers. Nevertheless this church was swept into the current of reform. Lodges of the Sons of Temperance and the Good Templars, mostly composed of Methodists and Baptists, were organized to promote total abstinence and prohibitory legislation. The public was frequently told that intemperance was "the cause of nearly nine-tenths of crimes and of untold suffering and ignorance. . . . It is a means of carrying thousands to drunkards' graves and drunkards' hell."[40] The way was prepared for the great prohibition wave which swept the state after 1880.

The importance which the churches attached to spiritual and moral uplift should not lead to the conclusion that the churchmen were gloomy saints altogether abjuring the pleasures of this world. It is true the churches were devoid of many attractions of later days. The utilitarian dogma that virtue and happiness, as well as sin and misery, were synonymous had not been proclaimed; it was still believed that the primrose path had its charms and that righteousness was to a degree the decree of an arbitrary God. The church was still simply a house of worship; there were no social halls, kitchens, and gymnasiums attached. Nevertheless, the church gathering was a more effective means of enjoying the delights of social intercourse than it is in our day of urban concentration and easy communications. It was the one certain means through which the farmer and his family could escape from the isolation of the farm. It was inevitable that on such an occasion social

[38] *Ibid.*, Oct. 4, 1867, Mar. 6, 1868, and Jan. 5, and Aug. 22, 1876.

[39] *Christian Index and Southwest Baptist*, Aug. 23, 1868.

[40] *Sou. Chr. Adv.*, Jan. 5, 1876. Cf. *Sumter News*, Mar. 20, 1873.

aims often took precedence over the religious. It was an open
scandal that the spiritual purposes of camp meetings and other
protracted sessions were often subordinated to the display of
new bonnets and dresses, bountiful dinners, and animated
chats on subjects removed from the religious message of the
day.

The church officially did not frown on certain forms of
conviviality. It imposed no fasts or pleasure-killing asceticism.
The ministers were notorious for their love of "good roast beef
and lamb and lemonade, if not disguised brandy smashers,"
and for their "strength and health, extended girth and ru-
bicund faces." One minister, who was no doubt exceptional,
is described as follows by a colleague: "His face is as fat as his
body. He eats!—yes, eats more heartily than ordinary men—
not ambrosia, but simple hog and hominy. He drinks; aye,
freely—but it is not sack and brandy; but simple water, tea and
coffee. He sleeps and that so soundly and sonorously that he
generally monopolizes all of that blessed commodity which
happens to be in the house at the time."[41] Most of the ministers wore no special dress; their sermons were illustrated from
everyday life and filled with amusing jokes and yarns. The
ritual was simple and colored with contemporary imagery.

Some aspects of church life betook of a carnival character
such as one usually associates with less puritanical faiths. A
large crowd gathered around the church. The ostensible purpose was to hear a sermon or the recitations of the Sunday
school pupils. But no special obligation to go within the
church was imposed, and the visitor could spend the morning
talking with friends and awaiting the dinner which the women
of the community would spread at one o'clock under the near-
by oaks. "The table, a long one," we are told of one of these
occasions, "was spread under umbrageous oaks. . . . The tim-

[41] Sou. Chr. Adv., Jan. 15, and Oct. 21, 1869.

bers literally groaned beneath the savory viands. Both the quality and the quantity seem to prove that hard times must surely be mythical."[42]

The Reconstruction period was not characterized by developments which tended to diminish or accentuate sectarian differences among the whites. Each sect maintained its definite dogmatic, ritualistic, and social traditions. All were united in a common dislike for Roman Catholicism without knowing much about that faith. Even the Episcopalians would tolerate nothing which suggested the "external and sensuous" rites of the Romanists.[43] At times they joined the other sects in union services. But generally they held apart, being suspicious of puritanism, vehemence and leveling tendencies. "They do not claim," said a Methodist bishop in derision, "to be more holy, but more genteel and respectable."[44] The Methodists, Baptists, and Presbyterians had much in common. They were puritanical, anti-ritualistic and tolerant of revivals. Frequently they met together in prayer meetings. But there were limits to their cordiality. The Presbyterians had a stiff-necked theology not subject to compromise. The Baptists and Methodists used similar methods in competing for the same class. The Methodists resented the tendency of the Baptists, because of their unique form of baptism, to claim theirs "to be the only church of Christ on earth."[45] On the other hand, the Baptists resented the Methodists' aggressive manners and assumption of moral superiority.

* * * * *

The internal development of the Negro churches was strikingly similar to those of the whites. For each white sect there was a corresponding Negro sect with approximately the same proportion of the race in it. The Baptist was the church of the

[42] *Ibid.*, July 11, 1876.
[43] *Diocesan Journal, 1866*, pp. 51-54.
[44] George Pierce in *Sou. Chr. Adv.*, Sept. 13, 1871.
[45] *Ibid.*, Aug. 4, 1875.

largest numbers of both races; the Episcopal was the church which attracted a small number of the genteel of both races.

White writers predicted that religious liberty would involve the Negroes in "the grossest paganism—obi-ism, fetishism of the lowest type, belief in false prophets, conjurors, sorcerers and other forms of African superstition."[46] But this never happened. The religious practices of the Negroes seldom got beyond an application of the imagery of the Bible to the culture which the race had acquired in South Carolina. Their religion was as native and as orthodox as that of the white Methodists and Baptists. Its exuberance, instead of being African paganism, was but a characteristic of American religion in an early stage of its development; if it was more strenuous than that of the white man, it was because the Negro was a more genuine type of early American, more darkened by the shadows of backwoods ignorance.

Perhaps the Negroes had a higher appreciation of the value of Christian orthodoxy than did the whites. They laid great stress on fine points of Biblical and theological interpretation. Northern visitors were surprised to find that Negro Baptists applied the restriction of the closed communion to them and that they observed funeral ceremonies and the Sabbath with such exactness. "All the colored people, whether church members or not," said a Northern lady, "had a blind devotion to religious restrictions."[47]

The Negro church members shared the moral convictions of the whites. Their numerous sins were not due to an unawareness of moral values. "They seem to have a true and even *delicate appreciation of right and wrong*," said acute New England critics. "None of their vices are practised unwittingly. They fully realize their moral responsibility. . . . Hell is a very vivid and palpable horror to their imagination, and heaven has

---

[46] *Report of Churches Damaged and Destroyed*, p. 9.

[47] Elizabeth H. Botume, *First Days amongst the Contrabands*, pp. 263-64.

more than ordinary attraction to the oppressed."[48]   The African Methodists were sincere when they joined the whites in condemning liquor, tobacco, dancing, and the playing of cards as contrary to the true spirit of Christianity."[49]

But it should not be concluded that the religions of the two races were alike in all respects. Differences in social and cultural level were bound to give opportunity for variations. The religion of the Negro was characterized by a higher degree of ignorance and emotionalism; but it also possessed startling advantages.

As a compensation for ignorance, the Negro was able to interpret inherited Christian experiences in terms of his own life. God, Jesus, Moses, Satan and other Biblical characters, in his interpretations, became immigrants to South Carolina, to be propitiated in very much the same manner as one pleased his neighbors. The landscape of heaven and hell was endowed with local features. This is revealed by the spirituals and other practices. In one hymn heaven was a place where there was no rainy weather, no sun to burn, no hard trials, "no whips a-crackin'."   In another Massa Jesus was represented as standing in front of the corn crib with the keys in his hands; that is, he guarded the plantation treasure house. To reach heaven one had to cross "de lonesome valley" and "one more river." Admiration of the flashy is revealed by the following couplet:

"Dere's a silver spade to dig my grave,
And a golden chain for to let me down."[50]

In accounting for the Ascension a preacher "pictured a windlass in heaven with a golden cord attached thereto, to one end of which the Savior was clinging, while beautiful angels, robed

[48] [Edward Everett Hale and W. C. Gannett], *North American Review*, CI (July, 1865), 11.

[49] *Minutes of the State Conference of* *the A. M. E. Church, 1871*, pp. 5, 19, 23 and 28.

[50] Thomas W. Higginson, *Army Life in a Black Regiment*, pp. 202-14.

in white, labored at cranks to wind him up."[51] That Jesus was not given a black face, in the manner in which the Virgin Mary once took on the style of every country and century, was not due to the Negro's lack of inventiveness; it was due to his deference to the white man's standards.[52]

The ceremony of baptism was a vivid illustration of how the Negro reduced a great spiritual experience to the consistencies of his own environment. The ceremony was as simple and devoid of color as the cabin in which the convert lived. There was a pool in a creek with banks as red or as black as the water within; there was the preacher in garments of black calico and candidates in ill-fitting dresses of white cotton; branches of oak and sweet gum formed the only cathedral arch above; the candidates entered the water with trepidation and came out screaming and with their garments clinging; and their was an audience, not from heaven but from the neighborhood, some mocking. Yet all this was far more satisfying than some splendid exotic ceremony.[53]

The vital force of Negro Christianity promoted the forgetting of the sorrows, poverty and sins of this world in order to contemplate the glories of heaven. This was not a unique virtue, but was a greater reality to Negroes than to most whites. Because of this the Negro was almost able to turn a funeral into a festival. A Northern lady found a mother who had lost a child "jubilant as if some great and unexpected good fortune had come to her." "You know, ma'am," said the mother, "the Big Massa want him [her]. Him bin a-callin' him fur a long time. 'Ma,' him say to me, 'don' you see bubba waitin' fur me?' . . . I knew w'en him say this, the Big Massa bin sen'

[51] [J. P. Green], *Recollections of the Carolinas*, pp. 125-26.

[52] The Reverend W. E. Johnston was accused of preaching at Fleming's Sheltor Church, Sumter County: "Christ is an African, was born in Africa and preached his first sermon in Africa. Mary his mother was a black woman, and Joseph his father an African and black man." —*Sumter Watchman*, Sept. 29, 1869.

[53] Descriptions of baptisms in *News*, Mar. 2, 1868, and in Elsie Clews Parsons, *Folk-Lore from the Sea Islands*, p. 205.

fur him."[54]   Religion was a relief for pain.   One day a visitor called at a cabin with dirt floor, no chimney and large holes in the roof.   Of a lean woman bent with age he inquired, "You live here all alone, Aunt Phillis?"   She answered simply as a child, "Me and Jesus."[55]

A notable feature of Negro religion was the power accorded the preachers.   Under slavery they were the only class which had gained experience as leaders.   During Reconstruction their importance was enhanced by their part in politics.   Their influence was not, as among the whites, overshadowed by the lawyer and business man.   So important have they remained that of the 290 names which appear in a biographical dictionary of notable colored persons published in 1919, 184 are those of ministers.[56]

The colored ministers proved to be more effective leaders of their flocks than their white brothers.   It is true that many were illiterate and brought reproach upon the church because of extravagant conduct.   But there were compensating qualities.   The chief of these was that they were not professionals. No distinct line was drawn between them and the rest of the community, and for this reason they could not be reproached with that ineffectiveness which men of the world find in a professionalized clergy.   In addition to being preachers they were farmers, artisans, traders, and politicians, community leaders in every respect.   This experience endowed them with a worldly craftiness which made them effective builders of churches and collectors of money.   They were often the richest members of their congregations—an accomplishment never unappreciated in a peasant community.   They were seldom pawns in the hands of their laymen, but were rulers of their neighborhoods.   Their lack of formal education was in a sense an asset.   Native qualities, not talents artificially fostered, were

[54] Botume, p. 104. Cf. *ibid.*, p. 252.
[55] [Hale and Gannett], *loc. cit.*, pp. 10-11. Cf. Botume, p. 85.
[56] A. B. Caldwell, *History of the American Negro, S. C. Edition.*

what they brought to the pulpit. Strength of avoirdupois and lungs, a voluble and graphic eloquence, and a naïve faith in the literal truth of the Bible, brought success. Congregations were not confused by unfamiliar doubts. The preachers were well versed in the Bible as it was written, sometimes adding comments of a startling originality.

"The black preachers," said Sir George Campbell, "seem to be a sort of Christian Brahmins among them [the Negroes], but still they are very democratic in their arrangements. The people like to have a large voice in all their religious affairs. These preachers . . . are rather a funny-looking set, with their black faces and white ties, but they seemed hearty and pleasant." After attending church in Charleston he attested to the effectiveness of the minister: "The preacher was as black as night—a typical Negro—and perhaps a little ridiculous in his manners; but I thought him a stirring and effective preacher. Every now and then during the sermon some of the congregation grunted out devout ejaculations in token of assent or by way of emphasizing the preacher's good points."[57] "If eloquence," affirmed another commentator, "must be measured by power to affect and persuade, then it is true that for natural eloquence colored preachers stand preëminent. The colored preacher is a philosopher and a consummate actor. He is thoroughly acquainted with his race. He knows how to excite each slumbering emotion of the soul."[58]

The funeral and related ceremonies were observed with much pomp and feeling. An observer[59] has written as follows of the funeral watch or "sitting up": "In the evening, a little after nine o'clock, the air was suddenly filled, as it seemed to me, with a strange, wild, screaming wail. . . . As I went up-

[57] *White and Black*, pp. 344, 361, 329.

[58] Prof. T. H. Keating, *A. M. E. Church Review*, I (1883), 139-44. Cf. G. M. Towle, *American Society*, II, 216-17; A. W. Nicholson, *Life of Alexander Bettis*, pp. 31-47; and J. M. Morgan, *Recollections of a Rebel Reefer*, pp. 324-25.

[59] H. W. Pearson, *Letters from Port Royal*, pp. 252-54. Cf. Botume, *op. cit.*, pp. 222-23.

stairs to bed there began, at first quite low, then swelling louder and louder with many voices, the strains of one of their wild, sad songs. . . . The night was wild and stormy, but above the tempest I could hear, as I woke from time to time, the strangely 'solemn, wildly sad strains' which were continued all the night through." Elaborate funerals were usual. The community always furnished a great crowd.[60]

The most unique manifestation of Negro religion was "the shout," a wild dance in which funerals, prayer meetings, and revivals often culminated. It occurred in its most perfect form on the sea islands immediately after the war, but modifications of it were found throughout the state and survived to the end of the century. It was dubbed a "regular frolic" difficult to distinguish from secular dancing and "idol worship," or a "savage heathenish dance" not tolerated by intelligent colored preachers.[61] But it was defended on the ground that the angels shouted in heaven and that it had Scriptural justification—"he in de Book" and "he dere-da in Matchew."[62]

"The benches are pushed back to the wall," said an anonymous writer in the New York *Nation,* "and old and young, men and women, sprucely dressed young men, grotesquely half-clad field hands—the women generally with gay handkerchiefs twisted about their heads and with short skirts—boys with tattered shirts and men's trousers, young girls barefooted, all stand up in the middle of the floor, and the progression is mainly due to a jerking, hitching motion, which agitates the entire shoulder, and soon brings out streams of perspiration. Sometimes they dance silently, sometimes as they shuffle they sing the chorus of the spiritual, and sometimes the song itself is also sung by the dancers. But more frequently a band, composed of some of the best singers and the tired shouters, stand

[60] Descriptions of funerals by Gabriel Manigault, *Land We Love,* V (July, 1868), p. 204, and by Elsie C. Parsons, *Folk-Lore from the Sea Islands,* pp. 214-15.

[61] *Letters and Diary of Laura M. Towne,* pp. 21-22.

[62] W. J. Allen, etc., *Slave Songs of the United States,* p. 13.

PRAYER MEETING IN A CONTRABAND CAMP

"Oh I'm gwine home to glory—won't yer go along wid me,
Whar de blessed angels beckon, an' de Lor' my Saviour be?"

Fridenberg Galleries

at the side of the room to 'base' the others, singing the body of the song and clapping their hands together or on the knees. Song and dance are alike extremely energetic, and often, when the shout lasts into the middle of the night, the monotonous thud, thud of the feet prevents sleep within half a mile of the praise-house."[63]

The animated character of Negro religious gatherings impressed observers. "The roads," said Whitelaw Reid, "were alive with a gaily-dressed throng of blacks, of both sexes and of all ages, wending their way, on foot, on horseback, in carts, and wagons, and even in a few cases in Northern trotting buggies, to Central Church."[64] The scene in the church yard was as spirited: "Overflowing all the church yard, flooding the road, . . . and backing up against the graves were the Negroes. . . . The woods back of the church were filled with carts and wagons; the horses were unharnessed, tied to the trees and fed while their owners were gathered in groups about the carts." The scene within the church was as follows: "Around them [the leaders] were a group of certainly the blackest faces, with the flattest noses and the woolliest heads, I ever saw—the mouth now and then broadening into a grin or breaking out in that low, oily, chuckling gabble of a laugh which no white man can ever imitate. Beyond them ranged all the colors and apparently all conditions. Some, black and stalwart, were dressed like quiet farm laborers. . . . Others lighter in color and slighter in build, were dressed in broadcloth, with flashy and gaudy pins, containing paste or Cape May diamonds. . . . On the other side of the church was a motley but brilliant army of bright-colored turbans wound around woolly heads, and tawdry bandanas, and hats of all shapes that have prevailed in the memory of this generation. . . ."

[63] May 23, 1867, cited *ibid.*, pp. 12-14. Cf. *Letters and Diary of Towne*, pp. 21-23; Higginson, *op. cit.*, pp. 17-18; Botume, p. 136; [Hale and Gannett], *loc. cit.*, pp. 17-18; and Elizabeth A. Coxe, *Memories of a S. C. Plantation*, p. 55.
[64] *After the War*, pp. 80-81, 99-102.

CHAPTER XVI

PROGRESS IN EDUCATION

EDUCATIONAL efforts during Reconstruction may be divided into three classes. There were those of the native whites, those of the Northern missionary societies and the Freedmen's Bureau, and those of the Radical state government.

The Civil War forced a gradual lessening of the educational efforts of the whites; the disasters of 1865 forced their practical abandonment. Immediately after the war physical distress was too great for extensive efforts toward the rehabilitation or improvement of existing schools. This was recognized by Northerners, and Governor Orr, in his message to the legislature of December 5, 1865, recommended that the usual appropriations for the free schools be discontinued.[1]

Soon, however, traditional institutions were reopened and educational aspirations previously confined to the North appeared. The constitutional convention of 1865 took notice of the need of public schools.[2] In 1866 the legislature instructed the governor to appoint a committee to look into the condition of the schools. This committee suggested improvements.[3] Meanwhile the newspapers called for action. An influential country journal said, "What wise legislation have we ever had upon the management of common schools? We look in vain for any. Tens of thousands have been squandered upon the veriest farce, yclept 'common schools.' We are too poor now

[1] *Senate Journal, Reg. Sess., 1865*, p. 38. Reuben Tomlinson, Superintendent of the schools of the Freedmen's Bureau, said that the state government was too crippled to assume the burdens of education. —*Courier*, Oct. 9, 1865.

[2] *Convention Journal*, p. 55. But there was no educational provision in the constitution of 1865.

[3] *House Journal, Ex. Sess., 1866*, p. 31; *ibid., Reg. Sess., 1866*, p. 88; and *Reports and Resolutions, 1866*, pp. 168-69.

to waste money. Yet, though so poor, we cannot afford to be ignorant."[4]

The upshot of these agitations was an appropriation from the legislature in 1866 of $25,000. During that year, twenty-two of the forty-five districts and parishes reporting had 313 schools taught by 362 teachers and attended by 2,245 students.[5] The imperfect school census of 1869 gave a fair notion of what the whites accomplished in education in the few years after the war in which they had control of public affairs. Excluding five counties from which there were no reports, this estimate revealed that only 8,255 children out of a white population of school age of 68,108 were in school. No public school for whites was reported in Georgetown and Colleton counties, while those of Darlington, Fairfield, and Union were described as few and primitive. Many of the schoolhouses which survived were one room log shacks. The subsidies from the state were so inadequate that many schools were only kept open through private subscriptions. Yet there were some good signs. The people were hopeful; some new buildings had been constructed; and Greenville and Charleston had more than one-fourth of their white children in school.[6] Had the whites been left in control of the government, it is likely that the legislature would have acted favorably on the promise of Governor Orr that the state would have an educational system superior to any which it had ever had.[7]

Heroic efforts were made to raise the South Carolina College from ruins. It had been converted into a hospital in 1862, but had escaped the fire of 1865. Governor Perry recommended to the legislature that it be reopened under the name of the University of South Carolina, with several professional

[4] *Fairfield Herald*, Jan. 25, 1867. Cf. *Courier*, Sept. 10, 1866, and Gen. D. H. Hill in *Land We Love*, I (May, 1866), 1-9.

[5] *Reports and Resolutions, 1866*, pp. 168-69.

[6] "First Annual Report of State Superintendent of Education," *ibid., 1869-1870*, pp. 404-6.

[7] *News*, Feb. 10, 1867.

schools, in addition to the traditional college of liberal arts. This recommendation was enacted into law on December 19, 1865,[8] and the "university" opened its doors the following month. But it was "practically nothing more than the college revived," since the board of trustees failed to provide the professional schools. But at the suggestion of Governor Orr, definite provisions were made for schools of law and medicine,[9] and the institution finally got under way with enlarged facilities and a very able faculty.

Yet it did not prosper. Funds were meager and the buildings continued in disrepair. It was ridiculed because of its unwieldy board of trustees of thirty-eight and its insistence on maintaining a medical school although there was already one in Charleston.[10] Its greatest weakness was its failure to attract students in sufficient numbers to lend dignity to the classes and provide the professors adequate salaries. There were only 48 students in 1866, 113 in 1868, and 65 in 1869.[11] Some people were "under the impression that the University would not continue its exercises,[12] due to unsettled political conditions. Others were too poor to attend or preferred sectarian colleges or those without the state. But had there been no interference from the Radicals, the institution would ultimately have prospered.

During the period in which the Radicals were in control of the schools, the whites were not neglectful of their educational needs. They supported academies for boys, seminaries for girls, and sectarian colleges for both sexes.

By 1870 there were seventeen academies scattered over the state attended by 650 boys. They fulfilled the purposes of the modern high schools, subjecting their students to intensive drills in mathematics, Latin, rhetoric, and Christian doctrine.

[8] *House Journal, Ex. Sess., 1865*, p. 18. See also legislative report in *Courier*, Dec. 4, 1865, and *Stat. S. C.*, XIII, 296-98.

[9] *Stat. S. C.*, XIII, 382-83.

[10] J. J. O'Connell, *Catholicity in the Carolinas and Georgia*, p. 223, and *News*, Jan. 7, and Sept. 2, 1867.

[11] Edwin L. Green, *A History of the University of S. C.*, p. 438.

[12] *News*, Oct. 23, 1868.

The most notable of these were the Methodist Conference School at Cokesbury, the Mt. Zion Institute at Winnsboro, and Porter's Academy at Charleston. The motives for their maintenance is illustrated by the history of Porter's. Feeling the need of education for the sons of former Confederates, the Reverend A. Toomer Porter set about the founding of a parochial academy. He got enough money from Northerners to open the school in 1867. In 1870 there were 259 students, many of them boarders from the interior of the state.[13] For many years his school was of great benefit to many whose education would otherwise have been neglected.

Young ladies attended seminaries in considerable numbers. These schools varied in size. Some were small and unostentatious, such as those supervised by Episcopal rectors. Those kept by French ladies were much sought after, due to the feeling that French was a necessity of polite culture, even if only a smattering of that language was ever assimilated. Those which enjoyed greatest distinction were kept by grand ladies of the old régime, who found some form of remunerative employment necessary. A school of this type was opened in Charleston in 1866 by the widow of Governor Allston. It was not long before a goodly number of students were attracted. Mrs. Allston was aided in the instruction by her daughter, a cousin, a French lady, and a professor from the College of Charleston who taught the mathematics and Latin. Although the instruction was not thorough, the students did develop the social graces, their principal concern.[14]

The most serious educational endeavors of the whites were centered in the College of Charleston and the colleges maintained by the several Protestant denominations. The College of Charleston enjoyed the distinction of being located in the cultural center of the state, and it gave its small number of

[13] *Episcopal Diocesan Journal, 1870,* p. 97.

[14] Elizabeth W. Allston Pringle, *Chronicles of Chicora Wood,* pp. 307-16.

students a type of instruction whose excellence was limited only by a narrow curriculum.

The most distinguished of the denominational colleges were Wofford, a Methodist institution at Spartanburg; Furman University maintained by the Baptists at Greenville; Erskine, the Reformed Presbyterian College at Due West; and the Lutheran College at Newberry. The special motive for the existence of these institutions was to inculcate Christianity, and, as has been pointed out elsewhere,[15] they succeeded in this endeavor. But this does not mean that the non-religious phases of higher education were neglected. They maintained the cause of education in the face of grave financial distress. Wofford never closed its doors during or after the war, because its faculty refused to surrender to want.[16] Furman was reopened in 1866 and maintained thereafter under distressing difficulties. The Methodists were able to collect sufficient funds to open Williamston College in 1872 and to reopen Columbia Female College in 1873.

The instruction afforded by these colleges was not inferior to that given by their successors of the present. Although the emphasis on religious teachings was too extensive to suit present standards, the curriculum narrow, and the library and laboratory facilities meager, one is impressed with the seriousness with which the ministers acting as professors taught Latin, the Bible, logic, and mathematics, and with the fact that these teachers substituted gifts of personality for what they lacked in scholarly experience. Such teachers as James C. Furman and Charles H. Judson of Furman, James H. Carlisle, Daniel A. Dupre and Whitefoord Smith of Wofford, and William Moffatt Grier of Erskine left lasting impressions upon their

[15] Simkins, "White Methodism in South Carolina during Reconstruction," *North Carolina Historical Review,* V (Jan., 1928), 61-63.

[16] "I have had," said the president, *Sou.* *Chr. Adv.,* Mar. 23, 1865, "the hardest time I have ever experienced in my life, but I am still inclined not to give up the interest if we [the faculty] can keep body and soul together."

students. Moreover, these colleges were not unaware of the cultural enthusiasms of the outside world. The students of Columbia Female College, for example, in addition to the traditional French, music, and Bible, found time for lessons in kindergarten training, calisthenics, telegraphy, photography, and typesetting.[17] That the young men students were alive to the world of Gladstone and Herbert Spencer, as well as to the traditions of the Old South, is proven by the subjects of their commencement orations. They were: "The Great Eclipse of August Next," "Fiction as an Instrument of Reform," "The Lost Cause," "Our Gallant Dead," and so on.[18]

It should not be inferred, however, that the educational facilities which the whites provided for themselves were sufficient to meet the needs of a progressive age. The girls' seminaries were amateurish. The colleges suffered from loss of endowments and the inability to attract adequate numbers of students. In spite of low tuition costs, the eleven colleges and universities of the state had only a combined total of 975 students in 1870.[19] The Spartanburg Female College was permanently closed and the Baptist Theological Seminary moved to a more promising field. The small enrollments were due to poverty and the necessity of the young men's devoting themselves to more practical concerns than the narrow literary instruction which the colleges afforded.

What the schools of lower grades supplied in quantity they lacked in quality. Ludwig Lewisohn has left the following description of one of them: "The village possessed one other school which charged a somewhat higher fee—two dollars a month, I think—and boasted an aristocratic flavor. It was kept by a broken-down gentleman of Huguenot extraction who was said to have been immensely wealthy and to have lived in a state of barbaric splendor before the Civil War. Major

---

[17] Advertisement in *Sou. Chr. Adv.*, Aug. 15, 1876.

[18] Taken at random from *News* and *Sou. Chr. Adv.*

[19] *Census of 1870*, I, 468.

Maury was a man prematurely old, slightly deaf and shaken by palsy. His features were almost hidden by harsh bunches of beard, and hair grew in long strands out of his ears and nostrils. He sat by the window, smoking a pipe and chewing tobacco at the same time. There, in a weary mechanical way, he heard the lessons which we were supposed to have prepared in the other bare room or on the porch of the windy and abandoned cottage. The ten or twelve pupils played and studied behind the sunken-eyed old man in a half-hearted kind of way; the manner and the mood of the place float to me across the years in images of chill discouragement and mouldering desolation."[20]

Under such conditions it is not surprising that the whites made little educational progress during the first fifteen or twenty years after the war. The number of white illiterates over twenty years of age rose from 14,792 in 1860 to 34,335 twenty years later.[21] This, taken in connection with the small number in college, leads to the conclusion that the state by 1880 had lost much of the culture which had given it distinction in 1860.

*   *   *   *   *

The coming of freedom forced the whites to revise earlier notions of Negro education. No longer did anyone favor the prohibition of literary instruction to that race. Influential white persons and organizations favored Negro education and approved certain aspects of the work of Northern missionaries, and some whites actually aided in this endeavor.

The state Baptist Convention of 1866 said that since no law stood in the way, it was "the plain duty of Christians to make efforts, or to foster and encourage efforts made, to enable the colored people to read. . . . By this means the former confidence of the Negro in the white man can be restored as a

---

[20] *Up Stream*, pp. 46-48.   [21] *Handbook of S. C., 1883*, pp. 535, 537.

counteracting influence to the perverting instructions of persons claiming to be the special friends of the Negro."[22] The legislature expressed its intention of making "additional provisions for the teaching of our colored people" in its plans for the revival of the common schools,[23] and Governor Orr said that he expected to recommend such provisions in the educational plans which he would present to the legislature of 1868. Certain individual leaders looked with favor on Negro schools. General James Chesnut, for example, said that the whites of his community "facilitated as far as possible the education of the colored people, with the belief that, if it were possible to educate them to a standard of intelligence, it was our highest interest as well as our bounden duty."[24] The superintendent of the schools of the Freedmen's Bureau, after visiting nine towns, reported in 1867 concerning the schools of his agency, "I question very much whether now half a dozen men of intelligence can be found in any of these places who would not deem it a public calamity to have these schools discontinued."[25]

A few of the whites actually aided Negro schools. Chesnut said that he established one on his estate and that what he did was not an unusual occurrence.[26] The Freedmen's Bureau reported instances of planters establishing schools to keep their laborers satisfied, and the Charleston school board undertook the support of the Morris Street School for the exclusive use of colored children.[27] Native whites showed a willingness to teach in Negro schools which would seem strange to later generations. About one half of the 405 native whites engaged in teaching in the public schools in 1869 were in schools for Negroes.

[22] *Convention Minutes, 1866*, pp. 226, 238-51. Cf. *Courier*, Sept. 20, 1866.

[23] *House Journal, Reg. Sess., 1866*, p. 88.

[24] *Ku-Klux Conspiracy, S. C.*, p. 461. Cf. James T. Bacon of Edgefield in *Courier*, July 14, 1866; and *ibid.*, July 18, 1867, and Apr. 4, 1869.

[25] Laura J. Webster, *Freedmen's Bureau in S. C.*, p. 133.

[26] *Ku-Klux Conspiracy*, p. 460. Cf. Elizabeth A. Coxe, *Memories of a S. C. Plantation*, p. 73.

[27] Webster, *op. cit.*, p. 133, and *News*, Apr. 2, 1869.

The most notable experiment in Negro education undertaken by native whites was the Franklin Street School, Charleston, which was opened in 1866 by the Reverend A. Toomer Porter with funds contributed largely by Northern Episcopalians.[28] The teaching corps was composed of local white women of the highest social standards. The Episcopalians were pleased with the school, seeing in it a means of checking the secession of the blacks from their church. During the six years of its existence it gave instruction to no less than three thousand children.[29]

There was, however, no general movement among the whites to establish Negro schools. General Charles H. Howard believed that, with a few exceptions, they were opposed to Negro education, believing that it would unfit the freedman for the work custom prescribed for him. There was, he added, no person sufficiently interested to make a move in the legislature embodying a plan for state aid to Negro education.[30] It was universally held that the Negro was biologically incapable of much educational progress. A white woman told a Northern teacher, "I do assure you that you might as well try to teach your horse or mule to read as to teach these niggers. They *can't* learn."[31] The school sponsored by the Reverend Mr. Porter would never have been opened had not the necessary money been furnished by Northerners. He soon closed this school and turned his energies to a project nearer his heart, a school for the sons of ex-Confederates.[32] Even the liberal minded were only in favor of elementary education for the Negroes, involving racial segregation and costing much less than that given whites. So advanced a thinker as Governor Orr

[28] President Johnson contributed $1,000.
[29] *News*, May 10, and July 19, 1867, and A. T. Porter, *Forty Years as Rector of the Church of the Holy Communion*, p. 16.
[30] *Report of the Joint Committee on Reconstruction*, Pt. III. p. 35.

[31] Botume, p. 4.
[32] In his *Led On! Step by Step*, p. 236, he naïvely declared, "I did not feel that my mission was to rescue *gamins*, who were no poorer than before the war."

only promised schools for the Negroes supported by the taxes they paid,[33] which would have meant a very meager outlay.

* * * * *

As soon as the victories of the Northern armies made the living of Northerners in South Carolina possible, educational missionaries entered the state to rescue it from the curse of literary ignorance. Exaggerated notions concerning the benighted condition of the people were held. A missionary naïvely remarked, "This state has not yet arrived at a state of civilization sufficiently advanced to provide windmills."[34] Moreover, it was felt that through education the evils which had overwhelmed the state would be eliminated. "This war," said the superintendent of the schools established in Charleston after the occupation, "is the result of the enslavement of the poor blacks and the ignorance of the poor whites. By educating everybody we will take care to prevent a war of races, which the old ignoblesse would bring about, if they dared and could, by prohibiting free schools and repealing the Holy Proclamation."[35] There was great hope that much could be accomplished. The aforementioned superintendent added, "Charleston leads the van; once arm in arm with Yeddo and Pekin, she nearly butted out her brains in a vain attempt to beat back the advancing car of progress; now arm in arm with New York and Boston she will, or she may be, the joint bearer of the 'banner with the strange device Excelsior.' " "New England," said the journal of a missionary society, "can furnish enough teachers to make a New England of the whole South, and, God helping, we will not pause in our work until the free school system . . . has been established from Maryland to Florida and all along the shores of the Gulf."[36]

[33] *News*, Feb. 15, 1867.
[34] E. S. Philbrick, in Elizabeth W. Pearson, *Letters from Port Royal*, p. 5.
[35] James Redpath, *Courier*, May 17, 1865. Cf. Henry Ward Beecher's Fort Sumter Address, *ibid.*, Apr. 5, 1865.
[36] *Freedmen's Journal*, cited by Luther P. Jackson, *Journal of Negro History*, VIII (Jan., 1923), 28.

In the history of education there has perhaps never been a people more willing to receive its benefits than the South Carolina Negroes when the tidings of this evangel were spread by the missionaries. "I have never found a community of blacks, never addressed them at public meetings or individually," said General Charles H. Howard, "where I did not find in them an eagerness to learn, either on their own part or especially for their children. Sometimes on plantations, when I urge the necessity of the blacks renewing their contracts for another year, they have given as the prominent reason why they wish to change their employers and go elsewhere, their desire to be near a village where they have a school for their children."[37] "The Negroes," said a correspondent of the *New York Herald* writing from Columbia, "certainly are very desirous of enlightenment, and the first use of their freedom, so far as my experience goes, is to learn to read. ... It is frequently the case that I see Negroes, who, by some means have learned to read, seated by the roadside teaching their less enlightened brethren and sisters the alphabet."[38] The first formal convention of the race ever held in the state declared, "Good schools for the thorough education of our children" should be established, since "an educated and intelligent people can neither be held in nor reduced to slavery."[39]

The educational efforts of the Northerners began among the Negroes of Port Royal soon after the capture of that area. During the late months of 1861 the Reverend Solomon Peck and others opened several schools. But they were not deemed sufficient. In February, 1862, Edward L. Pierce, an agent of the treasury department, and General Thomas W. Sherman, the commander of the area, issued a call to "the highly favored and philanthropic people" of the North to send volunteers to

---

[37] *Report of Joint Committee on Reconstruction*, Pt. III, pp. 34-35.

[38] Cited in Winnsboro *Tri-Weekly News* July 11, 1865.

[39] *Proceedings of the Colored People's Convention at Charleston, November. 1865*, pp. 9-10.

ZION SCHOOL FOR COLORED CHILDREN AT CHARLESTON

Harper's Weekly

teach "both old and young the rudiments of civilizations and Christianity." The response was the organization of freedmen's aid societies in Boston, New York, and Philadelphia, and the dispatch by them of forty-one men and twelve women teachers and labor superintendents to Port Royal on the following March 3. Two months later eight schools were in operation. Within a year this number had risen to thirty with three thousand students eager to get the advantage of "white sense." Officers were induced to conduct schools for their black soldiers, and many who had bought lands abandoned by the whites opened schools at their own expense. When the war ended, Port Royal schools had sixty teachers.[40]

In 1865 the opportunity to repeat throughout the state what had been done at Port Royal was open. In Charleston the army of occupation seized all school buildings, made James Redpath, who had written a popular biography of John Brown, superintendent of schools, and offered employment to all resident teachers who would take the oath of loyalty and such colored persons of the city as were deemed of sufficient education. Seventy-four of the eighty-three teachers employed were native whites. The freedmen's societies agreed to pay the teachers and furnish the necessary textbooks. Since provision was made for separate class rooms for the two races, some white students were attracted. As early as March 9, the new system was reported successful. The vagrant children had been removed from the streets and fifteen hundred students were attending classes. Two months later Redpath reported nine day schools in operation, with over three thousand students, and five night schools attended by five hundred adults.[41]

As soon as Federal garrisons were in possession of the interior of the state the freedmen's aid societies redoubled their

[40] [Hale and Gannett], *North American Review*, CI (Oct., 1865), 528-49; Pearson, *Letters from Port Royal*, pp. 5-7; and Webster, *Freedmen's Bureau in S. C.*, pp. 81-82.

[41] *Courier*, Mar. 9, Apr. 30, and May 17, 1865.

efforts. They assumed the burden of selecting the teachers and paying their salaries. At times they purchased or erected schools. From the confused statistics available,[42] it is apparent that the societies were in 1866 supporting sixty teachers who were instructing 3,587 students. Columbia had thirteen of their schools, Greenville six, and Anderson three. A year later they were supporting eighty schools which were attended by about 8,000. In 1869 they were supporting seventy schools with 137 teachers and 7,168 students.[43] After that year, due to the efforts of the state to establish a school system of its own, outside interest in the education of the freedmen declined. But Northern agencies to this day support some schools in the state.[44]

The educational efforts of the missionary societies were facilitated by the Freedmen's Bureau. Reuben Tomlinson, a native of Pennsylvania who had had experience with the Negroes of the sea islands, was appointed the Bureau's state superintendent of schools, and General O. O. Howard, the head of the Bureau, urged that all possible aid be given schools established by benevolent agencies. Tomlinson on assuming office in the fall of 1865 asserted that he acted in "no spirit of arrogance or self-sufficiency," but with the desire to help the state in its crippled condition.[45] Until the discontinuance of its educational activities in 1870, the Bureau did everything within

[42] Little distinction was made between the contributions of these societies and those of the Freedmen's Bureau, the direct tax commission, the local whites, and the freedmen themselves.

[43] *American Freedmen's Journal* cited in *Debow's Review*, N. S., II (Sept., 1866), 312; Report of the Freedmen's Bureau Superintendent of Education, *News*, Apr. 18, 1867; and *Report of Secretary of War, 1869-1870*, I, 518.

[44] They are the Penn School at St. Helena founded by Laura M. Towne in 1862; Avery Institute at Charleston founded in 1865; Brewer Institute at Greenwood founded in 1872; Benedict College at Columbia founded in 1871; Mather Industrial School at Beaufort founded in 1868; Claflin University at Orangeburg founded in 1869; Wallingford Academy at Charleston founded in 1865; Browning Industrial Home at Camden; Brainerd Institute at Chester founded in 1868; Laing Normal and Industrial School at Mount Pleasant founded in 1865; and Schofield Normal and Industrial School founded at Aiken in 1868. —Luther P. Jackson, *Journal of Negro History*, VIII (Jan., 1923), 28.

[45] *Courier*, Oct. 9, 1865.

its means to advance the schools of the state. It investigated needs, compiled statistics, instituted a system of examinations for teachers, kept the progress and needs of the schools before the nation, and after 1866 used a part of its appropriations for the repair and rent of school buildings. Nor, as is commonly supposed, did it fail to recognize the freedmen's need of industrial education. In 1869 Alvord, the Bureau's general superintendent of schools, proposed that they "be skilled in labor, be a producing class" as "a vantage ground from which to conquer prejudice and secure a hearty accord to equality of condition and capacity." The whites were encouraged to establish schools for the freedmen, and as soon as the Bureau realized that its seizure of school buildings caused more harm than good, this policy was abandoned.[46] The Bureau would have received white children in the schools had they been willing to associate with colored children and to accept the brand of patriotism offered. But of course they scorned this proffer. In 1867 there were only fifteen white children in the schools of the Bureau.[47]

The freedmen's aid societies and the Freedmen's Bureau did much to lift the pall of illiteracy which had been imposed upon the Negroes while slaves. Tomlinson believed that during 1866 as many as thirty thousand had been taught to read, and in 1870 the census reported that the rate of illiteracy among the blacks had declined to 81 per cent.[48] The type of work the schools were able to give under favorable conditions is revealed by the comments of the *Charleston Daily News* during the

[46] Alvord said that the opposition of the whites was "rather to the occupying of their public school houses by the Negroes than to their education."—*Report of Joint Committee on Reconstruction*, Pt. II, p. 251.

[47] *News*, Apr. 18, 1868. Two girls "of good Southern family" entered Miss Botume's school in 1867. But after two months they were withdrawn from the "nigger school" as the whites "made so much fuss."—Botume, pp. 257-58. A general discussion of the educational efforts of the Bureau is in Webster, pp. 129-37.

[48] *Ibid.*, p. 136, and *Report of the Commissioner of Education, 1897-1898*, II, 2487.

spring of 1867 on the schools of that city.[49]   At a public examination the students of one school "sang with expression," read well, exhibited excellent maps, and were "well dressed, neat and tidy." The students of another school were "well grounded" and the course of study adapted to their needs. The students of a third school "surpassed the hopes of its founders." Moreover, steps were taken to make the schools self-sustaining through the training of native colored teachers. That some progress was made in this work is attested by the fact that in 1869 forty-four teachers of this type were active in the schools of the state.[50]

In their methods of instruction the teachers showed a sense of realism not usually ascribed to "Yankee schoolma'ams." The interests of the students were excited by gifts of clothes and food. Their singing emotions were appealed to by use of standard hymns, spirituals, patriotic songs, and songs composed of the A B C's, as part of the class room instructions. Elaborate parades were organized proclaiming the advantages of universal education. The teachers were active in community life, teaching the Negroes domestic economy and manual work, as well as reading and writing. Nor did all the teachers tire of their work after brief services. Miss Martha Schofield gave forty-eight years of her life to teaching Negroes, Miss Abby D. Monroe gave forty-five years, and Miss Laura M. Towne thirty-eight years.

The manner in which the most devoted of these teachers faced their work is revealed by the experiences of Miss Towne and Miss Elizabeth Hyde Botume. Their initial difficulties seemed insurmountable. Their students were "real bullet-headed Negroes" who were heedless of discipline, spoke an unknown dialect, and thought a book was an object which through some occult influence imparted knowledge without

[49] Apr. 19, June 26 and 28, and July 18, 1867.

[50] Webster, p. 135, and *Reports and Resolutions, 1869-1870*, pp. 405-6.

effort of their own. An idea of their meager cultural experience is given by the answers which they gave to the following questions: "Who wrote the Ten Commandments?" "General Saxby [Saxton]"; "Columbus"; and "Uncle Sam." "Who is Jesus Christ?" "Massa Linkum." But difficulties were overcome. The teachers took advantage of their "eager, expectant scholars" for "book-larning." They saw that faces were washed, inspected cabins, ministered to the sick and became sympathetic toward the dialect and its peculiar songs. Sewing was taught, and interest stimulated by gifts of needles, thread, and clothing. "We are convinced," said the sagacious Miss Botume, "that plenty to eat would harmonize and Christianize them faster than hymns and sermons; and that needle and thread and soap and decent clothing were the best educators and would civilize them sooner than book learning." Their schools survive to this day, monuments to their able and devoted services.[51]

Of greater significance than the actual results accomplished was the influence which the schools enjoying Northern support exercised upon the Negro's attitudes. He was convinced that education was a principal means of emerging from the degradation of slavery. He was led to support enthusiastically universal education when he became the political master of the state; and, more important, he was made willing to take advantage of whatever schools have been provided for him. From 1869 through the second decade of the twentieth century, more Negroes than whites were always enrolled in the schools of the state.

But the weaknesses of the Northern-supported schools should be recognized. Their efforts were not sufficiently comprehensive, and they were not wholly beneficial.

This work reached only a small percentage of the colored

[51] *Letters and Diary of Laura M. Towne*, pp. 5 ff., and Botume, *First Days amongst the Contrabands*, pp. 43-95 ff.

population of school age. According to the reports of the county superintendent of education only 8,255 children were under instruction in 1868 out of a total colored population of school age of 100,711.[52] Moreover, the schools were not evenly distributed; they were best and most numerous in Charleston, Columbia, and near Beaufort.

With many of the teachers their mission was an emotional jaunt, to be abandoned as soon as abolitionist enthusiasm cooled through contact with the realities of Negro life. Representatives of this type were Mary Ames and Emily Bliss, two young Unitarian ladies of Springfield, Massachusetts. Moved by a desire to help the Negro, but without a definite notion of how this could be done, they entered the service of the Freedmen's Bureau and were sent to Edisto Island. Much to the delight of the Negroes they opened a school in an abandoned church. But the school was not a success. Attendance was irregular. The majority of the students were more attracted by the free clothes dispensed than by the desire to learn. Regular work was interrupted by an epidemic of smallpox and the desire of the teachers to spend time at a near-by beach to avoid the alleged dangers of the heat and the malaria. The result was that when the government told them that their services were no longer needed, the teachers showed no reluctance to return North. They had done little in their eighteen months' residence to raise the cultural level of the freedmen.[53]

The support which the Northern agencies gave the schools was not sufficiently lasting. By 1870 the Freedmen's Bureau had ceased educational activities and the enthusiasm of the private societies was on the wane. Thereafter only a few schools could be supported.[54] This neglect was excused on the theory that the state government was assuming the obligation of education.

[52] *Reports and Resolutions, 1869-1870,* pp. 504-5.
[53] Mary Ames, *A New England Woman's Diary in Dixie.*
[54] For facts on this point see Jackson, *loc. cit.,* pp. 22-32.

But this view was only partly justifiable, for the schools the state provided were insufficient for public needs and for a time at least were inferior to those supplanted.[55]

The zeal of many Negroes for schooling was often cooled by contact with the fatiguing exercises necessary if anything was to be learned. The desire of the race for education, said the *Charleston Daily News,* was "often vague and not infrequently erroneous."[56] "Thus," added this journal, "we not infrequently see great uncouth, unclean girls, eighteen and twenty years old, . . . the very beau ideal of the old style plantation hand, sitting unhappily on the hard bench in the school room, thumbing, soiling, and dog-earing an unfortunate Webster's spelling book; learning nothing and certainly not enjoying school." There were complaints over irregular attendance. Many children, said Redpath, "passed through the schools," only remaining "long enough to be taught three or four patriotic songs, to keep quiet, and to be decently clad."[57] The growth of a political consciousness checked the Negro's zeal for education. "Positions of trust," Miss Botume regretfully remarked, "were frequently given to those who could not read and write, while those who were studying were set aside. . . . They could not understand that education could help them to ways and means of which they knew nothing."[58]

It was inevitable that the teachers should become victims of prejudice; for they were conquerors attempting to bring an uplifting experience to an inferior caste. And by their blunders they added to these prejudices. In the beginning they assumed that the anti-equalitarian and anti-Yankee feelings of the white South Carolinian would vanish as soon as the New England brand of truth was available. When the whites refused to adopt their teachings, they used their influence over the Negro to teach him objectionable songs and a spirit of

[55] Opinion of Edward King, *Southern States of North America,* p. 463.
[56] Apr. 13, 1867.
[57] *Courier,* May 17, 1865.
[58] *Op. cit.,* p. 274.

political and social insubordination. Such doctrines created feelings among the whites which were long to remain an obstacle in the way of the educational advance of the Negro.[59]

The kind of education given the Negro was more suitable to a class industrially proficient than to a race which was just emerging from slavery. Not enough emphasis was laid upon the sort of industrial training which was necessary if the race were to emerge from its actual poverty and social degradation. The literary instruction imparted elevated the race into an unreal world and left it less adequately equipped for the problem of living than did the industrial training given the plantation slave.[60]

*   *   *   *   *

The constitution of 1868 was a notable departure in the educational history of the state. Not only was education mentioned for the first time in the organic law, but the state for the first time was given the outline of an educational system in keeping with the advanced thought of the age. The General Assembly was obligated to establish a system of universal education as soon as practical. Provision was made for compulsory attendance at public or private schools of all children, not physically incapacitated, between the ages of six and sixteen for a minimum period of twenty-four months, "after the system of public schools had been thoroughly and completely organized and facilities afforded the inhabitants of the State for the free education of their children." No less radical was the provision which declared that all schools "supported in whole or in part by public funds shall be free and open to all the children and youths of the State, without regard to race or color." The new system of administration provided for a state superintendent of education and for a school commissioner in

[59] White contempt is revealed in *Fairfield Herald*, Aug. 26, 1868.
[60] Rossa B. Cooley, *Homes of the Freed*, p. 178 and *passim*, is a criticism by a Northern teacher of a later generation of the Reconstruction schools.

each county. The state superintendent and the commissioners should constitute the state board of education. The counties were to be divided into school districts in each one of which one or more schools should be kept open for at least one month of the year. Support for the system was to be had through an annual tax on all property of the state and through a poll tax of one dollar on each male adult. The legislature was obligated to provide for the support of a state university, a normal school, an agricultural college, schools for the deaf, dumb and blind, and "as soon as practical" a reform school for juvenile offenders.[61]

In a series of acts[62] the legislature made detailed application of the constitutional mandates. It was provided that the state superintendent of education should hold office for four years and receive a salary of $2,500 per annum, plus traveling expenses. He was required to keep an office in the capital city where the school records should be kept. The county commissioners were given a salary of $1,000 each per annum, plus traveling expenses. Each commissioner was required to visit every school in his county during each school term, to advise teachers, to make reports to the state superintendent, and to see that the common branches of an English education were taught, together with "the history of the United States, the principles of the constitution and the laws of the United States and of this State, and good behavior." A board of county examiners was provided for each county. It was to be composed of the county commissioner and two other persons appointed by him who were "competent to teach a first grade school." Its duty was to examine and certify teachers. The counties were to be divided into school districts. The schools of each of these districts were placed in charge of three trustees. Their principal duty was to provide a school term of nine months

[61] Constitution of 1868, Art. X, and Convention Proceedings, pp. 685 ff.

[62] Stat. S. C., XIV (Sept. 15, 1868), 23-25; XIV (Feb. 16, 1870), 339-48; and XIV (Mar. 6, 1871), 574-84.

when funds were sufficient. Uniform textbooks were to be furnished the students of the state at 10 per cent above cost to those able to pay, while the trustees were authorized to furnish them free of charge to those unable to pay.[63] To provide revenue for the schools a one dollar tax was placed on all males and a two mill tax on all property. The revenue thus derived was to be apportioned among the counties on a basis of school attendance.

This law, said an authority on the comparative history of American education, "was sufficient to realize the ideal of the most radical schoolmen of the state. It, indeed, proposed a scheme in some particulars in advance of the large majority of the Northern states at this period."[64]

That such an ambitious law was impractical in a state laboring under the economic, political, and cultural difficulties of South Carolina in 1870, no sagacious person could have denied. A reading of the proceedings of the constitutional convention creates the impression that its authors were better acquainted with the educational possibilities of such highly socialized communities as Prussia and Massachusetts than with those of poverty stricken, caste-ridden and individualistic South Carolina. A state whose assessed property values had shrunk from $480,000,000 to $183,000,000 was called upon to support a system which if properly executed would have involved an expenditure of $900,000. The radical character in this demand is apparent when it is realized that only $74,400 had been spent by the state annually for common schools before the war, and that nine-tenths of this amount had been collected from taxes on slaves.[65] Under the new plan the white property owners were to pay a large tax for education of these self-same Negroes. But what provoked greater opposition was the intention of

---

[63] This was the first instance of the state-wide adoption of uniform textbooks by any American state.

[64] A. D. Mayo, *Annual Report of Commissioner of Education, 1904,* I, 1025.

[65] Estimate of a group of Democrats in *Ku-Klux Conspiracy, S. C.,* p. 1229.

the constitution-makers that ultimately the children of both races should be forced to attend the same schools.[66] Although the framers of this provision showed no desire to force the immediate adoption of their program,[67] the ugly conclusion which the whites drew from reading the constitution was that it intended making mixed schools a reality when the chance arose. Indeed the doctrinaire mulattoes and New Englanders of the convention, moved by revolutionary enthusiasms, imagined they saw the opportunity of freeing the state of race distinctions. "The most natural method of removing race distinctions," said Cardozo, "would be to allow children, when five or six years of age, to mingle in school together. . . . Under such training prejudices will eventually die out."[68] "We are laying," said B. F. Randolph, "the foundation of a new structure here. . . . We must decide whether we shall live together or not."

Moreover, the law had patent defects of an administrative character. The county commissioners were to be popularly elected. This would have been perhaps an excellent device if the educational system had been the outgrowth of local demands and practices. But in South Carolina it was an imposition on the counties from above, and the central administration should have kept the reins of authority. Another defect was that no law restrained the irresponsible legislative and executive authorities from using the school funds as they saw fit.

Because of these faults Justus K. Jillson, who for nine years served as state superintendent of education, was merely an "official clerk," with the privilege, it is true, of rebuking neglect and rascality, but without the power of removing or disciplining. His duties consisted principally of passing on to careless commissioners what portion of the school funds the

[66] That is, all who could not afford private schools.

[67] See speech of F. L. Cardozo, *Convention Proceedings*, p. 705.

[68] *Ibid.*, p. 901. Cf. *ibid.*, pp. 747, 685-98, 707.

administrators and legislators did not divert to improper uses, and of compiling such statistics as he could get from commissioners chronically indisposed to make proper reports. Many of these difficulties would have been obviated had the law concentrated all administrative powers in the hands of Jillson. He was honest, energetic, and thoroughly devoted to the welfare of the schools.

It was inevitable that Jillson's reports should have consisted largely of complaints. He complained of the slowness of the legislature in enacting adequate legislation, of the appropriation of only $50,000 in 1870 to inaugurate a system which required many times that amount, and of the diversion of educational funds to other purposes by state officials and county treasurers. In 1871 no textbooks could be distributed or school records purchased because of lack of money. "But little appropriation had been paid," remarked Jillson of that year, "and several of the unpaid balances of the previous year were yet due."[69] In 1872 the weary superintendent predicted the collapse of the schools because of mismanagement in the State House, and asked the legislature "in the name of humanity" to mend its ways. "Our whole state policy, as far as common education is concerned," he added, "has been, from the beginning, narrow and illiberal. . . . The education of the people has been of least consideration with the constituted authorities."[70] In May of that year he was forced to order a temporary closing of the schools because the state treasurer had refused to honor drafts on the school appropriations.[71] In 1874 the withholding of funds continued to be the chief complaint and, due to the low credit of the state, the superintendent found it impossible to borrow to secure the necessary supplies.[72] In his last report, that of 1875, he gave a long list of unpaid appropriations total-

[69] Reports and Resolutions, 1871-1872, pp. 55, 94-95.
[70] Ibid., 1872-1873, pp. 273-74.
[71] News, May 21 and 22, 1872.
[72] Reports and Resolutions, 1874-1875, pp. 340, 388-89.

ing $334,058.[73] "The legislature," remarked an authority in summary, "was either indifferent, ignorant or culpably insincere in its dealing with the public school interest during the entire period of Reconstruction."[74]

The inefficiency of the administration was reflected in the meager results accomplished. It is not surprising that there was an actual increase in illiterates between 1870 and 1880, that is, in the years following the abandonment of the field by Northern agencies and the inauguration of the public schools. The number of illiterates over ten years of age rose from 290,379 to 369,848.[75] Although the number enrolled in school increased from approximately 30,000 in 1870 to 123,085 in 1876,[76] it is probable that not more than half of these were in regular attendance. The official statistics took no account of attendance. Moreover, the school terms were short, varying from two and one-half to seven months.[77] Credit for much that was accomplished cannot be allowed the public authorities, for many of the so-called public schools were not public in the true sense because they were dependent upon private contributions.

The hopes of the constitution-makers that progress would be made in the direction of compulsory interracial schools ended in failure. Governors Orr and Scott and the school commissioners advised against the mixture of the races in the common schools and the Negroes never demanded that this be done.[78] No attempts were made in this direction by either Jillson or the legislature. But such an attempt was made at the Institution at Cedar Springs for the Deaf, Dumb and Blind and at the State University.

September 17, 1873, Jillson informed the Cedar Springs fac-

[73] Cited by R. Means Davis, *Handbook of S. C., 1883*, p. 455.

[74] A. D. Mayo, p. 1026.

[75] There was, however, a relative decline from 57.6 to 55.4.—*Annual Report of Commissioner of Education, 1897-1898*, II, 28-85.

[76] *Handbook of S. C., 1883*, p. 544.

[77] Mayo, p. 1030.

[78] *House Journal, Ex. Sess., 1868*, pp. 44-45, 62; and *Reports and Resolutions, 1869-1870*, pp. 466-83.

ulty that "colored pupils must not only be admitted into the institution on application, but that an earnest and faithful effort must be made to induce such to apply for admission." The colored pupils, he commanded, "must be domiciled in the same building, must eat at the same table, must be taught in the same classrooms and by the same teachers, and must receive the same attention, care and consideration as white pupils." The effect of this order was the resignation of the faculty and the closing of the school for three years. Efforts to get a new faculty failed. The institution was, however, reopened in 1876 under its former teachers. But separate quarters were provided for the two races.[79]

Against the advice of Orr, the legislature reorganized the University without making distinctions of race. Under act of March 3, 1869,[80] provision was made for the election of a new and smaller board of trustees, and the faculty was prohibited from making "any distinction in the admission of students, or the management of the University on account of race, color or creed." To stimulate the ingress of students, one was to be admitted free from each county, the fees of the others were reduced, and a preparatory school was authorized for those unfit to enter the college classes.

Much can be said in favor of these reforms. The institution since its reopening, as has been pointed out, had not prospered. There was, said Edward King, a real desire among a considerable number of Negroes, especially among state officials and legislators, to receive the advantages which only the principal educational institution of the state afforded.[81] Certainly it was reasonable for the men who were conducting the government of the state to consider themselves worthy of entering its university.

Moreover, the act of March 3, 1869, was applied slowly.

[79] John S. Reynolds, *Reconstruction in South Carolina*, 237-38.

[80] *Stat. S. C.*, XIV, 203-4.

[81] *Southern States of North America*, pp. 262-63.

The wisest counselors of the administration advised hesitation, and when several professors resigned, their places were filled by persons acceptable to the Conservatives. But the whites, with the act hanging over them and with the board of trustees made up of black and white Radicals, became more and more distrustful and gradually withdrew their patronage. Their distrust was increased when, on the resignation of additional professors, Northerners were appointed in their places. The final blow came when Henry E. Hayne, the colored secretary of state, was accepted as a student on October 7, 1873. Immediately the native white students resigned and the native professors resigned or were dismissed. This was followed by the matriculation of a goodly number of blacks and the adoption of the following ringing declaration by the board of trustees: "The board cannot regret that a spirit so hostile to the welfare of our state, as well as to the dictates of justice and the claims of common humanity will no longer be represented in the university, which is the common property of all our citizens without distinction of race."

The University enjoyed a fair degree of prosperity under Radical domination. No difficulty was experienced in securing a faculty of ability. Liberal appropriations were made for its support—$31,750 in 1873, with moderate increases in later years. An increased enrollment was insured through the distribution of 124 scholarships, the lowering of the requirements for admission, and the establishment of a preparatory department. A constructive innovation was the establishment in 1874 on the campus of the university of the first normal school which the state had ever known outside of Charleston.[82] But the university did not fulfill all expectations. Its appropriations were used improperly by the irresponsible rulers of the state.[83] The whites never became reconciled to co-education of the

[82] *Stat. S. C.*, XIV, 369.   [83] Jillson's statement in *Reports and Resolutions, 1873-1874*, p. 398.

races, and when they recovered power in 1877 they dismissed the colored students and imported professors, and reconstituted the institution along traditional lines in 1880.

In spite of many shortcomings there can be little doubt that during the nine years in which Jillson was superintendent of education much was accomplished toward giving the state a system of schools like that approved in most American states. At the beginning of his career that tenacious educator declared: "The education of *all* the children of *all* classes and castes is indispensable to the highest and best welfare of the community."[84] And these words were not without meaning to those to whom they were addressed. The legislature, faithful to principles of reform imported from New England, responded to the proddings of the superintendent. The very fact that it was irresponsible promoted an extravagance which benefited the schools.[85] In spite of rapacious treasury officials Jillson was able to spend a goodly portion of the school funds properly. In 1873 he was able to secure legislation to prevent their diversion.[86]

From year to year Jillson was able to report progress. When he took office in 1868, there were in the state some 30,000 students attending 400 schools taught by 500 teachers; when he left office in 1876 there were 123,035 students attending 2,776 schools taught by 3,068 teachers, and the school revenue was $457,260.[87] In view of the progress made we may well conclude that had the Radical government not been overthrown in 1877, it would have given the state a school system as good as that which took its place.

In spite of many glaring blunders it cannot be denied that the Radical government reconciled South Carolina to a system

[84] *Reports and Resolutions, 1870-1871,* p. 376.

[85] Between 1869 and 1876 the legislature appropriated $1,755,000 for school purposes in addition to the capitation tax. —Edgar W. Knight, *Influences of Reconstruction in Education,* p. 78.

[86] *Stat. S. C.,* XV, 354.

[87] *Annual Report of Commissioner of Education, 1880,* pp. 290-91, is a convenient summary of educational statistics for the ten years following 1869.

of schools open to all. "It was a great thing," says a historian of American education, "to commit the old commonwealth to the American ideal of universal education; to secure appropriations from the legislature even if they were not paid with regularity; to awaken into life a body of three thousand native teachers, however destitute many of them may have been of the higher qualifications for this great profession, and to make it possible for the people to tax themselves to the extent, in 1876, of $130,000 for the support of the district schools."[88]

The logic of circumstances induced those who came into power in 1877 to carry on Jillson's program. The educational laws remained in force, except those requiring mixed schools, compulsory attendance, and free textbooks. The two mill school tax was made a part of the constitution, and a state supported college for Negroes was established at Orangeburg.[89] Under the enlightened leadership of Hugh S. Thompson, the new state superintendent, popular prejudices against universal education were dispelled, and by 1880 the state was supporting a greater number of students and schools than in 1876.[90]

But of course the benefits of the new régime were intended primarily for the whites; the financial support given Negro schools immediately became less than that given white schools, and as the years passed this disparity became greater.[91]

[88] Mayo, p. 1031.

[89] *Acts of 1878*, pp. 571, 739, and *Acts of 1879*, p. 174.

[90] See again statistics in *Annual Report of Commissioner of Education, 1880*, pp. 290-91; see also Henry T. Thompson, *Establishment of the Public School System in S. C.*, pp. 18 ff.

[91] During the scholastic year 1894-95 thrice as much was spent by the state for the maintenance in school of each white child as was spent for each Negro child.—*Reports and Resolutions, 1897*, pp. 262, 274-75. By 1927 the expenditures for white schools had become eight times greater than those for Negro schools and the per capita expenditure nine times greater.—*Ibid.*, 1927, II, 69, 77.

Chapter XVII

OPPOSITION TO THE RADICAL GOVERNMENT

TURNING again to the political story, it is not to be supposed that the Radical government, composed of carpetbaggers, scalawags, and Negroes and maintained in office by the Federal government and the black vote, could be acceptable to the native whites. To them the constitutional convention of 1868 was the "great unlawful," the legislative assembly was unconstitutional, and its acts null and void. It was freely predicted that the Radical government could not last, that the colored man would lose his political power, and that the native whites, representing the wealth and intelligence of the state, would again be masters of the situation. But in spite of white protests the constitution of 1868 was carried into effect, and that year the state cast its electoral vote for Grant. In the effort to rid the state of Radical rule, white opposition assumed various forms.

The Ku-Klux Klan made its first appearance in South Carolina in 1868 as a minor factor in the attempt of the whites to intimidate the newly enfranchised black majority. Since other methods had not prevented the blacks from obtaining political power, the whites resorted to that type of local violence least amenable to the punishment of Federal authorities. The general purpose of the organization is made clear by the constitution which was used in York County. The members were obligated by oath to take "the side of justice, humanity, and constitutional liberty as bequeathed to us in its purity by our forefathers," to aid fellow members in sickness, distress, and pecuniary embarrassment, and to be of special protection to female friends, widows, and their households, and to oppose the principles of the Radical party. The penalty of death was provided for any member who revealed the secrets of the order. The members were required to become acquainted with designated signs and passwords and to provide themselves with arms and disguises.[1]

Rumors of the doings of this organization in other states appeared in the local press in the spring of 1868, and the leading newspaper affirmed that the organization existed at least in "the fancy of a few hairbrained youths."[2] In June, persons claiming to be members of the Klan sent Governor Scott a letter warning that unless he removed a certain local official, the Klan would "insure him a free ticket to Hell Station on the Devil's R. R.,"[3] and there were other rumors of "the coming of the K K K."[4]

As the fall election approached, Klan activities became more numerous and more definite. There was an organization in Abbeville County which some thought to be connected with similar organizations in Edgefield and Laurens. It was said that the organizations had as their purpose the destruction of the Radical party and the killing or banishment of its leaders.[5] Testimony taken by a legislative investigating committee[6] told of Klansmen disguised in false faces and white gowns going from door to door in order to whip prospective Negro voters. From Newberry came stories of "bands of persons generally disguised, having on false faces, and with white sheets around them" who rode along the streets at night threatening and abusing Negroes.[7] The committee reported that in Anderson County "the K K K are more daring and better organized" than in other counties,[8] and that in Edgefield "the Ku Klux

---

[1] This constitution was published in *Ku-Klux Conspiracy, S. C.,* pp. 1685-87.

[2] *News,* May 17, 1868.

[3] *Ibid.,* June 13, 1868.

[4] *Ibid.,* Aug. 1, 1868.

[5] W. K. Tolbert, *Ku-Klux Conspiracy, S. C.,* p. 1269; *News,* Feb. 24, 1869.

[6] Report on the Evidence and the Evidence Taken by the Committee of Investigation of the Third Congressional District, in *Reports and Resolutions, 1869-70,* pp. 615-1475.

[7] *Ibid.,* pp. 1033-1213, 618, 691, 738.

[8] *Ibid.,* p. 625.

is so strong and well organized that it had everything its way."[9] Witnesses before the congressional committee appointed to investigate irregularities in the fourth congressional district reported that in Laurens, Union, and York counties, and in the lower portion of Greenville, voters were visited by disguised men and warned not to vote the Republican ticket.[10] Comptroller-General Neagle said that the Klan had created a "perfect reign of terror" in York County.[11] Evidence more authentic was contained in the confessions of certain citizens of York. Several said they had joined an organization which required oaths, special grips, and the provision of arms, and which had officers bearing the Klan designations. They declared that the purpose of the order was to protect the whites against the Negroes.[12]

But one should not conclude that the Klan played an important part in South Carolina affairs in 1868. The most sensational murders of the year, those of State Senator B. F. Randolph and the white senator-elect, S. G. W. Dill, were perpetrated by undisguised persons obviously not Klansmen.[13] The Klan was organized in York County to protect the whites, and as soon as the period of anxiety was over it was forgotten.[14] The leaders of the Conservative clubs emphatically denied that there was any connection between their organizations and the Klan,[15] and there is no evidence to contradict this assertion. A leading citizen of Laurens testified that he was the leader of a band of fifteen or twenty young men, which had "signs and tokens of recognition," but that this organization had no connection with the Klan, and was abandoned as soon as the disturbed state of affairs was over.[16] After the election of 1868

[9] *Ibid.*, pp. 630-31.
[10] *House Misc. Doc.*, 41 *Cong.*, 2 *Sess.*, No. 17, Pt. 2, pp. 7, 8, 43-44.
[11] *Ibid.*, p. 47.
[12] J. W. Tomlinson, *Ku-Klux Conspiracy, S. C.*, pp. 1270-76, B. F. Briggs, *ibid.*, pp. 1456-60, John Caldwell, *ibid.*, p. 1725.

[13] *News*, July 10, Oct. 22, 1868.
[14] Briggs, *Ku-Klux Conspiracy, S. C.*, 1458.
[15] *News*, Feb. 27, Mar. 1, 25, 1869.
[16] B. W. Ball, *Ku-Klux Conspiracy, S. C.*, pp. 1328-29.

the state enjoyed a period of peace which gave the Klan and other organizations for violence no reason for existence. Having lost the election, the whites for the moment accepted Negro suffrage, and assumed the attitude that violent resistance to the government was futile and unwise.[17]

However, the government in Columbia was rapidly increasing the public debt, without constructive achievements, and bribery and corruption prevailed. Confronted with this situation, the Conservative press began to look forward to the election of 1870. Lamenting that the "smiling land" in which they lived was "at the mercy of a motley crew of vagabonds whose only principle is greed, and whose only policy is to plunder, while they may, the interests they have sworn to serve," the editors of the *Charleston Daily News,* on New Year's Day, 1870, urged that without distinction of color, religion, or class, the people should forget minor issues, organize upon a broad platform, and enter into a political campaign which, if successful, would make 1870 "The Year of the Happy Deliverance."[18]

Other papers followed in a like tone. The *Sumter Watchman* believed that the Radical party had found its life in the agitation of the Negro question, a question which the passage of the Fourteenth and Fifteenth amendments removed from politics. It was of the opinion that "the colored race . . . by a moderate and conciliatory policy might be induced to occupy the same platform with the white people of the state."[19] For securing concert of action the Columbia *Guardian* suggested a convention of the Conservative and anti-Radical newspapers "for the purpose of conferring together upon various subjects of public interest, . . . as well as to consult upon the policy proper to be adopted in the next political campaign."[20] This

[17] See *News,* Nov. 9, 12-14, 21, 1868.
[18] For a detailed study of the election of 1870 see R. H. Woody, "The South Carolina Election of 1870," *North Caro-* *lina Historical Review,* VIII (April, 1931), 168-86.
[19] *Sumter Watchman,* Feb. 16, 1870.
[20] *Courier,* Feb. 14, 1870.

convention met on March 16, 1870, and unanimously adopted resolutions recognizing the "legal rights of all citizens of the State, irrespective of color or former condition" to suffrage and office holding. The convention urged that a state convention be held June 15 to nominate a state ticket.[21]

When the convention of what came to be known as the Union Reform party met in Columbia, twenty-two of the thirty-one counties were represented by about 150 delegates; between twenty and thirty of them were Negroes.[22] The platform adopted declared that the Fifteenth Amendment ought to be fairly administered and faithfully obeyed as fundamental law; that the vast changes brought by the war should be "regarded as verities having the force and obligation of law"; and that the existing laws brought all into "entire harmony upon all questions of civil and political right."[23]

In the nominations made, two things were evident: (1) it was not a strictly Conservative convention, and (2) every effort was being made to conciliate the Negroes. Some in the convention opposed any nominations and others said the nominees should be Republicans.[24] But in the end Richard B. Carpenter, a Republican lawyer from Kentucky, was nominated for governor, and M. C. Butler, a Conservative of Edgefield, was selected as his running mate.[25]

The Conservative press was quick to give its support to the action of the convention, although there was some opposition to the idea of "Negro equality." Butler and James B. Kershaw were censured for declaring that "black and white are a common

[21] *News*, Mar. 18, 1870.

[22] *News, Courier*, June 16, 1870; R. B. Carpenter, *Ku-Klux Conspiracy, S. C.,* p. 259. The counties not represented were York, Georgetown, Williamsburg, Sumter, Oconee, Marlboro, Abbeville, Beaufort, and Clarendon.

[23] *Courier, News*, June 17, 1870. In 1868 there was determined opposition to qualified suffrage as advocated by the Democratic committee.—*Courier*, April 6, May 25, June 10, 1868.

[24] *News*, May 24, *News, Courier*, June 17, 1870.

[25] F. L. Cardozo was nominated for lieutenant-governor, but he would not accept. J. B. Kershaw said he would prefer an honest, capable colored man for lieutenant-governor to any friend of his own.

people" and should be united in all their purposes.[26] Edward McCrady, Sr., published a pamphlet denouncing the resolutions of the press conference. He was opposed to the recognition of the right of all races to the suffrage and to office; he feared that with political equality there would be social equality. He urged the Conservatives not to seek office or meddle with the politics of their conquerors but to maintain "the silent protest of unaggressive but unyielding principle. . . . Let education, agriculture, mechanics and commerce be our only politics. Around such well-doing, power, both physical and intellectual, must gradually accumulate, and will make its presence felt."[27]

Meanwhile the Radicals had not been idle. The state convention, which met in July and of which Robert B. Elliott was president, endorsed Scott's administration and nominated him for reëlection. Alonzo J. Ransier, a Negro from Charleston, was nominated for lieutenant governor.[28]

Each party entered into the campaign with energy. To the Radicals it was a struggle for existence; to the Reformers it was a plea for deliverance. Scott did not take the stump. Ransier, however, along with Elliott, Cardozo, Tomlinson, Chamberlin, and others, toured the state for the Radicals. The Reformers were equally active. Carpenter spoke in every county except one[29] and Butler in every county except four.[30] Candidates for the four congressional districts stumped their districts also. The Reformers denounced the Radical administration, charging that the public debt had been trebled, taxes increased, immigration prevented, the resources of the state left undeveloped, and education neglected. The Radicals, on the other hand, charged that the Union Reformers were Democrats sailing under false colors. They denied, in general, the

---

[26] *Sumter Watchman,* June 29, 1870.
[27] Edward McCrady, Sr., *A Review of the Resolutions of the Press Conference.*
[28] *News,* July 26, 28, 1870. Lemuel Boozer, a white man from Lexington County, who was elected lieutenant-governor in 1868, had resigned to become judge of the fifth circuit.
[29] Carpenter, *Ku-Klux Conspiracy, S. C.,* p. 229.
[30] Butler, *ibid.,* p. 1185.

accusation of corruption and dishonesty, tried to explain the state debt, and said they were going to give an economical, honest government, with equal rights to all.

Ex-Governor Orr came out against the Reformers. He pointed out that there was a colored majority of more than 25,000 voters and that the experience of the past five years had shown that the colored voters would sustain the Radical ticket. He proposed reform through the Radicals. "Suppose," he said, "one hundred of the most intelligent white citizens in each county had gone, in good faith and frank sincerity, into the Republican organization. Can it be doubted that their intelligence and moral strength would have secured honest nominees?"[31]

In the nomination of the Republican Carpenter, the Reformers made a bid for Radical votes. In addition, they tried in every way to win the Negro. Their platform endorsed the Fifteenth Amendment; Negroes were nominated for county offices; and eloquent speeches were made in an effort to tear down all barriers of prejudice.[32] According to the census of 1870, there were 62,547 white voters and 85,475 black voters in the state,[33] and it was hoped that enough colored voters would stay away from the polls to give the election to the Reformers if the whites turned out *en masse*.

Another activity which was expected to solidify the party and win Negro votes was the organizing of Union Reform Clubs in election precincts. This was begun in June. In August the executive committee of the Reformers announced a plan which called for a central committee, preferably composed of members of both races, at each county court house. The central committee was to organize the entire county, take charge of the voters on election day, and see that they "reach

[31] *Courier*, Aug. 17, 1870.
[32] *News*, July 4, 1870.
[33] *U. S. Census*, 1870, I, 619. Eleven counties, returning 39 legislators, had white majorities. They were: Spartanburg, Pickens, Horry, Greenville, Anderson, Oconee, Lexington, Chesterfield, Marion, York, and Lancaster.

ALL THE DIFFERENCE IN THE WORLD. Th.Nast

Harper's Weekly

A CARTOON FOR THE PRESIDENTIAL CAMPAIGN OF 1868

the polls, or remain away if unfavorable."[34]   The Reform Clubs were to counteract, so far as possible, the work of the Union League.   In July, 1870, Cardozo addressed the Grand Council of the Union League in Columbia, and during the succeeding campaign the League was moderately active.[35]

The Negro militia, organized in the spring and summer of 1870, played an important rôle in the campaign.   In April the *Charleston Daily News* carried the report that the colored citizens of Columbia were organizing into military companies— the Elliott Guards and the Neagle Rifles—and wondered if that action did not carry a political significance.[36]   Later, military companies were organized in Union, Laurens, Newberry, Edgefield, Kershaw, and Spartanburg counties.   Carpenter estimated that more than 20,000 colored people were armed and given ammunition near election time.[37]   This estimate was exaggerated, however, for the report of the adjutant general shows that between March 1 and October 27, 1870, only 7,222 stands of arms were issued.   Many, however, possessed private arms.   In addition to the arms issued, more than 88,000 rounds of ammunition were given out between May 15 and October 27 of that year.[38]   Colonel Joseph Crews, of Laurens County, received 620 rifle-muskets, 50 Winchesters, and 11,000 rounds of ammunition.[39]

Throughout the state the whites tried to organize militia companies, but their efforts were futile.   Some white companies were formed and their services tendered to the governor, but he refused to accept them.[40]   In Columbia a white company was accepted and rifles were issued, but in October it dis-

---

[34] *News,* Aug. 25, 1870.

[35] Carpenter, *Ku-Klux Conspiracy, S. C.,* p. 229; S. B. Hall, *A Shell in the Radical Camp,* I, Chap. VII, *passim.* Butler denounced the League vigorously. D. T. Corbin testified that the League was the chief organ of the Radical party used in getting a united Negro vote.—*Ku Klux Conspiracy, S. C., p.* 77.

[36] *News,* April 19, 1870.

[37] *Ku-Klux Conspiracy, S. C.,* p. 227.

[38] *Report of the adjutant general, Ku-Klux Conspiracy, S. C.,* 767-68.

[39] *Ibid.*

[40] C. H. Suber, *Ku-Klux Conspiracy,*

banded,[41] voluntarily, it was said, because it was assigned to a regiment commanded by a Negro colonel.[42]

The arming of the black militia naturally excited considerable race feeling, but it was believed that the blacks and their leaders had no thought of precipitating an armed conflict. Wade Hampton said that the arming of the militia created a "profound impression," but that in two interviews with Scott he had found him anxious for peace, realizing that a clash would be favorable to the whites.[43] The real purpose of the militia was to keep the Negroes in line for the coming election. They drilled frequently in the public squares of the towns and took great pride in their arms and "in ribbons and plumes and drums beating."[44] They listened to harangues of their own leaders and attended political meetings of both Reformers and Radicals, sometimes under arms, which were usually stacked near by. Butler testified that although he and his coadjutors made every effort to satisfy the people that no ill-feeling existed and that harmony was desired between the races, there was always more or less of a row at every political meeting.[45]

The chief activity of the militia was in the up-country. In the middle and lower counties, where the Radical majority was more certain, there seemed to be less racial antagonism. But in some up-country counties the whites had majorities, and there was a possibility that the border counties would be lost to the Radicals. The state constabulary, consisting of

S. C., p. 146; Gabriel Cannon, ibid., p. 765; David R. Duncan, ibid., p. 873. E. W. Seibels, secretary and treasurer of the Union Reform Party, testified that on various occasions he asked Scott to commission white militia and Scott "invariably refused."—Ibid., p. 119.

[41] News, Oct. 31, 1870.

[42] R. W. Shand, Ku-Klux Conspiracy, S. C., p. 969. The law under which these organizations were formed provided, "that there shall be no military organizations, or formations for the purpose of arming, drilling, exercising the manual of arms, or military manoeuvres, not authorized under this Act, and by the Commander-in-Chief."—Stat. S. C., XIV, 217.

[43] Ku-Klux Conspiracy, S. C., p. 1219.

[44] Butler, ibid., p. 1185.

[45] Ibid., pp. 1186-87, 1197-98.

about five hundred men of both races, was scattered in the up-country where it acted in a political capacity.[46]

The election, held October 19, passed without any serious disorder.[47] Special police were appointed in Charleston,[48] and Federal troops were garrisoned in Edgefield, Laurens, Newberry, Abbeville, and Union counties.[49] On November 10, when the final results of the election were known, it was found that the Radical candidates polled a total of 85,071, while the Reform candidates had only 51,537 votes—figures strangely resembling the white and colored vote of the state.[50]

Both parties charged that fraud and intimidation had been freely indulged in. Although the Ku-Klux policy of intimidation did not take a serious turn until after the election, when the whites saw they were defeated, the Ku-Klux undoubtedly played some part in the contest. There was evidence of Ku-Klux activities in Spartanburg County,[51] although in three of the four counties where the greatest violence and outrage was said to have been committed—Spartanburg, Union, York, and Laurens—Carpenter had received fewer votes than the Dem-

[46] *Reports and Resolutions, 1871-72*, pp. 12-14; *Reports and Resolutions, 1877-78*, report on the militia, constabulary, and armed force, *passim*. John B. Hubbard, chief of the constabulary, was constantly receiving reports of the political activities of his agents. The following from Joseph Crews, Laurens, July 8, 1870, is typical: " . . . Your letter of the 2d was received to-day enclosing $128 due me. It came in good time. We are going to have a hard campaign up here, and we must have more Constables. I will carry the election here with the militia if the Constables will work with me. I am giving out ammunition all the time. Tell Scott he is all right here now. Let me know how times are below."—Fraud Report, 1687.

[47] The right of suffrage was conferred upon "every male citizen of the United States, of the age of twenty-one years . . .

not laboring under the disabilities named in the Constitution, without distinction of race or color or former condition, who shall have been a resident of the State for one year, and in the County . . . for sixty days next preceding any general election," provided, that "no person while kept in any alms house or asylum, or of unsound mind, or confined in any public prison, shall be allowed to vote." *Stat. S. C.*, XIV, 393. No registration was required, although the Constitution provided that it should be the duty of the General Assembly to provide, "from time to time," for the registration of all electors. —Art. VIII, Sec. 3.

[48] *News*, Oct. 20, 1870.

[49] *Courier*, Oct. 13, 1870.

[50] *News, Courier*, Nov. 10, 1870.

[51] S. T. Poinier, *Ku-Klux Conspiracy, S. C.*, p. 39; Daniel Lipscomb, *ibid.*, p. 428; Tench Blackwell, *ibid.*, pp. 551-57.

ocratic presidential electors in 1868; only in Laurens was this not true.[52]

On the other side, evidence seemed to indicate that the Radicals were guilty not only of intimidation but also of fraud, made possible by their control of the election machinery. The *Charleston Daily News* thought that the Reformers had come to defeat through their failure to win the Negro vote.[53] C. H. Suber, a prominent lawyer of Newberry County, estimated that not more than five hundred Negroes voted the Reform ticket; nevertheless, he believed that many more would have voted it had the Radicals not intimidated voters.[54] Others were of the same opinion,[55] and Carpenter and Butler said that many Negroes were afraid to vote for them. Accounts of intimidation by Radicals were numerous. On the islands below Charleston the militia was out and armed on election day, and when a colored voter who was suspected of being a Reformer approached the polls, the militia was ordered to fall into line.[56] There was a near riot in Newberry when a colored man who had voted the Reform ticket was set upon by Negroes.[57] One manager of elections forced a Negro to vote the Radical ticket by threatening him with punishment by the law.[58]

General complaint was made because the election law provided that three commissioners of election in each county should be appointed by the governor without the confirmation of the senate. Commissioners were to appoint managers for each precinct.[59] A short time before the election, Carpenter had written to Grant, charging that of the 93 commissioners appointed, 24 were members of the legislature, a large majority were candidates for office, and all were, with few exceptions,

[52] *Ku-Klux Conspiracy*, Minority Report, pp. 581-83.

[53] *News*, Nov. 5, 1870.

[54] *Ku-Klux Conspiracy*, S. C., pp. 149, 157.

[55] *Ibid.*, p. 209.

[56] Carpenter, *ibid.*, p. 229.

[57] Suber, *ibid.*, p. 148. A similar incident occurred in Barnwell County.—Robert Aldrich, *ibid.*, p. 175.

[58] *Ibid.*

[59] *Stat. S. C.*, XIV, 393.

the corrupt tools of the existing administration.[60]   The commissioners and managers were all of one party,[61] except in a few instances where Radicals able to read could not be found.[62] It was said that the commissioners were careful to put polling places within convenient reach of the Negroes.   In the low-country they were placed on the banks of rivers where the colored population was very dense.   In some counties whites had to travel forty miles to the nearest precinct.[63]   In a few instances, too, the polls were changed from the regular voting places to the homes of Radicals.[64]   According to Seibels, some Radicals voted a dozen times; and women and children voted for sick husbands and brothers.[65]

A more serious charge was that the ballot boxes were tampered with while they were in the hands of the commissioners and managers.   The election law provided that the managers might keep the ballot boxes for three days following the election.   They were then to be turned over to the county commissioners who were to canvass the vote and make a report to the state board of canvassers within ten days.[66]   Orr admitted that "the present law certainly gives to persons so disposed the opportunity to commit fraud."   Corbin said it was "a very miserable machinery" and "some very glaring frauds were doubtless committed in some of the lower counties."   In Beaufort County the district attorney had convicted three Republicans charged with abstracting ballots and substituting others.[67] Seibels said that the commissioners and managers "committed fraud in a dozen different ways."   "I am certain," he added, "that if we had had any election at all we would have elected the members of the Reform party, or the Democratic party, in

---

[60] *Courier,* Oct. 5, 1870.

[61] Corbin, *Ku-Klux Conspiracy, S. C.,* 83; Seibels, *ibid.,* p. 123; Suber, *ibid.,* p. 151; Carpenter, *ibid.,* p. 240.

[62] Carpenter, *ibid.,* p. 240; I. D. Witherspoon, *ibid.,* p. 1513.

[63] Carpenter, *ibid.,* p. 228.

[64] John Genobles, *ibid.,* p. 360.

[65] *Ibid.,* p. 123.

[66] *Stat. S. C.,* XIV, 393, Sec. 17, 18.

[67] *Ku-Klux Conspiracy,* S. C., p. 82.

fourteen counties, perhaps more."[68]   In one precinct where
only six Reform votes were returned, forty-one men swore they
had voted the Reform ticket.[69]

In the four congressional districts, Radicals were declared
elected. Three of them, Joseph H. Rainey, R. C. DeLarge, and
Robert B. Elliott, were colored; A. S. Wallace, from the up-
country, was white. C. C. Bowen contested the seat of De-
Large. The congressional committee declared that DeLarge
"did not receive a majority of the votes legally cast" and was
not, therefore, entitled to retain his seat. Bowen, however, was
not admitted because he was thought to have tampered with
DeLarge's attorney, and because he was sheriff of Charleston
County and a member of the state legislature.[70]   In the contest
of I. G. McKissick against A. S. Wallace, the committee decided that there was "some reason for the belief that irregularities may have occurred in some localities," but the evidence
fell short of determining what effect those irregularities had
upon the actual vote of the district.[71]

No one doubted, however, that the Reformers were conclusively beaten. Said the *Charleston Daily News:* "The in-
geniously contrived frauds of the Radical party which have
defeated the Reform candidates in counties where a fair election would tell a widely different tale, do not, it must be confessed, account satisfactorily for the election of Governor Scott
by a majority of thirty or thirty-five thousand votes."[72]   Butler
admitted that even in a fair election his party would have been
defeated by some 15,000 votes,[73] and he was of the opinion that
Carpenter brought no Republican strength.[74]   The failure to
win the Negro, due to the belated concessions of the whites
and the solidifying effect of the militia and the Union League,

---

[68] *Ibid.,* p. 123.

[69] Carpenter, *ibid.,* p. 240.

[70] *Cong. Globe, 3 Sess., 42 Cong.,* Pt. 2,
pp. 689, 842.

[71] *Reports of Committees, House of
Rep., 42 Cong., 2 Sess., Report No. 66.*

[72] Nov. 5, 1870.

[73] *Ku-Klux Conspiracy, S. C.,* p. 1187.

[74] *Ibid.,* p. 1199.

inevitably meant defeat. Not until 1876, with different methods and new leaders, did an opposition party triumph.

It was thought useless to attempt to preserve the organization of the Reform party, although many felt that the party had a wholesome effect. Meeting in Columbia, November 11, 1870, the executive committee held a secret session. It was attended by the editor of the *Courier* who said in his paper, ". . . There was no despondency, but rather a renewed courage and devotion to the interests of the State. There was no retracing of the declarations made, or pledges given. . . . It may be, of course, that the name of the Union Reform movement, born of a particular crisis and occasion, may pass away, but means have been taken for an efficient and thorough organization, which, while it will keep the people of the State united, will enable them to make their voice efficient in such political mode as they may deem best suited."[75]

* * * * *

It was this defeat of the whites that led to the revival of the Ku-Klux Klan for its second, more extensive, and final period of operation in the state. Shortly before the October election Ku-Klux activities became evident in York, Spartanburg, and Union counties. A few cases of such actions were reported from the neighboring counties of Chester, Newberry, Fairfield, and Chesterfield, and there were isolated cases in Sumter and Clarendon. They reached their height in March and ceased by midsummer of 1871.

The evidence on the Klan in South Carolina leads to the conclusion that it took the form of haphazard associations which acted independently of any district, state, or regional organization. Such was the opinion of contemporaries well

[75] *Courier,* Nov. 14, 1870. For a detailed discussion of the Klan see Francis B. Simkins, "The Ku-Klux Klan in South Carolina, 1868-1871," *Journal of Negro History,* XII, 606.

acquainted with what was going on in the state,[76] and even the majority of the congressional committee appointed to investigate conditions did not allege that a general conspiracy existed.[77] The leaders of opinion, such men as Hampton, Butler, and James Chesnut, professed utter ignorance of the workings of the order.[78] The only general attempt made to organize the whites on lines similar to those of the Klan was the effort to establish the so-called Councils of Safety in the weeks following the election of 1870. Under the authority of some leaders of the Union Reform party, pamphlets were printed calling for the secret organization of the whites to preserve the peace, restore constitutional liberty, and if necessary use physical force "according to the recognized principles of the law of self-defense." But as the disorders which prompted the projection of this order no longer existed, in only two counties were Councils of Safety organized and the project was soon forgotten.[79] Only in the counties of York and Spartanburg is there evidence of the existence of a county organization of the Klan. Even the authority of the leaders in those counties was imperfectly recognized, and some of the most important raids were conducted without their knowledge.[80] The oaths administered were much less formal and dramatic than one familiar with the popular conception of the "hooded empire" might imagine: only those ceremonies of the order which were considered absolutely necessary for the accomplishment of the purpose of secret violence were bothered with. Confessed members, who had nothing to conceal because of the immunity from prosecution which had been guaranteed, manifested an

[76] Seibels, *Ku-Klux Conspiracy, S. C.*, p. 97; Butler, *ibid.*, pp. 1194-95; D. H. Chamberlain, *ibid.*, p. 50, would not affirm that there was a general conspiracy. Samuel G. Brown, *ibid.*, p. 1942, a klansman of intelligence, said that he never heard of a state chief of the order.

[77] *Ibid.*, Reports of Committee, pp. 28 ff.

[78] Butler's statement, *ibid.*, pp. 1185 ff.; Chesnut's, *ibid.*, p. 446; Hampton's, *ibid.*, p. 1228; Seibels', *ibid.*, pp. 101 ff.

[79] See testimony of Orr and Seibels on this subject, *ibid.*, pp. 2, 23-25, 102 ff.

[80] According to the confession of Klan Chief J. W. Mitchell, *ibid.*, p. 1939.

amazing ignorance of the forms of the order. This was due to the almost uniform ignorance of the rank and file and to the fact that the types of violence which the order accomplished could be carried out with little or no Ku-Klux formalities.

The Ku-Klux was most active in the counties of Spartanburg, Union, and York. The members usually did their work at night, attired in hoods, masks, and other regalia sufficient to disguise the wearer and calculated to impress the black man or Radical white that the wearer was a spirit from another world. But the victims usually regarded the disguise as artificial, which destroyed the desired impression of devils. The victims of the raids were insulted, frequently beaten severely or driven from the county; many were forced to renounce their political allegiance to the Radical party, and a number lost their lives. The Klan was at times guilty of wanton crimes for which there was hardly any palliation, and at times took the law into its hands. In two raids on the Union County jail, ten Negroes were shot to death by whites who accused the prisoners of the murder of a one-armed Confederate veteran. The Reverend A. W. Cummings, a Northerner who had been president of the Spartanburg Female College, compiled a list of 227 persons who he claimed were abused by masked men in Spartanburg County between the October election of 1870 and the following July 15. He asserted that some two hundred of this number had been beaten, seven wounded by gun fire, and four killed.[81] P. Q. Camp, a white office-holder, claimed that between September 2 and July 15 in the Limestone section of Spartanburg no less than 118 had been abused by the Klan in some fashion, of whom four were shot, sixty-seven whipped, and six had their ears cropped.[82] The United States army officer sent to York County to investigate conditions asserted that between December, 1870, and the following July, more than 300 persons were whipped in the

[81] Ibid., pp. 919-22.   [82] Ibid., pp. 897-98.

county, and six were murdered.[83]   He estimated that in a county which had a white voting population of 2,300 there was a Klan membership of 1,800.   So great was the fear of Klan activities that in certain disturbed areas three-fourths of the Negro population slept in the woods during the winter months.[84]

The South Carolina Klan was, for the most part, composed of low-type men, and did not enjoy among respectable contemporaries the esteem with which later generations have invested it.   The fact that it flourished most extensively in the hill counties of the state, where the uncultured whites were predominant, is an indication of the type of membership.   Ex-Governor Orr said that the crimes were committed by "reckless young men, without a great deal of standing in their community."[85]   A prominent citizen of Spartanburg characterized the Klansmen as "a set of drunken and lawless vagabonds."[86] The Democratic minority of the congressional investigating committee characterized those arrested in Spartanburg as "ignorant and without education to the last degree."[87]   The presiding judge of the United States court which tried Klansmen said to seventeen who pleaded guilty: "What is quite as appalling to the court as the horrible nature of these offenses is the utter absence on your part, and on the part of the others who have made confessions here, of any sense or feeling that you have done anything wrong.   Some of your comrades recite the circumstances of a brutal, unprovoked murder, done by themselves, with as little apparent horror as they would relate the incidents of a picnic."[88]

The fundamental cause of these activities was the desire of the whites to force the Negro into a position of political impotence and social subordination similar to that which the race

[83] Major Lewis Merrill, *Ku-Klux Conspiracy, S. C.*, pp. 1478-83.

[84] The testimony taken by the congressional committee is full of instances of whippings, assaults, etc., committed by the Klan.

[85] *Ibid.*, p. 7.

[86] Dr. John Winsmith, *ibid.*, p. 625.

[87] *Ibid.*, Reports of Committee, p. 520.

[88] Judge Hugh L. Bond, *ibid.*, p. 1981.

had occupied previous to Reconstruction. The agencies through which the blacks and their white friends exercised their citizenship were the militia, the Union League, and the ballot box, and it was mostly against Negroes attempting to carry on these functions that the Klan acted. It was the militiamen who were most frequently whipped and militia captains who received the most extreme punishment. Office-holders and voters were intimidated. Quite frequently the offenders were forced to promise that they would no longer support the Radical ticket; many in York and Spartanburg were forced to abjure their political faith by a statement published in local Democratic papers.[89] The Union League, which had been so largely responsible for the political organization of the Negroes, was much less provocative of Klan activities than the militia. Nevertheless, it was frequently mentioned as a cause of dissatisfaction. Great complaint was made because the League bound the Negro by an oath which virtually forced him to vote the Radical ticket. So conservative a newspaper as the *Yorkville Enquirer* charged the League "with the shameful state of things which now exist."[90] Accordingly, men who had been active in Leagues were often whipped, special examples were made of the presidents of these societies,[91] and many local chapters were broken up.

Although of less importance than the purely political motives, social and economic factors at times were the causes of Klan visits. White men living in adultery with Negro women and Negroes living in adultery with white women were whipped and driven from the community.[92] In Union, a Negro was killed and his step-daughter whipped because the latter caused embarrassment to a white family by having a child by one of its members.[93] In Spartanburg, a Negro

[89] Some 54 cards, for example, appeared in the *Carolina Spartan* (Spartanburg) between Jan. 5 and July 6, 1871.

[90] Feb. 9, 1871.

[91] For example, Elias Hill, of York, *Ku-Klux Conspiracy*, S. C., p. 1408.

[92] *Ibid.*, pp. 214, 1864-65.

[93] *Ibid.*, pp. 1051-52.

woman was whipped for "breaking the peace" between a white man and his wife.[94]   Negroes were whipped for refusing to work for whites; several Negroes of Spartanburg were mal-treated because they deserted farms to become railroad labor-ers.[95]   The prominent citizens of Spartanburg[96] were of the opinion that a primary motive for Klan activities was the desire of the lower class whites to remove the Negro as a competitor in labor, and especially in the renting of land.   The Klan activities were more violent in those upper rural counties, in which the mass of the white population had to work with their hands for a living, thereby coming into economic competition with the Negro.

In the achievement of its primary object of striking terror among the Negroes and white Radicals, the Klan was success-ful in the limited area in which it operated.   Except for the intervention of the national government, it is likely that the area of operation would have extended over the entire up-coun-try, and that the Radical government and its political organ-izations there would have been entirely uprooted.   The governor failed to execute the ample authority which the leg-islature had given him for the suppression of violence; the constabulary was forced to flee from the Ku-Klux areas;[97] and persons were afraid to make affidavits necessary to bring about convictions in the state courts.

The intervention of the national government came as a matter of course.   The Grant administration was definitely committed to the policy of maintaining the "reconstructed" governments in the South, and that government in South Car-olina seemed in imminent danger.   During 1870 and 1871 Con-gress passed a series of acts which placed the control of con-gressional elections under Federal jurisdiction, prohibited combinations which interfered with the free exercise of the

[94] *Ku-Klux Conspiracy, S. C.*, p. 1971.   [96] For example, Gabriel Cannon and
[95] *Ibid.*, pp. 27, 589.   Simpson Bobo, *ibid.*, pp. 762-63, 797.
                                                                     [97] S. T. Poinier, *ibid.*, p. 31.

rights of citizens, and gave the President authority to suspend the writ of habeas corpus in areas in which he believed the Federal law was set at defiance.[98] The President in a special message to Congress, March 23, 1871, told of "a condition of affairs which exists in some of the States . . . rendering life and property insecure and the carrying of mail and the collection of the revenue dangerous."[99] A delegation of the South Carolina legislature went to Washington to complain of the conduct of the Klan,[100] and a congressional committee soon proceeded to the South, a subcommittee being especially charged with the investigation of affairs in South Carolina. The investigations of the committee were supplemented by those of United States Attorney-General Akerman and the elaborate investigations of Major Lewis Merrill, an army officer sent to York. The result was that Grant issued on October 12, 1871, a proclamation that since "a condition of lawlessness and terror existed" in the nine counties of York, Newberry, Fairfield, Lancaster, Chester, Chesterfield, Spartanburg, Laurens, and Union[101] in the form of combinations and conspiracies which obstructed the execution of the law, he commanded that persons composing those combinations disperse. Five days later, asserting that the "insurgents" had not dispersed, and that they were in rebellion against the authority of the United States, he suspended the writ of habeas corpus in those counties.[102]

Immediately after the President's proclamation the Federal authorities began rounding up alleged Klansmen. The arrest of several hundred individuals was followed by a series of trials in the United States Circuit Court under indictments charging conspiracy to prevent the exercise of the rights of citizenship guaranteed by the Fourteenth and Fifteenth amendments. At

[98] See acts of May 31, 1870, and April 20, 1871.

[99] J. D. Richardson, *Messages and Papers of the Presidents*, VII, 127.

[100] Samuel Nuckles, a member of the delegation, tells the story of the trip in *Ku-Klux Conspiracy, S. C.*, p. 1159.

[101] By mistake Marion was included instead of Union. This was later corrected.

[102] Richardson, *Messages and Papers*, VII, 134-35, 138-39.

the Columbia session of the court in November and December, 1871, indictments against some five hundred persons were returned. The prosecution was conducted by the two ablest Radical lawyers in the state, District Attorney D. T. Corbin and Attorney-General Chamberlain. The defense was conducted by two of the most eminent lawyers of the North, Reverdy Johnson and Henry Stanbery. Five persons were convicted by juries composed almost entirely of Negroes. In addition to the five convictions, fifty pleaded guilty. The fifty-five were given sentences ranging from three months to five years, in addition to nominal fines.[103]

Rather weak efforts to secure the conviction of the others indicted were made at two subsequent sessions of the court. At the Charleston session of April, 1872, twenty-eight were convicted, although there were several failures to convict, due in part to the hesitancy of the court to accept the legality of the indictments. At the Columbia session of the following November, nine were convicted. At the three sessions only eighty-two were sentenced, a small part of those arrested and indicted.[104]

So thorough was the work of the Federal authorities that no more was heard of the Klan as an active organization after the summer of 1871. In the reports of the United States attorney-general there is no mention of it after 1872. In 1873 and 1874 *nolle prosequi* were entered in 1,091 cases pending before the Federal court in South Carolina.

*   *   *   *   *

The political campaign of 1872 was quite unlike that of 1870. The Union Reform party no longer existed and the Conservatives made no attempt to oppose the Radical candidates. The interesting thing is that the Radicals split into two factions and put out opposing candidates, thus reflecting the lack of

[103] The full stenographic report of these proceedings is in *Ku-Klux Conspiracy, S. C,.* pp. 1599-1900; it was also published separately.

[104] John S. Reynolds, *Reconstruction in South Carolina*, pp. 213-15.

harmony within the Radical party. At the same time the Radicals demonstrated their control of the voters. Neither faction of the Radicals attempted to make any sort of alliance with the Conservatives; it was almost purely a party battle, with the Conservatives approving neither group.[105]

Before the Radical nominations were made in the summer of 1872, it was clearly understood that there was a rift in the party. There had been a serious effort to impeach Scott, and even the administration papers were admitting that better men should be elected to the General Assembly. Good men in the legislature, they admitted, were the exception and not the rule; if the Radical party were to live it must remember that the taxpayers would not consent to their money's being wasted.[106] "There are good, honest Republicans in every county," and reform must begin within the Republican ranks, else the party would surrender its hold on the "popular heart."[107] The nominating convention was called to meet in Columbia in August to nominate state officials, one congressman-at-large, and seven presidential electors. It was thought that Speaker of the House Moses had "the inside track" for the governorship and would probably be nominated unless the Radical reformers mustered a strong force. "It is rumored that in case Moses is nominated, there will be another ticket put in the field with a Reform Republican at its head."[108]

When the convention met, division in the ranks was evident, for there were contesting delegations from the counties of Beaufort, Charleston, Chesterfield, Colleton, Lexington, and Union. The committee on credentials seated those favorable to Moses, and the roll of delegates contained the names of 33 white men and 115 colored.[109] After much bickering and bold

[105] For detailed study of election of 1872 see master's essay of R. H. Woody, in Duke University Library.

[106] Daily Union, March 15, April 16, May 11, July 20, 1872.

[107] Ibid., April 16, May 11, 1872.

[108] Fairfield Herald, Aug. 21, 1872.

[109] News, Aug. 22, 1872; Reynolds, Reconstruction in South Carolina, p. 222.

charges of bribery, Moses was nominated over S. W. Melton, Chamberlain, and Reuben Tomlinson. R. H. Gleaves, colored, was nominated for lieutenant governor.[110]

Meanwhile, the threatened bolt had occurred. Under the leadership of Orr about one-third of the convention withdrew. After speeches by Orr and others, Reuben Tomlinson was chosen to lead the Radical Bolters.

To the Bolters, Orr said, "If the white element choose to vote with us, well; if not, and they choose to put out their own ticket, let them take the responsibility."[111]   A number of Negroes were in the convention; and while they denounced the corrupt Republicans, they asserted firmly that they had no use for the Democrats. Tomlinson assured them that "we have not now, and will not make any alliance with the Democratic party."[112]   The platform of each Radical faction supported Grant and Wilson, and pledged the usual financial and administrative reforms.

Meeting in Columbia on August 27, immediately after the Radical conventions, the Conservative executive committee resolved, "That in the present state of parties in South Carolina we deem it unwise to nominate a Democratic State ticket, and decline therefore to call a convention of the people for that purpose."[113]   It was urged, however, that the party be organized in each county for local and legislative reform. Throughout the campaign the Conservatives had no plan except that of inaction, and the newspapers and people did not commit themselves to either wing of the Radical party. The Bolters denounced the abuses of Scott's administration, especially those connected with finances, and each side accused the other of all manner of fraud and evil purposes.

[110] *News, Courier*, Aug. 23, 24, 1872. The other nominees were: secretary of state, H. E. Hayne, colored; treasurer, F. L. Cardozo, colored; comptroller-general, S. L. Hoge; adjutant and inspector-general, H. W. Purvis, colored; superintendent of education, J. K. Jillson; attorney-general, S. W. Melton.

[111] *News, Courier*, Aug. 23, 24, 1872.

[112] *Courier*, Aug. 24, 1872.

[113] *News, Courier*, Aug. 28, 1872.

The Conservatives had no faith in the Bolters, their pledges, or their candidates. Many, like the *Edgefield Advertiser,* had "no choice in the tickets," and like the *Chester Reporter,* believed the contest was one between a "black dog and a monkey."[114] The *Fairfield Herald* could not see virtue in either candidate. Moses was a native South Carolinian "who jumped into the arms of Radicalism when it first made its appearance," while Tomlinson, "a carpetbagger who was wafted South," was an ex-state auditor, against whom "no whisper of corruption was breathed. . . . But from this can be gained no satisfactory idea of his fitness. . . . He belongs to a dangerous element in the State, the Carpetbaggers, and should be approached with great caution."[115] Indeed, said the *Edgefield Advertiser,* "the good people . . . simply look upon the entire contest as a struggle between thieves and plunderers, and have no preference between the combatants. . . . Let us pray!"[116]

Although the *Courier* thought it a mistake for the Conservatives not to nominate a ticket,[117] many Conservatives were determined to elect the best county and state officers on the Radical ticket.[118] The "Governor, Treasurer, Comptroller and Attorney-General are nearly powerless to achieve an effective and thorough reform without the aid of the Legislature," said the *Beaufort Republican.* "This body has been the chief seat of the all-pervading corruption of our government for the last four years. Here it must be arrested."[119]

Election day fell on October 16. The obnoxious election laws of 1870 had been amended to prevent fraud,[120] and the election passed off very quietly. The results showed that

[114] Quoted in *News,* Sept. 11, 1872.
[115] Sept. 4, 1872.
[116] Quoted in *Courier,* Sept. 26, 1872. The more prominent Bolters were: Orr, Tomlinson, Corbin, F. A. Sawyer, B. F. Whittemore, Timothy Hurley, C. C. Bowen (all white); W. J. Whipper, S. A. Swails, Robert Smalls, R. C. DeLarge, B. A. Boseman (all colored). Whitte-more, Hurley, Bowen, Whipper, and Swails would have discredited any reform party.
[117] Oct. 8, 1872.
[118] Winnsboro News, quoted in *Courier,* Oct. 5, 1872.
[119] Quoted in *Courier,* Oct. 5, 1872.
[120] *Stat. S. C.,* XV, 170-71.

Moses had carried the state with 69,838 votes as compared with Tomlinson's 36,533.[121]   To the state senate four Bolters and eight Conservatives were elected, a gain of three for the latter. Two constitutional amendments, one changing the election date and the other forbidding any increase in the state debt without a public vote, were ratified by large majorities.

The election indicated that the Conservatives had won in some local elections. The white vote was not heavy and seems to have been given generally to Tomlinson, for of the ten counties which he carried[122] eight were in the up-country, where there was a large white vote. The total vote cast was less by 30,217 than that of 1870, indicating that many whites, and no doubt a considerable number of Negroes, failed to vote.

* * * * *

Opposition to the Radical government as manifested in the elections of 1870 and 1872 and the Ku-Klux Klan of 1871 was either rendered ineffective at the ballot box or suppressed by the Federal government. But still further organized protest was evident in the taxpayers' conventions of 1871 and 1874.

From May 9 to 12, 1871, a taxpayers' convention was in session in Columbia.[123]   W. D. Porter was president and the delegates included leading Conservatives of the state. The principal object of the convention was the denunciation and prevention of "the fearful and unnecessary increase of the public debt" and the resultant "excessive taxation." Its work in regard to the public debt, taxation, railroad frauds, and so on, is discussed elsewhere.[124]   The convention deplored the work of the Klan and found the principal excuse for its existence in the inefficient and corrupt local government which the Radicals

---

[121] The congressmen elected were: R. H. Cain, colored, at large; Joseph H. Rainey, colored, first district; A. J. Ransier, colored, second district; R. B. Elliott, colored, third district; and A. S. Wallace, fourth district, defeated B. F. Perry.

[122] Anderson, Charleston, Greenville, Horry, Lancaster, Lexington, Oconee, Spartanburg, Union, and York. Charleston was no doubt carried through the manipulations of C. C. Bowen, a Bolter.

[123] See *Proceedings of the Taxpayers' Convention, 1871.*

[124] See above, pp. 156-58.

had set up. The committees appointed by the convention conferred with the governor in regard to the public debt and the local government. He promised reform and spoke favorably of proportional representation which would give the property owners a voice in the government. The convention adopted recommendations to be presented to the legislature, indicated means of financial retrenchment, denounced the railroad frauds and the general corruption of the government.

But no marked improvement was noted in affairs at Columbia. As a consequence, the executive committee and the president of the convention of 1871 called a second convention to meet in Columbia in February, 1874.[125] The convention was called only after "forbearance could find no further excuse. Not only have the promises given and the pledges made, been utterly and shamefully broken, but the career of corruption, of prodigal expenditure, and excessive taxation have gone forward with accelerated momentum, till it has driven us to the utmost limit of toleration. The property-holding and taxpaying people are not only in distress, but in despair. They see in the future nothing but ruin or revolution."[126] It was proposed to consider the condition of the state not "in the light of race, or color, or party, but simply and exclusively in the light of property-holding and non-property-holding";[127] the burden of the taxpayers was that the voting population of the state was divided by "a broad, distinct line," into two classes—the one property-holding and taxpaying, the other non-property-holding and non-taxpaying; secondly, the large, fixed majority of non-taxpayers had banded together and persistently refused to the taxpayers a fair representation for the protection of their property interests. Therefore, those who levied and expended the taxes neither contributed to them nor felt the weight of them.

[125] See *Proceedings of the Taxpayers' Convention, 1874.*
[126] Speech of W. D. Porter, president, to the Convention.
[127] *Ibid.*

Porter quoted a letter written by Chamberlain to W. L. Trenholm in 1871: "Three years have passed and the result is —what? Incompetency, dishonesty, corruption in all its forms . . . have put to flight the small remnant that oppose them, and now rule the party which rules the State." The convention proposed to memorialize the Congress of the United States for relief and protection against "flagrant misrule," to organize taxpayers' clubs in every county to oversee the doings of state and county officials, to "trace out the fraud and the offender, and do all in their power to bring the betrayers of the public trust to the bar of offended justice," and to encourage immigration. The taxpayers' clubs and the immigration policy are discussed elsewhere,[128] and the memorial to congress went unheeded, except that a committee of the legislature presented a counter-memorial. While the taxpayers' conventions may have prevented further mischief in the state government, no immediate results were apparent.

*   *   *   *   *

The gubernatorial contest of 1874 was similar to that of 1872 in that there was a demand for reform by a Radical faction which separated from the "Regulars." But unlike the campaign of 1872, the Bolters in 1874 sought to win the Conservative vote and in a large measure succeeded.

Everyone conceded the need for reform. In May, 1874, a convention of young Radicals resolved to "unload the thieves."[129] The reply of the legislature to the memorial of the taxpayers' convention acknowledged that the Republicans had "committed mistakes and errors in the past,"[130] and the speaker of the House in his valedictory in March, 1874, frankly admitted that "a change of things" was "absolutely and imperatively necessary for the preservation of our institutions and the stability of our government." He did insist, however, that the task

[128] See above, pp. 156, 242.
[129] *Union Herald*, May 23, 1874.

[130] *Reports and Resolutions, 1873-74*, pp. 983-90.

REPRESENTATIVE HAMILTON, REPUBLICAN OF BEAUFORT, WEEPING
OVER THE CORRUPTION OF HIS PARTY

of reforming the government rested mainly with the colored voters. "We, as a people, are blameless of misgovernment. It is owing to bad men, adventurers, persons who, after having reaped millions almost from our party, turn traitors and stab us in the dark. Ingratitude is the worst of crimes, and yet the men we have fostered, the men we have elevated and made rich, now speak of our corruption and venality, and charge us with every conceivable crime."[131]

In July, 1874, the Radical executive committee issued an address to the party in which it stated that "the pledges given ... in ... 1872 have not been fully redeemed, and that in many instances, sound policy has been discarded and reckless extravagance manifested. . . . The National Republican party admonishes us to at once retrace our steps, and vindicate . . . the integrity of Republicanism."[132]

When the Radical nominating convention met in Columbia on September 8, there was no thought of renominating Moses. After a five-day wrangle, featured by the public addresses of opposing candidates, Chamberlain was nominated over John T. Green by a vote of 72 to 40. R. H. Gleaves, the incumbent, was nominated for lieutenant governor over Martin R. Delany by a vote of 97 to 11.[133] The platform pledged the usual loyalty to the Republican party and to the interests of the state.

On October 2 there was a state convention in Charleston of "Independent" Radicals. The rules and the platform of the Regulars were adopted. But John T. Green and Martin R. Delany, the defeated candidates of the preceding convention, were nominated by the Independents for governor and lieutenant governor. The convention resolved that it was "not hostile to the domination of the Republican party in South Carolina, but it designed to maintain its integrity against the corrupt 'rings' which control it and at the same time protect the com-

---

[131] S. J. Lee in *House Journal, 1873-74*, pp. 551-52.

[132] *News and Courier*, July 24, 1874.

[133] *Ibid.*, Sept. 9-12, 14, 1874.

mon interests of the whole people." Furthermore, the Independents declared, "We cordially invite the whole people of the State to support the nominees of this Convention as the only means of preserving their common interests—especially requesting the Conservatives that have persistently declared that their desire was only for good government without regard to partisan politics to support the independents."[134]

Green was a native of the state. In 1868 he was elected judge of the third circuit and later was elected for a second term; in 1872 he was a candidate for attorney-general on the Bolters' ticket. He was regarded as an honorable man of some talent.[135] Delany was an intelligent black man, well-traveled and well-educated. As explorer, scientist, newspaper editor, officer in the army, member of the Freedmen's Bureau, he was perhaps the most unusual colored man in the state. With a hearty dislike for white carpetbaggers and what he considered their misdirection of his people, the ever fluent Delany was ready to denounce Chamberlain and his associates.[136]

As an honest native, Green won favor among the Conservatives. It was generally considered useless to nominate Conservative candidates, although a few papers in 1874 wanted a straight-out Conservative ticket. In September, while there was much talk of the Independents making nominations, James Chesnut, chairman of the executive committee of the state tax union, called a convention of "The citizens of South Carolina, in favor of honest and good government" to meet in Columbia, October 8. The delegates were to be selected under the auspices of the tax unions, not the Conservative or Dem-

[134] The leaders of the Independents were T. C. Dunn, E. W. M. Mackey, R. H. Cain, J. P. M. Epping, and W. A. Hayne.
[135] News and Courier, Oct. 5, 1874.
[136] News and Courier, Oct. 5, 1874; Aug. 24, Sept. 25, 1875; Feb. 19, 1876; F. A. Rollin, Life and Public Services of Martin R. Delany, passim. B. F. Perry said he had observed Delany for seven or eight years, and "I must say he has exhibited, in his speeches and addresses, more wisdom and prudence, more honor and patriotism, than any other Republican in South Carolina, white or black. I say this deliberately and after mature reflection."—News and Courier, Sept. 29, 1874.

ocratic party.[137]   The representatives of 29 counties met in the convention and endorsed the nominees of the Independents and adopted a platform of "Honesty and Economy in the administration of the State Government."[138]

After a state-wide canvass, the Independents were defeated by a vote of 68,818 to 80,403.[139]   The vote was the largest cast since 1868, indicating the increased participation of the whites.[140]

The reform movements of 1870, 1872, and 1874 had failed; the taxpayers' conventions and tax unions had failed; the Ku-Klux Klan had failed; appeals to Congress had failed; for two more years a Radical government was to remain in power.

[137] *News and Courier,* Sept. 16, 17, 1874.

[138] *Ibid.,* Oct. 9, 10, 1874.

[139] Judge Green was too ill to take the stump. He died in January, 1875, and had his ticket been elected Delany would have become governor largely through the vote of the white people. The Independents carried twelve counties: Anderson, Charleston, Chesterfield, Clarendon, Greenville, Horry, Lexington, Marion, Oconee, Pickens, Sumter, and Union. In this connection, the following is of interest: In 1860 Delany had attended the International Statistical Congress in London as a delegate from Canada. A. B. Longstreet, the only delegate from the United States and at that time president of the South Carolina College, withdrew from the Congress when Delany was introduced as a citizen of the United States.—See John Donald Wade, *Augustus Baldwin Longstreet,* p. 325.

[140] The vote for the years in which there were reform parties was as follows:

1870

Scott	85,071
Carpenter	51,537
Total	136,608

1872

Moses	69,838
Tomlinson	36,553
Total	106,391

1874

Chamberlain	80,403
Green	68,818
Total	149,221

Chapter XVIII

THE CAMPAIGN OF 1876

CHAMBERLAIN'S administration was emphatically one of reform. In accepting the nomination for governor, he stated that "no platform which does not commit us irrevocably and solemnly to the duty of reducing public expenditures to their lowest limits; of administering the public funds honestly in the public interests; of electing competent public officers; of filling the local offices of our counties and townships with honest and faithful incumbents; of guarding our language and our action so as to allay rather than rekindle the flames of past controversies; of directing the attention of our fellow-citizens to the hopes of the future rather than to the memories of the past, can bring to us party success or political honor."[1]

Similar declarations in the past had gone unheeded; but Chamberlain's inaugural address showed such an intimate knowledge of the condition of the state that corrupt Radicals were alarmed. Not only did the Governor denounce in the plainest terms the gross extravagance of the administrations of Scott and Moses, but he revealed a clear appreciation of the problems of Reconstruction: "The work which lies before us is serious beyond that which falls to the lot of most generations of men. It is nothing less than the reëstablishment of society in this State upon the foundation of absolute equality of civil and political rights. The evils attending our first steps in this work have drawn upon us the frowns of the whole world. Those who opposed the policy upon which our State was restored to her practical relations with the Union have already visited us with the verdict of absolute condemnation. . . . The

---

[1] *News and Courier*, July 6, 1876.

evils which surround us are such as might well have been predicted by a sagacious mind before they appeared. They are deplorable, but they will be transitory. . . ."[2]

It is not necessary to examine in detail the events of his administration.[3] Most of the reforms had to do with economy in finances. By repeated and urgent messages to the legislature and by the veto method, he sought to reduce taxes, safeguard the treasury, maintain the public credit, protect and support honest men in office, and carry on the government with efficiency and economy. His sincerity was unquestioned. He bespoke the aid of all parties; many Conservatives in the legislature supported his reform efforts. And well they might, for from the very first session it was plainly evident that the legislature was no better than it had been in the past and that reform measures would meet vigorous opposition from a well organized minority. Robert B. Elliott, speaker of the House, C. C. Bowen, B. F. Whittemore, W. J. Whipper, and others, while professing the greatest sympathy for reform, opposed Chamberlain at every point. The character and past history of these men reveal an easy explanation of their opposition; and the legislature had gone its extravagant and heedless way too long to be moved by reform pleas. The legislature attempted to remove from office Treasurer F. L. Cardozo, who was a friend and supporter of Chamberlain. During the first session Chamberlain wrote nineteen veto messages, and in no case did his opponents muster the two-thirds majority necessary to override the veto; the bills were made to conform to the wishes of the governor. During the second session of the legislature, the governor vetoed the tax and supply bill passed at the former session, and on occasion he did not hesitate to address letters to the ways and means or finance committee in which he presented schemes for retrenchment in appropriations.

[2] *House Journal, 1874-75,* message 1.
[3] For a documentary history favorable to Chamberlain, see Walter Allen, *Chamberlain's Administration in South Carolina.*

Not always successful but indicative of reform was the action taken against corrupt or incompetent officials. The circuit court rendered a verdict against former Treasurer Niles G. Parker for malfeasance in office resulting in a loss to the state of $225,000; James A. Bowley, Negro chairman of the committee on ways and means, was indicted for accepting a bribe from John B. Dennis, superintendent of the penitentiary, for including in the appropriation bill an $80,000 allowance for that institution; Robert Smalls, Negro senator from Beaufort, was tried for having counseled the clerks of the House and Senate to commit a breach of trust by certifying that a claim of Smalls for $2,250 had been passed and approved by the House; T. S. Cavender, auditor of Chesterfield County and a commissioner under the act for the settlement and payment of claims against the state, was removed from both offices by Chamberlain on a "grave suspicion" of fraud; Montgomery Moses, judge of the seventh judicial circuit, was impeached for "high crimes and misdemeanors" and removed from office; and the conduct of other judges was investigated. Chamberlain was very careful not to abuse the pardoning power as his predecessors had done,[4] and his appointees to public offices, especially county treasurers and trial justices, showed a notable improvement in character and ability over the appointees of Scott and Moses.

There appeared in the *News and Courier* of July 18, 1876, a summary of the accomplishments of Chamberlain's administration. The abuse of the pardoning power had been corrected; the character of the officers of the government improved; the settlement of the public debt maintained; the floating indebtedness of the state provided for in a way that resulted in a saving of at least $4,000,000; the tax laws amended so as to secure substantial uniformity and equality in the as-

[4] Scott granted 579 pardons in four years, Moses 457 in two years, Chamberlain 73 in seventeen months. *News and Courier,* July 7, 1876.

DANIEL HENRY CHAMBERLAIN, ATTORNEY-GENERAL,
1868-1872; GOVERNOR, 1874-1876

sessment of property; the contingent funds so reduced in amount that the savings in two years, upon the basis of the average of six previous years, were $101,260; legislative expenses reduced in a like manner at a saving of $350,810; legislative contingent expenses reduced so as to save the state $355,000; cost of public printing reduced from an annual average of $306,209 to $50,000; salaries of public officers reduced $30,000 a year; tax levy for current year reduced from 13½ mills to 11 mills; annual deficiencies reduced by more than $233,000; a total saving of $1,719,488. "This is the record of Governor Chamberlain as shown by hard figures and unmistakable facts. We have strained or exaggerated nothing."

Many of these reforms were accomplished in spite of the passive or active opposition of the Radical majority in the legislature. Only by diligent effort had the legislature been persuaded to sustain vetoes. Proposed reforms left unheeded by the legislature although reiterated in Chamberlain's message included a system of minority representation, the election by the people of justices of the peace and constables, and the registration of electors. And in one important action the legislature showed a total disregard of the wishes of the Governor and the press of the state. That was in the election of W. J. Whipper and F. J. Moses, Jr., as judges of the first and third judicial circuits respectively.

Taking advantages of the temporary absence of the governor in Greenville, the legislature on December 16, 1875, met in joint assembly to elect circuit judges. By substantial majorities Whipper was elected to the Charleston circuit and Moses to the Sumter circuit. That Chamberlain opposed such election was well known. In December, 1874, he had prevented Whipper's election, and in February, 1875, he had blocked the election of Moses.[5] Knowing that judicial elections were to

[5] *News and Courier,* Dec. 9, 11, 12, 1874; Jan. 30, Feb. 13, 15, 1875.

take place during the session, Chamberlain urged in his first message of the session, "Legal learning, a judicial spirit, and a high, unblemished personal character, should mark every man who shall be elected to sit in the seats of Harper and Dunkin, of O'Neall and Wardlaw. . . ."[6] Chamberlain characterized the election as "a horrible disaster. . . . This calamity is infinitely greater, in my judgment, than any which has yet fallen on this State."[7] In a letter to Grant the Governor said: "Unless the universal opinion of all who are familiar with his career is mistaken, he [Moses] is as infamous a character as ever in any age disgraced and prostituted public position. The character of W. J. Whipper . . . differs from that of Moses only in the extent to which opportunity has allowed him to exhibit it. The election of these two men to judicial office sends a thrill of horror through the State. . . ."[8] In declining an invitation of the New England Society of Charleston, Chamberlain said: "I cannot attend your supper tonight; but if there ever was an hour when the spirit of the Puritans, the spirit of undying, unconquerable enmity and defiance to wrong ought to animate their sons, it is this hour, here in South Carolina. The civilization of the Puritan and the Cavalier, of the Roundhead and the Huguenot, is in peril."[9]

On the ground that the incumbents of the first and third circuits, Reed and Shaw, who had been elected at the preceding session to fill unexpired terms, were legally elected for the full term of four years, Chamberlain refused to commission Whipper and Moses and proceeded to commission Reed and Shaw for full terms. This refusal was upheld by the Supreme Court in an action which Whipper brought to obtain possession of the bench.[10] Moses never attempted to take his seat. The election showed well the antagonism between the Governor

---

[6] *House Journal, 1875-76.*

[7] *News and Courier,* Dec. 20, 1875.

[8] Quoted in Allen, *Chamberlain's Administration,* pp. 228-29.

[9] *Ibid.,* pp. 200-201.

[10] 9 S. C. 5.

and the degraded legislature; and to many it indicated clearly that good government could not be exacted from the Radical party as then constituted.

Already had Chamberlain won the approval and qualified endorsement of a large portion of the press and populace of the state; he had been invited to social and literary gatherings and patriotic celebrations within the state, and had delivered addresses at Yale, and at the centennial celebrations of the Battle of Lexington and the Mecklenburg Declaration of Independence. On a visit to Charleston in November, 1875, he was received and toasted by the city and the chamber of commerce, and his address on the aims and policy of his administration was highly complimented by the press.[11]   And his refusal to sign the commissions of Moses and Whipper measurably increased his popularity. Public meetings in Charleston, Sumter, Barnwell, and elsewhere, lauded Chamberlain as eloquently as they denounced Moses, Whipper, Elliott, and the Radical legislature.   The leading bankers and merchants of Charleston thanked Chamberlain for his action.[12]

The election of Moses and Whipper meant a new turn in state politics. Chamberlain himself was quick to say that one immediate effect of their election would "obviously be the reorganization of the Democratic party within the State, as the only means left, in the judgment of its members, for opposing a solid and reliable front to this terrible crevasse of misgovernment and public debauchery."[13]   The *Union-Herald,* a Radical organ, said that the legislature had signed the death warrant of the party: "In that near and certain future, when in degradation and despair they learn the bitter lessons of adversity . . . they will see that no man, no party, no State, can resist the awful power of public opinion."[14]   Referring to the legislature an editorial in the *News and Courier,* December 21, said:

[11] See Allen, *Chamberlain's Administration*, Chap. X.

[12] *Ibid.*, Chap. XIII.

[13] *News and Courier,* Dec. 20, 1875.

[14] Quoted in *News and Courier,* Dec. 20, 1875.

"They have run over Governor Chamberlain, as they have run over any other Republican who strives to check them in their mad career. . . . They . . . *must make way for the Democratic* party. . . . The work of organization cannot begin too soon. . . . There is a heavy Radical majority in the State. . . . The State Democratic Committee should meet immediately."

*   *   *   *   *

Since the fall of 1868 there had been no Democratic organization worthy of the name. No strictly party ticket had been put out; the name Conservative was constantly used to designate the group opposed to the Radical government; and the Democrats, as an organization, had not cast their lot with any of the reform movements. But on December 23, 1875, Thomas Y. Simons, of Charleston, the South Carolina member of the National Democratic Executive Committee, summoned the members of the Democratic State Central Committee, which had been constituted in 1872 to carry the state for Greeley, to a meeting in Columbia on January 6. The committee earnestly advised the thorough reorganization of the Democratic party, but desired "to say emphatically that, in recommending its instant and comprehensive organization, their sole purpose is to obtain an honest and economical government . . . which shall maintain, without abridgement or change, the public rights and liberties of the whole people, and guarantee to all classes of citizens the blessings of freedom, justice and peace."

That statement met what was considered to be the view of the people. But there was a difference of opinion between the Coöperationists, who favored the fusion of the Conservatives and the better element of the Radical party led by Chamberlain, and the Straightouts who advocated a straightout Democratic ticket in 1876 with no thought of an alliance with the better class Radicals. In the fall of 1875, while the question of Democratic reorganization was under discussion, the *News and Courier*[15] said that the "balance of opinion" was "decidedly in favor of continuing the Conservative organization, strengthening and broadening it as much as possible. . . . With such an organization it will be practicable to support the Democratic candidates for President and Vice-President in 1876, without tying the State, hard and fast, to the Democratic nominations for State offices."

At a second meeting of the Democratic Executive Committee, February 22, in Columbia, the preponderance of feeling was in favor of a Straightout ticket as the most certain way of bringing out the entire white vote.[16] In March the Democratic clubs of Edgefield County passed a resolution: "We are sternly opposed to any fusion, coalition or compromise even with professedly honest Republicans."[17]

Meanwhile, the Democratic party was carrying its organization forward. There was never any opposition to a party reorganization; the difference of opinion was in regard to the policy of the party. Should it be independent or should it cooperate with honest Radicals? Some suggested that the name Conservative be retained, but after the Whipper-Moses election the term Democrat was generally used. The up-country took the lead in organizing county Democratic clubs, but by March, 1876, a census of Democrats in Charleston County was being taken, and a thorough registration of the voters was to precede the county convention.[18] "Some counties have been tardy in organization; but, upon the whole, the Democrats are in better condition to use their strength effectively than they were in any previous campaign. . . . They know that there is no present hope of obtaining good government in South Carolina through the Republican party. . . ."[19] Whether coöperative or independent action proved advisable, the party organization and

---

[15] Sept. 24, 1875.
[16] *News and Courier*, Feb. 24, 1876.
[17] *Ibid.*, Mar. 13, 1876.

[18] *Ibid.*, Mar. 17, 1876.
[19] *Ibid.*, Mar. 30, 1876.

discipline would be maintained. County delegates for the state Democratic convention to meet May 4, in Columbia, were to be elected in April, and such delegates would, of course, determine the action of the convention.

In addition to electing delegates to the National Democratic Convention and forming a new state executive committee of fifteen members, the May convention adopted a report recommending "the utmost vigor and zeal in perfecting a thorough and compact organization of the Democratic party. . . ." The *News and Courier* said the sentiment of the convention was "unquestionably in favor of nominating, in the summer, a full Democratic State ticket. . . . Such a nomination would arouse the whole state from the Blue Ridge to the Atlantic. This, however, is not the time . . . to decide who shall be nominated, and for what office. . . . The Democrats, it is easy to see, will stand together."[20]

*　*　*　*　*

The *News and Courier* had been one of the first and staunchest advocates of Chamberlain and his reform policy. A few days after the convention that paper defined the attitude of the Coöperationists toward the Governor, and gave the reasons for its objection to the scheme of the Straightouts: There was every likelihood that Chamberlain would be the candidate of his party. The stoutest opponents of Chamberlain said there would be no bolt in the party; the colored voting majority was 20,000 to 30,000; the colored population was massed in the lower counties and the Radical majority could be made whatever the commissioners and managers of election chose to make it; and add to the solid Radical vote the power to obtain Federal troops, the executive appointment of the managers of elections, the broad and undefined powers of the State Board of Canvassers, and what prospect was there that Chamberlain could be defeated? "It can be

[20] *News and Courier,* May 5, 6, 8, 1876.

done in only one way: *by armed force*. For that the people are not ready, and if they were ready such a course would end in disaster and ruin." What the *News and Courier* advised, then, was not to make Chamberlain the candidate of the Democrats but to let the Democrats waive a nomination for governor in case Chamberlain was nominated by the Republicans, the Democratic party to concentrate its efforts on the other state officers and the members of the legislature. "With Mr. Chamberlain as Governor, and a Conservative Democratic majority, or thereabouts, in the lower House, the State, in every sense of the word, would be safe. In attempting to gain more we might lose everything."[21] During the month of July, 1876, this paper ran a series of very strong articles on the reforms and record of Chamberlain.

As we have seen, the Governor had not only lost the support of a large element of his party but was carrying on a desperate fight against that element. When the state Republican convention met on April 12, in Columbia, before the adjournment of the legislature, for the purpose of electing delegates to the National Convention, a trial of strength took place. Arrayed against Chamberlain were United States Senator John J. Patterson; collector of the Port of Charleston, H. G. Worthington, speaker of the House, Robert B. Elliott; C. C. Bowen, sheriff of Charleston County; members of the legislature C. P. Leslie, B. F. Whittemore, S. A. Swails, and others. In the first skirmish Swails was elected temporary chairman, defeating Chamberlain by a vote of 80 to 40. From counties sending contesting delegations, the delegates opposing Chamberlain were seated. Confusion and disorder, with some threats of personal violence, marked the two sessions held on the 12th as well as the session of the 13th, which continued until seven o'clock in the morning.[22] The assault against the

[21] *Ibid.,* May 9, 1876. [22] *Ibid.,* April 11, 12, 1876.

Governor was led by R. B. Carpenter, one-time candidate for governor on the Union Reform ticket, then judge of the fifth judicial circuit by the will of the legislature. He said that Chamberlain when elected to office had turned his back upon his supporters and had ceased to represent the Republican party, and that Chamberlain "forgave his enemies [the Democrats], blessed them that cursed him, and prayed for those that despitefully used him. . . . He is no ordinary man. . . . He is bold, daring, and ambitious. If he were in France there would be a *coup d'état,* and he would be king, just as he has tried to be king of the Republican party here. . . . He has said that the men who have voted for two certain judges in this State are a gang of thieves. I did not vote for them. . . . But one hundred gentlemen in this hall did vote for them. . . ."[23]

It was four o'clock in the morning when Chamberlain began his masterful and eloquent reply which lasted one hour and thirty minutes. "He not only denied, but clearly disproved, every charge which Carpenter had brought against him. . . . As the speech progressed, the colored delegates gathered around the speaker; then they stood on chairs and desks to get a better view of him. Those who were nearest to him sat on the floor, looking up into his face with open-mouthed wonder at his terrible denunciation of his foes and his grand vindication of himself. Some of the Negroes were entirely carried away by his oration; they shouted with delight at the conclusion of some of the most effective passages; and as the Governor took his seat, pale and exhausted from over-exertion, all the enthusiasm of their fiery nature broke into one long-continued cry, and the name of 'Chamberlain, Chamberlain, our Chamberlain,' was echoed from every part of the Capitol."[24] Chamberlain was elected a delegate over Patterson by

---

[23] *Ibid.,* April 14, 1876.
[24] Correspondent of *N. Y. Times,* quoted in Allen, *Chamberlain's Administration,* pp. 260-61.

a vote of 89 to 32, and he was given a free hand at the National Republican Convention.[25]

*   *   *   *   *

With Chamberlain retaining a firm hold upon the party, his nomination for governor was almost certain; and with a division in the Democratic party between the Coöperationists and Straightouters, party politics reached an indeterminate stage. What made certain the rejection of Chamberlain by the Democrats and the nomination of a solid Democratic ticket was an event in Aiken County known as the Hamburg riot. Aiken and Edgefield counties were strongholds of the Straightouts and also the scenes of some very lawless conflicts between whites and blacks. In the summer of 1874 there had been a dangerous quarrel between a Negro militiaman and a party of white men,[26] and in December of that year, after a series of incendiary fires, the prominent men of the county adopted a resolution that "from and after today all parties, white or black, who may be caught in the act of firing any house . . . be dealt with in accordance with the precedents of lynch law. . . ."[27]

A second disturbance occurred in January, 1875. A committee of Edgefield citizens, including M. C. Butler, requested Chamberlain to withdraw the arms of a Negro militia company, captained by Ned Tennant. A short time later, Butler's house and everything in it was destroyed by fire. The incendiary confessed that Tennant hired him to do the deed, and a warrant was sworn out for Tennant, who escaped to the swamps but later gave up to protect his life. During the search for Tennant, two Negroes were mortally wounded and both whites and blacks were fired upon from ambush. Two agents sent by the Governor to investigate reported that the govern-

---

[25] For Chamberlain's speech and resolution, see News and Courier, April 14, 1876.

[26] Benjamin R. Tillman, The Struggle

of '76 (Speech at Anderson, S. C., 1909), pp. 42 ff.; News and Courier, Aug. 19, Sept. 23, 28, 1874.

[27] News and Courier, Dec. 9, 1874.

ment of the county constituted a "vast system of larceny," and
that there was a disturbing element in the minority of both
races. "Among the whites [is] a class of men who hold human
life at little value. . . . Among the colored people there is a
class who do not wish to labor, and are known as habitual
thieves or disturbers of the peace. . . ." On January 28 Chamberlain issued a proclamation disbanding all military organizations, including rifle and sabre clubs.[28] In May, six Negroes
were taken from the sheriff of Edgefield County by several
hundred men and shot to death. It was alleged that they were
responsible for the murder of a respectable couple in that
county. This indicates the temper of the people at the time of
the Hamburg affair.

On July 4, 1876, two young white men of Edgefield were
returning home through the town of Hamburg, then in Aiken,
formerly in Edgefield County. A militia company parading
in the streets prevented the passage of their buggy. After some
difficulty with the militia captain, Doc Adams, they were allowed to proceed. On complaint of the father of one of the
young men, the Negro trial justice in Hamburg, Prince Rivers,
issued a warrant for Doc Adams. At the trial, Adams was
arrested by the trial justice for contempt of court and the case
was continued until Saturday afternoon, July 8. At that time
M. C. Butler, who had been engaged to prosecute Adams, appeared at the office of the trial justice with his clients. But
Adams was not there. Butler then suggested that the case
might be arranged privately, and time was given him to see the
parties involved. Meanwhile, Prince Rivers learned that there
were two or three hundred armed white men in Hamburg who
demanded that the militia should surrender its arms. Rivers
sent for Butler, who had just returned from Augusta. After a
parley between Butler, Rivers, and Adams, in which Butler
refused to recede from his demand that the guns be surrendered

[28] *Ibid.*, Jan. 6, 20, 25, 28, Mar. 1, 1875.

THE HAMBURG RIOT, JULY, 1876

Harper's Weekly

and Adams refused to give up the arms, firing began between the whites and the militia. The militia had taken refuge in a brick building used as an armory. From this building the Negroes escaped by means of ladders and took refuge wherever they could find it. Their ammunition had already been exhausted. Meanwhile, one of the attacking party, McKie Meriwether, had been shot through the head and instantly killed. As the Negroes escaped from the armory, one, the town marshal, was killed, and later five of a party of about twenty-five captured Negroes were shot to death in cold blood. Several others were wounded.[29]

On July 13 the Governor addressed a letter to Senator T. J. Robertson in which he described the Hamburg affair: ". . . If you can find words to characterize its atrocity and barbarism, the triviality of the causes, and the murderous and inhuman spirit which marked it in all its stages, your power of language exceeds mine. . . ."[30] In a letter to the President he said:". . . The lines of race and political party were the lines which marked the respective parties to the affair at Hamburg. I mention this as a fact, and as, apparently, the most trustworthy index of the motives and aims which inspired those who brought on this conflict. . . . But the Hamburg massacre has produced another effect. It has . . . caused a firm belief on the part of most Republicans here that this affair at Ham-

---

[29] For accounts of the affair see voluminous testimony in *South Carolina in 1876. Testimony as to the denial of the elective franchise in South Carolina at the election of 1875* [sic] *and 1876.* 3 vols. Sen. Mis. Doc. No. 48. 44 Cong. 2 Sess. Hereafter cited *South Carolina in 1876.* See also *Recent Election in South Carolina. Testimony taken by the Select Committee on the Recent Election in South Carolina.* Ho. Mis. Doc. No. 31. 44 Cong., 2 Sess. Hereafter cited *Recent Election in South Carolina.* Benjamin R. Tillman, in *The Struggles of '76,* said:

"It had been the settled purpose of the leading white men of Edgefield to seize the first opportunity that the Negroes might offer to provoke a riot and teach the Negroes a lesson; as it was generally believed that nothing but bloodshed and a good deal of it could answer the purpose of redeeming the state. . . . It was our purpose to attend the trial to see that the young men had protection and, if any opportunity offered, to provoke a row, and if one did not offer, we were to make one."

[30] *News and Courier,* July 21, 1876.

burg is only the beginning of a series of similar race and party collisions in our State, the deliberate aim of which is believed by them to be the political subjugation and control of the State. They see, therefore, in this event what foreshadows a campaign of blood and violence, and such a campaign as is popularly known as a campaign conducted on the 'Mississippi plan'. . . . To be more specific, will the General Government exert itself vigorously to repress violence in this State during the present political campaign on the part of persons belonging to either political party, whenever that violence shall be beyond the control of the State authorities? . . ."[31]

The generality of the press very frankly condemned the Hamburg affair,[32] but Chamberlain was censored for giving the matter a political twist and indicating to Grant that troops might be needed. Said the *Southern Christian Advocate:* "The killing . . . was an outrage upon humanity which will find no apology outside the exasperated men who perpetrated the foul crime. . . . But the attempt to fasten upon the whites the responsibility for the inauguration of such collisions . . . is diabolically unjust."[33] Said the *News and Courier:* ". . . There is no disorder in South Carolina, or threat of disorder. . . . We have supported Governor Chamberlain's reform measures, and we have frankly expressed our opinions of the Hamburg riot, but we must protest against any move that wears the appearance of taking advantage of a local disturbance to prop up the waning fortunes of South Carolina Republicanism."[34]

* * * * *

On July 12, four days after the Hamburg affair, the Democratic State Executive Committee called a convention of the party to meet on August 15 in Columbia.[35] This indicated that the committee was determined to take decisive action without waiting for the decision of the Republican convention.

[31] *News and Courier,* Aug. 9, 1876.
[32] See *ibid.,* July 10 *et seq.*
[33] July 18, 1876.
[34] July 20, 1876.
[35] *News and Courier,* July 13, 1876.

The policy of the Coöperationists was to "Watch and Wait"; the Coöperationists believed that if the Republicans nominated Chamberlain, as it appeared they would, the Democrats should not put out a candidate for governor. The contest between the Coöperationists and the Straightouts was over the control of the August convention.

On July 19 the Democrats of Newberry County met and adopted the Straightout policy, the first in the state to take such definite and decisive action. The Edgefield convention, of which M. W. Gary was chairman, was not far behind. There "never assembled anywhere an equal number of more coldly furious men than composed this convention."[36] J. B. Kershaw, who had previously agreed with the *News and Courier* in opposing the Straightouts, changed his position the latter part of July. "I think the unhappy affair at Hamburg will be made such use of in the canvass that no alternative would probably have been left us than to 'take it straight'. . . . At all events it is a luxury once more to be able to put forward the men we like best. . . ."[37]

But the Coöperationists were not conceding defeat. Judge J. J. Maher, in declining to consider the nomination for governor, stated that unless the character and complexion of the legislature could be changed, no Democratic executive, even Kershaw or Hampton, could do as much for the state as Chamberlain.[38] George W. Williams, a wealthy merchant of Charleston, declined to consider the nomination: "We are not in a condition to enter into an excited political contest. I honestly believe that Governor Chamberlain can do more for South Carolina, in and out of the State, than any other man."[39] Meanwhile the *News and Courier's* special correspondent, R. Means Davis, was touring the state to ascertain the sentiment

[36] A. B. Williams, in Columbia *State*, Aug. 15, 1926.
[37] *News and Courier*, July 28, 1876.
[38] *Ibid.*, Aug. 7, 1876.
[39] *Ibid.*, July 28, 1876.

of the various counties.[40] On August 10 a poll of the state, by
counties, showed eighteen counties and eighty-nine delegates
for the Straightouts, six counties and forty-two delegates for
the Coöperationists, and seven counties with twenty-seven delegates as doubtful. This gave the Straightouts a majority of
five counties and twenty delegates.[41]

The Democratic state convention met the 15th of August
and was in session two days. The first test vote was in the
selection of a permanent president. G. D. Tillman of Edgefield nominated W. W. Harllee, a Straightouter, who defeated
C. H. Simonton of Charleston by a vote of 73 to 66. The vote
by counties indicated that it was not a sectional contest between
the up- and low-country; many counties split their vote.[42]
After a long secret session on August 17 the convention decided,
by a vote of 88 to 64, to make immediate nominations. M. C.
Butler nominated Hampton, who withdrew from the hall after
a short speech. John Bratton and ex-Governor John L. Manning were also nominated but withdrew in favor of Hampton.[43] Other state officers nominated were: lieutenant governor,
W. D. Simpson, of Laurens; secretary of state, R. M. Sims, of
York; attorney-general, James Connor, of Charleston; superintendent of education, Hugh S. Thompson, of Richland; comptroller-general, Johnson Hagood, of Barnwell; treasurer, S. L.
Leaphart, of Richland; and adjutant-general, E. W. Moise, of
Sumter. Connor and Moise had been opposed to Straightout

[40] Ibid., July 8, et seq.
[41] Williams in Columbia State, Aug. 22, 1926.
[42] News and Courier, Aug. 16, 1876.
[43] The nomination of Hampton had long been planned. On June 28 M. W. Gary had gone to Charleston to broach the nomination of Butler in the Charleston Journal of Commerce. On the way, he met Hampton and told him that his friends had decided to nominate him on the Straightout ticket. On July 8 Butler published a letter withdrawing his name and nominating Hampton. When the latter came to Columbia to the convention, A. C. Haskell organized a long torchlight procession so scheduled as to coincide with the meeting of the convention and turn the tide in favor of a Straightout policy which would result in the nomination of Hampton. It was well known that Hampton favored a Straightout ticket.— News and Courier, July 8, Aug. 10, 1876; U. R. Brooks, in State, Aug. 18, 1910; D. S. Henderson, in ibid., Sept. 22, 1911; W. P. Houseal in ibid., Dec. 12, 1926.

Top left: RICHARD HARVEY CAIN, PASTOR IN BROOKLYN, N. Y., 1861-1865; MEMBER OF THE CONSTITUTIONAL CONVENTION, 1868; EDITOR OF THE MISSIONARY RECORD; CONGRESS, 1873-1875, 1877-1879; BISHOP OF THE A. M. E. CHURCH, 1880-1887. *Top right:* MATTHEW CALBRAITH BUTLER, CANDIDATE FOR LIEUTENANT-GOVERNOR ON THE UNION REFORM TICKET, 1870; UNITED STATES SENATOR, 1877-1895. *Bottom left:* ALEXANDER CHEVES HASKELL, CHAIRMAN OF THE DEMOCRATIC EXECUTIVE COMMITTEE, 1876. *Bottom right:* FRANCIS W. DAWSON, EDITOR OF THE CHARLESTON DAILY NEWS AND THE CHARLESTON NEWS AND COURIER.

nominations and their acceptance of a place on the ticket indicated party unity. The candidates selected an executive committee constituted as follows: A. C. Haskell, chairman, John Bratton, J. D. Kennedy, T. B. Fraser, James A. Hoyt, J. Adger Smyth, R. O'Neale, Jr.

All factions of the Democratic party united in voicing approval of Wade Hampton. The *News and Courier,* while it opposed any nominations at the time, said that if Hampton should be the candidate, "none in the State will go farther than we will go to deserve success, if we cannot command it."[44] A citizen of Richland County, Hampton was graduated from the South Carolina College, served in both branches of the state legislature, resigned to take part in the Civil War as commander of "Hampton's Legion," and before 1865 became commander of Lee's cavalry with the rank of lieutenant general. In 1865 Hampton, although against his wish, was spontaneously put forward by the people for governor, and came within a few hundred votes of defeating James L. Orr, the regular candidate. With large plantations in Mississippi and South Carolina, he had possessed many slaves, but after the war he was one of the first in the state to advocate a restricted franchise for the Negro; he wanted the Negro to be dealt with kindly and justly. But he did not believe the whites would ever acquiesce in Negro rule. "I do not believe that the whites can now, or will, live under a rule where persons so entirely ignorant, so venal, so corrupt, have the management of their State government. . . . I think they will bear as long as they can but there will be a point beyond which they cannot bear."[45] As we shall see, Hampton was of a character and disposition that made him particularly acceptable in the campaign.

The Democratic platform was unexceptional. It accepted the Thirteenth, Fourteenth, and Fifteenth amendments and

[44] Aug. 10, 1876.   [45] Hampton in 1871. *Ku-Klux Conspiracy, S. C.,* pp. 1218 ff.

declared for Tilden and Hendricks. The Radical party was charged with "arraying race against race, creating disturbances and fomenting difficulties; with prostituting the elective franchise, tampering with the ballot box and holding unfair and fraudulent elections; with having accumulated an enormous debt . . . with levying exorbitant taxes. . . . We charge its legislation as demoralizing, partisan and disgraceful, and the venality and corruption which have characterized every branch of the Government, executive, legislative and judicial, have no parallel in the history of nations. . . . And to crown its disgraceful rule it has attempted to elevate to the bench two most corrupt and degraded men. . . . We, therefore, call upon our fellow citizens, irrespective of race or past party affiliation, to join with us. . . . We discountenance all disturbance of the peace . . . and earnestly call upon all of our fellow citizens, irrespective of party lines, to exercise forbearance and good will. . . . We demand a fair election and a fair count. . . .".

*   *   *   *   *

While the Democrats were organizing, county by county, Chamberlain was speaking throughout the state in an attempt to maintain his leadership. During July and August he spoke in about twenty counties in support of Hayes and Wheeler and his own administration. It was not a general party canvass under party auspices; the meetings were called at the request of Chamberlain.

It was during this canvass that the real spirit and force of the Democrats was felt. Chamberlain found that at some of his meetings there were more whites present than blacks. At several places the speakers were interfered with by armed whites, usually mounted; Democratic speakers took the liberty of addressing the crowd from the Radical platform. An example of this was the meeting at Edgefield on August 12. When Chamberlain, accompanied by T. J. Mackey and Robert Smalls, proceeded to Edgefield, he found five or six hundred white men in the town. They were apparently under the command of Butler and Gary, who ascended the stand with Chamberlain and announced that they intended to speak. "A glance at the crowd of white men who by this time covered the stand and swarmed around nearly three sides of it, besides climbing into the trees above our heads, all, so far as I could observe, heavily armed with pistols, displayed in many instances on the front of their persons, and even held in their hands, convinced me that any attempt to refuse the demand made, or even to abandon the meeting, would result in collision and bloodshed."[46] A division of time was granted. Chamberlain was frequently "interrupted by the crowd of white men with jeers and insults of every kind," and spoke under "great constraint and a consciousness that any word might precipitate a bloody collision." The speech of Butler, who followed, was not interrupted, and "was exceedingly violent and bitterly personal" towards Chamberlain, principally on account of his report of the Hamburg affair. After Mackey, Gary spoke. "In bitterness and violence of personal abuse," said Chamberlain, "I have certainly never heard or known its parallel."[47] Finally, the speakers' platform collapsed, and the Radicals withdrew.[48]

The Edgefield meeting was significant in view of the forthcoming Democratic convention, and it forecast the plan of the campaign. Similar meetings were held at Newberry, Abbeville, Midway, and Lancaster. At Abbeville, said Chamberlain, "mounted white men, marching in martial order, and under the command of officers or persons who gave orders which were obeyed, began to pour over the hill in front of the stand. . . . There were from eight hundred to one thousand mounted white men present. They came, as I know, from Edgefield County, and, as I was informed, from Newberry, Anderson, and Laurens counties, as well as from Abbeville County."

[46] Chamberlain to Haskell, Oct. 4, 1876. Quoted in Allen' *Chamberlain's Administration*, pp. 374 ff.

[47] *Ibid.*

[48] *News and Courier*, Aug. 14, 15, 1876.

There were repeated cries: "How about Hamburg?" Chamberlain replied, "Yes, I will tell you about Hamburg," whereupon he saw "a sudden crowding towards the stand by the mounted white men ... and heard distinctly the click of a considerable number of pistols." At Midway, the "meeting was addressed by two Democratic speakers, both of whom alluded to and described me and other Republican speakers present as 'buzzards,' 'plunderers,' 'adventurers,' and 'carrion crows.' "[49]

The Radical nominating convention met in Columbia on September 13, at the call of Robert B. Elliott, chairman of the state executive committee. The chief opponents of Chamberlain were Elliott, Bowen, Whipper, and at first, Patterson, who later nominated Chamberlain. Smalls, a Chamberlain supporter, was made president of the convention, and after a three-day discussion Chamberlain received the nomination by a vote of 88 to 32 over T. C. Dunn, then comptroller-general. Chamberlain accepted the nomination as significant of the desire of the party to carry out "the reforms demanded by the present condition of our public affairs." He urged the convention to put upon the ticket those who were in harmony with the principles and policy which he represented; without that he doubted if it would be worth while for him to enter the campaign. Furthermore, he wanted men nominated for the legislature who would not stand in the way of reform as had been the case for two years past. In order to conciliate party factions, however, the convention nominated three enemies of Chamberlain: R. H. Gleaves, renominated for lieutenant governor, Elliott, for attorney-general, and T. C. Dunn, renominated for comptroller-general. Chamberlain was severely criticized for consenting to run on a ticket with Elliott, the man who had led the legislature against him. During the campaign he defended his acceptance of Elliott on the ground that the "causes

[49] Chamberlain to Haskell, in Allen, *Chamberlain's Administration*, pp. 374 ff.

of his nomination were not his opposition to me or to reform, but his admitted ability for the position, his long record of political service to his party, and a desire . . . to conciliate an element of the party. . . ."[50] Another excuse for Elliott's nomination, said to have been given by Chamberlain himself, was that as attorney-general Elliott's opposition to reform would be less effective than as speaker of the House.[51] Undoubtedly Chamberlain laid himself open to much criticism by accepting Elliott; he later admitted as much.[52]

In contrast to the Democratic platform, the Radical platform was very specific in its reform pledges in regard to the bonded debt, taxation, legislative and court sessions, the reduction of salaries, fees and costs, and so on. The platform protested against "the practice now inaugurated by the Democratic party in this State of attending Republican meetings and by show of force and other forms of intimidation disturbing such meetings. . . ." And the Democratic party was charged with crimes and misdoings too long to enumerate.[53]

* * * * *

After a long struggle both Radicals and Democrats had now reached definite decisions. With a Straightout Democrat heading the ticket, the white population was for the first time in

[50] Chamberlain to Haskell, quoted in Allen, *Chamberlain's Administration*, p. 371.

[51] *Union Herald*, Sept. 22, 1876.

[52] "I made a grave mistake . . . I saw it then but not so clearly as now. . . . Elliott's bare presence on the ticket justly gave offense. . . . Unable to defeat me, he determined to foist himself on the ticket with me to cover his defeat. . . . I took the resolution unknown to any friends, to walk into the Convention and throw up my nomination. . . . I knew it would result in putting him off the ticket. I had actually risen in my office to go into the hall for this purpose when I was met at the door by a dozen or more of my most devoted colored supporters who came to congratulate me on *the surrender of Elliott in seeking to stand on a ticket with me!* I was disarmed of my purpose. . . . It was a mistake."—Chamberlain to William Lloyd Garrison, June 11, 1877. Quoted in Allen, *Chamberlain's Administration*, p. 505. Besides those mentioned, the nominees were F. L. Cardozo, treasurer, a loyal friend of Chamberlain; H. E. Hayne, secretary of state; James Kennedy, adjutant-general; and John R. Tolbert, superintendent of education. Gleaves, Elliott, Cardozo, and Hayne were colored. The Democratic ticket was quite superior.

[53] For proceedings of the convention, platform, etc., see *News and Courier*, Sept. 13, 14, 15, 16, 1876.

eight years united in a definite, fixed purpose. The Radicals, likewise, had completely eradicated signs of party dissensions which had existed in the campaigns of 1872 and 1874 and throughout Chamberlain's administration. Everyone knew, moreover, that there was a Negro majority of at least 20,000 in the state, and that, with few exceptions, the Negro ballot would be cast for the Radicals. How, then, could the Radical majority be turned into a minority?

The events at Hamburg and Edgefield definitely pointed the way, and the reorganization of the Democratic party added activity to hope. The nomination of Hampton and the careful organization of Democratic clubs seemed to arouse the entire state. Never before or since has South Carolina witnessed an election marked by so many forms of political activity, so much vigor and energy and zeal for a man and a party. A hope had appeared; a new crusade had begun. The Democrats must fight against great odds, odds that to some appeared insuperable, but with the progress of the campaign came new assurance of victory. It is to be noted that the Radical party showed no remarkable regeneration, expressed no unbounded zeal for a cause or a man; their enthusiasm paled into insignificance beside that of the Democrats.

The Democratic canvass opened at Anderson, in the up-country, on September 2, ten days before the Radical nominating convention. According to the press, fully 6,000 persons were present to listen to Hampton, W. D. Simpson, Gary, Samuel McGowan, J. D. Kennedy, and D. Wyatt Aiken. A procession, over a mile in length, consisted of 1,600 mounted men and a large number on foot.[54] As the campaign continued, first in the up-country where the white population was greater and then in the low-country, similar crowds and processions appeared. At a meeting in Abbeville in October on the same days as the Radical gathering, the procession was reported

[54] *Ibid.*, Sept. 4, 1876.

WADE HAMPTON, COMMANDER OF HAMPTON'S LEGION DURING THE CIVIL WAR; GOVERNOR, 1876-1879; MEMBER OF THE UNITED STATES SENATE, 1879-1891.

to be three miles long and to contain 3,000 mounted men, including 700 colored Democrats in uniform. There were three bands present and 200 women.[55]   A choir of young women sometimes furnished music and always there was a band. Special seats were reserved for women, who appeared in large numbers. Prayer was usually a feature of the meetings. Dramatic tableaux were used effectively on several occasions. Sometimes South Carolina was represented by "a bowed figure draped in robes of dense black and wrapped with chains." When Hampton approached the speakers' stand, the chains and mourning robes were cast aside and "a young woman in pure white stood tall and stately, head uplifted and eyes shining like stars." Or the prostrate figure of "South Carolina" might be raised to her feet by "Liberty," while "Justice," surrounded by thirty-seven girls representing the states of the Union, stood by with scales and sword. Crowds cheered while cannon roared a salute. At Orangeburg Hampton appeared in a chariot decorated with flowers and flags. Beneath a floral bower of laurel and roses sat Hampton while a guard of two hundred men rode with the chariot.

The day on which Hampton appeared was known as "Hampton Day." He was the hero of the hour. A powerful, athletic man, weighing well over two hundred pounds, he was a good-humored, self-confident, and fearless fighter. Aristocratic by birth and training, he was instinctively democratic in manner. Never brilliant or spectacular, he shunned attempts at lofty flights of oratory. After a delicate compliment to the women present, he would launch into a strong, clear campaign speech, largely directed to the Negroes. Although never excitable he was a man of intense feeling, but very practical and moderate when the time came for action. This first quality satisfied the feelings of white South Carolinians; the second the necessities of the times.

[55] *Ibid.*, Oct. 19, 1876.

The manner of the campaign indicated a very thorough and elaborate organization of the Democrats. The reorganization plans called for efficient county organizations. Democratic clubs were formed and a determined effort was made to get every white man, and as many Negroes as possible, to join. For example, the Barnwell County executive committee, of which Johnson Hagood, later candidate for comptroller-general, was chairman, drew up a plan of organization on August 1, fifteen days before the state convention. That county had already decided to run a Straightout county ticket. To obtain the full white vote, a committee of one was to call upon any white voter not a member of a Democratic club and "respectfully and cordially" invite him to join. Should anyone fail to respond to this invitation, a second committee of two members should "urge him by every consideration that can be presented, not to desert his kindred and country in this supreme effort at deliverance; and to tell him that his decision will determine whether we regard him as friend or foe. . . . Should this last appeal fail register that man as a radical and treat him as such."[56]

"The ordinary tactics of election," such as public speakings, barbecues, and meetings for discussion were to be avoided. The Democratic clubs were to meet at least twice a month, the transactions of the club to be made public only by its authority.[57]

Thus every white man was to be given ample opportunity to declare himself; no doubt many found it convenient to ally themselves with the Democrats even though at heart they were sympathetic with the Radicals. During the campaign several prominent Radicals, such as Judges T. H. Cooke, C. P. Townsend, and T. J. Mackey, came out for Hampton and spoke for him. It became customary to speak of the white Radicals who

[56] Manuscript in possession of J. C. Keel, Allendale, South Carolina.

[57] *Ibid.* For a more extreme plan of campaign drawn up by M. W. Gary of Edgefield, see Appendix.

went over to the Democrats as "crossing Jordan." Of three hundred white Radicals in Pickens County, it was reported that all but twenty had "crossed Jordan." White voters were almost solid for Hampton; it was said that Chamberlain, omitting office holders, did not have five hundred white supporters.[58]

During the campaign many of the Democrats, especially those in the rifle clubs, were attired in red shirts. For that reason it is frequently referred to as the "Red Shirt" campaign. This custom was said to have originated after the Hamburg affair when most of the members of the Sweetwater sabre club and others, indicted for murder and conspiracy to murder, were en route to Aiken to arrange bail. It was suggested that, though assembled as prisoners, they should wave the bloody shirt as a token of defiance. Accordingly the materials were purchased and the shirts made by ladies in Aiken. The red shirts were again worn on August 12 when Chamberlain spoke in Edgefield; they became a distinguishing uniform of the Democrats.[59]

* * * * *

Vastly more important than any formal organization were the rifle clubs organized in great number in the summer and fall of 1876. Just as the Negro militia and the state constabulary did much to carry the state for Scott in 1870, so did the rifle clubs exert a powerful influence for Hampton. The rifle clubs, or sabre clubs as they were usually called when mounted, were composed of white Democrats who were organized in armed companies, ostensibly for home protection and to prevent outbreaks of violence. The clubs were used for political purposes and the display of armed force intimidated many

[58] Williams, in Columbia *State*, Dec. 12, 1926; Hagood, in *South Carolina in 1876*, p. 550.

[59] Benjamin R. Tillman, *The Struggle of '76*, 34 ff.; D. S. Henderson in Columbia *State*, Sept. 22, 1911; U. R. Brooks in *ibid.*, Aug. 18, 1910. It became quite fashionable for women to wear red trimmings:

Red ribbons round their waists,
Red ribbons in their hair,
Red ribbons to their tastes,
Pinned to them everywhere.
—Columbia *Register*, Oct. 13, 1876.

voters. This was known as the "Mississippi Plan" and in South Carolina was sometimes referred to as the "Edgefield" or "shotgun" policy.

Rifle clubs were not new to the state. There had been a few companies during Scott's administration that were supplied with state arms. At that time rifle clubs were supposed to be for social purposes; dozens of charters were granted to companies, many of them Radical, as the names Grant and Wilson, Lincoln, Scott, Sherman, indicated.[60] In 1874 and again in 1875 the adjutant-general called the attention of the legislature to the fact that a large number of the state arms were in the possession of independent organizations which were entirely separate from the militia and not under the law that governed the militia. "I hold this to be very injurious to the perfection and good government of military bodies, and also one of the most dangerous elements of good and safe society. . . ."[61]

As early as the spring of 1876 Democratic leaders resolved to use violent methods if necessary. At that time M. W. Gary wrote to Mississippi leaders in regard to the plan of action by which they had "redeemed" their state the previous year.[62] Gary was an uncompromising Straightouter who was inclined to be violent both in speech and action. It was his friend Butler, "the hero of Hamburg," who nominated Hampton at the August convention. Each man on the Democratic state ticket was an ex-Confederate officer and was said to bear the scars of battle. Immediately after the nomination of Hampton, the number of clubs increased by about two hundred,[63] although it was said that very few of them were armed, that they were only Democratic clubs but were called rifle clubs after the excitement of the campaign.[64] It was admitted that they were organized for political purposes but were armed only for protec-

[60] See *Stat. S. C., 1870-74.*
[61] *Reports and Resolutions, 1874-75,* p. 632; *ibid., 1875-76,* pp. 667-68; *Stat. S. C.,* XV, 560-61.

[62] Henderson, in *State,* Sept. 22, 1911.
[63] Haskell, *South Carolina in 1876,* I, 828.
[64] *Ibid.,* p. 829.

MARTIN WITHERSPOON GARY, BOLD ADVOCATE OF
THE EDGEFIELD OR SHOTGUN POLICY OF 1876

tion. Almost every issue of the *News and Courier* carried notices of the formation of rifle clubs.[65]   In the latter part of October, H. V. Redfield, a correspondent of the *Cincinnati Commercial,* was writing: "There is no denying but what the whites have set out to carry this State according to the Mississippi plan. It is as plain to a man upon the ground as the light of the sun. They are determined to carry the election, and nothing but the presence of Federal troops will keep them . . . from doing it, and they may do it anyway."[66]

Chamberlain stated, October 4, that rifle organizations "exist in every county in the State, and that in many, if not most, of the counties they embrace a large majority of the white men between the ordinary limits of age for military duty, as well as a large number both below and above such limits . . . these organizations are armed, officered, drilled, to a considerable extent at least, in the manual and military movements appropriate . . . they have appeared in public . . . with their arms and under command of their officers . . . they serve as the basis of political organization. . . ."[67]   A later check showed at least 290 clubs in the state.[68]   The total number of members was put at 14,350.[69]   A general organization of the rifle clubs was formed under the following officers: General James Connor, Commander; Major Theodore G. Barker, Commander of the

---

[65] Week of Sept. 2-9 for example. Speaking of the Pendleton Club: "The club will be uniformed with red jackets, and will muster one hundred strong." Not all Red Shirts, of course, were members of rifle clubs.

[66] Quoted in the *News and Courier,* Nov. 1, 1876.

[67] See Appendix.   Letter to Haskell, quoted in Allen, *Chamberlain's Administration,* p. 383.

[68] Divided among the counties as follows: Abbeville, 13; Aiken, 10; Anderson, 20; Barnwell, 7; Beaufort, 24; Charleston, 20; Chester, 2; Colleton, 14; Darlington, 22; Edgefield, 35; Fairfield, 13; Georgetown, 1; Greenville, 4; Horry, 1; Kershaw, 15; Laurens, 15; Lexington, 6; Marlboro, 8; Newberry, 21; Oconee, 2; Orangeburg, 14; Pickens, 7; Richland, 5; Spartanburg, 1; Sumter, 4; Williamsburg, 4; York, 2. Five counties, Chesterfield, Clarendon, Lancaster, Marion, and Union had clubs but their location and commanders could not be definitely ascertained.—*South Carolina in 1876,* III, 509-10.

[69] *Ibid.*

Lower Division, and Colonel Samuel B. Pickens, Commander of the Upper Division.[70]

In regard to the rifle clubs there were two points of view, one held by the Democrats the other by the Radicals. To Chamberlain a "leading feature" of the canvass was the "constant attendance" upon the Democratic meetings of the clubs, "acting in their organized character and capacity." Yet in no instance had such clubs organized since December 1, 1874, been given authority for their existence by the governor, nor did any such organizations form any part of the military forces of the state. In fact, by the revised statutes they were plainly illegal, not only not authorized but actually forbidden. "But their organization is not more illegal than their objects. Those objects are disclosed by their conduct, and are no more doubtful than the fact of their existence. . . . You know, as I know, that the Republican voters of this State are not organized for successful resistance to the aggressions of the Democratic Rifle Clubs."[71]

The unhappy experiences of Chamberlain in his personal canvass in July and August were not easily forgotten. From the time of his nomination until October 14 there was no state canvass by his party. After that date the Radicals managed to hold one meeting in each county before the election, but the local leaders in the upper part of the state were afraid to go to the meetings. Chamberlain himself did not speak in the canvass, "simply because it was not considered safe. . . . I remained in Columbia constantly, for that and for no other reason."[72] "The exceedingly violent tone of the men who were chiefly responsible for inaugurating the straightout policy was one cause of fear"; another was the "policy of a division of time" which "was insisted upon by the democrats," and which

---

[70] C. Irvine Walker, *The Carolina Rifle Club*, p. 53.
[71] Letter to Haskell, Oct. 4, 1876.

Quoted in Allen, *Chamberlain's Administration*, pp. 383 ff.
[72] *South Carolina in 1876*, II, 24.

"amounted to simply giving up the meeting to them; and you could not get quiet, peaceable republicans to come out and expose themselves to such treatment after they had one or two experiences of it. . . . I think the purpose was to prevent me and others from making a thorough canvass. . . ."[73] Radical speakers were uncomfortable when they passed through groups of mounted men "drawn up in the line of battle" and "not a man smiled." The shouts and yells of men who galloped up and told the speaker it was no use to talk for Chamberlain and the Radical ticket or who demanded his picture "to scare rats away" meant disaster to any Radical gathering.[74]

On the other hand, Democratic partisans claimed that arms used in the rifle clubs were not for political purposes but were only for protection.[75] In Barnwell County the rifle clubs were not used for political purposes,[76] and Hampton did not see more than twenty pistols exhibited during the entire canvass.[77] "I can state that although I spoke at fifty-seven large meetings. . . . I never saw an organized armed body of men at any of those meetings." "I not only declared my disapprobation of any intimidation, but I said there should be none; that if there were any attempts made looking in that direction anywhere in the State, I should withdraw from the canvass; and, furthermore, that if any effort should be successful on the part of the democratic party to violate any of the pledges that I had made for them, I should resign my office."

Every effort was made to prevent a conflict between whites and blacks. Democratic leaders did not want a large force of Federal troops in the state. During the canvass two meetings of the state executive committee were held at which every county was represented. Instructions were given not to resort

[73] Ibid.
[74] See experience of Richard T. Greener, ibid., I, 230 ff.
[75] Haskell, chairman of the Democratic executive committee and a member of

three rifle clubs, in South Carolina in 1876, I, 824 ff.
[76] Hagood, ibid., pp. 549 ff.
[77] Ibid., p. 985.

to violence, threats, or any illegal means to secure votes. Polls were to be watched on election, but "there should not be one finger raised in violence, or any threat."[78] It was understood that there should be a show of strength "that it might have its moral and legitimate influence upon our adversaries," but no force should be used. Hagood said that he rode twenty miles and back one day to put a stop to rifle club demonstrations.[79] A circular issued by the executive committee of the party in Barnwell County stated that "Rioting before or at the polls, or race collisions brought about by the whites are deemed almost insane folly."[80]

The whites had some excuse for organizing for protection. Some serious difficulties took place in the state during the summer and fall of 1876. A strike of Negro agricultural laborers in Colleton County in May threatened the destruction of the crops and property of the planters. A more serious strike occurred among the rice field Negroes in Beaufort County along the Combahee River. In August, just at the time when it was absolutely necessary to gather the crop, about two hundred Negroes struck for an advance of 50 per cent in wages. Some other plantation hands who refused to join them were imprisoned in outhouses. The sheriff and a posse were overpowered, and the governor sent Robert Smalls, with a company of militia, to their aid. Before the ringleaders were arrested and the mob dispersed, the whites had collected for safety, and assistance had been offered from Charleston.

A riot of a political nature occurred in Charleston on the night of September 6. After the meeting of a club of colored Democrats, the leaders, for safety, were escorted home by a group of whites. On the way, they were attacked by a mob of Negroes and pistols were fired by both parties. Not until several whites and blacks had been wounded did the police get

---

[78] Haskell, *ibid.*, p. 837.
[79] *Ibid.*, p. 537.

[80] MS in possession of J. C. Keel, Allendale, South Carolina.

the affair under control. The next day one white man died from his wounds.[81] During the excitement the Carolina Rifle Club was drawn up before Hibernian Hall, but Major Barker would not allow it to proceed to the scene of battle on King Street. On September 9 Chamberlain issued a proclamation discountenancing and forbidding the presence upon the streets of armed bodies, whether organized or not. Meanwhile, Major Barker urged every white man to report to some rifle club or remain at call until the trouble was settled. And it is reported by an observer that for three months mounted men patrolled the streets from nine o'clock in the evening till sunrise.[82]

A more serious disturbance was a race riot at Ellenton in Aiken County. The trouble arose over the attempt of a white posse to arrest two Negroes who had attempted to rob the house of a white woman. The Negroes were pursued, one was overtaken, identified, and severely wounded when he attempted to escape. The second Negro attempted to escape and was said to have sought protection from a band of armed Negroes. A warrant for his arrest was issued by a colored trial justice, and when A. P. Brown and a posse of fourteen white men attempted to execute the warrant they were fired upon by Negroes. After a parley both parties agreed to disperse. Meanwhile, whites had been fired upon from ambush and one white man killed. The wreck of a Port Royal train was caused when Negroes tore up the track, and a mill and gin house were burnt. This was on Sunday night. By Monday morning one hundred white men had assembled, the number of whites increasing until it was estimated at from three to eight hundred. There were several groups of whites and blacks moving about the country under arms, the Negroes usually remaining in the vicinity of the swamps. In the conflicts which ensued, two

[81] *News and Courier*, Sept. 7, 1876. [82] *Ibid.*, Sept. 8, 11, 12, 1876; Williams, in *State*, Oct. 10, 1926.

white men were killed and eight wounded. Of the Negroes, fifteen were killed and two wounded. At least that was the current report. No one knows how many were killed; some estimated that between eighty and one hundred and twenty-five lost their lives. The riot was broken up by Federal troops, who were dispatched to Silverton and Rouse's Bridge in Aiken County, where most of the fighting took place. The whites were well armed and commanded by men like A. P. Butler and Johnson Hagood. The Negroes were armed but seemed to have no military organization. Had not the Federal troops interfered, the number of Negroes killed would probably have totaled several hundred.[83]

On October 16, five white men were killed and sixteen wounded by Negroes at a political meeting near Cainhoy in Charleston County. This was one of the few joint discussions of the campaign. Both sides had agreed to go unarmed, but after the speaking had begun a Negro fired a pistol into the air, and other Negroes rushed into an old building and into a swamp where guns were hidden. The whites took refuge in a brick building but were forced to retreat, and an old white man was knocked down and killed as he attempted to escape. The few whites who had pistols could not cope with the better armed Negroes and they retreated to Cainhoy. Upon the appeal of citizens of Charleston, a company of Federal soldiers was dispatched for protection.[84]

Meanwhile, on October 7, the Governor had issued a proclamation disbanding the rifle clubs. He commanded the "unlawful combinations and assemblages of persons" in Aiken and Barnwell counties to disperse. Also "combinations of men

---

[83] *News and Courier*, Oct. 3, 1876; Tillman, *The Struggle of '76*, pp. 56 ff.; Chamberlain in *N. Y. Tribune*, Oct. 25, 1876; Report of commanding officer of U. S. troops at Aiken, Sept. 23, 1876, cited in Allen, *Chamberlain's Administration*, pp. 416 ff.; *South Carolina in 1876*, I, II, III, *passim; Recent Election in South Carolina, passim.* It was at Chamberlain's request that troops were sent.

[84] *News and Courier*, Oct. 18, 24, 1876; Allen, *Chamberlain's Administration*, pp. 421-22.

commonly known as 'rifle clubs' " were ordered "forthwith to disband and cease to exist in any place and under any circumstances in the State." Should the proclamation be disregarded for the space of three days, he would appeal to the President.[85] On the same day the Democratic executive committee issued an address "To the People of the United States" in which it was stated that in "a period of profound peace" the Governor had declared it impossible to enforce the law in Aiken and Barnwell counties by the ordinary course of judicial proceedings. The charges of the Governor were declared "false and libelous." "Perfect peace and the profoundest quiet prevail. . . . We assert earnestly, with a full sense of our responsibility, that no condition of things exists in this State which justifies so extraordinary a proceeding on the part of Governor Chamberlain. Its sole object is to irritate and provoke collisions which may be the excuse for an appeal to the administration . . . to garrison the State. . . ."[86]

On October 9 a second address was issued by the Democratic committee. On the same day Chamberlain addressed the nation: ". . . I am at this moment in possession of authentic legal evidence to substantiate every fact and statement made by me. . . . And I further assert, upon my full official and personal responsibility, that the lawlessness, terrorism, and violence to which I have referred far exceed in extent and atrocity any statements yet made public. . . ." On October 26, the day set aside for religious services throughout the state at the sugges-

[85] *News and Courier*, Oct. 10, 1876.

[86] *News and Courier*, Oct. 9, 1876. A telegram from Chief Justice Moses stated: "I shall require very strong evidence to satisfy me that South Carolina is an armed camp." Associate Justice Willard, who had only been in the state for one week after a three months absence, stated: "I have seen no violence; on the contrary, as far as I have had intercourse with the gentlemen of your party, I have observed less disposition to excited statement and personal bitterness than during any of the previous political campaigns. . . . I am satisfied that it is the intention of the leading members of your party to prevent such a state of things, and I believe they have the ability to do so." Judges Mackey, Cooke, Shaw, Northrop, and Carpenter, said all was quiet in their circuits. *News and Courier*, Oct. 9, 11, 1876. Hampton sent telegrams to Butler and Hagood: "Use your influence to keep our people . . . from resistance to martial law."

tion of the Democratic executive committee, there appeared in the *News and Courier* an address by citizens of Charleston. This address, signed by the most eminent citizens,[87] declared that it was "not true" that the white people of the state were disloyal, that any counties were in "a state of insurrection or domestic violence . . . or that law and the process cannot be duly enforced," that "the few 'Rifle Clubs' " were "combinations of men against the law," and that in the recent race collisions the white people were the aggressors. It was true, declared the address, that there was in the state "a most active, earnest and excited canvass to overthrow corrupt rule," and that the rifle clubs were ordered to disband while the colored militia were allowed to remain in organization and in possession of their arms.

Meanwhile Chamberlain, stating that the rifle clubs had not disbanded, had appealed to Grant. On October 14, General W. T. Sherman, commanding the United States army, sent the following telegram to General T. H. Ruger, commanding the troops in South Carolina: "We are all back from California. If you want anything say so. I want all measures to originate with you. . . ." Ruger replied on the 16th: "Think I have troops sufficient. . . . Have nineteen companies . . . in stations of one to four companies. . . . If I need more troops I will ask for them. . . ."[88]

On the 17th Grant issued a proclamation commanding "all persons engaged in said unlawful and insurrectionary proceedings to disperse and retire peaceably to their respective abodes within three days." The same day, Cameron, secretary of war, instructed Sherman to order "all the available force in the

[87] They included S. Y. Tupper, president of the Chamber of Commerce, W. M. Wightman, Bishop of M. E. Church, South, W. B. W. Howe, Episcopal bishop of the Diocese of South Carolina, P. N. Lynch, Catholic bishop of Charleston, John Forrest, pastor First Presbyterian Church, J. L. Girardeau, professor in the theological seminary, and the pastors of seven other churches as well as eight bank presidents.

[88] Quoted in Henry T. Thompson, *Ousting the Carpetbagger from South Carolina*, p. 126.

military division of the Atlantic" to report to General Ruger at Columbia.[89]

Again Hampton sent telegrams urging the people to submit peaceably. On October 18 the Democratic executive committee issued an address to the people of the state: ". . . We make this declaration of our innocence. . . . We bow in perfect submission. . . ." The rifle clubs disbanded. At least they did not meet together publicly for display or military exercises. Actually, however, they retained their identity, although not formally recognizing their officers. They were frequently reorganized under new names: Allendale Mounted Baseball Club (with team of 150 members), Mother's Little Helpers, First Baptist Church Sewing Circle, Hampton and Tilden Musical Club—formerly the Columbia Flying Artillery.

Additional troops were sent into the state. All told, there were 16 companies distributed as follows: Charleston, 1; Columbia, 3; Yorkville, 1; Blackville, 2; Aiken, 3; Laurensville, 1; Edgefield, 2; Lancaster, 1; Marion, 1; Abbeville, 1.[90] Usually the troops were quite friendly with the whites. At Edgefield, the troops recently transferred from Atlanta were given an uproarious ovation by white men and women who cleverly assumed that the soldiers had come to protect them and the colored Democrats.[91]

*   *   *   *   *

Not only did rifle clubs exert a very persuasive influence over the Negro, but other organized efforts were made to get his vote. The Democratic platform called upon all citizens, "irrespective of race, color or previous condition," to rally with the party for the redemption of the state. Hampton, who since 1867 had favored qualified suffrage,[92] said that one reason for his nomination was that it would bring a "large number" of

[89] Quoted in Allen, *Chamberlain's Administration*, pp. 406-7.

[90] *Report of Sec. of War. 44 Cong., 2 Sess.*, I, 50, 52.

[91] Williams, in *State*, Sept. 26, 1926.

[92] *South Carolina in 1876*, III, 454.

colored voters to the support of the Democrats.[93]   There were
no Negroes in the Democratic nominating convention nor
were there any on the state ticket, but in several counties colored men were nominated for local offices or for the legislature.[94]

Early in the canvass, in fact before Hampton's nomination,
some counties with a Negro majority determined to elect a
Straightout ticket. In Barnwell, for example, it was estimated
that the Negro majority to be overcome was less than one thousand. Therefore, five hundred Negroes voting the Democratic
ticket or one thousand not voting would give the county to
the Straightouts. It is worth while to notice in detail the plan
of the Democrats to secure the necessary majority. "It is desirable that our attention be concentrated upon one thousand
selected Negroes . . . and that the other Negroes be let alone.
Those selected for our effort should not be party leaders, office
seekers or others who may expect to make out of the Radical
party. They should belong to the following classes: (1) Those
who have acquired property and pay taxes. (2) Those whose
relations to, and standing with, whites are best. (3) Those
who are poorest and most dependent upon the whites. (4) The
weaker characters generally. It is deemed best to operate upon
the individual Negro, and carefully avoid attempting to influence him in masses. . . . When your register of Negro voters
is complete, submit it to your club and require each member
to select such Negro or Negroes as he thinks he can influence.
. . . Make a separate list of those members who think they have
no influence with the Negro voters and detail each one to look
after one or more lukewarm or infirm white men in your precinct and see that they vote. There will be a list of Negroes
reported to your club, if the work is thoroughly done, who will
not vote with us, but will promise to stay away from the polls.

[93] *Ibid.*, p. 990. Hampton promised to   [94] Haskell, *South Carolina in 1876*, I,
protect the Negro in all his rights.   834.

To look after these and see that they adhere to their promise: enroll the white men of your precinct under the voting age, before the day of the election and assign each one to his Negro. ..."[95]

A very effective argument was that illustrated by resolutions adopted by Democratic clubs in Barnwell and Orangeburg counties and elsewhere. Club members promised not to rent land, or furnish a home, or give employment to Radical leaders and members of their family. Neither would they furnish any supplies, such as provisions, farm implements, stock, and so on, "except so far as contracts for the present year" were concerned. Nothing was to be purchased from, or sold to, any Radical leader or member of his family. Provided, however, that such resolutions were to become null and void, if by resolution of the club, such leaders ceased to be called Radical.[96]

Martin R. Delaney, a leading black man and candidate for lieutenant governor on the reform ticket of 1874, declared for Hampton. He said that he had but one duty left him, "to aid that effort which tends to bring about a union of the two races ... in one common interest in the State."[97] The colored Democrats were organized into clubs which were affiliated with the white clubs. It was said that the colored converts had steadily increased in number as well as in influence until sufficient to turn the scale in favor of the Democracy. It was thought "not prudent" to give the whole truth of the strength of the colored Democracy, but Abbeville had three or four colored clubs, the colored Democrats in Aiken numbered three hundred or four hundred, Anderson had several hundred colored Democrats, Barnwell, Chester, Colleton, Clarendon, etc., had a large number of colored clubs.[98] H. V. Redfield of the *Cin-*

[95] MS in possession of J. C. Keel, Allendale, South Carolina.
[96] *News and Courier*, Sept. 23, 1876;
Haskell, *South Carolina in 1876*, I, 834.
[97] *News and Courier*, Sept. 26, 1876.
[98] *Ibid.*, Oct. 13, 1876.

cinnati Commercial said that about seven thousand Negroes had been enrolled.[99]

But it was easier to get a Negro to declare for Hampton than it was to get his vote. Just as white Radicals were far more odious than colored Radicals to the Democrats, so were black Democrats far more odious to colored Radicals than white Democrats. Negro Democrats were protected by whites where possible; they were in constant danger of beatings and abuse. The Negro women who refused to hear Hampton speak were very bitter toward colored Democrats. Many who wished to join colored clubs were prevented by the threats and taunts of wives and female relatives. Women refused to wash their husbands' clothes or cook for them if they were Democrats. One Negro lawyer with a Tilden badge was run out of town after his landlady had requested him to move. Infuriated Negro women tore the red shirts from the backs of Negroes. One Negro shouted "Hurrah for Hampton" and the women tore his clothes off—"They didn't hurt me at all but just tore all my clothes off." Another was locked out by his wife—"said she wouldn't have any Democratic nigger sleep with her as long as she lived." It was not unusual for Negroes to be turned out of the church on account of their politics.[100] It is impossible to know how many Negroes voted for Hampton. It was said that the better class and more intelligent Negroes remained steadfast Republicans. "The few dozen or hundred that voted the Democratic ticket in Laurens were, as a rule, trifling, lazy, and careless fellows, who lived by tips from their white friends rather than by labor."[101] In Marion County it was said about four hundred Negroes went Democratic,[102] and between five and six hundred in Laurens County.[103] One intelligent Negro said that at least twelve

[99] Quoted in *ibid.*, Nov. 2, 1876.
[100] *South Carolina in 1876*, I, 592, 914, 939, 959, 960, 556, 560, 602, 605, 563, etc.

[101] W. W. Ball, *A Boy's Recollection of the Red Shirt Campaign*, p. 15.
[102] *South Carolina in 1876*, II, 595.
[103] *Ibid.*, pp. 173, 568.

thousand were enrolled to vote for Hampton and that about ten thousand did vote for him.[104] Chamberlain stated that as the result of inquiry and canvassing on the part of members of the Republican party who were interested in the question, he believed there were perhaps three thousand Negroes who voted for Hampton.[105] After Reconstruction the members of that group were known as "Hampton Democrats" and were allowed to vote in the Democratic primaries.

[104] S. L. Hutchens, colored lawyer, in *South Carolina in 1876*, I, 605.

[105] *South Carolina in 1876*, II, 40.

CHAPTER XIX

THE DUAL GOVERNMENT

A S to the election itself, little need be said. Both Democrats and Republicans claimed to have elected the state officials and a majority of the General Assembly; likewise each party charged the other with fraud. The Republicans, after throwing out the returns from certain counties, claimed 86,216 votes for Chamberlain as against 83,071 for Hampton; to Gleaves went 86,620 votes as against 82,521 for Simpson. The Democrats, on the other hand, threw out no returns and claimed 92,261 votes for Hampton as against 91,127 for Chamberlain. They claimed the defeat of Gleaves by a vote of 91,689 to 91,150.

That both parties committed fraud in various ways is not to be doubted; that adherents of the Democratic party were responsible for most of the fraud is equally certain. A study of the election returns proves little except that a full ballot was cast, and that in certain counties more ballots were cast than there were voters according to the state census of 1875. In all but the four counties of Charleston, Edgefield, Laurens, and Williamsburg, the voters were classified according to color. In only two counties did the colored vote exceed the census figures, the excess being 928; the excess of the white vote, on the other hand, was 3,505 in the counties in which the classification was made, and in the non-classified counties there was an estimated excess of 3,026. In four counties the white poll fell below the census figures by 328 votes; the Negro vote, however, fell below the census figures by 6,727 votes.[1]

Due to the presence at the polls of United States troops and to the expressed purpose of the Democrats to avoid riots and

[1] H. R. R. No. 175, Pt. 2, 44 Cong., 2 Sess., p. 62.

bloodshed, the election was attended with only minor disturbances. However, the troops did not prevent cheating at the polls. No one knows how many ballot boxes were stuffed, how many illegal voters cast ballots, or how many young white men of North Carolina and Georgia crossed into neighboring counties to aid the South Carolina Democrats. There are reputable white men living in South Carolina who boast of having voted 18 or 20 times in the election. Parties of white men on horseback cast their ballots at many polls. The bold actions of organized white men served not only to intimidate many election officials, but also to prevent Negroes from reaching the ballot box. In some counties, especially in Charleston and Beaufort, ardent Negro Republicans intimidated Democratic Negroes.[2]

[2] The testimony taken by committees investigating the election of 1876 proved beyond a doubt that fraud was committed in many ways. See index to *Recent Election in S. C.*, pp. 471-72; *S. C. in 1876*, index, p. xiii. A. B. Williams, a contemporary, writing many years later, says that the Democrats cheated, intimidated, bribed, bulldozed, and repeated where possible and that the Republicans did likewise. He describes it as a war and a revolution, a battle for life, where force and cunning displaced obedience to the law. He says that at many places U. S. soldiers who were relieved from duty late in the day changed clothes and voted for Hampton many times.— Columbia *State*, Feb. 13, 1927.

The greatest amount of fraud was in Edgefield and Laurens counties. At Edgefield, M. W. Gary, leading exponent of the Mississippi plan, had several hundred picked men with provisions and arms to take possession of the Court House and Masonic Hall. The Negroes were forced to vote at a small school house, and late in the day it was seen that it would be impossible for all the Negroes to vote before the poll closed. When a Negro leader with several hundred followers marched towards the Court House to vote, Gary ordered his men to pack the steps and corridors so that entrance would be impossible. When the Negroes protested to General Ruger, he asked Gary to let the Negroes vote. Gary refused and was reported to have replied: "By God, sir, I'll not do it. I will keep the compact I made with you this morning, that white men and Negroes should vote at separate boxes."—*Ibid.*, Aug. 18, 1910. See testimony in *S. C. in 1876*, p. xii. Thus a normally Republican county returned a Democratic majority of 3,134 out of a total of 9,374, which was 2,252 more votes than the total number of adult males in the preceding year. In Laurens County, the Democratic majority was 1,112 as against a Republican majority of 1,077 in 1874. For the election figures see H. R. R. No. 175, Pt. 2, 44 Cong. 2 Sess., p. 62; *S. C. in 1876*, III, 578. To catch the unwary Negro the Democrats counterfeited the Union Republican ticket in various ways. Some ballots were headed by the picture of Hayes and Wheeler but carried the name of no presidential candidate. Instead it carried the name of Hampton for governor along with Republican county candidates.

Since conflicting returns were reported and since both parties claimed the election, much depended upon the reports of the county canvassers and of the State Board of Canvassers. The commissioners of election were required to meet at each county seat on the Tuesday immediately following the election and organize as a county board of canvassers, and within ten days to make such statements of the votes "as the nature of the election required," and to transmit to the State Board of Canvassers any protests and all papers relating to the election. Duplicate statements were to be filed in the office of the county clerk and, if there were no clerk, then in the office of the secretary of state. Also three separate statements of the votes, containing the names of the persons voted for and the number of votes cast for each, were to be transmitted by mail to the governor, secretary of state, and comptroller-general.

The State Board of Canvassers at this time consisted of five persons: H. E. Hayne, secretary of state; F. L. Cardozo, treasurer; T. C. Dunn, comptroller-general; William Stone, attorney-general, and H. W. Purvis, adjutant and inspector-general. Three of these persons, Hayne, Cardozo, and Dunn, constituting a majority of the Board, were candidates for reëlection. This body was to meet on or before the tenth of November next after the general election, "for the purpose of canvassing the votes for all persons voted for at such election." The Board should then, "upon the certified copies of the statements made by the Board of county canvassers, proceed to make a statement of the whole number of votes given at such election for the various officers and for each of them voted for, distinguishing the several Counties in which they were given." They should certify such statements to be correct and upon such statements should "proceed to determine and declare what persons have been by the greatest number of votes duly elected. ... They shall have power, and it is made their duty, to decide all cases under protest or contest that may arise, when the power to do so does not, by the Constitution, reside in some other body." It was provided that in a contest for the election of a governor the Senate and the House, acting separately, should hear and determine the facts in the case.[3]

A contest of the election for governor was to be determined by the General Assembly under the provision of the constitution which provided: "In all elections held by the people under this constitution, the person or persons who shall receive the highest number of votes shall be declared elected."[4]

Very soon after the election it became known that, according to the returns or statements of the county boards of canvassers, Hampton had certainly received a majority of the votes for governor. It was also believed that the other candidates on the Democratic state ticket were elected; but as to the presidential electors there was great uncertainty, the chances being, apparently, that the Republican ticket had received a majority.

As to the election in the different counties for members of the legislature, it appeared that the Democrats had elected a majority of the members of the House; but the elections in Edgefield, Laurens, and Barnwell counties, in which the Democratic candidates had the majority, were contested, and it was feared and believed by many that the members of the State Board of Canvassers would assume judicial powers and give the certificates of election for those counties to the Republican candidates and thus give to that party the control of the organization of the House.

It was also feared and believed by many that the State Board would set aside, disregard, or ignore the returns of the county boards of canvassers for governor and lieutenant governor and

---

[3] *Stat. S. C.*, XIV, 395-97. Act approved Mar. 1, 1870. By the original act the state auditor and the chairman of the committee on privileges and elections were members of the Board, but the position of state auditor had been abolished and the chairman of the committee on privileges and elections did not serve on the Board. The Board should sit for ten days only; its determination should be delivered to the secretary of state.

[4] Art. VIII, Sec. 10.

the state ticket generally, and thus give a majority to Chamberlain and the other Republican candidates.

The Board met on Friday, November 10, organized, and adjourned until Saturday. On that day the Board unanimously resolved that the returns of the election of members of the General Assembly would be considered in connection with any protests or notice of contest that might be presented, "this having been the established practice of the Board heretofore." James Connor, Democratic candidate for attorney-general and counsel for the Democratic candidates, appeared before the Board with the following protests: that the state canvassers had no duties or powers in regard to the election of governor and lieutenant governor; that the Board had no right or duty in regard to the election of electors for president and vice-president and members of Congress, except to aggregate the vote of the respective counties, and certify what persons had received the greatest number of votes; that the function and duties of the Board in the contests for state offices were judicial, but that it was illegal for Cardozo, Dunn, and Hayne, candidates for reëlection, to hear and decide any contest and protest in regard to said offices; and that the Board could only aggregate the vote for members of the General Assembly and declare what persons had received the greatest number of votes for the Senate and House of Representatives, and certify such statements to the secretary of state, who should transmit a copy of such certified determination to each person declared to be elected.

To these protests the Board replied by resolving that it did not propose to canvass the returns for governor and lieutenant-governor, but that it had the right to hear protests as to the election of electors for president and vice-president and members of Congress, and that it was the opinion of the Board that the treasurer, secretary of state, and comptroller-general had the right to sit as members of the Board and determine all questions coming before them, "except that neither of the said officers shall vote upon his own election."[5]

This action was not satisfactory to the Democrats. On November 14, four days after the Board began its proceedings, the Democrats applied to the Supreme Court, which was then in session in Columbia, for two writs, one of prohibition to restrain the Board from exercising judicial functions, and one of mandamus to compel it to perform the merely ministerial functions of ascertaining from the returns which candidates had the highest number of votes and of then certifying the statements thereof to the secretary of state. An order was issued to the Board and secretary of state to show cause why writs of prohibition should not be issued. The return was made on the 16th by D. T. Corbin and R. B. Elliott, attorneys for the respondents, and on the 17th Chief Justice Moses issued a mandamus to the Board to aggregate the returns and ascertain the persons who had received the greatest number of votes for the offices for which they were candidates, and to certify their action in the premises to the court.[6]

On November 21 the Board submitted its report but at the same time protested against the claim that the Board was by law compelled to render account of its actions to the court. The Board stated that many allegations and evidences of fraud and other irregularities had been filed regarding the election in Edgefield, Barnwell, Laurens, and other counties. The Board reported that the face of the returns showed the election of two Democratic state officers,[6a] four Republican congressmen, three Republican state officers, enough Democratic members of the General Assembly to give that party a majority of one on joint

[5] For the minutes of the Board see *Recent Election in S. C.*, Appendix, pp. 67-78.

[6] This order applied to all officers voted for at the election, except governor and lieutenant-governor, which were not in question by the proceedings. Justice Wright dissented from that part of the order which required the Board to certify its action to the court.

[6a] But not if certain votes cast for John B. Tolbert were counted for John R. Tolbert, and certain votes cast for F. C. Dunn were counted for T. C. Dunn.

ballot, and all the Republican electors by majorities averaging about 816.[7]

The original petition for mandamus related to the different classes of officers voted for at the general election. On November 21 Chief Justice Moses ordered that the petition be considered and determined by the Court as if several separate petitions had been filed, and on November 22 the Chief Justice rendered a decision so far as related to the election of members of the General Assembly.[8] The Chief Justice stated that by the Constitution[9] "each house shall judge of the election, return, and qualification of its own members." The machinery by which the choice of the electors might be made known, so far as it primarily appeared from the evidence, was through the appointment of precinct managers, boards of county canvassers, and the State Board of Canvassers. The several "statements" submitted to the Board provided the means, not of "judging the election, return, and qualification of members of either house," but of ascertaining who were entitled to the certificates. It was not competent for the Board to determine, as the House only could, who was the chosen member. Therefore, the Court issued a writ of peremptory mandamus commanding the Board "to declare duly elected to the offices of senators and members of the house" the persons who by the certificates of the Board to the Court had received the greatest number of votes. The secretary of state was commanded to transmit copies of the record to each person declared to be elected and a copy to the governor and to cause a copy to be printed in one or more newspapers.

Meanwhile the State Board had met on the same day at 10:00 A.M., corrected the returns so as to elect T. C. Dunn and

[7] For the documents in the case and for the report of the Board see *Recent Election in S. C.,* Appendix, pp. 78-114.

[8] The necessity of an immediate decision prevented the court from declaring its views of the extent of the character of the powers of the Board, except as to the election of members to the General Assembly. The ten day limit of the duration of the Board was up on the 22nd.

[9] Art. II, Sec. 14.

Top left: JONATHAN JASPER WRIGHT, MEMBER OF THE STATE SENATE, 1868-1870; ASSOCIATE JUSTICE OF THE SUPREME COURT, 1870-1877. *Top right:* A. J. WILLARD, ASSOCIATE JUSTICE OF THE SUPREME COURT, 1868-1877; CHIEF JUSTICE, 1877-1880. *Bottom left:* ROBERT BROWN ELLIOTT, MEMBER OF THE CONSTITUTIONAL CONVENTION, 1868; STATE HOUSE OF REPRESENTATIVES, 1868-1870; CONGRESS, 1871-1874; SPEAKER OF THE HOUSE, 1875-1876; CANDIDATE FOR ATTORNEY GENERAL, 1876. *Bottom right:* WILLIAM HENRY WALLACE, BRIGADIER GENERAL, C. S. A., SPEAKER OF THE WALLACE HOUSE, 1876.

J. R. Tolbert, declared the election of the Republican electors, and excluded from the statement any determination of the vote from Edgefield and Laurens counties.[10] The Board then adjourned at 12:48 P.M., before the order of the Court was served. On November 24 the Supreme Court, when notified of the action of the Board, issued a rule to show cause why a writ of peremptory mandamus should not be issued to the secretary of state requiring him to certify as duly elected the persons who had received the greatest number of votes for members of the General Assembly. On the same day the Supreme Court ordered Hayne to show cause why he should not be attached for contempt for failure to obey the mandits of the Court. The order was returnable at 4:00 P.M.; the members of the Board petitioned for additional time. This was not granted, however, and on November 25 the members of the Board were adjudged in contempt of court and ordered to pay a fine of $1,500 and to be placed in the custody of the sheriff of Richland County for confinement in the county jail until discharged by the order of the Court.[11]

On November 27, two days later, the United States Circuit Court, presided over by Judge Hugh L. Bond, began sessions in Columbia. The members of the Board petitioned the Federal Court for writs of habeas corpus. The petition set forth the transactions of the Board of Canvassers and the action of the Supreme Court. It further declared that in canvassing the returns it was necessary, from the nature of the election, to determine and certify the election of presidential electors, members of Congress, and other officers voted for. Thus the petitioners were deprived of their liberty for acts done in pursuance of laws of the United States. Judge Bond held that it was

[10] The secretary of state and attorney-general voted to include the Laurens vote, and the secretary of state voted to include the Edgefield vote, because the testimony before the Board in regard to the elections in those counties was entirely *ex parte*.

[11] *Recent Election in S. C.*, Appendix, pp. 114-33.

competent for a Federal Court to issue the writ of habeas corpus in favor of those imprisoned for contempt by a state court, "where the acts of alleged contempt were committed in the performance of duties created by the constitution and laws of the United States." Judge Bond stated that the Board of Canvassers was clothed with discretionary powers which required it to discriminate the votes, that it was a part of the executive department and was in no wise subject to the control of the judicial department. The prisoners were released.[12]

There was much protest against the action of the Board of Canvassers in excluding from the returns the vote of Edgefield and Laurens counties. Hayne, as secretary of state, issued certificates of election to fifty-nine Republican members of the House and to fifty-seven Democrats, with eight vacancies from the two counties named. The Senate had a Republican majority of five with two vacancies from the same counties. According to law the votes for governor and lieutenant governor were to be canvassed by the General Assembly; the control of that body, therefore, was of the utmost importance. The legislature met on Tuesday, November 28. On the preceding night Federal troops, under the command of General Thomas H. Ruger, who was instructed by President Grant through the Secretary of War "to sustain Governor Chamberlain in his authority against domestic violence" had been placed in the hall of the State House.[13]

[12] *News and Courier*, Dec. 2, 14, 1876. Nothing further was done in this matter. Proceedings against the canvassers were never pressed to a judgment. The members of the Supreme Court were Chief Justice F. J. Moses, Sr., A. J. Willard, and J. J. Wright. Wright was colored. It is charged by P. L. Haworth in *The Hayes-Tilden Disputed Presidential Election* (p. 149) that the Court were willing tools of the Democrats. He evidently gets his opinion from Walter Allen in *Chamberlain's Administration in S. C.*, p. 429. The Court had always been viewed with the highest respect by the bar; and its members had been elected by the Radical majority of the legislature. It is difficult to believe that the Court was swayed by personal opinions. On the other hand, Judge Bond was commonly said to be sympathetic (at least as early as 1871) with the Republicans; he had arrived in Columbia several days before court and had stayed at Chamberlain's house. See *News and Courier*, Nov. 21, 1876.

[13] Allen, *Chamberlain's Administration*, p. 435; *News and Courier*, Nov. 28, 1876.

There was a great deal of excitement in Columbia. The Democrats had confidently predicted that they would control the organization of the House. About noon the Democratic members-elect of the House, including the five members from Edgefield and the three from Laurens counties, a total of sixty-four, proceeded in a body from Carolina Hall to the State House. The column was headed by the delegations from Edgefield and Laurens. They found the door of the State House guarded by troops. On their demand for admission, they were told by John B. Dennis, who claimed to be acting as sergeant-at-arms, that they could not enter unless they had certificates from the secretary of state. The delegations from Edgefield and Laurens presented certificates of election issued by the Supreme Court. An officer of the army said that persons with certificates either from the secretary of state or from the Supreme Court could enter. The Democratic members proceeded to the door of the House of Representatives. Meanwhile, the Republican members, unhindered, had organized by electing E. W. M. Mackey as speaker. The door-keeper of the House refused the Democrats admission, declaring the Supreme Court certificates to be insufficient. After reading a protest, the Democrats withdrew to Carolina Hall, where they organized by electing William H. Wallace speaker.

The next day the Mackey House unseated the five Democratic members from Barnwell County, whose election had been conceded by the Board of Canvassers, and who held the certificate of the secretary of state, and admitted the five defeated Republicans.[14]

The Senate, with Lieutenant Governor Gleaves in the chair, organized with all hold-over members, and every newly elected

[14] The Mackey House, as organized, contained only five white members. For accounts of these proceedings see *News and Courier*, Nov. 28, 29, 1876; H. R. R. No. 175, Pt. 2, 44 Cong., 2 Sess., pp. 100-4, 126-29, 138-40, for the official journals and other papers; speech of T. J. Robertson in the U. S. Senate, Jan. 29, 1877; Allen, *Chamberlain's Administration*, pp. 435 ff.; Reynolds, *Reconstruction in S. C.*, pp. 408 ff.

member who had a certificate, present. The Democratic claim-ants from Edgefield, Laurens, and Abbeville were present but were not allowed to vote. The usual message was sent to the House, the protests of the Democratic senators being entered upon the Journal.[15]

On November 30 the Wallace House, which had been aug-mented by two Republicans who had left the Mackey House, proceeded to the State House. Some of the Democrats with certificates from the secretary of state were admitted before the door-keepers seemed to realize what was happening. Then, in spite of the protests of the door-keepers, all the Democratic claimants, including those without certificates, entered. In a short time the Republican members appeared and Mackey ascended the speaker's stand and demanded that Wallace va-cate the chair. A scene of great confusion followed. Wallace declared that he was the lawful speaker and invited Mackey to retire. When two sergeant-at-arms ascended the stand to enforce the orders of Wallace and Mackey, a number of men, both Democrats and Republicans, crowded around and blood-shed seemed imminent. Trouble was averted, however, when a Democratic member moved the appointment of a committee to adjust matters.[16]

Thus was seen the singular spectacle of two speakers and two Houses conducting deliberations in the same hall. Mo-tions, suggestions, questions, and protests were heard by the respective speakers; neither speaker, however, recognized mem-bers of the other House. For more than four days this con-test endured. Both Democrats and Republicans did not dare to leave the hall for fear that they would not be allowed to reënter. Food furnished to the Wallace House by citizens of Columbia was sometimes shared with the Mackey House. At

---

[15] *News and Courier*, Nov. 30, 1876.
[16] It was said that A. C. Haskell, with two pistols under his cloak, stood behind Mackey, with the latter's knowledge. W.

P. Houseal, in Columbia *State*, Dec. 12, 1926; Williams, in *ibid.*, Feb. 27, 1927; Morgan, *Recollections of a Rebel Reefer*, pp. 365-68.

night the noise of dual debates subsided while the would-be legislators slept on the floor or the dusky members sang the songs of their race. After the first excitement had worn off, there was much good feeling between the opposing bodies; sometimes the whites joined in the songs of the Negroes, and when the hall was left in darkness because the gas bill was unpaid, the Democrats paid it.

General Ruger notified Wallace that on the next day, December 1 at twelve o'clock, the Democratic members from Edgefield and Laurens counties would be required to leave the hall. To this Hampton, Haskell, and Senator John B. Gordon of Georgia protested, and reminded Ruger that he had expressed his determination to exercise no supervisory control over the bodies claiming to be the House of Representatives. On December 1 General Ruger addressed a dispatch to W. T. Sherman, or the Secretary of War, in which he said he had "carefully abstained from interference with the organization of the House from the first." He stated that at the request of Chamberlain he had placed troops in the State House but that it was through a mistake that the soldiers had assisted in excluding from the hall the Democratic claimants when they had first appeared on November 28. His purpose, as he had previously explained to Chamberlain, was to have nothing to do with keeping the doors of the House—the soldiers were to be used to preserve the peace only.[17]

Ruger did not remove the Edgefield and Laurens members. However, on the afternoon of Sunday, December 3, Hampton received an anonymous letter stating that there was a plan to bring seventy-five or more members of the Hunkidori Club from Charleston to assist in removing the members from Laurens and Edgefield. The plan was to appoint as constables the roughs and bullies who constituted this club and station

[17] Correspondence cited in Reynolds, *Reconstruction in S. C.*, pp. 416-18.

them in the State House. An investigation revealed one hundred or more armed Hunkidoris in the State House.

When this plan became known, telegrams and couriers were sent to near-by counties summoning armed white men to Columbia to protect the Wallace House. Some telegrams were sent in code. A message to Greenville read: "Ship first train 200 chickens state fair with sufficient gaffs." When the "chickens" arrived most of them wore red shirts and the "gaffs" were not lacking. From Richland, Lexington, Fairfield, Sumter, and Newberry counties they came on horseback and on freight cars; by noon on Monday there were two or three thousand in town and by night there was double that number—enough to annihilate all Hunkidoris and troops too if necessary. They were armed and ready for an affray but they were held under very careful discipline.[18]

In the House, arrangements were made for effective resistance to any efforts to remove the Edgefield and Laurens members. It was said that a citizen of known courage and exceptional coolness was to take charge of any fight which might develop. Also it was arranged that on the first act of violence in the hall Mackey should be instantly shot to death.

On the morning of December 4, James L. Orr, a son of the former governor and a member of the Wallace House, moved that the House adjourn. Thereupon Wallace addressed the House, stated that he had "just been officially informed" that there were one hundred armed men ready to enter the hall for the purpose of ejecting certain members, and that the Chair distinctly understood if that force were resisted, the assistance of the military force would be invoked, "not for the purpose of upholding another body claiming to be the House of Representatives in South Carolina, but upon the ground that that force is under the Governor, and that the action of the

[18] *News and Courier,* Dec. 1, 2, 4, 1876; Williams, in Columbia *State,* Feb. 27, Mar. 6, 1927.

Top: THE TWO SPEAKERS, E. W. M. MACKEY AND W. H. WALLACE, PRE-
SIDING IN THE DUAL LEGISLATURE. *Bottom:* DEMOCRATIC MEMBERS
LEAVING THE DUAL HOUSE IN PURSUANCE OF A REQUEST OF SPEAKER
WALLACE, DECEMBER 4, 1876

military is in support of the executive authority of the State." It was insisted that the Wallace House was legal but that it was not essential to the legality of the House that it should sit in that particular hall. Therefore, "for the purpose of keeping the peace . . . we will repair to another hall and exercise the proper functions that appertain to this body." Some members of the Wallace House protested that they could maintain their position without violence, but eventually all retired to Carolina Hall where the session was resumed.[19]

On December 5 the Republican House and the Senate, the latter not having divided into Republican and Democratic groups, met in joint sessions, canvassed the vote for governor and lieutenant governor and declared Chamberlain and Gleaves elected by majorities of 3,145 and 4,099 votes respectively. The returns from Edgefield and Laurens were thrown out.[20]

The chief point at issue, of course, was the constitutionality of the rival houses. The Mackey House, acting upon the certificates issued to its members by the Board of Canvassers in contradiction of the order of the Supreme Court, organized with fifty-nine members.[21] This number, they claimed, constituted a quorum since the House, after the exclusion of the members from Edgefield and Laurens, consisted of only 116 members. Fifty-nine members would, therefore, constitute a quorum to do business. The Wallace House, on the other hand, organized with sixty-five members—one of them a Republican—present. Only fifty-seven of these had certificates of election from the secretary of state, the remaining eight presenting evidence of their membership by proceedings which had been held in the Supreme Court. If 116 members constituted the legislature, then the fifty-nine members of the Mackey

---

[19] *News and Courier*, Dec. 5; H. R. R. No. 175, Pt. 2, 44 Cong. 2 Sess., pp. 101, 142; Reynolds, *Reconstruction in S. C.*, pp. 419-21.

[20] *News and Courier*, Dec. 6, 1876;

H. R. R. No. 175, Pt. 2, 44 Cong. 2 Sess., pp. 114-21, 136-38.

[21] There were sixty members in the House, but one of them, a Democrat, was an observer only and refused to take part in the proceedings.

House constituted a constitutional majority. If, on the other hand, the legislature consisted of 124 members, as the Democrats contended, then the Wallace House with more than sixty-three members constituted a majority, provided that the eight members excluded by the Board of Canvassers but holding statements of election by the Supreme Court were admitted.

On December 2 the Democrats petitioned the Supreme Court for a mandamus commanding and enjoining Hayne, as secretary of state, and Mackey, speaker of the Mackey House, to deliver to the speaker of the Wallace House the returns of the managers of election. Hayne made return to the petition by saying that Mackey had been elected speaker and was in the chair acting as such, and that the returns had been delivered to him before Wallace made any demand for the returns or claimed to have been elected speaker. Mackey made a return in which he stated that he had been elected speaker, that the House had been lawfully organized, and that he had continued to act as speaker. The jurisdiction of the court was denied.

On December 6 the question was settled, in so far as it could be settled at that time, by a unanimous decision of the Supreme Court.

In rendering the decision of the court, Chief Justice Moses and also Associate Justice Willard in a concurring opinion affirmed that a mandamus might issue whenever a public officer was called upon to perform a ministerial act of a specific character, and, on demand, had refused its performance. The Court held that Wallace was the speaker of a legally constituted house; that sixty-three members, a majority of the constitutional number of 124 of which the House consisted, were present at the organization; and that the Supreme Court could confine the Board of Canvassers to the ministerial duty of certifying the results of the election as appeared prima facie upon the returns. It is worthy of note that Associate Justice Wright, in full concurrence with his colleagues, pointed out that if the Board had the right to throw out one county and thus defeat its representation, they could throw out one half or all of the counties and defeat an entire election.[22] While Wallace was adjudged speaker of the lawful House and entitled to the possession of the returns of the election for governor and lieutenant governor, it was reserved for further argument whether Hayne would be compelled by mandamus to issue the returns to Wallace after he had parted with them to Mackey. No mandamus could issue against Mackey for he was merely a private citizen.

Immediately after the decision of the Court the Wallace House appointed a committee to ascertain from General Ruger his attitude and purpose toward that body. Ruger replied that if the Wallace House should appear at the State House for the purpose of entering the hall of the House and should be denied admission "by those having charge of the doors, and such persons should apply to the officer in command of the troops . . . for assistance necessary to prevent you from entering, the present orders to the officer would require him to render such assistance."[23] In spite of Ruger's declaration that he would uphold the Mackey House, there was great rejoicing among the Democrats over the decision of the Supreme Court.

As we have seen, Chamberlain was inaugurated on December 7. In his address he declared: "Our greatest interest, our most commanding duty, now, is to stand firmly, each in his appointed place, against the aggressions and allurements of our political opponents."[24] That evening, Hampton declared in a speech: "The people have elected me Governor, and, by the

[22] *State, ex rel. Wallace,* v. *Hayne and Mackey.* 8 S. C. 367 ff. Moses stated that "on a day when everything was calm and serene; when the political atmosphere was pure; when there was no excitement in the country" the Court in the case of *Morton, Bliss and Co.* v. *The Comptroller-*

General, reported in 4 S. C. 430, had held that a quorum must constitute a majority of the legal House, i. e., 124 members.

[23] Quoted in Reynolds, *Reconstruction in S. C.,* p. 422.

[24] *News and Courier,* Dec. 8, 1876.

Eternal God, I will be Governor or we shall have a military governor."[25]

The Democrats did not recognize Chamberlain as governor. Not only was he sworn in by an illegal house but under no interpretation did the Mackey House contain a quorum. Upon the organization of the Wallace House, two members of the Mackey body, J. W. Westberry, of Sumter, and W. H. Reedish, of Orangeburg, seceded and took their seats in the Wallace House; on succeeding days Thomas Hamilton and N. B. Myers, of Beaufort, and J. S. Bridges, of Newberry, all of whom had qualified in the Mackey House, were sworn in, thus giving the Wallace House sixty-three members with certificates of election from the secretary of state.[26] Thus, no quorum existed in the Mackey House when Chamberlain was declared elected on December 5.

On December 10 the Wallace House adopted and sent to the Senate a concurrent resolution fixing December 14 as the day for tabulating the returns of the vote for governor and lieutenant governor, declaring the election, and inaugurating the two officers-elect. The Supreme Court had not issued a mandamus requiring Hayne to transmit the election returns to Speaker Wallace. However, J. S. Richardson, Democratic candidate for Congress from the first district who was contesting the election of J. H. Rainey, applied to Hayne for certified copies of the vote for governor in 1874 and in 1876. Hayne gave him the copies, and on both of the lists of returns certified, under the seal of the state, that they were correct. Thus, the

---

[25] As reported in *ibid.*, Dec. 8, 1876.

[26] *News and Courier*, Nov. 28-Dec. 7, 1876; speech of T. J. Robertson in U. S. Senate, Jan. 29, 1877; Columbia *State*, Oct. 14, 1911; Williams, in *ibid.*, Mar. 6, 1927, Houseal, in *ibid.*, Dec. 12, 1926. Democrats used every form of persuasion to induce members of the Mackey House to withdraw. It was said that Bridges was needed to make a quorum which Grant would recognize. Bridges' conversion was due to Dr. A. F. Langley, surgeon of the Prosperity Rifle Club and Bridges' family physician. The Doctor had no difficulty in showing Bridges his duty. He promised to look after Bridges' family professionally, and did so, as did his son after him. Williams, in *State*, Mar. 6, 1927.

Democrats had the returns for the entire vote for Hampton and Chamberlain including the vote of Edgefield and Laurens, certified to be correct by the secretary of state.[27] According to the returns, Hampton's majority was 1,134 and Simpson's majority 139. Although the Constitution required that the governor and lieutenant governor be sworn in by a justice of the Supreme Court, the House resolved not to embarrass any one of the justices; accordingly, Judge T. J. Mackey of the sixth circuit was invited to perform that duty.[28]

On December 15, Simpson addressed an official communication to the Senate requesting that body to unite with the Wallace House to put in full action the legislative power of the state. The communication was referred by the Senate to its judiciary committee, which never reported. It will be recalled that the Senate had never divided into two houses. The Democratic minority had protested against the Senate's recognition of the Mackey House, and soon after the organization of the two houses there was a movement to have the thirteen Democratic senators withdraw and set up a rival Senate. By admitting the senators from Edgefield, Laurens, and Abbeville, with one contestant from Darlington, they would have seventeen members, a constitutional quorum.[29] This was not done, however. Some of the Democrats insisted that their presence in the Senate was necessary for the safety of the judiciary. To many it seemed that the Democratic senators by recognizing Lieutenant Governor Gleaves as their presiding officer were sanctioning the claims of the Republicans. In fact, some Republicans suggested adjourning the legislature and leaving the Democrats without a Senate. Following Hampton's inauguration, he addressed a letter to Chamberlain requesting that he, as his "predecessor in office," deliver up "the great seal of the State, together with the possession of the State-house,

[27] *News and Courier*, Dec. 14, 1876.
[28] Chamberlain was sworn in by a probate judge of Richland County.
[29] *News and Courier*, Nov. 30, 1876.

the public records, and all other matters and things appertaining to said office." Chamberlain replied that he did not recognize any right of Hampton to make that demand and refused compliance therewith.[30]

The contest for the governorship was carried into the courts. On December 20, 1876, Chamberlain issued a pardon to Peter Smith, a convict confined in the state penitentiary. The superintendent refused to recognize the alleged pardon, and the prisoner applied to Judge R. B. Carpenter, of the fifth circuit, for a writ of habeas corpus.[31] After lengthy argument in the court, Carpenter rendered his decision of January 29, 1877. Following the precedent set by the Supreme Court in the case of *Wallace* v. *Hayne,* Carpenter held that the Mackey House was illegal, that even though it consisted of members of the House of Representatives it was without a quorum and that the only legal act which it could have performed would have been the adjournment from day to day. Not only was the Mackey House "simply illegal from being incomplete, but actively so, violating positive law and usurping the rightful authority of the House of Representatives." Furthermore, "all its acts were illegal and void"; therefore, "the attempted installation" of Chamberlain "was without lawful authority, and conferred no right whatever."

On the other hand, Carpenter decided that Hampton had not been legally installed by the General Assembly on December 14, since, in the first place, the election returns had not been delivered to Speaker Wallace by the secretary of state as the law required;[32] and since, in the second place, the attempted inauguration of Hampton took place in the presence of the House, without the concurrence of the Senate, and, "so far as appears by the pleadings and evidence, without its knowl-

[30] For the inaugural speech of Hampton see *News and Courier,* Dec. 15, 1876; for the Hampton-Chamberlain correspondence see *ibid.,* Dec. 19, 1876.

[31] It will be remembered that Carpenter was a staunch opponent of Chamberlain in the preceding political campaign.

[32] Art. III, Sec. 4 of the Constitution.

edge." Therefore it was held that there had been no legal qualification of Chamberlain's successor and that the attempted installation of Chamberlain, being illegal and void, "did not operate in law as a resignation of the office of governor which he held at that time." Chamberlain, then, was "lawfully in possession of the executive office."[33]

The case was appealed to the Supreme Court, but before it was heard two other judicial decisions adjudged Hampton to be governor. On the same day that Carpenter rendered his decision, January 29, Hampton granted a pardon to Amzi Rosborough, a prisoner confined in the Chester County jail. The sheriff denied the validity of the pardon and the case was heard by T. J. Mackey, judge of the sixth circuit.[34] The decision was rendered on February 3, 1877. Mackey found that the Constitution[35] declared "The person having the highest number of votes shall be Governor," that the law requiring the speaker to "open and publish" the returns "in the presence of both Houses" was simply directory, and the voluntary and wilful absence of the Senate did not invalidate such publication, and that Chamberlain, having refrained from contesting the said election in the manner prescribed by law,[36] was "estopped by his default from questioning in the courts the correctness of the sworn transcripts of the returns of the said election."[37] Hampton was declared governor and the prisoner discharged.

The second decision adjudging Hampton governor was rendered by the Supreme Court. On February 9, Hampton issued a pardon to Tilda Norris, a convict in the state penitentiary. The superintendent at the prison refused to recognize the pardon, and the case was duly brought before the Supreme

[33] *Recent Election in S. C.,* Appendix, pp. 197-206.

[34] Mackey, a Republican, had declared for Hampton in the campaign of 1876.

[35] Art. III, Sec. 4.

[36] *Stat. S. C.,* XIV, 396, provided that the Senate and House should hear and determine the facts in the contested election according to Art. VIII, Sec. 10 of the Constitution which provided that the person who received the highest number of votes was to be declared elected.

[37] *Recent Election in S. C.,* Appendix, pp. 221-26.

Court by the prisoner who applied for a writ of habeas corpus. After a long and able argument, in which exhaustive evidence was presented, Associate Justice Willard, with the concurrence of Associate Justice Wright,[38] filed an order releasing the prisoner. This order was signed on February 27. On March 1, a day before it was filed, Wright also filed a long opinion in which he revoked his signature to the above order and adjudged Chamberlain governor, since his successor had not been legally chosen and qualified. ·

On March 7, Justice Willard filed a statement of his conclusions.[39] Willard concluded that since Hampton had received the highest number of votes and since there was no contest before the General Assembly for possession of the office, Hampton was "at least" *de facto* governor, "without going through the regular form of installation." Chamberlain was "not entitled to be recognized as Governor holding over nor as Governor *de facto* against the person who received the highest number of votes" and who also had "entered upon the discharge of the duties of the office." "A pardon granted by one who is *de facto* Governor is valid, irrespective of his not having a perfect title or evidence of title to the office."[40]

Meanwhile the rival governments were carrying on independently. But all the while Hampton's position had become stronger, and Chamberlain's weaker; Chamberlain was sustained only by Federal troops. Early in December a temporary injunction restrained the two banks which were acting as repositories of the public funds, from paying out the deposits on order of Cardozo, Chamberlain's treasurer.[41] The plan was to "starve out" the Republicans. The Wallace House did

---

[38] Chief Justice Moses was mortally ill at the time.

[39] Which statement he had intended to express orally from the bench on March 2, but Justice Wright being absent "the Court was necessarily adjourned and no opportunity afforded for such statement."

[40] 8 S. C. 408. The prisoner was set free. On April 24, 1877, two weeks after Chamberlain had withdrawn from the executive office, Willard filed a lengthy opinion to this effect.—8 S. C. 471.

[41] *News and Courier*, Dec. 9, 1876.

S. CAROLINA
STATE
TREASURY

Leslie's Illustrated Newspaper

CHAMBERLAIN—"*Will you come down and fight, so that I can call in the troops to suppress you?*"
HAMPTON—"No!"
CHAMBERLAIN—"*Well, then, stay where you are.*"

not pass an appropriation bill because it could not get the concurrence of the Senate, but a resolution of that body authorized Hampton to call upon the taxpayers to contribute a sum not exceeding one-fourth of the tax last paid—the amount so contributed to be deducted from the contributors' future tax. The Mackey body and the Senate levied a tax of thirteen mills, but the county treasurers got less than $1,000.[42] On the other hand, Johnson Hagood, "acting Comptroller and Treasurer" for the Democrats said on March 1, 1877, that the contributions received by the Hampton government amounted to $119,-432.41, with $706.30 received as office fees. The disbursements amounted to $37,794.64—covering payments to the legislature, the judicial and executive departments, the state institutions and for contingent expenses.[43]

The Mackey body passed several acts of legislation, including "a bill to prevent and punish any person or persons for setting up . . . or maintaining a government of the State in opposition to the legitimate and lawful government." The Mackey House, together with the Republican members of the Senate, elected D. T. Corbin to succeed Senator T. J. Robertson in the United States Senate; the Wallace House and the Democratic Senators elected M. C. Butler for the same purpose. The Mackey House voted the usual gratuities to their speaker and clerk and $200 each to the members of the House and Senate. This money was procured by Cardozo from Corbin.[44]

After his inauguration, Hampton addressed circulars to prominent citizens in the counties. He asked that if any of the county offices were filled "by an incompetent person or anyone refusing to acknowledge the lawful government" that

[42] Reynolds, *Reconstruction in S. C.,* p. 434.

[43] *Ibid.,* p. 436. The report of the Comptroller-General on Nov. 26, 1877, showed the amount paid into the treasury from the 10 per cent contribution to be $135,805.93. *Reports and Resolutions, 1877-78.*

[44] It was said that Corbin used the money to bribe members to vote for him for the Senate.

the names of prospective officers, "possessing undoubted ability and integrity," be submitted.[45] By the middle of March it was said that the entire judiciary of the state was coöperating with the people in enforcing the actual fact of Hampton's governorship.[46]

Although Hampton had been adjudged governor and the Wallace House the lawful legislature by the Supreme Court, the Republicans refused to acknowledge the decrees of that tribunal. Chamberlain and the Republican state officials were maintained in their position by Federal troops. Everyone in the state knew that should the troops be withdrawn, Chamberlain's government would fall immediately. The contest, then, was carried to Washington.

South Carolina, of course, was one of the disputed states in the presidential election of 1876. The return of the Board of Canvassers indicated that the Republican presidential electors had been chosen. A proceeding in the nature of a *quo warranto* was instituted in the Supreme Court by the Democratic claimants against the Republican electors. The Democrats alleged that by comparing the statements of the county canvassers with the statements and returns of the precinct managers, they would have been elected. The proceeding was filed on December 2; three days later the defendants moved for a dismissal on the ground that the court had no jurisdiction; and on December 7 the defendants petitioned for a removal of the proceedings to the United States Circuit Court. The petition was not granted. On January 26, 1877, the Supreme Court unanimously decided that an action in the nature of *quo warranto* did not lie in the name of the state to determine the title to the office of elector; that an action to determine the title to an office could only be maintained by or in the name of the sovereign with whom the franchises and privileges of the office originated, and that the franchises and privileges of the

[45] *News and Courier*, Dec. 19, 1876.   [46] *Ibid.*, Mar. 14, 1877.

CONTEST CARRIED TO WASHINGTON

office of elector originated and were exercised under the constitution and laws of the United States and not under those of the state of South Carolina.[47]

In Washington, Senator John J. Patterson upheld the cause of Chamberlain, while Senator T. J. Robertson, who had been a Republican Senator since 1868, supported Hampton. Memorials and counter-memorials were laid before Congress; Senator John B. Gordon of Georgia offered a resolution declaring that the government represented by Hampton was the lawful government of the state. Senator Patterson did likewise on behalf of Chamberlain.

On the day following the adjournment of the Wallace House, December 22, Hampton addressed duplicate letters to Hayes and Tilden. He declared that "profound peace" existed throughout the state, that the course of judicial proceedings was unobstructed, and that the laws for the protection of the inhabitants "in all their rights of person, property, and citizenship" were being enforced in the courts. "While the people of this State" were "not wanting either in the spirit or means to maintain their rights of citizenship against the usurpers' power," he trusted that a solution might be had which would maintain the peace of the country and at the same time "do no violence to the constitutional safeguards of popular rights."[48]

In the meantime Congress and the country were much concerned with the outcome of the disputed presidential election. Committees and sub-committees visited the contested states and took voluminous testimony. The majority members of the House committee reported that the electoral vote of South Carolina belonged of right to Tilden and Hendricks; from the same testimony the minority members reported exactly opposite conclusions. The report of the Senate committee was just

---

[47] *Recent Election in S. C.*, Appendix, pp. 190-96; 8 S. C. 382, 400. The action by the Democrats had been brought in the name of the state and not of the United States.

[48] *News and Courier*, Dec. 30, 1876.

the reverse, with the majority report favorable to Hayes, the minority report favorable to Tilden. When the House and Senate met to count the electoral votes of South Carolina, February 26, 1877, two certificates were presented. That of the Hayes electors was certified by Chamberlain and Secretary of State Hayne; that from the Tilden "electors" was not certified by anyone, but in it the "electors" claimed to have received a majority of the votes cast, alleged that they had been wrongfully deprived of their rights by the Board of Canvassers, and referred to the mandamus and *quo warranto* proceedings already described. Objections were submitted against both returns and the case was referred to the Electoral Commission created by Congress.[49]

In the contest before the Commission the Democratic objectors did not attempt to prove that the Democratic electors had been chosen. They contended that the vote of the state ought not to be received because the legislature had failed to provide a registration law as required by the Constitution, that there was not a republican form of government in the state at the time of the election, and that Federal troops, without authority of law, and more than a thousand deputy United States marshals, appointed under an unconstitutional law, had interfered with the full and free exercise of the right of suffrage by the voters of the state.[50]

The Republican objectors confined themselves almost entirely to defending their own certificates and to combating the argument that the vote of the state ought to be thrown out. They contended that the constitutional provision requiring a registration was directory only, that the legislature had in effect complied with the requirement by enacting that a poll-list should be kept, that the Democratic position on the matter was

[49] *Proceedings of the Electoral Commission*, pp. 659-64.　　[50] *Ibid.*, pp. 666-78.

untenable because otherwise all elections and all government in South Carolina during the last eight years would be illegal and void, and that the state possessed a republican form of government as proved by the fact that it was represented in both Houses of Congress. They contended that the Commission was not competent to receive evidence regarding the use of troops and deputy marshals, but that both the troops and marshals had been used in accordance with the laws of the United States and under the direction of the President and the Attorney-General.[51] The Commission took substantially this same position in resolving to count the votes for Hayes.[52]

The outcome of the work of the Electoral Commission was the inauguration of Hayes. It had been understood by leading Democrats and those in close touch with the President that Hayes would follow a conciliatory policy toward the South; in fact, he had indicated as much in his speech of acceptance, but he refused to let anyone speak for him. The attitude of Hayes before his election was comparatively unknown, but certain leading Republicans were so close to him that in conferences with interested Democrats they, in effect, guaranteed that Hayes would, by a gradual process of non-interference and withdrawal of troops, allow the Republican governments in Louisiana and South Carolina to disappear.[53]

On March 4, Stanley Matthews, a close friend of Hayes, wrote to Chamberlain suggesting that an arrangement be arrived at which would "obviate the necessity of the use of Federal arms to support either government and leave that to stand which is able to stand by itself." To this letter was a postscript by William M. Evarts (to be Hayes' Secretary of State) in which he expressed a wish "to aid in a solution of the difficulties

[51] *Ibid.*, pp. 678-88
[52] *Ibid.*, p. 702.
[53] For a discussion of a "bargain" between the Democrats and Republicans see Haworth, *The Hayes-Tilden Disputed Election*, pp. 268-72. Hayes was not privy to any "bargain" or tacit agreement.

of the situation." Chamberlain, incensed, replied: "There are better ways than this to conciliate and pacify the South. Let the present administration . . . manifest a spirit of charity and sympathy for our opponents . . . in the thousand ways open to an administration, and peace will come. . . . To permit Hampton to reap the fruits of a campaign of murder, and fraud, so long as there remains power to prevent it, is to sanction such methods."[54]

Both Chamberlain and Hampton were invited to Washington for a conference with the President. This was on the 23d of March. On the 27th Chamberlain arrived in Washington and was followed two days later by Hampton. Interviews were had with the President, members of the Cabinet, and prominent public men. On March 31 Chamberlain, at the invitation of Evarts, wrote to the President his "views of the results to be expected to follow the withdrawal of the United States forces." Chamberlain objected that a withdrawal of the troops would be a withdrawal of support and aid against domestic violence, that the withdrawal would be a practical decision in favor of his opponent, and that it would place "all the agencies for maintaining the present lawful government of the State in the practical possession of the Democrats."

This letter was read at a meeting of the Cabinet on April 2; the following day it was determined in a Cabinet meeting that the troops should be withdrawn from the State House on April 10.[55]

Hayes immediately issued orders for the removal of the troops. Chamberlain returned to the state, issued an address, in which he denounced the action of the President but said that no effective means of resistance were left, and withdrew from office. The Republican state officials agreed with Chamberlain

[54] Quoted in Allen, *Chamberlain's Administration in S. C.*, pp. 469-71; *News and Courier*, Mar. 29, 1877.

[55] *News and Courier*, Mar. 25-April 5, 1877; Allen, *Chamberlain's Administration*, pp. 474-80.

in discontinuing the struggle, and on April 11, at twelve noon, the executive office was turned over to Hampton.[56]

[56] Allen, *Chamberlain's Administration*, pp. 480-86; *News and Courier*, April 5-15, 1877. Hampton always said that but for Hayes' "conscientiousness we should never have regained control of the State." Columbia *State*, Jan. 21, 1893. A reporter who saw Hampton soon after his return from Washington related the following: Upon being queried by Hayes as to what would happen if Chamberlain were recognized Hampton replied, "I told him that the first thing would be that every tax collector in the State would be hanged in twenty-four hours."—Williams, in Columbia *State*, Mar. 13, 1927. Chamberlain never forgave Hayes and the Republican politicians. See speech before Mass. Reform Club at Boston, Feb. 8, 1890, also Columbia *State*, July 10, 1893.

Chapter XX

THE HERITAGE OF RECONSTRUCTION

T
HE events which occurred in those twelve years between the April in which the Confederate armies surrendered and the April in which Chamberlain surrendered the State House have had a determining influence upon many phases of the history of the state. It is true that the restoration of white political supremacy resulted in the destruction of many characteristic institutions of the Reconstruction period. But these destroyed institutions have left vivid memories. The post-Reconstruction leaders have felt that their highest duty was to guard against their revival. Moreover, many institutions created during Reconstruction did not perish with the triumph of Hampton. They existed as the inevitable consequence of the revolution of 1865, and they were so firmly rooted that it was beyond the power of leaders to destroy them. Some of them were adjudged wholesome and have been fostered by the post-Reconstructionists with a diligence equal to that with which they have endeavored to prevent the revival of influences they deemed unwholesome.

The first concern of the victors of 1877 was to make certain that there would be no recurrence of the political experiences of Reconstruction. The personnel of the Radical régime must be reckoned with; the political and social importance of the Negro must be reduced to a minimum; and the supremacy of the white race must be maintained and justified.

After legislative investigations had made tolerably clear the extent of the guilt of the deposed public officials, the Democratic leaders resolved to make an example of a selected group. Chamberlain, Patterson, Neagle, Leslie, Parker, Kimpton, L.

Cass Carpenter, Cardozo, Smalls and a few others were indicted under the laws of the state. Carpenter, Cardozo and Smalls were tried and convicted before the court of general sessions for Richland County, and were sentenced on November 9, 1877. Carpenter was given two years in prison and a fine of $1,000; Cardozo was given two years in prison and a fine of $4,000; and Smalls was given three years in prison.[1] But circumstances halted further prosecutions. Many of those indicted fled beyond the borders of the state, and the prosecuting authorities experienced difficulties in apprehending them. The Democratic leaders were not inclined to go to extremes in matters not vital to their supremacy. There was little danger of the indicted Republicans again becoming vital forces in the political life of the state. The only real danger was the possibility of Federal intervention to restore Republicanism, and the Democratic leaders did not desire to stimulate this tendency by being guilty of acts which smacked of political persecution. Moreover, there were as many Democrats under indictment in the Federal courts for violating election laws as there were Republicans under indictment in the courts of the state. So when some of the fugitives from South Carolina justice approached members of the South Carolina delegation in Congress with compromise suggestions, they were willingly heard. It was agreed that steps should be taken to induce both the state and Federal governments to drop further prosecutions. Both the Governor of South Carolina and the President of the United States accepted this suggestion. The prosecution of the Republican leaders was dropped and Governor Simpson pardoned Carpenter, Smalls, and Cardozo before their sentences had been executed; in 1884 the United States district attorney for South Carolina formally withdrew from the Federal court the last of the election cases.[2]

---

[1] *American Annual Cyclopedia, 1877,* pp. 697-698.

[2] See letter of the attorney general of South Carolina to the United States dis-

The principals of the Reconstruction régime vanished from the public life of the state as completely as if they had been made to do long terms in the state penitentiary. Most of them removed from South Carolina; some secured minor Federal appointments, and others dropped completely from sight. It is not our purpose to trace in detail the later careers of these individuals, but it may be interesting to note briefly what the future held for them.

Of the ex-governors, Chamberlain was by far the most outstanding. He left South Carolina in 1877 and went to New York City where he engaged in a successful law practice. In 1883 he was a non-resident professor of constitutional law at Cornell. He made several return visits to South Carolina, where he was highly respected by many people. At one time he was appointed receiver of the South Carolina Railroad Company. It is worth noting that he became an independent in politics and deserted the Republican party to support Cleveland. Also he changed his attitude toward the Negro. In a speech before the Massachusetts Reform Club at Boston in 1890, he made the following statement:

I come from the South to-night. . . . I have mingled again during the last four months with the people whom I then knew so well. . . . I find that since 1876, both races in South Carolina have prospered. . . . I find the Negro more self-respecting, better provided with schools, far better, acquiring property more rapidly, more industrious, more ambitious for education and property, than he ever was before 1876. . . . I proclaim it because it is true. . . .

I do not exonerate the white race at the South from all past or present blame. There are wrongs done there to the Negro now, but I do say that the Negro has never known such an era of advancement and prosperity in all that benefits a citizen and freeman as the period since 1876, and if it be treason to say it, I reply, in historic words, "Make the most of it!"[3]

Years later Chamberlain was writing in an open letter to James Bryce that "the hope or dream of social or political equality," given to the Negro since emancipation, should be removed. And in regard to the truth of the physical repulsion on the part of whites toward blacks Chamberlain said, "I freely acknowledge the repulsion."[4]

After his term as governor, Franklin J. Moses, Jr., set up as a lawyer in Columbia, but he was soon a voluntary bankrupt with liabilities of $92,000. His property was sold by the sheriff.[5] He then drifted North where he began a career of petty crimes. On indictments for swindling individuals out of small sums of money, he was sentenced to three years in the Massachusetts State Prison. He served a short sentence in Detroit, and a six-months term in the Boston House of Correction for swindling Colonel Thomas Wentworth Higginson out of $34. Nor was he a stranger to the Tombs of New York City. His end came by asphyxiation in a rooming house in Winthrop, Massachusetts.[6]

Robert K. Scott returned to Napoleon, Ohio, in 1877, and engaged in the real estate business. In 1880 he was lodged in jail charged with first degree murder of a drunken companion of his son. He was found not guilty.[7]

The last employment of former Lieutenant Governor Ransier was that of a day laborer on the streets of Charleston. He died in 1882.[8] Lieutenant Governor Gleaves disappeared, although there is a tradition that he became a hotel waiter in

[3] Speech of Feb. 8, 1890, reported in Boston *Daily Post* and reprinted in pamphlet.
[4] *News and Courier*, Aug. 1, 1904. See also *Atlantic Monthly*, April, 1901, for article by Chamberlain on Reconstruction in South Carolina.
[5] *News and Courier*, Feb. 25, May 28, Oct. 5, 1875.
[6] *News and Courier*, Dec. 12, 1906; *The State*, Dec. 12, 1906, Mar. 16, 1907.
[7] *News and Courier*, Dec. 30, 1880.
[8] *Ibid.*, Aug. 12, 1882.

New York and at one time waited on Governor Wade
Hampton.

Of the speakers of the House, S. J. Lee moved to Charleston
where he became a busy criminal lawyer. Robert B. Elliott,
ex-congressman and ex-speaker, became a special agent of the
treasury department in New Orleans, and practised law until
his death in 1884.[9] E. W. M. Mackey, speaker of the Radical
house during the dual government, became assistant United
States attorney for South Carolina; he successfully contested
the election of M. P. O'Connor to the forty-seventh Congress
and was reëlected to the forty-eighth Congress, in which he
served until his death in 1884.[10]

The Democrats soon controlled the Supreme Court of the
state. Chief Justice Moses died in March, 1877.[11] Hampton
accepted the resignation of Associate Justice Wright in August
of that year.[12] In the summer of 1877, Justice Willard, who
appears to have been very favorable to the Democrats during
the contested election, was elected chief justice, a place he retained until July, 1880.[13]

The individuals who had been intimately connected with
the state treasury went North. Financial Agent Kimpton was
arrested in Massachusetts in 1878, but the governor refused to
deliver him on Hampton's requisition. Nothing more is known
of him.[14] Parker went into the laundry business in Escanaba,
Michigan. Cardozo went to Washington and became a clerk
in the auditing department of the treasury; later he became
principal of a Negro high school in the same city.[15]

Richard H. ("Daddy") Cain completed his congressional
term in 1879; the following year he was elected Bishop of the
African Methodist Episcopal church and continued in that

---

[9] *Biographical Congressional Directory,*
p. 627.
[10] *Ibid.,* p. 840; *News and Courier,* Jan.
29, 1884.
[11] *Ibid.,* Mar. 7, 1877.

[12] *Ibid.,* Feb. 20, 1885.
[13] *The State,* May 7, 1900.
[14] *Winnsboro News and Herald,* Aug.
21, Sept. 4, 1878.
[15] *The State,* Mar. 18, 1906.

position until his death in 1887.[16] L. Cass Carpenter moved to Colorado and became in turn supervisor of the 1880 census of that state, post-office inspector, insurance man, and lawyer. Robert Smalls represented South Carolina in Congress from 1875 to 1879 and from 1881 to 1887; after the expiration of his term in 1887 he was appointed collector of the port of Beaufort.[17] Both he and W. J. Whipper sat in the constitutional convention of 1895.

*   *   *   *   *

The elimination of the black constituency of these former leaders from the political life of the state was not so simple as that of getting rid of the leaders themselves. For five decades after 1877 the majority of the state's population was black. The Negroes did not easily forget the part they had played in politics, and potentially at least they remained loyal Republicans. But those who won the election of 1876 had the devices through which all the fruits of their victory would be conserved. "The lesson which the white people of the South learned at such bitter cost, and which they took to their hearts forever," remarks a recent historian of Reconstruction in the state, "is that the Negro must never again be allowed to gain an ascendency in politics; and that to prevent such a calamity, the whites must ever stand with united front, no matter what political differences they may have themselves."[18] After 1877 there was no disposition to keep Hampton's promise that he would protect the political rights of the Negroes. The seventeen Republican representatives in the legislature from Charleston were expelled, and Democrats, elected at special elections over which only Democrats officiated, were given their places. The election of 1878 was preceded by the abolition of voting precincts in

[16] *Biographical Congressional Directory,* p. 522; *A. M. E. Church Review,* III, 337-50.

[17] *Biographical Congressional Directory,* p. 1002.

[18] Henry T. Thompson, *Ousting the Carpet-bagger from South Carolina,* p. 166.

areas with large Republican majorities.[19]   This, it was alleged, compelled large numbers of Republicans to walk twenty miles or more in order to vote.   Governor Hampton in most instances refused to give Republicans representation on the boards of election.   Plans were made to revive the tactics of 1876. Members of the rifle clubs appeared at Republican meetings and the speakers were compelled to divide time with white orators.   Swails, the Republican leader of Williamsburg, was driven from that county by a white mob, and the Republicans of Edgefield dared not send representatives to the state convention of their party because of Democratic threats.   The Republican state convention, baffled, gave up hope; it made no nominations for state offices.   It contented itself with a denunciation of the actions of the Democrats.   Hampton was re-elected governor by a vote of 169,550 to 213.   The number of Republicans in the state Senate was reduced to five, the number in the House of Representatives to three.   All Democratic nominees for Congress were declared elected by increased majorities.[20]   In 1880 the Republican nominee for governor got only 4,277 votes to his opponent's 117,432, and only six Republicans were returned to the legislature.[21]   In 1882 a system of gerrymandering was adopted so as to make certain that the Republicans would control but one of the seven congressional seats. It provided for a colored majority of 25,198 in one district, slight colored majorities in four, and white majorities in two.[22] At the same session of the legislature a stringent registration law was adopted along with a curious voting device known as the Eight Box Law.   As many boxes as there were positions to be filled were placed at each polling place; each voter, unassisted, was required to place a separate ballot in each box.   It

[19] *Stat. S. C.*, XVI, 565-70.   Act of Mar. 22, 1878.
[20] Accounts of the election of 1878 in *American Annual Cyclopedia, 1878*, pp.
770-71, and in *Senate Report, 45 Cong., 3 Sess.*, No. 855.
[21] *American Annual Cyclopedia, 1880*, p. 670.
[22] *Stat. S. C.*, XVII, 1169.

was very likely that the great mass of Negro illiterates would invalidate their ballots by placing them in the wrong box.[23]

For the next fourteen years there were never more than eight Republicans in the legislature at one time; most of them were from Beaufort, the blackest county. During this period a few Negro Democrats were returned to the legislature from low-country counties, and three Negro Republicans won seats in Congress.[24] In the constitutional convention of 1895 there were five Negro delegates from Beaufort and one from Georgetown.

But white public opinion was not satisfied that the Negro should have even this small part in politics. The triumph of Ben Tillman in 1890 brought this sentiment to the fore. Tillman represented the common white man, the class which had contributed so much to the triumph of Hampton. He had done yeoman's service in the Hamburg riot. He desired that the last black face be banished from the public councils, and that, if possible, this be accomplished without the fraudulent practices and statutory makeshifts used in previous elections. He felt that a break in the political unity of the white race was inevitable, and perhaps desirable, provided white political supremacy was not endangered. He knew that because of the rude and radical character of his agitations he had created a bitterness which threatened this unity before the Negro had been absolutely excluded from politics. Would not the consequences be dire, he argued, if a disappointed white minority appealed to the Negro vote? When Alexander C. Haskell actually made such an appeal in a fruitless attempt to prevent Tillman from becoming governor, the doughty commoner saw red. He determined to have a new constitution which would disfranchise the Negro to the greatest possible degree under the limitations of national law.

[23] *Ibid.*, pp. 1117-1119.
[24] Robert Smalls in 1882 and 1884; Thomas E. Miller in 1890, and George W. Murray in 1893 and 1896.

Accordingly a Tillman-dominated constitutional convention met in 1895. Before it Tillman drew a lurid picture of the political potentialities of the Negro. He said, "We should guard against the possibility of this flood, which is now damned up, breaking loose; or, like the viper that is asleep, only to be warmed into life again and sting us whenever some white rascals, native or foreign, come here and mobilize the ignorant blacks. Therefore, the only thing that we can do as patriots and statesmen is to take from them every ballot that we can under the laws of the national government."[25]

As is well known, the suffrage restrictions adopted imposed rigid residence and poll tax requirements, and specified that the voter must be able to read and write a section of the constitution or should have paid a tax on as much as three hundred dollars worth of property. To accommodate those whites who could not fulfill the last-named requirement, all male persons of voting age who could read any section of the constitution submitted to them by the registration officer, or understand and explain it when read to them by the officer, could become life-long voters, and after January 1, 1898, the difficulties of the literacy test could be obviated by the provision which allowed the registration officers to exercise their discretion as to whether or not the prospective voters could in fact read and write.[26] Concerning the intent of the last named provision, Tillman made the following observations: "Some poisons in small doses are very salutary and valuable medicines. If you put it in here that a man must understand, and you vest the right to judge whether he understands in an officer, it is a constitutional act. The officer is responsible to his conscience and his God; he is responsible to nobody else. . . . It is just showing partiality perhaps [laughter], or discrimination."[27]

[25] *Journal of the Constitutional Convention of 1895*, pp. 463-64.

[26] Simkins, *The Tillman Movement in South Carolina*, pp. 212-15.

[27] *Journal of the Constitutional Convention of 1895*, p. 469.

The suffrage reforms instituted by Tillman have not had the desired effect. It is true that the Supreme Court of the United States has never declared them unconstitutional and that they have been followed by the complete elimination of the Negro from public life. In the legislatures of 1898 and 1900 there was only one Republican representative; since 1900 not a single Republican has been elected to the state legislature or to Congress, there has been no Republican candidate for governor, and the Republican presidential electors have polled insignificant votes. But it is likely that these results would have been accomplished had there been no constitutional restrictions on the suffrage. The Negro had already learned of the inconveniences and dangers of politics. Moreover, the evils of which Tillman complained have not been eliminated. The subterfuges of the Eight Box Law were no more pronounced than those he devised. The Negro still has the potential right to vote, and a few of them have always done so since 1895. Doubtless more of them would vote but for the prevalence of conditions inherited from the years immediately following Reconstruction. They know that the whites stand ready to use force to prevent them from exercising political privileges in large numbers. Cases of this type of violence have been recorded since 1895,[28] and everyone familiar with conditions in the rural counties knows that the possibility of violence is the principal reason why there are not more Negro voters.

The Negro issue still has a pronounced influence upon the political life of the state. To the whites the Negro vote is still "the viper that is asleep" ready "to be warmed into life and sting." They know that under the national constitution the Negroes have the same rights to the suffrage which they have, and they fear that sometime in the future the Negroes will be

[28] For example, the killing of the Negro postmaster at Lake City and the Phoenix Riot in 1898, and the expulsion in 1920 of Negro women applicants for registration. *International Yearbook, 1898,* pp. 719-20, and William Pickens, in *The Nation,* CXII (Mar. 23, 1920), 426-28.

able to circumvent restrictions. Consequently they have not felt inclined to act as freely in politics as Tillman hoped they would; they continue to adhere to the Democratic party with tenacity even when it champions distasteful men and measures. One of the principal tasks of the politician who seeks favor is to be sure that he is not touched by the damning taint of Negroism or Republicanism; his enemies stand ready to bring about his defeat by attributing, on the slightest evidence, this stigma to him.[29]

The issues of Reconstruction have affected the subsequent political history in another significant respect. The white masses did not forget the power they had displayed in 1876. They had pointed the way to Hampton's victory and then executed it. Afterwards they became angry with the manner in which Hampton and the clique which surrounded him seized the public offices for themselves. They were especially angry that General Gary, a cherished leader, was disappointed in his ambition to be governor or United States senator. Moreover, they were angered that the merchants of the towns, a class which came into prominence during Reconstruction, were able, through high prices and high interest rates on loans, to appropriate much of the profits of their farms. Consequently, when Ben Tillman, a farmer reared in the traditions of General Gary, voiced their complaints, they followed him enthusiastically and hurled Hampton and his coadjutors from office. Since that time it has been impossible for men not closely in touch with the plain white man to get public office in the state.

The whites followed their victories in politics by legislation which secured their position as a superior caste. The colored caste was precisely defined as composed of persons of one-

[29] For example, one of the reasons why Cole L. Blease, a politician who has profited much by accusing his enemies of Negroism, was defeated for the United States Senate in 1918 was because his principal newspaper opponent, the supposed enemy of such tactics, accused him of catering to the political ambitions of Negro university students.—*The State*, Aug. 27, 1918.

eighth or more Negro blood.[30] Marriage between the two castes was prohibited in 1879,[31] and rape was made a capital crime in 1878.[32] By the constitution of 1895 mixed schools were prohibited,[33] and in 1898 the races were required to ride in separate compartments on railroads.[34] In 1891 an attempt was made to put a check upon the mobility of Negro labor by the imposition of a prohibitive tax on emigration agents,[35] and in 1915 cotton manufacturing establishments were prohibited from employing the two races in the same operation.[36]

These and other laws in which the issue of race is not mentioned have usually been applied so as to discriminate against the Negro. The assumption of the equality of all men before the law has usually been flaunted whenever the issue of white supremacy has been involved. Juries have, in almost all cases, consisted exclusively of whites, and they have seldom turned a Negro free for an alleged crime against a white person and they have seldom convicted a white person for an alleged crime against a Negro. White public opinion has not always been content to let the law take its course in dealing with Negro culprits; since Reconstruction white mobs have lynched several scores of Negroes, and no one has been punished for these lawless acts. The law against the mixing of races in factories has made certain the exclusion of Negroes from most of the operations in cotton manufacture, the state's largest industry. The law against the mixing of races in schools has meant that Negro schools are very much inferior to those provided for the whites. The prohibition of the intermarriage of races has prevented colored women from getting the usual legal redresses against white men who betray their confidence.

The social restrictions which the whites have been able to impose on the blacks since Reconstruction are far more ex-

---

[30] *Constitution of 1895*, Art. III, Sec. 33.
[31] *Stat. S. C.*, XVII, 3.
[32] *Ibid.*, XVI, 175.
[33] Art. XI, Sec. 7.
[34] *Stat. S. C.*, XXII, 777.
[35] *Ibid.*, XX, 1048.
[36] *Ibid.*, XXIX, 79.

tensive than the statutes of the state indicate. Unwritten custom prescribes that the two races can have social relations only
on condition that the blacks acknowledge their inferiority. No
statute prohibits whites from teaching in Negro schools, but
the white who does so loses many of the privileges of his caste.
No law requires racial separation in street gatherings, but on
such occasions the invisible force of social distinction attracts
each race to groups of its own kind. Nowhere in South Carolina do members of the two races sit at the same table; all
whites would regard such a practice as a gross violation of
social propriety. They address all Negroes by their first names,
and the Negroes recognize their inferiority by replying with a
title. The familiarity tolerated between Negroes and white
children is broken when the child approaches maturity; social
relations are continued only on condition that the blacks
acknowledge their inferiority.

Fundamentally the conditions just described are a heritage
from the slave régime. The experiences of Reconstruction,
however, sharpened the distinctions between the races. During that period the blacks won many social privileges and became less tolerant of the white man's assumption of dominance.
But in no respect were they able to break through the hard
forms of caste. Consequently one of their greatest ambitions
has been to make themselves socially independent of the whites,
and an independent Negro society which gives the blacks a
maximum of social freedom has grown up. On the other
hand, the whites, unable to control the Negroes to the degree
they once did, have tended to make themselves free of the Negroes. They do many things for themselves which were once
done by black servants, and they are not as intimate or as sympathetic with the free Negroes as their grandfathers were with
the slaves.

The social maladjustments inherent in this sharpening of
race distinctions have tended to make both races dissatisfied

with each other. To escape the restraints of the color line the blacks have developed migratory habits. They move from farm to farm, from one employment to another, and often leave the state. Since 1880 the proportion of blacks in the state has declined from 60.7 per cent to less than one half. The whites have applauded this movement and in some instances regard the Negro as a social outcast. This view has been rudely expressed by demagogues and irresponsible mobs. But it has also found expression in more enlightened circles. The progressive and socially minded leaders of the whites have tended to grow more nationalistic. But their nationalism has little in common with the brand the carpet-baggers tried to impose. They wish to see South Carolina approximate the economic and social standards of the Northern and Western states, and they feel that the Negro is the great obstacle which stands in the way. His heritage of ignorance prevents the state from conforming to the educational standards of the nation; legislatures have been reluctant to adopt progressive measures because of the legal necessity of conferring part of their benefits on him; immigrants are unwilling to compete with his labor; political discussions, suffrage laws, and party organizations cannot conform to liberal and democratic standards because of him. Hence it is felt that the progress of the state can be best promoted by his elimination.

*   *   *   *   *

One consequence of Reconstruction has been the inability of the commonwealth to make significant contributions to the life of the nation. Since that dark period, its chief glory has been in recalling past achievements and in attaining material prosperity like that of Northern states. A heritage of disappointment and poverty has fostered a narrow utilitarianism which has left little room for the things of the spirit. The state has had little opportunity or inclination to assume the sort of leadership it exercised before the war. Its most trusted citizens have not been men of distinction. The first generation of post-Reconstruction leaders were the sons of great slaveholders. They had the polish but not the substance of their fathers. Their chief concern was to secure the emoluments of public office with which to mend their fortunes. The leaders who came after them were small-town merchants and lawyers or inexperienced men fresh from the farm. Those among them who achieved fame did so merely because they were picturesque and vehement.

Perhaps the most significant influence of Reconstruction has been the interpretation which has been put upon it. Writers have never tired of telling an interested public the story of this period. They have given it a sinister and an immense significance in the history of the commonwealth. They have painted in deep colors the horrors of the political events of the period, but have given little attention to important economic and social changes. The motives and actions of the Radical leaders have been shown in the most unfavorable light, while those of the Conservative leaders have been given most favorable interpretations. The result is that the white people have come to believe that the horrors and humiliations of Reconstruction were greater than those of the Civil War. Wade Hampton has become the hero of the state. His name is more affectionately revered than that of Calhoun. This is due primarily to his services in 1876, not to his career as a soldier.

The general character of the period has been portrayed in lurid colors. "Reconstruction," said Ben Tillman, "was this villainy, anarchy, misrule and robbery, and I cannot, in any word that I possess, paint it. There is no man on this floor [then] living in the country who dared during that dark period to leave his fireside without dread that when he returned he would find some harm to his family; and he dared not go forth without being armed, fearful of robbery. The sky was lit almost every night by the glare of burning dwellings and gin houses."[37] J. C. Sheppard, who represented another faction of the whites, agreed with Tillman in respect to Reconstruction, saying, "The record of the horrible crimes and disgusting debauchery which characterized the government, in all its departments, from 1868 to 1876, is here. No epitome can be made of it. In venality and corruption it was without parallel in the history of civilized government."[38]

Historians have confirmed the judgment of political leaders. "Ill-starred South Carolina," says a recent writer, "passed from bayonet rule to the government of those 'who robbed while they pretended to rule; who plundered while they professed to protect.' For there now began an orgy of corruption and crime, and the people of the state 'entered upon a period of mental anguish and material disaster unequalled in the annals of civilization.' . . . In fact, there was no state government, nor anything worthy of the name. . . ."[39] The government, says the most authoritative writer, was based on the suffrage of a "race incapable of forming any judgment upon the actions of men. . . . It naturally became a 'stench in the nostrils of decent people' and a disgrace to the country. The Federal bayonets removed, the power of the thieves destroyed, the so-called government fell to pieces of its own imbecility, came to naught of its own all-pervading corruption."[40]

The basest motives have been ascribed to those responsible for the inauguration of congressional reconstruction. It is asserted that had Lincoln lived "the South would have been spared a period, the horrors of which were even worse than those of the war";[41] he might even have paid for the loss of the slaves. But the leaders of Congress pretended "that they intended to restore free government when in truth their purposes were to humiliate the Southern whites and perpetuate party

[37] *Journal of the Constitutional Convention of 1895,* p. 462.

[38] *Ibid.,* p. 478.

[39] Henry T. Thompson, *op. cit.,* p. 53.

[40] Reynolds, *Reconstruction in South Carolina,* pp. 504, 514.

[41] Thompson, *op. cit.,* p. 13.

ascendency."[42] Thad Stevens has been made into an arch-villain worse than Sherman. His purpose, says the biographer of Hampton, "was irretrievably to destroy the dominant race in the South, and on its ruins to erect the rule of a population of hybrids." He was influenced in this action by his mulatto mistress. "He was dragged down in race sentiment to her level, and became as thoroughly saturated with hatred as she herself was. . . . Through his brain she forged the fetters, by his hand she fastened the manacles."[43]

On the other hand, the very best motives are ascribed to the local white leaders. The fact that they immediately recognized the abolition of slavery and the restoration of the Union is given emphasis, and the "black code" is interpreted as an effort to save civilization and to protect the Negro from his own folly.[44] It is asserted that "the two races of the South understood each other" and that had there been no outside interference white leaders would have promoted the very best interests of the blacks.[45] The Southern people, we are told, were right in their refusal to coöperate with the Reconstructionists, for in the absence of judicial determination they were proper in their belief that the measures taken by Congress to enfranchise the Negro were unconstitutional.[46] Although it is admitted "that even had the Negro government been administered honestly, effectively and economically the white people would not have acquiesced," this attitude is justified. Such acquiescence would have involved social equality. The political leaders of the day, we are reminded, "ate and drank, walked and rode, went to public places and ostensibly affiliated with Negroes." The patience of the whites under the afflictions of Reconstruction is extolled. Bad as was the course of Reconstruction, "conditions would have been far worse but for the

[42] Reynolds, *op. cit.,* p. 500.
[43] Edward L. Wells, *Hampton and Reconstruction,* pp. 79-82.
[44] Reynolds, *op. cit.,* p. 496.
[45] Thompson, *op. cit.,* pp. 26-27.
[46] Reynolds, *op. cit.,* pp. 501-6.

coolness, bravery and forbearance of the white people acting under the advice of wise and patriotic leaders." An almost idyllic portrait is drawn of General Gary, the most extreme of the white leaders. "Five feet eleven in height, with an elegant, well-proportioned form," says a recent historian, "he bore hi' self with an air of distinction. His face was that of a thinker and doer combined. . . . A member of the old aristocracy, he lived elegantly. . . . Among women, he was all gentleness and gallantry, enjoying their society, especially if they were beautiful and intellectual. There was just a faint fragrance of romance in the traditions around him."[47]

Most of the acts of the Radical government have been severely condemned. Of the constitution of 1868 the temporary chairman of the convention of 1895 said, "That constitution was made by aliens, Negroes and native whites without character, all enemies of South Carolina, and was designed to degrade our State, insult our people and overturn our civilization. It is a stain upon the reputation of South Carolina that she has voluntarily lived for eighteen years under that instrument."[48] The rule of Generals Sickles and Canby was said to have been "as brutish a tyranny as ever marked the course of any government whose agents and organs claimed to be civilized."[49] The Negroes and their leaders are held largely responsible for the crimes of the age. "Crimes among the Negroes were frequent," we are told, "and at the instigation of their leaders they passed to actual deeds of violence."[50] Chief State Constable Hubbard is described as one "who could be depended upon to do whatever underhand and brutal jobs were necessary to terrorize the whites."[51] The Republican leaders "from the first spread abroad false stories of killings and other outrages committed by the Southern whites on the Negroes, solely because the Ne-

[47] Claude G. Bowers, *The Tragic Era,* p. 503.
[48] *Journal of the Constitutional Convention of 1895,* pp. 1-2.

[49] Thompson, *op. cit.,* p. 98.
[50] *Ibid.,* p. 49.
[51] *Ibid.,* p. 46.

gross voted the Republican ticket; while, as a matter of fact, the restraint of the whites, remarkable in the face of the aggressiveness of the Negroes, alone prevented serious trouble between the races."[52] The governor has even been accused of creating riots. "The usual course before that [1875] in all such cases [riots]," says Congressman J. J. Hemphill, "had been for the Governor to work up these troubles into insurrections and have some Negroes killed and then appeal to the President for troops to suppress them."[53] The organization of the whites for armed resistance is justified. "No one who was not a citizen of the South in those days," says Professor R. Means Davis, "could appreciate the situation which gave rise to the Ku Klux. Something outside the law was needed to keep in check the Republican administration."[54] The schools were said to have been of little benefit. Reynolds says, "The school sessions were irregular, the teachers became discouraged, the white taxpayers were naturally disgusted, and the entire system had sunk into a state of disrepute and worthlessness. . . . The university was a fraud upon the state, as well as an imposition upon the taxpaying whites whose sons were excluded from its advantages."[55]

The conduct of the whites in 1876 has been the subject of elaborate defenses. Although Chamberlain's character and attainments are recognized by most writers as superior to those of his associates, it is felt that the whites acted wisely in not accepting him as their leader. From the time of the constitutional convention (1868) "till the last day of his occupancy of the state house his closest associates were among the lowest products of the Reconstruction period. . . . His partisanship was never modified sufficiently to cause any abatement of his servile submission to the behests of his party."[56] He was unable to bring lasting reforms because he could not control his party. His conduct after the Hamburg riot proved that he was un-

[52] Ibid., p. 82.
[53] In Hilary A. Herbert, *Why the Solid South*, pp. 105-6.
[54] Cited in Thompson, *op. cit.*, p. 54.
[55] *Op. cit.*, pp. 219, 509.
[56] *Ibid.*, pp. 507-10.

worthy of the support of respectable citizens. His account of that event was "a lurid partisan story for propaganda purposes in the North."[57] To Tillman he was "one of those swindlers" and an "infamous scoundrel."[58] Tillman frankly admits that illegal methods were used to effect Hampton's election. "By fraud and violence, if you please, we threw it [the Radical yoke] off." Those who admit that this is true feel that the methods used were justified. "Whatever may be said of the methods used by the whites," says Reynolds, "it must be said that the conduct of the Negroes, incited by their leaders, was quite as bad. Of actual intimidation there was much more visited upon colored Democrats than upon colored Republicans. . . . A careful study of the whole situation . . . must bring the conclusion that if fraudulent or otherwise illegal voting had been eliminated Hampton would still have been elected."[59]

The positive contributions of Reconstruction to the permanent life of the state were considerable. In notable instances political institutions created then have survived the uprooting following 1876. The principle of the equality of all men before the law was then grafted into the judicial practice of the state and it has not since been extirpated. The same is true of the right of all to attend state-supported schools and, potentially at least, to enjoy all political and civil liberties. Although the makers of the constitution of 1895 roundly attacked the constitution of 1868, the document they produced is scarcely more than a revision of the handiwork of the Radicals. Such notable parts of the constitution of 1868 as the provisions for the organization of the courts, the codes of judicial procedure, the systems of county government and school administration, the terms and manner of election of public officials, and the system of taxation were repeated in the constitution of 1895.

[57] Bowers, op. cit., p. 506.
[58] Journal of the Constitutional Convention of 1895, pp. 455-56.
[59] Op. cit., p. 504.

Except only in suffrage provisions and in declarations of rights are the two documents strikingly different.

Many of the innovations of Reconstruction in social and economic matters not directly affected by political changes have survived to this day. The winning by the Negroes of the liberty to manage their own church affairs is an achievement which still has a powerful influence upon the character of every community of the state. The system of land tenure and labor contracts devised during Reconstruction exists today with few modifications. The social adjustments then worked out are the basis of the comparative peace and contentment between the two races today. The Negro then learned that freedom had its obligations as well as its rights and that it was folly to aspire after many of the social privileges of the whites. The whites learned to tolerate the moderate aspirations of the Negroes. During Reconstruction the commercial towns and villages came into being. At present they dot the map of the state, forming its most important economic and social units.

In the years following the war, those attitudes of mind and action which are associated with the achievements of the New South had their inception. As early as 1865 there were hopes that the outcome of the war would bring new social and industrial opportunities. Most of these early hopes had immediate disappointment. But they were not given up, and the trials of those who cherished them were a sound experience. The leaders were shorn of romantic optimism. They became frugal, cautious, and practical. They were prepared to translate their hopes into practical achievements when the opportunity came. This opportunity was upon them as soon as the poverty caused by the war and the confusion caused by Reconstruction were things of the past. In the early eighties of the last century new industries, notably cotton mills, got under way, and by 1900 the state may be said to have regained what it had lost as the result of events following 1860. In 1900 its gross wealth was equal to that of 1860, and its people began to forget the glories and disappointments of the past in order to expect a future, if not of distinctive achievements, at least of material satisfaction and social progress.

APPENDIX

The following is General Martin W. Gary's plan of the campaign of 1876. This is copied from the original in the possession of Mr. F. B. Gary, Columbia, South Carolina, and is given to us through the courtesy of Mr. Gary and the Hon. John Gary Evans, Spartanburg, South Carolina. The rules here printed in italics were crossed out and marked "omit" in the original. These rules and the additional rules 28, 29, 30, 31, 32 and 33 are in General Gary's handwriting. This copy was afterwards corrected by D. R. Dureso, who acted as General Gary's secretary, and copies were furnished to the counties of the state.

No. 1
"Plan of the Campaign"
1876

1. That every Democrat in the Townships must be put upon the Roll of the Democratic Clubs. Nolens volens.

2. That a Roster must be made of every *white* and of *every negro* voter in the Townships and *returned immediately* to the County Executive Committee.

3. *That the Democratic Military Clubs are to be armed with rifles and pistols and such other arms as they may command. They are to be divided into two companies, one of the old men the other of the young; an experienced captain or commander to be placed over each of them. That each Company is to have a 1st and 2nd Lieutenant. That the number of ten privates is to be the unit of organization. That each Captain is to see that his men are well armed and provided with at least thirty rounds of ammunition. That the Captain of the young men is to provide a Baggage wagon, in which three days rations for*

*the horses and three days rations for the men are to be stored
on the day before the election in order that they may be prepared at a moments notice to move to any point in the County
when ordered by the Chairman of the Executive Committee.*

Election

4. We must get the three Commissioners of Election, who
are appointed by the Governor, as favorable to us as possible,
and we must demand that at least one reliable Democrat is on
the Commission and he must endeavor to get to be Chairman
of the Commission, and the clerk that is allowed them must be
a Democrat if we can possibly bring it about.

5. We must have at least one half of the managers of Election Democrats and as many more as we can get. We must
have the Chairman of the Board of Managers a Democrat by
all means. Also all the clerks to the managers of Precincts
must be Democrats.

6. We must have a duplicate of the result of the Election
made out for the benefit of the Executive Committee so soon as
the ballots are counted and forwarded at once by a courier, on
the night of the Election. There must be a Committee who
shall keep watch and guard over the ballot boxes to prevent
the Radicals from tampering with them in any way.

7. We must send a committee with a duplicate of the Election to Columbia in order to see to it that the State Canvassers
do not perpetrate any fraud upon us after the Election is held,
and see also that the Clerk of the Court files a copy of the returns of Election in accordance with Law.

8. *There must be at least two hundred select men, chosen
from the different Clubs, to go to Columbia in the event of a
refusal to seat the Democratic members elected, to compel and
enforce their rights to be seated at all hazards.*

9. Every Democrat must be at the polls by five o'clock in
the morning of the election, carry his dinner with him and

stay there until the votes are counted, unless the exigencies require him elsewhere.

10. It shall be the duty of each club to provide transportation to old and helpless voters and assist them to the Polls, and at same time see to it that all Democrats turn out and vote.

11. Every Democrat must be on the alert on the day of Election to see that negroes under age do not vote and that those who are properly entitled to vote do not repeat, and if they should discover that squads should leave the precincts and go in the direction of another precinct, they must follow them and challenge their vote at the next precinct.

12. Every Democrat must feel honor bound to control the vote of at least one negro, by intimidation, purchase, keeping him away or as each individual may determine, how he may best accomplish it.

13. We must attend every Radical meeting that we hear of whether they meet at night or in the day time. Democrats must go in as large numbers as they can get together, and well armed, behave at *first* with great courtesy and assure the ignorant negroes that you mean them no harm and so soon as their *leaders* or speakers begin to speak and make false statements of facts, tell them *then* and *there* to their faces, that they are liars, thieves and rascals, and are only trying to mislead the ignorant negroes and if you get a chance get upon the platform and address the negroes.

14. In speeches to negroes you must remember that *argument* has no effect upon them: They can only be influenced by their *fears,* superstition and cupidity. Do not attempt to flatter and persuade them. Tell them plainly of our wrongs and grievances, perpetrated upon us, by their rascally leaders. Prove to them that we can carry the election without them and if they coöperate with us, it will benefit them more than it will us. Treat them so as to show them, you are the superior race,

and that their natural position is that of subordination to the white man.

15. Let it be generally known that if any blood is shed, houses burnt, votes repeated, ballot boxes stuffed, false counting of votes, or any acts on their part that are in violation of *Law* and *Order!* that we will hold the leaders of the *Radical Party personally responsible,* whether they were present at the time of the commission of the offense or crime or not; beginning *first* with the white men, second the mulatto men and third with the black leaders. This should be proclaimed from one end of the country to the other, so that *every Radical* may know it, as the *certain, fixed* and *unalterable determination* of every Democrat in this county.

16. *"Never threaten a man individually if he deserves to be threatened, the necessities of the times require that he should die. A dead Radical is very harmless—a threatened Radical or one driven off by threats from the scene of his operations is often very troublesome, sometimes dangerous, always vindictive."*

17. Members of the Executive Committee and the leading members of the Party should visit the various Clubs and explain the Plan of the Campaign and such facts as are necessarily of such a nature as are not to be reduced to writing.

18. There should be at least five map meetings in the County, during the canvass, and the last one should be held at Edgefield C. H. on or about the middle of October.

19. The months of July and August ought to be devoted to speeches at the Club meetings or Township meetings, and speeches should then be made by the candidates and such other speakers as we can obtain.

20. At our map meetings we should invite distinguished men of this and other States to address our people.

21. *In the month of September we ought to begin to organize negro clubs, or pretend that we have organized them and*

write letters from different parts of the County giving the facts of organization out from prudential reasons, the names of the negroes are to be withheld. Those who join are to be taken on probation and are not to be taken into full fellowship, until they have proven their sincerity by voting our ticket.

22. In the nomination of candidates we should nominate those who will give their time, their money, their brains, their energies and if necessary lay down their lives to carry this election. Any attempt to run independent candidates must be prevented at any risk.

23. There should not be any assessment for money to carry on the campaign, before the month of October, when the cotton crop begins to mature and our people have an opportunity of raising money by its sale.

24. In voting for or nominating candidates for County, State or Federal offices, we must give the preference to native born *white South Carolinians* over Carpet baggers.

25. The watch word of our Campaign should be "fight the Devil with fire." That we are in favor of local self government, home rule by home folks and that we are determined to drive the carpet baggers from this State at all hazards.

26. That we must make the Campaign an aggressive one and prosecute it with great vigor and try and get up all the enthusiasm we can among the masses.

27. That harmony and concord should be preserved in our ranks. Personal considerations, must be given up for the good of the County. Success must be achieved at the sacrifice of everything except the *principles* of our Great Party.

The boys from 16 upwards are to be enrolled on the lists of our clubs.

28. In all processions the clubs must parade with banners, mottoes, etc. and keep together so as to make an imposing spectacle.

29. Every club must be uniformed in a red shirt and they

must be sure and wear it upon all public meetings and particularly on the day of election.

30. Secrecy should shroud all of transactions. Let not your left hand know what your right does.

31. Where ever there are two election precincts at the Court House the Democrats should remain mounted in order to move at once from one box to the other in case of any disturbances.

32. Where the negroes are largely in the majority a corps of challengers should be organized, with appropriate questions. You gain time by this.

33. Any member of the Party who fails to vote the ticket must be read out of the Party.

BIBLIOGRAPHY

Address of the Democratic white voters of Charleston to the Colored Voters of Charleston, the Seaboard and the State Generally. Charleston, 1868.

Adger, Robert, and others. Memorial with endorsement, report and order thereon. To Secretary of the Treasury. Charleston, 1865.

Allen, Walter. Governor Chamberlain's Administration in South Carolina. A Chapter of Reconstruction in the Southern States. New York and London, 1888.

Allen, W. J., and others, editors. Slave Songs of the United States. New York, 1867.

Alvord, J. W. Letters from the South relating to the Condition of the Freedmen. Addressed to Major General O. O. Howard, Commissioner, Bureau Refugees, Freedmen and Abandoned Lands. Washington, 1870.

American Annual Cyclopedia and Register of Important Events, The. New York, 1861-1902.

American Baptist Home Missionary Society, Annual Reports. Philadelphia, 1865-1877.

American Baptist Yearbook. Philadelphia, 1865-1877.

A. M. E. Church Review. Philadelphia, 1884-

Ames, Mary. From a New England Woman's Diary in Dixie in 1865. Norwood, Mass., 1906.

Andrews, Sidney. The South Since the War; as shown by fourteen weeks of travel and observation in Georgia and the Carolinas. Boston, 1866.

Annual Report of the Adjutant-General, on the operations of the freedmen's branch of his office, for the years 1873-78. 6 vols. Washington, 1873-78.

Annual Report of the Commissioner of Agriculture, 1865-1877. Washington.

Annual Report of the U. S. Commissioner of Education, 1870-. Washington.

Appeal to the Honorable the Senate of the United States, in behalf of the Conservative People of South Carolina, against the adoption by Congress of the New Constitution proposed for South Carolina. Columbia, 1868.

Archer, Henry P. Education in Charleston. Charleston Yearbook, 1886.

Armes, William Dallam. *See* Le Conte, Joseph.

Avary, Myrta Lockett. Dixie after the War. New York, 1906.

————. *See* Chesnut, Mary Boykin.

Baker, O. E. *See* Stine, O. C.

Ball, W. W. A Boy's Recollection of the Red Shirt Campaign. Columbia, 1911.

Bancroft, Frederic A. A Sketch of the Negro in Politics, especially in South Carolina and Mississippi. New York, 1885.

Barnwell, Joseph W. Dual State Governments, an address before the S. C. Historical Society, May 18th, 1880. Charleston, 1880.

Bellinger, Lucius. Stray-leaves from the Port-Folio of a Local Preacher. Macon, Ga., 1870.

Bettis, Alexander. *See* Nicholson, Alfred W.

Biographical Congressional Directory with an Outline History of the National Congress, 1774-1911. Washington, 1913. Extended to 1927. Washington, 1928.

Blue Ridge Railroad Company, South Carolina. Report of the chief engineer, July, 1871. Columbia, 1871.

Boddie, William Willis. History of Williamsburg County, South Carolina, 1705 until 1923. Columbia, 1923.

Botume, Elizabeth Hyde. First Days amongst the Contrabands. Boston, 1893.

Bowen, C. C. Right of Suffrage. Speech delivered in the House of Representatives, Jan. 29, 1869. Washington, 1869.

Bowen, Herbert W. Recollections Diplomatic and Undiplomatic. New York, 1926.

Bowers, Claude G. The Tragic Era. Boston, 1929.

Bratton, Theodore. Wanted—Leaders, A Study of Negro Development. New York, 1922.

Brawley, Benjamin. Social History of the American Negro. New York, 1912.

Broadus, John Albert. *See* Robertson, Archibald Thomas.

Brooks, U. R. South Carolina Bench and Bar. Vol. I. Columbia, 1908.

Brown, William Perry. A Sea-Island Romance. A Story of South Carolina after the War. New York, 1888.

Burgess, James M. Chronicles of St. Mark's Parish, Santee Circuit, and Williamsburg Township, South Carolina, 1731-1885. Columbia, 1888.

Campbell, Sir George. White and Black. The Outcome of a Visit to the United States. London and New York, 1879.

Campbell, James B. Remarks upon the affairs of the Savannah and Charleston Railroad Company, in the relations to South Carolina. Columbia, 1875.

——————. Two letters from the Hon. James B. Campbell, U. S. Senator elect from South Carolina, on Public Affairs, and our duties to the Colored Race. Published by the Democratic Central Executive Committee of South Carolina, n. p., 1868.

Capers, Henry D. The Life and Times of C. G. Memminger. Richmond, 1893.

Cardozo, Francis L. Address before the Grand Council of the Union Leagues at their annual meeting, held July 27, 1870. Columbia, 1870.

——————. Finances of the State of South Carolina. Columbia, 1873.

Carpenter, L. Cass. South Carolina before the national government; address to the President of the United States in behalf of free government in South Carolina and in reply to the memorialists from the so-called taxpayers' convention. Washington, 1874.

Census Reports. A Compendium of the Ninth Census: 1870. Washington, 1872.

——————. Abstract of the Eleventh Census: 1890. Washington, 1894.

——————. Negro Population in the United States, 1790-1915. Washington, 1918.

——————. Reports: 1860, 1870, 1880, 1890. Washington.

Centennial Edition of The Charleston News and Courier. Charleston, 1904.

Chamberlain, Daniel H. Arguments during the Ku-Klux Trials, at Columbia, S. C. Columbia, 1872.

——————. Dependent Pension Bills; and The Race Problem at the South. Speech before the Massachusetts Reform Club at Boston, Feb. 8, 1890. Boston, 1890.

——————. Financial Management of the Republican Administration of South Carolina, speech at the mass meeting in Chester, S. C., Aug. 19, 1870. Charleston, 1870.

—————. "The Race Problem," *New England Magazine,* Vol. LII.

—————. "Reconstruction and the Negro," *North American Review.* Vol. CXXVIII (1879).

—————. "Reconstruction in South Carolina," *Atlantic Monthly.* Vol. LXXXVII (April, 1901).

Charleston Year Book, The. Charleston, 1880-.

Chazal, Philip E. The Century in Phosphates and Fertilizers, a Sketch of the South Carolina Phosphate Industry. Charleston, 1904.

Chesnut, Mary Boykin. A Diary from Dixie, as written by Mary Boykin Chesnut, wife of James Chesnut, Jr., U. S. Senator from S. C., 1859-1861, and afterward an Aide to Jefferson Davis and a Brigadier-General in the Confederate Army. Edited by Isabella D. Martin and Myrta Lockett Avary. New York, 1905.

Christensen, A. M. H. Afro-American Folk Lore told round cabin fires on the Sea Islands of South Carolina. Boston, 1892.

Christian Index and South-Western Baptist. Atlanta.

Columbia, S. C. The Future Manufacturing and Commercial Centre of the South. Columbia, 1871.

Comettant, (Jean Pierre) Oscar. Voyage pittoresque et anecdotique dans le nord et le sud des États-unis d' Amérique. Paris, 1866.

Conyngham, Captain David P. Sherman's March through the South with sketches and incidents of the Campaign. New York, 1865.

Cook, Harvey T. Education in South Carolina under Baptist Control. Greenville, S. C., 1912.

—————. The Life Work of James Clement Furman. Greenville, S. C., 1926.

Cooley, Rossa B. Homes of the Freed, with an introduction by J. H. Dillard and four wood cuts by J. J. Lankes. New York, 1925.

Corbin, D. T. Speech delivered before a Republican mass meeting at Greenville, S. C., on the Fourth of July, 1872. n. p., n. d.

Coxe, Elizabeth Allen. Memories of a South Carolina Plantation during the War. Philadelphia, 1912.

Cromwell, John W. The Negro in American history; men and women eminent in the evolution of the American of African descent. Washington, 1914.

Cyclopedia of Eminent and Representative Men of the Carolinas of the Nineteenth Century. 2 vols. Madison, Wis., 1892.

Davidson, James Wood. The Living Writers of the South. New York, 1869.

Dawson, Warrington. Le Nègre aux États-Unis. Paris, 1912.

DeBow's Review. New Series. 1866-1870.

Delany, Martin R. See Rollin, Frank A.

Derrick, Samuel M. Centennial History of South Carolina Railroad. Columbia, 1930.

DuBois, W. E. B. "Reconstruction and its Benefits," *American Historical Review*, XV (1910).

Dictionary of American Biography. Edited by Allen Johnson and Dumas Malone. New York, 1929 et seq.

Diocesan Journal of the annual convention of the Protestant Episcopal Church of South Carolina. Charleston, 1859-1889.

Dixon, William Hepworth. White Conquest. 2 vols. London, 1875.

Dunning, William A. Reconstruction, Political and Economic. American Nation Series. New York, 1905.

Evans, Matilda A. Martha Schofield, Pioneer Negro Educator. Historical and philosophical review of Reconstruction period of South Carolina. Columbia, 1916.

Fleming, Walter L. A Documentary History of Reconstruction. 2 vols. Cleveland, 1906.

————. The Freedmen's Savings Bank; a Chapter in the Economic History of the Negro Race. Chapel Hill, N. C., 1927.

————. The Sequel to Appomattox: A Chronicle of the Reunion of the States. New Haven, 1921.

Fox, William F. Regimental Losses in the American Civil War, 1861-1865. Albany, N. Y., 1898.

[French, Justus Clement]. The Trip of the Steamer Oceanus to Fort Sumter and Charleston, S. C., comprising the incidents of the excursion, the appearance, at that time, of the city, and the entire programme of the exercises of re-raising the flag over the ruins of Fort Sumter, April 14, 1865. Brooklyn, 1865.

Furman, James Clement. See Cook, Harvey T.

Gannett, W. C. See Hale, Edward Everett.

Garrett, T. H. A History of the Saluda Baptist Association, etc. Richmond, 1896.

Garrison, Wendell Phillips, and Garrison, Francis Jackson. William Lloyd Garrison, 1805-1879. 4 vols. Boston and New York, 1885 and 1889.

Gary, Martin Witherspoon. Address delivered in the Senate of S. C., May 2, 1877, on Bill to Regulate the Rate of Interest. Columbia, 1877.

—————. Speech delivered in the Senate of S. C., May 25, 1877, on a Bill to make Appropriations. n. p., n. d.

—————. Speech on the Public Debt of the State of S. C. Delivered in the Senate Chamber. Columbia, 1878.

—————. Speech before the Taxpayers' Convention of S. C., at Columbia, on the 19th February, 1874. n. p., n. d.

Gaston, James McFadden. Hunting a Home in Brazil. New York, 1867(?).

Gibbs, James G. Who Burnt Columbia. Newberry, S. C., 1902.

Green, Edwin L. A History of the University of South Carolina. Columbia, 1916.

Green, James. Personal Recollections of Daniel Henry Chamberlain. Read before the Worcester Society of Antiquity, December 3, 1907, by his fellow-student and lifelong friend. Worcester, Mass., 1908.

[Green, John Paterson]. Recollections of the inhabitants, localities, superstitions, and Ku-Klux outrages of the Carolinas. By a "carpetbagger" who was born there. Cleveland, 1880.

Griffith, H[arrison] P[atillo]. Varioso: A Collection of Sketches, Essays and Verses. n. p., 1911.

Guerard, A. R. A Sketch of the History, Origin, and Development of the South Carolina Phosphates. Charleston, 1884.

H—————, Mr. and Mrs. J. C. Life of Maumer Juno of Charleston, S. C., A Sketch of Juno [Waller] Seymour. Atlanta, 1892.

[Hale, Edward Everett, and Gannett, W. C.] "The Freedmen at Port Royal," The North American Review, CI (July, 1865).

Hall, S. B. A Shell in the Radical Camp; or, An Exposition of the Frauds of the Republican party of South Carolina. Vol. I. Charleston, 1873.

Hamilton, J. G. de Roulhac. "Southern Legislation in Respect to Freedmen, 1865-1866," Studies in Southern History and Politics inscribed to William Archibald Dunning. New York, 1914.

Hammond, Harry. Report on the Cotton Production of the State of South Carolina, with a discussion of the General Agricultural Features of the State. In Report on the Cotton Production of the United States by Eugene W. Hilgard. House Mis. Doc., 47 Cong., 2 Sess., pt. 6. Washington, 1884. Census, 1880, Vol. 6.

[—————]. See South Carolina: Resources and Population, Institutions and Industries.

Hammond, M. B. The Cotton Industry. An Essay in American

Economic History, Part I. The Cotton Culture and the Cotton Trade. Publications of the American Economics Association. New Series, No. 1. New York, 1897.

Hampton, Wade. Free men! Free ballots!! Free schools!!! The pledges of Gen. Wade Hampton, Democratic candidate for governor, to the colored people of South Carolina, 1865-1876. n. p., n. d.

————. Reply of Wade Hampton, Governor of South Carolina, and others to the Chamberlain Memorial. [Written by LeRoy F. Youmans.] Columbia, 1877.

————. See Wells, Edward L.

Hardy, Iza D. Between Two Oceans; or Sketches of American Travel. London, 1884.

Harrison, W. P., editor. The Gospel Among the Slaves. A short account of missionary operations among the African Slaves of the Southern States. Nashville, 1893.

Haworth, Paul Leland. The Hayes-Tilden Disputed Presidential Election of 1876. Cleveland, 1906.

Henderson, D. S. Argument for Defendants in the Ellenton Cases. Tried May term, 1877, in the Circuit Court of the U. S. at Charleston, S. C., Augusta, Ga., n. d.

————. The White Man's Revolution in South Carolina. Address delivered at the unveiling of the McKie Meriwether monument, North Augusta, S. C., Feb. 16, 1916, n. p., n. d.

Henderson, P. E., Henderson, D. S., Jr., and Henderson, T. R. Life and Addresses of D. S. Henderson. Columbia, 1922.

Herbert, Hilary A. Why the Solid South, Or, Reconstruction and its Results. Baltimore, 1890.

Higginson, Thomas Wentworth. Army Life in a Black Regiment. Boston, 1870.

————. "Negro Spirituals," *Atlantic Monthly,* Vol XIX (June, 1867).

Historical and Descriptive Review of the State of South Carolina and of the Manufacturing and Mercantile Industries of the Cities of Columbia and Charleston, including many sketches of leading public and private citizens. Vol. II. New York, 1884.

Hitchcock, Henry. Marching with Sherman; Passages from the Letters and Campaign Diaries of Henry Hitchcock. Edited by M. A. DeWolfe Howe. New Haven, 1927.

Hoffman, Frederick Ludwig. Race Traits and Tendencies of the American Negro. New York, 1896.

Holland, Rupert Sargent. *See* Towne, Laura M.

Hollis, John Porter. The Early Period of Reconstruction in South Carolina. Johns Hopkins University Studies, Series XXIII. Baltimore, 1905.

Holmes, Francis S. Phosphate Rocks of South Carolina and the Great Carolina Marl Bed. Charleston, 1870.

House and Senate of the U. S. Miscellaneous Documents.

Howard, Oliver Otis. Autobiography. 2 vols. New York, 1907.

Hunt, W. R. Compilation of the acts, rules, forms and regulations relating to the District Courts, civil rights bill, etc. Columbia, 1866.

International Yearbook (1898).

Jackson, Luther P. "The Educational Efforts of the Freedmen's Bureau and the Freedmen's Aid Societies in South Carolina, 1862-1872," *Journal of Negro History,* VIII (Jan. 1923).

Jannet, Claudio. Les États-Unis contemporains; ou les moeurs, les institutions et les idées depuis la guerre de la sécession. Ouvrage précédé d'une Lettre de M. De. Play. 2nd. ed. Paris, 1876.

Jervey, Theodore D. The Slave Trade. Slavery and Color. Columbia, 1925.

Jones, F. D., and Mills, W. H., editors. History of the Presbyterian Church in South Carolina Since 1850. Columbia, 1926.

Jonveaux, Emile. L'Amérique actuelle. 2nd ed. Paris, 1870.

Journal of the Constitutional Convention of the People of South Carolina held at Columbia, S. C., beginning September 10th and ending December 4th, 1895. Columbia, 1895.

Journal of the Convention of the People of South Carolina, held in Columbia, S. C., September, 1865. Together with the Ordinances, Reports, Resolutions, etc. Columbia, 1865.

Journal of the House of Representatives of the State of South Carolina. Columbia.

Journal of the Senate of the State of South Carolina. Columbia.

Kennaway, John A. On Sherman's Track or, The South After the War. London, 1867.

King, Edward. The Southern States of North America. Hartford, Conn., and London, 1875.

Knight, Edgar Wallace. The Influence of Reconstruction on Education in the South. Teachers College, Columbia University Contributions to Education, No. 60. New York, 1913.

————————. "Reconstruction and Education in South Carolina," *The South Atlantic Quarterly.* Vols. XVIII-XIX (Oct.-Jan., 1919-1920).

Kohn, August. The Cotton Mills of South Carolina: a series of Observations and Facts as Published in the News and Courier. Charleston, 1907.

Ku-Klux Conspiracy, The. Report of the Joint Select Committee to inquire into the condition of affairs in the late insurrectionary States. Made to the two houses of Congress, Feb. 19, 1872. Vol. I of Ku-Klux Conspiracy. Senate Report, 42 Cong., 2 Sess., no. 41. Washington, 1872.

Ku-Klux Conspiracy, The. Testimony taken by the Joint Select Committee to inquire into the condition of affairs in the late insurrectionary states. Washington, 1872. Vols. III, IV, and V contain testimony taken by the committee in relation to South Carolina and the report of the trials in the U. S. Court held at Columbia. Cited as Ku-Klux Conspiracy, S. C.

Land We Love, The. A monthly magazine devoted to literature, military history and agriculture. Edited by D. H. Hill. Charlotte, N. C., 1866-1869.

Latham, Henry. White and Black. A Journal of a Three Months' Tour in the U. S. London, 1867.

Lathers, Richard. Address to President Grant, of Col. Richard Lathers, chairman of a committee of the Chamber of Commerce of Charleston, S. C., appointed to co-operate with the committee entrusted with the duty of presenting to the President and to Congress the memorial of the Tax-Payers' Convention of South Carolina. Charleston, 1874.

————————. Discursive Biographical Sketch, 1841-1902. Philadelphia, 1902.

————————. Reminiscences; sixty years of a busy life in South Carolina, Massachusetts, and New York. Edited by Alvin F. Sanborn. New York, 1907.

————————. South Carolina. The Condition and Prospects of the State. Confiscation of Private Property and Repudiation of the Public Debt. Delivered before the New England Society of Charleston on Forefathers' Day, December 22, 1873. Charleston, 1874.

————————. South Carolina, her wrongs and the remedy; remarks delivered at the opening of the Tax-Payers' Convention in Columbia, S. C., Tuesday, February 17, 1874. Charleston, 1874.

Lawrence, William H. The Centenary Souvenir, Containing a history of the Centenary Church, Charleston, and an account of the life and labors of Rev. R. V. Lawrence, father of the pastor of the Centenary Church. Charleston, 1885.

Leclerq, Jules [Joseph]. Un Été en Amérique, de l'Atlantique aux montagnes Rocheuses. Paris, 1877.

Le Conte, Joseph. Autobiography. Edited by William Dallam Armes. New York, 1903.

Leiding, Harriette Kershaw. Street Cries of An Old Southern City. Charleston, 1910.

Leland, John A. A Voice from South Carolina. Twelve chapters before Hampton. Two chapters after Hampton. With a journal of a reputed Ku Klux, and an appendix. Charleston, 1879.

Lewisohn, Ludwig. The Case of Mr. Crump. Paris, 1926.

—————. Cities and Men. New York and London, 1927.

—————. Up Stream, an American Chronicle. New York, 1922.

Littell's Living Age (1865).

Logan, John R[andolph]. Sketches, Historical and Biographical, of the Broad River and King's Mountain Baptist Associations, from 1800 to 1882. Shelby, N. C., 1887.

Landon, Fred. "The Kidnapping of Dr. Rufus Bratton," Journal of Negro History, Vol. X (July, 1925).

McCrady, Edward. Letter to Mark Reynolds, M. P., Charleston, June 4. 1870.

—————. A Review of the Resolutions of the Press Conference. Charleston, 1870.

McGlothlin, W. J. Baptist Beginnings in Education: A History of Furman University. Nashville, 1926.

Mackey, A. G. and T. J. The Political Record of Senator F. A. Sawyer and Congressman C. C. Bowen of So. Car. Charleston, 1869.

McPherson, Edward. The Political History of the United States during the period of Reconstruction, 1865 to 1870. Washington, 1871.

Macrae, David. The Americans at Home; pen and ink sketches of American Men, Manners and Institutions. 2 vols. Edinburgh, 1870.

Manigault, G. The United States Unmasked. A search into the causes of the rise and progress of these States, and an exposure of their present material and moral condition. With additions and corrections by the author. London, 1879.

Martin, Isabella D. *See* Chesnut, Mary Boykin.

Maxwell, E. J. Hampton's Campaign in South Carolina. A series of seven articles in the *South Atlantic Magazine.* Jan.-Aug., 1878. Wilmington, N. C.

Mayo, A. D. Annual Report of the Commissioner of Education, 1899-1900, I; 1904, I. Washington.

Mazyck, Arthur. Guide to Charleston Illustrated. Being a sketch of the History of Charleston, S. C. With some account of its present condition, etc. Charleston, n. d. (1875?).

Mims, Florence Adams. History of the Edgefield Baptist Church. Published in the Edgefield Advertiser in some 57 chapters and preserved in scrapbook.

Minutes of the Annual Conferences of the Methodist Episcopal Church, South. Nashville, 1860-1877.

Minutes of the Charleston Baptist Association. Charleston, 1865-1877.

Minutes of the State Baptist Convention of South Carolina, 1859-1877. Columbia and Greenville, S. C.

Minutes of the South Carolina Conference of the A. M. E. Church, 1865.

Mitchell, Broadus. William Gregg, Factory Master of the Old South. Chapel Hill, N. C., 1928.

—————. The Rise of the Cotton Mills in the South. Johns Hopkins University Studies, Series XXXIX, no. 2. Baltimore, 1921.

Mitchell, Edward P. Memoirs of an Editor. New York and London, 1924.

Mohler, Mark. "The Episcopal Church and National Reconciliation," *Political Science Quarterly,* Vol. XLI (Dec., 1926).

The Monthly Record. Charleston, 1870-1875. The official organ of the diocese of the Protestant Episcopal Church.

Morgan, James Morrison. Recollections of a Rebel Reefer. Boston and New York, 1917.

Nation, The. New York, 1865-.

National Baptist, The. Philadelphia, 1865-.

Nichols, George Ward. The Story of the Great March. From the Diary of a Staff Officer. New York, 1865.

Nicholson, Alfred W. Brief Sketch of the Life and Labors of Rev. Alexander Bettis. Also an account of the Founding and development of the Bettis Academy. Trenton, S. C., 1913.

Nordoff, Charles. The Freedmen of South Carolina: Some account of their appearance, character, condition and peculiar customs. Papers of the Day Series, No. 1. New York, 1863.

O'Connell, O. S. B., Rev. Dr. J. J. Catholicity in the Carolinas and Georgia. Leaves of its History, A. D. 1820-1878. New York, 1879.

O'Connor, Mary Doline. The Life and Letters of M. P. O'Connor, written and edited by his daughter. New York, 1893.

Orr, James L. His Reasons for Joining the Republican Party in South Carolina. n. p., 1870.

Our Women in the War. The Lives they lived; the Deaths they died. From the weekly *News and Courier*. Charleston, 1885.

Parker, Niles G. A Retrospective View. Speech in defense of his official acts as State treasurer. July 5, 1872. Columbia, 1872.

Parsons, Elsie Clews. Folk-Lore of the Sea-Islands, South Carolina. Memoirs of the American Folk-Lore Society, XVI. New York, 1923.

Payne, Daniel Alexander. Recollections of Seventy Years. Nashville, 1888.

Pearson, Elizabeth Ware, editor. Letters from Port Royal written at the time of the Civil War. Boston, 1906.

Peirce, Paul Skeels. The Freedmen's Bureau, a chapter in the history of Reconstruction. University of Iowa studies in Sociology, Economics, Politics, and History, III, No. 1. Iowa City, 1904.

Perry, Benjamin Franklin. Reminiscences of Public Men, with speeches and addresses, second series. Greenville, S. C., 1889.

Perry, Bliss. Life and Letters of Henry Lee Higginson. Boston, 1921.

Phillips, Ulrich B. Transportation in the Eastern Cotton Belt to 1860. New York, 1908.

Pierce, Edward L. "The Freedmen at Port Royal," *Atlantic Monthly,* Vol. XII (1863).

Pike, James Shepherd. The Prostrate State; South Carolina Under Negro Government. New York, 1874.

Poor, H. V. Manual of the Railroads of the U. S. New York, 1868-1880.

Porcher, F. A. The Last Chapter in the History of Reconstruction in South Carolina. In Southern Historical Society Papers, XII and XIII. 1884, 1885.

Porter, A. Toomer. Forty Years as Rector and Pastor at the Church of the Holy Communion, Charleston, S. C. Charleston, 1894.

—————. Led on! Step by Step. Scenes from clerical, military, educational, and plantation life in the South, 1828-1898. An autobiography. New York, 1899.

Porter, W. D. The Constitutionality of the Lawyers Test Oath. n. p., 1866.

Post, Louis. "A 'Carpetbagger' in South Carolina," *Journal of Negro History*, Vol. X (Jan. 1925).

Potwin, Marjorie. Cotton Mills of the Piedmont. Columbia University Studies, New York, 1927.

Powers, Stephen. Afoot and Alone; a walk from Sea to Sea by the Southern route, etc. Hartford, Conn., 1872.

Pringle, Elizabeth W. Allston. Chronicles of Chicora Wood. New York, 1923.

Proceedings. Agricultural Convention of South Carolina. Charleston, 1869.

Proceedings in the Ku-Klux Trials at Columbia, S. C., in the United States Circuit Court, November term, 1871. Printed from government copy. Columbia, 1872.

Proceedings of the Agricultural and Mechanical Society of South Carolina. 1869.

Proceedings of the Colored People's Convention of the State of South Carolina, held in Zion Church, Charleston, November, 1865. Together with the Declaration of rights and wrongs; an address to the people; a petition to the legislature, and a memorial to Congress. Charleston, 1865.

Proceedings of the Constitutional Convention of South Carolina, held at Charleston, S. C., beginning January 14th and ending March 17, 1868. Including the Debates and Proceedings. Reported by J. Woodruff, Phonographic Reporter. Two volumes in one. Published by order of the Convention. Charleston, 1868.

Proceedings of the Electoral Commission and of the two houses of Congress in joint meeting relative to the count of electoral votes cast December 6, 1876, for the presidential term commencing March 4, 1877. Washington, 1877.

Proceedings of the Stockholders of the South Carolina Railroad Company and of the Southwestern Bank. Report of the President and Directors. Report of the Superintendent. The 13 and 14 February, 1866. Charleston, 1866.

Proceedings of the Taxpapers' Convention of South Carolina, held at Columbia, beginning May 9th, and ending May 12, 1871. Charleston, 1871.

Proceedings of the Taxpayers' Convention of South Carolina, held at

Columbia, beginning February 17, and ending February 20, 1874. Charleston, 1874.

Ralph, Julian. Dixie, or Southern Scenes and Sketches. New York, 1896.

Ramage, B. James. Local Government and Free Schools in South Carolina. Johns Hopkins University Studies in History and Political Science. Vol. I. Baltimore, 1883.

Recent Election in South Carolina, The. Testimony taken by the Select Committee on Recent Election in South Carolina. House Misc. Doc. No. 31. 44 Cong., 2 Sess. Washington, 1877.

Reid, Whitelaw. After the War: A Southern Tour. May 1, 1865 to May 1, 1866. New York, 1866.

Religious Bodies, 1916. Bureau of the Census. Washington, 1919.

Rejoinder to the Reply of the Central Committee of the Republican Party of South Carolina to the Memorial of the Taxpayers' Convention. Charleston, 1874.

Reply to the Memorial of the Taxpayers' Convention, addressed to the Honorable the Senate and House of Representatives of the U. S. Columbia, 1872.

Reports of Cases heard and determined by the Supreme Court of South Carolina. 1868-1880. Vols. I-XIII. Annotated Edition. St. Paul, 1916.

Report of the Commission to investigate the indebtedness of the State, made to the General Assembly of South Carolina at the regular session of 1877-78. Columbia, 1878.

Report of the Committee on the Destruction of Churches in the Diocese of South Carolina during the late war presented to the Protestant Episcopal Convention, May, 1868. Charleston, 1868.

Report of the Joint Committee on Reconstruction at the First Session of the Thirty-Ninth Congress. Washington, 1866.

Report of the Joint Investigating Committee on Public Frauds and Election of Hon. J. J. Patterson to the United States Senate made to the General Assembly of South Carolina at the regular session of 1877-78. Columbia, 1878. Cited as Reports and Resolutions, 1877-78. Fraud Report.

Reports and Resolutions of the General Assembly of the State of South Carolina. Columbia.

Republican Party. Address of true Republican party . . . for campaign of 1872. n. p., n. d.

Respectful Remonstrance on behalf of the White People of South Carolina against the Constitution of the late Convention of that State, now submitted to Congress for Ratification. Columbia, 1868.

Reynolds, John S. Reconstruction in South Carolina, 1865-1877. Columbia, 1905.

Rhodes, James Ford. The History of the United States from the Compromise of 1850. 9 vols. New York, 1893-1919.

Richardson, James D. A Compilation of the Messages and Papers of the President. 10 vols. Washington, 1898.

Robertson, Archibald Thomas. Life and Letters of John Albert Broadus. Philadelphia, 1910.

[Robertson, Stephen T.] The Shadow of the War: A Story of the South in Reconstruction Times. Chicago, 1884.

Robertson, Thomas J. Government of South Carolina. Speech in U. S. Senate, Jan. 29, 1877. Washington, 1877.

Rollin, Frank A. Life and Public Services of Martin R. Delany. Boston, 1868. Second ed., Boston, 1883.

Rose, George. The Great Country; or, Impressions of America. London, 1868.

Rural Carolinian, The. 1869-1876. Charleston and Cokesbury, S. C. Edited by D. Wyatt Aiken and D. H. Jacques.

Sanborn, Alvin F. See Lathers, Richard.

Saunders, William. Through the Light Continent, or The United States in 1877-1878. London and New York, 1879.

Sawyer, Frederick A. Amnesty-Civil Rights. Remarks delivered in the Senate of the U. S., Dec. 21, 1871, Jan. 22, Feb. 7, 9, 1872. Washington, 1872.

Schurz, Carl. Reminiscences. 3 vols. New York, 1907, 1909.

Scott, Edwin J. Random Recollections of a Long Life, 1806 to 1876. Columbia, 1884.

Scott, W. A. The Repudiation of State Debts. New York, 1893.

Sharin, R. S. Letters on the Political Situation. Charleston, 1871.

Sherman, William T. Memoirs. 2 vols. New York, 1892.

Shipp, Albert M. The History of Methodism in South Carolina. Nashville, 1884.

Sickles, Daniel. Order annulling decree of chancery in South Carolina, and correspondence relating thereto. Charleston, 1867.

Simmons, W. J. Men of Mark; Eminent, Progressive and Rising. Cleveland, 1887.

Simkins, Francis B. "The Election of 1876 in South Carolina," *South Atlantic Quarterly,* Vol. XXI (July-Oct., 1922).

—————. "The Negro in South Carolina Law since 1865," *South Atlantic Quarterly,* Vol. XXI (Mar.-July, 1922).

—————. "The Ku-Klux Klan in South Carolina, 1868-1871," *Journal of Negro History,* Vol. XII (Oct., 1927).

—————. "The Problems of South Carolina Agriculture after the Civil War," *North Carolina Historical Review,* Vol. VII (Jan., 1930).

—————. "The Solution of Post-bellum Agriculture Problems in South Carolina," *North Carolina Historical Review,* Vol. VII (April, 1930).

—————. The Tillman Movement in South Carolina. Durham, N. C., 1926.

—————. "White Methodism in South Carolina during Reconstruction," *North Carolina Historical Review*, Vol. V (Jan., 1928).

[Simms, William Gilmore.] The Sack and Destruction of Columbia, S. C. Columbia, 1865.

—————. *See* Trent, William P.

Somers, Robert. The Southern States Since the War, 1870-1871. London and New York, 1871.

South in the Building of the Nation, The. 13 vols. Richmond, 1909-1913.

South Carolina Almanac for 1868. Charleston, 1868.

South Carolina Institute. Premium List Fair of 1870. Charleston, 1870.

South Carolina in 1876. Testimony as to the denial of the elective franchise in South Carolina at the elections of 1875 (sic.) and 1876. 3 vols. Senate Misc. Doc. No. 48, 44 Cong., 2 Sess. Washington, 1877.

South Carolina: Resources and Population, Institutions and Industries. Published by the State Board of Agriculture of South Carolina. Edited by Harry Hammond. Charleston, 1883.

South Carolina Women in the Confederacy. 2 vols. Columbia, S. C., 1903-7.

Southern Christian Advocate, The. Charleston, Augusta, Macon.

Southern Cultivator, The. Athens, Georgia.

Southern Presbyterian Review. Columbia.

Statutes of the State of South Carolina. 1861-1878. Vols. XIII-XVI. Columbia.

Statutes at Large of the United States.

Stearns, Charles. The Black Man of the South and the Rebels, or the Characteristics of the former, and the recent outrages of the later. New York and Boston, 1872.

Stine, O. C., and Baker, O. E. Atlas of American Agriculture, Pt. V, Sec. A. "Cotton." Washington, 1918.

Tanner, Benjamin T. An Apology for African Methodism. Baltimore, 1867.

Taylor, Alrutheus A. The Negro in South Carolina during the Reconstruction. Washington, 1924.

————. "Letter from Henry Wallace," *Journal of Negro History,* VII (July, 1922).

————. "Negro Congressmen a Generation After," *Journal of Negro History,* Vol. VII (April, 1922).

Thomas, J. P., Jr. Formation of Judicial and Political Sub-divisions in South Carolina, an essay read before the South Carolina Bar Association, Dec. 12, 1889. n. p., n. p., n. d.

Thomas, J. P. South Carolina in arms, arts, and the industries: a view of the past, present, and future of the commonwealth. New York, 1875.

Thomas, William Hannibal. The American Negro—What He Was, What He Is, and What He may become. New York and London, 1901.

Thomason, John Furman. Foundations of the Public Schools of South Carolina. Columbia, 1925.

Thompson, Henry T. The Establishment of the Public School System of South Carolina. Columbia, 1927.

————. Ousting the Carpetbagger from South Carolina. Columbia, 1926.

————. Henry Timrod. Columbia, 1926.

Thompson, James G. "The Original Carpet-bagger," *Journal of Negro History,* Vol. V (Jan., 1920).

Tillman, Benjamin R. The Struggle of '76. Speech at Anderson, S. C., 1909, n. p., n. d.

Tompkins, Daniel A. Cotton Mills, Commercial Features. Charlotte, N. C., 1899.

Towle, George Makepeace. American Society. 2 vols. London, 1870.

Towne, Laura M. The Letters and Diary of . . . written from the Sea Islands of South Carolina, 1862-1884. Edited by Rupert Sargent Holland. Cambridge, 1912.

[Townsend, Belton O'Neall]. "The Political Condition of South Carolina," "South Carolina Morals," and "South Carolina Society," *Atlantic Monthly,* Vol. XXXIX (Feb., April, June, 1877).

Trade and Commerce of Charleston, The. Charleston, 1873.

Trenholm, W. L. Local Reform in South Carolina. n. t. p.

——————. The South; an address delivered on the third anniversary of the Charleston Board of Trade, April 7, 1869. Charleston, 1869.

Trent, William P. William Gilmore Simms. American Men of Letters Series. Boston and New York, 1892.

Trescot, William Henry. "Letters on Reconstruction in South Carolina," *American Historical Review,* Vol. XV (April, 1910).

Trezevant, Dr. D. H. Burning of Columbia, S. C., a review of northern assertions and southern facts. Columbia, 1866.

Trip of the Steamer Oceanus. *See* French.

Trowbridge, J[ohn] T[ownsend]. The South, a tour of its Battle Fields and Ruined Cities, a journey through the desolated States, and talks with the people, etc. Hartford, Conn., 1866.

Two Diaries from Middle St. John's, Berkeley, South Carolina, February-May, 1865. Journals kept by Miss Susan R. Jervey and Miss Charlotte St. J. Ravenel, at Northhampton and Pooshee Plantations, and Reminiscences of Mrs. (Mary Rhodes) (Waring) Henagan with two contemporary reports from Federal Officials. Published by St. John's Hunting Club, 1921.

Union Reform Party. Platform and address of Executive Committee, 1870. n. p.

U. S. (2) military district: Circular. Showing the number of persons registered as voters in South Carolina, under the Reconstruction acts of Congress. 1868.

Van Deusen, John G. Economic Bases of Disunion in South Carolina. New York and London, 1928.

Vandiver, Louise Ayer. Traditions and History of Anderson County. Atlanta, 1928.

[Wagener, John A.] South Carolina: A Home for the Industrious Immigrant. Charleston, 1867.

Walker, C. Irvine. The Life of Lieutenant General Richard Heron Anderson of the Confederate States Army. Charleston, 1917.

——————. The Charleston Rifle Club. Charleston.

Wallace, David Duncan. The Historical Background of Religion in South Carolina. Annual address before the upper S. C. Conference Historical Society in Greenville, S. C., November 14, 1916, and before the S. C. Conference Historical Society in Florence, S. C., November 8, 1916, n. d., n. p.

—————. The South Carolina Constitution of 1895. Columbia, 1927.

Wallace, H. A. Communications to the Journal of Negro History, Vol. VII (1922).

War of the Rebellion. Official Records.

Webster, Laura Josephine. The Operation of the Freedmen's Bureau in South Carolina. Smith College Studies in History. Vol. I. Northampton, Mass., 1916.

Wells, Edward L. Hampton and Reconstruction. Columbia, 1907.

Whaley, William. Argument delivered before the Supreme Court, at Columbia, S. C., on the Negro Bond Question; against their validity. Calhoun vs. Calhoun. Charleston, 1869.

Whipper, W. J. Speech on a question of privilege, delivered before the House of Representatives of the state of South Carolina, January 18, 1876. n. p., n. d.

White, Andrew Dickson. Autobiography. 2 vols. New York, 1905.

[Williams, A. B.]. The Liberian Exodus. Charleston, 1878.

—————. Series of articles in the Sunday State (Columbia). 1926-1927.

Williams, J. F. Old and New Columbia. Columbia, 1929.

Williams, George Walton. History of Banking in S. C., from 1812 to 1900 and other papers. Charleston, 1903.

Williams, George Washington. History of the Negro Race in America from 1619 to 1880, etc. New York, 1883.

—————. A History of the Negro Troops in the War of the Rebellion 1861-1865 preceded by a view of the military services of Negroes in ancient and modern times. New York, 1888.

Williams, H. Historical sketch of the Young Carolina Association, 1873-1876. MS. Charleston Library Society.

Wilson, Robert, M.D., D.D. Half Forgotten By-Ways of the Old South. Columbia, 1928.

Woodson, Carter Godwin. The History of the Negro Church. Washington, 1921.

Woody, R. H. "Some Aspects of the Economic Condition of South Carolina after the Civil War," North Carolina Historical Review, Vol. VII (July, 1930).

——————. "The Labor and Immigration Problem in South Carolina during Reconstruction," *Mississippi Valley Historical Review,* Vol. XVIII (Sept., 1931).

——————. "The South Carolina Election of 1870," *North Carolina Historical Review,* Vol. VIII (April, 1931).

Woolson, Constance Fenimore. "Up the Ashley and Cooper Rivers," *Harper's Magazine,* Vol. LII (Dec., 1875).

Work, Monroe N., editor. "Materials from the Scrapbook of William A. Hayne," *Journal of Negro History,* Vol. VII (July, 1922).

Wright, C. D. The Phosphate Industry of the United States. Washington, 1893.

XIX Century, The. Charleston, 1869-.

Yelverton, Therese (Viscountess Avonmore) Teresina in America. 2 vols. London, 1875.

Youmans, LeRoy F. Sketch of the Life of Governor Andrew Gordon Magrath. Charleston, 1896.

Young, Edward. Labor in Europe and America. House Ex. Doc. No. 21. 44 Cong., 1 Sess. Washington, 1876.

Zincke, Foster Barham. Last Winter in the United States; being table talk collected during a tour through the Southern Confederation, the far West, the Rocky Mountains, etc. London, 1868.

NEWSPAPERS OF THE PERIOD

Beaufort Republican.

Carolina Spartan, Spartanburg.

Charleston Daily Courier. Cited as Courier.

Charleston Mercury.

Charleston Daily News. Cited as News.

News and Courier, Charleston, 1873-. A union of the Daily News and the Daily Courier.

Charleston Daily Republican.

Columbia Daily Herald.

Columbia Daily Phoenix.

Columbia Daily Union.

Columbia Daily Union-Herald.

Daily Register, Columbia.

Daily South Carolinian, Columbia.

Edgefield Advertiser.

Fairfield Herald, Winnsboro, S. C.

Fairfield News and Herald, Winnsboro, S. C.

Keowee Courier, Pickens, S. C.
New York Herald.
New York Sun.
New York Times.
New York World.
Orangeburg News.
Orangeburg Times.
Orangeburg News and Times.
Spartanburg Herald.
Sumter News.
Sumter Watchman.
State, The, Columbia.
Temperance Advocate, Camden and Columbia.
Winnsboro Daily and Tri-Weekly News.
Yorkville Enquirer.

INDEX

ABBEVILLE, Ku-Klux Klan in, 445; Chamberlain denounced in, 493; Hampton's visit to, 496; troops in, 509; Negro Democrats in, 511.

Academies, revival of, 418-19.

Adams, Doc, militia captain, 486.

Adger, Robert, connection of with Blue Ridge Railroad, 215.

African Methodist Episcopal Church, introduction of, 385-87.

Aftermath of Reconstruction, elimination of Radicals, 542-47; disfranchisement of Negroes, 547-55; interpretations of period, 556-61; positive contributions of, 562.

Agricultural and Mechanical Society, promotes immigration, 245; sessions of, 259; coöperates with Grange, 264; fairs of, 350.

Agriculture, decline of, 10, 225; problems of, 224; ambitions of Negroes in, 224-38; ambitions of whites in, 238-48; farm contracts, 249-57; rise in production, 257-59; organizations, 259-65; credit system, 273-77.

Aiken, provost courts in, 69; commercial advantages of, 267; troops in, 509; Negro Democrats in, 511.

Aiken, D. Wyatt, relief agent, 45; on immigration, 246; approves renting of lands, 255; editor of *Rural Carolinian,* 259; leader of the Grange, 262-64; on credit system, 277 n.; on living conditions, 319-20; on tobacco chewing, 322; speaks at Anderson, 496.

Aiken, William, on relief committee, 30; confers with President Johnson, 60; favors Blue Ridge Railroad, 210-11.

Akerman, Attorney General, investigates Ku-Klux Klan, 463.

Aldrich, A. P., opposes nullification of Ordinance of Secession, 38; opposes Sickles, 70-71: on Freedmen's Bureau, 215; literary address by, 351.

Alexander, E. P., establishes oil mill, 295.

Allen, J. M., on financial commission, 102; director of Greenville and Columbia Railroad, 206; director of Blue Ridge Railroad, 217.

Allston, Mrs., establishes seminary, 419.

Alvord, Superintendent, on Negro schools, 429.

American Bank Note Company, prints South Carolina bonds, 161.

Ames, Mary, distributes gifts, 226; educator, 432.

Anderson, position of Baptists in, 403; schools in, 428; Ku-Klux Klan in, 445; Hampton at, 496.

Anderson, Gen. R. H., in poverty, 18.

Andrews, Sidney, on Charleston ruins, 6-7; on misery of people, 20; on land hunger of Negroes, 228; on discontent of white farmers, 238; on means of transportation, 313; on hotels, 314; on Negro extravagance, 334.

Architecture, decay of, 328.

Armstrong, W. J., assaulted, 69.

Asbury, Bishop, 402.

Avery Institute, 117, 428 n.

Avonmore, Viscountess, on Charleston streets, 313; on destruction in Charleston, 315; on South Carolina gentlemen, 341.

BACHMAN, Rev. James, writings of, 353.

Bagging factory, 296.

Baker, Bishop, missionary efforts of, 376-77.

Baltimore Gazette, on trade, 268.

Bank of the State, law to close operations of, 150.

Banks, importance of, 270-73.

Banquets, 346-47.

Baptism, among Negroes, 411.

Baptists, Northern missionaries, 376-78; statistics of, 382, 385; independent Negro churches, 388-90; losses of, 397; revivals among, 399; moral discipline of, 403-5; social life of, 406-8; relations of with other sects, 408; Negro

on wage system, 254-55; on diversification, 260; on credit system, 274-75; on growth of towns, 278.

Hammond, James H., on manufactures, 288.

Hampton, Wade, interviewed by Perry, 36; on Negro suffrage, 41; nominated for governor in 1865, 43; appeal of for Negro vote, 83-84; policy of criticized, 85; its futility recognized, 86; chairman of Democrats, 108-9; conciliates Democrats, 110; on credit of state, 169-70; on emigration, 239-40; on Negro labor, 252; on Negro motives, 334; on militia, 452; on Ku-Klux Klan, 458; nominated for governor, 490; estimate of, 491; canvass of, 496-98; on peace, 503, 607 n., 509; vote for, 514, 517; protests action of Ruger, 525; determination of to be governor, 529-30; declared elected, 531; asks Chamberlain to surrender, 531; inaugurated, 533; supreme court in favor of, 533-34; levies taxes, 535-36; addresses Hayes and Tilden, 537; invited to Washington, 540; gains office, 541; fails to protect Negro vote, 547-48; reëlected, 548; defeat of, 552; a popular hero, 556, 558.

Hanckel, Rev. J. S., Episcopal agent, 381.

Harlee, W. W., nominated, 490.

Harmony Presbytery, on Sherman, 375.

Harrison, J. W., president of Blue Ridge Railroad, 209-14.

Hartwell, Gen. A. S., disciplines people of Orangeburg, 31.

Haskell, A. C., part of in Hampton's nomination, 490 n.; on Democratic executive committee, 491; bolts Democratic nominations, 549.

Hastie, W. S., sheriff of Charleston, 67.

Hatch, Lewis M., engages in phosphate mining, 305.

Haworth, P. L., on contested election, 522 n.

Hawthorne, O., buys mill, 302.

Hayes, President, withdraws troops, 539-541.

Hayes-Tilden election, South Carolina's part in, 536-539.

Hayne, Henry E., in legislature, 130; in University, 441; nominated for secretary of state, 466, 495; on State Board of Canvassers, 516-23.

Hayne, Paul H., poetry of, 352-53.

Hayne, W. A., an Independent, 472 n.

Haynesworth, Christopher, first Negro juror, 70.

Hemphill, J. J., on reconstruction, 560.

Hibernian Society, banquets of, 347-48.

Hickman, H. H., in charge of Graniteville mill, 302.

Higginson, Henry Lee, purchases plantation, 243.

Higginson, T. W., on swearing among Negroes, 362; victimized by Moses, 545.

Hill, Edward, Negro landowner, 256.

Hoge, Solomon L., on Supreme Court, 143; nominated for comptroller-general, 466.

Holidays, among whites, 349-50; among Negroes, 365-66.

Holmes, Francis S., agricultural experiments of, 259; promotes phosphate industry, 306; delivers lecture, 351; writings of, 353.

Holmes, J. H., director of Blue Ridge Railroad, 209.

Homes, of Negroes, 360-62.

Homestead law, in constitution of 1868, 100.

Hopkins, Bishop, on Southern churches, 380.

Horry County, carried by Democrats in 1868, 109.

Hotels, bad state of, 314; good, 343.

Howard, Gen. Charles H., on Negro schools, 424, 426, 428.

Howard, Gen. O. O., land policy of, 230.

Hoyt, James A., member of Democratic executive committee, 491.

Hubbard, John B., chief of constabulary, 453 n.; opinion of, 559.

Hucksters, 363-64.

Huger, Alfred, 20; in constitutional convention of 1865, 37.

Hunkidori Club, members of in Columbia, 525-26.

Hunting, widespread, 345.

Hurley, Timothy, estimate of, 125; lobbyist, 136; in Greenville and Columbia Ring, 204; a Bolter, 467 n.